The Jossey-Bass Handbook
of Nonprofit Leadership
and Management

Robert D. Herman
and Associates

The Jossey-Bass Handbook of Nonprofit Leadership and Management

Jossey-Bass Publishers • San Francisco

Substantial discounts on bulk quantities of Jossey-Bass books are available to corporations, professional associations, and other organizations. For details and discount information, contact the special sales department at Jossey-Bass Inc., Publishers. (415) 433-1740; Fax (415) 433-0499.

For sales outside the United States, please contact your local Simon & Schuster International Office.

Manufactured in the United States of America. Nearly all Jossey-Bass books and jackets are printed on recycled paper that contains at least 50 percent recycled waste, including 10 percent postconsumer waste. Many of our materials are also printed with vegetable-based inks; during the printing process these inks emit fewer volatile organic compounds (VOCs) than petroleum-based inks. VOCs contribute to the formation of smog.

Library of Congress Cataloging-in-Publication Data

The Jossey-Bass handbook of nonprofit leadership and management / Robert D. Herman and associates.
    p.   cm. — (The Jossey-Bass nonprofit sector series)
    Includes bibliographical references and index.
    ISBN 1-55542-651-4
    1. Nonprofit organizations—Management.   I. Herman, Robert D., date.   II. Series.
    HD62.6.H35   1994
    658'.048—dc20   93-47556
                                     CIP

FIRST EDITION
HB Printing   10 9 8 7 6 5 4 3   *Code 9446*

The Jossey-Bass
Nonprofit Sector Series

Contents

92345

Preface

Nonprofit organizations are different! They are unlike both business and government in certain fundamental ways, while similar in other ways. Nonprofit organizations, like businesses, rely on voluntary exchanges to obtain revenues and other resources. In business, customers supply the resources for the services they receive. Unlike businesses, nonprofit organizations (especially publicly supported charities) typically depend on one group (the donors) for the resources necessary to provide a different group (the clients or beneficiaries) with services. Indeed, one reason nonprofit organizations exist is that the services they offer would not be provided otherwise. This is the justification for the tax and other public policy preferences nonprofit organizations receive—they provide public goods that would otherwise not be provided, either by business or government.

A public good, in the economic sense, is one that has two special features: first, it costs no more to provide it to many than it does to a few; second, there is no easy way to prevent those who have not contributed to its provision from consuming it once it has been produced. (Economists call this the "free-rider" problem.) The production of public goods—clean water, for example—is typically the responsibility of government. In his 1988 book, *The Nonprofit Economy* (Harvard University Press), Burton Weisbrod argues that democratic governments are constrained to provide public goods at the level that satisfies the median voter, as preferences for and willingness to pay taxes in support of public goods varies. Thus, there is unsatisfied demand for some public goods, and nonprofit organizations are often created to meet such demands.

Nonprofit organizations, like governments, generally supply services with public-goods characteristics, but unlike governments, they cannot compel users to pay for those services. Moreover, nonprofit organizations, unlike governments, need not provide their services to all who meet eligibility requirements. Nonprofit organizations may serve particular interests. The particularism of nonprofit organizations enhances the articulation and advocacy of a wide range of values and causes. In this way nonprofit organizations contribute to pluralism and the strengthening of civic culture.

To summarize, nonprofit organizations are in some ways similar to and are yet different from both businesses and governments. The ways in which these similarities and differences are combined in nonprofits makes these organizations distinctively and importantly different.

This book is based on the premise that the distinctive character of nonprofits affects the leadership and management of such organizations. Those at the helms of organizations working in the nonprofit sector have become increasingly aware of the significance of their work in North American societies. The following factors are among the indicators of this growing importance: the number and strength of sector-serving organizations have increased in Canada and the United States over the last fifteen years; publications by and about nonprofits have proliferated; and the number of university programs devoted to research and teaching about philanthropy, voluntarism, and nonprofit management has grown as well.

As the sector in general has become more self-aware, interest in the distinctive leadership and management challenges facing nonprofit organizations has also increased. While the swelling volume of publications relating to voluntarism, philanthropy, and nonprofit management has served the nonprofit sector well in many ways, all too often expert advice on financial management, personnel procedures, communication methods, and organizational structure has only been available in fragmentary pieces published in far-flung periodicals. The need for a single volume that offers a comprehensive and thorough treatment of the functions, processes, and strategies of nonprofit organizational leadership and management has been apparent for some time. This handbook meets that need. In these pages a distinguished group of authors, all among the foremost experts in their fields, describe effective management practices—specifically as they apply to the needs of today's nonprofit leaders and managers.

Intended Audience

In that this handbook is designed to provide comprehensive and in-depth descriptions of effective leadership and management practices that apply throughout the nonprofit organization, we believe and intend the volume to be of utmost value to a wide range of practitioners. It will be especially useful to anyone who has come to management from a program service background, to anyone who has moved from a relatively specialized management niche into a more expanded position, and to everyone who seeks a solid core of support for the wide range of knowledge and skills that non-profit leadership requires. In addition to those in paid staff positions, this volume will benefit board members and other volunteer leaders who are interested in enlarging their understanding of the nature of nonprofit organizations. This handbook will also be useful to those, both in formal educational programs and in self-directed learning programs, who want to prepare for careers in nonprofit management. Finally, we believe that this book will be an important resource to those who work with nonprofit organizations as consultants, technical assistance providers, regulators, and funders.

Overview of the Contents

This handbook is organized into five parts. Part One is devoted to describing the context and institutions within which nonprofit organizations currently operate and the context in which they are likely to work in the near future. Nonprofit organizations have been shaped and will continue to be shaped by their historical roots, by societal and sector institutions, by laws and regulations, by political and economic forces, and by the increasing internationalization of the world. The chapters in Part One describe how these phenomena affect nonprofit organizations and their leadership and management. In Chapter One, Peter Dobkin Hall shows how the history of philanthropy and nonprofit organizations has influenced current practice. Jon Van Til, in Chapter Two, describes both how social institutions and developing sector institutions affect nonprofit organizations. In Chapter Three, Thomas Silk uses an illustrative case to clarify the crucial legal and regulatory issues affecting U.S. nonprofit organizations. The numbers, types, activities, and operations of nonprofit organizations are greatly influenced by political and economic events. In Chapter Four, Lester M. Salamon analyzes the impact of large-scale economic, political, and demographic forces and forecasts increasing commercialization for important parts of the nonprofit sector. Helmut K. Anheier and Kusuma Cunningham, in Chapter Five, describe how and why philanthropy, like much else, is becoming more internationalized. They provide an insightful review of the management issues often faced by organizations working in an international context.

Part Two covers key leadership issues in nonprofit organizations. Boards of directors of nonprofit organizations hold the prime leadership position and are expected to provide, at least in large part, leadership in defining their organization's missions and values. In Chapter Six, Nancy R. Axelrod analyzes the development of board leadership and tells how boards can fully meet their leadership obligations. In Chapter Seven, Dick Heimovics and I examine the crucial role of chief executives in nonprofit organizations and describe the board-centered external and political leadership skills of especially effective chief executives. One of the key leadership tasks facing boards and executives is that of strategically designing programs to most effectively achieve an organization's mission. John M. Bryson provides guidelines for the effective use of strategic planning by nonprofit organizations in Chapter Eight. In an era in which many businesses and government agencies (and too many nonprofit organizations as well) have been revealed as lacking all ethical sense, nonprofit leaders must meet the challenge of creating organizational cultures that uphold the highest ethical standards. In Chapter Nine, Thomas H. Jeavons offers important advice about how this can be achieved. Nonprofit leaders continually face questions of whether, when, and how to affect legislation relevant to their organizations' missions. Bob Smucker helps answer those questions in Chapter Ten. Nearly all nonprofit organizations undergo a major change at some time. In Chapter Eleven, Felice Davidson Perlmutter and Burton Gummer analyze types of transformations and describe how leaders can meet the challenges inherent in major organizational transformations.

The contributions in Part Three get at the heart of nonprofit organizational operations. Increasing numbers of nonprofit organizations have recognized the need to explicitly manage their exchanges with a wide variety of groups. Mel S. Moyer, in Chapter Twelve, provides nonprofit leaders with a thorough analysis of the uses of marketing. The great majority of nonprofit organizations rely on volunteers. In Chapter Thirteen, Jeffrey L. Brudney describes the issues and choices involved in designing and running effective volunteer programs. In Chapter Fourteen, Vic Murray and Bill Tassie consider the difficulties of evaluating organizational effectiveness and describe how nonprofit organizations can monitor and evaluate their performance. Contracting with governments is a fact of life for many nonprofit organizations. Steven Rathgeb Smith, in Chapter Fifteen, analyzes the many facets of government contracting and considers the ways in which nonprofit organizations can most effectively manage these relations. Governments and other funders are increasingly expecting better evidence about program outcomes. In Chapter Sixteen, John Clayton Thomas details how nonprofit organizations can use program evaluation methods to assess and improve the work they do.

Part Four covers the crucial topics of developing and managing financial resources. While an increasing number of publications offer advice on specific fundraising techniques, few of those publications deal with ways to integrate those techniques with the mission and culture of a nonprofit organization. In Chapter Seventeen, Robert E. Fogal not only tells how to design and manage the fundraising program but also provides perspective on integrating mission and moneymaking efforts. An increasingly important source of revenues for many nonprofit organizations is earned income. Cynthia W. Massarsky shows how a nonprofit organization can make better decisions about how to enhance various types of earned income in Chapter Eighteen. Robert N. Anthony and David W. Young, in Chapter Nineteen, cover the principles and management uses of financial accounting. In Chapter Twenty, David W. Young explains how nonprofit managers can use cost accounting data to better manage operations. One important way that nonprofit organizations can control both costs and exposure to losses is through better risk management. Charles Tremper, in Chapter Twenty-One, provides thorough and wonderfully readable guidelines for making decisions about various sorts of insurance in relation to an overall strategy of risk management.

Part Five includes four chapters on any nonprofit organization's most important asset—the people who, whether as employees or volunteers, make the organization what it is. In Chapter Twenty-Two, Stephen McCurley specifies how an organization can find, engage, and keep volunteers who are suited to its work. M. Sue Sturgeon, in Chapter Twenty-Three, describes the steps and best practices for selecting the right person for any given job opening. In Chapter Twenty-Four, Nancy E. Day explains how to establish and operate compensation and benefit plans to suit both the organization and the people who work in it. Nancy Macduff, in Chapter Twenty-Five, describes how nonprofit organizations can assess their training needs and then design and carry out appropriate programs for both paid and volunteer staff. In my conclusion to the book, I offer an assessment of the forces moving nonprofit organizations toward competition on the one hand and cooperation on the other. Along with a consideration of the trends that are likely to influence the survival and well-being of nonprofits, I make a case for the importance of building a more cooperative community of nonprofit organizations.

This handbook, then, contains practical, applicable guidelines for carrying out most facets of nonprofit organization management. It will, I hope and believe, be a standard reference, serving to inform leaders and managers for many years to come.

Acknowledgments

In a collective enterprise of this scope and magnitude, many people contributed. I want to acknowledge and thank all of the chapter authors. It is the excellence of their work that will make this book of exceptional value to the entire nonprofit sector, now and in the future. I greatly appreciate their cooperation and fine efforts. I also want to thank everyone who responded to my initial questionnaire asking for help in specifying the topics and possible authors for this book. While I could not follow all the advice I received, the suggestions and ideas that came back through those questionnaires greatly influenced the structure of the book.

I gratefully acknowledge the help of Linda Franta in preparing mailing lists, typing first drafts, and cleaning up my word processing efforts. My colleagues Ed Weaver and Beth Smith provided useful and timely advice and support. My thanks to them. Finally, I wish to thank Alan Shrader, senior acquisitions editor of the Nonprofit Sector Series, and everyone else at Jossey-Bass who helped in preparing this book.

Kansas City, Missouri   Robert D. Herman
July 1994

The Editor

Robert D. Herman is professor in the Cookingham Institute of Public Affairs, Bloch School of Business and Public Administration, University of Missouri, Kansas City, where he helped create and teaches in the nonprofit management program. He received his B.A. degree (1968) in economics from Kansas State University and his M.S. (1971) and Ph.D. (1976) degrees, both in organizational behavior, from Cornell University.

Herman's past research has concentrated on the effective leadership of nonprofit, charitable organizations, including chief executive–board relations. His current research focuses on investigations of nonprofit organization effectiveness.

Herman is past president of the Association of Voluntary Action Scholars (now known as the Association for Research on Nonprofit Organizations and Voluntary Action). He has also served on several boards of nonprofit organizations and works with nonprofit organizations in consulting and advisory capacities.

He is coauthor of *Executive Leadership* (with D. Heimovics, 1991), coeditor of *Nonprofit Boards of Directors* (with J. Van Til, 1989), and author of many articles on nonprofit leadership and governance.

The Contributors

Helmut K. Anheier is a member of the sociology department at Rutgers University and a research associate at the Institute for Policy Studies, Johns Hopkins University, where he co-directs the Johns Hopkins Comparative Nonprofit Sector Project. He has written widely on nonprofit sectors in nations beyond the United States. He is cofounder and editor of *Voluntas,* the international journal of research on nonprofit and voluntary organizations.

Robert N. Anthony is Ross Graham Walker Professor of Management Control, Emeritus, at the Harvard Business School. He received his D.B.A. degree (1952) from Harvard University. He is the author or coauthor of numerous books and journal articles on management control in general, and management control specifically in nonprofit organizations. His books have been translated into fifteen languages.

Nancy R. Axelrod is the president and founding executive of the National Center for Nonprofit Boards in Washington, D.C., whose mission is to improve the effectiveness of nonprofit organizations by strengthening their boards of directors. She previously served as vice president for the Association of Governing Boards of Universities and Colleges, where she designed and conducted educational programs for college and university trustees. Active in nonprofit governance for more than nineteen years, Axelrod has served as a board member, direct service volunteer, and board development consultant to numerous nonprofit organizations.

Jeffrey L. Brudney is professor of political science and director of the Doctor of Public Administration program at the University of Georgia. He received his Ph.D. degree (1978) in political science from the University of Michigan. He is the author of *Fostering Volunteer Programs in the Public Sector: Planning, Initiating, and Managing Voluntary Activities* (1990), winner of the John Grenzebach Award for Outstanding Research in Philanthropy for Education. Brudney is the author of numerous articles and reports on volunteers and volunteer programs, particularly as related to government, and is coauthor of *Applied Statistics for Public Administration* (with K. J. Meier, 1993).

John M. Bryson is professor of planning and public affairs in the Hubert H. Humphrey Institute of Public Affairs at the University of Minnesota. He is the author of the best-selling *Strategic Planning for Public and Nonprofit Organizations: A Guide to Strengthening and Sustaining Organizational Achievement* (1988) and of the audiocassette program *Getting Started on Strategic Planning* (1991). He is coauthor of *Leadership for the Common Good: Tackling Public Problems in a Shared-Power World* (with B. C. Crosby, 1992), which received the 1993 Terry McAdam Award for "outstanding contribution to the advancement of the nonprofit sector" from the Nonprofit Management Association. Bryson has served as a consultant to a wide range of nonprofit, public, and for-profit organizations.

Kusuma Cunningham is a graduate student in sociology at Purdue University, where she is completing her Ph.D. degree. Her areas of interest are the nonprofit sector, private voluntary organizations, developing countries, and international aid. She was previously a research assistant at the Institute for Policy Studies at Johns Hopkins University.

Nancy E. Day is assistant professor of human resources and organizational behavior at the Bloch School of Business and Public Administration at the University of Missouri, Kansas City. She received her Ph.D. degree (1987) in social psychology from the University of Kansas. Prior to entering academia she worked as a consultant with Lee & Burgess Associates, specializing in compensation programs and organizational development, and as a compensation analyst for the city of Overland Park, Kansas.

Robert E. Fogal is vice president of the Northern Region of the Ohio Presbyterian Retirement Services Foundation and editor in chief of *New Directions for Philanthropic Fund Raising*. He received his Ph.D. degree in folklore and ethnomusicology from Indiana University. He is a Certified Fund Raising Executive and was formerly director of the Fund Raising School at the Indiana University Center on Philanthropy. He has also been vice president for development at Otterbein College (Ohio) and director of development at Lancaster Theological Seminary (Pennsylvania).

Burton Gummer is professor of social welfare in the School of Social Welfare, Nelson A. Rockefeller College of Public Affairs and Policy, State University of New York, Albany. He received his Ph.D. degree from Bryn Mawr College. He is the author of *The Politics of Social Administration: Managing Organizational Politics in Social Agencies* (1990) and of a number of journal articles and book chapters on social administration, organizational behavior, and social planning. He is also the author of "Notes from the Management Literature," which is a regular feature of *Administration in Social Work.*

Peter Dobkin Hall is research scientist and director of the Project on the Changing Dimensions of Trusteeship at the Program on Nonprofit Organizations at Yale University. His work includes *The Organization of American Culture, 1700–1900: Institutions, Elites, and the Origins of American Nationality* (1992), *Inventing the Nonprofit Sector* (1992), and *Lives in Trust: The Fortunes of Dynastic Families in Late Twentieth Century America* (1992).

Dick Heimovics is Levitt Professor of Human Relations at the Bloch School of Business and Public Administration, University of Missouri, Kansas City, where he directs executive education programs. He received his Ph.D. degree (1975) from the University of Kansas. He is coauthor, with Robert D. Herman, of *Executive Leadership in Nonprofit Organizations: New Strategies for Shaping Executive-Board Dynamics* (1991) as well as author of many articles on organizational behavior and leadership.

Thomas H. Jeavons is director of the Center on Philanthropy and Nonprofit Leadership and assistant professor of public administration and philanthropic studies at Grand Valley State University in Allendale, Michigan. He received his Ph.D. degree (1992) in management and cultural studies from the Union Institute. He has served on the executive staff and on the boards of a number of nonprofit organizations.

Stephen McCurley is a partner in VMSystems, a consulting firm that specializes in providing technical assistance to volunteer-utilizing agencies. He previously served as director of field services for the National VOLUNTEER Center, now known as The Points of Light Foundation. He is a former national board member of the Association for Volunteer Administration. He is the author of eight books and more than eighty articles on volunteer management.

Nancy Macduff has twenty-five years of experience in the management of nonprofit and volunteer organizations. She served as executive director of a youth agency and program coordinator for a government-based volunteer program. She currently teaches college courses on volunteer management and administration. She is the author of several books and numerous articles on the management of nonprofit and volunteer programs. She is president of Macduff/ Bunt Associates, a training, consulting, and publishing company based in Walla Walla, Washington.

Cynthia W. Massarsky is president of CWM Marketing Group, a management consulting firm specializing in marketing and new business development for the nonprofit sector. She received her M.B.A. degree from Cornell University. Massarsky develops new business concepts or ventures; conducts strategic and long-range planning sessions; writes marketing, business, and program plans; analyzes financial and organizational risk; and conducts research. Prior to founding her own firm, Massarsky worked for Scholastic, Inc., Marlo Thomas's Free To Be Foundation, and the Foundation Center. She is the author of several articles on marketing and enterprise development for nonprofit organizations.

Mel S. Moyer is professor emeritus and senior scholar in the faculty of administrative studies at York University in Toronto, where he was the founding director of its Voluntary Sector Management Program. He is also an associate editor of *Nonprofit Management and Leadership*. He received his Ph.D. degree from Columbia University. He is the editor of *Managing Voluntary Organizations: Perspectives* (1983) and *Managing Voluntary Organizations: An Agenda for the Future* (1989).

Vic Murray is professor in the organizational behavior area of the faculty of administrative studies at York University, Toronto, where he is currently director of the Voluntary Sector Management Program. His research interests include organizational politics. His chapter in this book is based on a research project on the nature of patterns for judging organizational effectiveness in nonprofit organizations, funded by the Social Science and Humanities Research Council of Canada.

Felice Davidson Perlmutter is professor of social administration and chair of the administration/social planning graduate program at the School of Social Administration, Temple University. She received her Ph.D. degree from Bryn Mawr College and has been a Fulbright Scholar. She is the author of *Changing Hats: From Social Work Practice to Administration* and has published more than sixty book chapters and journal articles related to administration, mental health, and social policy. In addition to her involvement with social work administration, Perlmutter has been active in family dispute mediation and international research and teaching. She is a fellow of the American Orthopsychiatric Association and serves on the boards of several professional organizations.

Lester M. Salamon is professor at Johns Hopkins University and director of The Johns Hopkins Institute for Policy Studies. He received his Ph.D.

degree in government from Harvard University. From 1981 to 1986 he directed the Urban Institute's Nonprofit Sector Project, and between 1977 and 1980 he served as deputy associate director of the U.S. Office of Management and Budget. Prior to this, Salamon served on the faculties of Duke and Vanderbilt Universities.

Thomas Silk is the founder and senior partner of Silk, Adler & Colvin, a San Francisco law firm that restricts its practice to the representation of charitable and other nonprofit organizations, individual philanthropists, and corporations with regard to their charitable activities. Silk received his L.L.B. degree (1963) from the School of Law (Boalt Hall) at the University of California, Berkeley. From 1964 through 1968, Silk worked in Washington, D.C., for the U.S. Department of Justice, Tax Division, as appellate attorney and then as special assistant. He is currently adjunct professor at the University of San Francisco, where he developed and teaches a course in nonprofit law. Silk is also a lecturer at Boalt Hall, where he teaches a course in nonprofit law to law students and M.B.A. students. He serves as an adviser and consultant on nonprofit law in various countries in central and eastern Europe and in Asia.

Steven Rathgeb Smith is assistant professor of public policy and political science at the Sanford Institute of Public Policy, Duke University, where he is director of undergraduate studies and affiliated with the Center for the Study of Philanthropy and Voluntarism. He received his Ph.D. degree (1988) in political science from the Massachusetts Institute of Technology.

Bob Smucker, vice president of government relations for INDEPENDENT SECTOR since 1980, has worked with nonprofit organizations since 1957, including twenty-five years as a lobbyist at the local, state, and national levels. From 1957 until 1971 he worked in Pennsylvania with local mental health associations and with the Pennsylvania Mental Health Association. From 1971 to 1979 he was director of public policy for the National Mental Health Association, during which period he was centrally involved in the enactment of the 1976 lobby law that clarified and expanded the lobbying rights of nonprofit organizations. Smucker had principal staff responsibility for INDEPENDENT SECTOR's involvement in three Supreme Court decisions related to fundraising activities by nonprofit organizations, all of which were decided in favor of the First Amendment rights of nonprofit organizations. He is author of *The Nonprofit Lobbying Guide: Advocating Your Cause — And Getting Results* (1991).

M. Sue Sturgeon is president of HSC, Inc., in Overland Park, Kansas, which provides human resources and environmental consulting. She received her M.B.A. degree from Rockhurst College. From 1984 until 1992 she was director of corporate administrative services for the American Nurses Association.

Bill Tassie is a Ph.D. candidate in administrative studies at York University and an associate of York's Voluntary Sector Management Program. Tassie has several years' experience in business and government and has long consulted with government and nonprofit organizations. He received his M.B.A. degree from the University of Ottawa.

John Clayton Thomas is professor and director of the School of Public Administration and Urban Studies at Georgia State University. He received his Ph.D. degree in political science from Northwestern University. He has taught and conducted program evaluation research for almost twenty years. His latest book, coedited with H. V. Savitch, is *Big City Politics in Transition* (1991).

Charles Tremper is founding executive director of the Nonprofit Risk Management Center in Washington, D.C. He received his Ph.D. degree from the University of California, Los Angeles. He has taught at the National Law Center of George Washington University and the University of Nebraska College of Law. He has been a visiting scholar at Yale University's Program on Nonprofit Organizations, a Bush Foundation Fellow in Chile Development and Social Policy, and a senior research associate at the URSA Institute.

Jon Van Til is professor of urban studies and public policy at Rutgers University Camden College. His publications include *Living with Energy Shortfall: A Future for American Cities and Towns* (1982), which was selected by *Choice* as one of the outstanding academic books of the year, *Mapping the Third Sector* (1988), and *Critical Issues in American Philanthropy: Strengthening Theory and Practice* (1990). He served as editor of *Nonprofit and Voluntary Sector Quarterly* (previously *Journal of Voluntary Action Research*) from 1979 until 1993. Van Til serves as faculty consultant for the development of the nonprofit management program at the University of Colorado, Colorado Springs.

David W. Young is professor of accounting and control at Boston University School of Management, where he is also director of the Health Care Management Program. He currently serves as a commissioner and chair of the Massachusetts Hospital Payment System Advisory Commission. He received his D.B.A. degree (1977) from Harvard University. He has authored or coauthored many books and journal articles on health policy and management, and the management of nonprofit organizations.

The Jossey-Bass Handbook
of Nonprofit Leadership
and Management

PART ONE

❦

CONTEXT AND INSTITUTIONS

While individuals have probably always engaged in informal voluntary efforts, the establishment and character of formal nonprofit organizations are greatly affected by social, political, legal, and economic institutions. The United States and Canada have, by international standards, large nonprofit sectors of long standing. To fully understand contemporary nonprofit management and leadership practices and the ways in which institutional and social changes are likely to create new management and leadership challenges, we need to understand how institutions have shaped and influenced nonprofit organizations.

This part of the book includes five chapters that describe and analyze the following factors: the historical evolution of the U.S. nonprofit sector; the current cultural and social forces affecting the need for various sorts of nonprofit services; the legal and regulatory framework within which U.S. nonprofit organizations, particularly charities, must operate; the economic, political, and demographic trends that seem to be leading to increased commercialization of parts of the U.S. nonprofit sector; and how the increasingly international character of philanthropy affects the management of nonprofit organizations that operate internationally.

1

Historical Perspectives on Nonprofit Organizations

Peter Dobkin Hall

Nonprofit organizations comprise the newest and fastest growing category of organizations in America: the concept of charitable tax-exempt organizations as a unified and coherent "sector" dates back little more than twenty years. More than 90 percent of nonprofit organizations currently in existence were established since the Second World War.

Because their growth has been so rapid and because their impact has been so far-reaching—touching on every aspect of our lives and every level of institutions—nonprofits have been the focus of intense controversy as legislators, the courts, and the public have struggled to come to terms with this organizational revolution. At the same time, because the nonprofit universe has been in a process of emergence, those within it have themselves had to struggle to define and legitimate it.

Defining what nonprofits are and what they do is an extraordinarily difficult task. They vary enormously in scope and scale, ranging from community and neighborhood organizations with no assets and no employees through multibillion dollar foundations, universities, and health care complexes with thousands of employees. They vary enormously in what they do, from offering traditional charitable assistance to the needy to carrying out manufacturing and advanced research. Their sources of revenue follow

Note: The research on which this chapter is based was made possible through the generous support of the AAFRC Trust for Philanthropy, the Lilly Endowment, Rockefeller Archive Center, and the Program on Nonprofit Organizations, Yale University.

3

no clear pattern: some are traditional donative charities, others receive all their funds from government. Their modes of governance range from the autocracy of sole trustees selected from among the descendants of a charitable donor through broadly representative boards composed of *ex officio* elected officials or elected by members of organizations.

Nonprofits pose almost insuperable problems for anyone who would presume to relate their history. While elements of the "sector" — ideas about charity, philanthropic practices, and certain models of voluntary association — date back to biblical and classical times, other key aspects of it are entirely new. Tempting as it is to focus on the sector's remotest antecedents and to depict its development as unbroken, linear, and irresistible, such a treatment would do violence to its richness and complexity. More to the point, such an approach obscures the important connections between the evolution of nonprofits and the development of the state, the economy, and society.

Nonprofits are a new institutional form. Their emergence as a central feature of the polity represents a new configuration of public and private power. To grasp the history of nonprofits, we must strip away the selective and self-serving readings of the past, wishful thinking, unexamined assumptions, and folklore, which inevitably accompany the emergence of new institutional formations.

Colonial Antecedents

Although various components of today's nonprofits have their origins in the colonial period, neither philanthropy nor voluntary associations existed then in a recognizably modern form. Before the mid-eighteenth century, the fundamental ideological and legal infrastructure — notions of citizenship, political and economic rights, clearly demarcated public and private domains, and boundaries between church and state — that we consider absolutely central to modern civil society were entirely lacking. In such a setting, philanthropic and voluntary actions and institutions, even when they superficially resemble modern ones, were fundamentally different in meaning and motive.

While some colonies accepted English law and legal forms, primitive conditions, including the rarity of formal legal training, as well as limitations on the powers of colonial assemblies, particularly their inability to charter corporations, constrained the development of an American tradition of organized philanthropic and voluntary activity (Davis, 1917; Dodd, 1960; Hall, 1989). The New England colonies actively rejected English law and legal forms, regarding them as instruments of oppression and corruption. The practice of law was banned as inimical to the public interest, magistrates favored arbitration of disputes over adversary proceedings, the Common Law was rejected in favor of clearly stated commonsensical statutes and local customs, and equity — the jurisdiction under which trusts are enforceable — was considered wholly unnecessary. The adoption of English law and legal forms did not begin in any significant way before the 1790s.

And even then, it occurred in a selective fashion, framed by local and regional concerns (Nelson, 1975; Horowitz, 1977).

In most of the colonies, as in the Old World, the two central formal institutions framing the lives of all inhabitants were the co-joined interests of church and state. The family, which we now think of as a quintessentially private domain, was a public institution — a "little commonwealth" — in which were centered responsibilities for economic production, education, and social welfare. Not surprisingly, the polities of state, church, and family complemented one another: unlike the Old World, where church and state had the resources to retain officials to administer their affairs, the colonial governments depended on their power to levy labor from the populace for the construction of public works (primarily the building and maintenance of roads), for militia service, and for caring for the poor and dependent. The source of this labor was, of course, the family, to which all unmarried members of society were legally required to belong, and whose heads were held legally responsible for the behavior and conduct of their members. Families were required by law to provide for the basic literacy and religious training of their members and to provide them, usually through the apprenticeship system, with training in a craft or occupation. They were also required to provide care for poor and dependent relatives. Only if families lacked the resources to do so or if a poor and dependent person could not be proved to have a family, did public authorities assume responsibility — and when they did so, it was through paying a household to care for the needy.

While these practices — from neighbors pitching in to repair highways, drilling with the militia, or taking the poor and dependent into their homes — might superficially resemble voluntary action, perusal of the colonial statute books makes quite clear the coercive force framing these activities. In effect, constrained by their limited resources, the colonies had adopted the provisions of the Elizabethan Poor Law, which assigned responsibility for the care of the destitute to localities.

Although English philanthropists were generous with the colonies and the colonists themselves showed an early willingness to bequeath funds for charitable purposes, public institutions were invariably the recipients of this largesse. Thus, for example, when Boston merchant Robert Keayne (d. 1656) made charitable bequests in his will, the beneficiaries were the town of Boston (for "a Conduit and a Town House Comprising a Market Place, Court Room, Gallery, Library, Granary, and an Armory") and Harvard College (which received books and property) (Bailyn, 1964).

The situation of Harvard College, the oldest eleemosynary corporation in the colonies, illustrates well the anomalous status of all colonial corporations. First of all, under British law, all corporations were viewed as delegations of public authority — bodies empowered to do the public's business. Thus even from a legal perspective Harvard was not a private entity in the modern sense. Reinforcing its public character was the fact that it was governed by boards, the Fellows and the Overseers, composed of ministers of the tax-supported Congregational church and government officials sitting *ex officio*. Although its small endowment, given in part by benevolent colonists and in part by British friends, yielded a modest income, most of its revenues came from legislative grants and from tuitions and fees. Even after the Revolution, when merchants and lawyers began to replace clergymen on its boards and when individual gifts and bequests became more important than government funding, Harvard retained its public identity: the provisions of its charter, its professorial appointments, and even its curriculum were matters of legislative debate and concern. Not until 1865, when the senior members of the state senate were replaced as Overseers by elected alumni representatives, could Harvard be considered a private corporation in the modern sense (Morison, 1936; Foster, 1962; Harris, 1970; Story, 1980).

Only in the mid-eighteenth century did the political, economic, and legal conditions favorable to the development of voluntary associations and private philanthropy—elective government, market relationships, and conceptions of political and property rights—assume significance. This fundamental shift was due both to internal factors—such as the erosion of the authority of family, church, and government—and to external ones, especially the reintegration of the colonies into the British commercial system. Together, these encouraged the adoption of British legal forms, the growth of markets, individual entrepreneurship, and the growth of commercial interests, as well as the spread of radical political and economic ideas of the European Enlightenment (Deetz, 1977).

Religion played a key role in this transformation. The Great Awakening, a religious revival that swept the colonies between 1740 and 1760, was as much a social and political movement as a religious one. Throughout the colonies, ecclesiastical controversies quickly bloomed into full-blown struggles for political and economic dominance (Bushman, 1970). The evangelicals became the champions of popular liberties and stood at the forefront of revolutionary agitation by organizing voluntary associations like the Committees of Correspondence and the Sons of Liberty, which took the lead in resisting British rule. By the 1760s, Americans had begun to conceive of themselves as *citizens* possessed of political, economic, and religious *rights*.

Associational impulses were reinforced by secular models of collective action, attuned to European organizational development, which took root in cities like Boston, New York, and Philadelphia. When Benjamin Franklin traveled to England in the 1720s to refine his knowledge of printing, he became involved with London's burgeoning voluntary associations—most notably with the printers' guilds and the Freemasons. These became models for his "club for mutual improvement"—the Junto. A group of ambitious artisans who met weekly to debate morals, politics, and natural philosophy, the Juntos kept themselves informed of current events, learned to persuasively advance their ideas, and worked together to further their economic and political interests (Lemisch, 1961, pp. 73–74). Franklin and his friends quickly moved to the forefront of public life in Philadelphia.

Secret societies like the Junto and the Freemasons highlighted for Franklin and his contemporaries the potential power of organized collective action. It was but a short step from clublike mutual benefit associations to voluntary associations directed to broader public purposes. By the 1760s, Franklin and his friends had formed a subscription library, volunteer fire company, hospital, and academy—all of which became models for similar voluntary efforts in other colonies.

From an organizational standpoint, the American Revolution was a true watershed, fostering the convergence of various ideological impulses (evangelicalism and Enlightenment rationalism), organizational experiences (evangelical voluntarism and urban fraternalism), and organizational models (Freemasonry, urban clubs, covenanted congregations), and spreading them through the new nation. The war educated Americans both to their common interests and to the mechanisms through which those collective interests might be realized. While associations like the Sons of Liberty disappeared when the Revolution ended, their members regrouped into other associated bodies. Some were explicitly political, like the Society of the Cincinnati and such urban "benevolent" societies as Tammany Hall and the Ancient Order of Hibernians. Others claimed to be more disinterested, like the medical societies, which physicians who had served in the war took the lead in organizing.

Voluntary Associations in the New Republic

Although the Revolution brought many voluntary organizations into existence, it did little to allay the suspicions with which associations were viewed by most Americans. If the Americans feared the power of government, they feared even more the power of individuals associating to pursue their private interests (Madison, 1961, pp. 77–84). While favoring the right of individuals to associate for common purposes, Thomas Jefferson worried that such groups, if incorporated and empowered to hold property, would become the basis for new kinds of tyranny. Viewing all organizations as containing "some trace of human weakness, some grain of corruption, which cunning will discover, and wickedness will insensibly open, cultivate, and improve," Jefferson believed that associations, like government, should be limited in their powers and privileges (Jefferson, 1965a, p. 389). At the same time, he opposed the growth of the market economy, which he believed "begets subservience and venality, suffocates the germ of virtue, and prepares fit tools for the design of ambition" (p. 393).

Thus, the chartering of corporations, which had begun in earnest by the 1790s, was in no sense an endorsement of voluntary action. Because corporations were viewed as delegations of public authority rather than as private contracts, chartering served to restrict rather than to expand the domain of private action. This spirit is evident in Connecticut's 1792 act to provide Yale with renewed government support. To strengthen ties between church and state, the act added elected officials—the governor, lieutenant governor, and six senior members of the legislature's upper house—to Yale's governing board (which consisted of ten ministers of the state church). Under this new arrangement, wrote Yale president Ezra Stiles, "The clergy will have a particular & special Reason now to preach up for & recommend the Election of religious & undeistical Counsellors; & tho' now and then an un-principled Character may get into the Council, he may be hunted down in a future Election." The act, he concluded, "may be mutually beneficial by preserving a religious Magistracy & a more catholic Clergy" (Stiles, 1901, vol. II, pp. 457–458).

The economic institutions chartered in New England during this period had a similar intent. With charters granted only to politically and religiously reliable leaders, and with the state reserving to itself substantial blocks of stock and appointing a number of their directors, banks were unambiguously viewed by their supporters as public institutions and as pillars of orthodoxy (Purcell, 1963). The charters of many canal, turnpike, bridge, and manufacturing companies not only involved effective partnership with the state but also enjoyed the same privileges of tax exemption extended to eleemosynary institutions.

The states varied in their willingness to permit the establishment of corporations and private charities. While the New England states were willing to grant corporations extensive powers and to encourage the growth of charities, the southern states severely restricted both. In Virginia, for example, charitable corporations could not receive or manage endowments, their real estate was not tax exempt, nor were their students and faculties exempt from taxation and military duty. In 1792, Virginia affirmed its unofficial policy of discouraging private eleemosynary corporations by annulling the Statute of Charitable Uses and seizing the endowment funds held by the Anglican church, which were turned over to county authorities (Henning, 1821; Shepard, 1835; Hirchler, 1939). One jurist would affirm the wisdom of this act by condemning "the wretched policy of permitting the whole property of society to be swallowed up in the insatiable gulph of public charities" (Tucker, 1832).

Unlike New England, Virginia favored the creation of public agencies. As early as the 1770s, care for the insane was entrusted to an asylum that operated under the direct authority of the legislature (Henning, 1821, vol. IX, pp. 167–169). Jefferson's 1779 "Act to diffuse knowledge more generally through the mass of the people" stressed the government's responsibility for education and proposed a multi-tiered system of state-supported schools to provide equal opportunities for acquiring the rudiments, vocational, and classical education (Jefferson, 1965b, pp. 298–299). The University of Virginia, established in 1819, was a state institution, not a private one. Other southern states followed Virginia's lead.

The status of voluntary associations and private charities in the new states and territories—west of the Appalachians—reflected the conflicts in the older settlements (Hall, 1987). Although the original plan of government for the Northwest Territory, which was largely drafted by New Englanders, favored private initiatives, the admixture of southerners and northerners among the settlers, each with their own ideas about the permissible extent of private power, led first to intense struggles over the chartering of corporations and, subsequently, to the emergence of organizations that were neither clearly public or private. Ohio University, for example, had been originally chartered as a private corporation. With Jeffersonians in control of the new state, however, it was reorganized—with a board appointed by the governor, but with expectations that it would enjoy private support. This institution coexisted with colleges that were supported by religious denominations as well as ones that were owned by stockholders and supported by earned income. No purely private lay-governed, privately supported college would exist in Ohio until the end of the nineteenth century (Burns, 1905; Miller, 1918).

Privatizing the Voluntary Association

The establishment of the federal government created a genuinely national arena in which the advocates of divergent conceptions of public and private power could air their differences as they struggled to define republican government. Heated political controversies served as the catalysts for the emergence of a new kind of voluntary organization—the political party. The Federalists had taken the first steps in this direction in the 1780s, with the organization of the Society of the Cincinnati, an association of Continental Army officers headed by George Washington. The aristocratic cast of the society sparked a storm of controversy, in part because membership was to be passed by primogeniture, from original members to their eldest sons (Burke, 1784). To counter the power of this conservative group, its opponents began organizing "democratic societies," which eventually became the basis for a national political party headed by Thomas Jefferson.

Jefferson's Democratic Republican Party transformed the nature of democratic power itself. Before its emergence, the wealthy, learned, and respectable had ruled in the name of the people but were seldom accountable to them. Even where property qualifications did not restrict the ability to vote and run for office, the public had been unable to mobilize its political energies before the coming of party organizations. Their success, signaled by Jefferson's election as president in 1800, broke the ties between the state and associations that the Federalists had been trying to forge.

Turned out of office, the wealthy, learned, and respectable Federalists began to use voluntary associations as a counterforce to the electoral power of the democratic majority. Fancying themselves as "guardians of virtue," they were willing to use their wealth to influence public opinion. Recognizing the potential power of Federalist control of churches, schools, professional societies, and other voluntary associations, the Jeffersonians launched a series of attacks on established incorporated associations throughout the country.

The most famous of these struggles involved New Hampshire's efforts to take over Dartmouth College (Wyllie, 1959; Miller, 1961; Whitehead, 1976; Tobias, 1982). In 1816, the legislature passed a bill reorganizing the college, changing its name, and replacing its self-perpetuating board with a state-appointed one. The college was ordered to report annually to the governor and the state reserved to itself broad powers of oversight. When the old board of trustees contested the action, the New Hampshire Supreme Court upheld the state, drawing on the generally accepted doctrine that corporations, as creations of the legislature, were entirely subject to its will. The old trustees appealed and, in 1818, the case reached the United States Supreme Court.

In representing the old trustees, Daniel Webster conceded that the college's charter, like that of any corporation, was an act of government. But, he suggested, individuals had been encouraged by that grant of corporate powers to make donations and bequests to trustees of the institution. Though the use was public, Webster argued that this did not diminish the private character of the donated property: the gifts were made to the trustees and, as such, constituted private contracts between the trustees and the donors. The Constitution, he pointed out, specifically prohibited the states from passing laws impairing contractual obligations (Hofstadter and Smith, 1961, pp. 202–213).

The court, with a single dissent, accepted Webster's argument. The case, Chief Justice Marshall asserted, did not involve the corporate rights of the college. If it did, the New Hampshire legislature might "act according to its own judgment, unrestrained by any limitation of its power imposed by the Constitution of the United States." Rather, it involved the individual rights of the donors who had given property to Dartmouth's trustees. The charter, Marshall stated, was not a grant of political power, an establishment "of a civil institution to be employed in the administration of government," or a matter of government funds. It was, rather, "a contract to which the donors, the trustees, and the Crown (to whose rights and obligations New Hampshire succeeds) were the original parties" and, as such, as constitutionally protected (*Trustees of Dartmouth College,* 1819, p. 654).

The Dartmouth College case fundamentally redefined the nature of the corporation, transforming it from a delegation of public power over which the state could exercise control, to a private contract protected from government interference. While the Constitution had, through the Bill of Rights, defined and protected arenas of private action, these were domains of individual, not associational, action. Marshall's decision expanded these protections to include collective action and in doing so created a clearly defined distinction between public and private sectors.

Court rulings on charities and trusts followed a less affirmative course. In *Philadelphia Baptist Association* v. *Hart's Executors,* a key case decided in 1819, the Supreme Court upheld the power of states to restrict the charitable actions of testators and the powers of charitable corporations. Charities were not placed on a firm legal footing under federal law until 1844, when the Supreme Court heard the Girard Will Case (*Vidal* v. *Girard's Executors,* 1844; Ferguson, 1987). In this case, the court reversed the Hart ruling and upheld the validity of charitable trusts in states that had repealed the Elizabethan *Statute of Charitable Uses.* Although the decision in the Girard Will Case secured under federal law the right of individuals to create charitable trusts and of corporations to administer them, this decision did not affect particular states which chose to limit their activities.

Although Alexis de Tocqueville is frequently cited as an authority on the role of voluntary associations in early America, it seems clear in retrospect that he greatly exaggerated their importance. Although they were certainly central to economic, political, and cultural life in the Northeast, they were infinitely less so in the West and South, where public institutions were preferred (Tocqueville, 1945, vol. I, p. 378). Again, they were more important to certain social groups than to others, especially to those who for reasons of wealth, gender, religion, and race, could not influence public life through the electoral process (Tocqueville, 1945, vol. I, p. 187; Ginzberg, 1990; Scott, 1991). While voluntary associations and private philanthropy grew more important in the years before the Civil War, they represented only one of several modes of collective action—and at no time were they universally accepted throughout the country.

Two incidents in particular reveal the extent of American ambivalence about philanthropy in the ante bellum period. The first involved the half-million-dollar bequest made in 1835 by Englishman James Smithson for the establishment of an institution for the increase and diffusion of knowledge (Rhees, 1879). The bequest set off a decade of congressional debate. The first phase of the debate rehashed the previous half century of controversy over the legality of charitable trusts. The second phase centered on what kind of institution could best increase and diffuse knowledge, where such an institution should be located, and how it should be governed. Eventually it was decided to establish a federally chartered corporation, the Smithsonian Institution, governed by a board of elected and appointed federal officials. The establishment of the Smithsonian affirmed the tradition of public philanthropy—private funds devoted to public purposes through public instrumentalities.

The second incident involved President Franklin Pierce's veto of a bill to set aside ten million acres of federal lands for the support and relief of the insane throughout the United States. The bill had been passed by Congress in 1854, after years of lobbying by Dorothea Dix, the nation's leading advocate for the mentally ill. President Pierce, after a detailed review of the powers granted the federal government under the Constitution, vetoed the bill, declaring that, if passed, it would have the effect of transferring "to the Federal Government the charge of all the poor in all the states" and obligating the government "to provide hospitals and other local establishments for the care and cure of every species of human infirmity, and thus to assume all that duty of either public philanthropy or public necessity to the dependent, the orphan, the sick, or the needy which is now discharged by the States themselves or by corporate institutions or private endowments existing under the legislation of the States. The whole field of beneficence is thrown open to the care and culture of the Federal Government." "I cannot," he concluded, "find any authority in the Constitution for making the Federal Government the great almoner of public charity throughout the United States" (Pierce, 1898, vol. V, pp. 247–256). The compelling constitutional reasoning of Pierce's argument was persuasive — so much so that it became, until the Great Depression of the 1930s, the guidepost for opposition to efforts to bring the federal government into the domains of education, health, and social welfare. At the same time, it had the effect of powerfully affirming the role of private charity, which, in the absence of federal commitment, would have to assume far greater burdens than ever previously imagined.

Like the Revolution, the Civil War provided opportunities for further advancing the claims of private eleemosynary enterprise. The disastrous failure of the North's efforts during the early phases of the war — due, the friends of private enterprise argued, to democratic excesses that had, over the previous thirty years, deprived the North of its most talented officers — provided business and charitable elites with opportunities to transform the jerry-built prewar government into an effective and reasonably efficient administrative apparatus (Upton, 1907; Ambrose, 1962).

A model for this transformation was the United States Sanitary Commission, the private organization that assumed responsibility for providing medical care to the Union Army (Frederickson, 1965). Led by wealthy and educated urban professionals, it combined trained expertise with the enthusiasm and funds of volunteers, thousands of whom worked through local branches to raise funds and produce supplies and clothing. At the same time, the heroism of wealthy Harvard graduates like Colonel Robert Gould Shaw, leader of the famous Black regiment, the Massachusetts 54th, was used as an argument to advance the claims of the organized private sector and to legitimize the role of the elite that supported it (Higginson, 1866; Eliot, 1898 [1869]).

"Fighting the Wilderness, Moral and Physical": Private Institutions and the Search for Order

"As a people," Harvard's president Charles W. Eliot would declare in 1869, "we have but a halting faith in special training for high professional employments. The vulgar conceit that a Yankee can turn his hand to anything we insensibly carry into high places where it is preposterous and criminal. . . . Only after years of the bitterest experience, did we come to believe the professional training of a soldier to be of value in war" (Eliot, 1898 [1869], p. 38).

In statements of this kind, northern advocates of private power combined older notions of private responsibility for the public good with social Darwinism to forge a justification of the role of elites and the private institutions they supported. This redefinition pointed to vast new opportunities for extending the influence of private institutions (Eliot, 1898 [1869]; Hawkins, 1972).

From 1865 on, the advocates of private power concentrated their energies in two areas: building private business corporations capable of operating on a national scale and extending the scope, scale, and legal privileges of cultural infrastructure needed to sustain these enterprises. The two efforts were necessarily related. The ability to establish and operate large-scale business organizations required new kinds of trained manpower and new technologies, as well as the ability to gather and interpret social and economic information (Buck, 1965; Haskell, 1977; Ross, 1991). These were needs that the colleges could best supply. But to meet these needs, higher education needed the support of private wealth to expand facilities, to recruit students nationally and faculty internationally, to create new curricula, and to develop new fields for teaching and research.

University administrators and reform-minded business people sought one another out, with dramatically successful results (Sears, 1922, pp. 23–24). Businessmen became so involved with the affairs of the major universities — all of which were private — that it was hardly an exaggeration to claim, as Thorstein Veblen did, that "men of affairs have taken over direction of the pursuit of knowledge" (Veblen, 1918, p. 57). University training became essential for the pursuit of careers in the larger business corporations. And businessmen were active in the founding of professional organizations like the American Social Science Association, the American Statistical Association, and the American Economic Association, which brought together nonprofit and for-profit institution builders in contexts of mutual concern.

It was during this period that a coherent rationale for the role of private institutions in the democratic state was finally articulated and, more important, translated into legislation. In 1874, Harvard's Eliot, defending the university's tax exemption to the Massachusetts General Court, presented a detailed economic analysis of benefits the public received from private charitable institutions (Eliot, 1988 [1874], pp. 369–394). It was so persuasive that the legislature raised the ceiling on the amount of charitable property that could be exempted from taxation, and also increased the range of exempt institutions to include any "educational, charitable, benevolent, or religious purpose," including "any antiquarian, historical, literary, scientific, medical, artistic, monumental, or musical" purpose. "Any missionary enterprise," with either foreign or domestic objects, was granted exemption, as were organizations "encouraging athletic exercises and yachting," libraries and reading rooms, and "societies of Freemasons, Odd Fellows, Knights of Pythias and other charitable or social bodies of a like character and purpose" ("An Act Concerning . . . ," 1874, pp. 412–414). The Massachusetts law became a model for those seeking to extend the privileges of private institutions (*"Yale University* v. *Town of New Haven,"* 1899; "An Act in Relation to . . . ," 1893, p. 1748).

Despite their successes in the Northeast, however, the advocates of civil privatism were neither unopposed nor universally successful. Outside the Northeast, public rather than private institutions continued to be the preferred vehicle for delivering cultural, educational, health, and social services (Ely, 1894).

Despite opposition and criticism, private philanthropy and the use of private charitable corporations grew enormously in the last decades of the nineteenth century. Big business and private wealth underwrote the growth of universities, libraries, hospitals, museums, social welfare organizations, professional societies, and private clubs. At the same time, the middle and lower classes supported labor unions, mutual benefit societies, fraternal organizations, volunteer fire companies, building and loan associations, and even cooperatively owned nonprofit businesses. Growing awareness of urban poverty among the middle and upper classes encouraged the establishment of charitable organizations of every sort, ranging from traditional funds for the relief of the sick, poor, and disabled to new forms of nonprofit activity, such as the settlement houses and charity organization societies (Bremner, 1956, 1980; Davis, 1967; Huggins, 1971; Katz, 1986). With the rise of the "social gospel," Protestant churches, which had until the 1860s restricted themselves primarily to spiritual matters, became active in charitable affairs and in social, economic, and political reform efforts (Cross, 1967; Smith-Rosenberg, 1971). And a host of nonpartisan organizations promoting good government, civil service reform, and economic development became actively involved in the political process.

No less important than the private organizations directed to the reform of society was the rise of new kinds of cultural organizations whose primary constituencies were the well-to-do. The establishment and professionalization of museums and symphony orchestras (as well as the growth of the academic specialties that legitimated their activities) played a major role in recasting the nature of urban culture, transforming the market for artistic products, and reshaping the identity of the nation's upper classes (Fox, 1963; Horowitz, 1976; McCarthy, 1982; DiMaggio, 1986, 1990; Bender, 1987).

By the 1880s, charitable activity itself became subject to the trend toward rationalization that was affecting business, as reformers attempted to make benevolence more effective through the creation of charity organization societies and state charity commissions, which oversaw the administration of public and private charitable activities (Warner, 1908; Katz, 1986).

While social and economic turbulence increased in the last quarter of the nineteenth century—and along with it criticism of business, the wealthy, and the institutions they supported—so too did the intensity of efforts by the propertied classes to deal with these problems. Andrew Carnegie was the most influential and articulate promoter of new ideas about philanthropy (Wall, 1970). A series of essays written in the late 1880s stated a new doctrine of benevolence, which was based on an acknowledgment of the extent to which industrialism had altered fundamental assumptions about political and economic life. The concentration of wealth and power in the hands of a few was, in Carnegie's view, the inevitable consequence of advanced industrial development. This process, which advanced to the forefront men "with a genius for affairs," was not a bad thing as long as the process did not become "clogged by layers of prescription" (Carnegie, 1886a).

If capitalism were to be self-renewing, means must be created to ensure that traditional equality of condition, which was no longer possible in the industrial setting, be replaced by equality of opportunity. This involved not only confiscatory taxation — which in ensuring that great fortunes could not be passed on, would prevent the formation of classes — but also proactive philanthropy, which would ensure the continuation of the competitive processes that underlay the progress of the race. "The best means of benefiting the community," Carnegie urged his fellow millionaires, "is to place within its reach the ladders upon which the aspiring can rise" (Carnegie, 1889, p. 663).

At the same time, Carnegie attacked traditional charity, which not only failed to get at the root causes of poverty, but which actually perpetuated it. "It were better for mankind that the millions of the rich were thrown into the sea," Carnegie wrote, "than so spent as to encourage the slothful, the drunken, the unworthy. Of every thousand dollars spent in so-called charity today, it is probable that nine hundred and fifty dollars is unwisely spent — so spent, indeed, as to produce the very evils which it hopes to mitigate or cure" (1889, p. 661). In Carnegie's view, the responsibility for remedying the evils of the industrial economy lay with those who had created it — the "men with a genius for affairs," who, if the system were to survive, had to be willing to wisely administer their wealth, devoting it to "institutions of various kinds, which will improve the general condition of the people; in this manner returning their surplus wealth to the mass of their fellows in the forms best calculated to do them lasting good" (1889, p. 663).

As sensible as Carnegie's ideas seemed to many of his contemporaries, the means of carrying them out were not immediately apparent. At first, he and those he influenced, like John D. Rockefeller, tried parcelling out their fortunes to particular kinds of institutions — libraries, churches, universities. But these rather traditional objects were not suited to addressing problems faced by American society at the turn of the century. Nor did they solve the dilemmas of fortunes that were accumulating more quickly than they could be given away. Addressing these problems would require a new kind of charitable instrument — the grant-making foundation.

Carnegie and his contemporaries proceeded cautiously in moving toward the foundation form (Karl and Katz, 1981b). Although some states permitted great latitude to the founders of charitable trusts, others, like New

York, imposed restrictions on charitable donors. In addition, the hostile political climate encouraged the wealthy to be cautious about creating new charitable instruments. It is perhaps for this reason that credit for establishing the first foundation of the modern type—an open-ended endowment devoted "to the good of mankind," which carried out its charitable purposes by giving money to institutions rather than operating them, and which entrusted decision making to staffs of experts—went not to "robber barons" like Carnegie or Rockefeller, but to a lesser-known figure, Margaret Olivia Slocum Sage. The controversy surrounding the Rockefeller Foundation exemplified the suspicions that many Americans had about the wealthy and their philanthropic intentions (Fosdick, 1952). Despite Rockefeller's willingness to have his $100 million foundation run by a publicly appointed board, it was denounced by leading Americans of every political stripe (Collier and Horowitz, 1976).

The new foundations, particularly Sage and Rockefeller, were unusual, both in the broad discretion granted their trustees and in their explicit goals of reforming social, economic, and political life. These lofty ends were to be achieved not by direct political action, but by studying conditions, making findings available to influential citizens, and by mobilizing public opinion to bring about change. This relationship between academic experts, influential private groups, and government would become the paradigm of a new kind of political process—one based on policy rather than politics (Lagemann, 1989; Karl and Katz, 1981a, 1987; Smith, 1991). These relationships were fostered through the creation of operating foundations like the Brookings Institution (1916), and the Twentieth Century Fund (1919), which address themselves directly to public policy questions. Foundation-supported intermediary organizations like the National Research Council, the Social Science Research Council, the American Council of Learned Societies, and the National Bureau of Economic Research became important players in the public policy process. And grants to universities had a profound impact on the growth of new disciplines capable of engaging the social, economic, and political challenges of the new urban and industrial order (Laski, 1930; Karl, 1969, 1976; Alchon, 1985; Katz, 1985).

Foundations were not the only new charitable instruments to be created as the new century began. While the grant-making entities created by Sage, Carnegie, and Rockefeller enabled very wealthy individuals to affect society, other entities—the community chest and the community foundation—served to democratize philanthropy. Created with the intention of broadening the base of charitable giving and, at the same time, ensuring that funds went to organizations that genuinely served their communities, the first community chest was established in Cleveland, Ohio, in 1913 (Cutlip, 1965; Hall, 1989). The following year, Clevelanders organized the first community foundation, a device which, by placing charitable trusts under central management, enabled persons of relatively modest means to establish such funds (Hammack, 1989; Magat, 1989).

Thus, despite controversy, in the early decades of the twentieth century, a paradigm for the resolution of the nation's social and economic problems began to take shape. Large bureaucratic institutions guided by scientifically trained experts would be the most efficient mechanisms for achieving the social, economic, and political goals of reform. To sustain democratic and Christian traditions, Americans were urged to become "efficient instruments" of the national purpose by accepting large hierarchical organizations, specialization, and inherent inequality of condition (Croly, 1909). These institutions would substitute for equality of condition equality of opportunity and, suffused with an ethos of service, would invest social, economic, and political life with a sense of common purpose. The new order would take the form of a moral equivalent of war, in which individuals attained their positions according to ability and talent and in which differentials of position and power, as well as high degrees of specialization and interdependence, would become recognized as essential to the pursuit of collective goals. World War I crystallized these possibilities.

"Government by People Outside of Government," 1900–1935

Mobilization for World War I was an experiment in public-private partnership. Even before American entry into the war, the preparedness movement was training elite businessmen and professionals as officers, while the Red Cross, the American Friends Service Committee, and other private groups were operating ambulance corps to assist the British, Canadian, and French armies. Once the United States entered the war, industrial production, transportation, food, finance, and other crucial domains were coordinated by quasi-public bodies staffed by "dollar-a-year" men—volunteers from big businesses. The war provided the impetus for national fundraising efforts: the community chest was transformed from a midwestern oddity to a national charitable force, while the Red Cross energetically solicited private corporations and individuals.

The war experience provided the basis for more ambitious—and less contentious—attempts to combine public and private initiative. The leader of this effort was Herbert Hoover, a millionaire mining engineer turned public servant, who, as administrator of European food relief during and after the war, had seen the horrors of social upheaval firsthand. Hoover's book, *American Individualism* (1922), which set forth his vision of a "New Era," summarized the previous half-century of social thought by business reformers (Heald, 1970; Hawley, 1974, 1977; Johnson, 1983, pp. 203–260). Beginning with a candid acknowledgment of the "great inequalities and injustices" caused by modern industry, Hoover believed that equality of opportunity, combined with an ethos of service and cooperation that acknowledged the interdependence of all Americans, could lead to a new social and economic order.

Accepting the post of secretary of commerce from President Harding, Hoover strove through the 1920s to implement his vision of "self-government by the people outside of government." This effort, based on "voluntary co-operation within the community," was extolled as the best means of perfecting the social organizations, caring for those in distress, and advancing knowledge, scientific research, education, and, most important, economic life (Hoover, 1922, pp. 4–5). In this "associative state," government would act as umpire and nexus for the exchange of information, using "promotional conferences, expert enquiries, and cooperating committees" rather than legal coercion or arbitrary controls. "Like the private groupings to which it was tied," government agencies "would be staffed by men of talent, vision, and expertise, and committed to nourishing individualism and local initiative rather than supplanting them" (Hawley, 1977, pp. 132–133).

Hoover's ideas formed the basis for the first phase of Franklin Roosevelt's New Deal, the National Recovery Administration (NRA), which was in its essentials, a formalization of the voluntaristic and associational relationship between business, charity, and government that Hoover had built during the 1920s. Intended to revive industrial and business activity and to reduce unemployment, the NRA was based on the principle of industrial self-regulation, operating under government supervision through a system of fair competition codes. Based on the fair trade codes that had been developed by associationists under Hoover's leadership, these collective security arrangements were designed to prevent wage and price cutting, which in turn would enable corporations to maintain employment levels and intrafirm benefits packages, and to support nonprofit welfare agencies.

Even with the NRA, the resources of the private sector were inadequate to the massive challenges of the Great Depression. The economic crisis of the thirties was national and international in scope, while most foundations and private social welfare agencies operated on a local level. In the end, their dependence on business proved to be a handicap rather than an advantage, for the business of the corporations was to make money. When pressed, welfare and benefits programs were often the first areas in which savings were sought by cost cutters. Some firms acted very quickly both to curtail benefits programs and to lay off workers, while others struggled to maintain their commitments to their employees. But ultimately, as Bethlehem Steel's Charles Schwab admitted, "None of us can escape the inexorable law of the balance sheet" (Brody, 1980, p. 73).

As the inadequacies of the private sector grew more evident, the federal government turned increasingly to direct action. Nevertheless, private charitable enterprise remained important. Private think tanks like the Brookings Institution played a vital role in helping to draft new public initiatives like the Social Security Act. The big foundations underwrote research of vital importance to the framing of the emerging welfare state. And, on the local level, private charities served as important conduits for public assistance. Despite his rhetorical assaults on "economic royalists," Roosevelt did not entirely rule out a charitable role for big business (Heald, 1970). While New Deal legislation dramatically increased the tax burden for corporations and for the wealthy, it also provided major incentives for large-scale giving. These incentives were further enhanced in 1943, when income taxation became universal.

Nonprofits and the Welfare State, 1950–1990

Although conventional wisdom has suggested that the expanding scope and scale of government discouraged the growth of private nonprofit enterprise, it appears that big government actually fueled explosive growth in the population of charitable tax-exempt organizations. Numbering only 12,500 in 1940 and 50,000 in 1950, by 1967, there were 309,000 secular nonprofits; by 1977, there were 790,000, and by 1989, just under a million—an eighty-fold increase in forty years.[1] (By contrast, the number of business corporations during the same period increased from 473,000 to 3,000,000—a mere sevenfold increase). Government policies played a crucial role in the growth, not only indirectly through creating incentives to individuals and firms for contributing to private organizations serving governmental ends, but also directly, through grants and contracts (Webber and Wildavsky, 1986, pp. 494ff). By the 1970s, it was estimated that direct government support to charitable tax-exempt organizations ranged from 35 percent to 55 percent of total annual revenues (Salamon, 1987, pp. 29–49). In retrospect, it seems quite clear that the American welfare state, rather than involving the elaboration of a vast bureaucracy concerned with delivering cultural, educational, health, and social services, encouraged the development of a private infrastructure to implement its purposes.

The interplay of forces in the creation of this distinctly Americanized version of the welfare state was extraordinarily complex. Changes in foreign policy, economic philosophy, tax and budgeting practices, legal doctrines, conceptions of the social role of corporations, and demographic factors all played important roles. First, the war and postwar years internationalized the outlook of Americans, not only bringing into sharp focus the confrontation between the capitalist democracies and totalitarianism but also underlining the need for altering the ways in which the nation would find revenues to sustain its role as the free world's political and economic leader. Traditionally—except in wartime—government spending had been limited by the amount of available revenues. The urgent tasks of maintaining international security and domestic economic stability and of keeping the country poised for military mobilization altered this relationship. As policy commitments replaced available revenues as the foundation of the federal budgetary process, Keynesian economic theory pointed to the ways in which taxing, spending, and borrowing could be used to influence the economic activities from which government drew its revenues. The highly progressive tax rates of the postwar years were accompanied by loopholes that encouraged the transfer of private resources into activities—for-profit and nonprofit—that government economic planners deemed necessary to the national purpose.

The introduction of tax policies designed to channel the enormous post-war increases in individual and corporate income into savings, investment, and charitable giving coincided with the aging of the founders of many of America's great twentieth-century industrial fortunes. This produced an enormous increase in the number and importance of foundations. Numbering only 203 in 1929, the population of foundations with assets exceeding a million dollars grew to 2,058 by 1959—with the vast majority of these established within the decade. In 1929, their assets represented only 10.7 percent of the total property controlled by charitable tax-exempt organizations; by 1973, their share was 21.7 percent (Wood, Struthers & Company, 1932, p. 6; Andrews, 1950, p. 70; Copeland, 1977, pp. 143–155; Odendahl, 1986). According to most commentators, this growth was a response to steeply progressive income and estate taxes. Foundations enabled the wealthy to avoid taxation while maintaining control of their enterprises (MacDonald, 1956, pp. 36ff; Nielsen, 1972).

The growing importance of foundations established by business wealth was accompanied by changes in the corporations' understanding of their place in the polity. World War II encouraged closer ties between business and government. Despite some wariness, the prospect of the United States as the dominant world power sustained the public-private partnership that developed during the war. Surely a major factor in this was the parallel growth of foreign policy activism in government and the internationalist orientation of business. The growing influence of Keynesian economic thought also helped business and government leaders to recognize their common stake in domestic and international economic stability. Pax Americana transformed the federal government into the largest single consumer of the nation's goods and services and into the undisputed controller of the country's economic life—facts that could not be ignored by managers concerned with stability and with reliable short-term returns on investment.

Government's assumption of a central role in national economic, social, and political stabilization—the planning function that had previously been assumed by a coalition of private groups—proved to be increasingly acceptable to the business community, both as it became apparent that America's struggle with the Soviet Union would be a long-term commitment requiring a high degree of national unity and as Dwight David Eisenhower's probusiness administration allayed fears about Washington's leftward drift. The acceptability of the enlarged federal role was further enhanced by the fact that it remained dependent on universities, foundations, think tanks, and business groups like the Business Advisory Council, the Conference Board, the Committee for Economic Development, and the Business Roundtable. These organizations, which promoted active public service by business managers and academic experts, became the basis for a privatized policy establishment (Mills, 1956; Domhoff, 1967, 1970; Burch, 1981).

The federal government's ties to nonprofit enterprise paralleled its ties to big business, as government dollars became the largest source of revenues for charitable tax-exempt organizations in the fields of culture, education, health, and social welfare. Beginning in the early 1940s, when basic and applied research became crucial to the war effort, government became the largest single contributor to the incomes of private universities. This role became permanent in the postwar effort to defend the peace and with the establishment of the National Science Foundation and the National Institutes of Health, all of which made grants on a massive scale to private hospitals and universities. The passage of the GI Bill in 1944 and its renewal in 1952, together with the 1958 National Defense Education Act, provided massive indirect subsidies to private institutions through federal underwriting of student aid. The Hospital Construction Act of 1945 and the postwar encouragement of the growth of private nonprofit health insurance plans transformed the federal government into a major actor in the health care field, though still acting largely through the organizations of the private sector (Starr, 1982; Fox, 1986; Stevens, 1989). Federal funding of charitable tax-exempt institutions grew still further in the 1960s, with the intensification of international rivalries in arms and space exploration and with the War on Poverty.

Inventing the Nonprofit Sector, 1950–1980

A combination of factors led legislators to take notice of the proliferation of charitable tax-exempt organizations by the early 1950s. The universalization of income taxation and high tax rates during the Korean War increased congressional sensitivity to individuals and institutions taking advantage of tax "loopholes." The press did its part in calling attention to these in its reportage of the settlement of the Ford estate, as well as a series of scandalous — though technically legal — arrangements between business, foundations, and universities that exempted their earnings from taxation. Although most charitable tax-exempt organizations were apolitical, a few — notably large foundations like Ford, Carnegie, and Rockefeller — were either identified with liberal causes such as civil rights or with internationalist foreign policy initiatives to which many conservatives, Republican and Democrat, took exception. Finally, a broad range of private institutions became the targets of politicians who were building their careers on rooting out communist subversion.

In April of 1952, the Select (Cox) Committee of the House of Representatives began an investigation of "educational and philanthropic foundations and other comparable organizations which are exempt from federal taxation to determine whether they were using their resources for the purposes for which they were established, and especially to determine which such foundations and organizations are using their resources for un-American and subversive activities or for purposes not in the interest or tradition of the United States" (Select Committee, 1953, p. 1). The committee heard testimony from a host of witnesses, ranging from professional anti-communists through foundation and university leaders. Its final report, submitted to Congress in January of 1953, ringingly endorsed the loyalty of the foundations. "So far as we can ascertain," it declared, "there is little basis for the belief expressed in some quarters that foundation funds are being diverted from their intended use" (Select Committee, 1953, p. 6). It concluded by recommending better public reporting and a reexamination of pertinent tax laws to encourage private individuals to make greater gifts to "these meritorious institutions" (p. 13).

Unhappy with the Cox Committee's conclusions, Congressman B. Carroll Reece pushed for a continuation of its work. In April of 1954, the House authorized the Special Committee to Investigate Tax-Exempt Foundations and Comparable Organizations (the Reece Committee). Unlike its predecessor, which limited its attention to generalities, the Reece Committee mounted a comprehensive enquiry into both the motives for establishing foundations and their influence on public life. Areas of interest included the use of foundations as mechanisms of tax avoidance and dynastic control, their influence on the social sciences, their power to influence public opinion and policy through selective patronage of academic research, failures of fiduciary responsibility, the rising power of foundation bureaucrats, foundation influence on the press and broadcasting, and, last but not least, the foundations' role in promoting internationalist foreign policy and supporting subversive activities.

While the Reece Committee, after lengthy proceedings, found philanthropy blameless of supporting communism, they challenged traditional American institutions in a more profound and disturbing way: vast private fortunes, preserved by being incorporated as perpetual charitable trusts and in which donors retained considerable control, were administered by a "guild" of managers—the "philanthropoids"—who used their power to control research, education, and the media. Their influence over government involved not only control of the information on which the public and politicians based their actions but also control of the experts who advised and implemented public policy. Though the foundations' promotion of internationalism and moral relativism concerned the committee, the more central threat, in its view, involved the simple fact of concentrated power. Even if benign, it posed a threat to democratic government (Special Committee, 1954, pp. 1–14).

Generally dismissed as an artifact of McCarthyism, the Reece Committee's report raised serious questions about the proliferation of charitable tax-exempt organizations, the lack of government oversight and regulation of their activities, and the extent to which they served private rather than public interests. Most important, the report underscored both the lack of knowledge about the tax-exempt universe and its vulnerability to future regulatory efforts.

Mindful of these issues, foundation leaders set about preparing for future congressional assaults by trying to create a public record of their activities (Andrews, 1973, pp. 131ff). Initiatives took several forms. In 1955, the Ford Foundation made its first grants to encourage scholarly investigations of the role of philanthropy in American life (*Report of the Princeton Conference*, 1956). In the same year, the Carnegie Corporation and the Russell Sage Foundation began planning the establishment of "a new organization [which] would be a strategic gathering place for knowledge about foundations"—the Foundation Library Center. The Center's activities included the publication of a comprehensive directory of foundations and a bimonthly magazine, *Foundation News* (Andrews, 1973, pp. 175–194).

These modest efforts encountered resistance in the philanthropic community. While Carnegie and Russell Sage took the lead, other foundations, large and small, were reluctant to support the Foundation Center, fearing that public knowledge of their activities would only fuel public hostility. Nonetheless, the center, under F. Emerson Andrews' leadership, succeeded in creating an institutional basis for the growth of self-awareness among charitable tax-exempt organizations. This would ultimately lead not only to the establishment of agencies that could more effectively defend the interests of foundations but also to a thoroughgoing reconceptualization of the place of these organizations in the democratic polity.

These efforts came none too soon. In July of 1959, the Senate Finance Committee recommended a liberalization of tax code provisions affecting unlimited deductions for charitable contributions. A minority on the committee—which included senators Russell Long, Albert Gore, Eugene McCarthy, and Clinton Anderson—issued a sharply worded report charging that "this bill is designed specifically to encourage a proliferation of foundations which would be established by individuals and families." "The tax base is being dangerously eroded by many forces," the minority warned, "among them tax-exempt trusts and foundations. Not only is the tax base being eroded, but even more harmful social and political consequences may result from concentrating, and holding in a few hands and in perpetuity, control over large fortunes and business enterprises. The attendant inequities resulting from the tax treatment of contributions, particularly in the form of capital, to foundations are being magnified daily."

Noting that 87 percent of the 13,000 foundations had been created since 1940 and that approximately 1,200 new ones were being created every year, the minority report warned that "at present rates of establishment, substantial control of our economy may soon rest in the 'dead hands' of such organizations." The minority report urged that "the social, political, and economic implications of the growth of foundations should be thoroughly studied," underlining the dangers of wealth "removed from ostensible ownership and from the free choices presented by the marketplace and by the democratic processes of a free government, free economy, and a free society" (U.S. Senate, 1961, pp. 7–8).

In May of 1961, Texas Congressman Wright Patman took up the challenge suggested by the minority report, taking the floor of the House to deliver a series of speeches on foundations and other tax-exempt organizations (Sherill, 1969). Over the course of the decade, Patman directed a steady stream of highly publicized criticism at philanthropy.[2] Though touching on many aspects of foundation activity, the central theme was discontent with the fundamental inequities of the tax system.

Through the sixties, Patman's concerns came to be shared by a number of economists and tax policy experts in the Department of the Treasury, who were beginning to question unexamined assumptions about the efficiency of the current tax system, particularly with regard to the charitable deduction. The Department of Treasury's report on foundations, issued in 1965, recommended major changes in the rules governing foundations, including prohibitions against business dealings between donors and foundations, limits on foundations' control of voting in businesses they controlled, restrictions on the deductibility of donor-controlled gifts, and regulation of the number of years donors and their families could sit on governing boards (Treasury Department, 1965; U.S. House, Committee on Ways and Means, 1965; "Treasury Report," 1965, p. 29; Myers, 1965, pp. 51–54). These concerns attracted increasing attention in the late 1960s, as rising taxes and inflation increased public tax sensitivity and stimulated new demands for tax reform.[3] In response, Congress began hearings on tax-exempt organizations in February of 1969.

In their appearances before Congress, leaders of the big foundations were unanimous in their opposition to any form of increased regulation.[4] They dismissed reported abuses of the tax exemption, defended the "honored place" of foundations, and warned that governmental control would "have far reaching and extremely dangerous consequences for the American pluralistic system." In their testimony, foundation leaders not only misjudged the level of congressional concern, but, more seriously, failed to grasp the fundamental shift in the language and concepts of public policy which framed it.

The 1969 Tax Reform Act, as finally passed, proved to be far less draconian than many had feared. Though comprehensive, the bill was also unclear in many areas. It would take several years for the Congress, the Treasury Department, and officials of tax-exempt organizations to negotiate what the bill really meant and how it was to be applied.[5] More than anything else, the act again underlined the urgent need for more knowledge about the rapidly growing tax-exempt universe. Further, it made painfully clear that quoting Tocqueville to Congress would no longer serve as an effective defense; the defenders of organized philanthropy would have to learn the technical language of law and economics that had become the language of public policy.

John D. Rockefeller III was one of the few philanthropic leaders to recognize how significantly philanthropy had changed since the war. He urged philanthropy and government to work together to reevaluate the place of foundations in modern society.[6] Rockefeller's call for a public-private partnership in the drafting policies affecting "private initiative in the public interest" acknowledged the complexities and uncertainties of the relationship between government and the private sectors that had developed since the war. At the same time, he recognized the unprecedented proliferation of voluntary organizations and was moving toward suggesting that they constituted a "second American Revolution" (Rockefeller, 1973).

The current hostility to foundations and other tax-exempt organizations did not end with the passage of the 1969 Tax Reform. Through the early seventies, Congress and the Treasury Department continued to joust with organized philanthropy (Suhrke, 1972, 1973a). In the fall of 1973, the Subcommittee on Foundations of the Senate Finance Committee, chaired by Indiana's Vance Hartke, began a series of "panel discussions" on the issue (Suhrke, 1973b). Hartke was outspokenly hostile and disdainful to foundation representatives. His only positive comments came in response to the suggestion that a national commission on philanthropy be formed to gather reliable information about foundations.

Unknown to most of the foundation world, steps were already under way to do just that — and then some. During the 1969 congressional hearings, John D. Rockefeller III had formulated the Commission on Foundations and Private Philanthropy (the Peterson Commission) — a group of prominent citizens who, with staff support, undertook a survey of foundations and their activities.[7] The Commission's most important contribution was to broaden thinking about philanthropy beyond foundations. It acknowledged that private initiative included not only grantmakers, but a broad range of voluntary groups supported by a mix of public and private funds. From the government's standpoint, this was hardly a startling insight: tax law treated all charitable tax-exempt organizations, donors and donees, as a unified class, even though it made increasingly elaborate regulatory distinctions between different types of agencies. But, in the context of the ways in which philanthropy had conceived of its tasks, it was very new indeed.

Soon after the Peterson Commission disbanded, Rockefeller and his associates initiated conversations with Congressman Wilbur Mills, Treasury Department officials, and others, with regard to convening "a group of knowledgeable and concerned individuals to review and make recommendations in regard to tax incentives in the philanthropic field" and other matters relating to the well-being of "the whole private nonprofit sector."[8] Mills's positive response led to organization of a Committee on Tax Incentives, with Rockefeller's support, under the direction of Rockefeller's associate Datus Smith and Washington tax lawyer Leonard Silverstein.[9]

Scholarship played a key role in reframing ideas about philanthropy in ways that addressed public policy concerns. The 501(c)(3) Group, a loose network of tax lawyers and top officials of national donee organizations — to which Silverstein and Smith belonged — began searching for economists interested in studying charitable giving.[10] Eventually, they found Harvard professor Martin S. Feldstein, who had done important work on the economics of health care in the 1960s. Early in 1973, Feldstein was retained to conduct a general analysis of the rationale of the current tax treatment and its effects on private philanthropy.

Feldstein found strong connections between tax incentives and giving and suggested a compelling and credible rationale for the tax treatment of nonprofits; in this, his work accelerated the efforts of Rockefeller's Committee on Tax Incentives. By the end of the summer of 1973, the committee had been reorganized as a joint effort supported by Congress, the Treasury Department, and the private sector. A prestigious group was empaneled — exquisitely balanced in terms of geographical origins, party affiliation, gender, race, occupation, and religion — under the chairmanship of John Filer, a corporate lawyer and corporate executive officer of Aetna insurance company.[11] This group, aided by a distinguished panel of experts including economists, sociologists, tax attorneys, and specialists in nongovernmental organizations, was given a broad mandate to examine policy considerations respecting the present system of incentives to private philanthropic giving, issues relating to the treatment of private contributors, methods of supervising, regulating, and classifying charitable institutions, and alternatives to existing philanthropic institutions and practices.

Although many in the world of philanthropy privately questioned the work of the Filer Commission, its efforts could not be ignored. Its comprehensive multidisciplinary survey of every aspect of charitable tax-exempt organizations described and analyzed the role of nonprofits as employers, as sources of essential health, educational, welfare, and cultural services, and as forces in political life. It also carefully considered the regulatory and tax issues affecting their well-being. Most important, the commission's work gave substance to what, up to then, had been only an idea: that charitable tax-exempt organizations comprised a coherent and cohesive "sector" of American political, economic, and social life. This unified conception of nonprofits as part of a "Third," "Independent," or "nonprofit" — or, as the commission preferred to call it, "voluntary" — sector lay the groundwork for establishing organizations that could give unified expression to common interests. The results of the Filer Commission's work were published by the Department of the Treasury in seven weighty volumes in 1977.[12]

Although the commission's recommendation of the establishment of a permanent agency — modeled on the British Charities Commission — within the Department of Treasury failed to materialize, other means were quickly devised to promote the idea that all charitable tax-exempt organizations, regardless of the particular activities in which they were engaged, constituted a coherent and cohesive "sector." Undiscouraged, a group of Filer Commission veterans worked to organize a private group, INDEPENDENT SECTOR (IS), to serve as a "common meeting ground" for all elements and all viewpoints within the charitable universe, to gather information about the sector, and to represent its interests to the public (Coalition, 1979; INDEPENDENT SECTOR, 1980).

Nonprofits in the Postliberal Era

The formation of IS was an effort to institutionalize the idea that all charitable tax-exempt organizations were part of a distinctive and coherent domain of organizations — to, in effect, invent the nonprofit sector. Overlooking the enormous diversity in what nonprofits did and how they did it, IS sought to recruit a membership that would cut across industry lines, to represent to the public the distinctive attributes of nonprofit enterprise, and to promote research focused on the commonalities linking nonprofits and the public policies that would favor its growth. IS also became the most active promoter of programs devoted to the professional training of managers for nonprofit organizations.

IS's efforts received a boost from the election of Ronald Reagan. The new president, who proclaimed himself a friend of private initiative, set about increasing the responsibilities of private sector initiatives by proposing cutbacks in federal spending and encouraging localities and voluntary groups to "take up the slack." Both Reagan and his successor, George Bush, promoted efforts to stimulate higher levels of private giving and voluntary commitment — Reagan through his Task Force on Private Initiatives and Bush through his "Thousand Points of Light" initiative (President's Task Force on Private Sector Initiatives, 1982a, 1982b; *Corporate Community Involvement,* 1982; Olasky, 1983). Ironically, all of these efforts, which were framed by a belief that the nation's nonprofits were primarily supported by individual and corporate giving and by the labor of volunteers, utterly failed to grasp the changes that had swept the nonprofit sector over the previous thirty years.

The reality was that by 1980, government itself was the largest single source of nonprofit revenues and that the Reagan budget proposals, if implemented, would cripple the very organizations the President hoped to strengthen (Salamon and Abramson, 1981). Not only were nonprofits far less dependent on donated revenues than generally supposed, a large and growing proportion of these "charitable tax-exempt" entities were not directed to traditional charitable, educational, or religious purposes. They were essentially commercial enterprises, often operating in competition with for-profit firms, but by the grace of the tax code, they enjoyed the benefits of tax exemption (Hansmann, 1980; Weisbrod, 1988).

If the organizations comprising the nonprofit sector in 1980 bore little resemblance to traditional donative charitable entities, a variety of forces over the course of the next ten years pushed them even further from common stereotypes. Even organizations that had resembled traditional charities before the Reagan era were compelled by a combination of federal budget cuts, weakened tax incentives for giving, and economic uncertainties, to move away from dependence on donations and toward a variety of earned-income strategies. At the same time, fundraising itself became enormously more sophisticated, as technological advances made it possible for some organizations to use direct mail and telemarketing techniques on an unprecedented scale.

Negotiating the increasingly challenging financial and regulatory environments of the 1980s and employing sophisticated administrative and technological strategies naturally required far higher levels of expertise than volunteers could muster. Although some nonprofit industries, such as education and health care, had been professionally managed for decades, by the end of the Reagan era, professionalization had penetrated every area in which nonprofits operated, including religion. Although managerial professionalization often improved organizational performance, it also tended to diminish the role of boards of trustees and other groups of volunteers on which organizations had traditionally depended for support.

Whatever commonalities nonprofits may have shared at the beginning of the Reagan era were further eroded over the decade by the differential impact of public policies, economic forces, and strategic adaptations on the various nonprofit industries. Nowhere was this more evident than in the field of health care, where federal policies both promoted an astronomical escalation in health care costs and encouraged the evolution of new organizational forms to handle the health care burden. Because government had made health care a potential source of profits, many hospitals either became for-profit companies or found themselves competing with such firms. Many hospitals accommodated to the new environment by restructuring themselves as hybrid organizations, integrating for-profit and nonprofit components. By the end of the 1980s, economic pressures had forced almost all small voluntary hospitals out of existence. And though the surviving nonprofit hospitals continued to consider themselves as charitable enterprises, only a tiny fraction of their income came from donations and they provided a diminishing amount of services to the needy.

Human and social services followed a very different path. A combination of federal and state policies, undergirded by court decisions ordering the deinstitutionalization of the disabled, promoted the privatization of social and human services (Gronbjerg, 1991a, 1991b; Stone, 1992; Lipsky and Smith, 1993). This led to the growth of an enormous nonprofit human services industry that was entirely dependent on various forms of government funding. In one state, the industry was structured around a single firm—a nonprofit holding company that owned real estate and provided financial services for more than two hundred provider agencies. The company was governed by an insider board composed of executive directors of provider agencies and advocacy groups—with no public representation. Operating in every one of the state's municipalities, the political clout wielded by this organization was such that it could extract hundreds of millions of dollars from the legislature annually—and could mobilize thousands of supporters on the rare occasions that its interests were threatened. With huge amounts of money being dispensed with a minimum of oversight, such privatized human services enterprises carried with them an enormous potential for corruption and client abuse.

While federal dollars became less available to most nonprofits during the Reagan era, presidential jawboning brought forth unprecedented amounts of corporate funds. Some of this money was distributed through traditional philanthrophic vehicles, such as company foundations. But most of it, reflecting the public relations and marketing concerns of donor firms, tended to go to high-profile programs — to the arts and to athletic events — that enhanced corporate visibility. Cause-related marketing, involving tie-ins between the sale of products and contributions to nonprofit organizations, became an increasingly important part of corporate "giving" during the 1980s. Businesses also began to make major commitments to education reform, both through traditional grants and through more innovative programs in which companies "adopted" public schools or sent executives into classrooms as mentors.

The increasing involvement of business in nonprofit activity was part of a broader phenomenon of vastly greater public participation and support (Bailey, 1990; Independent Sector, 1990). Before the 1960s, support and guidance for nonprofits tended to be exercised by small groups of established community leaders, most of whom were male, Protestant, and northern European in origin. The availability of higher education and economic growth in the decades following the Second World War fueled large-scale social mobility, propelling non–northern European and non-Protestants into positions of leadership in business, politics, and the nonprofit sector. They brought with them a variety of new perspectives on communities, their needs, and how best to meet them. Client groups have also become more vocal, demanding both a voice in shaping organizational policies and representation on governing boards.

At the same time, mergers, buyouts, and the decline of older manufacturing industries transformed local economies across the country. By 1990, the core businesses in American communities were less likely to be locally owned than they had been a generation earlier — and top executives were less likely to have enduring ties to the communities in which they worked. This does not appear to have diminished the willingness of executives to serve and support nonprofits. Indeed, board service, like corporate contributions, had become very much a part of contemporary corporate culture (Useem, 1984; Galaskiewicz, 1985). But it did tend to alter the standards by which nonprofits were managed and their degree of commitment to communities and their traditions.

The increasing diversity of backgrounds and viewpoints of community leaders produced major tensions within organizations like United Way, which had, in the past, been able to set communities' charitable agendas. United Way's monopoly on workplace giving was challenged by employees who demanded greater control of the use of their donations and by other federated giving campaigns which supported less conventional causes and programs (Polivy, 1982, 1988; Millar, 1989, Brilliant, 1990). Diversity also produced conflict among board members and between boards and managers over organizational missions, goals, and strategies. This has fueled growing attention to the recruitment, training, and counseling of nonprofit boards (Hall, 1992).

Summary

In the 1980s, nonprofits finally achieved the centrality they had always claimed to hold. As the nation's fastest growing organizational domain, they touched the lives of almost all Americans — as donors, as board members, as employees, as clients, as consumers, as citizens. But the price of success was increasing public scrutiny.

There had always been scandals in the world of charity but, like the charities themselves, they had generally had no more than a local impact. But with the enormous growth in the scope, scale, and resources of some nonprofit enterprises during the 1980s and 1990s, they attracted national attention. The Covenant House scandal, in which the founder-CEO had misused the organization's funds and sexually abused its clients; the United Way scandal, which set in motion a national outcry over the perks and pay of nonprofit executives; an assortment of scandals involving televangelists who had misused their organizations' nonprofit status for personal gain; scandals involving Blue Cross organizations in several states — all served to erode the credibility of nonprofits and to attract journalistic and legislative scrutiny.

At the same time, the financial pressures on states and municipalities produced a decreasing willingness to accept nonprofits' claims of devotion to public service at face value. In a number of states, legislatures passed laws attempting to regulate charitable fundraising. In others, local authorities successfully challenged the tax exemptions of nonprofits. In 1985, the Pennsylvania Supreme Court imposed a "charitableness test," which made the tax exemptions of nonprofit hospitals contingent on demonstrable services to the communities in which they were located (*West Allegheny Hospital*, 1982; *Hospital Utilization Project*, 1985). Efforts to expand this test to other forms of nonprofit activity have achieved some success and, as financial pressures on localities increase, it seems likely to be applied in other states.

While it is probable that nonprofit enterprise will continue to grow and flourish in the future, it seems inevitable that as this happens, legal, regulatory, and popular conceptions of charity and philanthropy will have to painfully adjust to the rapidly changing realities of what nonprofits are, what they do, and how they conduct their activities. Nonprofits also will have to confront and shed many illusions about themselves — particularly the notion that their high purposes exempt them from responsibilities as corporate citizens — and, very likely, they will have to concede to public demands for greater accountability.

The challenge of increasing domestic responsibilities for nonprofits is matched by the internationalization of nonprofit activity. Although American nonprofits have for decades been active in international relief and development, these activities have been matched or exceeded by the proliferation of indigenous nongovernmental organizations in the Third World. At the same time, the collapse of communism in the U.S.S.R. and Eastern Europe has opened new vistas to those who see nonprofits as an essential component of the effort to construct market economies and political democracies. The European community is also making major commitments to policies that will favor the growth of nongovernmental organizations (James, 1989; Hodgkinson, 1990; Joseph, 1989; Bailey, 1989; Greene, 1989).

For nonprofits, the future presents a daunting combination of unparalleled challenges and opportunities and intense conflict and controversy. History can provide no guide to those who will be piloting nonprofit enterprises through these troubled waters. But perhaps it can show that what we now call the nonprofit sector has always been contested ground—precisely because its nature and extent involve fundamental questions about the nature of human institutions, the possibilities of political, economic, and social organization, and the quality of our values and moral imagination.

Notes

1. Exact figures on the number of charitable tax-exempt organizations in existence before 1967, when the IRS began counting them, are elusive. In testifying to the Cox Committee in 1952, Norman Sugerman, Assistant Commissioner of Internal Revenue, estimated the number of nonreligious charitable tax-exempt organizations as having been 12,500 in 1939; 27,500 in 1946; and 32,000 in 1950 (U.S. House of Representatives, 1954, p. 64). Figures for the period 1967–1985 are from Burton Weisbrod's *The Nonprofit Economy* (1988, pp. 169–170). Figures for 1985–1989 are from "The Nonprofit World" (1990, p. 8).

2. *U.S. Congress. The Power and Influence of Large Foundations.* 87th Cong., 1st sess., Vol. 107, pt. 73 (May 2, 1961), H. Doc. 6560; (May 3, 1961) H. Docs. 6780–6781; and *Foundations Fail to Give Adequate Financial Reports,* (May 8, 1961), H. Docs. 7053–7063. See also, *IRS Needs Sharper Tools,* (August 7, 1961), H. Docs. 13751–13756. Patman's subsequent reports include *Tax-Exempt Foundations and Charitable Trusts: Their Impact on Our Economy,* Chairman's Report to the Select Committee on Small Business, House of Representatives, 87th Cong., Dec. 31, 1962 (Washington, D.C.: Government Printing Office, 1962); *Tax-Exempt Foundations and Charitable Trusts: Their Impact on Our Economy,* Second Installment, Subcommittee Chairman's Report to Subcommittee No. 1, Select Committee on Small Business, House of Representatives, 88th Cong., Oct. 16, 1963 (Washington, D.C.: Government Printing Office, 1963); *Tax-Exempt Foundations: Their Impact on Small Business,* Third Installment, Hearings Before Subcommittee No. 1 on Foundations, Select Committee on Small Business, House of Representatives, 88th Cong., 2nd sess., Mar. 20, 1964 (Washington, D.C.: Government Printing Office, 1964); *Tax-Exempt Foundations and Charitable Trusts: Their Impact on Our Economy,* Fourth Installment, Dec. 21, 1966; *Tax-Exempt Foundations and Charitable Trusts: Their Impact on Our Economy,* Fifth Installment, Apr.

28, 1967; *Tax-Exempt Foundations: Their Impact on Small Business*, Hearings Before Subcommittee No. 1 of the Select Committee on Small Business, House of Representatives, 90th Cong., 1st sess. (1967); *Tax-Exempt Foundations and Charitable Trusts: Their Impact on Our Economy*, Sixth Installment, Mar. 26, 1968.

3. In *The Rich and the Super-Rich* (1968), Ferdinand Lundberg devoted over seventy pages to discussing Patman's findings.

4. The testimony of foundation leaders and other friendly witnesses can be found in *Foundations and the Tax Bill: Testimony on Title I of the Tax Reform Act of 1969 Submitted by Witnesses Appearing Before the United States Senate Finance Committee, October 1969* (New York: The Foundation Center, 1969) and in *Hearings Before the Committee on Ways and Means,* House of Representatives, 91st Cong., Part 1 (Feb. 18, 19, 20, 1969) (Washington, D.C.: Government Printing Office, 1969). The published testimony of the hearings, because they are edited and because they seldom reveal the jockeying behind the various positions taken by witnesses, only provide a partial documentation of the tension and turmoil in the world of philanthropy during this period.

 Three sources prove especially useful in reconstructing the events of 1969 and interpreting their meaning. First, *Foundation News,* which had come under the control of the Council on Foundations, presented a number of important pieces on the 1969 Tax Reform Act (TRA69) hearings and the foundations' strategizing. These include "Ways and Means Hearings on the Foundations," 1969, *10*(3), 93–96; "House Ways and Means Report," 1969, *10*(4), 139; "A Program of Self-Regulation by Philanthropic Foundations," 1969, *10*(6), 213–215; "National Leaders Support Foundations," 1969, *10*(6), 217–221; Robert D. Calkins, "The Role of the Philanthropic Foundation," 1970, *11*(1), 1–13.

 Second, *Nonprofit Report* (now *The Philanthropy Monthly*), an independent newsletter focusing on public policy issues affecting philanthropy, provided insightful, if opinionated, coverage of the hearings. Especially useful articles include "Foundation Associations and Tax Reform," "Treasury Testimony on Tax Reform," and "Report–Interview: Background on the Treasury Proposals," 1969, *2*(5); "Foundations Urged to be United in Own Defense," "The Private Sector Is in Trouble — Dana Creel," and "Mills Announces Proposed Tax Reforms," 1969, *2*(6); "Pifer Finds Mills Proposals 'Shocking,'" 1969, *2*(7); "House Responds to 'Taxpayers Revolt,'" and "The Tax Reform Act of 1969," 1969, *2*(8); "Senate Hearings on Tax Reform," "Kennedy and Cohen Testify for Nixon Administration," "Javits Critical of Foundation-Related Reforms," and "Open Letter to Senator Russell B. Long," 1969, *2*(9); "Senate Finance Committee and Tax Reform" and "Mr. Bundy Isn't Overly Concerned," 1969, *2*(11); "The Christmas Tree Act of 1969" and "Senator Kennedy Lists the 'Secret Provisions' of the Tax Reform Bill," 1969, *2*(12).

Finally, the files of John D. Rockefeller III and his associates and the working files of the Council on Foundations, both of which are at the Rockefeller Archive Center, not only abundantly document the internal debate within the world of philanthropy about how to best respond to Congress but also contain unedited stenographic transcriptions of much of the congressional testimony. In addition, both collections contain extensive clipping files from national and local newspapers' and periodicals' coverage of the hearings.

5. Clarification of the meaning of TRA69 was carried out through an intricate and protracted set of negotiations between congressional staffers, led by Lawrence Woodworth, Treasury Department officials, representatives from the Council on Foundations, and tax lawyers in private practice — like former Assistant IRS Commissioner Norman Sugerman and D.C. lawyer and lobbyist Leonard Silverstein — who operated in the Treasury/foundation industry network. On this, see memoranda and correspondence in the Council on Foundations files at the Rockefeller Archive Center, Filer, Box 4. Also useful are the articles in *Foundation News* and *Non-Profit Report* published in 1970–71 that sought to interpret the technical provisions of the Act.

6. John D. Rockefeller III had been thinking along these lines as early as the mid-1960s; see "Thoughts on Philanthropy" (at the Rockefeller Archive Center: Fam, RG3, JDR3, Box 370, "Philanthropy" — JDR3rd/Book). His ideas were much stimulated by Alan Pifer's May 1968 speech, "The Foundation in the Year 2000," ("Thoughts on Philanthropy"). Pifer helped Rockefeller understand the fluidity of circumstances and the necessity for philanthropy to be able to respond to extraordinary change with flexibility — a view very much in contrast to the rigidity and defensiveness of most philanthropoids and wealthy donors in this period. Rockefeller acknowledged his intellectual debt to Pifer by appointing him to the Filer Commission. He was the only foundation executive so honored.

7. The final report by the Commission on Foundations and Private Philanthropy appeared in published form as *Foundations, Private Giving, and Public Policy* (University of Chicago Press, 1970). On the Commission's activities, see "The Role of Foundations in Society: Two Studies," *Non-Profit Report,* 1969, *2*(5), 8–9, and "The Peterson Study: The Role of Foundations in the U.S.," 1969, *2*(8), 13. See also Andrews, *Foundation Watcher* (1973), pp. 255–256. The papers of John D. Rockefeller III and his associate Datus Smith contain extensive material on the establishment of the commission and its activities.

8. John D. Rockefeller III to Wilbur Mills, Nov. 1, 1972; Mills to Rockefeller, Nov. 8, 1972; and Datus Smith to Mills, Nov. 13, 1972 (Rockefeller Archive Center: Fam, RG3, JDR3rd, Box 369, "Committee on Tax Incentives").

9. Memorandum from Datus Smith to John D. Rockefeller III, "Com-

mittee on Tax Incentives," Dec. 7, 1972 (see Note 8 for citation information). This memo summarizes the group's thinking about the committee's purposes, composition, program, and budget. Evidently, the
effort was originally conceived as a modest effort—budgeted at only
$80,000. By the time it completed its work in 1978, the committee—
better known as the Filer Commission—would have raised and spent
over $2 million. The original list of members was compiled by Rocke-
feller's staff and congressional staffer Lawrence Woodworth. On Woodworth's involvement, see Datus Smith to Lawrence Woodworth, Chief
of Staff, Joint Committee on Internal Revenue Taxation, Nov. 13,
1972 (Rockefeller Archive Center: Fam, RG3, JDR3rd, Box 369,
"Commission on Philanthropy"). Interestingly, none of the twenty-five
proposed members were foundation executives.

10.   I am grateful to Hayden W. Smith for his account of the origins of
the 501(c)(3) Group, of which he was a member from the early seventies until it disbanded in 1987. According to Smith, the founders included Charles Sampson of United Way, Jack Schwartz of the American Association of Fundraising Counsel (AAFRC), John Leslie of the
American College Public Relations Association (now CASE), and tax
lawyers Connie Tytell and Stan Whitehorn. Hayden Smith was interviewed by the author on Dec. 13, 1989.

11.   Memorandum from William Howard Beasley III to Mr. [William]
Simon, "Advisory Group on Private Philanthropy," May 11, 1973;
memorandum from Porter McKeever to Howard Bolton and Leonard
Silverstein, "Subject: John Filer," July 16, 1973; and memorandum
from Leonard L. Silverstein to Commission on Private Philanthropy
Advisory Committee, untitled (to apprise the Advisory Committee of
developments since its Aug. 13 meeting), Aug. 1973 (Rockefeller Archive Center: Fam, RG3, JDR3rd Confidential Files, Box 14, "Commission on Philanthropy"). This important summary of the Filer Commission's preliminary discussions specifically details the range of its
informational needs and policy concerns. Porter McKeever, author
of the first memo, had replaced Datus Smith as Rockefeller's point man
on the philanthropy front. He would be a key background figure in
the Filer Commission's activities and in institutionalizing its legacy with
the formation of INDEPENDENT SECTOR.

The papers of the Filer Commission, donated by executive director Leonard Silverstein to INDEPENDENT SECTOR, are not available to
researchers. However, the papers of John D. Rockefeller III and his
associates and the working files of the Council on Foundations—all of
which are at the Rockefeller Archive Center—cover the ground pretty
well.

12.   The first volume, Report of the Commission on Private Philanthropy
and Public Needs, *Giving in America: Toward a Stronger Voluntary Sector*
(Washington, D.C.: Commission on Private Philanthropy and Pub-

lic Needs) was published in 1975. The six volumes of research papers were put out by the Department of the Treasury in 1977 as *Research Papers Sponsored by the Commission on Private Philanthropy and Public Needs.*

References

Alchon, G. *The Invisible Hand of Planning: Capitalism, Social Science, and the State in the 1920s.* Princeton, N.J.: Princeton University Press, 1985.

Ambrose, S. E. *Halleck: Lincoln's Chief of Staff.* Baton Rouge: Louisiana State University Press, 1962.

Andrews, F. E. *Philanthropic Giving.* New York: Russell Sage Foundation, 1950.

Andrews, F. E. *Corporation Giving.* New York: Russell Sage Foundation, 1952.

Andrews, F. E. *Foundation Watcher.* Lancaster, Pa.: Franklin & Marshall College, 1973.

"An Act Concerning Associations for Religious, Charitable, Educational and Other Purposes." In *Acts and Resolves Passed by the General Court of Massachusetts in the Year 1874.* Boston: Wright & Potter, 1874.

"An Act in Relation to the Exemption of the Real Property of Religious, Charitable, and Educational Corporations from Taxation." In *Laws of the State of New York Passed at the One Hundred Sixteenth Session of the Legislature.* Albany, N.Y.: James B. Lyon, Printer, 1893.

Bailey, A. L. "Leaders of Philanthropy Call on Foundations to Join Forces, Seek Solutions to Global Ills." *Chronicle of Philanthropy,* 1989, *2*(3), 1, 4–8.

Bailey, A. L. "Big Gains in Giving to Charity." *Chronicle of Philanthropy,* 1990, *3*(1), 1, 16–18.

Bailyn, B. (ed.). *The Apologia of Robert Keayne: The Self-Portrait of a Puritan Merchant.* New York: HarperCollins, 1964.

Bender, T. *New York Intellect: A History of Intellectual Life in New York City.* New York: Knopf, 1987.

Bremner, R. M. *From the Depths: The Discovery of Poverty in the United States.* New York: New York University Press, 1956.

Bremner, R. M. *The Public Good: Philanthropy and Welfare in the Civil War Era.* New York: Knopf, 1980.

Brilliant, E. *The United Way: Dilemmas of Organized Charity.* New York: Columbia University Press, 1990.

Brody, D. "The Rise and Decline of Welfare Capitalism." In D. Brody (ed.), *Workers in Industrial America: Essays on the Twentieth Century Struggle.* New York: Oxford University Press, 1980.

Buck, P. (ed.). *The Social Sciences at Harvard.* Cambridge, Mass.: Harvard University Press, 1965.

Burch, P. *Elites in American Society.* New York: Holmes & Meier, 1981.

Burke, A. *Considerations on the Society of Order of Cincinnati Lately Instituted by the Major-Generals, Brigadier-Generals, and Other Officers of the American Army.* Philadelphia: Robert Bell, 1784.

Burns, J. J. *Educational History of Ohio.* Columbus, Ohio: Historical Publishing Company, 1905.

Bushman, R. *From Puritan to Yankee: Character and the Social Order in Connecticut, 1690–1765.* New York: Norton, 1970.

Carnegie, A. "An Employer's View of the Labor Question." *Forum,* 1886a, *1,* 114–125.

Carnegie, A. "Results of the Labor Struggle." *Forum,* 1886b, *1,* 538–551.

Carnegie, A. "Wealth." *North American Review,* 1889, *148,* 653–664 and *149,* 682–698.

Coalition of National Voluntary Organizations and National Council on Philanthropy. *To Preserve an Independent Sector: Organizing Committee Report.* Washington, D.C.: Coalition of National Voluntary Organizations, 1979.

Collier, P., and Horowitz, D. *The Rockefellers: An American Dynasty.* Troy, Mo.: Holt, Rinehart & Winston, 1976.

Commission on Foundations and Private Philanthropy. *Foundations, Private Giving, and Public Policy.* Chicago: University of Chicago Press, 1970.

Commission on Private Philanthropy and Public Needs. *Giving in America: Toward a Stronger Voluntary Sector.* Washington, D.C.: Department of the Treasury, 1975.

Commission on Private Philanthropy and Public Needs. *Research Papers Sponsored by the Commission on Private Philanthropy and Public Needs.* Washington, D.C.: Department of the Treasury, 1977.

Copeland, J. "Financial Data from Form 990 Returns for Exempt Charitable, Religious, and Educational Organizations and Private Foundations." In *Research Papers Sponsored by the Commission on Private Philanthropy and Public Needs.* Washington, D.C.: Government Printing Office, 1977.

Corporate Community Involvement. New York: Citizen's Forum on Self-Government/National Municipal League, 1982.

Croly, H. *The Promise of American Life.* New York: Macmillan, 1909.

Cross, R. D. (ed.). *The Church and the City.* Indianapolis: Bobbs-Merrill, 1967.

Cutlip, S. M. *Fund Raising in the United States: Its Role in America's Philanthropy.* New Brunswick, N.J.: Rutgers University Press, 1965.

Davis, A. F. *Spearheads for Reform: The Social Settlements and the Progressive Movement.* New York: Oxford University Press, 1967.

Davis, J. S. *Essays in the Earlier History of American Corporations.* Cambridge, Mass.: Harvard University Press, 1917.

Deetz, J. *In Small Things Remembered: The Archaeology of Early American Life.* Garden City, N.Y.: Doubleday, 1977.

DiMaggio, P. J. "Cultural Entrepreneurship in Nineteenth-Century Boston." In P. DiMaggio (ed.), *Nonprofit Enterprise in the Arts: Studies in Mission and Constraint.* New York: Oxford University Press, 1986.

DiMaggio, P. J. "Class Authority and Cultural Entrepreneurship: The Problem of Chicago." Working paper no. 155. New Haven, Conn.: Program on Nonprofit Organizations, Yale University, 1990.

Dodd, E. M. *American Business Corporations until 1860, with Special Reference to Massachusetts.* Cambridge, Mass.: Harvard University Press, 1960.

Domhoff, G. W. *Who Rules America?* Englewood Cliffs, N.J.: Prentice-Hall, 1967.

Domhoff, G. W. *The Higher Circles: The Governing Class in America.* New York: Random House, 1970.

Eliot, C. W. "The New Education." *Atlantic Monthly,* 1869, *23,* 203–220, 358–367.

Eliot, C. W. "The Exemption from Taxation of Church Property, and the Property of Educational, Literary, and Charitable Institutions." In *19th Century Legal Treatises* (microfiche #36778). Woodbridge, Conn.: Research Publications, 1988. (Originally published 1874.)

Eliot, C. W. "Inaugural Address as President of Harvard" (1869). In C. W. Eliot (ed.), *Educational Reform: Essays and Addresses.* New York: Century, 1898.

Ely, R. "The Universities and the Churches." In *One Hundred and Seventh Report of the Regents, 1893.* Albany: University of the State of New York, 1894.

Ferguson, R. A. "The Girard Will Case: Charity and Inheritance in the City of Brotherly Love." In J. Salzman (ed.), *Philanthropy and American Society: Selected Papers.* New York: Center for American Culture Studies, 1987.

Fosdick, R. B. *The Story of the Rockefeller Foundation .* New York: Harper-Collins, 1952.

Foster, M. S. *"Out of Smalle Beginnings . . . ": An Economic History of Harvard College in the Puritan Period.* Cambridge, Mass.: Harvard University Press, 1962.

Fox, D. M. *Engines of Culture: Philanthropy and Art Museums.* Madison: State Historical Society of Wisconsin, 1963.

Fox, D. M. *Health Policies, Health Politics: The British and American Experience.* Princeton, N.J.: Princeton University Press, 1986.

Frederickson, G. M. *The Inner Civil War: Northern Intellectuals and the Crisis of the Union.* New York: HarperCollins, 1965.

Galaskiewicz, J. *Social Organization of an Urban Grants Economy: A Study of Business Philanthropy and Nonprofit Organizations.* San Diego, Calif.: Academic Press, 1985.

Ginzberg, L. D. *Women and the Work of Benevolence: Morality, Politics, and Class in the Nineteenth-Century United States.* New Haven, Conn.: Yale University Press, 1990.

Greene, S. G. "For U.S. Philanthropy, Opportunity in the Turmoil of Eastern Europe." *Chronicle of Philanthropy,* 1989, *2*(4), 1, 10.

Gronbjerg, K. "How Nonprofit Human Service Organizations Manage Their Funding Sources: Key Findings and Policy Implications. *Nonprofit Management and Leadership,* 1991a, *2*(1), 159–175.

Gronbjerg, K. "Managing Grants and Contracts: The Case of Four Nonprofit Social Service Studies." *Nonprofit and Voluntary Sector Quarterly,* 1991b, *20*(2), 5–24.

Hall, P. D. "Cultures of Trusteeship in the United States." In *Inventing the Nonprofit Sector and Other Essays on Philanthropy, Voluntarism, and Nonprofit Organizations.* Baltimore, Md.: Johns Hopkins University Press, 1992.

Hall, P. D. "The Spirit of the Ordinance of 1787: Organizational Values, Voluntary Associations, and Higher Education in Ohio, 1803–1830." In P. H. Mattingly and E. W. Stevens, Jr. (eds.), ". . . *Schools and the Means of Education Shall Forever Be Encouraged.*" Athens: Ohio University Libraries, 1987.

Hall, P. D. "Organizational Values and the Origins of the Corporation in Connecticut, 1760–1860." In Association for the Study of Connecticut History, *Three Hundred Fifty Years: Legal and Constitutional Development in Connecticut, 1638–1988.* Willimantic: Connecticut Studies Center, 1989.

Hammack, D. M. "Community Foundations: The Delicate Question of Purpose." In R. Magat (ed.), *An Agile Servant: Community Leadership by Community Foundations.* New York: Foundation Center, 1989.

Hansmann, H. "The Role of Nonprofit Enterprise." *Yale Law Journal,* 1980, *89,* 835–901.

Harris, S. E. *The Economics of Harvard.* New York: McGraw-Hill, 1970.

Haskell, T. *The Emergence of Professional Social Science: The American Social Science Association and the Nineteenth-Century Crisis of Authority.* Urbana: University of Illinois Press, 1977.

Hawkins, H. *Between Harvard and America: The Educational Leadership of Charles W. Eliot.* New York: Oxford University Press, 1972.

Hawley, E. W. (ed.). *Herbert Hoover as Secretary of Commerce: Studies in New Era Thought and Practice.* Iowa City: University of Iowa Press, 1974.

Hawley, E. W. "Herbert Hoover, the Commerce Secretariat, and the Vision of an 'Associative State.'" In E. J. Perkins (ed.), *Men and Organizations.* New York: Putnam's, 1977.

Heald, M. *The Social Responsibilities of Business: Company and Community, 1900–1960.* Cleveland, Ohio: Case Western Reserve University Press, 1970.

Henning, W. W. *The Statutes at Large: Being a Collection of All the Laws from the First Session of the Legislature, in the Year 1619.* Richmond, Va.: Privately printed, 1821.

Higginson, T. W. *The Harvard Memorial Biographies.* Cambridge, Mass.: Sever & Francis, 1866.

Hirchler, E. S. "A Survey of Charitable Trusts in Virginia." *Virginia Law Review,* 1939, *25,* 109–116.

Hodgkinson, V. (ed.). *The Nonprofit Sector (NGOs) in the United States and Abroad: Cross-Cultural Perspectives—1990 Spring Research Forum Working Papers.* Washington, D.C.: INDEPENDENT SECTOR, 1990.

Hofstadter, R., and Smith, W. (eds.). *American Higher Education: A Documentary History.* Chicago: University of Chicago Press, 1961.

Hoover, H. C. *American Individualism.* New York: Doubleday, Doran, 1922.

Horowitz, H. L. *Culture and the City: Cultural Philanthropy in Chicago, 1880–1917.* Chicago: University of Chicago Press, 1976.

Horowitz, M. J. *The Transformation of American Law, 1780–1860.* Cambridge, Mass.: Harvard University Press, 1977.

Hospital Utilization Project, Appellant v. *Commonwealth of Pennsylvania,* 507 *Pennsylvania Rpts.* 1, 487 A.2d 1306 (1985).

Huggins, N. *Protestants Against Poverty: Boston's Charities, 1870–1900.* Westport, Conn.: Greenwood Press, 1971.

INDEPENDENT SECTOR. *Program Plan (as Amended and Approved by the Membership, Oct. 24, 1980).* Washington, D.C.: INDEPENDENT SECTOR, 1980.

INDEPENDENT SECTOR. *Giving and Volunteering in the United States, 1990.* Washington, D.C.: INDEPENDENT SECTOR, 1990.

James, E. (ed.). *The Nonprofit Sector in International Perspective: Studies in Comparative Culture and Policy.* New York: Oxford University Press, 1989.

Jefferson, T. "Notes on the State of Virginia." In A. Koch (ed.), *The American Enlightenment.* New York: George Brziller, 1965a.

Jefferson, T. "Systematic Plan of General Education." In A. Koch (ed.), *The American Enlightenment.* New York: George Braziller, 1965b.

Johnson, P. *Modern Times.* New York: HarperCollins, 1983.

Joseph, J. *The Charitable Impulse: Wealth and Social Conscience in Communities and Cultures Outside the United States.* New York: Foundation Center, 1989.

Karl, B. D. "Presidential Planning and Social Science Research: Mr. Hoover's Experts." *Perspectives in American History,* 1969, pp. 347–409.

Karl, B. D. "Philanthropy, Policy Planning, and the Bureaucratization of the Democratic Ideal." *Daedalus,* 1976, Fall, pp. 129–149.

Karl, B. D., and Katz, S. N. "The American Private Foundation and the Public Sphere, 1890–1930." *Minerva,* 1981a, *19,* 236–270.

Karl, B. D., and Katz, S. N. "The Legitimation of the Philanthropic Foundation in the United States, 1890–1930." Paper presented at the Shelby Collum Davis Center, Princeton University, Jan. 30, 1981b.

Karl, B. D., and Katz, S. N. "Foundations and Ruling Class Elites." *Daedalus,* 1987, *116*(1), 1–40.

Katz, M. B. *In the Shadow of the Poorhouse: A Social History of Welfare in America.* New York: Basic Books, 1986.

Katz, S. N. "Grantmaking and Research in the United States, 1933–1983." *Proceedings of the American Philosophical Society,* 1985, *129*(1), 1–19.

Lagemann, E. C. *The Politics of Knowledge: The Carnegie Corporation, Philanthropy, and Public Policy.* Middletown, Conn.: Wesleyan University Press, 1989.

Laski, H. J. "Foundations, Universities, and Research." In *The Dangers of Obedience and Other Essays.* New York: HarperCollins, 1930.

Lemisch, L. J. (ed.). *Benjamin Franklin: The Autobiography and Other Writings.* New York: New American Library, 1961.

Lipsky, M., and Smith, S. R. *Nonprofits for Hire.* Cambridge, Mass.: Harvard University Press, 1993.

Lundberg, F. *The Rich and the Super-Rich: A Study in the Power of Money Today.* New York: Lyle Stuart, 1968.

McCarthy, K. *Noblesse Oblige: Charity and Cultural Philanthropy in Chicago, 1849–1929.* Chicago: University of Chicago Press, 1982.

MacDonald, E. *The Ford Foundation: The Men and the Millions.* New York: Reynal, 1956.

Madison, J. "No. 10." In *The Federalist Papers.* New York: New American Library, 1961.

Magat, R. (ed.). *An Agile Servant: Community Leadership by Community Foundations.* New York: Foundation Center, 1989.

Millar, B. "United Ways and the Charities They Support Will Face Fast-Paced, Dramatic Changes in the 1990s, Report Says." *Chronicle of Philanthropy,* 1989, *2*(4), 1, 8–9.

Miller, E. A. *The History of Educational Legislation in Ohio from 1803 to 1850.* Columbus, Ohio: F. J. Heer Printing Company, 1918.

Miller, H. S. *The Legal Foundations of American Philanthropy, 1776–1844.* Madison: Historical Society of Wisconsin, 1961.

Mills, C. W. *The Power Elite.* New York: Oxford University Press, 1956.

Morison, S. E. *Three Centuries of Harvard.* Cambridge, Mass.: Harvard University Press, 1936.

Myers, J. H. "Foundations and Tax Legislation." *Foundation News,* 1965, *6*(3), 51–54.

Nelson, W. E. *The Americanization of the Common Law: The Impact of Legal Change on Massachusetts Society, 1760–1830.* Cambridge, Mass.: Harvard University Press, 1975.

Nielsen, W. *The Big Foundations.* New York: Columbia University Press, 1972.

"The Nonprofit World: A Statistical Portrait." *Chronicle of Philanthropy,* 1990, *2*(6), 8.

Odendahl, T. (ed.). *America's Wealthy and the Future of Foundations.* New York: Foundation Center, 1986.

Odendahl, T. *Charity Begins at Home: Generosity and Self-Interest Among the Philanthropic Elite.* New York: Basic Books, 1990.

Olasky, M. "Reagan's Second Thoughts on Corporate Giving." *Fortune,* Sept. 20, 1983, pp. 130–136.

Philadelphia Baptist Association v. *Hart's Executors,* 4 *Wheaton* 518.

Pierce, F. "Veto Message, May 3, 1854." In J. D. Richardson (ed.), *A Compilation of the Messages and Papers of the Presidents of the United States, 1789–1897.* Washington, D.C.: Published by the Authority of Congress, 1898.

Polivy, D. K. "The United Way: Understanding How It Works Is the First Step to Effecting Change." In C. Milofsky (ed.), *Community Organizations: Studies in Resource Mobilization and Exchange.* New York: Oxford University Press, 1988.

Polivy, D. K. "A Study of Admissions Policies and Practices of Eight Local United Way Organizations." Working paper no. 49. New Haven: Program on Nonprofit Organizations, Yale University, 1982.

President's Task Force on Private Sector Initiatives (Verity Commission). *Building Partnerships.* Washington, D.C.: Government Printing Office, 1982a.

President's Task Force on Private Sector Initiatives. *Investing in America: Initiatives for Community and Economic Development.* Washington, D.C.: Government Printing Office, 1982b.

Purcell, R. *Connecticut in Transition, 1775-1818.* Middletown, Conn.: Wesleyan University Press, 1963.

Report of the Princeton Conference on the History of Philanthropy. New York: Russell Sage Foundation, 1956.

Rhees, W. J. (ed.). *The Smithsonian Institution: Documents Relative to Its Origin and History.* Smithsonian Miscellaneous Collections XVII, Publ. no. 328. Washington, D.C.: Smithsonian Institution, 1879.

Rockefeller, J. D., III. *The Second American Revolution: Some Personal Observations.* New York: HarperCollins, 1973.

Ross, D. *The Origins of American Social Science.* New York: Cambridge University Press, 1991.

Salamon, L. "Of Market Failure, Voluntary Failure, and Third Party Government: Toward a Theory of Government-Nonprofit Relations in the Modern Welfare State." In S. A. Ostrander, S. Langdon, and J. Van Til (eds.), *Shifting the Debate: Public/Private Sector Relations in the Modern Welfare State.* New Brunswick, N.J.: Transaction Books, 1987.

Salamon, L., and Abramson, A. *The Federal Government and the Nonprofit Sector: Implications of the Reagan Budget Proposals.* Washington, D.C.: Urban Institute, 1981.

Scott, A. F. *Natural Allies: Women's Associations in American History.* Urbana: University of Illinois Press, 1991.

Sears, J. B. *Philanthropy in the History of American Higher Education.* Washington, D.C.: Bureau of Education, Department of the Interior, 1922.

Select Committee to Investigate Foundations. *Final Report.* 82nd Cong., 2nd sess., 1953. H.R. 2514.

Shepard, S. *Statutes at Large of Virginia, from Oct. Session 1792 to Dec. Session 1806, Inclusive, in Three Volumes.* Richmond, Va.: Privately printed, 1835.

Sherill, R. "'The Last of the Great Populists' Takes on the Foundations, the Banks, the Federal Reserve, the Treasury." *New York Times Magazine,* Mar. 16, 1969, pp. 24-25, 105-118.

Smith, J. A. *The Idea Brokers: Think Tanks and the Rise of the Policy Elite.* New York: Free Press, 1991.

Smith-Rosenberg, C. *Religion and the Rise of the American City: The New York City Mission Movement, 1812-1870.* Ithaca, N.Y.: Cornell University Press, 1971.

Special Committee to Investigate Foundations and Comparable Organizations (Reece Committee). *Tax-Exempt Foundations.* 83rd Cong., 2nd sess., 1954. H.R. 2681.

Starr, P. *The Social Transformation of American Medicine.* New York: Basic Books, 1982.

Stevens, R. *In Sickness and in Wealth: American Hospitals in the Twentieth Century*. New York: Basic Books, 1989.

Stiles, E. *Literary Diary*. New York: Henry Holt, 1901.

Stone, M. M. "Issues of Nonprofit Governance in a State-Dominated Environment: A Historical Case Study." Working paper no. 185. New Haven, Conn.: Program on Nonprofit Organizations, Yale University, 1992.

Story, R. *The Forging of an Aristocracy: Harvard and Boston's Upper Class, 1800–1870*. Middletown, Conn.: Wesleyan University Press, 1980.

Suhrke, H. C. "Foundation Replies: 'Dear Mr. Patman.'" *Nonprofit Report,* 1972, *5*(9), 1, 4–8.

Suhrke, H. C. "Peril in Treasury's Tax Proposals." *Nonprofit Report,* 1973a, *6*(5), 1, 4–8.

Suhrke, H. C. "Foundations on the Senate Griddle." *Nonprofit Report,* 1973b, *6*(10), 1, 4–7.

Tobias, M. *Old Dartmouth on Trial*. New York: New York University Press, 1982.

Tocqueville, A. de. *Democracy in America*. New York: Knopf, 1945. (Originally published 1835–1840.)

Treasury Department. *Report on Private Foundations, Printed for Use of the House Committee on Ways and Means, February 2, 1965*. Washington, D.C.: Government Printing Office, 1965.

"Treasury Report." *Foundation News,* 1965, *6*(2), 29.

Trustees of Dartmouth College v. *Woodward,* 4 Wheaton 625 (1819).

Tucker, H. St. G. *Gallego's Executor* v. *The Attorney General, 3 Leigh* 462 (1832).

U.S. House of Representatives. Committee on Ways and Means. *Written Statements by Interested Individuals and Organizations on Treasury Department Report on Private Foundations Issued on Feb. 2, 1965*. 89th Cong., 1st sess., 1965.

U.S. House of Representatives. *Hearings Before the Select Committee to Investigate Foundations and Comparable Organizations*. 82nd Cong., 2nd sess., 1954.

U.S. Senate. *Limitation on Deduction in Case of Contributions by Individuals for Benefit of Churches, Educational Organizations, and Hospitals: Report Together with Minority and Supplemental Views*. 87th Cong., 1st sess., 1961, S. Rept. 585, 7–8.

Upton, E. *Military Policy of the United States*. Washington, D.C.: Government Printing Office, 1907.

Useem, M. *The Inner Circle: Large Corporations and the Rise of Business Political Activity in the United States and the United Kingdom*. New York: Oxford University Press, 1984.

Veblen, T. *The Higher Learning in America*. New York: B. W. Huebsch, 1918.

Vidal v. *Girard's Executors,* 2 *How* 27, 11 L. Ed. 205 (1844).

Wall, J. F. *Andrew Carnegie*. New York: Oxford University Press, 1970.

Warner, A. G. *American Charities*. New York: Thomas Y. Crowell, 1908.

Webber, C., and Wildavsky, A. *A History of Taxation and Expenditure in the Western World*. New York: Simon & Schuster, 1986.

Weisbrod, B. *The Nonprofit Economy.* Cambridge, Mass.: Harvard University Press, 1988.

West Allegheny Hospital, Appellant v. *Board of Property Assessment,* 500 *Pennsylvania Reports* 236, 455 A.2d 1170 (1982).

Whitehead, J. S. *The Separation of College and State.* New Haven, Conn.: Yale University Press, 1976.

Wood, Struthers & Company. *The Trusteeship of Charitable Endowments.* New York: Macmillan, 1932.

Wyllie, I. G. "The Search for an American Law of Charity." *Mississippi Valley Historical Review,* 1959, *46,* 203–221.

"Yale University v. *Town of New Haven." Connecticut Reports,* 1899, p. 71.

2

Nonprofit Organizations and Social Institutions

Jon Van Til

The work of nonprofit managers takes place within organizations identified by society as voluntary, charitable, or nonprofit, as Peter Dobkin Hall well explains in Chapter One. The task of this chapter is to look at the ways in which the work of nonprofit managers forms an important part of the institutional life of society.

The concept of "institution" should not be seen to be as offputting. An institution is simply an aspect of society that relates to meaning in a special way. An institution organizes meaning; indeed it manifests it. It makes clear to those who live in a society just what it is that their society values most highly. Among the basic institutions of Victorian England, as Gilbert and Sullivan put it, were "the army, the navy, the church and the stage." In our own time and place, a list might include the family, the church, the workplace, and the mall. And maybe the nonprofit organization, as well, although this latter is a relative newcomer to the primary ranks of institutional life.

In this chapter, I will treat the nonprofit organization as an institution, one surrounded by and subject to the influence of other institutions. I will examine the institutional environment within which the nonprofit organization exists; I will seek to enumerate the principal institutional actors who perform within nonprofit organizations; and I will endeavor to clarify the mission of the nonprofit organization manager in fulfilling the institutional role of the nonprofit organization.

Note: I am grateful for the helpful comments of Joanne Carr and Linda Dugger on an earlier draft.

At the Beginning: The Human Side of Nonprofit Institutions

It all begins, Susan Ostrander and Paul Schervish (1990) remind us, with the simplest of human choices: how do we spend our time and money? If some of our time is spent in advancing the work of nonprofit organizations, and some of our money is spent in making sure those organizations can survive, then we may have chosen to do less fishing than we might have otherwise done, or bought a less fancy fishing pole (or traveled to a less remote river) than we might have otherwise afforded.

But then it all depends, doesn't it? If volunteers spend their time showing a group of youngsters how to fish, they might be doing all the fishing they really wanted to. And if the donor's money is spent to support a nonprofit organization that allows youth to fish, then the donor's money may still have gone for the purchase of poles or the transport to fish-laden waters. Such is the transformational power of the individual act of giving: it allows us to do things we would have done only for ourselves, and makes the same action into something that benefits others as well.

And that is what makes an institution: the pulling together by people in a way that makes collective meaning out of actions that are important to them. Which is not to say that everything that gets done under the name of nonprofit organization is institutional, or even of value. The work of nonprofit organizations can be subverted by people as weak, devious, and malevolent as those who scheme, from time to time, in the halls of governments and corporations. (Perhaps the most dramatic example of the perversion of nonprofit organizations involves their use by the Hitler government. For a full review of this experience, see Bauer, 1990. For a more recent examination of the follies and foibles committed in the name of the third sector, see the 1993 seven-part investigative report in the Philadelphia Inquirer by Gaul and Borowski.)

How things look depends a lot on where we're looking from. Nonprofit administrators see the world, quite naturally, from the perspective of their own organizations. And from that perspective they, like other executives, see most immediately the structure of their own organization. Demanding as the tasks of managing any organization are, executives can hardly focus all their attention upon it. Students of organizational life observe that the best administrators practice, by a combination of preference and necessity, a "mixed scanning" approach (compare Etzioni, 1968, pp. 284–285) that keeps in at least a soft focus distant specks on the organization's environment as well as the more immediate troubles directly at the executive's desk. Organizational scholar Henry Mintzberg (1980) identifies the variety of roles played by the successful executive, which include directing, motivating, coordinating, innovating, serving as an external spokesperson and gladiator, and managing crises. If nonprofit administrators are truly to be effective, they need to recognize that their organization is linked in myriad ways to the world outside it. Theirs, like any other organization, exists in a complex net of relations with other organizations and institutions, each of which affects each other in some way.

Sociologist Talcott Parsons provided a way of seeing this nesting of all organizational life in the context of broader social forces when he noted that any organization must meet four challenges if it is to survive. These challenges, in everyday language rather than the jargon used by Parsons, may be seen as:

1. The need to meet basic life challenges
2. The need to meet goals shared with others
3. The need to secure resources adequate to sustain the organization
4. The need to relate to other organizations as each organization pursues its particular tasks

These challenges are so important that all societies create institutions to provide for them. Thus (and paralleling the list above):

1. Family and community structures develop to meet basic needs for meaning and support.
2. Political institutions emerge to define and articulate public goals.
3. Economic institutions exist to develop resources.
4. Social institutions exist to harmonize the various actions of organizations.

These categories of institutions are often thought of as "sectors" in society. Think of it this way: we divide our institutions into four major sectors to accomplish our societal tasks. Corporations and businesses (the first sector) make most of our products and hire most of our labor; this sector provides jobs that amount to 80 percent of our payrolls. Government (the second sector) provides a military capacity and a number of ancillary regulatory and welfare services; it meets about 13 percent of our national payrolls. Voluntary and nonprofit organizations (the third sector) address a number of educational, charitable, and membership purposes; their payrolls amount to more than 7 percent of the national total and are supplemented by much valuable voluntary effort as well. Finally, households and other informal community organizations (such as neighbors, kin, and so on) perform the lion's share of home management and child raising, though usually without the transfer of cash.

To the nonprofit organization administrator, these sectors and the various cultural, political, economic, and social forces that form them should be seen as part of the organization's environmental field, the arena within which it seeks to operate effectively. The first substantive section of this chapter will focus on the environment of nonprofits.

The ability to scan the environment, however, is just one part of the administrator's task. In order to be effective, nonprofit managers also need to understand the workings of the nonprofit sector—the immediate organizational world inhabited by their organization. This sector, sometimes called the "third sector," includes the many givers, intermediaries, and regulators that impinge upon the nonprofit organization. And, as Ostrander and Schervish remind us, it also includes that all important member of the sector, the beneficiary who receives the services provided by the organization.

The Environment of Nonprofit Management

Nonprofit organizations are powerfully influenced by the culture within which they exist. Thus, it has been contended that the role of nonprofits is unique to the American experience, where a frontier mentality gave rise to a distrust of both government and business as institutions capable of solving human problems. Recent research, however, has blasted this view as itself a cultural myth, finding that voluntarism and nonprofit organizations have been used in many cultures over the sweep of human history (see Lohmann, 1992; Gidron, Kramer, and Salamon, 1992).

The fact that voluntarism exists in other societies, however, does not detract from the fact that it has been, and continues to be, an important force in American life. It reflects forces of local activism that are important in American history and represents a considerable strength in the American way of life.

The basic cultural carriers in any society are the family, the church, and the school. This is as true in a contemporary democratic society as it is in a totalitarian one, as the Nazi celebration of "Kinder, Küche, and Kirche" (children, kitchen, and church) reminds us. Each of these cultural institutions shapes and influences the scope and scale of the nonprofit organization in many important ways.

The Family

The 1992 presidential election is close enough in the collective memories of Americans to be recalled as the time when "family values" surfaced as a political issue. As erstwhile candidates for the highest offices in the land sought to clarify their thoughts regarding the pregnancy of a fictional television character (the "Murphy Brown" episode), nonprofit managers found a minefield of issues confronting their own work.

Some of these issues dealt with the family directly: Could teenagers be advised about, or provided with, abortion services without their parents' knowledge or consent? Should schools offer instruction on the use of condoms as well as outfit their students with this particular form of birth control technology? Should community organizations take a stand in favor of the normative superiority of the married two-parent family in preference to "alternate" forms of family life?

Other issues affected the nonprofit organization more indirectly, though often requiring at least as much delicacy to resolve: Should the needs of parents be given special consideration at the workplace when children's emergencies arose? Should the ire of the Catholic Church be risked when partnerships are proposed with pro-choice organizations, such as Planned Parenthood? Should welfare reform plans requiring recipients to work be supported?

Lurking behind these issues was a fundamental social fact: the family as an institutional force in society is in the process of being fundamentally reshaped. For some, this reshaping means the emergence of a "post-modern family," as Stacey (1990) calls it. "No longer is there a single culturally dominant family pattern to which the majority of Americans conform and most of the rest aspire. Instead, we uneasily inhabit a multiplicity of family and household arrangements, frequently reconstituted in response to changing personal and occupational circumstances" (Marien, 1992, p. 132). For others, this reshaping means the disappearance of the father as a presence. A clear majority of children born to low-income parents do not issue into families headed by a married couple. Throughout society as a whole, 25 percent of all children are born into a status until recently identified by society as "illegitimate" (Marriott, 1992).

For the nonprofit administrator, the decline of the family means a dramatic increase in responsibility, and sometimes in funding as well. For the Westbridge Center in Phoenix, which receives badly troubled children for a care package that includes "round-the-clock, one-on-one supervision, as well as psychiatric treatment and counseling" delivered on a campuslike residential setting, client fees may approach $400 per day. The city of Philadelphia sent a twelve-year-old youth there in 1991 after he threatened suicide, violence, and fire, and his mother relinquished care of him. Six months later his sister was sent to join him in the care of the center. Yearly bills to the nonprofit Westbridge Center were defrayed by the taxpayers of Philadelphia, and amounted to $273,650 per year (Purdy, 1992).

The implications of these cultural changes in the family are clear for nonprofit organizations: these organizations are increasingly expected to perform functions formerly reserved to the family. The social service agency provides day care; the school instills values and breakfast as well as instruction; the university offers its students as tutors and hallway monitors; the counselor valiantly seeks to substitute for father, and increasingly, in the crack-infested areas of the metropolis, mother as well. And the bill for these services mount, no matter how cost-effective the nonprofit organization. The fourth sector (family, church, and school) is simply not performing its functions in our modern society, and it is to voluntarism and nonprofit organization (the third sector) that society increasingly turns to raise, and control, its youth.

Religion

A second institutional keeper of the cultural flame are religious institutions. Themselves prominent members of the nonprofit community, such institutions manifest by their doctrine and practice basic values of a society: conceptions of behavior, thought, and attitude that are transmitted from generation to generation as the elements of life properly lived.

Nonprofit administrators must recognize the role that religious values and institutions play in their communities. Religious leaders articulate underlying values and concerns of their communities with a particular sensitivity, though certainly not with a unanimity of view. The interplay of the different theological conceptions, social values, and organizational structures of the religious sphere assure a lively and compelling social process. No nonprofit manager should be without an appreciation of this mosaic, nor lose track of the various ways in which the religious culture will affect perceptions of the work of nonprofit agencies.

Education

The third major cultural force at play in any society involves education, both formal and informal. By education I mean more than formal schooling, and the massive institutional structure that aims to provide such. Education also includes the many ways by which individuals seek to think about the world, to participate in what some have called the "learning society." Such institutions as the mass media as well as informal learning environments, such as community associations, should be included in our expanded view of education.

Many schools and colleges are moving in this direction as they develop new programs to assist students in learning the values of civic and voluntary participation. As Hall (1992) has noted, schools convey important orientations toward service by their curricula. If they put a value on service that even approaches the weight they give football and other collective sports endeavors, schools might be able to assist students in learning that we live in the kind of society in which we all rise or fall together. As a collection of programs begins to emerge under the rubric of "national service," nonprofit managers will have many opportunities to assist young Americans in finding appropriate placements in their agencies and communities.

At the same time, the outcomes of formal education appear to be in decline. Measured aptitudes are falling, as indicated by the Educational Testing Service, and observers report on a malaise that grips schools at every level. Meanwhile, comparative testing shows an increasing advantage being secured by students in many countries overseas. Assisting schools in achieving their daunting goal of educating youngsters is becoming a more widely shared community responsibility, and one that nonprofit managers will increasingly be called upon to assist.

As the challenge of enhancing education is increasingly recognized as a society need, many nonprofit managers will choose to monitor the state of education as a cultural element in their communities. Are they perceived as well-educated individuals? Do their organizations have a "learning style" congruent to those prevalent in their communities? Are their organizations seen as being "willing to learn"? Will they take advantage of the change to assist in the improvement of education as a community process, say, by playing an active role in encouraging service learning? All of these factors will affect the success of individual nonprofit organizations in the communities they seek to serve.

Social and Demographic Conditions

We live in an age of troubling paradox. The triumph of democracy and capitalism is celebrated globally, but electoral participation declines and living standards stagnate. The morning paper cites the weekly poll on presidential preference, but "none of the above" rises as the candidate of choice. The blessings of "being an American" are ritually cited, but the connectedness of individuals, and especially youth, seems increasingly to recede before the lures of mass consumption and private indulgence.

It is imperative that nonprofit organization managers understand the ways in which their work is affected by the powerful social forces abroad in our world. This is a time of great turbulence, of great change. Indeed, the time has come, as a young political scientist named Woodrow Wilson foresaw a century ago, when our country has awakened "surprised to find herself grown old—a country crowded, strained, perplexed." In such a situation, Wilson observed, it will be necessary for America "to pull herself together, adopt a new regimen of life, husband her resources, concentrate her strength, steady her methods, sober her views, restrict her vagaries, trust her best, not her average, members. That will be the time of change" (quoted in Schlesinger, 1992, pp. 14ff.).

Among the pressing challenges presented in this time of change are those of poverty, racism, alienation, and incapacity. Let us review each of these forces briefly, and tie them to the work of nonprofit organizations.

Poverty and Economic Malaise

An important part of the time of change through which we are presently living is that living standards, for the large majority of Americans, have ceased to grow. Both within our cities and in myriad small towns and rural areas, poverty is actually increasing. Even within the seemingly placid suburban areas inhabited by the new majority of Americans, structural unemployment annually removes hundreds of thousands of heads of households from positions formerly viewed as secure.

Within many urban areas, life proceeds at standards that may be called at best "third world," with few human needs assured in a chaos of crime, housing decay, and hunger. Federal poverty statistics show a rise in the percentage of Americans living in poverty since 1978, and the staggering total of one in five American children now live in a condition of poverty (Ropers, 1991, p. 45).

Even for those not living below the poverty line, economic insecurity has become a fact of life in an era of permanent and recurring recession. Consumer confidence remains shaken, and employee confidence has been riddled by major corporations' daily announcements of layoffs and reductions in force.

Racism

For the one in five of Americans who belong to a minority group, and especially the one in eight who identify themselves as black Americans, life contiues to unfold beneath the ever-present threat of white racism and racial discrimination, however subtle. A significant proportion (some estimate as many as one-half) of the black population has been relegated to a condition of multigenerational undereducation, unemployment, and societal alienation. For those who have escaped poverty, the specter of personal and social slight remains an ever-present threat.

Many black Americans find their lives confined to urban areas that provide them with few opportunities for education, employment, or health care. Gary, Indiana, East St. Louis, vast stretches of North Philadelphia—and other such "Type 2" cities, as Robert Catlin calls them—provide a nearly impossible situation for the staging of social stability or mobility (see Catlin, 1993).

Alienation

The alienation of the ghetto dweller is not unique in American society. With the loss of the employer's commitment to the provision of job security has come the loss of the worker's commitment to the provision of a quality job. With the loss of religious participation has come a loss in the individual's ability to find meaning and connection in everyday life. With the transformation of politics into late-night television entertainment has come the loss of individual participation in community problem solving. With the decline of the urban, and even suburban, community has come the privatization inherent in what Robert Reich has called our "zip-code society."

Alienation, as Hegelian philosophy reminds us, is multiple: from society, from others, from self, and ultimately from meaning itself. Americans have become deeply cynical about every element of their lives, and this cynicism is increasing. As Kanter and Mirvis write: "The number of people who say 'What I think doesn't count anymore.' 'The people running the country don't really care what happens to me,' 'The rich get richer and the poor get poorer,' and 'Most people with power try to take advantage of people such as myself' has doubled over the last two decades. The average figure for those expressing disaffection on a combination of these items increased from 29 percent in 1966 to over 60 percent today" (1989, p. 6).

Incapacity

A fourth collection of social problems clusters around questions of personal incapacity. As society becomes more complex and the literacy required to perform even its most minimal functions increases, a growing number of individuals find themselves faced with one or another set of personal incapacities. These incapacities may be physical (such as the disability following upon an automobile accident or an assault with a deadly weapon) or mental (such as infantile disability resultant from the mother's prenatal drug use or a degraded physiochemical environment).

The enhancement of social and economic opportunities for disabled individuals has become the goal of ambitious legislation and a growing social change agenda. With all this movement, the bottom line is a sense in society that many individuals are being left behind through no fault of their own, and that something must be done to assure their living as normal a life as possible, in spite of their characteristics.

Government, Politics, and Law

A player that looms larger than it perhaps deserves in American life is our system of government — laden with the historic lore of freedom from the colonial domination of the old world and the manifold blessings of democracy. From another perspective, government may be seen as being, in the United States, a quite closely confined and limited tool for action and change. Supported by tax rates that appear stingy in comparison with those of other developed nations, and heavily focused upon the delivery of military capacity abroad and public safety at home, government in America more resembles Hobbes's "watchman" than it does the cradle-to-grave service provider of the Scandinavian welfare state.

Despite these limits, however, governmental institutions (which include political parties and the framework of laws created by government) affect, directly and indirectly, the daily work of the nonprofit manager.

Directly, government affects the nonprofit world because it decides which nonprofit organizations it will recognize as eligible for tax deductions and which ones it will select as contracting partners in the delivery of publicly mandated services. Indirectly, government affects the nonprofit world because its very choice of which services to provide channels the opportunities for services a nonprofit might provide.

Welfare Mix

A government's choices regarding the degree to which it will provide social service programs vitally affect the size and scale of the nation's nonprofit sector. If a government chooses to provide the full range of services of the modern welfare state — services that may include free health care, access to subsidized education at all levels, and guaranteed employment—the range of services provided by voluntary organizations will be limited. If, on the other hand, that government chooses to provide only a limited range of services—for example, health care only to the poor and aged, free education only through the secondary level, and little or no guaranteed employment—then the nonprofit sector will be provided a more open field for the development of its programs.

The British have come to identify this problem as "the welfare mix": Which services does government provide? Which are offered by nonprofits? Which are left to the economic marketplace? The American response may best be identified as that of a reluctant and limited welfare state. Our history shows that we adopt welfare programs a generation or more after they are pioneered in Western Europe, and usually only under the pressure of a looming economic catastrophe, such as the Great Depression of the 1930s or the long decline of the late 1980s and early 1990s (still euphemistically referred to as "the recession").

The preferred American response has been to provide two levels of services directly: (1) to those in poverty, a set of services designed to provide a minimum level of food, shelter, and educational opportunity; (2) to those no longer able to work owing to advanced age, a more lavish set of programs designed to assure adequacy of income and health care. This "dual welfare system" (on the one hand, Aid to Families with Dependent Children, Food Stamps, and Medicaid; and on the other hand, Social Security and Medicare) is provided with quite different dispositions. Assistance aimed at the poor is given grudgingly, with frequent checks for eligibility and cheating. Assistance provided to those who have been employed throughout their lifetimes is typically provided as a right, and not a privilege, and carries none of the stigma typically associated with the receipt of welfare, food stamps, or Medicaid.

Within the boundaries of the welfare mix, nonprofit entrepreneurs conduct a constant search for niches in which to place nonprofit organizations. Few nonprofits choose to provide income directly (a government monopoly), but many provide the services government provides only sporadically, such as health care, housing, and higher education. Large numbers of nonprofit organizations also present themselves as potential providers of services that government chooses to fund but not provide directly itself—services like sheltering the homeless, feeding the hungry, and counseling those without family support.

The welfare mix is always under pressure to change. Democrats and Republicans differ sharply as to its proper form. With the election of Ronald Reagan to the presidency in 1980, for instance, the die was cast for a considerable reduction in welfare state funding, almost entirely taken from the housing budget. A direct result of this policy choice was the drastic increase in homelessness that accompanied the reduction in federal spending on housing from $29 billion to $15 billion during the Reagan years (Piven and Cloward, 1982).

As party domination of national and state governments shift, and as new problems come to dominate the national agenda, one can anticipate a never-ending shift in the content of the welfare mix. From a strategic point of view, nonprofit managers cannot afford to ignore these processes and must seek to anticipate and plan for the implications they will have for the organizations they serve.

Certification

Government not only affects the reach of nonprofit organizations by preempting certain service areas, it also sets the stage for nonprofit action by certifying those organizations it will recognize as tax exempt. By controlling this identification, government determines which nonprofits can inform their supporters that donations are tax deductible. The deductibility of such contributions effectively socializes the individual charitable contribution, assuring that each donor's gift is "matched" by the taxpaying citizenry as a whole. (At a 33 percent tax rate, the donation of $1,000 to a charitable organization, for instance, costs the donor $667 in after-tax dollars, while the remaining $333 that is deducted from the giver's tax liability is effectively paid by every other taxpayer in the country.)

By ceding government the power to certify organizations as exempt, nonprofit organizations also cede a good deal of their sometimes-claimed "independence." As the Reagan administration's effort to regulate the charities allowed into its federated giving drives indicates, governments often have strong likes and dislikes when it comes to nonprofit organizations. Having the ability to certify these organizations allows a considerable restriction of their independence.

Moreover, allowing the deduction of charitable donations further advances the ability of government to support the organizations it approves. When an individual's gift is effectively matched by all taxpayers, as explained above, the power of the wealthy giver is magnified at the expense of those of lesser wealth.

Regulation

In addition to certifying nonprofit organizations, various governments at every level, from federal to local, regulate the work of nonprofits in a variety of ways. In some cases this regulation accompanies the provisions of contracts between government and nonprofits. In others, regulations are part of the public responsibility to assure for the general health and welfare.

Behind many regulations stand important community values. Thus, what may appear to one person to be a reasonable regulation may seem to another to be undue harassment. The members of the suburban church congregation who offered meals to the homeless in a suburban Philadelphia county, for example, found their work declared illegal by an Upper Darby township regulation requiring that food served outdoors be cooked in regulated and inspected kitchens. Project organizers pointed out that other mass feeding occurred routinely in the suburban town in such events as backyard picnics, for example. They questioned the application of the regulation to their activity, noting that it was not being applied to more reputable and influential township residents. As a result of their advocacy, the homeless feeding project continued.

Nonprofits and the Economy

A final set of institutional actors and outcomes that must centrally concern the nonprofit administrator are those of the economic order — regional, national, and global. Nonprofit managers need to be alert to matters of productivity, distribution, and globalization in their work.

Productivity

Productivity issues are those most commonly thought of in terms of "growth." When the economy grows, people tend to feel hopeful and optimistic. When it stagnates, people tend to feel as though they are being left behind.

Nonprofit organizations are directly influenced by these sentiments, for they affect levels of charitable giving, and they also affect the range and magnitude of problems that are brought to nonprofits for succor and resolution. In times of growth, nonprofits may find a bit of a surplus in their operating budgets. In times of stagnation or decline, however, they face double trouble: a greater range of needs waiting at their doors, but also shrinking resources, both from public and charitable sources, with which to fund the staff and services required.

Distribution

How society distributes its wealth and income also critically affects the work of nonprofit organizations. The long sweep of human history has shown a reduction of patterns of inequality in the distribution of income since the inception of the Industrial Revolution. This pattern continued in the United States through most of the twentieth century, but has been reversed since 1980. Since that date, the rich have increased their wealth and income, while the middle and working classes have stagnated and the poor have lost. This "reverse Robin Hood" pattern, especially in the recessionary years of the late 1980s and early 1990s, has made the work of nonprofit organizations particularly perilous.

When a society begins to blame its poor for not only inducing their own poverty but also for costing its wealthier members more in the way of crime, services, and education, a nasty downward cycle confronts nonprofit organizations. The issues of distribution are certainly important to monitor, and confront, if a vital nonprofit sector is to be sustained.

Globalization, Including Mass Media

A third economic force that needs the monitoring of the nonprofit manager is that of the onrushing global economy. We have never before lived as fully in one world as we do today. The transnationalization of economic life has many implications: (1) It reduces the prospect of world war, since corporations are powerful in every government and do their work globally—they do not want to fight themselves; (2) it creates a single financial market that makes all national economies interdependent; (3) it creates the possibility for international problem solving in a world whose problems (like AIDS or abortion—in an age of RU-486—for example) know no borders; (4) it opens the possibility for the creation of a transnational philanthropic system, in which, for example, Japanese-owned corporations that do business in the United States participate in the support of American nonprofit organizations.

Among the forces that have been globalized are those of the mass media. With their hunger to report sensational news, events of fleeting interest in a local community may flash for a few moments upon the TV screens of the world, whereas world leaders are known to monitor Cable News Network (CNN) on a constant basis, even directly from their own offices.

For the nonprofit organization leader, the transnational media means that a particularly dramatic case may lead to transitory international attention, and perhaps some checks in tomorrow's mail. But it also means that a transgression will be noted, and possibly punished with a swift sword. Thus, a Father Ritter of Covenant House, accused of sexual misconduct with a youthful client, is quickly removed from office. And a William Aramony of United Way of America, found to have abused the perquisites of his office in a variety of hardly less sensational ways, is as quickly removed from a position he had secured over decades using political skills to match those of a medieval potentate.

One world—one economy—one information system. It is a new world, and one nonprofit managers need to understand and exploit, at least for the appropriate interests and values of their organization and the interests it represents.

Major Players on the Nonprofit Stage

This chapter has thus far reviewed the environmental field within which nonprofit organizations are sited. The second part of the chapter deals with the sector itself, its principal players and their roles.

The "third sector," as I prefer to call it, is a world of thoughts and dreams, individuals and groups, needs and solutions. Its principal actors are givers, intermediaries, regulators, nonprofit organizations, beneficiaries, and customers.

Givers are those who join with others in meeting their own and others' perceived needs by means of voluntary organization. For the giver, it is not enough to rely on the benefits provided by the other main sectors of society. There is an additional level of involvement that is perceived, and that involves joining with others of like mind in supporting the work of a voluntary or nonprofit organization.

Givers rely, like the rest of us, on the other three sectors. They are citizens who vote, complain about government inaction, and enjoy the blessings of governmental services. They are also persons who live in families, and enjoy the joys and frustrations occasioned by that venerable human institution. And they make their livings, or seek to, within the confines of the world of economic organizations.

But there is something that the three other sectors are not able to provide that these individuals seek by involvement in the third sector. Perhaps they volunteer, as more than half of the American population does on a regular basis, in assisting persons who may require their assistance, whether it be a group of youngsters in a town swim team or a group of homeless persons thankful to receive a hot meal on a regular basis.

Givers also make financial contributions to nonprofit organizations. Sometimes these gifts are large, such as the $100 million gift made by a New Jersey industrialist to a regional public college in 1992; sometimes these gifts are small, such as the quarter you may have placed in a UNICEF tin carried by a trick-or-treater last Halloween. The varieties of giving, and the attitudes underlying them, is increasingly the subject of an emerging subfield of "fund raising" (see Burlingame, 1992).

The question of the attitude underlying giving has long concerned social scientists. After many studies of the subject, it appears clear that giving is performed for a variety of motives. Some are largely altruistic: some people find it rewarding to assist others without receiving any evident reward themselves. But, of course, they do receive a psychic reward in the form of their feeling of having done the right thing. So have they acted entirely without concern for their own well-being?

Other gifts come with strings attached, such as the aforementioned gift of $100 million by industrialist Henry Rowan to Glassboro State College. A substantial piece of the gift was earmarked to provide tuition and educational programs for the employees of the company Rowan owns. In return, and apparently unsolicited by Rowan, officials of the College and the state of New Jersey rushed to enact a name change of Glassboro State: to Rowan College of New Jersey.

During the Nixon presidency, Americans learned about the laundering of money. Had they been more attuned to the history of philanthropy, they might have been more ready for these revelations. Giving to nonprofit organizations involves a transformative process: money made in the first sector (business) is not spent in the fourth sector (the household) for personal use, but is rather donated to the third sector (a certified nonprofit organization), where it receives an immediate reward from the second sector (government) in the form of forgiveness of taxation.

Thus is raised the question of "tainted money." The argument goes as follows: a fair amount of money that individuals make in the world of corporate business comes to them as a result of ethically dubious activity. What is to assure that this money is somehow purified when it is offered to a nonprofit organization, especially when a third of it returns to the donor in the form of a tax deduction? Cases in point often chosen are Andrew Carnegie and John D. Rockefeller, neither of whom was known for particularly humane treatment of their employees or their competitors.

In opposition comes the standard response of the successful nonprofit administrator: "Tainted money? 'Taint enough of it around for my organization!" A variety of ethical dilemmas are thus suggested: Should nonprofit organizations participate with corporations in "cause-related marketing" schemes? Should nonprofit organizations accept donations from donors who make their profits from legal but addictive drugs, such as tobacco and alcoholic beverages? Should fundraising advisers work on contracts that provide them a fixed share of the moneys that are raised by campaigns they counsel? Should educational institutions accept funding when it is accompanied by specific requests for board control or program revision?

Since we live in a world in which the alchemic transformation of dross to gold has been shown to be a problematic process at best, it is the advice of this author that nonprofit managers examine these questions fully and deeply before they accept a donation. At least they should be as sophisticated as the young lady from Kent in the somewhat bawdy rhyme. Remember the lady from Kent? She knew what it meant, but she went . . .

Intermediaries

Very little is accomplished without the use of intermediaries in the modern world. In the nonprofit organizational world, intermediaries are those who link the money and time of donors with the needs the organization themselves seek to meet. These intermediaries are variously known as consultants, trainers, counselors, and program officers. They work for their own firms, support centers, fundraising firms, "sector-serving organizations," and foundations. They apply a good deal of the grease to the tracks of American philanthropy and voluntarism.

Of all these intermediary institutions, the foundation is the most visible. Typically established by an individual of considerable wealth, the foundation provides support through its program for a wide range of nonprofit organizations.

Nonprofit organization managers, as a matter of professional course, get to know the lay of the foundation land. Particularly, they learn that foundations come in three major varieties: national, regional, and community. National foundations support programs that are seen to have a particular impact on a pressing problem of broad concern to the foundation, the solution of which might be applicable in other parts of the country or world.

Regional foundations support programs that are seen to have a particular impact on problems of the region, typically one that was identified by the donor himself. Community foundations draw support from many local donors and seek to enhance the social capacity of organizations in a particular city or metropolitan area.

Foundations operate in the context of an etiquette of "giving and getting" that differs quite considerably from the rough and tumble of daily organizational contact. Historically, foundations sought to create an aura of refined dignity in their offices and processes, with the "grant-seeker" typically left to play the role of humble supplicant. In more recent times, foundation officers have come to recognize that the grant-seeker is its very life blood, in that a foundation is only as good as the programs it is able to attract to it. Considerable effort has been devoted, in many foundations, to reducing the perceived distance between seeker and grantor. And, in many cases, the sheer volume of queries and prospectuses that reach a foundation officer gives a glimpse of the position as an often paper-glutted office rather than a last bastion of corporate gentility.

Organizations such as INDEPENDENT SECTOR, the Council on Foundations, the National Society of Fund Raising Executives, and literally hundreds of associations of like-minded nonprofit organizations serve as the "trade associations" of the sector. They share information on legislation, grants opportunities, societal trends, and research, as these pertain to the interests of their members. They assert the interests of their members in the legislative process, and they engage in public relations campaigns aimed at convincing Americans that the work of nonprofit organizations is of considerable value and merit.

University-based centers on voluntarism, philanthropy, and nonprofit organizations, of which there are now more than thirty (Wish, 1993), provide educational, training, and research service to those aspiring to enter the field of nonprofit management and to those already established in positions in the field. Typically funded by a major regional foundation in their area, these centers are beginning to develop degree programs (usually at the M.A. level) and to otherwise secure their rather perilous niches in the tottering structure of American higher education.

Closer to the firing line of everyday organizational give and take is the office of the support, or technical assistance, provider. Typically this is an individual, "mom-and-pop," or small-group venture, which lives and dies on the basis of accumulating and discharging the responsibilities of many short-term contracts. Consultants strive to project the image of "taking charge" and providing important services to organizations that reach out to them for assistance. The aristocrats of the consultant trade are the "fundraising counsel," a fascinating group of individuals who adopt both the elan of the old-line foundation and a kind of locker-room camaraderie based on having located, and secured for their clients, a considerable amount of philanthropic wealth.

Regulators are few and far between in the nonprofit sector (Gaul and Borowski, 1993). But when they enter the scene, the sector trembles. Principal among this group are (1) state agencies of taxation, (2) nonprofit organizations that serve as sector monitors, (3) program evaluators, and (4) congressional subcommittees. The work of these three bodies, taken as a whole, yields only a sporadic product.

The process by which an organization receives tax exemption tends to be a one-time review, conducted in full rigor only before the organization moves into a fully operational mode. Once the exemption is granted, the major requirement of tax agencies involves the completion of an annual form, the "990," which is at best a perfunctory reporting device. Few are the nonprofit organizations whose exempt status is questioned after initial certification, assuming the annual filing of the 990.

Sector monitoring organizations, like the Better Business Bureau (BBB) and the Charities Information Bureau, are similarly noteworthy for the limits of the services they provide. Some, like the BBB, respond to individual complaints and queries regarding the legitimacy of the practices of nonprofit organizations. Others compute data on the proportion of agency funding that actually reaches the intended beneficiaries of the nonprofits' service. Typically, however, a bogus charity does not begin to suffer before its malevolence reaches the press and courtroom. (An example here is the fundraising work of the Philadelphia businessman whose for-profit company claimed to be raising money for the American Foundation for AIDS Research [AmFAR]. As reported in the *Philadelphia Inquirer* of July 23, 1992, the scheme worked as follows: "[The businessman] sold in excess of 25,000 canisters to between 75 and 100 professional fundraisers in 'several' states. The fundraisers, in turn, hired individual 'representatives' who were to place and service the bright yellow canisters in stores. The fundraisers were to pay the representatives 25 percent of the money in the can, keep 20 percent for themselves and send 55 percent to [the businessman], who was to forward 10 percent of the original gross recepts to AmFAR." At this writing, the scheme is being investigated by the attorneys general of four states.)

Program evaluators are required by most federal grants, and some foundations. Their work is intended to assure the funder that the recipient organization has indeed delivered the service promised in the initial proposal. The work of a professional evaluation consultant is often of great value to the delivery of the program, providing an ongoing "formative" contribution to the program as well as a formal "summative" report. However, the evaluation component is typically cast as a part of the program, rather than as an external review, and is therefore not properly seen as a purely regulatory device.

The form of regulation that strikes the deepest fear in the nonprofit organization's heart is that of the congressional subcommittee. As detailed by several historians, and particularly Peter Dobkin Hall (1992), this process raises, from time to time, the threat of removing the charitable deduction for nonprofit organizations. Thus, in the 1950s, Congressman Wright Patman led a series of hearings that eventuated the recasting of foundation practice, requiring all foundations to provide at least a fixed proportion of their assets in annual contributions. And in the 1980s, Congressman J. J. Pickle raised the specter of removing tax exemption as a means of coping with the increasingly intractable federal budget deficit. When the specter of changes in federal tax codes present itself, the national and regional structure of sector-serving organizations mobilizes for action. While some argue that such change would be beneficial, the typical response of the sector servers is that disaster is impending. The net effect of this process, however, is never one of thoroughgoing regulation, but rather of sporadic intervention. Most of the time the nonprofit sector pursues its various ends in American life in a self-regulated, or even unregulated, fashion.

Nonprofit and Charitable Organizations

Over a million nonprofit organizations exist in the United States, employing approximately 10 percent of the total number of workers in the United States. These denizens of the third sector constitute an army over half the size of government. They comprise a formidable array of society's institutional forces, providing religious, educational, social, health, and cultural services.

The work of nonprofit organizations involves three major forms of activity: (1) service, (2) advocacy, and (3) member benefit. These activity forms are elaborated in the work of Smith (1992), among others. Service assists individuals in need with the resolution of their immediate and pressing problems. Advocacy defines a set of policies that other institutions, including governmental and corporate structures, might follow to more fully achieve a just and humane society. Member benefit provides the collective structure within which association members can enjoy both colleagueship and the articulation of common interests.

Nonprofit organizations as an institutional force is the subject of a number of useful volumes. Among these works are those of Lohmann (1992), Hall (1992), Wolch (1990), O'Neill (1989), Van Til (1988), O'Connell (1983), and Douglas (1983). These volumes, as well as the present one, belong in a prominent place on the reading shelf of every nonprofit manager. They document, in considerable detail, the rapid expansion of the nonprofit sector in American life over the past half-century; they also show the ways in which nonprofit organizations have come to stand as institutions unto themselves in American life: Boy Scouts and Girl Scouts, the Catholic Church and PTL, the Brookings Institution and the Heritage Foundation, Blue Cross and the Mayo Clinic, Yale and Amherst, the Ford Foundation and the Getty Trust, the National Football League and the Motion Picture Academy of America . . . and on and on.

Beneficiaries

Who benefits from the activity of nonprofit organizations? A beginning list might go as follows:

1. Those who directly receive services from the nonprofit organization
2. Those in whose name the nonprofit organization advocates
3. Members of the nonprofit organization who receive direct membership benefits
4. Staff members employed by the nonprofit organization
5. Those who enjoy the benefits of nonprofit organizations as consumers or customers
6. Members of the general public who find a higher quality of life available to them as a result of the work of the nonprofit organization

In an intriguing recent presentation, historian Rudolph Bauer (1993) suggested that volunteers tend to treat nonprofit organizations as though they were providers of charitable service, while board members tend to see them as though they were political organizations. Meanwhile, staff members behave as though the same organization is a business. In this way, Bauer observes, a "third sector" organization tends to take on the coloration of business (first sector), politics (second sector), and community (fourth sector). It all depends on one's point of view, which itself is determined by one's role within the organization!

Summary: A Couple of Big Questions

The nonprofit sector arises as an institutional response to societal disquiet and need. Its leaders proffer the obligatory citation to Tocqueville in their encomiums and routinely observe the importance of the third sector in American pluralism. But do nonprofit organizations serve as tools of a democratic process, or are they too often simply tax-free businesses in disguise, another form of organization out to preserve advantage in an age of grab and greed? And what of the role of individual voluntary action in the modern mass society: how does it contribute to the values of participation in a strong democracy?

The role of the nonprofit sector as an institutional contributor to the building of a viable democratic society is a question that requires continuing attention. While it has been probed in the literature on an intermittent basis by Etzioni, O'Connell, Van Til, and Wolch, among others, it is clear that the relationship with democratic theory and institutions is considered as at best a question of secondary importance by many in the field. Such issues as management capacity, fundraising strategems, and public relations predominate in professional conferences and literature, including this handbook. How voluntary action and nonprofit organization may serve to expand the democratic horizon are questions that typically are not advanced onto the usual nonprofit agenda.

Nonprofit organization leaders will be well advised to take the work they do in a manner both serious and clear-minded. At stake is the success of their organizations and the welfare of their clients and members. But also in the balance stands the very health of the nonprofit sector as an institutional actor in the precarious process of contemporary society. Nonprofit managers will do well to understand this institutional field, and the importance of their own role within it.

References

Bauer, R. "Voluntarism, Nongovernmental Organizations, and Public Policy in the Third Reich." *Nonprofit and Voluntary Sector Quarterly,* 1990, *19,* 199–214.

Bauer, R. Plenary presentation to Conference on Well-Being in Europe and the Third Sector, Barcelona, Spain, May 1993.

Burlingame, D. (ed.). *The Responsibilities of Wealth.* Bloomington: Indiana University Press, 1992.

Catlin, R. *Racial Politics in Urban Planning: Gary, Indiana 1980–1990.* Lexington: University of Kentucky Press, 1993.

Douglas, J. *Why Charity?* Beverly Hills, Calif.: Sage, 1983.

Etzioni, A. *The Active Society.* New York: Free Press, 1968.

Gaul, G. M., and Borowski, N. A. *Free Ride: The Tax Exempt Economy.* Kansas City, Mo.: Andrews and McMeel, 1993.

Gidron, B., Kramer, R., and Salamon, L. *Government and the Third Sector: Emerging Relationships in Welfare States.* San Francisco: Jossey-Bass, 1992.

Hall, P. D. *Inventing the Nonprofit Sector and Other Essays on Philanthropy, Voluntarism, and Nonprofit Organizations.* Baltimore, Md.: Johns Hopkins University Press, 1992.

Kanter, D. L., and Mirvis, P. H. *The Cynical Americans: Living and Working in an Age of Discontent and Disillusion.* San Francisco: Jossey-Bass, 1989.

Lohmann, R. *The Commons: New Perspectives on Nonprofit Organizations and Voluntary Action.* San Francisco: Jossey-Bass, 1992.

Marien, M. *Future Survey Annual 1992.* Bethesda, Md.: Publisher, 1992.

Marriott, M. "Fathers Find That Child Support Means Owing More Than Money." *New York Times,* July 20, 1992.

Mintzberg, H. *The Nature of Managerial Work.* Englewood Cliffs, N.J.: Prentice-Hall, 1980.

O'Connell, B. (ed.). *America's Voluntary Spirit.* New York: Foundation Center, 1983.

O'Neill, M. *The Third America: The Emergence of the Nonprofit Sector in the United States.* San Francisco: Jossey-Bass, 1989.

Ostrander, S., and Schervish, P. "Giving and Getting: Philanthropy as a Social Relation." In J. Van Til and Associates, *Critical Issues in American*

Philanthropy: Strengthening Theory and Practice. San Francisco: Jossey-Bass, 1990.

Piven, F. F., and Cloward, R. *The New Class War: Reagan's Attack on the Welfare State and its Consequences.* New York: Pantheon, 1982.

Purdy, M. "Philadelphia's Troubled—and Costly—Children." *Philadelphia Inquirer,* May 24, 1992.

Ropers, R. *Persistent Poverty: The American Dream Turned Nightmare.* New York: Plenum, 1991.

Schlesinger, A. M., Jr. "Faded Glory." *New York Times Magazine,* July 12, 1992, p. 14.

Smith, D. R. "A Neglected Type of Voluntary Nonprofit Organization: Exploration of the Semiformal, Fluid-Membership Organization." *Nonprofit and Voluntary Sector Quarterly,* 1992, *21,* 251–270.

Stacey, J. *Brave New Families: Stories of Domestic Upheaval in Late Twentieth Century America.* New York: Basic Books, 1990.

Van Til, J. *Mapping the Third Sector: Voluntarism in a Changing Social Economy.* New York: Foundation Center, 1988.

Wish, N. B. "Colleges Offering More Nonprofit Graduate Programs." *NonProfit Times,* June 1993, pp. 22–23.

Wolch, J. *The Shadow State.* New York: Foundation Center, 1990.

3

The Legal Framework
of the Nonprofit Sector
in the United States

Thomas Silk

> Non-profit, non-business, non-governmental are all negatives.
> One cannot, however, define anything by what it is not. What,
> then, is it that all these institutions do? They all have in com-
> mon — and this is a recent realization — that their purpose is to
> change human lives [Drucker, 1989, p. 198].

Several years ago at a legal conference in Moscow, I was approached by
a Russian lawyer who was trying to make sense of the interplay of laws
that govern the charitable sector in the United States. What was needed,
he suggested, was not more detailed treatments of state corporation and trust
laws or federal and state tax laws pertaining to the charitable sector. What
was missing, he said, was an overview with practical detail, a "bird's-eye
and worm's-eye view" of U.S. charitable law. This chapter is based on the
paper I wrote in response to that request. It takes the form of a case study
and commentary featuring a hypothetical charitable advocacy organization
which, although fictional, is a composite of many existing organizations.
The case study provides the basis for the subsequent commentary on legal
and regulatory issues that are frequently encountered during the life cycle
of a charitable organization in the United States. To allow consideration
of a broad range of legal issues, the case study considers the growth and
development of a large and successful charitable organization.

Case Study

Pre-Formation

Jim and Beth Rankin received their doctorates in oceanography in 1965. After graduation, they taught marine science at neighboring universities and conducted academic research. They formed a discussion group with their colleagues, which met weekly. In the first year, the group included about twenty people who discussed their research findings about the ocean environment. It soon became apparent to the members of the group that the oceans were threatened and that citizens as well as social institutions, including the federal and state governments, were blissfully unaware of the threat and its significance. Existing environmental organizations were concerned with other issues pertaining to land and air and had not yet begun to consider marine issues.

In 1967 the Rankins decided to do something about the problem. They expanded their discussion group to fifty members, and they enlisted the aid of their colleagues in giving speeches about the environmental threat to the oceans to any local organizations that would listen. Their goal was clear and entirely lacking in modesty: to change the attitude and behavior of people toward the oceans. Changes in the policies of government and business, they believed, would follow in time.

The Rankins began to encounter a pleasant but persistent problem. After they gave a speech, members of the audience would ask where they could contribute money to support their work. By this time, the Rankins had come to think of themselves primarily as organizers rather than as academics. They decided to form a new nonprofit environmental organization to protect the oceans.

Formation

Name. The Rankins wanted a name that was dramatic. They considered many names and settled on the international distress signal, SOS, as an acronym for Save Our Seas, only to learn that another organization in a distant state was already using that name. They kept returning to the idea that the problem was global in scope and that water comprises more than two thirds of our planet. Late one night the name came to them: Planet Water.

Incorporation. With the help of an attorney, Planet Water was incorporated in California in 1969 as a nonprofit corporation. Its purpose, as stated in its articles of incorporation, is to encourage and promote the environmental protection of the oceans. The articles were signed by the Rankins and were mailed to California's secretary of state for filing. Within a week, the Rankins were notified that the document had been accepted and filed. They opened a bank account for Planet Water with $1,000 that they had managed to save from their salaries.

The bylaws of Planet Water provide for a voting membership of all individuals who pay dues. They also make provision for a fifteen-person board of directors elected by the members for three-year terms.

Tax Exemption. Next, Planet Water applied simultaneously to the Internal Revenue Service and to the California Franchise Tax Board for federal and state tax exemption as a charitable organization.

In those applications, the Rankins described the purpose and intended activities of Planet Water and included a proposed budget listing the anticipated receipts and expenditures of Planet Water for the next three years. The California Franchise Tax Board exemption was issued in two months. Three months later the IRS exemption was in hand.

Operation

Program. Since its formation, Planet Water's activities have become extensive. All are reviewed each year by its board of directors. Old programs are continued or dropped, and new ones added, and all are tested by whether they advance the goals of oceanic environmental education and constituency building.

Research has become an important component of its program. Planet Water has designed and is conducting a five-year study of San Francisco Bay and of Chesapeake Bay for the purpose of developing a scientific baseline against which to measure the environmental health of those bodies of water. Both studies are funded by the federal government.

Planet Water conducts an extensive public education program. It offers a training course in marine environmental policy issues for volunteers. There are about 425 volunteers, each of whom makes a commitment to give ten speeches a year. Planet Water publishes, in seven languages, a quarterly magazine and widely popular books that are filled with handsome photographs and informative articles on ocean themes. It has produced numerous related television programs.

Children are not overlooked. Planet Water publishes an ocean science curriculum for elementary school teachers. It commissions and publishes books for children designed to acquaint them with the world's oceans, and each summer it operates a sea camp for children at eight coastal locations. After a flurry of publicity in the national press about the killing of dolphins, Planet Water launched an "adopt-a-dolphin" campaign, which has resulted in the formation of Dolphin Clubs for schoolchildren across America.

Active in lobbying nationally and internationally, Planet Water has been credited with contributing significantly to the International Whaling Commission's global ban on whaling and the enactment of the Clean Water Act and the Ocean Dumping Ban Act.

Planet Water also makes modest grants in support of water-related environmental activities of other groups, both foreign and domestic.

Membership. Planet Water now has 300,000 members worldwide, who pay annual dues of $25. They receive a quarterly magazine and are invited to attend the annual meeting at which the Rankins, who serve as co-executive directors, report on the current status and future prospects of Planet Water. It has chapters in major coastal cities in the United States and affiliates in twelve other countries. Members vote by mail for directors to fill terms that have expired.

Governing Body. The governing body of Planet Water is its board of directors. Except for the Rankins, who are paid as staff members and who have been elected to the board on a continuing basis over the years, the fifteen board members serve without compensation. They are, however, reimbursed for their travel, meal, and lodging expenses in connection with attending board meetings. The board meets quarterly, in January, April, July, and October. At the July meeting the board reviews the goals and objectives of the organization and makes, usually on recommendation of the Rankins, the modifications it believes to be suitable. At the October meeting, the board reviews and approves the program and financial budget for each quarter of the next year. At the following year's meetings, the primary task of the board, apart from developing the budget for the new year, is to review the program and financial performance of the organization in comparison with the budget, to consider policy issues put before them by the co-executive directors, and to approve grants.

Between board meetings, policy decisions are made by an executive committee consisting of the four officers who are also board members. The day-to-day management decisions are made by the Rankins in accordance with the program and financial budget approved by the board of directors.

Staff. The paid staff of Planet Water now consists of 312 people, ranging from accountants to zoologists. When employees are hired, they are given three documents: a letter containing a description of their duties and their salary, a personnel policy describing the health plan and retirement and other benefits, and an evaluation form. Each year the board of directors reviews and sets the salary and benefits for the Rankins.

The compensation for all other employees is decided annually by the co-executive directors, subject to review and approval by the board. In determining the appropriate amount of salary and benefits, the Rankins rely on an annual compensation survey published by a national nonprofit management organization. From that survey, they determine the range within which other nonprofit organizations of comparable size pay their employees for performing comparable tasks. The amount paid to the employee within that range by Planet Water will depend upon how well the employee has fared in the evaluation.

Finances. The finances of Planet Water, which were precarious indeed at the beginning, have now stabilized. Its annual revenues are about $20,000,000, made up of dues and fees (40 percent), book sales (16 percent), individual contributions (13 percent), government contracts (8 percent), royalty income (7 percent), investment income (6 percent), joint venture income (5 percent), foundation grants (4 percent), and corporate contributions (1 percent).

Dues and fees are paid by members and participants. At $25 each, 300,000 members generate dues of $7,500,000. Parents of the 2,000 children who attend the summer sea camp pay a fee of $200.

The source of the income from book sales is Planet Water's extensive program of publishing educational books on the ocean environment.

Individual contributions are derived mainly from direct mail campaigns. Each year, Planet Water conducts four campaigns, reaching 20 million households. The core of the solicitation for funds is often a copy of a recent Planet Water advertisement in the *New York Times* dramatizing the consequences of an oil spill or other environmental catastrophe at sea. Over the years, as the public has learned more about the effective work of Planet Water, the amount of bequests has also increased.

The government contracts include, in addition to the bay studies, the designation of Planet Water as portkeeper of four coastal ports, to monitor compliance with restrictions on the discharge of pollutants into the waters of those ports by shipping, industry, and local governments.

Planet Water receives extensive royalty income. It licenses the use of its name and logo to approved manufacturers of over 100 products, ranging from t-shirts to windsurfers, in return for a 3 percent fee or royalty based on the gross receipts from sales.

Planet Water's fund balance is now $5,000,000. Investment decisions are made by the board of directors on recommendation of the finance committee. The funds of Planet Water available for investment are allocated equally among four outside investment managers. Once a year, the committee meets with its advisers to review their investment performance. The board of directors has instituted a policy of replacing, every third year, the investment adviser with the poorest performance record.

Planet Water is also engaged in a joint venture with a commercial organization. They are partners in the design, manufacturing, and marketing of submersible vehicles that are used to gather data on pollution beneath the ocean surface. The vehicles are also sold to the public for recreational use.

Grants from foundations have increased each year, although they remain a small percentage of overall receipts. The amount of corporate contributions has not improved in recent years.

Compliance

Each year Planet Water must submit reports to tax and regulatory agencies.

Annually, at the federal level, Planet Water must file a report with the Internal Revenue Service, setting forth its receipts and expenditures, explaining the general nature of its activities, disclosing the name of each large contributor and each director, officer, top official, highly compensated employee, and consultant. The report discloses the salaries and benefits provided to highly compensated employees.

Each year, at the state level, Planet Water must file similar reports with the California Franchise Tax Board and the Registry of Charitable Trusts. Also, it must disclose the names of its current officers to the secretary of state.

At the local level, Planet Water must file an annual form with the City and County of San Francisco, to qualify for an exemption from property tax on any land, buildings, and office equipment that it owns in San Francisco. Planet Water must describe the nature of its property and explain how it is used in carrying out its charitable purpose.

Each quarter during the year, Planet Water must file with federal and state tax authorities a form that describes the amount of income and other taxes it has withheld from the salaries of its employees and paid to the tax authorities.

Finally, Planet Water must comply with separate charitable solicitation laws imposed by most states and by some cities, which require that all charitable organizations that raise funds in their area must register and report on a periodic basis with the appropriate authority.

Termination

The board of directors does not plan to terminate Planet Water. The directors believe there is a continuing need for its work. Its goals, they have concluded, are not likely to be realized in the foreseeable future.

In a recent interview, Beth Rankin was asked how she would know when Planet Water had accomplished its mission. "No one is more aware than I am," she said, "that the changes in public attitudes toward the environment have not been due solely to our modest efforts. We happened upon an idea whose time had come. On the other hand, I am convinced that we have made some difference. But there is still a long way to go. I will know that we have reached our goal," she concluded, "when the act of polluting water that belongs to everyone is every bit as socially unacceptable as fouling the water you serve in your own home."

Commentary

Pre-Formation

For several years, the Rankins met regularly with colleagues and gave speeches about environmental threats to the oceans. In many countries, such meetings and public speeches would be regulated by government. In America, however, the Bill of Rights to the U.S. Constitution limits government regulation of speech and the related right of association. Private meetings and speech may not be regulated. Public speech and meetings may not be regulated as to content, but reasonable restrictions as to time, place, and manner may be imposed. The early environmental activities of the Rankins and their colleagues, therefore, proceeded lawfully, despite the absence of government knowledge or authorization. Government involvement did not occur until the Rankins decided to conduct their activities within a formal legal entity.

Formation

The Rankins were not required to form a charitable organization, or any organization at all, in order to advocate for environmental preservation. It was, rather, the benefits of charitable status and the corporate form that led them to choose this approach. Had they wanted to operate without governmental oversight and without legal formalities, they would have been entirely free to do so, but they would have had to forego the accompanying benefits. The benefits are both symbolic and practical. A formal organization would have its own separate identity, which would symbolize their mission and could survive their retirement or death. Moreover, the corporation, rather than the Rankins as individuals, would be legally responsible for the project's acts and omissions.

The tax benefits of forming a separate charitable organization are even more significant. A tax-exempt charity, as the name implies, generally pays no tax on its income. Of equal importance, charities may offer potential donors not only the satisfaction of contributing to a good cause but also the ability to lower their income tax bills. This is because individuals and corporate taxpayers who contribute to charitable organizations may, under the federal tax system and those of many states, reduce, by the amount of their contributions, the income base on which their tax is calculated.

The formation of legal entities is regulated, in almost all instances, by state law rather than by federal law. In California, the Rankins would have three legal entities to choose from: a nonprofit public benefit corporation, a charitable trust, or an unincorporated nonprofit association. The association form is seldom used, because its few rules contain little protection against liability and leave many operational questions unanswered. The nonprofit corporation has largely replaced the more ancient legal form, the charitable trust, as the entity of choice for new nonprofit organizations. This has come about because charitable trusts are largely creatures of case law, while nonprofit corporations are creatures of statutory law. Modern statutory rules governing organizational formation, operation, and termination contain protections against liability and provide comprehensive legal guidance to the directors and members of nonprofit corporations but not to trustees of charitable trusts.

Name. The Rankins were not able to use their initial choice of name, SOS, because another charitable organization was already using it. Had they attempted to use that name, both the government and the other charity could have taken steps to prevent it.

No state will allow the formation of a new corporation whose name is deceptively similar to that of another organization. Moreover, the civil law of unfair competition allows an existing organization to prevent a new organization from using a name that exploits the value which the prior organization has given to the name. To avoid name-related problems, new organizations commonly search the state corporation registry and, with increasing frequency, the federal trademark registry as well, before a name is finally chosen. After the name has been chosen and the organization has been formed, registering that name for protection under the federal and state trademark laws is becoming standard practice.

Incorporation. A common term for the enabling document of a nonprofit corporation in the United States is "articles of incorporation." State practice varies, however, and other terms (such as "constitution," "certificate," "charter," and "organic document") are still encountered.

In California the content of articles of incorporation is largely standardized by statute. Articles generally contain the name of the organization, the law under which it is being incorporated (for example, the Nonprofit Public Benefit Corporation Law), its purposes, the manner in which the net assets are to be distributed in the event of dissolution, and the name of the incorporator or incorporators. California law requires only one incorporator. However many incorporators there are, they need not be U.S. citizens or even residents.

The incorporator submits the articles to the secretary of state, together with the minimum state income tax prepayment (which is refunded, with interest, if the corporation later receives tax-exempt status). The secretary of state reviews the articles of incorporation for form, but not for content. If the articles are correct in form, they will be accepted for filing and given a corporate number. The corporation's legal existence begins on the date on which the articles are accepted for filing by the secretary of state.

Once the articles have been filed and returned, the individuals who have incorporated the organization then adopt its bylaws. The bylaws prescribe the organizational rules that, so long as they are not inconsistent with state law, govern the corporation. They usually contain various sections describing the board of directors (its powers, the term of office and manner of election of the directors, and the rules for conducting meetings), the members, if any (their rights and duties and rules for members' meetings), the duties of officers, and other similar matters relating to the formal government of the corporation. At the same meeting, the incorporators will usually elect the first board of directors and the officers and authorize the opening of a bank account, specifying which individuals have authority to withdraw funds.

The next step is, commonly, to visit the local office of a bank and to open the new charity's bank account. Banks generally require evidence of the organization's legal existence (here, the file-stamped articles) and of the connection between the organization and those who will manage the bank account (usually, a resolution adopted by the board of directors appointing signatories on the bank account).

State law requires that minutes — a written record of a meeting — be made of all meetings of the organization's board of directors and committees. There is no requirement that the minutes be filed with any governmental agency. They must be produced, however, if they are requested in connection with any audit of the organization by a governmental agency.

The bylaws are effective as soon as they are adopted by the incorporators. It is not necessary to obtain the approval of any governmental agency.

Tax Exemption. The revenues of nonprofit organizations are generally exempt from federal income tax. Business revenues are a major exception. If the nonprofit organization is actively engaged in a business whose conduct is unrelated to its exempt purpose, then it is taxable on the net receipts from that activity at the same rates that apply to a business corporation. There are many exceptions and exclusions, however, to the scope and coverage of that complex tax. It does not apply, for example, to passive investment income, such as most types of dividends, interest, rents, and royalties.

California law is substantially the same: a nonprofit organization is exempt from state income tax except on its unrelated business income. In both jurisdictions the exemption process entails the filing of an application for exemption and a review by the tax agency of the proposed purposes and activities of the nonprofit organization. It is in this review that the content of the charitable organization is scrutinized for the first time by any governmental agency.

The exercise of discretion by the Internal Revenue Service is reviewable internally and in court. Federal law gives an organization extensive opportunities to challenge a proposed determination by the IRS that it fails to qualify as charitable. The initial determination is usually made at a regional office of the IRS. The organization may appeal the adverse proposed determination administratively, within the IRS, at the regional and national levels. If those appeals do not succeed, the organization may file an action in federal court, where a neutral judge will review the administrative proceedings and make an independent determination as to whether the organization qualifies as charitable.

When Planet Water applied for tax-exempt status, it represented to the Internal Revenue Service and the Franchise Tax Board that it fit the statutory definition of a charitable organization. The statutory definition (contained in a federal statute — Section 501(c)(3) of the Internal Revenue Code — and, also, in corresponding provisions of the laws of many states) requires that a tax-exempt charitable organization be formed only for certain permitted purposes: religious, charitable, scientific, testing for public safety, literary, educational, fostering national or international amateur sports competition, or the prevention of cruelty to children or animals. It must be organized exclusively for one or more of those purposes; that is, its governing document must limit its activities to proper goals. And it must be operated exclusively for one or more of those purposes. Thus, it may not engage in activities that serve other purposes, except to an insubstantial degree.

The federal statute explicitly prohibits certain activities by tax-exempt charitable organizations. No part of a charity's net earnings may be regularly diverted to the benefit of any private person or entity. This means that the charitable organization's funds must be used to carry out its charitable program and may not be paid to individuals except as reasonable compensation for necessary services performed for the charity or as fair and reasonable payment for the use or acquisition of property required by the organization.

The federal statute bars a charity from engaging in electioneering — activity in support of, or in opposition to, a candidate for public office — and it also provides that no substantial part of a tax-exempt charity's activities may involve attempts to influence legislation. Except for churches, charities that are broadly publicly supported (as opposed to charities that are supported chiefly by a single family or business entity) may make expenditures to influence legislation amounting to 20 percent of their total expenditures in any taxable year, subject to a maximum of $1,000,000 per year for the largest organizations. Since Planet Water intended to work for the passage of proenvironment legislation, it notified the Internal Revenue Service, in its application for tax exemption, that it would engage in lobbying activity to the extent permitted by law.

Although American tax-exempt charitable organizations are subject to these limits on their political activity, they are nonetheless free to engage in activities that, in many other countries, would be considered political indeed. For example, Planet Water has sponsored rallies, parades, and other law-abiding demonstrations opposing the pollution of the oceans. It regularly buys full-page advertisements in major newspapers to advocate its views. It has led international consumer boycotts of products that endanger marine life. The activities of Planet Water in attempting to change the attitudes and behavior of all sectors of society — business, government, nonprofit, and citizens — are intended to target power relationships between and within those sectors. Its activities are political in the most fundamental sense. So long as it refrains from involvement in campaigns for public office and complies with the limits on its lobbying expenditures, however, the political activities of Planet Water — like those of other American charities — are limited only by the willingness of its supporters to finance them.

Operations

Program. Planet Water receives donations from the public and grants from other charities, but most of its income is generated by its own activities, including publications and government contracts. It is entirely legal and proper in the United States for a charitable organization to charge a reasonable fee for goods or services it provides. However, its activities must be conducted in a noncommercial manner, and the conduct of those activities (not just the use to which the proceeds are put) must be substantially related to the accomplishment of the charity's exempt purpose. If not, the organization may be taxed on the proceeds of the activity at corporate rates. Furthermore, an organization's tax exemption may be revoked if its unrelated business activities are so extensive in comparison with its charitable activities that the organization fails to carry out a charitable program reasonably commensurate with its financial resources.

During its annual review of Planet Water's programs, the board of directors examines each program to determine whether it satisfies these standards. In considering Planet Water's magazine, for example, the board determined that the magazine helps Planet Water to advance its educational purposes by informing a wide audience about marine issues. But is it improperly commercial? Like many commercial publications, the magazine is well designed and filled with color photographs. But these graphic techniques help the magazine to convey its message more effectively. The magazine is distributed through conventional commercial channels, including subscriptions and newsstand sales. But it is also made available at reduced rates to schools, libraries, and other public facilities. Moreover, the board has decided to continue to distribute foreign language editions of the magazine, even though their costs far exceed the revenues derived from them, in order to reach a global audience with information about the global problem of marine pollution. The board concluded that publishing and distributing the magazine contributes substantially to the accomplishment of Planet Water's exempt purposes and that the magazine is not operated in a commercial manner.

In a market economy, the success of a business enterprise depends not only on the decisions made by its directors, officers, and staff, but also on whether investors are willing to risk their money on the enterprise and on whether consumers are willing to buy the goods or services it produces. The economic dynamics of much of the charitable sector are similar. Planet Water will survive only if the public supports it, whether with volunteer time, donations of money, or purchases of the educational materials and services that Planet Water provides. Planet Water's staff and board, therefore, are constantly concerned with improving Planet Water's performance and level of response of the public in the organization itself, as well as in the marine issues it advocates.

In recent years, Planet Water has received, with increasing frequency, requests for grants from individuals and other smaller and sometimes informal environmental groups. After extensive consideration, the board of directors decided that an important part of Planet Water's mission was to support informal citizen-based environmental activity related to the oceans. The board agreed to set aside 5 percent of Planet Water's annual revenues to fund this effort. Each year the board grants a total of $1,000,000, usually in amounts of $5,000 or less.

Planet Water has adopted a written grants procedure which provides that it will consider proposals for support of emerging charitable organizations and informal groups engaged in activities to preserve oceans, lakes, and rivers. The written proposal must describe the problem to which the organization or group is responding, and it must also contain a description of the activities the grantee intends to conduct, including a budget that shows, in detail, how the money requested will be spent to carry out those activities. The staff of Planet Water reviews all proposals received and recommends to the board of directors those that it believes should be funded. The Board considers them at its quarterly meetings. Planet Water receives far more proposals than it is able to fund, even with $250,000 available each quarter. Last year, the staff recommended to the board only one out of every ten proposals it received. The board, in turn, funded about 80 percent of the proposals recommended to it by the staff.

Once a grant is approved, the staff sends a letter to the grantee, advising it of the grant award and enclosing a check. The grantee is required to submit periodic written reports to Planet Water, explaining how the grant is being spent and how those expenditures are consistent with the representations made by the grantee in its proposal.

When Planet Water received its federal tax exemption as a charitable organization, it also was classified by the IRS as a public charity, based on its representation that it would have a broad base of financial support. As a public charity, Planet Water is not limited in making grants to organizations that have achieved formal recognition of their charitable and tax-exempt status. It may make grants to support any activity that furthers its own charitable purposes, whether that activity is conducted by a formal charitable organization, an informal group, a business, or an individual. If the grantee is not a formal charity, however, Planet Water must restrict the grant to charitable purposes and must require written reports so that it can be assured that the grant was used for a proper charitable purpose and not for a personal or business purpose. So long as it adheres to these standards, Planet Water may make grants abroad as well as in the United States.

Membership. Planet Water's bylaws provide that a member of the corporation is anyone whose current dues are paid. Over 300,000 people around the world have paid their annual dues for the current year and have the right, under the bylaws, to vote for members of the board of directors. They also receive Planet Water's magazine.

Planet Water is not required by law to have voting members. California law permits a public benefit corporation like Planet Water to operate with only a board of directors, and most of them do so, often giving donors the honorary title of "member." Vacancies on the boards of such corporations are filled by the vote of the remaining directors rather than by members.

Planet Water's members are more than honorary, however, because they have the right to vote for directors. California law gives such members the right not only to vote for directors but also to nominate them. The consent of the membership is required if the board wants to remove a director. Planet Water's members also have the rights to receive annual reports on its finances; to inspect and copy its tax returns, minutes, and other records; to vote on the manner in which its assets will be distributed upon dissolution, termination, or merger with another corporation; to receive written notice a reasonable time in advance of any membership meeting; to sue to protect the charity against wrongful acts by its directors; to vote on amendments to the charity's articles of incorporation; and to vote on bylaw amendments that would affect their rights as members.

Despite the presence of these rights, however, voting members of a public benefit corporation are not personally responsible for the charity's debts, liabilities, or other obligations. And members are not personally liable for improper actions of directors, unless the member personally benefits from such an act.

Unlike stockholders of a business, voting members of a public benefit corporation do not own the corporation, nor do they have any right to its assets. Their rights have to do with governance and access to information about the organization. The corporation's assets are held in charitable trust, for the benefit of the public.

Governing Body. Asked to say whether the board or the staff ran Planet Water, an impartial observer would probably say that the staff did. After all, the board meets only four times a year, and then only to set policy, to adopt a budget, and to make grants. But under the law, it is the board who is responsible for the operations of the organization. The organizational role of the staff is to carry out the policies set by the board.

State law defines the responsibilities of Planet Water's directors in broad terms. Like directors of other public benefit corporations in California, they must act in good faith, in the best interest of the charity, with the same degree of thoughtfulness that a reasonable person would apply to the decision-making process. In traditional legal terms, directors owe the corporation a duty of loyalty and a duty of care. If directors adhere to this standard in performing their duties as directors, they will not be penalized personally for acts or omissions that turn out later to have been mistaken.

The distinction between board responsibility and staff management can produce unexpected results. Suppose, for example, that the staff member in charge of payroll fails to pay the employment taxes on time, and the government assesses fines and penalties against Planet Water. The attorney general of California will automatically demand that the individual members of the board of directors, not the employee, personally reimburse Planet Water for the charitable dollars lost to the organization due to the payment of those fines. This is because, under the law, it is the directors, rather than the staff, who are responsible for the acts of the organization. So long as the directors can demonstrate that they acted responsibly (by, for example, requiring the staff to keep and monitor a calendar of all filing dates), they will probably not be penalized.

The day-to-day decisions about Planet Water's operations are made by its co-executive directors and other senior staff members. They consult with the executive committee on major decisions between board meetings, but the board is generally not involved in these decisions except to ratify actions previously authorized by the executive committee. The board, with fifteen members who are geographically dispersed, is simply too cumbersome a body to respond quickly. State law generally leaves the organization free to decide how many directors it will have (California law requires a minimum of one director). As an organization becomes larger, however, the size of its board of directors tends to follow suit, since the practice is to bring people onto the board who are resourceful and who are in a position to contribute expertise or other resources, including money.

Directors, as we have seen, owe a duty of loyalty to the charity: they must put the best interests of the charitable organization before any personal benefit to themselves. But a charity is not prohibited from dealing with a board member in his or her professional capacity. Planet Water's board, for example, includes its attorney, Susan Cohen; Larry Yee, who owns the public relations agency that produces Planet Water's advocacy advertisements and direct mail appeals; and Jim and Beth Rankin, its founders and co-directors—all of whom are compensated for the professional services they render. Rather than bar a charity from benefiting from the expertise of its board members, California law allows such transactions, so long as the interested director—that is, the director with a financial stake in the transaction—discloses all the material facts to the other directors and they alone decide that the benefit to the corporation outweighs the benefit to the individual director.

At least four of Planet Water's fifteen directors were interested directors. California law permits such interested directors to serve on the board, but only if they make up no more than 49 percent. In practice, the founders of a new organization may have difficulty attracting a sufficient number of outside directors. The hope of the founders is that their cause will have sufficient public appeal that the increase in activities will lead to greater outside recognition and an expansion of the number of resourceful supporters who will be willing to volunteer time to serve as board members and in other capacities.

Some foundations follow a policy of refusing to make grants to organizations that have employees on their boards. The laudable purpose of that policy is to strengthen the independence of the board. The unfortunate consequence, however, is that deserving charities may be disqualified simply because they are at an early stage in their development.

Staff. A charitable organization is not exempt from the extensive body of federal, state, and local labor law regulating employment. Planet Water must comply with laws requiring that the amount of wages paid to employees meet a certain minimum standard. It must pay the employees additional compensation if they work more than an eight-hour day or a forty-hour week. California and San Francisco have stronger antidiscrimination laws than the federal government. Those laws, taken together, prohibit Planet Water from discriminating on the basis of race, religion, national origin, sex, sexual preference, physical or mental disability, and age, in the hiring, promotion, or termination of employees.

One type of law applies only to employees of a charitable organization: laws limiting the amount of compensation that an employee may receive. Federal and state laws prohibit the payment of excessive compensation to employees of charitable organizations. The compensation they receive must be reasonable in relation to the services that they perform. There is, by comparison, no such restriction on the amount of compensation that may be received by employees of business organizations.

An individual who wants to engage in a particular activity must take this limitation into account when deciding whether to conduct that activity as a charity or as a business. For example, suppose that a teacher wants to form a school to teach foreign languages, and suppose further that the salary range for language teachers in nonprofit schools in her area is $20,000 to $40,000. If the teacher wants her school to be a charity, she must be content with receiving a salary within that range. On the other hand, she is free to form her school as a business, instead, and to receive as much compensation as her business can generate.

Finances. Except for joint venture income, the sources of financing for Planet Water are fairly representative of a large nonprofit environmental organization. The amount and types of funds received will differ, of course, from organization to organization. A large performing arts organization, such as a symphony orchestra or an opera, would typically receive much of its support from ticket sales, but significant amounts would also come from government and foundation grants, individual and corporate contributions, and investment income. A charitable organization providing a social service, such as housing advice to the poor, would in the past have been supported primarily by government grants. Due to reduced government funding, however, that organization would now be supported, at a reduced level, by foundation and corporate grants and individual contributions.

Most of Planet Water's income is exempt from federal and California income taxes. Even the income that may appear to be commercial in nature—from book sales, government contracts, royalties, and investments—will probably qualify as tax-free to Planet Water. Commercial income that requires no significant activity on the part of the charity to produce it, such as the investment and royalty income, is not subject to the unrelated business tax. The commercial income that does require sustained activity, such as the sale of books or the performance of government contracts, qualifies for that reason as business income. Since the activities of publishing environ-

mental books and conducting environmental research further the purpose
of Planet Water, they generate related business income, which is not subject to the tax imposed on unrelated business income.

The joint venture income, from the sale for recreational use of the
submersible vehicles, would be taxed as unrelated business income. Income
from the sale or rental of such vehicles for environmental research purposes
would probably be treated as related income because of its connection to
Planet Water's purposes and would, therefore, not be subject to tax.

The direct mail campaign is a form of solicitation for charitable contributions. There is, as yet, no federal regulation of such solicitation. There
is an enormous diversity of laws at the state and local level, however. In
California alone, more than two hundred cities and counties have enacted
laws regulating charitable solicitations. Before Planet Water solicits funds
either by mail or door-to-door, it must review the laws of the particular localities and states where it will be soliciting. Those rules commonly require
a charity to register with a governmental agency and to disclose its program
and its finances. Charities, like businesses and individuals, may not obtain
money by fraud or misrepresentation. The government may not regulate
charitable solicitation without restriction. Charitable fundraising is an exercise of constitutionally protected free speech, and in recent decisions the
Supreme Court has struck down state and local laws regulating charitable
solicitation on the ground that they were unduly burdensome of free speech.

The investment of charitable funds is regulated primarily at the state
level. Most states require the governing body of the charity to make its assets productive. This means that the surplus funds of the charity must be
invested prudently and may not be allowed to lie idle. For example, members of the board of directors of a California charitable foundation were fined
by a court because they allowed foundation funds to remain in a non-interest-
bearing checking account in excess of the amount needed to meet current
expenditures. The court required them to pay to the foundation the amount
of interest that the foundation would have received had its excess funds been
deposited in a savings account.

State laws do not ordinarily specify which types of investments a
charitable organization must choose. California does, however, regulate the
process by which the choice is made: it requires the directors to exercise
reasonable and prudent judgment. In addition, many states have laws that,
like California's, protect the members of boards of directors from liability
that might otherwise arise as a consequence of unwise investment decisions,
so long as the decisions are made on the basis of advice from a competent
professional investment manager.

Compliance

Government review of a charitable organization occurs most commonly in
connection with the annual reports filed by a charity. Random audits are

made of those reports. In recent years, sophisticated computer programs have been designed by tax and charitable regulatory agencies. Those programs are applied to the reports to identify legal compliance issues from the information contained in them. An organization may also be selected for audit because of a complaint made by an individual or because a newspaper article describing improper charitable activity comes to the attention of the government agency.

If a charitable organization's report is selected for audit, a government auditor may schedule a visit to the office of the organization. The auditor is empowered to examine any document and to interview any person connected with the charitable organization. Despite this extensive audit power, most charitable organizations have never been audited by any government organization. When they do occur, most audits take no more than a few days, assuming no serious violation of law is uncovered. In most cases, the result of an audit is a "no change" letter, indicating that the organization is in compliance with the laws and regulations of the governmental agency conducting the audit.

Termination

The determination of when a charitable organization should end its existence is ordinarily a private matter, made not by the state, but by the governing body of the organization.

The government has extensive powers in the event of abuse, but the exercise of those powers is surrounded with important protections.

On the federal level, for example, the Internal Revenue Service has the power to in effect terminate the existence of a nonprofit organization by proposing to revoke its tax exemption. Revocation is proper only if specific violations of law have occurred, such as failing to conduct legitimate charitable activities, conducting activities in a manner that confers an improper economic benefit on an individual, or engaging in excessive lobbying or electioneering. In the event of a proposed revocation, the organization has extensive rights to present evidence and to oppose that action within the Internal Revenue Service. If the IRS is unpersuaded, the organization can challenge the proposed IRS action in court.

At the state level, the powers of the tax agency and the protections of the organization are similar. In addition, the state attorney general has extensive powers to investigate the activities of a charitable organization to assure that they comply with the law. The attorney general, however, has no power to act against the organization on his or her own. If that office discovers violations of law and decides to impose penalties over the charity's objections, the attorney general must take the charity to court. The court, not the attorney general, will decide, after a full trial, whether the organization has violated the law; whether a penalty or other remedy should be imposed under the law; and, if so, what the appropriate remedy or penalty should be. Nevertheless, due to the cost of litigation and the potential of harmful adverse publicity, most disputes between charities and states' attorneys general are resolved by settlement rather than by litigation.

If the organization voluntarily dissolves or terminates and has money or property, those assets must, in California and in most other states, be distributed by the organization to another charitable organization with similar purposes. The attorney general reviews all proposed terminations to assure that charities comply with this rule. For example, if Planet Water's directors voted to end the organization's existence, they could distribute its assets only to other charitable tax-exempt organizations whose purpose was to protect and preserve marine life and the oceans in general. If they wanted to distribute a portion of Planet Water's assets to organizations working on other important social problems, such as homelessness, the attorney general would step in to prevent it. This is because, under the law of charitable trusts, a charity's assets must be used for the purpose stated in its governing document, unless that purpose becomes illegal, impossible, or, in some states, impracticable. Environmental protection, Planet Water's purpose, will, no doubt, remain viable for the foreseeable future.

Reference

Drucker, P. F. *The New Realities*. New York: HarperCollins, 1989.

4

The Nonprofit Sector and the Evolution of the American Welfare State

Lester M. Salamon

> The future of the voluntary agency is indissolubly tied to the future of the welfare state, and both are increasingly perceived to be in crisis [Kramer, 1981, p. 270].

Two alternative paradigms vie for the attention of scholars and practitioners in defining the role of the voluntary sector in the provision of social welfare services: the paradigm of competition and the paradigm of partnership. The paradigm of competition is the paradigm of the law, of economic theory, and of conservative social thought. Stressing the uniqueness of the voluntary sector, it posits an inherent conflict between voluntary organizations and the state and views the growth of the latter as a threat to the viability of the former (see, for example, Nisbet, 1953; Berger and Neuhaus, 1977; Weisbrod, 1977). The paradigm of partnership is the paradigm of practice and of liberal pragmatism. Acknowledging the special characteristics of the voluntary sector, it stresses instead the areas of overlap and potential cooperation between voluntary organizations and the institutions of the state.

In previous work I have examined the applicability of these two paradigms to the realities of the American welfare state as it had evolved through the early 1980s (Salamon, 1982, 1985, 1987a, 1987b; Salamon and Abramson, 1982). This work revealed that an elaborate partnership between

Note: This chapter draws on Lester M. Salamon, "The Voluntary Sector and the Future of the Welfare State," *Nonprofit and Voluntary Sector Quarterly,* 1989, *18*(1), 11–24.

government and the voluntary sector forms the core of the modern welfare state and constitutes the principal financial fact of life of the modern voluntary sector. However, recent developments have challenged this partnership in rather fundamental ways. In response, some (for example, Butler, 1985) have beckoned the nonprofit sector back to its essentially voluntary roots in line with the "paradigm of competition," while others (such as Crimmins, 1985) have nudged it toward a more entrepreneurial future. What is lacking is an assessment that relates the future of the voluntary sector to recent trends in the modern welfare state, although Gilbert (1983) has made a significant start toward this goal. It is the purpose of this chapter to outline at least the major components of such an assessment.

The central conclusion of the chapter is that powerful forces are leading the voluntary sector away from its recent role as a partner in public service. But rather than leading the sector toward a more charitable mode of operation, they are leading it instead toward greater integration into the private, market economy. To help the reader understand this development, the discussion in this paper is divided into four parts. I begin by reviewing three major conclusions that flow from my earlier work on the recent pattern of government-nonprofit relations in the American welfare state. Next I explore some of the salient trends in the operation of the American welfare state. Third, I examine the implications of these trends for the future character and role of the voluntary sector. Finally, I examine the implications of these developments for nonprofit managers.

Prevailing Realities

The central fact of life of the American welfare state as it had evolved by the 1970s was a widespread pattern of partnership between government and the voluntary sector. Facing major new responsibilities in a context of continued public hostility to the bureaucratic state, government at all levels turned extensively to existing and newly created private nonprofit organizations to help it carry out expanded welfare-state functions. As a consequence, through direct and indirect grants and third-party payments, government support easily surpassed private charity as the major source of private nonprofit sector income. For example, data I generated in the early 1980s revealed that, in 1981, 40 percent of the income of a wide array of private nonprofit human service agencies, exclusive of hospitals and higher education institutions, came from government, as opposed to 30 percent from fees and 20 percent from private charity (Salamon, 1984, 1987b). No wonder the Commission on Private Philanthropy and Public Needs (the Filer Commission) concluded in 1975 that "government has emerged in the United States as a major 'philanthropist,' *the* major philanthropist in a number of the principal, traditional areas of philanthropy" (Commission, 1975, p. 85).

This partnership between government and the nonprofit sector was not, moreover, simply a recent development, as some accounts of the sector suggest. Rather, its roots lay deep in American history. Summarizing the historical record, Waldemar Nielsen points out that "collaboration, not separation or antagonism, between government and the Third Sector . . . has been the predominant characteristic" through much of our history (1979, p. 47).

Not only does this pattern of partnership have deep historical roots, it also has a strong theoretical rationale. Unfortunately, this rationale has been obscured by prevailing theories of the welfare state and of the voluntary sector, which emphasize, respectively, a hierarchically structured state and a voluntary sector filling in for "market failures" where government has yet to act. But as I have argued elsewhere (Salamon, 1987a), these theories overlook the fragmented character of the American state, its widespread reliance on third parties to carry out public functions, and inherent weaknesses in the voluntary sector and the state that make collaboration between government and the voluntary sector a productive partnership for both.

This is not to say that the resulting partnership between government and the nonprofit sector worked perfectly. Relationships between government and the voluntary sector evolved in ad hoc fashion in the United States, with little opportunity to spell out clearly who was expected to do what and with what degree of oversight and control. What is more, the proliferation of programs in the 1960s created a serious managerial challenge that persists to this day. Nevertheless, the system remains fundamentally sound as a basis on which to design public action.

Recent Trends

For a variety of reasons, this collaborative pattern seems very much on the defensive. Important developments now under way seem likely to change the character of the voluntary sector in fundamental ways and unseat the partnership between government and the nonprofit sector from its primary place as the central organizing principle of the American welfare state. This section examines five of these developments.

Resource Constraints

The most obvious change in the operation of the American welfare state in recent years has been the imposition of a significant restraint on its provision of resources. While the Reagan administration was far less successful than it had hoped to be in reducing budgetary outlays for human service programs, it did manage to halt a twenty-year pattern of rapid growth, and the Bush administration generally continued to hold the line. Thus, after adjustment for inflation, federal spending on a wide array of human service programs as of fiscal year (FY) 1990 was a mere 5 percent above the level it had reached in FY 1980, and most of this was due to growth in health expenditures. Indeed, if we exclude the two major federal health programs,

Medicare and Medicaid, spending on the remaining human service programs was 7 percent lower in 1990 than it had been in FY 1980 (Salamon and Abramson, 1992). Inevitably, this decline translated into fiscal constraints on the private nonprofit sector. Excluding Medicare and Medicaid, nonprofit organizations ended up in FY 1990 with about 10 percent less federal support than they had received in FY 1980, and thus a considerable period of rapid growth was reversed. With rare exceptions, the states were not able to compensate for the federal restraint. On the contrary, in many areas federal contraction brought state contraction along with it (Nathan, Doolittle, and Associates, 1987; Salamon, Musselwhite, and De Vita, 1986).

Perhaps even more significant than the cuts in federal social welfare spending achieved during the Reagan-Bush era is the legacy of restraint imposed by the federal budget deficit created during this period. Although estimates of the size of the future deficit vary widely, the drag on federal spending is considerable. The one potentially countervailing factor is the splintering of the Soviet bloc following 1989 and the possibility that this creates to reduce defense spending and free up resources for social programs. Given the size of the deficit, however, even under this scenario there is little basis for optimism about the potential for major domestic spending increases in the foreseeable future.

From Categorical Aid to Universal Entitlements

In addition to the overall pattern of restraint, important changes have taken place in the composition of social welfare spending. In particular, the retrenchment hit hardest on the so-called discretionary spending programs and the means-tested welfare programs aimed at the poor and near poor. In contrast, the so-called entitlement programs, especially those targeted at the middle class, experienced considerable growth. In the process, a significant shift occurred in the structure of federal welfare spending—away from categorical programs aimed at the needy toward general entitlement programs available to significant portions of the middle class.

A comparison of federal spending for Social Security, Medicare, and other retirement programs—the major entitlement programs—to other domestic spending demonstrates this shift clearly (see Table 4.1). After adjustment for inflation, federal spending on the entitlement programs increased 38 percent between FY 1980 and FY 1990, while spending on the rest of the domestic budget declined by 10 percent. In this ten-year period, spending on these middle-class entitlement programs therefore increased from 47 percent of the domestic budget to 57 percent.

To be sure, the Reagan administration made efforts to cut back on entitlement payments to middle-income groups under a number of federal programs, including food stamps and college student aid. But some of these changes have been reversed, and coverage under other programs had been extended. For example, coverage under the federal government's Medicaid

Table 4.1. Growth of Federal Entitlement and
Other Domestic Programs, Fiscal Year 1980–1990.

Program	Fiscal Year 1980 Outlays	Fiscal Year 1990 Outlays (in FY 1980 dollars)	Percent Change 1980–1990
Entitlements:			
Social Security	$118.5	$154.8	+31
Medicare	32.1	61.0	+90
Other retirement	31.7	35.5	+12
Subtotal, entitlements	182.3	251.4	+38
Other domestic programs	208.1	186.6	−10
Total domestic programs	$390.4	$438.0	+12
Entitlements as a percentage of domestic programs	46.7	57.4	

Source: Computed from figures in U.S. Office of Management and Budget, 1991.

program, which originally was limited to welfare recipients, was recently expanded to allow states to cover the aged poor as well as pregnant women and children under five years of age in families whose income is 85 percent above the poverty line, whether the families are on welfare or not (Pear, 1988). Reflecting these changes and other developments, Medicaid expenditures have continued to grow despite rather vigorous cost-control efforts. More generally, the recent reality has been one not of across-the-board restraint but of cutbacks falling most heavily on the most vulnerable, while support for the broad middle class has experienced considerable growth.

From Producer Subsidies to Consumer Subsidies

A third important trend in the structure of the American welfare state is a marked shift in emphasis away from aid delivered through producers of services to aid delivered through consumers. This trend is only the most recent manifestation of a broader pattern of government operation, of which government reliance on nonprofit organizations is one part. This pattern involves the transformation of government from a direct producer of services into a financier or arranger of services provided by others (Salamon, 1981). Paying nongovernmental third parties, including nonprofit organizations, to deliver publicly financed services has been one way of accomplishing this transformation. Paying consumers of services directly and letting them decide what provider to use is simply a more extreme version of the same idea.

While the shift from producer subsidies to consumer subsidies or vouchers is rooted in the broad movement toward third-party government, it has more proximate origins in the recent efforts by conservatives to "privatize" the public sector. As one advocate (Butler, 1985, p. 43) has observed,

"From the privatizers' perspective, the voucher is a useful device to make private-sector alternatives financially available to low-income citizens." According to advocates of privatization, the great advantage of vouchers is that they rely on the market rather than on the government or the producer to determine the allocation of resources, and thus they presumably increase efficiency and cut the important political link tying service providers, politicians, and bureaucrats together in support of public expenditures (Butler, 1985; Savas, 1987). This same line of argument has recently been endorsed as well by a group of progovernment moderates who view reliance on market-oriented incentives as a useful way to help "reinvent government" (Osborne and Graebler, 1992), a view that gained considerable currency early in the Clinton administration.

The extent of the shift toward voucher-type arrangements is quite striking. Looking only at federal assistance to the nonprofit sector, Table 4.2 shows that the amount of federal aid that reached nonprofit organizations through voucher payments to individuals grew between FY 1980 and FY 1986 from 53 percent of all federal assistance to 70 percent. During this same period, producer subsidies that nonprofits received from the federal government — either directly or via state and local governments — fell from 47 percent of the total to 30 percent. In other words, a significant shift took place in the basic structure of federal assistance.

Table 4.2. Changes in the Form of Federal Assistance to
Nonprofit Organizations Between Fiscal Year 1980 and Fiscal Year 1986.

	Percent of Total Support	
Form	FY 1980	FY 1986
Producer subsidies	47	30
Consumer subsidies	53	70
Total	100	100

Source: Computed from data in U.S. Office of Management and Budget, 1988.

In addition to the expansion of voucher-type programs and the contraction of direct-service programs, increased reliance is being put on so-called tax expenditures to subsidize human services. Like voucher payments to individuals, tax expenditures — that is, exemptions in the tax law for certain kinds of activities — channel government aid through the consumers of services. The main difference between tax expenditures and voucher payments is that the former operate through the tax system rather than the expenditure side of the budget. Not incidentally, they also tend to deliver their benefits disproportionately to the better-off, whose tax liabilities are more substantial to start with. Thus, in the field of day care, while the real value of federal spending for the Title XX social services program (the chief producer subsidy for day care as well as other social services) declined from

$2.7 billion in FY 1980 to the equivalent of $2.0 billion in FY 1987, the federal tax credit for child and dependent care expenses increased more than 400 percent in inflation-adjusted terms, from $700 million in FY 1980 to $3.2 billion in FY 1987 (U.S. Office of Management and Budget, 1988). In other words, by 1987 the federal government was "spending" more on day care through consumer subsidies in the tax system than it was spending on day care and more than a dozen other social services through the producer payments provided by the Social Services Block Grant. Further shifts in the pattern of government support for day care are evident in state efforts to switch day-care funding for welfare recipients from the Social Services Block Grant, a producer-oriented discretionary program whose funding levels have been declining, to the Aid to Families with Dependent Children Program (AFDC), an entitlement program whose funding levels have proved harder to cut. These and similar developments in other fields add up to a significant overall trend that, while relatively unheralded, has important implications for the evolution of government-nonprofit relations.

Demographic Developments

Beyond these programmatic shifts, important changes have also occurred in the basic demography of the welfare state and in the demands for its services. Some of these demographic changes are manifest in the trends noted earlier. Others have yet to make their full effects felt. Four of these changes seem particularly likely to have significant long-term consequences.

One of the most dramatic changes confronting the American welfare state is the continued growth in the number and proportion of elderly persons. Between 1960 and 1980, the number of persons aged sixty-five and older increased by 50 percent, while the overall population grew by just over 25 percent. If this trend continues over the next forty to fifty years, the proportion of the population that is sixty-five and older will double. Moreover, among the elderly, the proportion that is over seventy-five is also projected to grow, so that it will reach 50 percent of the elderly over the next forty to fifty years. This demographic fact of life has already found expression in the growth of federal support to the elderly. Given the potent political power that the elderly can wield, there is every reason to expect continued pressures for expansion of the welfare-state benefits they receive.

Another recent change that has powerful implications for the character of the American welfare state is the transformation in the role of women. While this transformation has many dimensions, one of the most important is the surge in female labor force participation. Between 1960 and 1980, the labor force participation rate of women increased from 30.5 percent to 50.1 percent. Even more dramatic, the labor force participation rate for married women with children under the age of six rose from 18.6 percent in 1960 to 45.1 percent in 1980. That same year, the labor force participation rate for separated women with children under six reached 55.2 percent. For divorced women with children under six it grew to 68.3 percent. Aside from its social and economic effects, this development signals a substantial increase in the need for day care.

Significant changes have also occurred in family structure. In 1960, there was one divorce for every four marriages. By 1980, there was one divorce for every two marriages. During this period, the number of children involved in divorces almost tripled, from 463,000 in 1960 to almost 1.2 million in 1980. Since divorce typically brings a significant loss in economic status, this development suggests increased demands on existing human services. What is more, a very significant increase also occurred in the proportion of births to unmarried women. Between 1960 and 1980, the proportion of such births jumped from 5.3 percent to over 18 percent. Among nonwhites, it rose from 22 percent to 48 percent. Although the proportion of births to unmarried women was lower among whites, the absolute number of such births was almost equal — 320,000 whites and 346,000 nonwhites for a total of 666,000 as of 1980, compared to 224,000 twenty years earlier (U.S. Census Bureau, 1986).

The fourth recent demographic development of great importance to the evolution of the American welfare state has been the emergence of a sizable cadre of hard-core inner-city poor persons, which some scholars perceive as a veritable urban underclass. As University of Chicago sociologist William Julius Wilson has put it:

> Regardless of which term is used, one cannot deny that there is a heterogeneous grouping of inner-city families and individuals whose behavior contrasts sharply with that of mainstream America. . . . Today's ghetto neighborhoods are populated almost exclusively by the most disadvantaged segments of the black urban community, that heterogeneous grouping of families and individuals who are outside the mainstream of the American occupational system. Included in this group are individuals who lack training and skills and either experience long-term unemployment or are not members of the labor force, individuals who are engaged in street crime and other forms of aberrant behavior, and families that experience long-term spells of poverty and/or welfare dependency. . . . The term ghetto underclass . . . suggests that a fundamental social transformation has taken place in ghetto neighborhoods, and the groups represented by this term are collectively different from and much more socially isolated than those that lived in these communities in earlier years [1987, pp. 7–8, 143].

From Cultural to Economic Explanations of Poverty

One further development in the evolution of the American welfare state worth mentioning involves a significant change in our thinking about the causes and solutions of poverty. The key aspect of this change is a loss of faith in the traditional dogma of professional social work, with its emphasis on case-work and individualized services as a cure for poverty and distress. During the 1960s, this doctrine was translated into public policy through the 1962 amendments to the Social Security Act and, later, through portions of the Economic Opportunity Act. The central premise of this doctrine was that poverty was the product of a "culture of poverty" that could be broken only by the provision of a variety of supportive services. Attention consequently focused on the individual, whose maladjustment or aberrant behavior was perceived as being largely responsible for the persistence of poverty.

Whether this "services strategy" received a fair test or not, it now enjoys little sustained support either from the left or from the right. Conservatives view the growth of supportive services during the 1960s as at best wasteful and at worse destructive of the work ethic and the value of self-reliance. Liberals now question the tendency of the culture of poverty theory to degenerate into a new form of "blaming the victim," because of its tendency to focus on the behavior of the poor, rather than broader social and economic circumstances, as the principal cause of poverty.

This latter critique has gained added force as awareness has grown of the impact of international economic changes on the availability of traditional manufacturing jobs in the United States. Now that unionized production workers—not just racially stereotyped ghetto dwellers—have found themselves exposed to structural unemployment and distress, attention has come increasingly to focus on the underlying economic causes of poverty. Even some presumably cultural phenomena, such as the rise of households headed by females and out-of-wedlock births among blacks, have been reinterpreted in strongly economic terms that emphasize the negative impact of chronic joblessness on stable family life. According to this line of thought, what accounts for the deterioration of black family life in urban ghettos is not lax morals or a deteriorating sense of responsibility but a concrete decline in the pool of marriageable—that is, employed—black men (Wilson, 1987).

Implications for the Nonprofit Sector

The changes in the American welfare state just outlined have important implications for the evolution of the private, nonprofit sector. Of course, how these implications play out depends on factors that are difficult to predict. But some of the main pressures in the system are already evident.

Overall Sector Growth

One of the most obvious yet often overlooked implications of the trends just discussed is that the private nonprofit sector is not likely to wither away in the foreseeable future. The prevailing demographic trends alone suggest a significant increase in the demand for the kinds of services that nonprofit organizations have traditionally provided, including day care, nursing home care, family counseling, and hospital services. Moreover, the demand is growing not only among the poor—the traditional target group of charitable organizations—but also among the broad middle class. That is the meaning of the jump in labor force participation rates among women with children under six, the growth in the numbers of elderly people, the continued rise in income support and medical assistance spending, and other, similar trends. Assuming a reasonable degree of responsiveness and efficiency on the part of nonprofit providers, there is every reason to expect that the nonprofit sector will capture a significant share of the expanded "business" that seems likely to result. At the same time, the growth seems likely to be concentrated in particular portions of the sector—the portions in which growing demand coincides with growing resources. Most likely, this coincidence will occur in the areas of services for the aged, health care, the arts and recreation, and day care for children.

Commercialization

If there is thus reason to expect considerable growth in the size and scale of the nonprofit sector in the foreseeable future, there is also reason to expect that this growth will lead to greater integration of the voluntary sector into the market economy. In part, this development reflects the expansion of the paying market for human services as a product of the demographic developments detailed earlier. In part, it also reflects the shift in government human service expenditures for the poor from producer subsidies to consumer subsidies. By explicit design, this shift moves the provision of human services even for the poor into a commercial-type market.

One important consequence of this development, which Neil Gilbert has chronicled in *Capitalism and the Welfare State,* is the "penetration of profit-oriented agencies into the welfare state" (1983, p. 23). As I have shown elsewhere, this development has become epidemic in such fields as specialty hospital care, home health, nursing home care, and social services (Salamon, 1993). Equally important, however, is the penetration of the mechanics of the market into the operation of nonprofit organizations. This penetration is evident in the growth of fee-for-service income in the funding structure of the nonprofit sector.

Like the expansion of government support, such commercial income is by no means a new phenomenon for nonprofit organizations. For example, in the early 1900s, the Charities Aid Society of New York operated both a wood yard and a laundry that charged fees for their services and generated income for the organization (Brandt, 1907). Similar examples are evident in the settlement house movement of the Progressive Era. But it is clear that the scale of such support has grown substantially in recent years. For example, a survey I conducted in the mid-1980s revealed that private nonprofit human service agencies, exclusive of hospitals and higher education institutions, already received 30 percent of their income from service fees as of 1981, more than from all sources of private giving combined (Salamon, 1984; De Vita and Salamon, 1987). This figure was even higher among some types of organizations, such as institutional care facilities and arts organizations. Perhaps even more significantly, a larger proportion of these nonprofit agencies received income from service fees than from any other single income source.

As government support declined in the early 1980s, moreover, nonprofit organizations turned increasingly to fees and service charges to finance their activities. In fact, such receipts accounted for 75 percent of the replacement income that the nonprofit sector generated in the early 1980s, enabling the sector to overcome its loss of government support and post an overall gain in income.

The developments discussed earlier suggest strongly that this trend is likely not only to continue but to accelerate. In the process, it seems likely that the same process of transformation that affected the nonprofit hospital between 1885 and 1915 is affecting a broad array of nonprofit human service agencies today. As historian David Rosner has noted, that transformation involved a switch from small community institutions to large bureaucratic organizations staffed by professionals, supported by fees, oriented to paying customers, and "focused less on patients' overall social and moral well-being and more on their physical needs alone" (1982, p. 6). Whether other segments of the nonprofit sector will join hospitals in becoming "once charitable enterprises" is hard to tell, but the pressures in that direction are unmistakable.

Reorganization of Assistance to the Needy

While it thus seems likely that a significant share of the activity of traditional human service agencies will assume an increasingly commercial cast, both subsidized and unsubsidized, it is also possible that other institutions will assume increased responsibility for the traditional charitable mission of the nonprofit sector. In other words, while nonprofit organizations move increasingly toward the higher end of the human service market, other institutions may be developing a sense of responsibility and a service rationale targeted on those left behind. These developments are even more speculative and uncertain than the ones just identified, but some of the main lines of potential evolution are beginning to be visible.

The key to this change is the growing realization that the traditional skills of the human service sector may be increasingly irrelevant to the problems facing the urban poor. As long as the prevailing conceptions attributed a significant share of the responsibility for poverty to the personal maladjustments of the poor, traditional social work practice and traditional social welfare agencies had a significant role to play in the alleviation of poverty. But, as newer conceptions that attribute poverty more clearly to the maladjustments of the economy take hold, new solutions seem called for. In this emerging view, the solution to social distress is identical to the solution to economic distress—access to a decent job. Under these circumstances, the employer rather than the social worker becomes the pivot of social policy.

Fortunately, trends in the labor market are creating a powerful economic incentive for business to take an interest in the job situation of the urban poor. These trends suggest the real possibility of a significant shortage of trained labor in the years immediately ahead (U.S. Department of Labor, 1988). As one educator recently put it, "For the first time in our history, we are facing a situation where we can no longer afford the economic luxury of throwaway kids. We could never afford the moral luxury of throwaway kids, but only recently have the economic costs become prohibitive" (Hornbeck, 1988).

To the extent that these observations prove correct, they suggest a reorientation of antipoverty and charitable activity toward the preparation of skilled workers for the labor market. Private, nonprofit organizations may play a role in this effort, but, except for the community development corporations, these organizations have a limited track record in this area. More likely is an increase in partnership arrangements involving the business community and the public school system. Equally likely is increased reliance on penal institutions and the criminal justice system generally to ease the transition of the inner-city poor into the work force of the future. Finally, business enterprises themselves will play an increasing role, utilizing on-the-job training and employment guarantees to tighten the link between the inner-city poor and the world of work.

For-Profit–Nonprofit Competition and the Challenge to Tax Exemption

Taken together, the developments just cited will further intensify the competition between the for-profit and nonprofit sectors and weaken the traditional rationale for nonprofit tax-exempt status. Of course, increased competition between the sectors and loss of tax-exempt status do not necessarily go hand in hand. Competition between for-profit and nonprofit organizations does not need to provoke a challenge to the tax-exempt status of the nonprofit sector. While tax-exempt status gives nonprofit organizations certain advantages, it also exacts certain costs, such as limitations on the generation and distribution of profit. Thus, it is quite conceivable that the competition between nonprofit and for-profit organizations will increase without posing a serious challenge to the tax-exempt status of the sector. However, for this to occur, the sector will have to clarify the relative advantages and disadvantages of tax-exempt status and develop a rationale for tax exemption that takes into account the sector's changing role.

Implications for Nonprofit Managers

Not only do the changes identified above have implications for the nonprofit sector; they also have implications for the individual nonprofit manager. Four such implications seem especially deserving of comment.

Market Savvy

In the first place, in light of the trends elaborated above, it is clear that non-profit managers must increasingly add to their already large repertoire of skills a more sophisticated awareness of the market trends in the fields in which they are operating. As their organizations become more sensitive financially to shifts in consumer demand and to competitive pressures arising from other providers, nonprofit managers must find ways to stay on top of the market conditions facing them. Increasing use of advertising, market surveys, "industry analyses," and the like will consequently be necessary as managers seek to define and maintain a suitable market niche for their organizations.

Personnel Management Challenges

The pressures pushing nonprofit managers to take more account of market forces will also put special strains on human resource management within nonprofit organizations. As these organizations go "upscale" in client focus, they will likely encounter pressures from staff to upgrade pay and other working conditions. At the same time, the pressures of competition will force nonprofit organizations to seek cost-cutting possibilities, perhaps by keeping wage rates for nonprofessional staff low. To the extent this occurs, however, it will reduce one of the principal advantages of the nonprofit sector as a place to work — the relative "flatness" of nonprofit organizations, the relative lack of strict hierarchy, and the resulting sense of solidarity among workers who consider themselves participants in a shared mission.

Similar tensions may also arise between paid staff and volunteers. The more nonprofits become engaged in fee-for-service work, the more the rationale for volunteers to give their time to the organization for free will be strained. To be sure, hospitals have escaped this dilemma and retain a significant voluntary corps, but the task of defining and promoting the role of the volunteer still seems likely to become more problematic for nonprofit managers in the world that seems destined to lie ahead for them.

The Threat to Organizational Missions

Underlying these marketing and personnel management pressures is a more basic challenge. This is the fundamental challenge of maintaining a distinctive sense of organizational mission. Mission orientation is, in a sense, the fundamental distinguishing characteristic of nonprofit organizations. Where for-profit organizations acquire their organizational *raison d'être* fundamentally from the pursuit of profit, nonprofit organizations get theirs from the pursuit of a mission, a purpose that binds the agency's personnel, supporters, and beneficiaries together in common purpose. The most important task of a manager in such organizations is to protect and embody the agency's mission while adapting as necessary to the pressures of the external world. A manager who makes it possible for an agency to survive as an organization but at the cost of undermining its central mission inevitably purchases short-term victory at the cost of long-term viability. So, too, however, a manager who holds so rigidly to a particular conception of an agency's mission and modus operandi that he or she fails to adjust to external realities can end up with no organization to protect over the long run. The successful manager is the one who strikes a reasonable balance between these internal and external pressures.

What the analysis presented here suggests, however, is that this balance is likely to grow increasingly hard to achieve for nonprofit managers in the years ahead as the pressures to adapt to the market grow increasingly intense. While becoming more "market savvy," therefore, nonprofit managers will have to take care to nourish the sense of "mission" within their agencies.

Preserving the Advocacy Role

Among the missions of the nonprofit sector likely to be placed under particular strain by the developments outlined here is the advocacy role these organizations have traditionally performed. One of the great strengths of the nonprofit sector is its function as a source of criticism of government and the market sector, and hence as a source of innovation in policy. As organizations become more enmeshed in the competitive market economy, it is likely that their managers will lose both the time and the incentive for this kind of advocacy work. This is so because advocacy can often lead to adverse publicity, in addition to absorbing the time and energy of agency staff. Nonprofit managers struggling to attract clients to their agencies may therefore be inclined to downplay their advocacy role, lest they antagonize potential customers or dissipate agency energies in "do-good" causes that do little for the "bottom line." Some observers of nonprofit social service agencies have argued that this is precisely what happened to them as professional social workers, committed to "case work," took over from an earlier breed of community organizers (Cloward and Epstein, 1965). It seems reasonable that the commercialization of the nonprofit sector may intensify this tendency, furthering the transformation of nonprofit organizations into service providers rather than policy innovators and social critics.

Summary

Whether these implications will materialize as predicted here depends, of course, on the speed with which the developments outlined above proceeds, and on the way nonprofit managers react to them. Properly fortified with a sense of the mission of the nonprofit sector and the values that are critical to its continuance, nonprofit managers may fend off some of the pressures that are looming. But this will require a high level of self-consciousness within the sector and a concerted effort to revitalize the value base on which the sector rests. While there is only very limited evidence that such a development may be in prospect, some encouraging signs are apparent—in the renewed calls to service on the part of the Clinton administration and in the surge in nonprofit activity that is apparent at the international level (Salamon, forthcoming). Whatever the reaction, however, it seems clear that the first step must be to understand the basic trends that are at work.

References

Abramson, A. J., and Salamon, L. M. *The Nonprofit Sector and the New Federal Budget.* Washington, D.C.: Urban Institute, 1986.

Berger, P. L., and Neuhaus, R. J. *To Empower People: The Role of Mediating Structures in Public Policy.* Washington, D.C.: American Enterprise Institute, 1977.

Brandt, L. *The Charity Organization Society of the City of New York: 1882–1907.* Twenty-fifth Annual Report. New York: Charity Organization Society, 1907.

Butler, S. *Privatizing Federal Spending: A Strategy to Eliminate the Deficit.* New York: Universe Books, 1985.

Cloward, R. A., and Epstein, I. "Private Social Welfare's Disengagement from the Poor: The Case of Family Adjustment Agencies." In M. N. Zald (ed.), *Social Welfare Institutions: A Sociological Reader.* New York: Wiley, 1965.

Commission on Private Philanthropy and Public Needs. *Giving in America: Toward a Strong Voluntary Sector.* Washington, D.C.: Department of the Treasury, 1975.

Crimmins, L. *Enterprise in the Nonprofit Sector.* Washington, D.C.: Fund for Livable Places, 1985.

De Vita, C., and Salamon, L. M. "Commercial Activities in Nonprofit Human Service Organizations." Paper presented at the Independent Sector Spring Research Forum, New York, Mar. 19–20, 1987.

Gilbert, N. *Capitalism and the Welfare State: Dilemmas of Social Benevolence.* New Haven: Yale University Press, 1983.

Hornbeck, D. "Speech to Private Industry Councils," Annapolis, Md., Mar. 1, 1988.

Kramer, R. M. *Voluntary Agencies in the Welfare State.* Berkeley: University of California Press, 1981.

Nathan, R. P., Doolittle, F. C., and Associates. *Reagan and the States.* Princeton, N.J.: Princeton University Press, 1987.

Nielsen, W. *The Endangered Sector.* New York: Columbia University Press, 1979.

Nisbet, R. *The Quest for Community: A Study in the Ethics of Order and Freedom.* New York: Oxford University Press, 1953.

Osborne, D., and Graebler, T. *Reinventing Government.* Reading, Mass.: Addison-Wesley, 1992.

Pear, R. "Expanded Right to Medicaid Shatters the Link to Welfare." *New York Times,* Mar. 6, 1988, pp. 1, 32.

Rosner, D. *A Once Charitable Enterprise: Hospitals and Health Care in Brooklyn and New York, 1885–1915.* New York: Cambridge University Press, 1982.

Salamon, L. M. "Rethinking Public Management: Third-Party Government and the Changing Forms of Government Action." *Public Policy,* 1981, *29*(3), 255–275.

Salamon, L. M. "The Nonprofit Sector." In J. L. Palmer and I. Sawhill (eds.), *The Reagan Revolution.* Cambridge, Mass.: Ballinger, 1982.

Salamon, L. M. "Nonprofits: The Results Are Coming In." *Foundation News,* July/Aug. 1984.

Salamon, L. M. "Government and the Voluntary Sector in an Era of Retrenchment: The American Experience." *Journal of Public Policy,* 1985, *6,* 1–20.

Salamon, L. M. "Of Market Failure, Voluntary Failure, and Third-Party Government: Toward a Theory of Government–Nonprofit Relations in the Modern Welfare State." *Journal of Voluntary Action Research,* 1987a, *16*(1–2), 29–49.

Salamon, L. M. "Partners in Public Service: Government and the Voluntary Sector in the American Welfare State." In W. Powell (ed.), *The Nonprofit Sector: A Research Handbook.* New Haven, Conn.: Yale University Press, 1987b.

Salamon, L. M. "The Marketization of Welfare: Changing Nonprofit and For-Profit Roles in the American Welfare State." *Social Service Review,* 1993, *67*(1), 16–39.

Salamon, L. M. "The Global Associational Revolution: The Rise of the Nonprofit Sector on the World Scene." *Foreign Affairs,* forthcoming.

Salamon, L. M., and Abramson, A. J. *The Federal Budget and the Nonprofit Sector.* Washington, D.C.: Urban Institute Press, 1982.

Salamon, L. M., and Abramson, A. J. *The Federal Budget and the Nonprofit Sector: Fiscal Year 1993.* Baltimore: Institute for Policy Studies, Johns Hopkins University Press, 1992.

Salamon, L. M., Musselwhite, J. G., and De Vita, C. J. "Partners in Public Service: Government and the Nonprofit Sector in the American Welfare State." Paper presented at the Independent Sector Spring Research Forum, New York, Mar. 1986.

Savas, E. S. *Privatization: The Key to Better Government.* Chatham, N.J.: Chatham House, 1987.

U.S. Census Bureau. *Statistical Abstract of the United States, 1986.* Washington, D.C.: U.S. Government Printing Office, 1986.

U.S. Department of Labor. *Workforce 2000.* Washington, D.C.: U.S. Department of Labor, 1988.

U.S. Office of Management and Budget. *Special Analyses, Budget of the United States Government: Fiscal Year 1980.* Washington, D.C.: U.S. Government Printing Office, 1980.

U.S. Office of Management and Budget. *Special Analyses, Budget of the U.S. Government: Fiscal Year 1989.* Washington, D.C.: U.S. Government Printing Office, 1988.

U.S. Office of Management and Budget. *Budget of the United States Government: Fiscal Year 1992.* Washington, D.C.: U.S. Government Printing Office, 1991.

Weisbrod, B. *The Voluntary Nonprofit Sector: An Economic Analysis.* Lexington, Mass.: Heath, 1977.

Wilson, W. J. *The Truly Disadvantaged: The Inner City, the Underclass, and Public Policy.* Chicago: University of Chicago Press, 1987.

5

Internationalization
of the Nonprofit Sector

Helmut K. Anheier
Kusuma Cunningham

The internationalization of the nonprofit sector is certainly not a recent phenomenon. For centuries, "operating across borders" has been deeply imprinted in the objectives of many religious (nonprofit) organizations, and, indeed, institutions linked to the Catholic Church, Islam, or Judaism precede the emergence of both the modern nation state and the modern business firm. Religious institutions present some of the earliest examples of nonprofit organizations working in different political, economic, and cultural systems. Monastic orders, missionary societies, or Islamic schools and universities are cases in point. Today, the increased internationalization of the nonprofit sector is, however, rarely discussed in reference to its religious roots (see Smith, 1990); rather than this, the internationalization of modern nonprofit sectors is a process that began in the nineteenth century, that has achieved much momentum since 1945, and that will most likely lead to significant growth rates in the future. What is new, therefore, is not internationalization itself; it is its size, scope, and form.

The 1992–93 *Nonprofit Almanac* (Hodgkinson, Weitzman, Toppe, and Noga, 1992), a basic source of quantitative information on the nonprofit sector, lists a total of 3,077 nonprofit organizations with a primary focus on international affairs. These organizations represent 0.7 percent of all nonprofit organizations operating in the United States, which makes the field "International, foreign affairs" one of the smallest, together with areas such as "environment" and "civil rights." To be sure, this number does not include any organization that carries out some international activity. The Ford

Foundation, for example, would not be classified under the label "international" because the bulk of its activities are domestic, even though the foundation has a significant grant-making program overseas and maintains offices in sixteen countries. Included, however, are organizations like Catholic Relief Services, Africare, Technoserve, and the Save the Children Federation.

While the overall proportion of international nonprofit organizations may be small, the area has nonetheless shown some of the highest growth rates in the sector: between 1987 and 1989, for example, the increase in the number of nonprofit organizations focusing primarily on international issues was 58 percent, as opposed to 17.8 percent for the sector as a whole. Even though some of the increases may be attributed to improved reporting and coverage, the largest registered was in the area of "international human rights issues," with 442 percent; followed by "promotion of international understanding," at 97.5 percent; and "international development and relief services," with about 85 percent (Hodgkinson, Weitzman, Toppe, and Noga, 1992, pp. 195–196, 322).

Data provided by the *Yearbook of International Organizations* (Union of International Associations, 1992) point in the same direction at the international level. The *Yearbook* includes a wide range of international bodies such as membership organizations, operating and grant-making foundations, internationally oriented national organizations, subsidiary and internal bodies, religious orders and secular institutes, and more. It shows a global increase in international organizations between 1977 and 1992 of about 122 percent. In the United States, a growth rate of 92 percent during the same period indicates the significant expansion of nongovernmental organizations (NGOs) internationally. The total increase in Canadian international organizations amounted to 96 percent also, and in Japan to 99 percent. Increases in Europe were on average somewhat higher (107 percent), and the bulk of relative growth occurred in the developing world: in Africa, 164 percent, and 142 percent in Asia.

In 1981, over 1,700 private development organizations were registered in the *Directory of Nongovernmental Organizations* in OECD countries, one of the first attempts to record nonprofit organizations operating internationally to foster development in the third world. In 1990 over 2,500 NGOs were included in this directory on the basis of a total list of some 4,000, which represents a total increase of about 50 percent (OECD, 1991). In Japan, a country where until very recently few international nonprofit organizations existed, 131 such organizations were listed in 1985 and 257 in 1990 in the OECD *Directory*. In Canada the directory lists about 215 developmental NGOs (OECD, 1991).

Nonprofit, or nongovernmental, organizations have also gained in relation to the international financing of development activities and relief efforts. The amounts of funds raised by NGOs and channelled through them to the developing countries have increased significantly. In 1981 grants by NGOs amounted to $2 billion and by 1989 had increased to more than $4 billion.

As a portion of total official assistance from the developed to the developing world, it increased from 1.5 percent to 3.8 percent during the same period (OECD, 1991). The U.S. has led other members of the OECD in total official and private contributions to nonprofit organizations for activities overseas. The 300 larger NGOs registered with the U.S. government (AID) received about $1.09 billion in public funds and were able to raise about $3.6 billion in private contributions in 1990. NGOs account for approximately 13.5 percent of total development assistance funds in the United States, a proportion likely to increase in the future (AID, 1992).

The Rise of NGOs

Two types of nonprofit organizations are at the center of the sector's internationalization: humanitarian relief and private-development assistance organizations, and interest associations. Though somewhat imprecisely, these very different types of organizations are summarily referred to as nongovernmental organizations, or NGOs.

The emergence of humanitarian organizations in the nineteenth century is closely related to two developments that occurred at about the same time in the United States and in Protestant European countries: First, the evangelical revival of the mid-nineteenth century led to an increase in missionary activities and in the number of missionary societies operating overseas. Second, in contrast to the autocratic state in most of continental Europe, the liberal state in the United Kingdom and the United States allowed the institutionalization of special interest in the form of associations. The founding of the Foreign Anti-Slavery Society in London (1823), the World's Evangelical Alliance (1846), the World Alliance of Young Men's Christian Association (1855), and the Red Cross (1863/1880) are important events in the initial development of the modern international nonprofit sector.

In the second half of the nineteenth century, the number of international nonprofit organizations continued to increase. By the 1920s, about a thousand international NGOs existed. Much of this increase was no longer due to religion and basic humanitarian concerns. After the "boom" in creating missionary societies and humanitarian associations ended at the beginning of this century, academic and scholarly associations contributed to the growth of the sector, particularly in the field of medicine and the natural sciences. The brief period of economic prosperity in the 1920s increased the need for international business and professional associations. The Depression and World War II, however, delayed the full development of this type of international nonprofit organization, and it was not until the 1950s that business and professional associations became more important actors: they represent about 12.5 percent of all new international nonprofit organizations founded between 1945 and the early 1980s, yet they accounted for only 3.3 percent of all pre-1914 organizations.

NGOs played an important role in the formation of the modern world of international relations. Not only did NGOs participate alongside governments in the first international human rights conferences, they also helped bring about a system of international contracts and agreements that paved the way for the establishment of the League of Nations. While the league did not officially recognize NGOs as parties to treaties, a modus operandi developed that allowed representatives to participate, speak, and introduce resolutions in plenary sessions and meetings. This form of informal participation proved increasingly difficult as the international climate deteriorated in the 1930s. As relations among governments worsened, the role of NGOs became politicized and controversial.

This mixed record was one important reason why the Founding Conference of the United Nations in San Francisco in 1945 decided to establish a formal consultative status for NGOs. We should also take into account that 42 U.S. NGOs participated in an official advisory role to the U.N. conference, and that an additional 240 U.S. NGOs enjoyed "observer status." The significant presence of U.S. NGOs in San Francisco, which by far outnumbered the state delegations, aroused the critique of the Soviet Union. The Soviets preferred a much-reduced role of NGOs in the future international world order and argued against the proliferation of special interests.

The modern history of international NGOs began as part of the history of the emergent cold war. While the United States favored a more extensive participation of NGOs in the new world body, the Soviet Union argued for limited involvement. Article 71 of the U.N. Charter represents a compromise between the U.S. and Soviet positions in the sense that NGOs are excluded from all central political and security-related U.N. operations and restricted to social and economic matters under the Economic and Social Council. In turn, the charter guarantees NGOs a consultative role. Other international organizations, like the European Communities and the Organization for Economic Cooperation and Development, essentially followed the United Nations in developing similar models of NGO participation.

The role of NGOs in the U.N. system has changed significantly since the founding period of the 1950s. Until the 1970s most of the recently independent countries of Africa and Asia shared the distrust socialist regimes had for NGOs. However, to the extent to which the Third World was able to organize its own interests relatively independent of either the U.S. or Soviet spheres of influence, attitudes toward NGOs became more positive. This development coincided with the first major economic crises since World War II and the beginning of a disillusionment with the role of the state in the process of development. Ironically, distrust previously aimed at NGOs was now redirected toward the state; and particular interests represented by NGOs were now seen as more universalistic and impartial than some Third World governments themselves. This changed perspective about NGOs was prevalent in the Third World as well as in North America and Europe, and it paved the way for their popularity in the 1980s and 1990s (see below).

NGOs maintain consultative status with specialized U.N. organizations, and not with the U.N. in general. About 130 NGOs are linked with the World Health Organization, such as the League of Red Cross Societies. Similar committees exist for the U.N. High Commission for Refugees, the Drug Control Program, the United Nations Educational, Scientific, and Cultural Organization (UNESCO), and the U.N. Development Program. Several hundred NGOs are tied into the U.N. news and information system. Together with governmental and intergovernmental representatives, NGOs are part of a global interorganizational network, in which policies are discussed and formulated.

Many important social and political issues were first brought to the attention of the U.N. and other international bodies through the lobbying activities of NGOs, and much less so through the regular political channels of member states. Examples are fundamental equity issues of social and economic development, concerns for democracy, participation, human rights, and the environment. The 1992 United Nations Conference on Environment and Development ("Earth Summit") in Rio de Janeiro, Brazil, witnessed not only the historically largest gathering of heads of states (118) but also the highest participation of NGOs in an international, intergovernmental conference. Over a thousand NGOs were accredited to the conference, ranging from the Aspen Institute, the National Audubon Society, and the Environmental and Energy Studies Institute in the United States, to the Environmental Resource Center in Kenya, the International Indigenous Commission in Switzerland, and the International Institute for Environment and Development in the United Kingdom.

The Earth Summit in Rio de Janeiro underlined a general tendency in international policy arenas: the rise of NGOs to become an accepted and increasingly integrated part of an international policy network. In this way, NGOs replicate at the international level the development of complex national policy networks — among government agencies, corporate representatives, and nonprofit organizations — to formulate and implement domestic policies (Laumann and Knoke, 1987). NGOs are basic ingredients of an emerging international society of organizations.

NGOs and Development

Industrialized countries' interest in providing aid through NGOs to the developing world can be largely explained by the poor performance of many Third World governments in bringing about equitable and sustainable development. NGOs are seen as an alternative to state-led and state-dominated development. The planned development efforts after colonialism had not had the intended effects among the world's poorer countries. Many of the countries are still in the grips of poverty and in a continued state of dependence on foreign assistance. Some African countries depend to over 50 percent of their GDP on international financial assistance in one form or another. Many developing countries are victims of excessive corruption and other forms of distributional inefficiencies, thereby causing a severe obstacle to developmental efforts through planned governmental intervention.

At the same time there is a strong emphasis on human resources development, or "human capital formation." The realization that investment in capital-intensive technology has not resulted in "trickle down" development has added to the growing consensus among planners that it is time to take seriously the "basic needs approach" to development (Toye, 1987). International agencies such as the World Bank and OECD see a potential in NGOs to help negate the harmful effects of macroeconomic policies on poor and disadvantaged groups by promoting local reforms and institution building (World Bank, 1989; OECD, 1988b, 1990). Simultaneously many Western governments see the activities of NGOs as a contribution to civil society, thereby strengthening democratic traditions in Third World countries.

U.S. Development Assistance and NGOs

Although the pattern of relief and development assistance financing between NGOs and the U.S. government emerged during the immediate post–World War II era, the biggest push came in the 1970s. At that time, the U.S. Congress promoted the "new directions" approach in development assistance as part of revamping the politicized and negative image of U.S. activities abroad. Congress tried to promote a humanitarian image of its foreign aid programs and espoused a basic human needs approach to development activities. In doing so, Congress emphasized that NGOs were ideal conduits for delivering these kinds of services. Thus the 1973 "new directions" legislation was a very important step that led to the growth of the NGOs involved in developmental efforts.

In the 1960s, total development assistance funds channelled through NGOs amounted to $282.2 million. In the 1970s, it increased to $643.5 million, and to $1.09 billion in the 1980s. Currently, the U.S. AID funds to NGOs cover a wide range of activities: agriculture, rural development, nutrition, population planning, health, child services, education and human resources, economic support, disaster relief, and technical assistance.

According to Congressional legislation, in order to be eligible for government development assistance, NGOs must register with U.S. AID, and they are required to come up with 20 percent of financial support from non–U.S. government sources. Table 5.1 provides a summary of funding flows to U.S. NGOs for 1990. Government funding includes "freight and food" as well as grants and contracts from U.S. AID and other U.S. government agencies. "Freight and food" supports the overseas shipments of donated goods, clothing, food, books, medical and other equipment and supplies, and any other resources necessary to support NGO relief efforts and development projects. "PL 480" finances food aid programs and authorizes the donation of U.S. commodities for nutritional, development, and emergency relief purposes as well as feeding programs. U.S. AID grants and

Table 5.1. Summary of Funds for
Private Voluntary Organizations in the United States.

U.S. Government	Dollars	Non–U.S. Government	Dollars
AID freight & food	98,600,086	Other international organizations and governments	179,918,835
AID PL 480 food	255,370,200	In-kind contributions	565,806,234
U.S. AID grants & contracts	490,094,131	Private contributions	2,109,644,936
Other U.S. government grants & contracts	252,971,200	Private revenue	791,648,092
Total	$1,097,035,617	Total	$3,647,018,097

Note: Data report on the 301 NGOs registered at U.S. AID.
Source: Agency for International Development, 1992, p. 82.

contracts fund direct service delivery as well as technical assistance and training. Non–U.S. government funding comes from several sources, such as international organizations and multilateral institutions, individual donations, private fundraising, and endowments, as well as revenue from sales of goods and services.

Table 5.1 shows that total U.S. government funding to NGOs amounted to $1.1 billion, whereas private contributions to NGOs amounted to nearly $3.6 billion. Note that this figure includes private contributions to only the 301 registered NGOs. (There are no accurate data on the total number of U.S. NGOs operating and the extent of their financial support from private and public contributions.) Overall, NGOs received less than 30 percent of their revenue from government. There are, however, significant variations in the extent of government support, and larger NGOs such as Catholic Relief Service, World Vision, and CARE receive between 60 percent and 80 percent of revenues from the public sector. The pattern of NGO financing seems characteristic for the general pattern of third party government in the United States, by which government delegates public tasks to private nonprofit organizations (Salamon, 1987). Over the years, U.S. government funding for NGOs has increased considerably.

Largely in response to the alleged failure of public-sector programs in many developing countries to bring about sustained development, the international aid community has developed a favorable attitude toward NGOs and refers to their flexibility and ability to reach the grassroots as well as to their low-cost, participatory management style. However, whether NGOs are in fact able to meet such high expectations is increasingly doubtful. Judith Tendler's study (1982) of NGOs operating in Latin American countries concludes that NGOs do not necessarily reach the poorest segments of the population, nor are they successful in ensuring sustainable projects. Moreover, increased government funding has many in the development field concerned about the nature and direction of NGO goals and direction. They fear that NGOs are being co-opted to comply with the government's agenda for development, and that NGOs may lose some of their creativity and initiative.

From the perspective of the host country governments, there is a certain ambiguity to the entry and proliferation of international NGOs funded by donor countries. On the one hand, NGOs seem to relieve some of the host government's burden in performing service delivery functions and promoting development. But on the other hand, as Bratton (1989) has noted, they tend to react negatively if NGOs become an alternative mechanism to reallocate development assistance away from governments. In such situations, autocratic governments may fear that they are no longer in control of the developmental agenda.

International Philanthropy

The activities of foundations such as the Ford Foundation and the Rockefeller Foundation in Africa, Latin America, and Asia are among the earliest examples of international philanthropy by the United States. Such activities peaked during the independence period of the 1960s, when U.S. foundations established and helped create universities and research institutions in the newly independent countries. Legal changes in the United States and changing economic conditions, in particular the relative devaluation of the U.S. dollar, make it impossible now for foundations to engage in large-scale development activities. Instead, U.S. foundations like Ford see their role in facilitating and initiating, rather than implementing institution building in the Third World.

The large U.S. foundations were formed at a time when great industrial fortunes were being amassed by relatively few. There was also popular discontent and a growing belief that education, research, and scientific experimentation would lead to the amelioration of social problems. According to Arnove (1980), from the very beginning the giant philanthropic foundations were also involved in extending the "benefits" of Western science and technology, as well as Western value systems, abroad. They did this by investing heavily in higher education, research, and scientific institutions all over the world; by doing so they hoped to be able to influence cultural and social policies, and did indeed have a powerful impact on international development assistance and related policy initiatives.

Foundation Giving

According to the survey reported by the Foundation Center on Giving (Renz, 1991), the 100 largest foundations give a total of about $2.4 billion, out of which about 4.4 percent, or $109 million, goes toward international activities. Of the total number of grants made in this category, 812, or about 3.5

percent, are to international activities. And among the 372 other foundations with a total of about $789 million, $17 million, or 2.2 percent of the funds, are given to international activities. Out of the total number of grants made, about 548 are international grants, amounting to only 2.3 percent of the total. International activities are defined as constituting the following categories: peace, security, and arms control; exchange programs; development and relief services; research; policy and management; and "other." In Canada, the Foundation Directory (McClintock, 1991) lists close to sixty foundations that are focusing on international activities.

Individual Giving

At the end of the 1980s, data on individual giving noted an increase in the area of international affairs, especially in the area of peace, security, and arms control (Renz, 1991). And according to the *Annual Report on Philanthropy* (Weber, 1991), giving to organizations involved in international affairs, including projects on international peace and security, amounted to an estimated $2.23 billion, an increase of nearly 30 percent compared to the previous year, which was estimated at $1.71 billion. This estimate of giving to international affairs is projected from a survey of organizations conducted by the American Association of Fundraising Counsel (AAFRC) Trust for Philanthropy as well as data supplied by other organizations.

One of the most important reasons for this surge in individual giving to international causes is the end of the cold war, which has led to revelations of new needs and opportunities for private philanthropy in Eastern Europe. Not surprisingly churches and religious groups have been major players in the field. In 1990, the American Catholic Church, for example, launched a multimillion-dollar campaign over the next three years to assist churches in the former communist bloc countries. Many other churches have launched their own campaigns and are putting considerable effort into this endeavor.

International Philanthropy in the United States

While we have some data on the funds for developmental and humanitarian activities flowing out of the United States, we do not have any accurate figures of such foreign-country funds flowing into the United States. There are two reasons for this. First, funds flowing into the United States for charitable purposes are likely to be rather small in comparison to out-flowing philanthropic funds. Second, no central agency documents donations from abroad. With the exception of organizations like the German Marshall Fund or the Friedrich-Ebert Foundation, which operate grant programs in the United States, most of the funds from other countries enter the United States indirectly via the establishment of foundations by multinational corporations. Japanese corporations have established foundations in the United States and are making visible philanthropic gestures, particularly to the communities in which they have a presence.

Japanese business leaders assume that practicing "corporate citizenship" is important to promoting cultural integration. According to Yamamoto and Amenomori (1989), the concentration of Japan's philanthropic giving in scientific and technological research can be attributed to the fact that tax incentives for contributions have been available to donors of grants to organizations designated as "experimental research corporations" (*shiken kenkyu hojin*). The definition of what may be "experimental research corporations" has been expanded over the years to include other categories, such as scholarships, environmental protection, and the like.

Japanese philanthropy had to overcome restrictive domestic tax treatment. For example, tax laws specifically imposed restrictions against contributions concerned with humanities and the social sciences. However, recently there have been significant changes in the tax laws toward private foundations and corporate giving programs. The reasons are largely found at the international level, in which Japan was charged with trying to escape from sharing responsibility in the global community and was asked to promote closer intercultural links as part of open market policies. According to the new tax incentive scheme, there are tax deductions available to organizations promoting "international understanding" of Japan and as well as "overseas contribution tax deduction." These tax deductible contributions are to be channelled through public interest corporations such as the *Keidenran,* the Federation of Economic Organizations that created the 1 percent club. Member companies of the club pledge to donate at least one percent of their pretax profit for charitable purposes. *Keidenran* recently also created the Council for Better Corporate Citizenship, as a mechanism through which corporations can make tax deductible donations to overseas recipients (Amenomori, 1993).

Contributions coming from Japan are mainly from corporate foundations. One reason for the predominance of corporate foundations in Japan is the incorporation process, which is often exceedingly time-consuming and expensive. For a nonprofit organization to incorporate, it needs the approval of several different government ministries. According to London (1991), the time between an organization's applying for tax-deductible status to its final approval is typically one-and-a-half years; the actual time taken may be anywhere between six months and three years. It also depends on what type of contributions the organization intends to make and who is sponsoring it.

Another reason is that several government agencies have set very high minimum capital requirements for establishing a foundation — typically as high as 200 or 300 million yen ($1.4–2.1 million). However, this requirement may be relaxed, depending on what the contribution is intended for (London, 1991). In any case, the Japanese tax system does not encourage individual giving, unlike the tax system in the United States.

It is estimated that Japanese giving in the United States was $30 million in 1985 and $300 million in 1990—a dramatic increase in a five-year period. According to Delwin Roy (1992), president of the Hitachi Foundation, Japanese corporations now account for nearly 5 percent of total corporate giving in the United States, which is estimated at $6 billion total. During the same time period the number of Japanese foundations in the United States increased from three to twenty-five. The most important observation, according to Roy, is that this performance has made Japanese-funded philanthropic activity the most rapidly growing component of overall charitable activity conducted in the United States.

Management of NGOs

Research on nonprofit management has long emphasized the complex environment in which nonprofit organizations operate (Herman and Heimovics, 1991). Nonprofit organizations have to reconcile the demand of multiple constituencies, such as board members, clients, and donors (Powell and Friedkin, 1987). This complex management task is made even more precarious for nonprofit organizations operating internationally and in different social, cultural, and political settings. For international advocacy organizations, Young (1992) argues that they are successful if they adopt organizational structures and strategies that accommodate the problems associated with international operations. These are cultural diversity, geographical distance in operations, economic barriers, and political fragmentation. Young finds that decentralized and federated structures appear more successful over time than both centralized organizations and hierarchical federations in meeting the challenges of international environments.

Of course, organizations vary to the extent to which they are able, willing, or formed to find a match between organizational structure and environment. U.S. AID sponsored a study of AID-funded NGOs and their operations, both in the United States and in the developing world (Biddle, 1984). The study was able to identify several management problems that seemed characteristic across a wide range of projects and countries: insufficient institutional planning, weaknesses in fundraising, suboptimal financial planning, poor human resource management, inefficient headquarters–field office relations, lack of project evaluation, bad information management and lack of data processing facilities, administrative difficulties, and inefficiencies in project implementation. We will briefly discuss some of them.

Lack of Institutional Planning

Nearly 75 percent of the respondents mentioned that some aspect of planning was a problem. Many NGO members complained that because NGOs do not have long-term planning, they deal with challenges on an ad hoc basis and "move from one crisis to the other." The need to secure funding opportunities means that NGOs frequently opt for working in the area where there is funding available rather than where there is demand for their services. This results in a serious lack of a "strategic focus" to their programs. They are unable to set clear goals and priorities in terms of funds and activities needed to meet the demand for their services.

Some of the main reasons cited to explain difficulty and resistance to institutional planning was that planning establishes rigid frameworks that prevent adaptation and flexibility—which are seen as characteristics of NGOs. Institutional planning is more complicated to implement when dealing with diversified international operations. The program staff are geographically separated from the planning staff; the political context may be full of uncertainties; government policies may be ambiguous, and local as well as international funding uncertain.

The Management of Fundraising

Nearly 49 percent of the respondents mentioned that obtaining a secure financial base had become increasingly difficult—not only because of scarcer resources and increased competition but also because NGOs are moving away from direct relief and rehabilitation to working toward institutional development and policy reform. This has created problems for fundraising. It is not always easy to justify complex development goals to a potential constituency of donors. Some NGOs fear losing their funding base unless they make direct emotional appeals to the public (see also Smith, 1990).

Besides this, NGOs may not be able to obtain strong support and help toward fundraising from their boards; many staff felt that boards interfere too frequently in daily operational matters. Twenty-two percent of the respondents felt that relations with the board in matters of fundraising were not always smooth sailing. Another problem was that NGOs are generally reluctant to use professional fundraising experts. They fear that professionals would not have the same values as those within the NGO community. Recently, however, there has been a growing trend toward hiring professional fund raisers.

Financial Planning

Most NGOs face considerable problems in the field of financial planning. Nearly 34 percent of the respondents alluded to budgeting as a problem in allocating funds to competing priorities. Not only the delays and uncertainties of obtaining available funds in an international financial environment contribute to this problem but also the complexity of different sources and types of funds, which, combined with donor preferences and restrictions, has created a complicated financial system. Few NGOs have the capacity to track the variables at work in a financial system that would allow them to predict financial outcomes with a degree of certainty. As a result, NGOs seek stable funding from a few sources, and few follow a strategy by which they try to optimize return across several funding arenas under conditions of uncertainty.

Management of Human Resources. Human resources involves a whole range of problems, such as recruitment, salary, training, and technical and managerial skills. However, this situation has currently improved; as the NGOs have matured and gained in stature, they have become highly professional and are able to recruit well-trained and educated staff. Yet finding experienced people willing and able to work overseas at often noncompetitive wages remains a problem. As a consequence, managerial and technical competence at the field level may be lacking. Still, for many organizations, due to budgetary pressures, there is a tendency to hire junior staff and rely on "hands on" training to substitute for experience. Budgetary pressures also reduce the ability of NGOs to finance programs suited to their special needs.

Headquarters/Field Staff Relations. At least 26 percent of the respondents felt that management difficulties flowed from the geographical separation of operations. Communication becomes difficult and lack of information creates managerial distrust and need for action; as a result many NGOs have developed centralized management styles. But the growing influence of semi-autonomous indigenous and local organizations in the field has brought additional problems of coordination and responsibility. Frequently, however, managers at headquarters are faced with the problems of weak local accounting systems, inexperienced staff, high turnover, and low job security at the field level.

Project Evaluation and Information Management. Many NGOs recognize that one of their weaknesses is the lack of proper evaluation of their projects. This is only partially due to budgetary or staff constraints, which make it difficult to devote time and resources for evaluation. In other cases, these difficulties serve as a protective shield to maintain the myth of the cost-effective, responsive, and participatory NGOs.

Administrative Difficulties. Government procedures and regulations in grant management tend to be complex. Many NGOs wish for technical assistance and help in the interpretation of AID rules and regulations. Changes in federal policies with regard to procurement or financial management policy may create uncertainties for NGOs. However large, well-established NGOs are better equipped to cope with this problem than small, newly established ones.

Professionalization. Although managers may be well versed in project design and evaluation, when it comes to project implementation at the field level, managers frequently find that there is a greater need for training in day-to-day project management, contracting, procurement, listening skills, and training. The rapid growth of the NGO community over the last two decades has also brought about some dramatic changes in all aspects of the NGO operations, including the management culture of the NGOs. Universities are now offering curricula that define an area of study as prerequisite for entering the field.

Increased growth has brought along with it increased professionalization. The managers of NGOs may no longer see themselves as primarily guided by idealistic notions. They see themselves as development professionals. Those entering the profession are no longer generalists, but well-trained specialists. Increased professionalization brings with it, however, a greater potential for bureaucratization and a certain rigidity — a loss of flexibility.

As NGOs move into more complex areas of development such as promoting institutional development and policy reform, they are also beginning to borrow terminologies and techniques from the corporate culture, such as "strategic management," "risk taking," "marketing a product," and "participatory management." The traditional ideology of NGOs, as exemplified in Dichter (1987), stresses group processes and popular participation: team building, problem solving, facilitation skills, active listening skills, conflict resolution, and coalition building skills.

The term "participatory management" has become increasingly popular among the development community. Although it is a simple sounding term and makes sense intuitively, there is much debate as to what it means and how it can best be effectively practiced. Even though the notion of participatory development has its roots in socialist thinking of the nineteenth century, it entered current management debates via the theology of liberation in Latin America and the secular NGO community in OECD countries. It is now given considerable importance and attention by development experts as well as multilateral institutions such as the World Bank, which in 1992 hosted a three-day workshop on participatory management. Development experts are also learning to build on indigenous traditions, which often include elements of cooperation and mutual self-help, in addressing the public goods problem in communities within developing countries.

Future Trends

In recent years NGOs have become major actors in an emerging international society of organizations. Three trends are part of this on-going development: the emergence of local NGOs in developing countries, the increased prominence of Japanese foundations, and the European Association Statute that will make it possible for nonprofit organizations to operate as pan-European associations (6 and Kuti, 1992).

Developmental NGOs have changed somewhat over the last decade as these organizations have matured and are asked to be more accountable. At the same time, NGOs are faced with competition for financial resources, not only because of the growth in the number of such organizations seeking funding but also specifically because of growth in an unexpected area, namely southern NGOs, which is to say, nongovernmental organizations based in the developing countries. The southern NGOs have grown so rapidly that it is conceivable that they pose some challenges to the northern NGOs (Fisher, 1993).

As Dichter (1989) points out, the trend among the southern and northern NGOs is toward a "shift in responsibilities." In the future, donor agencies may bypass established "northern" NGOs and deal directly with those in the south. Not many solutions exist to this possible dilemma, except that U.S. NGOs could maintain their comparative advantages in terms of research, education, institution building, and environmental protection, and their traditional forte—emergency and disaster relief.

Global interconnectedness and a highly competitive international economic environment will bring new opportunities and new challenges to the NGO community. NGOs, with their years of experience in developing countries, may be useful in initiating commercial activity in those areas. For example, NGOs are now intermediaries between the U.S. government and the local populations of some developing countries. In the future, NGOs may also act as intermediaries between private business interests and potential markets in developing countries. Another related factor to the globalization of the economy is the increasing numbers and scope of corporate philanthropic activities. The notion of a "good corporate citizen," which Japanese corporations are currently being asked to abide by (Koike, 1992), may become one of the yardsticks for measuring the success or failure of global corporations.

References

Agency for International Development. *Implementation of "New Directions" in Development Assistance: Report to the Committee on International Relations on Implementation of Legislative Reforms in the Foreign Assistance Act of 1973.* Washington, D.C.: AID, 1975.

Agency for International Development. *Voluntary Foreign Aid Programs: Report of American Voluntary Agencies Engaged in Overseas Relief and Development Registered with the Agency for International Development.* Washington, D.C.: AID, 1992.

Agency for International Development. Advisory Committee on Voluntary Foreign Aid, 1990 Report. *Responding to Change: Private Voluntarism and International Development.* Washington, D.C.: AID, 1990.

Agency for International Development. Office of Private and Voluntary Cooperation, Bureau for Food for Peace and Voluntary Assistance. *The AID-NGO Partnership: Sharing Goals and Resources in the Work of Development.* Washington, D.C.: AID, 1987.

Amenomori, T. "Defining the Nonprofit Sector: Japan." Working papers of the Johns Hopkins Comparative Nonprofit Sector Project, no 15. Baltimore: Johns Hopkins University Press, 1993.

Arnove, R. F. (ed.). *Philanthropy and Cultural Imperialism: The Foundations at Home and Abroad.* Boston, Mass.: G. K. Hall, 1980.

Biddle, S. C. "The Management Needs of Private Voluntary Organizations." In *A Report Prepared for the Office of Private and Voluntary Cooperation, AID.* Washington, D.C.: Agency for International Development, 1984.

Bratton, M. "The Politics of Government-NGO Relations in Africa." *World Development,* 1989, *17*(4), 569–587.

Dichter, T. W. "The Contexts and Cultures in Which NGOs Manage." *AID Technical Paper.* Washington, D.C.: Agency for International Development, 1987.

Dichter, T. W. *Issues Critical to a Shift in Responsibilities Between U.S. PVOs and Southern NGOs: Paper presented to the Advisory Committee on Voluntary Foreign Aid.* Washington, D.C.: AID, 1989.

Fisher, J. *The Road to Rio: Sustainable Development and the Nongovernmental Movement in the Third World.* Westport, Conn.: Praeger, 1993.

Herman, R. D., and Heimovics, R. D. *Executive Leadership in Nonprofit Organizations: New Strategies for Shaping Executive-Board Dynamics.* San Francisco: Jossey-Bass, 1991.

Hodgkinson, V., Weitzman, M., Toppe, C. M., and Noga, S. M. *Nonprofit Almanac 1992-93: Dimensions of the Independent Sector.* San Francisco: Jossey-Bass, 1992.

Inside Japanese Support. Rockville, Md.: TAFT Publications, 1992.

Koike, I. "Japanese Giving at the Grassroots." *Foundation News,* 1992, Jan./ Feb., pp. 41–43.

Laumann, E. O., and Knoke, D. *The Organizational State: Social Choice in National Policy Domains.* Madison: University of Wisconsin Press, 1987.

London, N. *Japanese Corporate Philanthropy.* New York: Oxford University Press, 1991.

McClintock, N. (ed.). *Canadian Directory to Foundations.* Toronto, Canada: Canadian Center for Philanthropy, 1991.

Organization for Economic Cooperation and Development. *Directory of Nongovernmental Organizations in OECD Member Countries.* Paris: OECD, 1981.

Organization for Economic Cooperation and Development. *Development Cooperation 1988 Report.* Paris: OECD, 1988a.

Organization for Economic Cooperation and Development. *Voluntary Aid for Development: The Role of Nongovernmental Organizations.* Paris: OECD, 1988b.

Organization for Economic Cooperation and Development. *Development Cooperation 1989 Report.* Paris: OECD, 1989.

Organization for Economic Cooperation and Development. *Development Cooperation 1990 Report.* Paris: OECD, 1990.

Organization for Economic Cooperation and Development. *Directory of Nongovernmental Organizations in OECD Member Countries.* Paris: OECD, 1991.

Powell, W., and Friedkin, R. "Organizational Change in Nonprofit Organizations." In W. Powell (ed.), *The Nonprofit Sector: A Research Handbook.* New Haven, Conn.: Yale University Press, 1987.

Renz, L. *Foundation Giving: Yearbook of Facts and Figures on Private, Corporate and Community Foundations, 1991 Edition.* New York: Foundation Center, 1991.

Roy, D. "Japanese Philanthropy in the U.S.: The 1990s and Beyond." Speech given by the president of the Hitachi Foundation at NOVA University, Fort Lauderdale, Florida, 1992.

Salamon, L. M. "Partners in Public Service: The Scope and Theory of Government-Nonprofit Relations." In W. Powell (ed.), *The Nonprofit Sector: A Research Handbook.* New Haven, Conn.: Yale University Press, 1987.

6, P., and Kuti, E. "Into the European Community: Impacts of Future Membership on Hungary's Nonprofit Sector." Paper presented at the Arnova Conference, Yale University, New Haven, Conn., Oct. 1992.

Smith, B. *More than Altruism: The Politics of Private Foreign Aid.* Princeton, N.J.: Princeton University Press, 1990.

Tendler, J. *Turning Private Voluntary Organizations into Developmental Agencies: Questions for Evaluation.* AID Program Evaluation Discussion Paper 12. Washington, D.C.: AID, 1982.

Toye, J. "Development Theory and the Issues for the Future." In L. Emmerij (ed.), *Development Policies and the Crisis of the 1980s.* Paris: Organization for Economic Cooperation and Development, 1987.

Union of International Associations. *Yearbook of International Organizations, 1992–93.* Munich, Germany: K. G. Saur Verlag GmbH, 1992.

Weber, N. (ed.). *Giving USA: The Annual Report on Philanthropy for the Year 1990.* New York: Joanne Hayes, 1991.

World Bank. *The World Bank Development Report.* Oxford: Oxford University Press, 1989.

Yamamoto, T., and Amenomori, T. *Japanese Private Philanthropy in an Interdependent World: The JCIE Papers.* New York: Japan Center for International Exchange, 1989.

Young, D. "Organizing Principles for International Advocacy Associations." *Voluntas,* 1992, *3*(1), 1-28.

PART TWO

KEY LEADERSHIP ISSUES

Governance and leadership are important areas in which nonprofit organizations differ fundamentally from businesses and government agencies. Boards of directors (or trustees) of nonprofit organizations are legally responsible for the conduct of organizational affairs and are expected to provide leadership in defining their organizations' missions and values. Experience and systematic research have shown that the chief executives of nonprofit organizations typically play central leadership roles as well.

The six chapters in this part of the book collectively examine the leadership roles that boards and chief executives are expected to enact in nonprofit organizations, the difficulties that sometimes prevent boards or executives from carrying out their prescribed roles, and the strategies and techniques that have been found useful in enhancing the leadership effectiveness of both boards and executives. One chapter focuses on the board side of the board–chief executive leadership equation and another examines the chief executive side of that relationship. In addition, other chapters highlight the leadership roles of boards and executives (as well as other participants) in strategic planning, creating and maintaining ethical organizational culture, advocating for legislative or regulatory actions pertaining to organizational missions, and managing organizational transformations.

6

Board Leadership and Board Development

Nancy R. Axelrod

One of the distinctive features of the nonprofit sector in the United States is the way in which it is governed. The responsibility for governing most nonprofit organizations is vested not in stock owners, government officials, or professional managers, but with volunteer leaders from diverse backgrounds who serve as members of boards of directors. Nonprofit board members are guided in the exercise of their organizational responsibilities by legal requirements that range from the organization's articles of incorporation and bylaws to state nonprofit corporation laws to federal tax and civil rights laws. While external agencies such as state attorneys general and the Internal Revenue Service exert some regulatory control, most of the responsibility for self-regulation, accountability, and ethical practice rests on the shoulders of the millions of lay individuals who serve on boards.

The nonprofit board has always been important, but greater national attention is being focused on its role than ever before. This scrutiny has been precipitated by escalating demands for the services that nonprofits provide, intense competition for funds from private and public sources to finance these services, and growing recognition that the success of nonprofit organizations in delivering these services will be influenced by the effectiveness of their leaders.

Governance has become a central issue as nonprofit organizations face increasing attention from the media and government. The serious and well-publicized weaknesses exposed in the financial, management, and governance practices of some nonprofits serve to undermine the public's confidence in the sector as a whole. Nothing can do more to restore waning confidence than the actions governing boards can take to assure the public that they understand their role as stewards and guardians and that they are committed to holding their organizations accountable.

In *Fulfilling the Public Trust: Ten Ways to Help Nonprofit Boards Maintain Accountability,* Peter Bell, president of the Edna McConnell Clark Foundation and chairperson of CARE, notes: "Boards that hold themselves and their organizations to high standards of accountability start with individual members who are committed to giving the time and quality attention for responsible trusteeship. These board members view their service on nonprofit boards as a public trust that requires establishing a framework for accountability and exercising governance within that framework. What motivates them is not fear of the consequences from falling short, but satisfaction at the prospect of effectively advancing the social purposes of their organizations. While accountability demands discipline, board members will experience its proper exercise as less confining than liberating" (1993, p. 18).

The Board's Basic Responsibilities

It is the board that is ultimately responsible for ensuring that the organization it governs fulfills its mission. The board also has the duty to conserve and protect the assets of the organization and to ensure that it operates in accordance with the state and federal laws that affect its operations. While the personal liability of directors and officers varies from state to state, individual board members remain personally liable for a breach of their duties of care, loyalty, and obedience to their organizations. Consider the following observations from an article titled "Board Members and Risk: A Primer on Protection from Liability," which appeared in *Board Member* in 1992: "Although Directors and Officers coverage shields board members from certain kinds of risk, it is only one such vehicle. The key way a board member can guard against liability is by being a good board member. Acting responsibly as a trustee or director is never a guarantee against lawsuits but is still the best prevention. Leifer and Glomb, in *The Legal Responsibilities of Nonprofit Boards* (1992, p. 41), say it well: 'Clearly the best way for a board member to avoid personal liability is to avoid conduct that breeds liability'" (p. 13).

An overriding responsibility of the nonprofit board is that of *fiduciary,* which involves a duty to act for the good of others. Unlike the governing board of a for-profit corporation, which is accountable to the owners or shareholders of the corporation, the governing board of the nonprofit organized and operated for charitable purposes is accountable to the public. In return for exemption from taxes and freedom from excessive government regulation, the organization is expected to serve the public benefit and its board is expected to function as guardian or steward to safeguard the public interest.

While the fiduciary role is fundamentally the same for most nonprofit boards, each board's specific responsibilities vary according to several factors. These include the organization's size and scope, its developmental stage, the method of selecting board members, and whether the organization is managed primarily by staff or by volunteers. For example, the founding board of a newly established, local community agency managed primarily by volunteers may be expected to help more with running the organization than the board of a large, mature, well-staffed health agency that provides research and patient care services throughout the country.

The majority of nonprofit boards are expected to carry out the following responsibilities:

1. *To determine the organization's mission and purpose.* One of the board's most important responsibilities is to establish the mission of the organization. A clear sense of mission — why the organization exists and what it seeks to accomplish — is an integral part of any organization's foundation. New and more experienced board members alike need to be familiar with the current mission statement in order to make wise decisions. The board must continually monitor whether its own policy decisions as well as the organization's programs and services reflect this mission.

A mission statement is not a static document. The board should review the mission periodically to determine whether it needs to be updated, revised, or even reaffirmed. Changing social, demographic, and environmental conditions can alter an organization's original reasons for existence. If midcourse adjustments are needed, the board needs to be engaged in redrawing and approving a new mission statement that reflects these changes.

2. *To select and support the chief executive.* The quality of the leadership that the organization is able to attract and retain in its chief executive will also contribute to how well the organization fulfills its mission. While other people may be invited to assist with or participate in the selection of the new executive, it is the board's job to make the final decision.

An unprofessional or incompetent search for an executive will reflect poorly on the organization's image. Worse yet, it can cost the board the loss of good candidates. The board's success in hiring the best person to serve as the chief executive will be a function of several factors, including the board's understanding of the organization's current strengths, needs, and goals for the future; a clear description of the duties of the chief executive; and a systematic search that casts a wide net for the most qualified candidates.

Executive searches take considerable time, and rapid turnover in this position is costly and disruptive for the entire organization. Executives cannot be expected to stay forever, but as long as the board has confidence in an executive, it has the obligation to do what it can to support and retain its leader. To help the executive serve as the agent who carries out the board's policies, the board must allow the executive to assume responsibility and assert leadership. The necessary climate of trust and cooperation can develop when the board outlines its expectations of the chief executive, takes at least some responsibility for difficult but unpopular decisions that have to be made, and stays attuned to the executive's need for renewal and professional development.

3. *To review the executive's performance.* Once the board selects an executive, it then has an obligation to review that person's performance on a regular basis and to provide constructive feedback on strengths as well as weaknesses. In *Board Assessment of the Chief Executive: A Responsibility Essential to Good Governance,* author John Nason says, "One of the most important responsibilities of the board is to assess the progress and health of the organization, which requires an appraisal of the performance both of the chief executive and of the board itself" (1990, p. 2).

The precise form of executive evaluation will vary. While Nason offers methods of and criteria for assessment, he warns that "no single or perfect formula exists for assessment, no single or perfect rating instrument. Many rating lists used to evaluate chief executives are inadequate." Regardless of the method used, Nason advises boards to "do it; do it in a humane and sensitive way; and make it a constructive, regular exercise for the chief executive, for the board, and for the organization" (p. 12).

Regular assessment of the chief executive produces additional benefits. While the effectiveness of the executive tends to be interrelated with the effectiveness of the board, the division of labor between the two is not always clear. An executive evaluation can provide an opportunity to stop and take stock of the executive's role, as distinct from that of the board.

Second, a regular assessment process reduces the likelihood that evaluation will be conducted only when problems or a crisis occur. The purpose of an assessment is not to conduct a popularity contest, but ultimately to strengthen the performance of the chief executive. The best time to establish evaluation procedures is when the new executive is hired.

4. *To plan for the future.* A board that devotes most of its time to administrative, operational issues cannot give adequate attention to the strategic issues that will profoundly affect the organization's growth and success. In order to make wise policy decisions for the future, the board must take the time to consider where the organization is going and how it is going to get there.

One of the board's responsibilities is to ensure that the organization engages in a multiyear planning process — one that looks beyond the present. A good planning process will consider such questions as the adequacy of the mission statement, the changes in the external environment that have affected the organization, and ways that the organization can meet new opportunities and challenges. Staff members, other volunteers, and consultants may be enlisted to help with the strategic planning process, but it is the board's responsibility to make sure that it is being done and to approve and adopt the final plan.

5. *To approve and monitor the organization's programs and services.* While the board must delegate to staff the responsibility for administering programs,

it cannot abdicate its responsibility for making sure that these programs advance the mission of the organization, and are conducted effectively and efficiently.

To make decisions about allocating finite resources among competing priorities the board must learn to ask the right questions to determine what the organization can do best. The answers to these questions will help the board consider the strengths and weaknesses of existing programs, which programs should be modified or discontinued altogether, and what new programs should be adopted.

In *Board Assessment of the Organization: How Are We Doing?* (1992, p. 11), author Peter Szanton offers some key questions that board members should ask to assess programs and services:

If we were starting today, would we do it this way?
Do our actions match our mission statement?
How are we like and unlike the best in our field?
What do our intended beneficiaries think of our performance?
How are the next five years likely to be different?

6. *To provide sound financial management.* One of the ways a nonprofit board serves the public trust is to ensure that income is managed properly, that assets are guarded, and that adequate financial resources are secured to support the organization. This cannot be accomplished unless the board receives timely, accurate, intelligible financial reports on a regular basis that reveal the financial condition of the organization.

All of the members of the board are expected to participate in financial decision making. In *Understanding Nonprofit Financial Statements: A Primer for Board Members,* John Paul Dalsimer notes, "Even though one [board] member is usually elected treasurer, and many boards have a finance committee (and staff who maintain records), each board member must receive financial statements, review them, and ask questions about anything that is unclear. Reviewing financial statements is an integral part of fulfilling board financial responsibility" (1991, p. 2).

One of the ways that the board exercises its responsibility for financial oversight is by developing and approving the annual operating budget. Financial reports should help the board monitor the budget's implementation and track expenditures and revenues. Boards also carry out their financial responsibilities by implementing sound financial controls and requiring an annual audit by an independent account.

7. *To enlist financial resources.* The board must also make sure that the organization has adequate financial resources to carry out its mission. Board members are expected to take an active role as fund raisers for those nonprofit organizations that depend on private contributions from individuals, foundations, and corporations. Regardless of the amount of time the chief executive or the development officer spends in fundraising, individual board

members can help raise funds in a variety of ways. In *Fund Raising and the Nonprofit Board Member,* Fisher Howe assures that "every board member can do something useful to support the fund-raising effort, employing his or her own skills and interests" (1989, p. 6). Howe suggests, for example, that in addition to making an annual contribution themselves, board members can provide names of key prospects, help with the cultivation of a prospective donor, and accompany a member of the staff when soliciting a corporate or foundation donor.

Not all nonprofit organizations depend on grants and donations to support their operations. Whether or not the organization derives its revenue from voluntary contributions, government contracts, or earned income from its services, the board is ultimately responsible for ensuring that it has the required finances to support its program. Even before helping to actually generate revenue, boards undertake this responsibility by approving the financing strategy.

8. *To advance the organization's public image.* Since nonprofit boards are often composed of individuals from the community the organization serves, its members can be in the best position to offer perspective to the organization, and to communicate to others why that organization exists and how it serves that community. This is a two-way process at best. As the bridge between the organization and its external environment, individual board members are also in an ideal position to listen to what the community says about the role and effectiveness of the organization.

In *The Board's Role in Public Relations and Communications,* Joyce Fitzpatrick reminds us that "board members can place the organization's work in context with other business, political, demographic, and social trends. They should initiate strategic alliances with other organizations and fight insularity. They must be the advocates of members, clients and donors to help their organizations become truly customer-driven" (1993, p. 13).

The board should ensure that a public relations strategy is in place to communicate the organization's purposes and accomplishments, and to enlist support for its activities. A board also needs to have a policy in place to handle crises that may catapult the organization into the media and jeopardize its integrity. In these cases, a host of decisions may have to be made such as who serves as the spokesman for the organization, whether interim leadership must be put into place, and how the board can protect the public interest during any leadership transitions that may result.

9. *To strengthen its own effectiveness as a board.* In addition to its responsibilities in evaluating the performance of the chief executive, a board needs to develop the capacity to assess periodically its own performance as a governing body. According to Richard T. Ingram, author of *Ten Basic Responsibilities of Nonprofit Boards,* boards should occasionally "stand back from their usual preoccupations and reflect on how the board is meeting its responsibilities. This process should look at how its membership composition, member se-

lection process, organization or structure, and overall performance can be strengthened" (1989, p. 13).

A board can also strengthen its effectiveness by establishing a systematic selection process to add qualified individuals to its membership and an orientation process to educate these new members. After the orientation program, learning should never end, because one of the few certainties in the nonprofit world is that things will continue to change. The board needs to establish a program of continuing education or "board development" that keeps board members informed of the work of the organization, changes in the field in which the organization is operating, and the evolving role of the board.

Using Board Development to Apply Theory to Practice

The growing interest in nonprofit boards has encouraged more research on the actual behaviors of boards, the variables that affect board operation and performance, and the characteristics that seem to make some boards more effective than others. This interest is manifested in dramatic increases in the literature, consulting, and folklore that prescribe what boards are supposed to do to carry out their significant role as nonprofit leaders. Much of this activity is fueled by board and staff members who are hungry for thoughtful guidelines for good practice and advice on the art and science of good governance. This demand resulted in the creation of the National Center for Nonprofit Boards (NCNB) in Washington, D.C., which was established in 1988 as the first national organization dedicated exclusively to improving the effectiveness of organizations throughout the nonprofit sector by strengthening their governing boards. As NCNB has grown, so has the amount of information available on board members and the organizations they serve. Two related facts have become increasingly obvious: the hunger for information about governance issues is immense and growing, and the need for governing boards to be informed, engaged, and effective has never been greater.

Perhaps a more compelling issue for those who serve on and work with boards is how to apply the theory of what the board is supposed to do. While many nonprofit organizations are run exclusively by volunteers, a large number are eventually managed by paid staff. These staff members often have significant expectations—realistic and unrealistic—about how board members can help their organizations. It is ironic that the growing number of nonprofit management programs that purport to educate those who aspire to run nonprofit organizations often exclude governance from the curriculum.

New and more experienced board members also approach their positions with a wide array of expectations about what it means to be a trustee and how they can best serve their organization. And yet most individuals who serve on boards do not receive any formal preparation for their role. While the executive staff of nonprofit organizations are increasingly recognized as legitimate participants in leadership and management training, board members are rarely provided with opportunities to develop and sharpen their governance skills.

How can governing boards, typically made up of busy part-time volunteers, who are not engaged in the daily management of their organizations, discharge their significant responsibilities? And how can chief executives, who may or may not come to their positions with experience in working with boards, assist in this process?

Many factors influence the competence with which a board carries out its responsibilities, including the quality and commitment of those selected to serve on the board. The quality and potential contribution of candidates persuaded to serve on a nonprofit board, however, will not automatically create an effective board. Adequate resources must be channeled into the recruitment, education, and retention of board members. This process, typically referred to as "board development," represents the educational component of trusteeship. It consists of a cluster of activities, directed at individual board members and the board as a whole (as well as the staff who work closely with the board), that are designed to help the board carry out its work.

The following are some of the characteristics of a meaningful board development program:

1. *It is a continuing process rather than a single event.* More boards are participating in retreats or special workshops expressly for the purpose of reviewing and clarifying their collective role and responsibilities. As helpful as these may be, a single program is unlikely to provide the continuing education to keep the board informed of the issues and trends that may affect the organization's mission, direction, and delivery system. Board development is most successful when it is approached as a means to help board members periodically review their performance, learn from their mistakes, and attend to their continuing education needs as policy makers.

2. *The board chairperson and the chief executive are committed to it.* While the chief executive needs to devote adequate time to educating and enlisting board members, the board cannot relinquish its own responsibility to manage itself. Some nonprofit boards have reaffirmed this principle by charging a standing committee of the board with the responsibility to select, orient, provide continuing education for, and evaluate board members. In some cases, these tasks are entrusted to the nominating committee, if the board has one; other nonprofit boards establish a separate committee on board development to attend to them. Consultants and senior staff may also be involved in the board development process, but without the ongoing support and attention of the board chair or the chief executive, the return on investment in such efforts will be minimal.

3. *The board is willing to invest in its own development.* In a three-year study of the characteristics and behaviors that distinguish strong boards of

higher education from weak ones, Chait, Holland, and Taylor report that at least one competency of stronger boards relates to the "educational dimension": "Effective boards take the necessary steps to ensure that trustees are well informed about the institution and about the board's roles, responsibilities, and performance. As self-directed learners, strong boards consciously create opportunities for trustee education; regularly seek feedback on the board's performance; and pause periodically for self-reflection, especially to examine the board's mistakes" (1991, p. 26).

Speakers, retreats, workshops, and other educational opportunities often require time and dollars. A board that is not willing to invest resources in board development is unlikely to practice it.

These specific kinds of board development activities will be most helpful to board members:

1. *Orientation for new board members.* The process of orienting new board members actually begins when they are invited to serve on the board. This is a good time to describe the goals of the organization, the role of the board, and most important, the expectations of individual members. Once an individual has agreed to serve, he or she is entitled to a more detailed education on the nature of the organization, some of which will be acquired in the course of board service. In *Six Keys to Recruiting, Orienting, and Involving Nonprofit Board Members,* Judith Grummon Nelson points out that "even old board hands — those who have served on boards of other organizations — will need orientation in your organization, and indeed may understand the value of such a process even more keenly than do first-timers. In an event, all new board members should be invited to go through an orientation process, which should be made as convenient, time-effective, and entertaining as possible" (1991, p. 35).

Organizations that provide formal board orientation programs often deluge individuals with information on the organization and touch lightly, if at all, on the role of the board. Nelson reminds us that board members "need to know the strengths and weaknesses of your nonprofit, how they can contribute and work hard for its benefit, and learn what the organization expects of them" (p. 36).

2. *Retreats, workshops, and conferences.* The professional development of board members can be pursued during special events such as retreats, as well as in sessions within board meetings devoted to exploring single topics in depth or learning from experts. Individual board members might also attend workshops and conferences on governance-related matters hosted by other organizations.

3. *Keeping job descriptions current.* The description of the board found in most bylaws tends to be brief and rather vague. The board should have a separate statement that defines its role and responsibilities. This more explicit statement of the board's responsibilities can be an excellent recruit-

ment and orientation tool for new board members. This description should reflect the changes that occur in the organization and its leaders over time. If it is carefully crafted by the board and reviewed on a regular basis, it also provides a useful tool for the board to use in periodically reviewing and clarifying its role.

4. *Developing a systematic selection process for new board members.* While a thoughtful, systematic process of identifying and selecting qualified board members is undoubtedly a lever for building a good board, this continues to be a haphazard procedure in far too many nonprofit organizations. Not all boards have a committee structure. For those that do, the nominating committee represents one of the most important and influential vehicles for creating an effective board. A good nominating committee can assess current strengths and weaknesses in the board's composition, identify the desirable characteristics of candidates, cast a wide net for nominees, and develop an aggressive plan to recruit the best candidates. Boards that do not have the authority to fill their own vacancies may have to be a bit more resourceful in educating and influencing those who decide who to invite to join the board.

5. *Maintaining a governance information system.* Board members generally receive vast quantities of information to digest prior to board and committee meetings. Frequently, much of the material attached to the agenda for these meetings is not tailored to the business of the board. Furthermore, the administrative data that many boards receive may be completely unrelated to the *governance* information they need as decision makers.

Board members, chief executives, and staff who work with the board have a joint responsibility to design a governance information system that meets the needs of the board. This can be accomplished by making the following determinations: What information does the board need to do its job? How often does it want this information? And in what form does it need this information? In addition, board members should be contacted between meetings with updates on key activities and events, requests for help when appropriate, and information about problems before they may surface in the media.

6. *Conducting periodic self-assessments.* While board members often comment on their work before, during, or immediately following board or committee meetings, their observations, objections, plaudits, or suggestions are unlikely to be taken into account. One of the ways that a board can strengthen its performance as a governing body is to periodically assess its own performance. This process is likely to be more constructive if it is the subject of a separate, well-planned meeting or retreat for the express purpose of helping the board assess its strengths and needs.

In *Self-Assessment for Nonprofit Governing Boards* (Slesinger, 1991, p. 1), the following six potential outcomes of a meaningful self-assessment process are identified:

- Identify important areas of board operation that need improvement.
- Measure progress toward existing plans, goals, and objectives of the board.
- Shape the future operations of the board.
- Define the criteria for an effective and successful board of directors.
- Build trust, respect, and communication among board members.
- Enable individual board members to work more effectively as part of a team.

When assessments are planned and conducted effectively, board members often show a remarkable willingness to offer suggestions and ideas for improving the board's performance.

7. *Providing opportunities for the board to observe and participate directly in the organization's services.* Another important way to provide continuing education to the board is to provide opportunities for interaction between board members, members of the staff, and the community the organization serves. This can be accomplished by inviting board members to participate in key events, by scheduling social activities in conjunction with board meetings, and by giving board members the chance to observe the work of the organization. This interaction can also help educate others in the organization about the role and composition of the board.

Why Is Board Development Neglected?

If nonprofit organizations were to invest more board and staff time, and some modest expenditures, into the orientation and continuing education of the board, the results would be significant. And yet board development is usually not regarded as a priority by a nonprofit until a major problem or even a crisis occurs. Many nonprofits carefully woo new members to serve, and then abandon them to fend for themselves in deciphering their role. Other longer-serving board members are often uncertain about the overall role of the board and their responsibilities as individual members. What are the barriers to developing adequate board development programs?

Perhaps the most overriding one is the relentless pace of business. In day-to-day operations, many nonprofits are overwhelmed with dire financial needs and overworked staff and volunteers. The time and dollars that must be channeled into board development are often put on hold to attend to the immediate and the urgent.

A second reason is a general uncertainty as to how to proceed. Herman and Heimovics (1991) have noted in their study of effective chief executive officers that a distinguishing variable associated with successful executive directors is their ability to work with and through their boards. Many executives, however, come to their positions *without* the experience of working with a corporate entity like a governing board. They may assume that once individuals accept the invitation to join a board, they automatically know what they are supposed to do. Or they may underestimate the time it will take to attract, develop, and retain effective board members.

A third reason is a fear of change. For many executives and managers the concept of a strong active board holds all the charm of root canal work. They may be reluctant to educate and engage the board for fear that they will breed meddlesome, intrusive board members who begin to act more like surrogate administrators than policy makers. And for some busy board members, the fear that they have no spare time in their busy lives for board development becomes a self-fulfilling prophecy.

A fourth reason that systematic attention to board development may be deferred relates to the burgeoning literature on boards. Too much of it suggests quick fixes and bromides to cure ailing boards. A growing portion of the literature is beginning to respond to the tremendous hunger for practical governance tools to help board and staff members work together more effectively. But while publications can help provide standards for good practice and strategies for building better boards, they will never replace the time that an organization's leaders must invest in making it happen.

Nonprofit boards have contributed to the diversity and vitality that distinguish the sector, and they will continue to make decisions involving millions of dollars every day. Cyril Houle has astutely observed that "a good board is a victory, not a gift" (1989, p. 165). Nonprofit organizations that have achieved this victory have invested wisely. The nonprofit sector's growth and success will continue to depend on the recruitment, education, and retention of qualified individuals to serve on nonprofit boards.

The Board's Governing Role Versus the Staff's Managing Role

One of the best things that a board can do for the nonprofit it governs is to look ahead. More than anyone else connected with the organization, board members should be addressing such questions as these about the organization's future: Have our purposes and our mission changed? What kind of organization should we be in the next several years? What steps need to be taken to achieve that vision?

Unfortunately, many boards neglect these core issues. Either they devote most of their time to operational matters or they rely exclusively on the executive to chart the course for the future. Neither of these governance styles is likely to give the board sufficient time to determine where the organization should go and how it can get there.

One of the conventional pieces of wisdom in nonprofit governance is the adage that policy should be made by the board and implemented by the staff. While the underlying principle is sound, the aphorism itself is an oversimplification. In *The Board Member's Book*, Brian O'Connell states the following objection: "The worst illusion ever perpetrated in the nonprofit field is that the board of directors makes policy and the staff carries it out.

This is just not so. The board, with the help of the staff, makes policy, and the board, with the help of the staff, carries it out. Unless volunteers are committed and involved in the action phase of the organization, the agency cannot develop and, in fact, should not be characterized as a voluntary organization. Also, it is naive to assume that the staff doesn't have considerable influence—usually too much—on policy formulation" (1985, p. 44).

"Governance is too complicated and too dynamic to be reduced to some inviolate division of labor," notes Richard Chait in *How to Help Your Board Govern More and Manage Less* (1993, p. 2). Certainly, most would agree that as a policy-making body, the board must delegate much of the implementation of the policies it formulates to the executive and his or her administrative team. However, practically speaking, both executive and board may have to get involved in policy and administration.

Most effective chief executives are active in recommending as well as implementing policy objectives. And board members are often expected to play an active role in such policy execution activities as raising funds and friends for the organization. Furthermore, in young organizations with little or no staff, or those that are run predominantly by volunteers, board members must often assist with numerous administrative tasks.

Policy and administration are often interconnected. An administrative matter may be transformed into a governance issue if it has policy implications. For example, boards are appropriately advised to delegate to the chief executive the supervision of staff below the chief executive. But a board may have to get involved in the adjudication of a personnel issue involving a staff member if there are not adequate personnel policies in place to resolve the matter in a legal and ethical manner.

The board that keeps its fingers in operational matters is often a symptom of an underlying problem. A board that regularly gets involved in personnel matters is likely to reflect a management deficiency, such as the absence of sound internal policies and practices for the staff. A board that chronically meddles in administrative concerns may also indicate a weak or ineffective administration (or a loss of confidence in the executive's leadership). Or it may merely reflect the misguided zeal of individual board members who perceive their role to be running the organization rather than making sure that it is well run.

Individual board members may be tempted to turn their attention to the operational rather than the strategic, because their knowledge, skills, and experience are often with the former. The fact is that many board members are professional staff members from other organizations who have been selected because they are good at running things. It is not easy to move from the role of practitioner or administrator to the more detached role of board member and policy maker.

Concomitantly, some executives may inadvertently steer the board's attention to the day-to-day administrative detail rather than the big picture. Chait suggests that "boards that concentrate on trivia frequently do so not by design but by default, as a direct result of the chief executive's failure to engage trustees' attention on crucial questions. To the degree that chief executives explicitly direct the board's attention to issues with significant stakes, boards are far less likely to focus on minutiae" (1993, p. 4).

There are at least two problems that are likely to result from a board that spends most of its time "micromanaging." Board members who regularly interfere in the work that the chief executive and other staff members were hired to do can lower staff morale and productivity. At some nonprofit organizations, a chronic ritual of confrontation between the board and the staff over turf has severely eroded the governance process.

But the second reason is perhaps even more significant. A board that devotes most of its attention to day-to-day operational issues is likely to have little time left for the issues that will have the greatest impact on the organization's future. Chait suggests that the central issues related to governance include "the organization's mission, values, or direction; its long-term performance; the conservation and expansion of institutional assets; and the processes used to identify, discuss, and decide matters of strategic or symbolic significance" (1993, p. 2).

An inactive "rubber-stamp" board that delegates everything to the chief executive is just as dangerous as the board that is overinvolved. It not only neglects the strategic issues, it abdicates its responsibility for oversight.

In *Governing Boards: Their Nature and Nurture,* Cyril Houle counsels, "The normal day-to-day relationship between the board and the executive is that of a responsible partnership. Neither of the two can mark out any one institutional activity as its central concern, nor can it permit itself to be denied authority over any such activity. Even if the board relieves the executive of responsibility for some function, he still has the obligation to consider it to be part of the whole program and to warn the board when he believes that the function is not being adequately performed" (1989, p. 86).

There may always be a certain degree of creative tension between boards and executives. While even the best relationships might not be characterized as mutual love, the most successful teams seem to be able to support each other, while challenging one another when necessary.

Situational Variables Affecting the Board's Role

It is impossible and misleading to ascribe monolithic characteristics to the more than one million nonprofit boards in the United States. The board's precise responsibilities and the culture in which it operates will often depend on distinct organizational and leadership variables that vary from institution to institution.

Perhaps one of the most important variables is the age of the organization. For example, the founding board of a newly established organization with little or no staff is likely to play more of an administrative role than the board of a more established organization. Even when the organization is fortunate enough to start with paid staff, in its early days it may need a good deal of hands-on help from its board members in developing the systems, programs, and services that more mature organizations already have in place.

Some of the most difficult transitions in governance occur as nonprofit organizations grow. Board experts as well as organizational development theorists are increasingly recognizing the impact of developmental stages in an organization's life cycle on the role and behavior of governing boards. For example, many nonprofit organizations begin as all-volunteer organizations. As they grow and mature, the role of their boards may also change to accommodate paid staff and new leadership needs. The organization's particular stage of development will also influence the kinds of board members it will be able to recruit.

Karl Mathiasen has observed that many nonprofit boards pass through three very different and distinct stages. In *Board Passages: Three Key Stages in a Nonprofit Board's Life Cycle,* Mathiasen observes that "the roles, functions, and membership [of the board] need to be altered to meet the new challenges the nonprofit organization confronts. Many of these changes in board roles, functions, and membership are predictable because they are natural consequences of organizational growth" (1990, p. 2).

The size and scope of the organization may also affect the role of its board. A small, local organization with little or no staff may well depend on its board for much of the technical expertise it needs, whereas the board of a larger, staff-driven organization serving a broader constituency is more likely to rely on its professional staff to manage programs and provide administration and accounting support to the organization.

A common growing pain experienced by many nonprofits occurs when the organization begins to exceed the capacities of its original founders. The processes of building up the institution and introducing new leadership to help it fulfill its mission usually reflect growth and progress. Nevertheless, founding board and staff members may feel reluctant to see changes in the organization they helped to create.

The way the board's members are selected may affect the group's manner of governing. Not all nonprofit boards retain the authority to fill their own vacancies. When individuals or entities outside of the organization have the authority to select some or all of the members of the board, this may affect board composition and the nature of individual board members' commitment. For example, a government official or the member of the organization may select people to serve on the board who will represent specific interests. If the selection process is driven largely by political considerations, the board may end up with members who are not prepared to serve as leaders. Regardless of the method of selection, board members who perceive their role exclusively as representational may prevent the board from exerting leadership on behalf of the welfare of the organization as a whole. The composition of the board may also affect the way in which its members contribute to the specific needs of the organization. For example, a board made up of individuals who have been involved in the organization as direct service volunteers for special events may raise funds in a very different manner than a board composed of corporate CEOs.

The board's composition is also likely to influence the way in which the board and staff relate to each other. For example, in a paper entitled "Conflicting Managerial Cultures in Nonprofit Organizations" (1988), Peter Dobkin Hall examines conflicts that arise over goals and managerial cultures between professional managers on nonprofit staffs and the professional business managers who often serve on nonprofits' boards.

The leadership styles of the chief executive and board chairperson — and the chemistry between them — can influence the board's role significantly. In *The Role of the Board Chairperson,* Eugene Dorsey cautions, "It's essential that the two key people in a nonprofit organization understand with great clarity what their roles and responsibilities are, and what kind of power they exert" (1992, p. 2). As an experienced chairperson, Dorsey observes, "The kind of relationship that the chairperson establishes with the board and the chief executive officer can immensely influence the effectiveness of the organization. If he or she can energize the board and establish a harmonious and productive relationship with the chief executive officer, things happen. Staff and board work together to serve the mission of the organization. Goals and objectives are set and met" (1992, p. 1).

A leadership transition or crisis may also influence the role of the board. When a new executive takes office, the board may actively engage in oversight until it is sure that the executive is managing well. Likewise, when a chief executive departs suddenly following a financial, management, or personal problem, the board may move in to work more closely in day-to-day management to fill the leadership vacuum and protect the organization until a suitable successor, interim or permanent, is appointed. This is understandable given the loss of confidence of the board and the organization's publics. It can be problematical, however, if the board is unable to relinquish this role once the new staff leadership is in place and ready to assume this responsibility.

Summary

One of the distinctive features of the U.S. nonprofit sector is that the responsibility for governance rests with volunteer leaders who serve as members of boards of directors. The correlation between organizational effectiveness and governing board strength is difficult to quantify, but today there is strong empirical belief that a board can have a profound effect on the success of the organization it governs — if not on its very survival.

A nonprofit governing board is ultimately responsible for ensuring that the organization it governs fulfills its mission. In its role as fiduciary, the board of a nonprofit organization established for charitable purposes is accountable to the public interest it serves. Most nonprofit boards are entrusted with the following basic responsibilities: determining the organization's mission and purpose, selecting and supporting the chief executive, reviewing the executive's performance, planning for the future, approving and monitoring the organization's programs and services, providing sound financial management, enlisting financial resources, advancing the organization's public image, and strengthening the board's own effectiveness as a governing body.

Since the quality and commitment of those selected to serve will not automatically result in an effective board, adequate resources must be channeled into the recruitment, education, and retention of board members. "Board development" consists of a series of educational activities designed to help board members clarify and carry out their responsibilities. It is integral to building an effective board, but it is often neglected by nonprofit leaders because of the press of other business or the perceived danger of encouraging board members to meddle in the day-to-day activities of the organization. Successful board development programs are characterized by regular and systematic efforts to keep the board informed; a commitment from the chief executive and the board chairperson to the process; and a willingness on the board's part to review its own performance.

While board members and chief executives have to be involved in both policy formulation and policy execution, most boards can best serve their organizations by focusing on the strategic issues that will have the greatest impact on the organization's future. In practice, the actual responsibilities of the board will be influenced by the organization's age, size, and scope; the method of selecting board members; the composition of the board; the leadership styles of and relationship between the chief executive and board chairperson; and the inevitable cycles in leadership transitions.

References

Bell, P. D. *Fulfilling the Public Trust: Ten Ways to Help Nonprofit Boards Maintain Accountability.* Washington, D.C.: National Center for Nonprofit Boards, 1993.

"Board Members and Risk: A Primer on Protection from Liability." *Board Member,* 1992, *1*(6), 13.

Chait, R. P., Holland, T. P., and Taylor, B. E. *The Effective Board of Trustees.* New York: Macmillan, 1991.

Chait, R. P. *How to Help Your Board Govern More and Manage Less.* Washington, D.C.: National Center for Nonprofit Boards, 1993.

Dalsimer, J. P. *Understanding Nonprofit Financial Statements: A Primer for Board Members.* Washington, D.C.: National Center for Nonprofit Boards, 1991.

Dorsey, E. C. *The Role of the Board Chairperson.* Washington, D.C.: National Center for Nonprofit Boards, 1992.

Fitzpatrick, J. L. *The Board's Role in Public Relations and Communications.* Washington, D.C.: National Center for Nonprofit Boards, 1993.

Hall, P. D. "Conflicting Managerial Cultures in Nonprofit Organizations." Occasional paper, Program on Nonprofit Organizations. New Haven, Conn.: Yale University, 1988.

Herman, R. D., and Heimovics, R. D. *Executive Leadership in Nonprofit Organizations: New Strategies for Shaping Executive-Board Dynamics.* San Francisco: Jossey-Bass, 1991.

Houle, C. O. *Governing Boards: Their Nature and Nurture.* A publication of the National Center for Nonprofit Boards. San Francisco: Jossey-Bass, 1989.

Howe, F. *Fund Raising and the Nonprofit Board Member.* Washington, D.C.: National Center for Nonprofit Boards, 1989.

Ingram, R. T. *Ten Basic Responsibilities of Nonprofit Boards.* Washington, D.C.: National Center for Nonprofit Boards, 1989.

Leifer, J. C., and Glomb, M. B. *The Legal Obligations of Nonprofit Boards: A Guidebook for Board Members.* Washington, D.C.: National Center for Nonprofit Boards, 1992.

Mathiasen, K. *Board Passages: Three Key Stages in a Nonprofit Board's Life Cycle.* Washington, D.C.: National Center for Nonprofit Boards, 1990.

Nason, J. W. *Board Assessment of the Chief Executive: A Responsibility Essential to Good Governance.* Washington, D.C.: National Center for Nonprofit Boards, 1990.

Nelson, J. G. *Six Keys to Recruiting, Orienting, and Involving Nonprofit Board Members.* Washington, D.C.: National Center for Nonprofit Boards, 1991.

O'Connell, B. *The Board Member's Book.* New York: Foundation Center, 1985.

Slesinger, L. H. *Self-Assessment for Nonprofit Governing Boards.* Washington, D.C.: National Center for Nonprofit Boards, 1991.

Szanton, P. L. *Board Assessment of the Organization: How Are We Doing?* Washington, D.C.: National Center for Nonprofit Boards, 1992.

7

Executive Leadership

Robert D. Herman
Dick Heimovics

Nonprofit organizations are distinctive forms of organization, differing in fundamental ways from business and government. Like businesses, nonprofit organizations engage in voluntary exchanges to obtain revenues and other resources, and like governments, they usually provide services with public goods characteristics. Robert Payton (1988) has suggested that philanthropy is voluntary (private) action for public purposes. Nonprofit organizations — particularly those classed as 501(c)(3) publicly supported charities in the U.S. Internal Revenue Code — are the chief instruments for actualizing philanthropy.

We believe the distinctive character of nonprofit organizations creates special challenges for the leadership of such organizations. Leaders of nonprofit organizations must *integrate* the realms of mission, resource acquisition, and strategy. The choice of a mission for an organization depends on the potential for acquisition of sufficient resources to carry out that mission. Conversely, the acquisition of certain kinds of resources can influence the mission an organization chooses to undertake. Any mission, no matter how "great a cause" it may be, is likely to fail if the organization lacks necessary and sufficient resources to pursue it. Moreover, decisions about strategies for acquiring resources must be consistent with the mission and ethical values of the organization. Actions in one realm affect the other realms. The leadership challenge is to see that decisions and actions in one realm are not only consistent with those in other realms but that they are also mutually reinforcing.

While we recognize that leadership does not and cannot occur only at the top of an organization, we also recognize that organization-wide leadership is fundamentally the responsibility of those at the top. For nonprofit organizations such system-level leadership is the responsibility of the chief executive and the board. In fact, the chief executive–board relationship is crucial to effective organization leadership. Since Nancy Axelrod's chapter focuses on board leadership, our chapter will focus on executive leadership — both in relation to the organization and in relation to the board.

The chief executive position in nonprofit organizations is usually demanding and difficult. While this observation is unsurprising, we believe the demands and difficulties can be more effectively met if CEOs both understand and develop the skills to focus on the essential relationships and tasks. In the following pages we first describe the psychological centrality of CEOs. In spite of the formal hierarchical structure that puts the CEO as subordinate to the board, the day-to-day reality — as it is experienced by CEOs, board members, and staff — is that CEOs are expected to accept the central leadership role in nonprofit organizations. This often requires that CEOs take responsibility for enabling their boards to carry out the boards' duties.

We go on to describe the specific board-centered leadership skills that characterize especially effective chief executives. Next, we address the importance of executive leadership in the external environment. Here we develop strategies for leadership across the boundaries. We continue by exploring recent research on the "political" skills of especially effective CEOs and providing guidelines for thinking and acting in politically effective ways. Our closing summary emphasizes that the essence of effective executive leadership is an external orientation in which the strategies pursued are directed at the tasks of mission accomplishment and resource acquisition.

Executive Centrality

Like other formal organizations, a nonprofit organization is typically understood as necessarily hierarchical, with the board of directors in the superior position. The board is seen as defining mission, establishing policies, overseeing programs, and using performance standards to assess financial and program achievements. The chief executive is hired to assist the board and works at the board's pleasure. This conception is the application of what organizational theorists have labeled the "purposive-rational" model (Pfeffer, 1982) or the "managed systems" model (Elmore, 1978) to nonprofit organizations. This model, generally derived from Weber's description of bureaucracy (Gerth and Mills, 1946), conceives of organizations as goal-directed instruments under the control of rational decision makers where responsibility and authority are hierarchically arranged. This rational, managed-systems model is also the commonplace or conventional "theory" of many organizational participants. It is how, many people believe, organizations do and should work.

Much of the substantial normative literature on nonprofit boards accepts this conventional model (for example, Alexander, 1980; Bower, 1980; Conrad and Glenn, 1976; Swanson, 1978), putting the board at the top of the hierarchy and at the center of leadership responsibility. Based on a legal requirement and a moral assumption, the normative literature has advanced a *heroic* ideal (Herman, 1989) for nonprofit boards. United States law holds that a nonprofit board is ultimately responsible for the affairs and conduct of the organization. The moral assumption is that the board conducts the organization's affairs as a steward of the public interest, in a manner consistent with the wishes and needs of the larger community.

Notwithstanding the wide dissemination of this normative model, the actual performance of boards often falls short of the ideal. Middleton's (1987) thorough review of the empirical literature shows that nonprofit boards seldom completely fulfill their assigned duties and roles. Consequently, the notion that chief executives are simply agents of the board cannot be supported. Recognizing that the relationship between boards and chief executives is more complex than the normative model envisions, many people have invoked a "partnership" or "team" metaphor to describe (and prescribe) the executive-board relationship. Such terms are more appropriate than the conventional model's depiction of the relation as superior-subordinate. However, the partnership and team conceptions remain misleading. Middleton uses the phrase "strange loops and tangled hierarchies" to describe more accurately the complex board-executive relationship (p. 149). Boards retain their legal and hierarchical superiority (and sometimes must exercise it), while executives typically have greater information, expertise, and a greater stake in and identification with the organization. Thus, both parties are dependent on the other, but they are not exactly equals. This complex, interdependent relation is not fundamentally changed even when nonprofit organizations adopt the "corporate model" of designating the chief executive "president" and giving her or him a vote in board decisions.

The complex board-executive relationship can be better understood and new, more effective standards and practices relating to the board-executive working relationship developed, if other organizational models are used. We have found that a "social constructionist model" of organizations provides very important insights about the chief executive's organizational role and about the dynamics of effective executive-board relations. In contrast to the managed systems model, the social constructionist perspective abandons assumptions of hierarchically imposed order and rationality, emphasizing that what an organization is and does emerges from the interaction of participants as they attempt to arrange organizational practices and routines to fit their perceptions, needs and interests. The social constructionist model recognizes that official or intended goals, structures, and procedures may exist only on paper. Actual goals, structures, and procedures emerge and change as participants interact and socially construct the meaning of ongoing events.

In interviews with nonprofit CEOs we asked them to fully describe two critical events in their organizations, one of which turned out successfully and one unsuccessfully. We then asked the CEOs, board presidents, and senior staff to assess the extent to which the skills and abilities and the hard work and effort of each party (that is, the CEO, the board, and the staff) as well as good or bad luck affected the outcome of each critical event.

In the successful critical events, all participants (the chief executives, the board presidents, and the staff) credited the executives with contributing the most, through their skills and their hard work, to that outcome. In successful events, the chief executives assign much more credit to their boards than the board presidents do. In the unsuccessful critical events, the executives assign more blame to themselves than to others or bad luck. This is atypical. Laboratory studies have repeatedly confirmed the "self-serving" hypothesis — that individuals see themselves as causes of successful outcomes and others or luck as responsible for failure. Board presidents and staff, consistent with the self-serving hypothesis, saw the chief executive as most responsible, assigning less responsibility to themselves or to luck. In short, all (including chief executives themselves) see the executive as centrally responsible for what happens in nonprofit organizations (see Heimovics and Herman, 1990, for a thorough report).

We have had several occasions to present and discuss this empirical support for our concept of executive psychological centrality. The nonprofit chief executives to whom we have presented our results have always confirmed that their experience matches our finding. But, what does the reality of executive centrality imply for more effective action?

We believe two implications are indicated. One, since chief executives are going to be held responsible, they should take full control, running things as they think best. The board then becomes either the proverbial rubber stamp or a combination rubber stamp and cash cow. Obviously, there are many instances of this manipulative pattern. Alternatively, since chief executives are going to be held responsible and since they accept responsibility for mission accomplishment and public stewardship, they should work to see that boards fulfill their legal, organizational, and public roles. We believe this second implication the much wiser choice. It is not only consistent with legal and ethical duties, but it is also more likely to enhance organizational effectiveness.

We are not advocating that chief executives dominate or "demote" their boards. Boards, in addition to their legal and moral duties, can contribute a great deal to achieving their organizations' missions. What our results and experience demonstrate is that chief executives can seldom expect boards to do their best unless chief executives, recognizing their centrality, accept the responsibility to develop, promote, and enable their boards' effective functioning.

Board-Centered Leadership Skills of Effective Executives

We have come to the view expressed above—that chief executives often must enable and develop their boards' abilities to carry out their duties and responsibilities—largely as a result of our research on the leadership skills of effective nonprofit chief executives. We wanted to determine what behaviors or skills distinguished especially effective nonprofit chief executives from others. We selected a sample of especially effective chief executives by asking several knowledgeable participants in a metropolitan nonprofit sector to identify those executives they judged to be highly effective. The nominators held positions—such as heads of foundations, federated funding agencies, technical assistance providers, and coalitional organizations—that required them to make and act on judgments of executive effectiveness. Chief executives who received at least two independent nominations as highly effective were included in the effective sample. A comparison sample was selected from among those executives who received no nominations and who had held their position for at least eighteen months. Executives from both the effective and comparison samples were interviewed, using the critical event approach, by interviewers unaware of the sample distinction or the research hypotheses. The interviews were tape recorded and transcribed.

We analyzed the interviews by training raters to note the presence of various leadership behaviors (using an inventory developed by Quinn [1983] based on Yukl's analysis [1981]). Recognizing that a CEO's relationships with the board and staff would probably differ, we had the raters determine executive leadership in relation to each (see Herman and Heimovics, 1990, for a technical report on this research).

The results confirmed the importance of distinguishing between executive leadership in relation to the board and to the staff. Analysis showed that executive leadership in relation to staff and in relation to the board are independent and distinct factors. Effective and comparison executives differed little in leadership with their staffs. The most important finding was that the effective executives provided significantly more leadership to their boards. This does not mean that the effective executives ordered their boards around. Rather, as the descriptions of their behavior in the critical events showed, the effective executives took responsibility for supporting and facilitating their board's work. The effective executives value and respect their boards. As a result they see their boards as at the center of their work. Their leadership is board-centered. We found the following behaviors specifically characterized the board-centered leadership of the especially effective executives.

1. *Facilitating interaction in board relationships.* The effective chief executive is aware of and works to see that board members engage in satisfying and productive interaction, with each other and with the executive. The executive is skilled at listening (that is, at hearing the concerns behind the words) and at helping the board resolve differences.

2. *Showing consideration and respect toward board members.* The effective executive knows that board service is an exchange and seeks to be aware of the needs of individual board members. The executive also works with the board president to find assignments that meet those needs.

3. *Envisioning change and innovation for the organization with the board.* Given their psychological centrality and their centrality in information flows, chief executives are in the best position to monitor and understand the organization's position in a changing environment. However, appropriate response to this external flux requires that board members be apprised of the trends, forces, and unexpected occurrences that could call for adaptation or innovation. The executive encourages the board to examine new opportunities, to look for better ways of doing things and better things to do. In short, the executive challenges the board consistently to think and rethink the connections among mission, money (and other resources), and strategy.

4. *Providing useful and helpful information to the board.* In addition to the usual routine information, such as financial statements, budget reports, and program service data, boards need relevant and timely information that can aid in decision making. Since the executive will have access to a great deal of information, of all kinds and quality, he or she must find ways of separating the important from the trivial and of communicating the important to the board. One key rule followed by effective executives is *no surprises.* The temptation to hide or delay bad news is understandable, but it must be resisted. Effective executives realize that problems are inevitable and know that by sharing the bad news, solutions are more likely to be found.

5. *Initiating and maintaining structure for the board.* Like other work groups, boards require the materials, schedules, and work plans necessary to achieve their tasks. Effective executives take responsibility to work with the board president and other members to develop and maintain consistent procedures. In many effective organizations the board has annual objectives. It is important that the chief executive support the work of the board in reaching those objectives.

6. *Promoting board accomplishments and productivity.* The effective executive helps to set and maintain high standards (about attendance, effort, and giving). Through the board president and committee chairpersons, the executive encourages board members to complete tasks and meet deadlines.

Executives who have learned these key board-centered leadership skills have hardworking, effective boards. The board-centered executive is likely to be effective because he or she has grasped that the work of the board is critical in adapting to and affecting the constraints and opportunities in the environment. In short, the effective executive knows that leadership is not solely an internal activity.

Leadership Across the Boundaries: Impact in the External World

As other chapters in this volume demonstrate, the complexity and unpredictability of the world in which nonprofit, charitable organizations operate is great and seemingly continually increasing. Such change and unpredictability make the challenge of integrating mission, resource acquisition, and strategy even greater and require that chief executives effectively engage in leadership across the boundaries. Our research, in conjunction with that of others, suggests four specific strategies for enhancing external impact.

Spend Time on External Relations

Spending time on external relations may seem too obvious to deserve mention. However, both systematic evidence and experience show that routine activities and the inevitable day-to-day office problems can easily absorb nearly all an executive's time. Executives must learn to delegate much of the management of internal affairs and focus on the external. Dollinger (1984) found that small business owners/managers who spent more time on boundary-spanning or external activities were more successful.

Develop an Informal Information Network

Information about what happened in the past (such as is found in financial statements and program evaluations) is important, but information about what might happen in the future (whether that future is next week or next year) is even more important. Information on possible futures is much more likely to be widely scattered, partial, and ambiguous. To acquire, evaluate, and integrate this "soft" information, executives (and others) need to communicate with those in government agencies, foundations, accrediting bodies, professional associations, similar nonprofit organizations, and so forth. They must attend meetings and lunches, breakfasts and legislative sessions.

Important, useful information is more likely to flow when the parties are more than acquaintances. Face-to-face communication helps to build reciprocal credibility and trust. A successful network is built and sustained when people are willing and able to understand and accept the interests of others, and it requires exchanging reliable information without violating confidentiality. It means not only investing time but also helping others with their concerns in exchange for help with your own. As Huff (1985) observes, a network is important for more than sharing information. Networks are also deeply involved in making sense of an often rapidly changing field. Different kinds of information are available from different parts of an organization's environment. Information gleaned from a professional associate will be different from that available from a corporate giving officer. Both are likely to be important to a particular policy or program delivery issue. The network, as a collectivity, has an important role in defining emerging issues and in pointing the way to new program practices.

Know Your Agenda

Strategic planning, as John Bryson's very helpful chapter in this volume demonstrates, provides organizations with a rational process for deriving specific goals and objectives from their missions. Thus the strategic plan structures the executive's work. Both Kotter (1982) and Huff (1985) have found that executives supplement the strategic plan with agenda that are both more immediate and more long range. The executive's agenda, whether taken directly from the plan or consistently supplemental to it, provides a short list of goals or outcomes that the executive sees as crucial. Knowing and using the agenda to focus work offers a basis for effectively allocating time and effort. A limited, focused agenda also helps to bring order and direction in a complex and rapidly changing environment. Concentrating on the agenda also allows the executive to use external interactions to advance those goals. Huff (1985) has described three strategies effective executives often employ in advancing their agenda as dramatizing events, "laying a bread crumb trail," and simplifying.

Dramatizing events entails calling attention to the relationship between networking events and the executive's agenda. For example, an executive who wants to add staff fluent in Spanish to expand services to Spanish-speaking communities might send clippings about growth in the city's Latino population and its service needs to board members. The executive also might feature a digest of such stories in the organization's newsletter and see that the newsletter goes to regular funders. The key is to dramatically or memorably connect public issues to the organization's agenda.

Another good example of how to dramatize events comes from the chief executive of an agency serving the developmentally disabled. She encouraged a friend who taught creative writing at a local university to engage a class in developing a story about a day in the life of her agency. The story was included in the materials made available to those attending an annual banquet and awards dinner for the organization. The story was presented to many stakeholders and others to give them a "real feel for the work of the agency." Clearly, the executive director had additional uses for the story. The description skillfully catalogued the creative work of a staff constrained by limited resources. Copies of the story became part of the publicity program of the agency and were conveniently included in reports to funders and in grant applications.

Just as dramatizing external events is a way of focusing attention, so is the "laying of a bread crumb trail." Over time, through various communications, a chief executive points the way to an important decision. As Huff (1985, p. 175) puts it, organizational action requires that an executive edit his or her concerns "into a smaller number of items that can be comprehended by others. Repetition of these concerns is almost always necessary to gain the attention of others and convince them of serious intent." Such a strategy is probably widely applicable, but we find it especially germane in executive-board relations.

Consider, for instance, the strategy of the chief executive of an organization that operates group homes for the mentally ill. The organization's original facility, called "Tracy House," was an old building in great need of repair. Operations at the house did not quite break even. Surpluses from the operation of other facilities covered the shortfall. The executive, based on what he was hearing from the network of licensing, funding, and accrediting bodies, believed that new standards would require modifications that, combined with no growth in state daily rates, would mean operating the facility at an increasing deficit. So he began laying out a bread crumb trail for board members, both formally in board meetings and informally in conversations in other settings.

Part of his problem was that a few board members had a strong emotional attachment to Tracy House; they had personally painted it and made repairs to meet licensing standards. Instead of pointing out again that the Tracy House was decrepit, he provided an update on the state funding prospects, noting the financial implications for each facility, which made the burden of carrying the home's deficit obvious. Some time later, he mentioned the possibility of federal housing funds becoming available for group home construction, observing that this would permit the organization to "get out from under" Tracy House. In this way, when the decision was finally taken to sell Tracy House, it was a foregone conclusion. The trail of markers not only defined and focused the issue, it also brought everyone to the same conclusion, making what could have been a painful decision easy.

The last strategy identified by Huff is to keep things as simple as possible. A complex and interdependent world enhances the tendency for inaction and drift. Before we can make a decision about X, we have to see what happens with Y, and Y depends on what A and B do. To make decisions and take action, individuals must risk simplifying the situation. As Huff observes, behaving as though the situation is simpler than you know it to be helps bring about more simplicity. Acting in relation to the agenda is an important way of simplifying, or creating order in a disorderly world.

Improvise and Accept Multiple, Partial Solutions

The point of leadership across the boundary is to position the organization in the larger environment and match its capabilities with the demands for its services and the resources available. Of course, the inevitable fact is that neither organizational capabilities nor environmental demands and resources are static. A short, clear agenda and the strategies to carry it out provide a compass pointing the way to where the executive, who has integrated to the greatest extent possible the preferences of the stakeholders, wants to go.

The metaphor of the compass, however, is not complete because the executive (reflecting the stakeholders' varying preferences) wants to go to several places. For example, the agenda might include increasing total revenues, diversifying revenue sources, acquiring a new facility, and expanding a particular program. Not only are these different goals, but there are likely to be different paths to each. Furthermore, the most direct path to one may make paths to the others longer or more difficult to find. Finding the combination of paths that most efficiently leads to all goals may often be beyond calculation, particularly when the environment keeps changing. The upshot is that executives must sometimes be willing and able to improvise, to take an unexpected path when it presents itself.

Sometimes chief executives find they cannot, at least within a crucial period, reach a goal in exactly the form imagined. As Huff (1985, p. 167) observes, an "administrator's ability to perceive issues is almost always bigger than the ability to act on issues. As a result, the administrator often must be content to work on a small part of the larger whole." That is, sometimes the organization may have to go someplace a little different from what was at one time imagined because that is where the only available path leads. Huff suggests that a "specific action should rarely be taken unless it is compatible with several different issues" (p. 168). Or, in the terms of our metaphor, an action that leads to movement on paths to two or three places at once is particularly useful.

For an especially compelling illustration of this sort of creative leadership, let us look at the case of a nonprofit organization that required a facility with large spaces. For several years the organization used an old warehouse that a business corporation provided for free. However, the corporation made it clear that it was interested in selling the warehouse and that the organization might have to relocate. As a few years passed and the corporation lacked success in selling the warehouse and had little apparent necessity for doing so, the issue of obtaining a suitable, more permanent facility was increasingly put on the back burner. One day the chief executive received a call from a corporate officer saying that a tentative agreement to sell the warehouse had been reached and that the organization would have to vacate in six months. The first thing the chief executive did was to call the board. Staff were also quickly informed to avoid the spread of rumors. The chief executive found that many board members and staff assumed that the organization should try to find another old warehouse. However, the executive knew that old warehouses had several disadvantages: high energy costs, lack of parking, inaccessibility, and so forth. The executive thought this was an excellent opportunity to rethink what sort of facility would be most appropriate.

After conferring with the board chairman and other key board members, a facility planning committee was formed. The executive was interested in connecting the facility issue to other agenda issues, especially those of enhancing collaboration with other community organizations and adding a demonstration day-care program for children. As the facility planning committee identified alternative ways of securing a replacement facility and the costs associated with each, a board member suggested the executive meet with an official from a local community college. While the community college was not in the same service field as the organization, the community college had enough money available through a bond issue to construct a new building, but not enough money to finish and equip the building. Following quick negotiations the organization agreed to provide funds to finish and equip the facility in exchange for a ten-year lease of two floors at a very low rental rate. This solution, though not perfect, moved the organization along on several agenda issues simultaneously. This progress was achieved because the executive worked with and through the board and linked action on one issue with progress on others. (An extensive treatment of both board-centered leadership skills and of boundary-spanning leadership can be found in Herman and Heimovics, 1991.)

In emphasizing the importance of externally oriented leadership we do not intend to suggest that internal operations can be ignored by chief executives. As the chapters in Parts Three, Four, and Five of this volume attest, designing, implementing, and improving the various internal systems and procedures are important and challenging. We believe that nearly all executives and boards are well aware of the importance of these issues. What seems to us to be less well comprehended is the importance of understanding and influencing, when possible, people and systems beyond the organization's boundaries. Effective executive leadership beyond the boundaries is based on a "political" orientation and on political skills. In the next section we define what we mean by a political orientation, describe recent research that finds effective executives are more politically skillful than others, and suggest how executives can enhance their political acumen.

Using the Political Frame

Our studies have shown that not only do successful executives provide significantly more leadership for their boards than those not deemed especially effective, they also work with and through their boards to position their organization in its environment. Special effort is extended externally across the boundaries of the organization to manage the organization's dependence on those factors that determine the availability of the resources to carry out the mission and to establish the legitimacy of the organization. In short, effective executives boundary-span to seek and act upon opportunities in the environment to help shape the future health and direction of the organization.

Why do some executives engage in more external and board-centered actions than other executives? A continuation of our research reported above helps answer the question (see Heimovics, Herman, and Coughlin, 1993, for more details about this study). Effective executives are more likely to "frame" their orientations toward external events in political ways than are executives judged to be less effective. This political orientation helps explain how effective executives work "entrepreneurially" to find resources and revitalize missions for their organizations. Effective chief executive officers use a political frame to understand and deal with the challenges of resource dependency faced by their organizations.

A multiple frame analysis for understanding organizations and leadership developed by Bolman and Deal (1991) forms the basis for our examination of the political orientation of the effective executive. Bolman and Deal identify four distinct organizational perspectives, or "frames," that leaders may adopt to understand the many realities of organizational life: structural, human resource, political, and symbolic. Knowledge of these frames, their various strengths, and their appropriate use, according to Bolman and Deal, can help leaders understand and intervene in their organizations more effectively. The following brief discussion summarizes these frames.

In the structural frame, clarity in goal setting and role expectations provides order and continuity in organizations. Clear procedures and policies, and the view of the organization as a rational and hierarchical system, are characteristic of this frame. Adherence to accepted standards, conformity to rules, and the creation of administrative systems confer upon the organization its form and logic. Allowing procedures (for example, personnel systems and board performance standards) to define individual and organizational effectiveness is also characteristic of this frame, as is the emphasis on certainty in mission and clarity of direction. Leaders who rely strongly on the structural frame "see" effectiveness as largely determined by clear procedures and clear goals.

According to the human resource frame, people are the most valuable resource of any organization. The effective leader, as defined by this frame, searches for an important balance between the goals of the organization and the hopes and aspirations of its members by attending to individual hopes, feelings, and preferences, valuing relationships and feelings, and advocating effective delegation. Nonprofit leaders who use this frame believe in delegation because it not only "empowers" others to take initiative but it also provides opportunities for personal growth and development. This frame defines problems and issues in interpersonal terms and encourages open communication, team building, and collaboration.

The political frame assumes ongoing conflict or tension—over the allocation of scarce resources or the resolution of differences—most often triggered by the need to bargain or negotiate to acquire or allocate resources. As viewed by the political frame, conflict resolution skills are necessary to build alliances and networks with prominent actors or stakeholders to influence decisions about the allocation of resources. The informal realities of organizational life include the influence of coalitions and interest groups. Politically oriented leaders not only understand how interest groups and coalitions evolve, they also can influence the impact of these groups upon the organization. Those who use the political frame exercise their personal and organizational power and are sensitive to external factors that may influence internal decisions and policies.

According to the symbolic frame, realities of organizational life are socially construed. Organizations are cultural and historical systems of shared meaning wherein group membership determines individual interpretations of organizational phenomena. Organizational structure, politics, and human relations are inventions of the cultural and historical system. Leaders evoke ceremonies, rituals, or artifacts to create a unifying system of beliefs. This frame calls for charismatic leaders to arouse "visions of a preferred organizational future" and evoke emotional responses to enhance an organization's identity, transforming it to a higher plane of performance and value (Bass, 1985).

Our research on the use of frames began by revisiting the critical incident interviews that served as the source of data for our prior research about board-centered behaviors and psychological centrality of the chief executive. Two coders, unaware of differences in the two samples and the hypotheses of this aspect of our research, read and coded the transcribed interviews to determine which frames were used by the chief executives. Analysis revealed that the structural frame was the dominant frame for both the effective and comparison executives. The substantial reliance on the structural frame may be a reflection of the attention of both groups of executives to aspects of events that may be relatively close at hand, immediately demanding, and perhaps amenable to actions.

The use of the political frame differed significantly, however, between effective and comparison executives. Comparison executives not only use the political frame less, they seem to differentiate little in their use of the political frame. The comparison executives are almost twice as likely to employ the structural frame and 70 percent more likely to use the human resource frame than the political frame. By contrast the political frame was the second most dominant frame for the effective executives, who are almost as likely to use it as the structural frame.

We are particularly confident about our findings of the substantial use of the political frame by effective executives. Most of the critical events described by both groups of executives occurred in the environment external to their organizations. Both effective and comparison executives were more likely to choose an external event than an internal event to describe as critical. Examples of environmental events were usually incidents that dealt with the challenges of resource dependency, such as mergers, alliances, fundraising strategies, legislative lobbying, collaboration with other agencies, relations with government officials, new program developments, or program decline. We distinguished these kinds of events from internal critical events, such as a personnel action or problems with implementing an administrative system or procedure.

We then analyzed the data by location of events to determine if this variable explained differences in frame use. Again we found significant differences between our two groups of executives in the political frame. Comparison executives were substantially less likely to rely on the political frame than were the effective executives when dealing with events in the external environment of the organization, where the political frame is assumed to be most important.

We also found that effective executives not only rely more on the political frame, but they also deal with events in more cognitively complex ways than do those not deemed to be especially effective. In other words, effective executives integrate and employ multiple frames and do not rely on single perspectives, as the comparison executives do. We suspect that the use of multiple frames by effective executives contributes to a deeper understanding of the complexities and volatility of the leadership challenges faced in the fast-changing and complicated environment of nonprofit organizations. Environmentally induced events are characteristically turbulent, fast changing, and uncertain.

Most service-providing nonprofit organizations are highly dependent on a wide variety of external organizations, ranging from state and local government administrators and politicians, accrediting bodies and federated funding organizations, to foundation and corporate boards. All these groups represent power centers whose actions can directly affect the mission and vitality of those nonprofit organizations that depend on them. The ability of nonprofit executives to understand and act politically, as well as through other frames, in relation to complex sets of interrelated actors helps explain why some executives are more effective than others.

Summary

Nonprofit leaders continually face the challenge of integrating mission, money (and acquisition of other resources), and strategy. Both boards and chief executives play crucial and interdependent roles in meeting this continuing challenge. Both must ask, "How well are we collectively meeting our responsibilities — to define and refine the organization's mission, to secure the resources necessary to achieve our mission, and to select and implement strategies appropriate to and effective in mission accomplishment and resource acquisition?" Chief executives must ask this question not only of themselves but also in relation to their boards. Are their boards meeting these responsibilities? If the answer is yes, a chief executive will surely want to understand how this happy state of affairs has been achieved and take pains to see that it is maintained. If the answer is no, a chief executive will want to consider the following four fundamental executive leadership strategies. Our research suggests that executives who use these strategies are more likely to lead organizations that effectively meet their responsibilities.

Effective executives accept and act on their psychological centrality. Our research shows that chief executives, board members, and others regard the chief executive as primarily responsible for the conduct of organizational affairs.

This is, we think, a fact of life in nonprofit organizations, however strongly we or others might want it to be otherwise. This fact implies that chief executives must often accept the responsibility for enabling their boards to carry out their leadership roles.

Effective executives provide board-centered leadership. Boards can make a difference in how nonprofit organizations meet the challenge of integrating mission, money, and strategy. Boards are much more likely to be active, effective bodies when they are supported by a chief executive who, recognizing his or her psychological centrality, is willing and able to serve the board as enabler and facilitator.

Effective executives emphasize leadership beyond their organizations' boundaries. Given the extensive dependence of nonprofit organizations on their external environments, executives generally recognize the importance of "networking" and other external activities for understanding the changes in that environment. Beyond the information value of external relations, some executives recognize the importance and value of affecting events in the environment. Exercising external leadership is difficult and demanding, since executives often can bring little, if any, financial or political power to bear. The leadership resources they are likely to have in greater abundance are expertise, trustworthiness, the moral stature of their organizations, and skills in coalition building and conflict resolution.

Effective executives think and act in political ways. Effective executives are realists. They recognize and accept that their organizations and the larger world are composed of groups with differing interests. As such, an important part of the leadership role is that of building coalitions, bargaining, and resolving conflicts. Politically astute executives are not immoral or manipulative. However, they are comfortable with the fact that interests differ and sometimes conflict. They are also comfortable with and skilled at negotiating, compromising, and forming alliances.

These four executive leadership strategies are highly interrelated. An executive who enhances his or her board-centered leadership skills will also likely become more attentive to externally oriented leadership. An executive who becomes more active in and skilled at leadership in the external environment will likely develop more politically oriented ways of thinking and behaving. Obviously, these skills are increments to a solid base of other knowledge and skills, such as those of program services, financial management, human resource management, fundraising, planning, evaluation, and the like. These board-centered, external, and political leadership skills are what distinguish especially effective nonprofit chief executives.

References

Alexander, J. G. "Planning and Management in Nonprofit Organizations." In T. D. Connors (ed.), *The Nonprofit Organization Handbook.* New York: McGraw-Hill, 1980.

Bass, B. M. *Leadership and Performance Beyond Expectations.* New York: Free Press, 1985.

Bolman, L. G., and Deal, T. E. *Reframing Organizations: Artistry, Choice, and Organizations.* San Francisco: Jossey-Bass, 1991.

Bower, M. "The Will to Manage the Philanthropic Organization." In T. D. Connors (ed.), *The Nonprofit Organization Handbook.* New York: McGraw-Hill, 1980.

Conrad, W., and Glenn, W. E. *The Effective Voluntary Board of Directors: What It Is and How It Works.* Chicago: Swallow Press, 1976.

Dollinger, M. J. "Environmental Boundary Spanning and Information Processing Effects on Organizational Performance." *Academy of Management Journal,* 1984, *27,* 351–368.

Elmore, R. F. "Organizational Models of Social Program Implementation. *Public Policy,* 1978, *26,* 185–228.

Gerth, H. H., and Mills, C. W. (trans. and eds.). *From Max Weber: Essays in Sociology.* New York: Oxford University Press, 1946.

Heimovics, R. D., and Herman, R. D. "Responsibility for Critical Events in Nonprofit Organizations." *Nonprofit and Voluntary Sector Quarterly,* 1990, *19*(1), 59–72.

Heimovics, R. D., Herman, R. D., and Coughlin, C.L.J. "Executive Leadership and Resource Dependence in Nonprofit Organizations: A Frame Analysis." *Public Administration Review,* 1993, *53*(5), 419–427.

Herman, R. D. "Concluding Thoughts on Closing the Board Gap." In R. D. Herman and J. Van Til (eds.), *Nonprofit Boards of Directors: Analyses and Applications.* New Brunswick, N.J.: Transaction, 1989.

Herman, R. D., and Heimovics, R. D. "An Investigation of Leadership Skill Differences in Chief Executives of Nonprofit Organizations." *American Review of Public Administration,* 1990, *20*(2), 107–124.

Herman, R. D., and Heimovics, R. D. *Executive Leadership in Nonprofit Organizations: New Strategies for Shaping Executive-Board Dynamics.* San Francisco: Jossey-Bass, 1991.

Huff, A. S. "Managerial Implications of the Emerging Paradigm." In Y. S. Lincoln (ed.), *Organizational Theory and Inquiry: The Paradigm Revolution.* Beverly Hills, Calif.: Sage, 1985.

Kotter, J. P. *The General Managers.* New York: Free Press, 1982.

Middleton, M. "Nonprofit Boards of Directors: Beyond the Governance Function." In W. W. Powell (ed.), *The Nonprofit Sector: A Research Handbook.* New Haven, Conn.: Yale University Press, 1987.

Payton, R. *Philanthropy: Voluntary Action for the Public Good.* New York: Macmillan, 1988.

Pfeffer, J. "Size, Composition and Function of Hospital Boards of Directors: A Study of Organization-Environment Linkage." *Administrative Science Quarterly,* 1973, *19,* 349–364.

Pfeffer, J. *Organizations and Organization Theory.* Boston: Pitman, 1982.

Pfeffer, J., and Salancik, G. R. *The External Control of Organizations: A Resource Dependence Perspective.* New York: HarperCollins, 1978.

Provan, K. C. "Board Power and Organizational Effectiveness Among Human Service Agencies." *Academy of Management Journal,* 1980, *23,* 221–236.

Quinn, R. E. "Applying the Competing Values Approach to Leadership: Toward an Integrative Framework." In J. G. Hunt and others (eds.), *Managerial Work and Leadership: International Perspectives.* New York: Pergamon, 1983.

Swanson, A. *The Determinative Team.* Hicksville, N.Y.: Exposition Press, 1978.

Yukl, G. A. *Leadership in Organizations.* Englewood Cliffs, N.J.: Prentice-Hall, 1981.

8

Strategic Planning and Action Planning for Nonprofit Organizations

John M. Bryson

This chapter will cover strategic planning and action planning for nonprofit organizations. The strategic planning process encompasses broad policy and direction setting, internal and external assessments, attention to key stakeholders, the identification of key issues, development of strategies to deal with each issue, decision making, action, and continuous monitoring of results. Action planning involves the creation of work programs designed to implement strategic plans. Strategic planning thus conceptually subsumes action planning, but action planning deserves attention in its own right, since the good intentions of strategic planning are likely to fail without adequate emphasis to implementation.

Strategic thought and action are increasingly important to the continued viability and effectiveness of nonprofit organizations of all sorts. Without strategic planning and work programs that assure adequate follow-through, these organizations are unlikely to meet successfully the numerous challenges that face them. Strategic planning is likely to embrace consideration of a broad agenda of potential issues and strategies, but to focus on a narrowed domain for action. The thinking will be broad, but the action will be targeted and specific in order to make the most progress against the most important issues.

Benefits and Uses of Strategic and Action Planning

Effective strategic and action planning can help nonprofit organizations

- Think strategically
- Clarify future direction
- Make today's decisions in light of their future consequences
- Meet mandates facing the organization and further fulfillment of the organization's mission
- Develop a coherent and defensible basis for decision making
- Exercise maximum discretion in the areas under organizational control
- Address major issues and solve major organizational problems
- Improve organizational performance
- Deal effectively and rapidly with changing circumstances
- Build teamwork and expertise
- Improve organizational credibility and enhance organizational legitimacy

While there is no guarantee that strategic and action planning will produce these benefits, an increasing number of case examples and studies indicate that they can help as long as key leaders and decision makers want planning to work and are willing to invest the necessary time, resources, and attention (Bryson, 1988; Bryson and Einsweiler, 1988; Stone and Brush, 1992). It is important to emphasize, however, that any planning process is worthwhile only insofar as it helps key decision makers *think* and *act* wisely. Strategic and action planning are not ends in themselves, but merely sets of concepts, procedures, and tools to help decision makers make important decisions and take important actions. Indeed, if any planning process gets in the way of wise thought and action, the process should be scrapped — not the thinking and acting!

What Is Strategic Planning?

With that caution in mind, let us proceed to a more detailed exploration of strategic planning. Strategic planning is "*a disciplined effort to produce fundamental decisions and actions that shape and guide what an organization (or other entity) is, what it does, and why it does it*" (Bryson, 1988, p. 5). These decisions typically concern the organization's mandates, mission, product or service level and mix, cost, financing, management, or organizational design.

What does strategic planning look like? Its most basic formal requirement is a series of discussions and decisions among key decision makers about what is truly important for the organization. And those discussions are the big innovation that strategic planning brings to most organizations, because in most organizations key decision makers rarely get together to talk about what is truly important. They may come together periodically at board or staff meetings, but usually to discuss relatively trivial matters, such as the organization's sick leave policy or the assignment of parking spaces. Or they may attend the same social functions, but there, too, it is rare to have a sustained discussion of organizationally relevant, important matters.

When they do gather to engage in strategic planning, key decision makers need a reasonably structured process to help them identify and resolve the most important issues their organizations face. Reasonable structure is needed to provide for order, deliberation, and participation. One such process that has proved effective in practice is outlined in Figure 8.1. The process consists of the following eight steps: (1) development of an initial agreement (or the "plan for planning"), (2) identification of mandates, (3) clarification of mission and values, (4) external environmental assessment, (5) internal environmental assessment, (6) strategic issue identification, (7) strategy development, and (8) preparation of a description of the organization in the future (or its "vision of success"). These eight steps should lead to actions, results, and evaluation.

It is important to emphasize that action, results, and evaluative judgments should emerge at each step in the process. In other words, implementation and evaluation should not wait until the "end" of the process, but should be an integral and ongoing part of the process. It is also important to emphasize that the eight steps are unlikely to be carried out in a rigid sequence. Rather, each step represents an occasion or occasions for discussion by key decision makers and/or members of the strategic planning team. The process is more iterative than linear, as understandings developed in one step inform subsequent steps, and then are reevaluated and revised and fed back through the process again.

As Hubert Humphrey once observed, "When in doubt, talk." And, indeed, the fundamental technology of strategic planning is talk (Bryson and Crosby, 1989), in part because there is so much that is unclear and open to question as organizations explore who they should be, what they should do, and why they should do it (Stone and Brush, 1992). The sections that follow detail the key processes in this kind of exploration.

Step 1: Development of an Initial Agreement

The first step is to negotiate agreement with key internal (and perhaps external) decision makers and/or opinion leaders concerning the overall strategic planning effort and key planning steps. The support and commitment of key decision makers are vital if strategic planning in an organization is to succeed (Olsen and Eadie, 1982). Further, the involvement of key decision makers outside the organization usually is crucial to the success of strategies if implementation will involve multiple parties and organizations (Bryson and Crosby, 1992).

Some person or group must initiate the negotiation process. One of the initiator's first tasks is to identify exactly who the key decision makers are. The next task is to identify which persons, groups, units, or organizations should be involved in the effort. The initial agreement will be negotiated with at least some of these decision makers, groups, units, or organizations.

The agreement itself should cover the purpose of the effort; preferred steps in the process; the form and timing of reports; the role, functions, and membership of any group or committee empowered to oversee the effort; commitments of necessary resources to proceed with the effort; and the role, functions, and membership of the strategic planning team. In subsequent discussion, we will assume that a strategic planning team has been formed as a result of the initial agreement.

An important feature of the discussions leading up to the agreement should be attention to the "givens," or that which is not up for discussion, at least at the beginning of the process. These givens might include certain aspects of the organization's charter and mission, specific products or services, service areas, target markets, and so on. There are two points to keep in mind: If everything has to be taken as a given, then there is no point to engaging in strategic planning. On the other hand, if everything is up for grabs, people may become quite fearful and perhaps even paralyzed by the prospect of change.

Step 2: Identification and Clarification of Mandates

Step 2 is to identify and clarify the formal and informal mandates placed on the organization. These are the *musts* confronting the organization, and may be either formal or informal in nature. The *formal* ones typically are embodied in externally imposed legislation, regulations, guidelines, ordinances, contracts, and so on, or else may be contained in organizational charters and governing board prescriptions and proscriptions. For example, nonprofit organizations that are in the social service business often rely on government funds to perform their work. Along with the funds typically comes a host of government mandates. The *informal* mandates are basically political and are embedded in the expectations of key external, and perhaps internal, stakeholders. For example, equal opportunity employment legislation is not likely to be embraced by an organization in a truly *affirmative* way until an important internal constituency demands it (Nelson and Hummer, 1989).

Actually, it is surprising how few organizations know precisely what they are mandated to do and not do. Typically, few members of any organization have ever read the relevant legislation, ordinances, charters, articles, and contracts that outline the organization's formal mandates. It may not be surprising, then, that most organizations—at least in the author's experience—make one or both of two fundamental mistakes. Either they believe they are more tightly constrained in their actions than they are, or they assume that if they are not explicitly told to do something, they are not allowed to do it.

Step 3: Development and Clarification of Mission and Values

The third step is the development and clarification of the nonprofit organization's mission and values. An organization's mission, in tandem with its

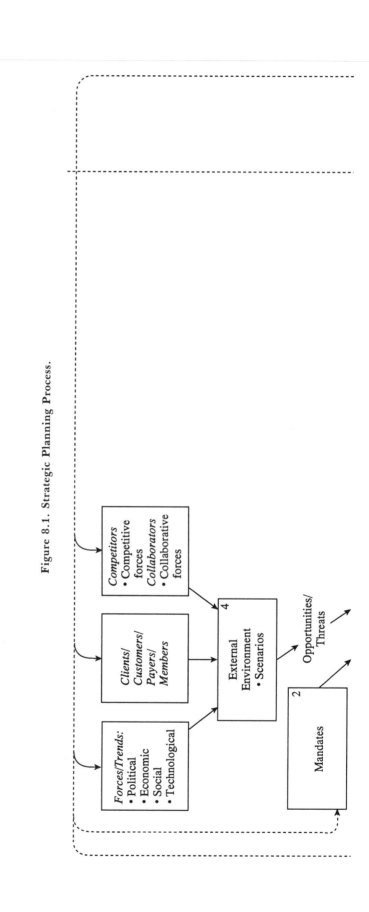

Figure 8.1. Strategic Planning Process.

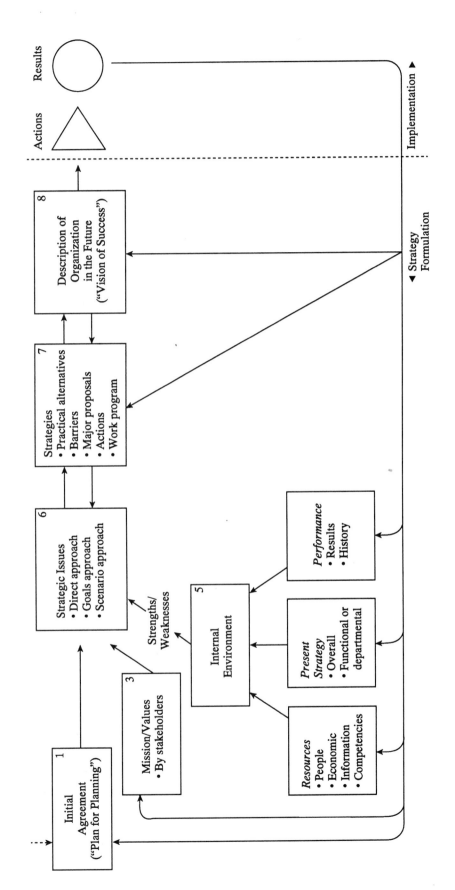

Results

Actions

Implementation ▶

1
Initial Agreement ("Plan for Planning")

3
Mission/Values
• By stakeholders

5
Internal Environment

Strengths/ Weaknesses

6
Strategic Issues
• Direct approach
• Goals approach
• Scenario approach

7
Strategies
• Practical alternatives
• Barriers
• Major proposals
• Actions
• Work program

8
Description of Organization in the Future ("Vision of Success")

◀ Strategy Formulation

Performance
• Results
• History

Present Strategy
• Overall
• Functional or departmental

Resources
• People
• Economic
• Information
• Competencies

Source: Adapted from Bryson, 1988, pp. 50–51.

mandates, provides its raison d'être — the social justification for its existence. For a nonprofit organization, this means there must be identifiable social or political needs that the organization seeks to fill. In particular, nonprofit organizations basically must serve some important public purpose that would not otherwise be served. Viewed in this light, nonprofit organizations must always be seen as a means to an end, not as ends in and of themselves. In other words, nonprofit organizations are externally justified.

Specification of an organization's mission, however, does not serve solely to justify the organization's existence. The clarification of purpose can eliminate a great deal of unnecessary conflict in an organization and can help channel discussion and activity productively. Agreement on purposes defines the arenas within which the organization will compete and, at least in broad outline, charts the future course of the organization. Moreover, an important and socially justifiable mission is a source of inspiration to key stakeholders, particularly employees. Indeed, it is doubtful if any organization ever achieved greatness or excellence without a basic consensus among its key stakeholders on an inspiring mission.

Prior to development of a mission statement, an organization should complete a stakeholder analysis. A *stakeholder* is defined as any person, group, or organization that can place a claim on an organization's attention, resources, or output, or that is affected by that output. Examples of a nonprofit organization's stakeholders might include clients, service recipients, or customers; employees and direct service volunteers; the chief executive officer; the board of directors; members; third-party payers or funders; other nonprofit organizations providing complementary services or involved as co-venturers in projects; public, nonprofit, or for-profit competitors; banks holding mortgages or notes; and suppliers. Attention to stakeholder concerns is crucial because the key to organizational success in the nonprofit sector (or any sector, for that matter) is the satisfaction of key stakeholders — according to their criteria for satisfaction.

A complete stakeholder analysis will require the strategic planning team to identify who the organization's stakeholders are, what their "stake" in the organization or its output is, what their criteria are for judging the performance of the organization, how well the organization performs against those criteria, how the stakeholders influence the organization, and, in general, how important the various stakeholders are. A complete stakeholder analysis also should identify what the organization needs from its various stakeholders — for example, money, staff, or political support. A stakeholder analysis will help clarify whether the organization needs to have different missions — and perhaps different strategies — for different stakeholders.

After completing the stakeholder analysis, a strategic planning team can proceed to develop a mission statement by responding to six questions. First, *who are we as an organization?* This question can be a surprisingly difficult question for a strategic planning team to answer succinctly (Dutton and Dukerich, 1991). Second, in general, *what are the basic social or political needs we exist to fill, or what are the basic social problems we exist to address?* Again, the answer to this question provides the justification for the organization's existence. Third, in general, *how do we recognize or anticipate and respond to these needs or problems?* This query should reveal whether the organization is active or passive, what it does to stay in touch with the needs or problems it is supposed to fill or address, and, in general, what it does to make sure it does not become an end in itself.

Further, the answer to the third question will tell organizational members whether they will be praised or punished for bringing back "bad news" to the organization concerning troubling events in the environment or critical evaluations by key stakeholders. Too many organizations "shoot the messenger" instead of attending to the message. Organizational members need to know that they will not be punished for bringing back important, but troubling, information; otherwise, they will simply keep their mouths shut and the organization will not have the benefit of useful feedback.

The fourth question is *how should we respond to our key stakeholders?* What value-added will we provide for key stakeholders? What will we do that makes them glad we exist, happy to support our continued efforts, and willing to go to bat for us when we need them? Fifth, *what is our philosophy and what are our core values?* Clarity about philosophy and core values will help an organization maintain its integrity (Covey, 1991). Furthermore, since only those strategies in keeping with an organization's philosophy and values are likely to work, the response to this question also helps the organization choose effective strategies (Pfeiffer, Goodstein, and Nolen, 1986). And finally, *what makes us distinctive or unique?* If there is nothing unique or distinctive about the organization, then perhaps it shouldn't exist. Perhaps some nonprofit competitor is better able to do the job. Or if there is no nonprofit competitor, perhaps there is a way for a government or for-profit organizations to step in and provide what is needed within the product or service domain.

The mission statement itself might be very short—perhaps not more than a paragraph or a slogan. But development of the mission statement should grow out of lengthy discussions in response to these six questions. Complete answers to these questions may serve as a basic outline for a description of the organization in the future, or of its "vision of success," the last step in the process. But considerable intermediate work is necessary before a complete vision of success can be articulated.

Step 4: External Environmental Assessment

In Step 4 the planning team explores the environment outside the organization in order to identify the opportunities and threats the organization faces. Basically, the "outside" factors are those the organizational does not control, while the "inside" factors are those mostly controlled by the organization (Pfeffer and Salancik, 1978). Opportunities and threats can be discovered by monitoring a variety of political, economic, social, and technological forces and trends. PESTs can be an especially appropriate acronym for these forces and trends because organizations typically must change in response to them, and the change can be quite painful. Unfortunately, organizations all too often focus only on the negative, or threatening, aspects of these changes, and not on the opportunities they present (de Bono, 1985; Jackson and Dutton, 1987; Dutton, forthcoming).

Besides monitoring PESTs, the strategic planning team also should monitor various stakeholder groups, including clients, customers, payers, members, competitors, and collaborators. Attention also should be paid to the forces favoring both competition and collaboration in the environment. The organization might construct various scenarios to explore alternative futures in the external environment, a practice typical of private-sector strategic planning (Linneman and Klein, 1983).

Members of an organization's governing board—particularly if they are elected—often are better at identifying and assessing external threats and opportunities than the organization's employees. This is partly owing to a governing board's responsibility for relating an organization to its external environment and vice versa (Thompson, 1967; Carver, 1990). Unfortunately, neither governing boards nor employees usually do a systematic or effective job of external scanning. As a result, most organizations are like ships trying to navigate troubled or treacherous waters without benefit of human lookouts, radar, or sonar equipment.

Because of this, both employees and governing board members should rely on a relatively formal external assessment process. The technology of external assessment is fairly simple, and allows organizations—cheaply, pragmatically, and effectively—to keep tabs on what is happening in the larger world that is likely to have an effect on the organization and the pursuit of its mission. In its simplest form, external assessment is a three-part function (Pflaum and Delmont, 1987):

1. Identification of key issues and trends that pose actual or potential threats or opportunities
2. Analysis and interpretation of the issues and trends
3. Creation of information that is useful for decision making, including, for example, reports, discussion papers, presentations, and decision packages

Step 5: Internal Environmental Assessment

To identify internal strengths and weaknesses, the organization might monitor resources (inputs), present strategy (process), and performance (outputs). Most organizations have volumes of information on their inputs, such as salaries, supplies, physical plant, and full-time equivalent (FTE) personnel. They tend to have a less clear idea of their present strategy, either overall or by function. And typically they can say little, if anything, about outputs, let alone the effects those outputs have on clients, customers, or payers. For example, many nonprofit organizations involved with social services have a difficult time demonstrating that their efforts have provided demonstrable benefits to clients. The funders of these programs can be expected to be resistant to future funding requests when clear client benefits are not evident to justify continued funding.

The relative absence of performance information presents problems both for the organization and for its stakeholders. Stakeholders will judge the worth of an organization according to how well the organization does against the criteria the stakeholders—and not necessarily the organization—wish to use. For external stakeholders in particular, these criteria typically relate to performance. If the organization cannot demonstrate its effectiveness against the stakeholders' criteria, then regardless of any "inherent" worth of the organization, stakeholders are likely to withdraw their support.

The absence of performance information may also create, and harden, major organizational conflicts. This is because without performance criteria and information, there is no way to evaluate the relative effectiveness of alternative strategies, resource allocations, organizational designs, and distributions of power. As a result, organizational conflicts are likely to occur more often than they should, serve narrow partisan interests, and be resolved in ways that do not further the organization's mission. The difficulties of measuring performance are well known (Flynn, 1986; Patton, 1986). But regardless of the difficulties, the organization will be continually challenged to demonstrate effective performance to its stakeholders.

Step 6: Strategic Issue Identification

Together, the first five elements of the process lead to the sixth, the identification of strategic issues. *Strategic issues* are fundamental policy questions affecting the organization's mandates, mission and values, product or service level and mix, clients, users or payers, cost, financing, management, or organizational design. Usually, it is vital that strategic issues be dealt with expeditiously and effectively if the organization is to survive and prosper. An organization that does not respond to a strategic issue can expect undesirable results from a threat, a missed opportunity, or both.

Two examples can help illustrate this point. The first comes from a recent plan by a major inner-city American Red Cross chapter. The issues faced by this organization are presented in Exhibit 8.1.

The second example is presented in Figure 8.2, and consists of the interconnected set of issues facing a North American religious community and service order for men. The issues are organized according to their "precedence" (Nutt and Backoff, 1992). In other words, issues at the beginning of a string of arrows should be dealt with first in order to set the stage for dealing with issues later in the chain of arrows. For example, the order's strategic planning team believes that finding important starting points for

Exhibit 8.1. Strategic Issues Facing an American Red Cross Chapter.

Finance/Revenue Issue:

How can the Chapter achieve financial independence and stability and secure sufficient resources to support services necessary for the execution of our mission?

Community Needs and Involvement Issue:

How can the Chapter successfully monitor changing community needs and develop effective responses (short- and long-range) appropriate to our mission and priorities?

Human Resource Issue:

How can the Chapter recruit, train, and retrain a sufficient number of qualified people with diverse backgrounds to address our paid and volunteer staff service needs?

Organizational/Structural Issue:

What organizational structure will best serve the Chapter in meeting current and future community needs through the provision of quality, cost-effective services?

Communications/Visibility Issue:

How can we enhance Chapter visibility and inform the public of our mission and services and the resources we need to carry them out?

National Issue:

How can we more effectively educate the national sector of the American Red Cross on the attitudes of local funders, exert greater influence on them to respond to our need for increased financial accountability, and better identify the local benefits derived from the national sector through our fair share contributions?

Service Effectiveness Issue:

How should we evaluate our service methods and results to (1) assess efficiency in providing mandated services, (2) measure effectiveness in addressing needs of targeted community populations, and (3) ensure that marginal services will be strengthened or discontinued?

United Way Issue:

How can we strengthen our relationship with the United Way based on mutual understanding of our respective organizational missions and requirements for client and community service?

Source: 1989 Strategic Plan of the Greater Minneapolis Area Chapter of the American Red Cross. Used by permission.

---

making ministries more effective involves clarifying the order's assumptions and core values and its governance and management processes and structures. Options for addressing some of the issues are indicated by bullet points.

Strategic planning focuses on achievement of the best "fit" between an organization and its environment. Attention to mandates and the external environment, therefore, can be thought of as planning from the "outside in." Attention to mission and values and the internal environment can be considered planning from the "inside out." Effective strategies deal with the issues that arise on the boundaries between inside and outside.

The iterative nature of the strategic planning process often becomes apparent in this step when participants find that information created or discussed in earlier steps presents itself again as strategic issues. For example, many strategic planning teams begin with the belief that they know what their organization's mission is. They often find out in this step, however, that one of the key issues their organization faces is determination of exactly what its mission ought to be. In other words, the organization's present mission is found to be inappropriate — given the team members' new understanding of the situation the organization faces — and a new mission must be created.

Strategic issues, virtually by definition, involve conflicts of one sort or another. The conflicts may involve ends (what), means (how), philosophy (why), location (where), timing (when), and who might be advantaged or disadvantaged by different ways of resolving the issue (who). In order for the issues to be raised and resolved effectively, the organization must be prepared to deal with the almost inevitable conflicts that will occur.

A statement of a strategic issue should contain three elements. First, the issue should be described succinctly, preferably in a single paragraph. The issue itself should be framed as a question that the organization can do something about. If the organization can't do anything about it, it's not an issue — at least for the organization (Wildavsky, 1979). An organization's attention is limited enough without wasting it on issues it cannot resolve.

Second, the factors that make the issue a fundamental policy question should be listed. In particular, what is it about mandates, mission, values, internal strengths or weaknesses, and external opportunities and threats that make this a strategic issue? Listing these factors will become useful in the next step, strategy development. Every effective strategy will build on strengths and take advantage of opportunities while it minimizes or overcomes weaknesses and threats. The framing of strategic issues therefore is very important because the framing will contain the basis for the issues' resolution.

Finally, the planning team should prepare a statement of the consequences of failure to address the issue. A review of the consequences will inform judgments of just how strategic, or important, various issues are. For instance, if no consequences will ensue from failure to address an issue, it's not an issue — or at least it's not a strategic issue. At the other extreme, if the organization will be destroyed by failure to address an issue, or will miss a gigantic and valuable opportunity, the issue clearly is *very* strategic, and should be dealt with immediately. The strategic issue identification step therefore is aimed at focusing organizational attention on what is truly important for the survival, prosperity, and effectiveness of the organization.

There are four basic approaches to the identification of strategic issues: the direct approach, the indirect approach, the goals approach, and the scenario, or "vision of success," approach (see also Barry, 1986). Which approach is likely to work best depends on the specific situation the organization faces. The *direct approach* involves going straight from a review of mandates and mission and strengths, weaknesses, opportunities, and threats (SWOTs) to the identification of strategic issues. It is the best choice if there is no agree-

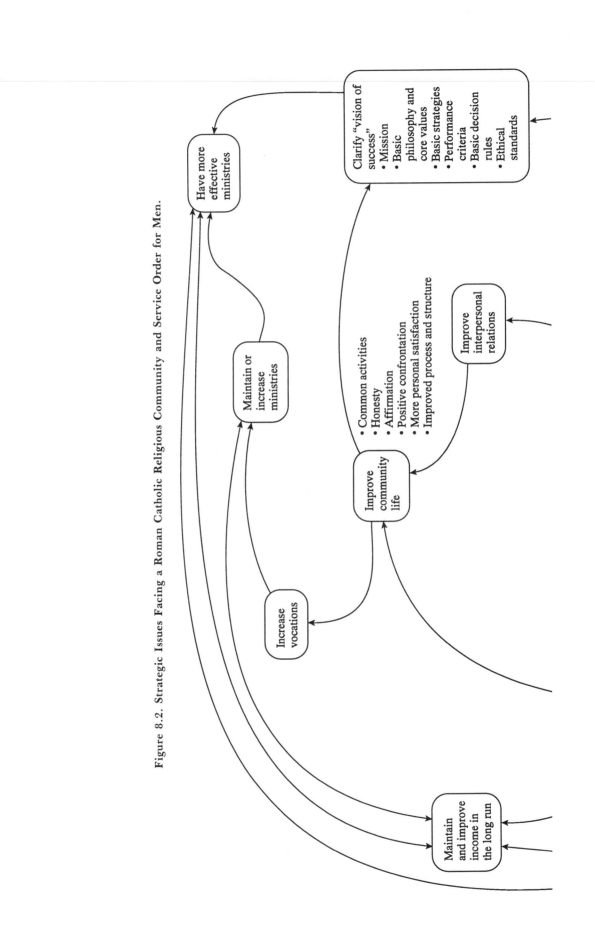

Figure 8.2. Strategic Issues Facing a Roman Catholic Religious Community and Service Order for Men.

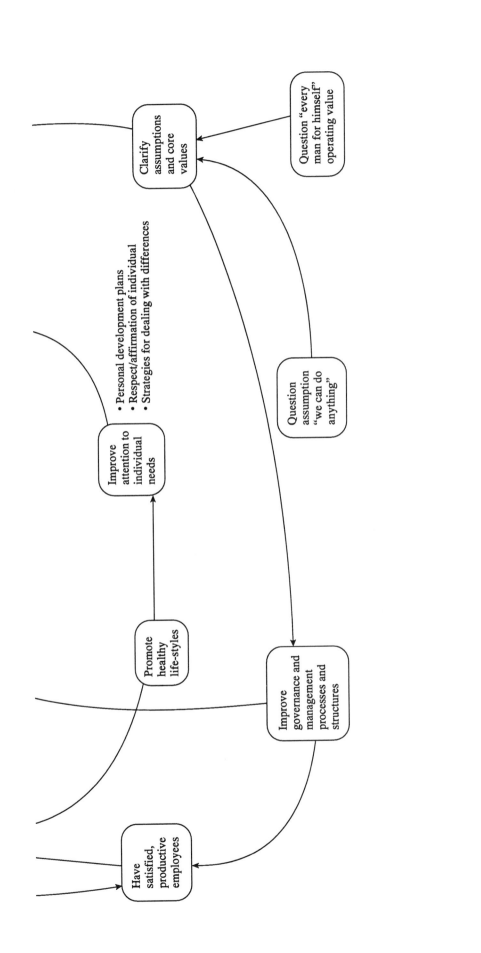

ment on goals, or if the goals on which there is agreement are too abstract to be useful. In other words, the approach works best when there is no preexisting explicit value congruence. The direct approach also is best if no preexisting vision of success exists and if developing a consensually based vision would be too difficult. This approach also works best when no hierarchical authority can impose goals on other actors. And finally, the direct approach is best when the environment is so turbulent that limited actions in response to issues seem preferable to development of goals and objectives or visions that may be rendered obsolete quickly. The direct approach, in other words, can work in highly pluralistic, partisan, politicized, and relatively fragmented situations — as long as there is a "dominant coalition" strong enough and interested enough to make it work.

The *indirect approach* is a variant of the direct approach, and it applies in the same situations. The indirect approach is particularly useful when time is short because it can be used to identify strategic issues and response strategies in an expeditious way. The approach works as follows:

1. A stakeholder analysis is completed, a draft mission statement is formulated, a SWOT analysis is performed, and any other necessary or desirable background studies are prepared or reviewed. (This step would be the same for the direct approach; the next two steps are what differentiates the indirect approach from the direct approach.)

2. The analyses are reviewed and options for action are created that would address the specific results of the analyses. Each option is placed on a separate half-sheet of white paper called a "snow card" (see Bryson, 1988, pp. 126–128; Nutt and Backoff, 1992, pp. 257–258). Specifically, (a) possible organizational actions are generated that would either keep or make stakeholders happy according to the criteria the stakeholders use to judge the organization's performance. A separate snow card is prepared for each action, indicating the stakeholder for which the action represents a response. (b) Similarly, actions are formulated that might keep the organization strong where it is strong, take advantage of opportunities, or minimize or overcome weaknesses and threats. The snow cards for these options should indicate whether the actions represent a response to a strength, weakness, opportunity, or threat. (c) Finally, possible actions stated or implied by the applicable mandates and mission are created for consideration, as are options that might be considered based on background studies included in the external and internal assessment phases. Again, the cards developed for these options should indicate the feature of the organization's situation to which the action responds, and whether the card is a consequence of mandates, mission, or specific reports or studies.

3. Once all these various options have been identified and noted on snow cards, they are taped to a wall and grouped in categories that make sense. The categories represent "portfolios" of options that embody an ac-

tion theme, such as how to improve customer or client service, how to better manage volunteers, how to enhance financial stability, and so on. These action themes are likely to be strategic issue areas for the organization (Eden and Huxham, 1986; Eden, 1989). The issues have been formulated *indirectly* through first positing possible actions that might deal with the results of stakeholder, SWOT, and other analyses, and secondly formulating the action themes — or issue areas — that tie those portfolios together.

The *goals approach* is more in line with conventional planning theory, which stipulates that an organization should establish goals and objectives for itself and then develop strategies to achieve those goals and objectives. This approach can work if there is fairly broad and deep agreement on the organization's goals and objectives — and if those goals and objectives themselves are detailed and specific enough to guide the development of strategies. The approach also can be expected to work when there is a hierarchical authority structure with leaders at the top who can impose goals on the rest of the system. The strategic issues then will involve how best to translate goals and objectives into actions. This approach is more likely to work in a single-function nonprofit organization than in multiorganizational, multifunctional situations.

Finally, there is the *scenario* or *vision of success* approach, whereby the organization develops a "best" or "ideal" picture of itself in the future as it successfully fulfills its mission and achieves success. The strategic issues then concern how the organization should change from the way it is now to the way it would look and behave if it embodied its vision. The vision-of-success approach is most useful if it will be difficult to identify strategic issues directly; if no detailed and specific agreed-upon goals and objectives exist and if developing them will be difficult; and if drastic change is likely to be necessary. As conception precedes perception (May, 1969), development of a vision can provide the concepts that enable organizational members to see necessary changes.

Step 7: Strategy Development

A *strategy* is defined as a *pattern* of purposes, policies, programs, actions, decisions, and/or resource allocations that define what an organization is, what it does, and why it does it. Strategies can vary by level, function, and time frame. The strategies in strategic planning are designed to deal with the issues.

This definition is purposely broad, in order to focus attention on the creation of consistency across *rhetoric* (what people say), *choices* (what people decide and are willing to pay for), and *actions* (what people do). Effective strategy formulation and implementation processes will link rhetoric, choices, and actions into a coherent and consistent pattern across levels, functions, and time (P. Bromiley, personal communication, 1986).

The American Red Cross chapter referred to earlier developed thirty-five specific strategies to deal with the strategic issues they identified. These strategies were organized into seven themes, or strategic directions:

- Ensure ongoing excellence in program development and delivery.
- Maximize the Chapter's ability to secure necessary resources.
- Improve the effectiveness of communications with key audiences.
- Strengthen the paid and volunteer work force.
- Adapt the organizational structure to meet changing community needs.
- Strengthen relationships with the United Way based on mutual understanding of respective organizational missions and requirements for client and community service.
- Maximize Chapter influence in policy making and administration of the American National Red Cross.

The write-ups of the specific strategies included the following elements:

- Rationale for the strategy recommendation
- Compatibility with Chapter mission
- Expected results or outcomes
- Implementation responsibilities and required time
- Impacts on relationships with other organizations
- Resource requirements
- Other factors affecting strategy success
- Advantages of the strategy and opportunities it presents or takes advantage of
- Disadvantages of the strategy, including risks

These write-ups contribute directly to preparation of action plans for implementation.

One valuable approach to strategy development involves a five-part process. (Other valuable approaches will be found in Friend and Hickling, 1987; Bryson, 1988; Bryson and Crosby, 1992; Rosenhead, 1989; and Nutt and Backoff, 1992.) Strategy development begins with identification of practical alternatives, dreams, or visions for resolving the strategic issues. It is of course important to be practical, but if the organization is unwilling to entertain at least some "dreams" or "visions" for resolving its strategic issues, it probably shouldn't be engaged in strategic planning. In other words, if the organization is only willing to consider minor variations on existing strategic themes, then it probably is wasting its time on strategic planning. After completing a strategic planning process, an organization may decide that minor variations are the best choice, but if it *begins* the process with that assumption, it is wasting its time with strategic planning.

Next, the planning team should enumerate the barriers to achieving those alternatives, dreams, or visions, and not focus directly on their achievement. To focus on barriers at this point is not typical of most strategic planning processes. But doing so is one way of assuring that any strategies developed deal with implementation difficulties directly and in advance, rather than haphazardly and after the fact.

Once alternatives, dreams, and visions, along with barriers to their realization, are listed, the team develops major proposals for achieving the alternatives, dreams, or visions directly, or else indirectly through overcoming the barriers. (Alternatively, the team might solicit proposals from key organizational units, various stakeholder groups, task forces, or selected individuals.) As an example of a barrier to be overcome, many nonprofit organizations need to enhance organizational capacities for action before they undertake major strategic planning efforts. Capacity enhancements may involve filling key board or staff positions, correcting cash flow or financial control problems, or acquiring needed staff training. Fixing problems such as these will improve the organization's ability to think and act strategically.

After major proposals are submitted, two final tasks remain in order to develop effective strategies. Actions that need to be taken over the next two to three years to implement the major proposals must be identified. And finally, a detailed work program to implement the actions must be spelled out for the next six months to a year. These final two steps will be covered in more detail in the section on action planning.

Another valuable approach to the development of strategies flows out of the indirect approach to the identification of strategic issues. In the indirect approach, the issues consist of portfolios of possible actions. Strategies then become the options actually chosen for action from the portfolios. Those chosen may then need to be elaborated, supplemented, and rationalized into coherent patterns that merge rhetoric, choices, and actions (Eden, 1989).

An effective strategy must meet several criteria. It must be technically workable, politically acceptable to key stakeholders, and in accord with the organization's philosophy and core values. Further, it should be ethical and legal. It must also deal with the strategic issue it was supposed to address. All too often strategies are developed that are technically, politically, ethically, and legally impeccable, but that do not deal with the issues they were supposed to address. These strategies therefore are virtually useless.

Step 8: Description of the Organization in the Future

In the final step in the process, the organization develops a description of what it should look like as it successfully implements its strategies and achieves its full potential. This description is the organization's "vision of success" (Taylor, 1984). Few organizations have such a description or vision, yet the importance of such descriptions has long been recognized by well-managed companies (Ouchi, 1981; Peters and Waterman, 1982) and organizational psychologists (Locke, Shaw, Saari, and Latham, 1981). Typically included in such descriptions are the organization's mission, its basic strategies, its performance criteria, some important decision rules, and the ethical standards expected of all employees.

Such descriptions, to the extent that they are widely known and agreed to in the organization, allow organizational members to know what is expected of them without constant direct managerial oversight. Members are freed to act on their own initiative on the organization's behalf to an extent not otherwise possible. The result should be a mobilization and direction of members' energy toward pursuit of the organization's purposes, and a reduced need for direct supervision.

Visions of success should be short—not more than several pages—and inspiring. People are inspired by a clear and forceful vision delivered with heartfelt conviction. Inspirational visions—such as Dr. Martin Luther King, Jr.'s "I Have a Dream" speech—have the following attributes: they focus on a better future; encourage hopes and dreams; appeal to common values; state positive outcomes; emphasize the strength of a unified group; use word pictures, images, and metaphors; and communicate enthusiasm and excitement (Kouzes and Posner, 1987).

Some might question why development of a vision of success comes last in the process rather than much earlier. There are two basic answers to this question. First, development of a vision doesn't have to come last for all organizations. Some organizations—as was suggested above in the discussion of mission development and strategic issue identification—are able to develop a fairly clearly articulated vision of success much earlier in the process.

But second, most organizations will not be able to develop a vision of success until they've gone through several iterations of strategic planning—if they are able to develop a vision at all. A challenging yet achievable vision embodies the tension between what an organization *wants* and what it *can have.* Often several cycles of strategic planning are necessary before organizational members know what they want, what they can have, and what the difference is between the two. A vision that motivates people will be challenging enough to spur action, yet not so impossible to achieve that it de-motivates and demoralizes people. Most organizations, in other words, will find that their vision of success is likely to serve more as a guide for strategy implementation, and less as a guide for strategy formulation.

Further, for most organizations, development of a vision of success is not *necessary* in order to produce marked improvements in performance. Most organizations can demonstrate a substantial improvement in effectiveness if they simply identify and resolve satisfactorily a few strategic issues. Most organizations most of the time simply do not address what is truly important; just gathering key decision makers to deal with a few important matters in a timely and effective way would enhance organizational performance substantially.

Our review of the eight-step process and, in particular, of the four different approaches to the identification of strategic issues, should make it clear that goals and visions may be inserted at various places in the process. In many cases, detailed and specific goals will not emerge until the end of the strategy development step. The goals and objectives developed then will embody the desired directions and values of the strategies (the goals) and milestones along the way toward their achievement (the objectives). Alternatively, there may be widely shared and agreed-upon strategic goals in place at the beginning of the planning process. These goals can be used to guide the development of strategic issues and subsequent strategies. Or perhaps suitable goals are not available to guide the process from the beginning, but it may be possible and desirable to develop them after strategic issues are identified. These goals then can guide the development of strategies to deal with the issues.

Similarly, visions of success usually cannot be identified until the end of the eight-step process. But there are organizations and circumstances in which visions can be developed that will guide the strategic planning process. Alternatively, visions (or scenarios) may be used to guide the identification of issues and/or subsequent strategies. The general point is that there is no one "best way" to use goals or visions in strategic planning. The process must be tailored to fit specific circumstances — the goals and visions should be used in ways that are appropriate to those circumstances.

Action Planning

Action planning is necessary to ensure that selected proposals or options for dealing with the issues actually are implemented. Action plans detail the specific means by which strategies will be implemented and strategic objectives reached. Action plans typically incorporate the following five factors (Morrissey, Below, and Acomb, 1987, pp. 63–64):

- The specific steps or actions required
- Who will be held accountable for seeing that each step or action is completed
- When these steps or actions are to be carried out
- What resources need to be allocated in order to carry them out
- What feedback mechanisms are needed to monitor progress within each action step

Action plans may be formatted with the help of the graphic aids such as that reproduced in Figure 8.3. In addition, it is particularly important that action plans be coordinated with the organizational budgeting process to make sure adequate financial resources are available to support implementation efforts. Further advice may be found in Frame, 1987; Friend and Hickling, 1987; Morrisey, Below, and Acomb, 1987; and Nutt and Backoff, 1992.

Figure 8.3. Action Plan Format.

Objective:

Action Plan

Action Steps	Accountability		Schedule		Resources		Feedback Mechanisms
	Primary	Others	Start	Complete	Dollars	Time	

Source: The Executive Guide to Operational Planning by George L. Morrisey, Patrick J. Below, and Betty L. Acomb. San Francisco: Jossey-Bass. Copyright © 1988. Permission to reproduce hereby granted.

Application of Strategic and Action
Planning Across Levels and Functions

It is relatively easy to take a group of key decision makers through a strategic planning process. The eight steps outlined above make the process of strategic thinking and acting fairly orderly and allow a reasonable number of people to participate in the process.

What is more difficult is the application of strategic and action planning across levels and functions of a large nonprofit organization. One possible way to do so is outlined in Figure 8.4. The application is based on the system used by the 3M Corporation (Tita and Allio, 1984). The system's first cycle consists of "bottom up" development of strategic plans within a framework established by the board, CEO, and management team, followed by reviews and reconciliations at each succeeding level. In the second cycle, operating or action plans are developed to implement the strategic plans. Depending on the situation, decisions at the top of the organizational hierarchy may or may not require governing board approval, which explains why the line depicting the process flow shows two possible paths at the top.

Strategic planning may be used in three different ways. First, it may be used infrequently to develop "grand strategy" to guide the organization for a substantial period of time, such as four to five years. Development of grand strategy is not undertaken on a yearly basis, both because of the amount of effort likely to be involved and because it takes time to implement grand strategy. Second, strategic planning can be used on a yearly basis to identify important issues that need to be addressed as part of implementing grand strategy and that presage development of the next grand strategy. Figure 8.4 outlines this second use of strategic planning. Finally, strategic planning can be used to address issues that are completely disconnected from routine planning exercises. These are issues—often emergencies or crises—that just happen and must be addressed strategically if the organization is to survive and prosper.

While the "rational" approach to strategic planning would seem to suggest that the grand strategy ought to be developed first, followed by the initiation of yearly rounds of strategic planning within the framework of the grand strategy, the usual sequence is the reverse. Typically, organizations engage in strategic planning because they are faced with fairly immediate and serious difficulties, and they decide to give strategic planning a try. If it works, they move toward an annual strategic planning exercise. Finally, they may pursue development of grand strategy on a periodic basis.

Some Important Details and Caveats

Although the steps of the strategic and action planning processes are laid out here in a linear, sequential manner, it must be emphasized that the process in practice is iterative. Participants typically rethink what they have done

Figure 8.4. Adaptation of 3M's Strategic Planning System to a Nonprofit Organization.

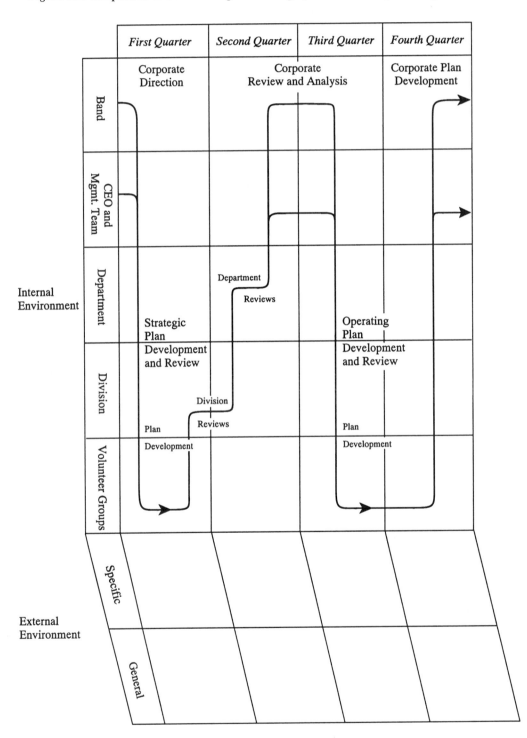

several times before they reach final decisions. Moreover, the process doesn't always begin at the beginning. Instead, organizations typically find themselves confronted with a strategic issue or external mandate that leads them to engage in strategic planning (Stone and Brush, 1992). Once engaged, the organization is likely to go back and begin at the beginning. In addition, implementation usually begins before all of the planning is complete. As soon as useful actions are identified, they are taken — as long as they don't jeopardize future actions that might prove valuable.

Furthermore, from a linear, sequential perspective, the eight-step process should result in decisions and actions to implement the strategies, and subsequent evaluation of results. As indicated above, however, implementation typically doesn't — and shouldn't — wait until the eight steps have been completed. For example, if the organization's mission needs to be redrafted, then it should be. If the SWOT analysis turns up weaknesses or threats that need to be addressed immediately, they should be. If aspects of a strategy can be implemented without awaiting further developments, they should be. And so on. As noted earlier, strategic thinking *and* acting are important, and all of the thinking doesn't have to occur before any actions are taken.

The process is applicable to all or most nonprofit organizations. The only general requirements are a "dominant coalition" willing to sponsor and follow the process (Thompson, 1967), and a process champion willing to push it.

Many organizational strategic planning teams that are familiar with, and believe in, the process should be able to complete it in three major segments: (1) a two- or three-day retreat, (2) follow-up work by individuals or teams on issues identified at the retreat, and (3) an additional half-day meeting scheduled three to four weeks later to review the resulting strategic plan. Responsibility for preparing the plan can be delegated to a planner assigned to work with the team, or the organization's chief executive may choose to draft the plan himself or herself. Additional time might be needed for further reviews and sign-offs by key decision makers. Additional time also might be necessary to secure information or advice for specific parts of the plan, especially recommended strategies.

If the organization is fairly large, specific linkages will be necessary to join the process to different functions, levels, and budgets in the organization so that the process will be orderly and integrated. Different organizations will rely on different methods of ensuring that necessary integrations occur. One effective way to achieve such a linkage across levels and functions below the board level is to appoint the heads of all functional departments to the strategic planning team — indeed, to make *them* the strategic planning team. Each department head then can be sure that his or her department's information and interests are represented in strategy formulation, and can oversee strategy implementation in that department. Care must be taken, of course, to ensure that the board's policy-making role and responsibilities are respected. For example, the board may demand to sign off on what the strategic issues are, to choose or ratify selected strategies to deal with the issues, and to have periodic updates on strategy implementation efforts.

In any event, whichever key decision makers are involved, they might wish to form themselves into a permanent strategic planning committee (of the board or staff) or cabinet (of the staff). There is much to recommend this approach — if it appears workable for the organization — as it emphasizes the role of policy makers and/or line managers as strategic planners and the role of strategic planners as facilitators of decision making by the key decision makers. Pragmatic and effective strategies and plans are likely to result. Temporary task forces, strategic planning committees, or a cabinet can work, but whatever the arrangement, there is no substitute for the support and direct involvement of key decision makers in the process.

Why Strategic Planning Is Here to Stay

Many managers are likely to groan at the prospect of having yet another new management technique foisted upon them. They have seen cost-benefit analysis, planning-programming-budgeting systems, zero-based budgeting, management by objectives, total quality management, and a host of other techniques trumpeted by their inventors, various authors, and cadres of management consultants. All too often, they have also seen the techniques fall by the wayside after a burst of initial enthusiasm by their adoptors. The managers frequently, and justifiably, feel as if they are the victims of some sort of perverse management hazing (P. Eckhert, personal communication, 1985).

Strategic planning, however, is not just a passing fad, at least strategic planning of the sort proposed here. The reason is that the strategic planning process presented in this chapter builds on the nature of *political* decision making. So many of the other management techniques have failed because they have ignored, or tried to circumvent, or even tried to contradict the political nature of life in most organizations. Too many planners and managers — at least in my experience — just do not understand that such a quest is almost guaranteed to be quixotic.

Most of these new management innovations have tried to improve organizational decision making and operations by trying to impose a formal rationality on systems that are not rational — at least in the conventional meaning of that word. Most organizations are *politically rational,* and any technique that is likely to work well in such organizations must accept and build on the nature of political rationality (Wildavsky, 1979; Bolman and Deal, 1991).

Let us pursue this point further by contrasting two different kinds of decision making — the "rational" planning model and political decision making (Bryson, 1988; Bryson and Crosby, 1992). The rational planning model is presented in Figure 8.5. It is a rational-deductive approach to decision making that begins with a primary goal (or goals), from which are deduced policies, programs, and actions to achieve the goals. If there is a traditional planning theology, this model is one of its icons. Indeed, if there were a planning Moses, Figure 8.5 would have been etched on his tablets when he came down from the Mount.

Figure 8.5. Rational Planning.

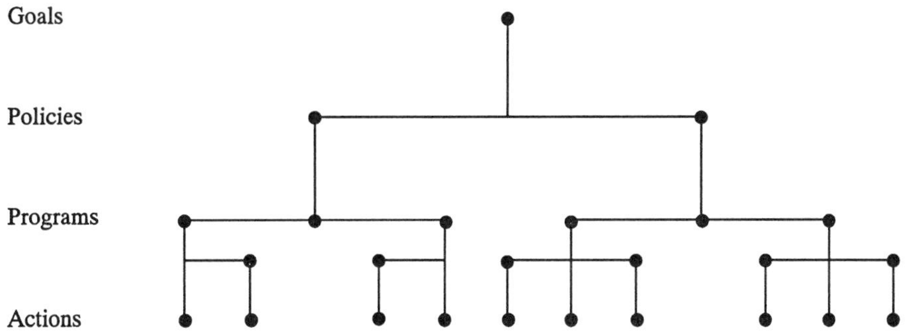

Source: Bryson, 1988, p. 67. Used by permission.

But now let us examine a fundamental assumption of the rational planning model: that in the fragmented, shared power settings that characterize many nonprofit organizations there will be a *consensus,* or at least strong agreement, on goals, policies, programs, and actions necessary to achieve organizational aims. The assumption just does not hold. Only in fairly centralized, authoritarian, and quasi-military bureaucracies will the assumption hold—maybe.

Now, let us examine a model that contrasts sharply with the rational planning model—the political decision-making model presented in Figure 8.6. This model is inductive, not rational-deductive. It begins with issues, which by definition involve conflict, not consensus. The conflicts may be over ends, means, timing, location, political advantage, philosophy, or reasons—and the conflicts may be severe. As efforts proceed to resolve the issues, policies and programs emerge that address the issues and that are politically rational—that is, they are politically acceptable to involved or affected parties. Over time, more general policies may be formulated to capture, frame, shape, guide, or interpret the policies and programs developed to deal with the issues. The various policies and programs are in effect treaties among the various stakeholder groups and, while they may not exactly record a consensus, at least they represent a reasonable level of agreement among stakeholders (Pfeffer and Salancik, 1978).

Now, recall that the heart of the strategic planning process discussed in this chapter is the identification and resolution of strategic—important—

Figure 8.6. Political Decision Making.

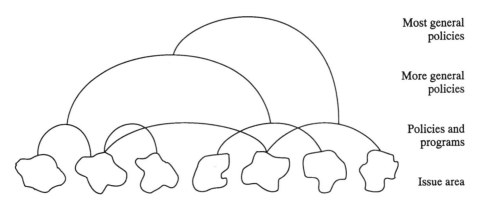

Source: Bryson, 1988, p. 68. Used by permission.

issues. The process, in other words, accepts political decision making's emphasis on issues and seeks to inform the formulation and resolution of those issues. Effective strategic planning therefore should make political decision makers more effective, and, if practiced consistently, might even make their professional lives easier. Since every key decision maker in a large (and often small) nonprofit organization is, in effect, a political decision maker, strategic planning can help these people and their organizations. Strategic planning therefore is an innovation that will last in nonprofit organizations. It will last because it accepts and builds on the nature of political decision making—and if done well, it actually improves political decisions, programs, and policies.

Now, having drawn a sharp distinction between the rational planning model and political decision making, it must be emphasized that the two models are not inherently antithetical. They may simply need to be sequenced properly. The political decision-making model is necessary to work out a consensus on what programs and policies will best resolve key issues. The rational planning model can then be used to recast that consensus in the form of goals, policies, programs, and actions. While the planning and decision making that go into the formulation of a strategic plan may look fairly sloppy to an outsider, once a consensus is reached on what to do, the resulting strategic plan can be rewritten in a form that looks perfectly rational. The advantage of the strategic planning process outlined in this chapter is that it doesn't presume consensus where consensus doesn't exist.

What It Takes to Initiate and Succeed with Strategic Planning

As experience with strategic planning grows, it appears reasonable to conclude that any organization that wishes to engage in strategic planning should have (1) a process sponsor or sponsors in positions of power and authority to legitimize the process and demand that it be pursued; (2) a process champion or champions to push the process along on a day-to-day basis; (3) a strategic planning team; (4) an expectation that there will be disruptions and delays; (5) a willingness to be flexible about what constitutes a strategic plan; (6) an ability to pull in information and people at key points for important discussions, decisions, and actions; and (7) a willingness to construct and consider arguments geared to very different evaluative criteria, in particular, those of technical workability, political acceptability to key stakeholders, and ethical and legal defensibility (Bryson and Roering, 1988).

Different nonprofit organizations will choose different criteria to judge the effectiveness of their strategic planning efforts. At a minimum, their efforts should be judged according to the extent to which they (1) focus the attention of key decision makers on what is important for their organizations, (2) help set priorities for action, and (3) generate those actions.

Nonprofit organizations also may choose to institutionalize strategic planning as an ongoing management practice. If key people are willing to make the effort, the following elements of a strategic planning system can be integrated and institutionalized as a strategic planning system: (1) an effective policy-making body; (2) a formal or informal cabinet of managers; (3) an agreed-upon, vibrant, and inspiring mission statement; (4) policy objectives that are widely supported; (5) periodic situation analyses, such as SWOT exercises; (6) periodic strategic issue identification exercises; (7) strategic issue management practices, such as the use of task forces and preparation of option papers and decision packages; (8) more formal multicriteria proposal evaluation procedures; and (9) action planning procedures and protocols that assure strategies are implemented and evaluated.

Summary

This chapter has outlined an eight-step process for promoting strategic thinking and acting in nonprofit organizations. The steps are (1) development of an initial agreement concerning the strategic planning effort (or the "plan for planning"), (2) identification of mandates, (3) clarification of mission and values, (4) assessment of the external environment, (5) assessment of the internal environment, (6) identification of strategic issues, (7) development of strategy, and (8) preparation of a description of the organization in the future (or its "vision of success"). Following these eight steps come actions, results, and evaluation—all of which should emerge as well in each step of the process. Furthermore, while the process is presented here in a linear, sequential fashion, typically it proceeds iteratively, as groups continuously rethink connections among the various elements in the process on their way to formulation of effective strategies.

Strategic planning is a management innovation that is likely to persist because, unlike many other recent innovations, it accepts and builds on the nature of *political* decision making. The raising and resolution of important issues is the heart of political decision making, just as it is the heart of strategic planning. Strategic planning seeks to improve on the rawest forms of political decision making, however, by assuring that issues are raised and resolved in ways that benefit the nonprofit organization and its key stakeholders. The prospects may thereby be enhanced for improved organizational achievement and pursuit of the public purposes that must justify the existence of any nonprofit organization.

References

Barry, B. W. *Strategic Planning Workbook for Nonprofit Organizations.* St. Paul, Minn.: Amherst H. Wilder Foundation, 1986.

Bolman, L. G., and Deal, T. *Reframing Organizations: Artistry, Choice, and Leadership.* San Francisco, Calif.: Jossey-Bass, 1991.

Bryant, J. *Problem Management.* New York: Wiley, 1989.

Bryson, J. M. *Strategic Planning for Public and Nonprofit Organizations: A Guide to Strengthening and Sustaining Organizational Achievement.* San Francisco, Calif.: Jossey-Bass, 1988.

Bryson, J. M., and Crosby, B. C. "The Design and Use of Strategic Planning Arenas." *Planning Outlook,* 1989, *32*(1), 5–13.

Bryson, J. M., and Crosby, B. C. *Leadership for the Common Good.* San Francisco, Calif.: Jossey-Bass, 1992.

Bryson, J. M., and Einsweiler, R. C. (eds.). *Strategic Planning — Threats and Opportunities for Planners.* Chicago: Planners Press, 1988.

Bryson, J. M., and Roering, W. D. "Initiation of Strategic Planning by Governments." *Public Administration Review,* 1988, *48,* 995–1004.

Carver, J. *Boards That Make a Difference: A New Design for Leadership in Nonprofit and Public Organizations.* San Francisco, Calif.: Jossey-Bass, 1990.

Covey, S. *Principle-Centered Leadership.* New York: Summit Books, 1991.

de Bono, E. *Six Thinking Hats.* Boston, Mass.: Little, Brown, 1985.

Dutton, J. "The Making of Organizational Opportunities," forthcoming.

Dutton, J., and Dukerich, J. "Keeping an Eye on the Mirror." *Academy of Management Journal,* 1991, *34*(3), 517–554.

Eden, C. "Using Cognitive Mapping for Strategic Options Development and Analysis." In J. Rosenhead (ed.), *Rational Analysis for a Problematic World.* New York: Wiley, 1989.

Eden, C., and Huxham, C. "Action-Oriented Strategic Management." *Journal of the Operational Research Society,* 1986, *39*(10), 889–899.

Flynn, N. "Performance Measurement in Public Sector Services." *Policy and Politics,* 1986, *14*(3), 389–404.

Frame, J. D. *Managing Projects in Organizations: How to Make the Best Use of Time, Techniques, and People.* San Francisco, Calif.: Jossey-Bass, 1987.

Friend, J. K., and Hickling, A. *Planning Under Pressure: The Strategic Choice Approach.* Oxford, England: Pergamon, 1987.

Jackson, S., and Dutton, J. "Discerning Threats and Opportunities." *Administrative Science Quarterly,* 1987, *33,* 370–387.

Kouzes, J. M., and Posner, B. Z. *The Leadership Challenge: How to Get Extraordinary Things Done in Organizations.* San Francisco, Calif.: Jossey-Bass, 1987.

Linneman, R. E., and Klein, H. E. "The Use of Multiple Scenarios by U.S. Industrial Companies: A Comparison Study, 1977–1988." *Long-Range Planning,* 1983, *16*(6), 94–101.

Locke, E. A., Shaw, K. N., Saari, L. M., and Latham, G. P. "Goal Setting and Task Performance, 1969–1980." *Psychological Bulletin,* 1981, *90,* 125–152.

May, R. *Love and Will.* New York: Norton, 1969.

Morrissey, G. L., Below, P. J., and Acomb, B. L. *The Executive Guide to Operational Planning.* San Francisco, Calif.: Jossey-Bass, 1987.

Nelson, B., and Hummer, A. "The Origins of the YWCA's Anti-Racism Campaign." Minneapolis, Minn.: Center on Women and Public Policy, Hubert H. Humphrey Institute of Public Affairs, University of Minnesota, 1989.

Nutt, P. C., and Backoff, R. W. *Strategic Management for Public and Third-Sector Organizations: A Handbook for Leaders.* San Francisco, Calif.: Jossey-Bass, 1992.

Olsen, J. B., and Eadie, D. C. *The Game Plan: Governance with Foresight.* Washington, D.C.: Council of State Planning Agencies, 1982.

Ouchi, W. *Theory Z: How American Business Can Meet the Japanese Challenge.* Reading, Mass.: Addison-Wesley, 1981.

Patton, M. Q. *Utilization-Focused Evaluation.* (2nd ed.) Newbury Park, Calif.: Sage, 1986.

Peters, T. J., and Waterman, R. H., Jr. *In Search of Excellence: Lessons from America's Best-Run Companies.* New York: HarperCollins, 1982.

Pfeffer, J., and Salancik, G. *The External Control of Organizations: A Resource Dependence Perspective.* New York: HarperCollins, 1978.

Pfeiffer, J. W., Goodstein, L. D., and Nolen, T. M. *Applied Strategic Planning: A How to Do It Guide.* San Diego, Calif.: University Associates, 1986.

Pflaum, A., and Delmont, T. "External Scanning: A Tool for Planners." *Journal of the American Planning Association,* 1987, *53*(1), 56–67.

Rosenhead, J. (ed.) *Rational Analysis for a Problematic World.* New York: Wiley, 1989.

Stone, M. M., and Brush, C. G. "Planning in Nonprofit Organizations and Entrepreneurial Firms: An Assessment of Empirical Research and a New Interpretation." Paper presented at the Academy of Management Meetings, Las Vegas, Nev., Aug. 1992.

Taylor, B. "Strategic Planning—Which Style Do You Need?" *Long-Range Planning,* 1984, *17,* 51–62.

Thompson, J. D. *Organizations in Action.* New York: McGraw-Hill, 1967.

Tita, M. A., and Allio, R. J. "3M's Strategy System—Planning in an Innovative Organization." *Planning Review,* 1984, *12*(5), 10–15.

Wildavsky, A. *Speaking Truth to Power.* Boston, Mass.: Little, Brown, 1979.

9

Ethics in Nonprofit Management: Creating a Culture of Integrity

Thomas H. Jeavons

In the mid-1970s in the aftermath of the Watergate scandal there was a surge of interest in "professional ethics." This was particularly true for lawyers, but it involved other professionals as well. (It should be recalled that almost all those convicted of crimes in the Watergate scandal were lawyers, some from the most prestigious law schools.) There was also some skepticism in the larger public at the time, however, about how sincere this new interest in ethics was.

This skepticism was perhaps best captured in a Doonesbury comic strip of that era. The first frame showed a professor at the front of a class making some basic point about ethical judgment, followed by a student raising his hand. The next frame showed the professor calling on the student, who asks, "Should we be taking notes? Is this going to be on the exam?"

In a pointed, albeit humorous way this comic strip highlights two key assumptions about ethics and the consideration of ethical matters that are unfortunately too often operative among professionals (and aspiring professionals) of all types. The first is the belief that careful, skilled thinking about these matters, ethical matters, is more the business of philosophers and academics than practitioners. In the imagery and language of the cartoon, ethical questions are not seen as the "important stuff" on which we should take notes and expect to be tested in professional schools — which is to say, they are not matters we assume to be essential concerns in professional practice.

The second assumption is found among many who believe, even while they admit the importance of ethical questions and issues, that these questions and issues may be isolated and dealt with as discrete concerns in professional practice, apart from others. This perspective may be exemplified in the tendency to have one course on ethics in a professional program, or to have one or two sessions in courses on other subjects take up ethical issues — rather than work to ensure that the ethical implications of all subjects and of every aspect of professional practice are dealt with wherever they might arise in a professional education.

I lift up these two assumptions at the beginning of this chapter on ethics in nonprofit management because they are both, I believe, false; and they both certainly undermine the maintenance of appropriate ethical standards and behavior in the management and operation of nonprofit organizations. (Indeed, this is true for organizations of any kind.)

The analysis that follows begins, in fact, with two quite opposite assumptions. The first is that reflecting critically and actively on ethical issues is an obligation of every "professional," including nonprofit managers. The capacity for and inclination to socially responsive, historically grounded, critical, ethical judgment should be one of the outcomes of any sound professional education program, and one of the capacities of a "professional" as "reflective practitioner" (Schön, 1983, 1987). The second is that a concern for the ethical content or implications of one's decisions and actions is salient in every aspect of professional practice and — in the context of the considerations of this volume — in relation to every facet of the life of nonprofit organizations.

Indeed, I will argue here, as the title for this chapter implies, that we are most likely to see consistently ethical behavior among nonprofit managers and organizations only where an emphasis on ethical values and behavior is deeply embedded in the cultures of these organizations. So, building and reinforcing that kind of organizational culture becomes a primary responsibility for those concerned that ethical practice be a hallmark of all the functions, including the management, of their organization.

An Overview of This Chapter

The argument that will be proffered and supported in this chapter claims first that ethical behavior in and by nonprofit organizations cannot be assured simply by employing encouraging rhetoric about ethics, nor just be establishing specific rules for ethical behavior. This point can be readily demonstrated by examining the historical record and the common experience of most managers and organizational analysts. Most people with any significant experience in organizational life know there is often a marked disparity between rhetoric and practice in organizational behavior. They also know that rules (about ethics and other matters) can be, and frequently are, followed "in the letter" while being totally ignored or even violated "in the spirit."

Thus, the claim to be argued here is that ethical behavior will be assured only by creating an organizational culture where key ethical ideals and expectations are incorporated in the "core values" (Schein, 1985) of an organization and thus permeate its operations. This process will almost certainly involve the use of appropriate rhetoric about values. More important, though, it must involve modeling of the key values in the behavior of key individuals in an organization, and reinforcement of those values through the organization's structures and reward systems.

Additionally, I will argue that because of the unique historical and societal dimensions of their character and function, expectations about what constitutes ethical behavior in and by nonprofit, and especially by philanthropic, organizations differ from expectations placed on other organizations. Specifically, the question of trustworthiness goes to the core of the reason for the existence of these organizations and their ability to satisfy public expectations. The very existence of most nonprofit organizations, their capacity to garner resources — and so to survive and carry out their missions — depends on their moral standing and integrity (see Hansmann, 1987; Douglas, 1987; Ostrander and Schervish, 1990; and Jeavons, 1992a).

There exists in this context, I would contend, an *implicit social contract* undergirding the presence and function of private nonprofit, especially philanthropic, organizations in our society. These organizations are given a special standing, and even certain legal advantages over other private organizations, on the basis of the promise that they will serve the public good. The public expects these organizations to be motivated by and adhere to such a commitment in their performance. The public also expects that these organizations will honor a set of widely accepted moral and humanitarian values — deriving from these organization's historical and philosophical roots — and that they will (virtually) never act in a self-serving manner.

Accordingly, if the managers of nonprofit, especially philanthropic, organizations wish to ensure the ethical behavior of their organizations, staffs, and themselves, they need to work at creating and maintaining organizational cultures that accept and honor in practice (as fundamental) a set of "core values" that are in continuity with the historic philosophical and religious roots of the voluntary sector and that meet the public's current expectations. In this context we need to see that trust is the essential lifeblood of the nonprofit sector — trust that nonprofits will fulfill this implicit social contract. And to ensure that this trust is sustained, I will argue, five core values must permeate these organizations, shaping their ethics. These values are integrity, openness, accountability, service, and charity (in the original sense of that term).

To understand this argument we must begin by considering what ethics are and are not. We will look at a number of definitions of *ethics,* with a particular eye toward the origins, character, and purposes of ethical norms or standards. Then we need to examine more closely the kinds of ethical norms that are usually applied to nonprofit and philanthropic organizations in American culture, the factors that have shaped these norms, and the purposes they serve.

Having formed a well-grounded perspective on the norms or standards for ethical behavior in and by nonprofit organizations, we next need to ask how such behavior can be assured. What is the relationship between values and behavior? Assuming that an organization does ascribe to the "right" values, how can one help ensure that those values are captured and reflected in all aspects of its operations, by all its members?

In essence, this is to ask about the integrity of an organization; about how to make certain that it is—and will continue to be—what it claims to be. Specifically, how can one make certain that there will be continuity between the values an organization claims to represent and the purposes it says it intends to serve, on the one hand, and its actual operation, on the other? Finally, I want to conclude this chapter with some specific suggestions about how a "culture of integrity" can be created and sustained in nonprofit organizations—for assuming that nonprofit organizations intend to act ethically, it is only by creating and sustaining such an organizational culture that this intention is likely to be fulfilled in consistently ethical behavior. Let us begin, then, by examining the nature of "ethics" and "ethical behavior."

What Are "Ethics"?

As a field of study or discipline, "ethics" refers to "the study of moral topics, including moral issues, moral responsibilities, and moral ideals of character."* In a normative sense, "ethics" may be seen simply to refer to "justified moral standards"—which is to say, not just what people do believe about how they should act, but what they *should* believe. As this chapter is directed more to practitioners of management and other "lay people" than to scholars and philosophers, however, we probably need to think more about more common uses of the term *ethics*.

Webster's New World Dictionary of the American Language (2nd College Edition, 1970) defines ethics as "the system or code of morals of a particular person, religion, group, profession, etc." The *Oxford English Dictionary* (Compact Edition, 1971) notes the derivation of the word *ethics* from the Greek term *ethos,* meaning "custom, usage, manner or habit," and goes on to offer the following definitions (for *ethics*): "the moral principles by which a person is guided" and "the rules of conduct recognized in certain associations or departments of human life." The derivation of the term and the differences we see in these common definitions highlight two facets of the origins and purposes of ethics that we might examine.

*Note: I am indebted for this definition, and for much of the formulation of the material that follows on ethical theory, to Mike W. Martin, professor of philosophy at Chapman University. His critical reading of an early draft of this chapter was immensely helpful.

One set of issues to be considered has to do with the derivations of and justifications for specific ethical systems or values. To explore these topics and the types of ethical theories—rights ethics, duty ethics, utilitarianism, virtue ethics—is not useful here as it would take us far from my intended focus on foundational questions about *applied* issues in the ethics of nonprofit management. An exploration of the foundations of moral theory, while potentially fascinating, is simply too complex and time-consuming to pursue here.

On the other hand, the etymology and definitions of *ethics* also remind us that much of what we typically think about as ethical principles or judgments, especially when our concern is application and practice, are not derived in any case from philosophical absolutes, but rather from the reference point of social or community standards. To play with the words, *ethics* (as we commonly use the term) may be as much a matter of "ethos"—what is expected or socially acceptable, what is customary—as a matter of indisputable moral vision. Of course, these two aspects of ethics are often intertwined; what a particular community views as ethically acceptable will often be determined by what its members believe that some source of absolute moral authority (God, perhaps) requires.

Understanding this about the origins and meaning of "ethics" makes it clear that when we raise and examine questions about ethics—ethics generally, professional ethics, the ethics of nonprofit managers, or the ethics of the behavior of nonprofit organizations—there are two reference points we need always to bear in mind in our considerations: one a point of moral absolutes, and another of community standard and expectations. For our purposes, when we think about the ethics of nonprofit organizations and their management, I believe we should be asking two kinds of questions: First, What are we morally obligated to do and not do? Second, What does society require or expect of us? Moreover, ethical questions should be considered in that order, giving preference to moral obligations over customary ones.

Professional Ethics

If ethics are, as one volume observes, "a set of rules that apply to human beings over the totality of their interrelationships with one another, and that take precedence over all other rules" (Gellerman, Frankel, and Ladenson, 1990, p. 41), then we need to ask, How are such rules more specifically defined by and applied to particular spheres of professional activity?

Some scholars claim that one of the elements that define a "profession" (as opposed to other kinds of work) is that every specific profession involves a commitment to a publicly articulated set of goals and *social and societal purposes* for that profession's practice, and to standards for and approaches to that practice, which should be shared by all its practitioners. It is because they meet societal needs with special expertise, it is argued, that professions are given certain privileges—like self-regulation, control over standards for training and entry into practice, and (thus) control over their own markets and competition. These prerogatives are provided in exchange for the profession's commitment (implicit, at least) to meet public needs and serve the public good (see Larson, 1977; Bellah and others, 1985; and Van Til, 1988). Interestingly, here we have another implicit social contract. A classic paradigm for this is the medical profession and doctors with their Hippocratic Oath and the other specific expectations about their obligations to society in the provision of medical care.

Following this line of reasoning, one commentator on "professional values" argues that in our culture "professionals are viewed as morally committed to pursuing the dominant value that defines the goals of their professional practice. . . . They are expected to pursue such goals on a social as well as individual level. . . . And they are expected to do so even when self-interest may have to be sacrificed in that pursuit" (Alan Goldman, cited in Gellerman, Frankel, Ladenson, 1990, p. 5).

Now it may not be immediately clear what "the dominant value" that defines the goals of the practice of management generally is (or should be). Still, it can be argued that the dominant value that should define the practice of management of nonprofit, especially philanthropic, organizations is "morally responsible service." Such organizations were or are usually created specifically to provide services, and generally (as I will soon show) for situations where the establishment of trust in the integrity and commitment of the service-delivering agency is a paramount concern.

In sum, the claim being made here is that professional ethics for nonprofit management and in the operation of nonprofit agencies require the articulation and internalization of standards for behavior and ways of being for those agencies and their managers that adequately reflect the sector's origins in the moral, often religious, spheres of our culture, and meet the current, morally justifiable expectations of our society. Before moving on to look closely at those origins and expectations and the standards for behavior they necessitate, however, I want to note briefly how this perspective contrasts with some more general current views of the purposes of professional ethics— because those current views are especially dangerous if they are adopted in the nonprofit world.

Misunderstanding Professional Ethics

One commonly articulated view of the rationale and purposes for ethical behavior in professional practice is that it is simply "good for business." I would not dispute this, and believe it can be demonstrated that it is (generally) true, as Washington claimed, that "honesty [and other ethical behavior] is the best policy." What is clear, however, is that this utilitarian perspective does not provide an adequate underpinning for behaving ethically. Yet, this is often the only, or at least the most prominent rationale or motivation given for the development and practice of "sound business ethics."

One advertisement appearing regularly over the last year for a prestigious business school's seminars on ethics says that the reasons for learning—and, presumably, practicing—"good business ethics" is to "build stable, profitable relationships, strengthen employee loyalty . . . [and] avoid litigation." One would hope that all these results would ensue for the ethical organization, but we need to ask, How well does the focus on these goals hold up as the rationale or motivation for behaving ethically?

What if lying about something that has recently occurred is more likely to help one's firm avoid litigation than telling the truth? Is lying acceptable then? What if misusing funds to provide extra perquisites for employees is more effective in gaining their loyalty than using funds properly? What if there are cases where "more stable, profitable relationships" can be better secured through bribery or deceit than through honest competition? The point to recognize here is that when commitments to or judgments about ethical behavior are based primarily on utilitarian, cost/benefit calculations, they will be weak indeed.

It is easy to fall into the trap of arguing for the practical benefits of ethical behavior as the primary justification for adhering to ethical standards. But, as the examples just cited point out, such a justification is easily undermined. Ironically it is most easily undermined in just those situations where sound ethical choices may be most difficult to discern and most important to make.

One advantage nonprofit, especially philanthropic, organizations have in this sphere is that they can—and should—root their judgments about and commitments to ethical behavior in the moral traditions from which the nonprofit sector sprang. As one recent article reminds us, "Institutions that enunciate, transmit, and defend ethical values fall within the boundaries of [the nonprofit] sector. Educational, religious, and advocacy organizations constitute a majority of [the] membership and have shaped the sector itself" (Mason, 1992a). Moreover, as the recent INDEPENDENT SECTOR monograph *Ethics and the Nation's Voluntary and Philanthropic Community* notes, "Those who presume to serve the public good assume a public trust" (1991, p. 1).

Understanding, then, that ethical judgments must be based on firmer moral and social considerations, let us look more closely at the particular ethical values—and the character of the public trust—that can and should shape the ethical perspectives of nonprofit managers, whatever the practical advantages (or disadvantages) of ethical behavior may be.

Core Values and Their Origins in the Voluntary Sector

Many explanations have been offered for the origins and use of the nonprofit organizational form. Scholars differ as to which explanations are most adequate or serviceable. (For a very useful discussion of this question see Hansmann, 1987, or Van Til, 1988.) The one of these explanations that rings truest to many people's experience, however, revolves around what economists and some organizational theorists call "contract failure" and an "agency problem." Simply put, this suggests that private nonprofits are created or exist to provide services, first, where governments cannot or will not provide the service for some reason, and then, where those who want a service provided either (a) will not be in a position to see that what they want to have done or to have happen will occur, or (b), because of the nature of the service to be provided, are unable to judge the quality of that service. In such circumstances, it is argued, people create or use private nonprofit — rather than for-profit — organizations because they feel nonprofit organizations will have less incentive to cheat consumers and supporters. That is, they believe this type of organization is less likely to provide lesser amounts or lower quality of services because its board and managers have little opportunity to enrich themselves by that behavior.

It is also important to recognize that in these cases the people paying for the services provided are often *not* the consumers of the services. Rather they may be donors. This being the case, they want to work through an organization that, as an "agent," they can expect to provide a service for someone else as they, the donors, would themselves provide it if they could. Consequently, they seek an agent they believe to be highly committed to providing that service for others. Crassly put, they want an agent that is involved "for the cause," not "for the money."

A quick analysis of both these situations tells us what is likely to be the most important and desirable ethical quality of nonprofit organizations, at least in the public's eyes. In these circumstances trust is a key consideration. That being so, we can project what kinds of operational ethical values will need to be evident in organizations that have earned and deserve the public's trust. Among the most central, as I have already mentioned, are integrity, openness, accountability, and service.

Also on that earlier list, though, is "charity," in the original sense of the term — from the Latin *caritas*. Obviously there are some nonprofit organizations that would not be expected to be "charitable" as that word is usually used — "generous" or "eleemosynary." Most people do not expect these to be characteristics of trade associations, for example. Still, the majority of those organizations that populate the nonprofit or voluntary sector are service providers dependent in some way on the philanthropic traditions and practices of our society. They are expected in that context to be "caring" organizations, willing to put the public good and the welfare of others above their own gain and comfort.

It is important to understand how this last expectation is a *moral* quality — ascribed to such organizations and assumed by them as a result of their historical and sociological functions in our society. The fact is nonprofit philanthropic and service organizations occupy a distinctive place in American society because of their origins — largely in religious or other idealistic voluntary associations — and because they have traditionally been vehicles for preserving, transmitting, or promoting social values. As a result of

both their historical development and their contemporary roles, these organizations carry much of the burden of mediating civic, moral, and spiritual
values in the public realm and from one generation to the next (Curti, 1958;
Parsons, 1960). In this light they are objects of special moral expectations
that they will be charitable, caring organizations.

There are, thus, ethical qualities or values that are essential in the
character and behavior of nonprofit, especially philanthropic, organizations.
They are expected to be — and should be — organizations that demonstrate
integrity, openness, accountability, service, and a caring demeanor. And
what is required of managers of these organizations is that they give special
attention to seeing that these ethical values are reflected in every aspect of
these organizations. This requires that the managers model ethical qualities
in their own behavior as well as articulate and foster them as ideals for others.
Considering more carefully the meaning of these values in organizational
behavior should allow us to see better how managers can undertake these
responsibilities and work toward creating a culture of integrity.

Ethical Management in Ethical Organizations

It will be useful at this point to consider each of the key ethical attributes
of nonprofit managers and their organizations more fully. In this process we
should undertake an analysis at two levels — the individual and the organizational — asking, for example, What does it mean for a manager to do his or
her work with integrity, and for an organization to operate with integrity?

It is important to say here that I cannot, in this section, try to present
an exhaustive analysis or numerous illustrations of how these ethical qualities would be evident in each of the many aspects of the operations and management of nonprofit organizations. Authors of other chapters in this volume
that address those different aspects of nonprofit management discuss ethical
questions and offer considerations of ethical issues specifically relevant to
different facets of the work of nonprofit organizations. At this point, my intention is to offer a broader context within which to think further in ethical
terms about the material presented in the other chapters. Ideally, the relationship between this chapter, focused specifically on ethics, and those chapters addressing various facets of nonprofit management, should constitute
a dialogue about ethical concerns.

Integrity

It may be most useful to describe integrity as "honesty writ large." That is
to say, integrity has to do with continuity between appearance and reality,
between intention and action, between promise and performance, in every
aspect of a person's or an organization's existence. If trust is the most crucial quality in the operation of nonprofit organizations, if these organizations being "trustworthy" is one of the most basic expectations the public

holds for them, then "integrity" in this sense becomes a fundamental ethical characteristic they need to possess.

At the organizational level, integrity is most obviously demonstrated to be present or absent by comparing an organization's own literature — fundraising materials, reports, statements of missions and values — with its actual program priorities and performance. For instance, an organization that claims to be in existence to serve the poor, but regularly spends large amounts of resources on enlarging itself, enhancing its own image before the public, or improving the comfort or security levels of its staff must be suspect. So, too, we should wonder about educational institutions that say they are devoted to providing the best education possible to students, but spend more of their resources on things intended to improve their own status — for example, image enhancing athletics, high-profile research projects, or "star" faculty members — rather than on facilities and activities for teaching and learning.

This is not to say that staff in such organizations should not have reasonable salaries and benefits; that being in the public eye for fundraising purposes is not important to support the work to be done; or that an organization might not be able to improve its service delivery by growing. But it is to say that a careful examination of budgets, allocations of staff time, and the application of other resources too often show that nonprofit and philanthropic organizations that were created and claim to be serving the public good are giving more attention to caring for and improving themselves than others. Moreover, the public is sensitive to these issues. If we need proof of this, we would do well to recall the controversies involving United Way of America or some television ministries in the late 1980s and early 1990s.

In the late 1980s, at a time when it might even have been said that greed was a socially acceptable value, the PTL Ministries, a nonprofit corporation involving an evangelical Christian broadcasting operation and theme park, became embroiled in an enormous controversy. While the initial problems related to the sexual indiscretions of the organization's head, Jim Bakker, what finally brought the wrath of the public (and the IRS) down on the operation was the wanton waste, misdirection, and misuse of donated funds. The wildly excessive salaries and opulent life-style of Jim Bakker and his wife Tammy Faye, supported by donations from people who thought they were giving to the good works of a ministry, were so embarrassing as to damage the credibility and fundraising efforts of a wide range of legitimate Christian ministries, simply through guilt by association.

In an event even more injurious to the credibility of charities more generally, in the spring of 1992 it was revealed that the head of the United Way of America was receiving a salary of almost $500,000, traveling about the world first-class, and setting up subsidiary organizations run by his friends and relatives. When the millions of small donors to local United Ways found out that a portion of their gifts were going to support a lavish life-style for an executive of a charitable organization, most were again outraged. Despite the massive efforts of local United Ways to explain that only a tiny portion of income went to the national organization, which was a legally separate entity, the giving to local United Ways (and hence to their member agencies) in the following year fell significantly. Once more a great many ethical and efficient charitable organizations found themselves tarnished with guilt by association.

Dramatic disparities between the ethical or practical promise (implicit or explicit) and the performance of one charitable organization may precipitate difficulties for the entire nonprofit sector. As one economist studying the nonprofit sector has observed, "Whenever any nonprofit is found to have abused its trusted position, the reputation of trustworthy nonprofits also suffers. . . . Nonprofits that do not act opportunistically, as well as those who do, will find it increasingly difficult to obtain resources" (Weisbrod, 1988, p. 13).

A specific operational example of the kind of behavior that raises such issues about integrity can be drawn from a recently completed study of relief and development agencies (Jeavons, 1992b). One of the agencies studied engaged in practices that are not illegal, but would certainly cause questions in the minds of donors (and others)—if they became aware of them.

First, this agency sometimes uses what are called "representational" images in their fundraising materials. That is to say, a brochure will tell a story about a family or person in need, often desperate need, and include pictures of their plight that are quite striking. It turns out, though, that sometimes this story is actually a composite of stories of a number of people in the impoverished area, put together for maximum effect; or the pictures are not of the particular persons or family mentioned at all, but rather are the most moving pictures the agency could find. Now, the needs are real, and the stories and pictures convey the needs quite effectively; but this approach lacks integrity—the stories and pictures finally are not true.

Some argue that this is morally wrong because, simply enough, it is a form of dishonesty, regardless of the fact that it raises money for a good purpose. Even those within this organization admitted that if donors became aware of this practice there could be problems. The donors' expectations of high moral standards for such an organization would be violated.

Second, this same agency often makes general appeals by producing brochures featuring projects for which it can most easily raise money, with the brochures giving the strong impression the money raised will go to those particular projects. But in fact those projects are fully funded from other sources, and the donations are used for other purposes. Again, this is done in a way that ensures there is no illegality, but neither is there any integrity. One is left to wonder, in such an organizational climate, what other normal ethical standards are allowed to slide, and how well are the funds that are raised being used?

If one is inclined to think that these kinds of decisions can be seen purely as matters of strategic operational choice, one needs to see the contrast between this organization and other relief and development agencies studied. In a number of the others there are specific rules against using "representational images," and policies that require donors to be consulted before their gifts are used for projects other than the ones for which they were solicited. The managers in those agencies described their standards and policies as points of pride, as conscious choices made to uphold the ethical character of their organizations and their work. And those managers pointed out that it was vital to maintain the highest moral standards in all facets of their operations, lest the willingness to compromise at one point become the beginning of a lowering of standards more generally. This, in fact, points us back to examining the meaning of integrity at the individual level for managers and management.

"Integrity" may have different meanings for different individuals, but in the context of professional ethics it must mean doing one's job as honestly and as fully in adherence to one's professed principles as possible. Careful observers of organizational behavior have noted that managers and leaders in organizations, or particular parts of organizations, tend to have a significant effect in setting behavioral standards, either as a matter of personal influence, or because of their control of reward systems, or for both reasons. The manager who wants her or his employees to deal honestly with others had better deal honestly with them, and, further, had better reward honesty and discourage any dishonesty. If the manager is willing to cut corners, tell "little" lies, or act in self-serving ways, it becomes more likely the employees too will see this as acceptable behavior, at least within the work setting. So the manager who wants the organization she or he oversees to be known for its integrity, and to be trustworthy, must begin by being completely trustworthy in her or his dealings with all those who are part of the organization, and make it clear that similar behavior is expected of all those people.

Put more simply, integrity must be one of the hallmarks of nonprofit management. It is an ethical obligation, both as a matter of morality, because it is right, and as a matter of societal necessity, because the public expects nonprofit organizations to do these things. Failing to embody and uphold the highest standards for personal and organizational integrity can have enormous consequences for nonprofit managers and their agencies or institutions.

Openness

It would be inaccurate to call the quality of openness a "moral" value, at least within the context of the most common value systems of American culture. So the claim to be made about openness as an ethical value is not based so much on moral absolutes — as may be the case for integrity — as on social values and expectations. In this context, we might think of openness as a "derivative virtue."

In any case, in the history and practice of philanthropy in America, for an organization or individual to try to hide their philanthropic endeavors from public view has almost always been to raise profound skepticism about the motivation for and character of those endeavors. In colloquial terms, the public's attitude here has been, "If they are really doing good, why would they be reluctant (or embarrassed) to have us see what they are doing?"

This is especially true for organizations. It is possible to put forth a reasonable argument, even one based on religious grounds (see Matthew 6:2–4 or the Mishneh Torah), for individuals "doing good works" anonymously or in secret. However, for organizations that operate in the public sphere, especially in areas of service or advocacy that can have an impact on public policy or community life, it is hard to argue convincingly for secrecy. Indeed, it may be crucial for these organizations to conduct their business in a way that is open to public scrutiny.

One reason for this is that, if nothing else, openness undergirds other ethical behavior. The organization that does operate openly cannot afford to cut other ethical corners. If one looks at the case just considered of the relief and development agencies, it is clear that the one that engaged in questionable tactics would not be able to operate in this way and retain its donor base if its practices were open to the scrutiny of outsiders.

Another reason for this is historical. There have long been critical questions raised about the roles philanthropic and service organizations play in shaping people's and communities' lives. (See, for instance, Griffin, 1957, or Nielsen, 1985.) This is, in part, because some of these organizations appear to have had ulterior motives — for example, intentions of "social control" or protection of the interests of the privileged, embedded in their work. It is clear, for instance, that some of the impetus for legislation regulating the operation of foundations (in 1969) came from supposedly philanthropic entities being formed and using their tax-exempt status as a way to protect family fortunes from taxation while still controlling family businesses (Bremner, 1988). And more recent scandals in the conduct of nonprofit organizations reinforce the case to be made for their being subject to public scrutiny.

In addition, from the point of view of those who are concerned about the continuing vitality of nonprofit organizations and who recognize that maintaining a climate of trust is essential to that vitality, we should see that operating openly is one of the best ways to build trust. Organizations that wish to engage people's support and good faith can find no better way to do so than to do good works well, and then welcome the inquiries and inspection of anyone interested in their methods.

What is more, the same kind of logic applies to those who would lead these organizations, in terms of their leadership and management style. In the effort to build the support and commitment of staff, volunteers, and donors, a manager's willingness to talk openly and honestly about rationales for programs, the reasons for and ways in which decisions are made, and approaches to problem solving can be invaluable. Additionally, many nonprofits (as voluntary associations) come out of a rich populist democratic tradition in American culture, and it can be argued that they really ought to be operated in an open and democratic manner to represent and further that tradition—that this may be another significant part of their role and social obligation in this society. (For a very helpful discussion of these issues, see Van Til, 1988.)

All this is finally to say that openness in the business of decision making, in matters of raising and allocating resources, and, more generally, in the manner of their operation should be seen as a key ethical value for nonprofit organizations and their managers. Moreover, openness is, of course, a necessary prerequisite to accountability, which is the next core value we should examine.

Accountability

Not only is it important for nonprofit organizations, especially philanthropic ones, to be open about the things they do, and how and why they do them, it is also important that they be ready to explain and generally be accountable for their choices. This is an extension of the implicit social contract of privilege and trust these organizations enjoy in our society.

Looked at (again) in contractual terms, we should see that these organizations are granted the right to solicit tax-deductible contributions, or at least are granted tax-exempt status, on the assumption that they are serving the public good and will put their resources to work as directly and efficiently as possible on behalf of the causes or people they claim to serve. Indeed, the character and language of the legal discourse about these issues—employing terms like "public benefit" or "mutual benefit" organizations—confirms these assumptions (see, for example, Simon, 1987). From this implicit social contract derives a clear ethical obligation to perform according to promise and, as with all contracts, to be subject to evaluation and ready to answer for a failure to perform.

In accepting the privilege of tax exemption and the right to solicit tax-deductible contributions, the public benefit agencies and philanthropic organizations also accept an obligation to be ready to answer not only to their membership but to the broader public as well, for the way they use resources that would otherwise have gone into the public treasury. And while the level of public support is not nearly as great for "mutual benefit" organizations—which are exempt but cannot receive deductible contributions—their exempt status is based in part on the expectation that they will also, at the least, be answerable to their membership in pursuing the articulated mission of their organizations.

All of this is to say that in social and contractual terms, all nonprofit organizations have an ethical responsibility to be accountable to their supporters, their members, and their donors; and some, the public benefit organizations, have an even larger responsibility to be accountable to the broader public for the ways in which they undertake to fulfill their philanthropic purposes. We would do well to note here that a confirmation of the growing public expectations in this regard (and some organizations' recognition of those expectations) can be found in the growth in recent years of "watch-dog" groups like the National Charities Information Bureau, the Better Business Bureau's section on nonprofit organizations, and the Evangelical Council for Financial Accountability. In addition, more and more states are passing laws to mandate financial disclosure and regulate fundraising practices of nonprofits.

How does this obligation of accountability extend to nonprofit managers? In much the same way as the obligations of integrity and openness do. First, if this is a quality managers and leaders want to see reflected in their organization, it is one they had better model in their own behavior. It then becomes an expectation that they can articulate credibly to others.

Second, managers can establish this commitment most firmly by making sure they hold themselves accountable to their organization's board, and work to build a board that will hold them accountable for their performance. Much of the most useful recent literature on board/executive relationships has pointed out that a full and vital partnership between executives and managers is essential for there to be effective leadership in nonprofit organizations (Drucker, 1990; Herman and Heimovics, 1991; Middleton, 1987). Ironically, one of the things this may require of an executive is that he or she encourage (or even educate) a board to play a more active role in evaluating the manager's — and the organization's — performance. Yet in this way, if the board is representative of, or at least in touch with, the needs and feelings of the larger community, then the manager is soliciting oversight and feedback from those the organization should serve. And in this the manager is modeling a quality she or he should hope to encourage in all staff — constructive accountability and receptivity to constructive criticism.

Service

The grounds for the ethical obligation here are virtually identical with those for accountability. Nonprofit organizations, especially public benefit organizations, exist and are granted specific privileges (as noted above) with the explicit understanding that they are committed in some way to *serve* the public good. Those that are classified as "mutual benefit" organizations — which include trade associations, fraternal organizations, and such — are not beholden in the same way to serve "the public" in the broadest sense, but they are still certainly expected to serve their membership. The point being that service, service to people or service to a cause, is at the heart of the reason for being of all these organizations.

The social contract extended to these organizations assumes that they will primarily devote themselves to service. In operating under the privileges they have been granted, these organizations acknowledge their ethical obligation to be service oriented. Moreover, in accepting the support — membership dues, donations, volunteers' time — of people who sustain them, these organizations reinforce their ethical obligations in this regard.

This ethical obligation to service should be manifest in the conduct of managers in a number of ways. Many people now make a career of work in the nonprofit sector. We could not have a meaningful discussion, as we do in this book, of nonprofit management as a "profession" if people did not commit themselves to and build careers in this area. But while this creates the ground for our discussion of professional ethics, it also creates a context in which managers can easily work with as much concern for their own advancement as for the people or cause their organization is supposed to serve.

To say that nonprofit managers should make the ethical obligation of service a primary concern is to say that they must give precedence to fulfilling the mission of their organization over possibilities for advancing their own status and careers. This is *not* to say that managers are required to sacrifice themselves — their health, their basic financial security, or their personal well being — for the benefit of their organization. Nonprofit organizations, especially cause-oriented ones, are notorious for exploiting and burning out their staff in the name of noble ideals (see Greene, 1991). Rather it is to say that the undergirding values of the nonprofit sector are altruistic, and while it is fine to be concerned for one's own career and fulfillment in one's work in nonprofit organizations, it is never acceptable for managers to advance themselves at the expense of the people and causes they have promised to serve.

In addition, observation suggests that the willingness of managers and leaders to see themselves as servants of others may be crucial to focusing others in an organization on that organization's commitment to service. Here the notion of "servant leadership" (Greenleaf, 1977) takes on both profound significance and immediate salience.

"Charity"

Finally, the last, but certainly not least important ethical obligation of nonprofit, especially philanthropic, organizations is to charity, in the original sense of the term. The word "charity" comes from the Latin *caritas*. This means more than giving to those in need. It originally was translated as "love"; not romantic love, but the love of neighbor and committed concern for the welfare of others illustrated in the parable of the Good Samaritan. It meant caring, putting the welfare of others on a par with one's own, being generous with one's own resources, not out of a sense of pity but out of a sense of relationship with and concern for others.

It can surely be argued that for nonprofit organizations an ethical obligation to "charity" in this sense derives from reciprocity. That is, many of these organizations depend on the generosity of their supporters for their existence, and ought to display such generosity themselves. Furthermore, at least in the case of the philanthropic organizations, the motivation of most of their supporters rests in no small way on a belief that these organizations are committed to caring for others. As I noted in earlier discussion of the origins of nonprofit organizations and the voluntary sector, the basis of much of these organizations' support is the expectation that they will be vehicles for building a more caring, more just society.

This expectation is manifest in an interesting range of phenomena. For instance, the preference of many clients and supporters of social service agencies for private nonprofit groups appears to be based on an assumption that they will provide services in a more personal, more caring way than a government agency. In industries where potential employees—for example, teachers, nurses, or social workers—might work for either government or private organizations, the preference of some for private nonprofits is often explained in terms of their expectation (or experience) of these organizations as more caring work environments. And this expectation is certainly confirmed by the public indignation that is often evident when an organization that is itself the beneficiary of charity turns around and acts in uncaring ways.

Once more, the way in which this expectation applies to the ethics of management seems obvious. An uncaring or mean-spirited manager can undermine the caring quality of an organization as fast as any negative influence imaginable. If one wants the participants in an organization to treat its clients (and one another) with love and respect, it is hardly likely that treating the participants coldly or with indifference will help that occur. Managers and leaders help set the tone of an organization's life—whether they intend to or not—and that tone is almost certainly going to be reflected in the way that organization—and all its staff—interacts at every level with its various constituencies.

Finally, we should see again, as we noted before, that the organizations of the nonprofit sector have been seen as having a special role in transmitting civic, social, and ethical values in our society from one generation to the next. If that is true, then we have yet another reason to be concerned that these organizations reflect the highest ideals for a caring society. And it is clear that some managers do see their responsibilities in this light. Discussing the kind of "witness" his organization wants to make to all those who deal with it, the president of a Christian relief and development agency said, "We have a major challenge in living up to our commitment [to care for people]; not just for children eight thousand miles away, but also for the people at our elbow" (Jeavons, 1992b, p. 265).

From Ideals to Operative Values

If we can agree, then, that these five concepts or ideals—integrity, openness, accountability, service, and charity—may describe key ethical qualities and obligations of nonprofit organizations and their managers, we are still left to ask how these ideals get translated into behavior.

At the individual level this may be easy. If one assumes that people can choose what to value and choose to embody those values in their actions, then for individuals, ethical behavior is a matter of choice and will. If this is the case, then the managers of nonprofit organizations simply need to choose to act with integrity, to be open and accountable in their work, to make commitment to service and charity a cornerstone for their decision making and interaction with others. They need to do these things because they are the right things to do; because that is what the public that supports (or can harm) their organization expects (or even demands) of them; and because the failure to uphold these obligations can have very significant negative consequences for their organizations and others. However, this still leaves open the question of how these ethical ideals become the operational values of an organization as a whole.

At this point we need to turn to the work that has been done over the last several years on "organizational culture." This field offers some valuable insights to our discussion. In particular, I want to draw heavily on the careful research and analysis of Edgar Schein in his book, *Organizational Culture and Leadership* (1985).

Much of the thinking about organizational culture has tended to focus, often somewhat shallowly, on "rites and rituals" of organizational life (see Deal and Kennedy, 1982; Peters and Waterman, 1982). Schein takes a different tack, arguing that an excessive focus on what he calls "the manifestations of culture" will obscure the fact that very similar rituals, conventions, or regular practices in various companies are undertaken for very different reasons. Thus, he claims, to understand organizational culture one must focus on the essential values these visible practices are meant to express. These values are "the substance of culture," in Schein's view.

There are in fact, Schein suggests, some values that represent the basic assumptions of a group of people—as, for instance, the membership of an organization—about the way the world is and how they, as a group, can function most successfully in it. These "core values" will shape the organization's behavior, not only by dictating what are right or acceptable responses to different kinds of situations but also by shaping the way those situations are perceived, by influencing what people see as important or unimportant information. Note that these ideas are reinforced by other scholars of organizations who argue that the most effective (and "unobtrusive") controls on the behavior of individuals in organizations may be achieved by shaping (or selecting people for) their basic "premises" about organizational or professional goals and practices (Perrow, 1986).

In this vein, Schein argues that leaders or managers can shape the direction, character, and operations of an organization most fundamentally and effectively by shaping the core values of the participants within it, or selecting new participants who share those values. Indeed, he claims that "there is a possibility—underemphasized in leadership research—that the only things of real importance that leaders do is to create and manage culture"

(1985, p. 2). The implications of this for people who are concerned about creating and maintaining organizations that behave ethically is obvious.

The connection between the ethical behavior of managers and the maintenance of the highest ethical standards of behavior by nonprofit organizations is manifest in those managers' capability to create a culture of integrity. Such a culture is one wherein the ethical ideals we have been discussing come to be accepted as "givens," and where the expectation that these ideals will be honored in the life and work of the organization permeates every participant's thinking. This can only occur where these ethical values are both articulated and modeled by those in positions of responsibility and leadership. In this way leaders and managers can shape the core values of an organization as a whole—and the individuals within it—around these ethical ideals.

One realm where such a dynamic may be observed most readily is in some religious service organizations that maintain a strong commitment to honoring very clear and sometimes constricting ethical ideals in their operations while still competing successfully for donor support in a highly competitive market. (For a more detailed description of these groups, see Jeavons, 1992b.)

Creating and Maintaining a Culture of Integrity

Finally we must see that clear, strong commitments to ethical ideals and behavior on the part of managers is a prerequisite to creating organizational cultures of integrity in nonprofits that will enable the organizations themselves to behave ethically. The importance of the example of leadership in this process cannot be overemphasized. As one commentator has observed, "CEOs . . . are ultimately accountable for [their] organization's ethical posture. . . . No organization can rise above the ethical level of its manager" (Mason, 1992b, p. 30).

Clearly, a manager who tells others about the importance of behaving ethically while behaving otherwise him- or herself is likely to have little positive influence on the organization. In fact, such a manager is likely to have a destructive influence, generating cynicism about and indifference to ethical concerns throughout the organization. And ultimately a manager whose own behavior models all the best of these values but who does not talk about their significance for the organization's life may still have a less positive influence than is needed.

Still, even where the management of an organization is consistent in both preaching and practicing the right values, more will probably be needed to create and sustain a culture of integrity. Organizational structures and reward systems must also support and encourage ethical behavior among all employees and volunteers. People's best intentions can be undermined or confused by organizational structures and processes that lead them to make choices that have negative ethical consequences.

One has to wonder, for instance, how often in nonprofit service agencies of various types reports of problems with their programs or relationships to their clients are stifled, or mistakes that could reveal ways to improve their service are never mentioned — because their staffs (and volunteers) are rewarded only for successes. As in many organizations that are hierarchically ordered, some nonprofits have a tendency to punish the bearers of bad news — and even reward the bearers of false news, so long as it is good. That tends to leave the organization less able to perform its mission and encourages employees to be less than honest about policies and programs that are failing. The leadership and management of nonprofit organizations must put in place systems that reward participants for honesty in every form, even forms that lead to the revelation of difficulties and deficiencies of the organization.

Similarly, one has to wonder about organizations that constantly emphasize short-term goals and focus solely on raw numbers (of dollars raised) in evaluating and rewarding development efforts, rather than asking questions about the quality of relationships with donors and other potentially positive effects of fundraising — such as its educational impact. Where these kinds of emphases and reward systems dominate, what is the impact on fundraisers' approaches to donors? Are they as honest and caring as they should be? What is the effect on individual and organizational reporting? Is the information about fundraising costs and results as complete and fully revealing as it should be?

These kinds of questions about the relationship between reward systems and structures and ethical behavior become even more complex, but no less important, when the behaviors at issue are not so simple — whether the truth is being told, for example — and when more subtle matters are involved — such as whether an organization is exploiting its employees or whether it is being true to the values it claims to represent.

By way of example, I recently worked with an organization claiming that one of its core values is that it "values people . . . [and] does not permit the accomplishment of goals at the expense of people." However, the organization has a structure for and approach to fundraising that emphasizes continually increasing the number of dollars raised and reducing administrative costs without consideration for the effects of such goals and policies on the relationships among staff or between donors and staff. Rewards in the organization — both raises and promotions — are distributed in a highly competitive system according to an assessment of performance based almost solely on quantitative measures. The outcome is that managers tend to exploit staff to achieve "more impressive" results, in direct contradiction to articulated values.

We could look as well at the case of United Way of America, mentioned earlier. How did an organization that was formed specifically to serve and support local United Ways and to promote a philosophy of service and giving come to be an example of self-serving, empire-building management practices? In part, at least, this seems to have been a result of organizational structures that insulated the management from the constituencies they were supposed to be serving, making them less aware of and accountable to the people the organization most needs to hear — that is, local United Ways' donors and clients.

In addition, the staff leadership seemed to spend most of its time with, and came to pattern itself after, business leaders — in the effort to gain support and resources from them. However, in the process, the United Way of America's executive leadership came to think like for-profit corporate executives, and appears to have come to believe that organizational growth was an end worth pursuing in itself for United Way of America. That particular strategies for attaining this end were undermining United Way's stated mission was overlooked. The result was a questionable use of donated funds, a clear abuse of public trust, and some erosion of the very spirit of giving and volunteering the organization was suppose to promote.

The point is that organizational structures and processes, and systems of rewards and disincentives, must be put in place to reinforce whatever rhetoric about ethical values an organization puts forth; and all this must be supported by the managers and leaders of the organization demonstrating personal commitment to those ethical values in their own behavior. The creation and maintenance of an organizational culture of integrity — one where integrity, openness, accountability, service, and charity consistently predominate; one that will lead to consistently ethical behavior on the part of nonprofit organizations — cannot be achieved absent these elements in an organization's life.

Summary

This chapter has demonstrated that ethical questions and issues must be primary concerns of *all* nonprofit managers, and that these issues and questions are salient in *all* aspects of the operation of nonprofit organizations. It has been argued that the ethical values most important for nonprofit managers and organizations to honor and exhibit center on the qualities of integrity, openness, accountability, service, and charity. We have seen how these particular ethical ideals are prescribed for nonprofit organizations by virtue of the distinctive history of the voluntary and nonprofit sector and the roles that these organizations play in American society. It is crucial that nonprofit organizations embody these ethical ideals in practice, both because ethical conduct and character is what moral duty requires — it is right — and because the public expects this of nonprofit organizations that say they are serving the public good. Only in this way can nonprofits fulfill the implicit social contract that supports their existence in our society.

It is important to note the educational implications of this. The last decade has seen the emergence of a number of programs around the country to educate people specifically for the work of managing nonprofit organizations. How much attention do these programs give to helping those people understand the special history and unique roles and expectations that should shape the way these organizations function and are managed? Some would say not enough. Those being educated to take on the responsibilities of management and leadership in nonprofit organizations must be taught sound approaches to, as well as the profound importance of, careful, responsible reflection on the ethical issues embedded in the various facets of the life of these organizations.

Managing an organization so that key ethical values will be consistently embodied in the organization's life requires more than rhetoric. It requires that managers demonstrate these values through their own conduct in their professional lives and service. It also requires that they create and maintain organizational structures and dynamics by which ethical conduct is rewarded and unethical conduct, in any manifestation, is discouraged. This has to involve an examination of all organizational systems and structures, from fundraising strategies to human resources policies to accounting systems, to ensure that those structures and systems do not generate pressures on personnel to ignore or violate the standards and assumptions for ethical behavior espoused in broader contexts. The chapters that follow will offer more illustrations of how ethical questions arise and come into play in specific facets of the work of nonprofit organizations and their managers.

The vital significance of these matters cannot be overemphasized. The lifeblood of the nonprofit sector is trust. Without trust on the part of donors, clients, and the larger public, nonprofit organizations will not be able to do the important work, to fulfill the crucial roles, which are theirs in our society. And nothing will erode this foundation of trust—for the good nonprofits as well as the bad—as quickly as new (or continuing) scandals involving unethical behavior by nonprofit organizations and their managers.

When the temptation to cut an ethical corner, tell a little lie, not bother with *full* disclosure, or let the ends justify the means arises, it is essential that the leadership and management of nonprofit organizations understand the implications of such actions and refuse to compromise on upholding rigorous ethical standards. We have to remember that, ultimately, noble ends are never served by ignoble means. We have to understand that inevitably our "ethical chickens will come home to roost."

Nonprofit, especially philanthropic, organizations have special responsibilities to serve the public good in our society; to do the right thing—for those in need and for important causes and those who care about them—because it is right. This represents the ethical and essential foundation of the nonprofit sector. Without this foundation intact, it is quite likely the sector will—and probably should—disappear from our society. Attention to ethical concerns must therefore continue to be a primary concern of every nonprofit manager.

References

Bellah, R. N., and others. *Habits of the Heart: Individualism and Commitment in American Life.* Berkeley, Calif.: University of California Press, 1985.

Bremner, R. H. *American Philanthropy.* (2nd ed.) Chicago: University of Chicago Press, 1988.

Curti, M. "American Philanthropy and the National Character." *American Quarterly,* 1958, *10,* 420–437.

Deal, T. E., and Kennedy, A. A. *Corporate Cultures: The Rites and Rituals of Corporate Life.* Reading, Mass.: Addison-Wesley, 1982.

Douglas, J. "Political Theories of Nonprofit Organization." In W. Powell (ed.), *The Nonprofit Sector: A Research Handbook.* New Haven, Conn.: Yale University Press, 1987.

Drucker, P. F. *Managing the Nonprofit Organization.* New York: HarperCollins, 1990.

Gellerman, W., Frankel, M. S., and Ladenson, R. (eds.). *Values and Ethics in Organization and Human Systems Development.* San Francisco, Calif.: Jossey-Bass, 1990.

Goldman, A. H. "Professional Values and the Problem of Regulation." *Business and Professional Ethics Journal,* n.d., *5*(2), 47–59.

Greene, S. G. "Poor Pay Threatens Leadership." *Chronicle of Philanthropy,* Mar. 26, 1991, pp. 28–31.

Greenleaf, R. K. *Servant Leadership.* Ramsey, N.J.: Paulist Press, 1977.

Griffin, C. S. "Religious Benevolence as Social Control, 1815–1860." *Mississippi Historical Review,* 1957, *44*(3), 423–444.

Hansmann, H. "Economic Theories of the Nonprofit Sector." In W. Powell (ed.), *The Nonprofit Sector: A Research Handbook.* New Haven, Conn.: Yale University Press, 1987.

Herman, R. D., and Heimovics, R. D. *Executive Leadership in Nonprofit Organizations: New Strategies for Shaping Executive-Board Dynamics.* San Francisco, Calif.: Jossey-Bass, 1991.

INDEPENDENT SECTOR. *Ethics and the Nation's Voluntary and Philanthropic Community.* Washington, D.C.: INDEPENDENT SECTOR, 1991.

Jeavons, T. H. "When Management Is the Message: Relating Values to Management Practice in Nonprofit Organizations." *Nonprofit Management & Leadership,* 1992a, *2*(4), 403–421.

Jeavons, T. H. *When the Bottom Line Is Faithfulness: An Examination of the Place, Functions and Management of Christian Service Organizations.* Ph.D. dissertation, Union Institute, 1992b.

Larson, M. S. *The Rise of Professionalism: A Sociological Analysis.* Berkeley, Calif.: University of California Press, 1977.

Mason, D. E. "Keepers of the Springs: Why Ethics Make Good Sense for Nonprofit Leaders." *Nonprofit World,* 1992a, *10*(2), 25–27.

Mason, D. E. "Ethics and the Nonprofit Leader." *Nonprofit World,* 1992b, *10*(4), 30–32.

Middleton, M. "Nonprofit Boards of Directors: Beyond the Governance Function." In W. Powell (ed.), *The Nonprofit Sector: A Research Handbook.* New Haven, Conn.: Yale University Press, 1987.

Nielsen, W. *The Golden Donors: A New Anatomy of the Great Foundations.* New York: Dutton, 1985.

Ostrander, S. A., and Schervish, P. G. "Giving and Getting: Philanthropy as a Social Relation." In J. Van Til and Associates, *Critical Issues in American Philanthropy: Strengthening Theory and Practice.* San Francisco, Calif.: Jossey-Bass, 1990.

Parsons, T. *Structures and Process in Modern Societies.* Glencoe, Ill.: Free Press, 1960.

Perrow, C. *Complex Organizations: A Critical Essay.* (3rd ed.) New York: Random House, 1986.

Peters, T. J., and Waterman, R. *In Search of Excellence.* New York: Harper-Collins, 1982.

Schein, E. *Organizational Culture and Leadership.* (2nd ed.) San Francisco, Calif.: Jossey-Bass, 1985.

Schön, D. A. *The Reflective Practitioner.* San Francisco, Calif.: Jossey-Bass, 1983.

Schön, D. A. *Educating the Reflective Practitioner: Toward a New Design for Teaching and Learning in the Professions.* San Francisco, Calif.: Jossey-Bass, 1987.

Simon, J. G. "The Tax Treatment of Nonprofit Organizations: A Review of Federal and State Policies." In W. Powell (ed.), *The Nonprofit Sector: A Research Handbook.* New Haven, Conn.: Yale University Press, 1987.

Van Til, J. *Mapping the Third Sector.* New Brunswick, N.J.: Transaction Press, 1988.

Weisbrod, B. *The Nonprofit Economy.* Cambridge, Mass.: Harvard University Press, 1988.

10

Nonprofit Lobbying

Bob Smucker

Most nonprofit programs are affected directly or indirectly by legislation. Whether a group's concern is conquering cancer, preserving the ozone layer, saving neighborhood schools, providing famine relief, or championing the rights of children, women, or minorities, decisions affecting those issues and programs are made by legislators in Washington, D.C., and in state capitols, city councils, and county governments throughout the nation. Their decisions affect not only public policy central to programs carried out by nonprofits but also the funding. It is a little-known fact that while private giving makes up 18 percent of all charitable income, government is the source of 31 percent, according to *America's Nonprofit Sector: A Primer,* by Lester M. Salamon (1992).

The importance of government decisions on nonprofit programs and the funding of those programs argues strongly for the development by nonprofits of lobbying skills and knowledge of the laws governing nonprofit lobbying. However, managers of nonprofits and their boards of directors have been slow to recognize and act on this point. Many still doubt that lobbying is a proper nonprofit activity, or even legal.

The law is absolutely clear about the legality of lobbying. In fact, the law has always permitted some lobbying by nonprofits, although prior to 1976 the amount of lobbying permitted was very ambiguous. In 1976, legislation was passed that clarified and vastly expanded the amount of lobbying nonprofits can conduct. Equally important, on August 31, 1990, the Internal Revenue Service promulgated regulations that supported both the spirit

and the intent of the 1976 law. Together the law and the regulations provide more lobbying leeway than 99 percent of all nonprofits will ever need — or
want.

The point that the law is generous in the amount of lobbying permitted is evidenced by the fact that of the 6,600 publicly supported charitable
nonprofits that have elected to come under this law, only two spent the maximum amount permitted ($1 million), according to 1992 data from the In-
ternal Revenue Service. Those IRS data list organizations by name, city,
state, and amount spent on lobbying under the 1976 law.

Although lobbying is both a legal and an essential nonprofit activity,
volunteers and staff often are inclined to place lobbying at the very bottom
of the list of abilities they want to develop. In addition to the question of
legality, they may believe that it is too complex to master, perhaps a bit
tainted, or they may assign it low priority simply because they already have
a number of well-honed skills that they can immediately put to work for
their organizations. Once involved in the process, however, most find that
lobbying is not difficult to learn and the organizing skills they possess are
easily transferred to influencing legislation for the people they serve. And
most discover that, far from being disreputable or illegal, lobbying is a perfectly legitimate, reasonable, and personally rewarding way of fulfilling their
organization's public purposes.

The primary purpose of this chapter is to provide information regarding
the generous lobbying limits permitted to nonprofits under the law. The lobbying process and how-to lobbying information are described briefly here,
but have been addressed more exhaustively in other publications, such as
The Dance of Legislation, (1973) by Eric Redman, and *The Giant Killers,* (1986)
by Michael Pertschuck, which give lively descriptions of how nonprofits and
other groups have successfully affected legislation. *The Nonprofit Lobbying Guide:
Advocating Your Cause and Getting Results,* (1991) by Bob Smucker, provides
how-to information, and also gives, in lay language, answers to a number
of technical questions regarding lobbying by nonprofits. (Most of the material in this chapter was taken from that book and is used here with the permission of Jossey-Bass, Publishers.)

Anyone Can Lobby

The personnel manager of a large midwestern manufacturing company once
told me that job descriptions, even for junior executives, are often drawn
up by well-intentioned but unknowing staff to include requirements so
demanding that not even the president of the company could fulfill them.
How-to information can suffer from the same problem. Often, it doesn't distinguish between what you have to know and all the other things that could
be helpful but are not absolutely essential.

All your organization needs as you start lobbying is a staff person or volunteer who has a little knowledge of lobbying techniques; has an elementary

understanding of how the legislative process works in whatever body you are planning to lobby, whether Congress, the state legislature, county government, or the city council; can organize a government relations committee that will consider the legislative issues your organization may want to tackle; can organize volunteers to form a legislative network; and has a passing knowledge of the law governing lobbying by nonprofits.

Much of the information you need to start lobbying probably is readily available in your own community. A number of nonprofits, civic organizations, and public-spirited citizens have been lobbying for years and would be complimented if your group asked them for help in understanding the areas just described. The League of Women Voters is one such organization; others include environmental organizations and most of the major health groups (such as the heart, lung, cancer, mental health, and mental retardation associations), whose staff members often have considerable lobbying knowledge and would probably have affiliates in your community.

Lobbying Law

Before you start lobbying, you should know a little about the law governing lobbying by nonprofits. The 1976 lobby law and regulations provide very generous lobbying limits. You should know what the law says about how much of your organization's annual expenditures can go for lobbying and what activities are defined as lobbying; but the most important point to keep in mind is that the law permits ample room for all the lobbying your group will probably want to undertake. It is very simple for a nonprofit to elect to come under the provisions of that law.

If you have questions about whether the amount of lobbying you want to conduct is within the law, discuss it with other nonprofits that lobby extensively, as well as with your attorney. But remember that attorneys almost always err on the side of extreme caution in counseling nonprofits about lobbying. If you ask your lawyer for advice, be certain that he or she not only knows the lobby law well (only a few do), but, even more important, also is familiar with the experience of organizations that have lobbied under the law. Many groups have found plenty of legal latitude for lobbying, without jeopardizing their tax-exempt status.

The Legislative Process and Your Lobbyist

It is important to have a volunteer or staff person in your organization who knows the basics of how your legislature works, because you will need that information in order to focus your efforts. For example, you may be trying to block legislation averse to your group, help support pending legislation backed by your organization, or arrange the introduction of legislation vital to your group. In the typical legislature, to achieve any of these aims, you will have to gain the support of the committee designated to consider your issue. It follows that you will need to know something about the composition of that committee. For example, if you are seeking to have legislation introduced, it is usually possible to recruit a committee member to introduce your bill. But you won't want just any member. You will want a person of influence, and that usually means a senior committee member whose party is in the majority and therefore controls the committee.

It is, incidentally, helpful to know that many decisions on legislation are made in a last-minute frenzy as legislators prepare to adjourn for the legislative session. The lobbyist (whether a volunteer or a paid staff member) who is following your issue in the legislature should have enough understanding of how the legislative process works that your group can make the right move at the right place and time. Your lobbyist needs to recognize, for example, whether this is the last chance to modify your bill or if you still have a reasonable chance to effect the changes you want in the other house of the legislature. A lobbyist who knows (among other things) who would be the best legislators to introduce your bill and how and when decisions are made in your legislature is referred to as an *inside lobbyist*.

Having a seasoned insider available to your organization can save you enormous time and effort. Perhaps volunteers or staff people bring such experience to your group from their work with other nonprofits. If not, such groups as the League of Women Voters can help your group develop an understanding of how your legislature really works. Former legislators or those currently in office can also be very helpful. Nationally, the Advocacy Institute and INDEPENDENT SECTOR, both of Washington, D.C., among other organizations, can provide how-to information about lobbying by nonprofits.

If you have the funds, it is possible to hire a good, experienced lobbying consultant. If you choose that route, check with other nonprofits whose opinions you value highly and who have used consultants to lobby. The best way of being certain that you are getting the right person is to check his or her track record with other groups. Consultants should be pleased to give you the names of groups for which they have lobbied.

The Government Relations Committee and the Legislative Network

Your organization will need to set up a government relations committee to consider how your group's program can be furthered by legislative initiatives. The committee will also establish legislative priorities and provide direction for the group's lobbying efforts. A strong government relations committee that represents a broad cross section of your community can add immeasurably to the impact of your lobbying efforts. In using a government relations committee, it is enormously important to hold firmly to one top legislative priority, rather than follow the more common route of trying to work on many issues at once.

A nonprofit's principal lobbying power resides in its ability to enlist as many of its members as possible in supporting its legislation. To achieve that objective, most groups set up a legislative network to mobilize their grass-roots network. At the minimum, your network should assign *one* volunteer, capable of enlisting others in his or her community, as a contact person for *each* member of the legislative committee(s) that will act on your bill. If there are twenty members of a legislative committee that will act on your bill, twenty contact persons should be recruited.

Establishing and maintaining the network takes time and commitment because it is tedious, time-consuming work. It is easy to put off establishing a network and even easier to neglect it once it is set up. A nonprofit neglects its network at great risk, however. Without a network, there may be no chance to mobilize broad support on short notice. That kind of quick mobilization may be needed repeatedly during a legislative campaign.

In short, you need very little to get started. As we have seen, it helps to know a little about the law governing lobbying, and to have a volunteer or a staff person who has an elementary understanding of basic lobbying techniques and of the lobbying process, as well as some organizing skills. It's helpful to have a government relations committee and critically important to have a legislative network, and as in all activities that involve people, common sense helps immeasurably. Most important, don't be put off by the amount of technical information in this chapter. Just go ahead. Get started, and keep in mind that lobbying and legislative process are not nearly as complicated or difficult as lobbyists would have you believe.

The 1976 Lobby Law and 1990 Internal Revenue Service Regulations: An Overview

The landmark legislation enacted into law in 1976 clarified and greatly expanded the extent to which nonprofits could lobby without jeopardizing their tax-exempt status. That legislation, Section 1307 of Public Law 94-455, recognized lobbying as an entirely proper function of nonprofits and ended the longstanding uncertainty about the legality of lobbying by groups that are tax exempt under Section 501(c)(3) of the Internal Revenue Code. Briefly, Section 501(c)(3) nonprofit organizations are those that are organized for specific public benefit purposes. These are the only U.S. nonprofit organizations that are both exempt from federal income taxes and to which contributions by individuals (and other taxpayers) may be deductible from their tax liability. (Public Law 94-455 resulted in Internal Revenue Code Sections 4911 and 501[h]. Section 4911 includes information on how much can be spent on lobbying. Section 501[h] provides information on electing to come under the provisions of Public Law 94-455.)

It took a full fourteen years for the Internal Revenue Service to issue final regulations under the 1976 lobby law, but the regulations were worth the wait. While there was some stormy debate between nonprofits and the IRS regarding earlier proposed regulations, the final version, issued on August 31, 1990, is faithful to the 1976 law. There is clear consensus in the nonprofit community that the regulations provide a framework that is both flexible and workable for charities' efforts on legislation. In every critical area, the regulations reflect responsiveness to (although not complete acceptance of) the criticisms and suggestions offered by nonprofits during the long process that led to the final outcome.

In understanding the 1976 lobby law, it helps to know that for a nonprofit electing to come under the law, lobbying is only the expenditure of money by the organization for the purpose of attempting to influence legislation. Where there is no expenditure by the organization for lobbying, there is no lobbying by the organization. Therefore, lobbying by a volunteer for a nonprofit is not counted as a lobbying expenditure to the organization and *is not* lobbying. If, however, the volunteer is reimbursed by the nonprofit for out-of-pocket expenditures, then the reimbursed funds do count as a lobbying expenditure. But it's important to keep in mind the point that *lobbying occurs only when there is an expenditure of funds* for an activity that meets the other criteria for lobbying.

It is also helpful in understanding the 1976 law to recognize that it defines two kinds of lobbying: direct lobbying and grass-roots lobbying. To oversimplify, "direct lobbying" means communications that your organization has about legislation (1) with legislators or government officials who participate in the formulation of legislation and (2) with its own members. Direct lobbying would include visiting a congressperson about a bill and being in touch with your organization's members and urging them to contact legislators. "Grass-roots lobbying" refers to any attempt to influence legislation by affecting the opinion of the general public. The ceiling for a nonprofit's spending on grass-roots lobbying is one-fourth of the total allowable lobbying expenditures.

Sometimes groups confuse grass-roots lobbying of the general public with urging their members to lobby. They mistakenly think that contacting their members (who may number hundreds of thousands) to urge them, in turn, to contact members of the legislature constitutes grass-roots lobbying, simply because those members are at the grass-roots level. Only when an organization is trying to reach *beyond* its members to get action from the general public does grass-roots lobbying occur.

Don't be deterred by all the detail in the following description of the 1976 law. Keep in mind that the law is very generous. It provides all the lobbying latitude that ninety-nine out of a hundred groups will ever need. The details included here will help provide the assurance you may need that many of your activities in the legislative arena are not lobbying under the 1976 lobby law.

Virtually all of the information that follows is drawn from materials written for INDEPENDENT SECTOR by Walter B. Slocombe of Caplin & Drysdale, Washington, D.C. It is an overview of the lobbying latitude permitted to 501(c)(3) organizations under the 1976 law and regulations.

Public Charity Lobbying: An Overview

The 1990 regulations are effective for an organization's first tax year following their (the regulations') publication; that took place on August 31, 1990. Public charities that have elected to come under the 1976 lobby law need to familiarize themselves with the regulations, so that they will know what activities will and will not count against the statutory limits, and so that they can correctly calculate the amounts they treat as spending for lobbying. Private foundations are affected. This is because the regulations (1) elaborate the standards that foundations must meet to comply with the general ban on lobbying by private foundations and (2) establish guidelines for grants by private foundations to public charities that elect to come under the law.

Public charities that have any degree of involvement in public policy issues also have an interest in the regulations, even if they have not elected to be covered by them. This is partly because public charities need to decide whether to make that election, now that its effects are clearer, and partly because, although the regulations nominally apply to public charities only if they have so elected, the standards set forth in the regulations may affect the application of the old "substantiality" standard, to which nonelecting charities will remain subject.

The general rule of Section 501(c)(3), to which all organizations exempt under that provision are subject unless they elect to come under the 1976 lobby law, is that "no substantial part" of their activities may be that of attempting to influence legislation. Although the provision has been in the IRS code since 1934 and has occasionally been applied by the courts, there has never been a clear definition of the point at which lobbying becomes substantial or, indeed, of what activities related to public policy and to controversial subjects constitute attempts to influence legislation. In particular, the IRS position is that spending, as a share of budget, is far from the sole measure of whether a nonelecting group's lobbying is substantial; such factors as absolute amount spent, impact, public prominence, and unpaid volunteer work also enter into the determination.

To clarify and liberalize the rules for lobbying by charities, Sections 501(h) and 4911 were added to the code in 1976, as a result of the enactment of the 1976 lobby law. In outline, the provisions permit most public charities (but not churches, their integrated auxiliaries, or a convention or association of churches) to elect to have their legislative efforts governed by the specific rules of Sections 501(h) and 4911, instead of the vague "substantiality" standard. To that end, the 1976 legislation both sets financial limits for lobbying activities and defines the activities that count against those limits.

What Are the Main Elements of the 1976 Law?

Exclusions from Lobbying

Critical to the 1976 law are the provisions declaring that many expenditures that have some relationship to public policy and legislative issues are not treated as lobbying and so are permitted without limit. These include expenditures for the following:

1. Communications to members of an organization that discuss legislation but do not urge action by the members.
2. Making available the results of a "nonpartisan analysis, study, or research" on a legislative issue that presents a sufficiently full and fair exposition of the pertinent facts to enable the audience to form an independent opinion. (The regulations make clear that research and analysis need not be "neutral" or "objective" to fall within this "nonpartisan" exclusion. The exclusion is available to research and analysis that take direct positions on the merits of legislation, as long as the organization presents facts fully and fairly, makes the material generally available, and does not include a direct call to the reader to contact legislators.)
3. Responding to written requests from a legislative body (not just a single legislator) for technical advice on pending legislation.
4. So-called self-defense activity — that is, lobbying legislators (but not the general public) on matters that may affect the organization's own existence, powers, exempt status, and similar matters. (Lobbying for programs in the organization's field, however, is not self-defense lobbying.)
5. Discussion of broad social, economic, and similar policy issues whose resolution would require legislation, as long as there is no discussion of specific legislative measures.

Permitted Levels of Spending for Lobbying

The second key element of the 1976 law is that it unequivocally declares that activities that do constitute active lobbying are permitted, provided only that they fall within the spending ceilings established by the law. The spending ceilings are based on percentages of the charity's budget for the year, beginning at 20 percent of the first $500,000 and ending at 5 percent of expenditures over $1.5 million. (Strictly speaking, the base is the charity's exempt-purpose expenditures, which include all payments for the organization's programs and exempt purposes but exclude costs of investment management, unrelated businesses, and certain fundraising costs.) There is an overall maximum ceiling of $1 million a year. The effect of the sliding-scale ceilings is that an organization reaches the maximum permissible ceiling when its exempt-purpose expenditures reach $17 million. Expenditures for grass-roots lobbying — that is, attempting "to influence legislation through an attempt to affect the opinions of the general public or any segment thereof" — are limited to one-quarter of the overall ceiling, as already stated. Amounts spent on lobbying in excess of that level must be for direct lobbying — that is, for communications made directly to legislators and their staffs and to executive-branch officials who participate in the formulation of legislation. (As previously described, communications with an organization's members that urge them to contact legislators are also treated as direct, rather than grass-roots, lobbying. The total and grass-roots ceilings at various exempt-purpose expenditure levels are shown in Table 10.1.) Since the amount that may be spent on grass-roots lobbying is limited to one-quarter of the overall lobbying limit, if an organization's total lobbying limit is $100,000, then it may spend the full $100,000 on direct lobbying or it may spend up to $25,000 on grass-roots lobbying and the rest on direct lobbying. Even if it chooses to spend nothing on direct lobbying, it will still be limited to $25,000 on grass-roots lobbying.

Table 10.1. Lobbying Ceilings Under the 1976 Lobby Law.

Exempt-Purpose Expenditures	Total Lobbying Expenditures	Amount of Total Allowable for Grass-Roots Lobbying
Up to $500,000	20% of exempt-purpose expenditures	One-quarter
$500,000–$1 million	$100,000 + 15% of excess over $500,000	$25,000 + 3.75% of excess over $500,000
$1 million–$1.5 million	$175,000 + 10% of excess over $1 million	$43,750 + 2.5% of excess over $1 million
$15 million–$17 million	$225,000 + 5% of excess over $1.5 million	$56,250 + 1.25% of excess over $1.5 million
Over $17 million	$1 million	$250,000

Flexible Sanctions

A third important element of the 1976 legislation was the establishment of a new and more flexible system of sanctions, to replace the "death sentence" of loss of exemption as the principal sanction for violation of the "substantiality" standard. (Since 1976, Congress has added additional sanctions, beyond loss of exemption, for nonelecting organizations that violate that standard — a 5 percent excise tax on excessive lobbying spending, and a similar tax on managers who willfully and unreasonably agree to lobbying expenditures, knowing that these are likely to cause loss of exemption.) The initial sanction for public charities under the 1976 law that spend more than either the overall or the grass-roots limit is a 25 percent excise tax on the lobbying spending in any year in excess of the ceiling. (If both ceilings are exceeded, the tax is on the greater of the two excess amounts.) Loss of exemption is an available sanction only if spending normally exceeds 150 percent of either the overall or the grass-roots limit, generally determined by aggregating both spending and limits over a four-year period.

What Spending Counts Against the Limits?

There is considerable uncertainty about what activity counts against the "substantiality" standard, but the standard, under the 1976 lobby law, is strictly financial. The only factor that must be taken into account is the cost of communications for direct or grass-roots lobbying, including the cost of preparing the communication (such as staff time, facilities, and allocable overhead).

Elements Required for a Lobbying Communication

To be a direct lobbying communication, and therefore to count against the direct lobbying dollar limits, a communication must refer to specific legislation and reflect a point of view on its merits. "Specific legislation" includes a specific measure that has not yet been introduced, but it does not include general concepts for solving problems that have not yet been distilled into legislative proposals.

To be a grass-roots lobbying communication, subject to the lower ceiling, in most cases, a communication must, apart from referring to specific legislation and reflecting a view on it, encourage recipients to contact legislators. Under the regulations, such a call to action exists only when the material directly tells its audience to contact legislators; provides a legislator's address, phone number, or similar information; provides a petition, postcard, or other prepared message to be sent to the legislator; or identifies one or more legislators as opposing the organization's views, being undecided, being recipients' representative(s), or being a member of the committee that will consider the legislation. Under these rules, a public charity (except in the narrow case of "highly publicized legislation," to be discussed) can make any public statement it likes about a legislative issue, without having the costs counted against its grass-roots lobbying limit — as long as it avoids calls to action. The broad freedom that this rule gives charities to discuss issues freely, as long as they forgo calls to action, is shown by an example in the regulations. It concerns a mass-media advertisement that the IRS says would not normally be considered grass-roots lobbying because it lacks such a call. The sample advertisement reads as follows: "The State Assembly is considering a bill to make gun ownership illegal. This outrageous legislation would violate your constitutional rights and the rights of other law abiding citizens. If this legislation is passed, you and your family will be criminals if you want to exercise your right to protect yourselves."

Special Rule for Paid Mass-Media
Messages Close to Votes on "Famous" Bills

There is one exception to the rule stating that a public communication about legislation must include a call to action in order to be considered lobbying, and that exception will affect very few nonprofits. The regulations eliminate the "call to action" requirement in a narrowly defined set of cases involving mass-media advertising just before a vote on certain legislation that has elicited a high degree of public awareness. These regulations apply — and communications can be considered grass-roots lobbying, even without a call to the public to communicate with legislators about the legislation — only when all the following conditions are met:

1. The legislation in question has received so much publicity that its pending or its general terms, purpose, or effect are known to a significant element of the general public, not just to the particular interest groups directly affected. The degree of publicity given the legislation is a factor here, but there must be more than just publicity; there must also be general public knowledge about the particular legislation.

2. The public charity has bought paid advertising in the mass media (meaning television, radio, billboards, or general-circulation newspapers and magazines). Direct mail and the organization's own media outlets are not considered paid media, except for radio and television broadcasting by the organization itself and organization-published periodicals that have a circulation of 100,000, more than half of which is outside the organization's membership.

3. The advertising appears within two weeks before a vote will be taken in a full house or full committee (not just a subcommittee).

4. The advertisement *refers directly to the legislation* (as in the gun control ad above) but does not include a call to action, as defined under the general standards. (If the ad includes a call to action, it is grass-roots lobbying without the special "mass media" rules.) Or the advertisement *states a view on the general subject* of the legislation and urges the public to communicate with legislators about that subject. (To carry on the handgun example, such an ad might say, "Let your state representative know you want to protect your right to keep and bear arms" — without referring directly to the pending bill.)

Even when all these conditions are present, the organization can avoid counting the ad as a lobbying cost if it can show that it has customarily run such ads without regard to the timing of legislation, or that the particular ad's timing was unrelated to the upcoming legislative action (as may be the case when television ads are bought under conditions that allow the station to determine when they run). This special rule for ads on highly publicized and well-known legislation affect few if any activities that are not directly and consciously aimed at legislative results. Even in those cases, of course, the activity is permitted within financial ceilings.

Special Rules for Referenda, Initiatives, and Similar Procedures

In general, legislative messages aimed at the public as a whole are grass-roots lobbying if they meet the "call to action" standard. The final regulations, however, recognize that in the case of referenda, initiatives, and similar procedures, the public is itself the legislature. Accordingly, communications to the public that refer to such measures and that take a stand on them are treated as direct lobbying of a legislature — subject only to the higher ceiling. The effect of these rules is that communications (newspaper ads, for example) that refer to a ballot measure and reflect a view on it are direct lobbying, whether or not they explicitly tell people how to vote.

The rule gives public charities important flexibility to be active in referendum efforts, which would have been impractical if they had been forced to count against the lower grass-roots lobbying limits.

When Does Later Use of Materials
Cause Their Costs to Be Counted as Lobbying?

The costs of a lobbying communication include the costs of the staff and facilities needed to prepare it, not just the costs of paper and ink or videotape. An issue of concern to many groups, especially those doing research on public policy issues, has been the possibility that research costs might be treated as costs of preparing to lobby, if the published results of the research were later referred to and used in lobbying. The final regulations on this so-called subsequent use issues should greatly ease organizations' concerns that their lobbying spending will be boosted unexpectedly because materials they have prepared are later used in lobbying — whether the use is by the organization itself, by a related organization, or by a third party. This is because costs of materials that are not themselves used for lobbying need to be counted as lobbying support costs (on the basis of their later use in lobbying) *only* in cases in which all of the following conditions exist:

1. The materials both refer to and reflect a view on specific legislation. (They do not, however, in their initial format, include a call to action. If the materials do include such a call, their public circulation would itself be grass-roots lobbying.) Materials — such as raw research data — that do not meet this test are entirely outside the "subsequent use" rules.

2. The lobbying use occurs within six months of payment for the materials. Therefore, lobbying use more than six months after a research project is complete cannot affect the organization's lobbying costs. In any case, only the most recent six months of spending potentially represents a lobbying cost. There is no risk that, because of some lobbying use of research results more than six months after a project is finished, years of accumulated research spending will be treated as lobbying costs.

3. The organization fails to make a substantial nonlobbying distribution of the materials before the lobbying use. If the materials are "nonpartisan, analysis, study, or research," a nonlobbying distribution qualifies as "substantial" (and therefore excludes all the costs from lobbying treatment) if it conforms to the normal distribution pattern for similar materials, as followed by that organization and similar ones. For other materials, the

nonlobbying distribution must be at least as extensive as the lobbying distribution. This rule means that, by seeing that research-and-analysis materials that take positions on legislation are first distributed to the public in normal ways, an organization can prevent their costs from being treated as lobbying costs, even if the materials are later used in lobbying by the organization itself or by an affiliate.

4. The organization's primary purpose in creating the materials was to use them in lobbying rather than for some nonlobbying goal. When the lobbying use is by an unrelated organization, not only must there be clear and convincing evidence of such a lobbying purpose, but that evidence must also include evidence of collusion and cooperation with the organization using the material for lobbying.

For private foundations making grants to public charities that spend the money on materials later used in lobbying, there is another layer of protection. Even if the grantee violates the "subsequent use" rules, the grantor foundation can be taxed on the grant as a lobbying expenditure only if the private foundation had a primary lobbying purpose in making the grant or if the grant-making foundation knew or should reasonably have known of the grantee's lobbying purpose.

The cumulative effect of these safeguards is that a research organization can readily avoid any risk of unexpected lobbying expenses. Only costs that are less than six months old can be at issue. Even in theory, the problem can arise only in the case of material that takes a position on specific legislation. Even for such materials, there is a safe harbor for distributions that follow the normal patterns of dissemination. In any event, an organization can avoid having costs for materials later used in lobbying treated as grass-roots lobbying cost if the primary purpose of incurring the cost was a nonlobbying objective. If the later use is by an unrelated organization, there must be clear and convincing evidence that the organization developed the research for the purpose of lobbying.

Does Electing to Be Governed by the New Regulations Complicate Receiving Grants from Foundations?

Private foundations may not elect to come under the 1976 law, and they remain absolutely prohibited from making expenditures for lobbying purposes. Therefore, some foundations have been concerned about their ability to make grants to nonprofits that explicitly adopt programs of lobbying by electing to come under the 1976 lobby law, and some nonprofits have worried that making an election under the 1976 law will scare off foundation funders.

The regulations — which codify and even liberalize long-established IRS policy — meet these concerns by setting up a highly protective system for grants by private foundations to public charities that elect to come under the 1976 law. Under these rules, a foundation may, without tax liability, make a general-purpose grant to a public charity that lobbies, whether or not the public charity has elected. A private foundation may also make a grant to support a specific project that includes lobbying, as long as its own grant is less than the amount budgeted for the nonlobbying parts of the project. For example, if a specific project has a $200,000 budget, of which $20,000 is to be spent for lobbying, a private foundation can give the project up to $180,000 because that is the part of the project budget allocated to nonlobbying uses. The fact that other private foundations have already made grants for the project need not be taken into account in considering how much a private foundation can give.

The regulations make clear that a foundation can rely on statements by the prospective grantee regarding how much the project will spend on lobbying, unless the foundation knows or has reason to know that the statements are false. The regulations also make clear that as long as the granting foundation complies with these standards when it makes the grant, it will not be held to have made a taxable lobbying expenditure if the public charity violates the assurances it gave when seeking the grant.

When Will a Public Charity's Transfers to a Lobbying Organization Be Counted as Lobbying Expenditures?

If a public charity pays another organization or an individual to do lobbying for it, the payment counts against its direct or grass-roots lobbying ceiling according to the character of the work done. The regulations also seek to prevent evasion of the limits by public charities that provide funds to other organizations not subject to the Section 501(c)(3) lobbying limits — such as, presumably, a related organization exempt under Section 501(c)(4) — to increase the resources available for the recipient's lobbying efforts. In such a case, the funds transferred are deemed to have been paid for grass-roots lobbying, to the extent of the transferee's grass-roots lobbying expenditures; any remaining amount is treated as having been paid for direct lobbying, to the extent of the transferee's direct lobbying expenditures.

This rule is subject to some very important qualifications, however. There is no lobbying expenditure when a public charity makes a grant to a noncharity and the grant's use is expressly limited to a specific educational or otherwise charitable purpose and when records demonstrate that use. The regulations also make clear that the rule does not apply when the public charity is getting fair market value for the money it transfers. Thus, if a 501(c)(3) organization pays rent at fair market value to a 501(c)(4) group, or if the 501(c)(3) group pays to a 501(c)(4) group its proper portion of the costs of a shared employee, the rule does not apply because the 501(c)(3) group is getting full value from the 501(c)(4) group.

These transfer rules protect public charities that engage in normal and legitimate transactions with related (or unrelated) entities. Such charities need only follow the substantive and accounting procedures that are required in any case for general tax purposes, without regard to the special lobbying provisions.

What Accounting Is Required for Lobbying Expenditures?

All Section 501(c)(3) organizations—whether or not they elect to come under the 1976 lobby law—must report on their annual IRS Form 990 the total amount of their lobbying expenditures. The only additional requirement for electing organizations is that they must break the expenditures down by direct and grass-roots activities. Both classes of organizations must maintain records to support the entries on the return—showing, for example, the basis for computing the overhead allocated to lobbying activities.

Organizations that have not elected are required to state whether they attempted to influence public opinion through the use of volunteers, and if so, to give a detailed description of the activities. There is no such requirement for electing organizations, which should give substantial additional incentives to nonprofits to elect.

How Are Expenditures Treated That Have Both Lobbying and Nonlobbying Purposes?

Sometimes a public charity wants to distribute a communication that has both lobbying and nonlobbying messages, such as a mass mailing that calls for readers to contact legislators about pending legislation and also asks them for contributions to the organization. In general, the regulations permit allocation between the lobbying and nonlobbying aspects of such mixed-purpose communications; but, to reflect the special solicitude that is extended to communications with members, treatment of such communications is more generous.

The details are beyond the scope of this overview, but the general situation is as follows. First, costs of communications with members may be allocated, as between lobbying and any other bona fide nonlobbying purpose (education, fundraising, or advocacy on nonlegislative issues), in any reasonable basis. An attempt to allocate to lobbying only the particular words actually urging legislative action—and not the material explaining the legislative issue and the organization's position—will be rejected as unreasonable. Second, costs for part-lobbying communications to nonmembers (including even the membership share, if the communications go primarily to nonmembers) can be allocated to nonlobbying purposes only to the extent that they do not address the "same specific subject" as the legislative message in the communication. The "same specific subject" is rather broadly defined to include activities that would be affected by legislation addressed elsewhere in the message, as well as the background and consequences of the legislation and activities affected by it. Nevertheless, fundraising and providing general information about the organization are not treated as being on the "same specific subject" as a legislative message. Therefore, expenses attributable to those goals would not be considered lobbying costs. Allocation of expenditures away from lobbying is also permitted for the parts of a communication that discuss distinct aspects of a broad problem, one feature of which would be affected by the legislation addressed elsewhere in the communication.

Organizations that have extensive and expensive direct-mail operations aimed at current contributors (who are members) and prospects (who are not) will need to review their mailings to ensure that they do not inadvertently make large grass-roots lobbying expenditures. Similarly, groups that routinely send legislative alerts to nonmembers may want to make them distinct publications, rather than combining them with general communications.

When Are Several Nonprofits Treated on an Aggregate Basis?

In general, ceiling determinations and lobbying expenditure calculations are made on a separate basis for each legally distinct 501(c)(3) organization. Only if two or more organizations are subject to common control through interlocking majorities on their boards (or to common control by a third organization), or if one organization is required by its governing instrument to follow the legislative decisions of another, are the organizations aggregated under a single ceiling, with aggregate computations of expenditures. The requirement to follow legislative decisions must be express and not merely implied.

For Further Information

The preceding analysis is intended to give interested volunteers and staff members an overview, in lay language, of the 1976 lobby law. No guide, however, can adequately substitute for official information. Those wishing to make their own analyses will find the following additional sources to be of value:

- U.S. Internal Revenue Code of 1986, as amended, especially Sections 501(a), 501(c)(3), 501(h), and 4911.
- Public Law 94-455, The Tax Reform Act of 1976, approved October 4, 1976 (specifically, Section 1307, "Lobbying by Public Charities").
- House Report 94-1210, "Influencing Legislation by Public Charities," June 2, 1976, to accompany House Report 13500. (H.R. 13500 became Section 1307 of Public Law 94-455.)
- Senate Report 94-938, Part 2, supplemental report on additional amendment to House Report 10612, July 20, 1976. (H.R. 10612 became Public Law 94-455.)
- House Report 94-1515, conference report on House Report 10612, September 13, 1976.

- "Final Regulations on Lobbying by Public Charities and Private Foundations," *Federal Register,* Aug. 31, 1990, p. 35579.

Election Procedure for Nonprofits

The process for electing to come under the 1976 lobby law (Public Law 94-455) is very simple, which no doubt partly accounts for the fact that as of 1993, about 6,600 nonprofits, large and small, have chosen to do so since 1976. Those eligible to so elect are nonprofits exempt from taxation by Section 501(c)(3) of the Internal Revenue Code. The legislation does not apply to churches, their integrated auxiliaries, or a convention or association of churches. Private foundations also are not eligible, although they may make grants to nonprofits that do elect.

If a nonprofit does not elect to take advantage of the generous lobbying provisions under the 1976 lobby law, it remains subject to the vague "insubstantial" rule that has been in the tax code since 1934. Under that provision, if a charity engages in more than "insubstantial" lobbying, it loses its Section 501(c)(3) status and its right to receive tax-deductible charitable contributions. Unfortunately, "insubstantial" has never been defined under the law, with the result that nonprofits that do lobby but have not elected to come under the 1976 law cannot be certain how much lobbying they may conduct without jeopardizing their tax-exempt status. Many nonprofits have followed the questionable guideline that the allocation of 5 percent of their total annual expenditures to lobbying is not substantial and is therefore within the law. They have assumed that 5 percent of their *expenditures* is permissible because of a 1955 Sixth Circuit Court of Appeals ruling to the effect that attempts to influence legislation that constitute 5 percent of total *activities* are not substantial.

There is good reason to doubt that the "5 percent test" should be relied on. It was called into question by a 1972 ruling, which rejected a percentage test in determining what constituted substantial lobbying. In that case, the Tenth Circuit Court of Appeals supported a "facts and circumstances" test instead of a percentage test. In a 1974 ruling, the Claims Court stated that a percentage test was deemed inappropriate for determining whether lobbying activities are substantial. It was found that an exempt organization enjoying considerable prestige and influence could be considered as having a substantial impact on the legislative process, solely on the basis of making a single official position statement—an activity that would be considered negligible if measured according to a percentage standard of time expended. It is clearly in the interest of every nonprofit that lobbies more than a nominal amount to consider electing to come under the provisions of the 1976 law.

The law makes the process for electing very easy. A nonprofit's governing body—that is, its executive committee, board of directors, other representatives, or total membership, according to the constitution or bylaws of the particular nonprofit — may elect to have the organization come under the law. An authorized officer or trustee signs the one-page Internal Revenue Service Form 5768 and checks the box marked "Election." Regardless of the actual date of election, the nonprofit is considered to have come under the provisions of the law as of the start of the tax year during which it files the election.

The nonprofit automatically continues under the provisions of the 1976 law unless it chooses to revoke that election. It can do that by having its governing body vote on revocation and by having an authorized officer or trustee sign another Form 5768. The revocation becomes effective at the start of the tax year that *follows* the date of the revocation. In other words, revocation can only be prospective.

A new nonprofit may elect to come under the lobby law even before it is determined to be eligible by the IRS. It simply submits Form 5768 at the time it submits its "Application for Recognition of Exemption" (Form 1023). The nonprofit's employer identification number, which is requested at the top of the form, is listed on the nonprofit's "Employer Quarterly Federal Tax Return" (Form 941).

One final important note: some nonprofits have been reluctant to come under the 1976 lobby law for fear that taking this action will serve as a "red flag" to the IRS and prompt an audit of lobbying activities. Fortunately, this is not the case. The Internal Revenue Service, in an October 7, 1988, letter to attorneys representing INDEPENDENT SECTOR, made clear that it does not plan to single out nonprofit organizations that elect to come under the provisions of the 1976 law. (Earlier, the Internal Revenue Service had furnished each IRS region with a listing of organizations that had elected to come under the 1976 law, and that action had raised fears among some nonprofits that the IRS planned to target for audit the lobbying activities of those nonprofits that had elected.) In the letter, the IRS representative said, "As I stated above, our intent has been, and continues to be, one of encouragement [of nonprofit organizations] to make the election. Accordingly, I am taking steps to see that the IR Manual provision on this is revised. I have instructed that the IR Manual clarify that the filing of an election is a neutral factor for audit selection purposes. This change should eliminate the perception and concerns expressed in your letter." In compliance with that promise, the Internal Revenue Manual now states, "Experience also suggests that organizations that have made the election [under the 1976 lobby law] are usually in compliance with the restrictions on legislative activities, so they do not appear to justify an effort to examine solely on this issue." When Congress was debating the 1976 lobby law, before its enactment, there was clear evidence that Congress fully intended the law to encourage nonprofits to lobby and not to discourage them by singling them out for audit. These facts should reassure nonprofit groups that they will not be targeted for lobbying audits if they elect to be covered under the 1976 law.

Summary

The programs and funding of services of particular interest to nonprofits are closely linked to the decisions of legislatures and government executive offices in Washington, D.C., and in state capitols, city councils, and county seats throughout the nation. It is very important therefore that volunteers and staff of nonprofits understand how to affect the outcome of those decisions and how lobbying can open that door.

You need to know only a little about the following to get started lobbying: (1) the lobbying process; (2) organizing your group's government relations committee; (3) setting up a legislative network; (4) the law governing lobbying by nonprofits. Also, it is important to have the help of a volunteer or staff person who has at least a beginning understanding of basic lobbying techniques and the lobbying process as well as nonprofit organizing skills. A number of publications provide helpful information regarding nonprofit lobbying process and the law affecting such lobbying.

The information provided in this chapter on the lobbying latitude under the law is somewhat complex and may tend to discourage those who think they must understand it before they start lobbying. In candor, you really don't have to master the information. It is provided more as a useful resource than a mountain you must climb before you can safely enter the lobbying arena. The main point is that the 1976 lobby law provides extraordinarily generous nonprofit lobbying limits — more than ninety-nine out of a hundred organizations that lobby will ever need — or want. So don't be put off by the somewhat complex information regarding the law. Go ahead. Get started, and keep in mind that lobbying is often a nonprofit's best service.

References

Pertschuck, M. *The Giant Killers.* New York: Norton, 1986.

Redman, E. *The Dance of Legislation.* New York: Simon & Schuster, 1973.

Salamon, L. *America's Nonprofit Sector: A Primer.* Washington, D.C.: Foundation Center, 1992.

Smucker, B. *The Nonprofit Lobbying Guide: Advocating Your Cause — And Getting Results.* San Francisco, Calif.: Jossey-Bass, 1991.

11

Managing Organizational Transformations

Felice Davidson Perlmutter
Burton Gummer

Leadership in the nonprofit sector is facing serious challenges as many organizations struggle not only to remain vital and effective but just to survive. In this chapter we focus on a specific challenge—that of managing organizational transformation, a process often necessary to assure both the survival and relevance of those organizations we lead. Heimovics and Herman's research suggests that "what is 'real' for the major actors of these organizations is the central position of final responsibility with the chief executive" (1990, p. 68). Accordingly, it is our assumption that leadership is a proactive function and that executives, indeed, bear final responsibility for the decisions made in their organizations. The specific illustrations in this discussion will be from the human services. However, the issues they address are of general interest to all nonprofit organizations.

Organizational transformation is a complex and fascinating challenge that requires a broad systems perspective because during the process of change internal and external factors mesh to create a sticky wicket. The challenge becomes one of retaining control—of managing, and not being managed by, organizational transformation. All too often executives find out after the fact that unanticipated changes have occurred and that they have reacted inappropriately to critical issues. For example, when management information systems (MIS) first appeared in the human services, executives were ill prepared to deal with them. Thus, a major social agency hired a consultant to install an MIS at a cost of $2 million. The consultant, an ethical professional, was most uncomfortable with this assignment because he was given no direction regarding the administrative design or the system's needs; his major concern was that by designing this system, he would, necessarily, be creating an administrative structure. Executive staff did not understand the problem; they only knew that if they did not spend the money in that fiscal year, it would be lost. Not surprisingly, within two years it became clear that adequate thought had not been given to this problem, and the system was totally redesigned at an even greater cost. Had the management team been proactive, rather than reactive, it would have anticipated its requirements and managed a transformation whose consequences would have been more lasting and more positive. The rapid development of new technologies demands constant vigilance since many of these innovations potentially can have a great impact on nonprofit organizations.

The call from many executives of human service organizations is for more skills and knowledge in dealing with the multiple demands of their work (Perlmutter and Adams, 1992). In addressing the problem of organizational transformation, we hope to add to the repertoire of strategies that will empower executive decision makers to meet the demand for change.

A Working Definition of Organizational Transformation

Implicit in the concept of organizational transformation is the idea of *change*. Since there are many kinds and degrees of change, ranging from small to large, from short term to long term, any discussion of organizational change must begin with a specification of the level of change. Small changes are those that do not affect the structural form of the organization; they are cosmetic in the sense that they affect the organization's appearance but not its core structural features. For example, job titles may change, but the functions performed may remain the same; funding sources and levels may change, but the distribution of funds within the organization may remain the same; standard measures may be used to judge organizational effectiveness and efficiency, even when a program is so unusual as to be far from "standard."

Big changes, by contrast, are fundamental in nature. They transform what Haveman (1992) calls the organization's "core form," what Selznick (1957) calls the organization's "character," and what we think of as the essential competence of the organization—that which identifies it and marks it as unique or indispensable. The implication for management is that it is necessary to continuously examine the accelerated changing needs of society in order to redesign organizational structure so that any major change is compatible with the agency's mission.

This notion is distinctly different from that which focuses solely on organizational efficiency or effectiveness. Core organizational changes can be viewed as the managerial version of Kuhn's (1962) notion of "paradigm shifts" in the natural sciences. For much of this century core organizational changes—whether in the public, for-profit, or nonprofit sectors—have been few and far between. In the profit sector, Alfred P. Sloan's multidivisional corporate form at General Motors became the paradigm for the automobile industry for over fifty years. In the public sector, the structure of federal-state relations, and the federal involvement in social programs developed by the New Deal, lasted more than forty years. Interestingly, these models are both currently the focus of major transformations as General Motors and other industry giants, such as Sears and IBM, are downsizing, and as the pressure on the federal government to decentralize and privatize many of its functions, first introduced by Nixon's New Federalism, continues to grow (Levine, 1986).

In sum, we define organizational transformation as a catapulting circumstance that affects the fundamental essence and operations of the organization. This change in state is not an evolutionary process, a case of expected development. However, the essential aspect of this concept of transformation is that the organization must continue to serve its fundamental objectives and retain its unique mission; if it abandons its mission we are no longer discussing organizational transformation, but the death of an old entity and the birth of a new one (Perlmutter, 1971).

The Context of Organizational Transformation

Since organizational transformation does not occur in a vacuum, it is essential to understand the context that stimulates the change before we begin our exploration of the nature of this transformation and how to manage the process. In a model of social agency development, Perlmutter (1969) proposes that *the changing external environment* is central in shaping an agency's development. "Although external socioeconomic conditions are not part of the internal agency system, an analysis of changing historical circumstances is essential to an understanding of the agency. . . . The initial motivation to organize a voluntary social service agency is determined by these external conditions; . . . and the [agency's] life cycle . . . can be understood only in relation to the external conditions" (p. 469).

The present discussion of external context highlights two variables: time and space. Both are complex constructs that yield important information concerning how a society conducts itself. The issue of "the pace of time" is of interest because it highlights relative differences in conception among societies. In late twentieth century America we are experiencing what appears to be continuously accelerating time pressures. As early as the 1970s, this phenomenon was noted by an executive of a nonprofit family service agency who came into administration "when there was still the usual rhythm of going on year to year, and changes, if they occurred, took about two to four years and you had a lot of time to get used to them. I don't believe that there is any place in the country that such a rhythm is possible today, at least if one is going to survive" (Perlmutter, 1980, p. 62). These observations confirm the trenchant insights of Emery and Trist (1965). Their concept of "turbulent fields" sought to explain the rapidly shifting and uncertain environments that were beginning to impact organizations. While these authors identified three other types of environments in which organizations operate, these were certainly simpler. What is distinctive about the concept of a "turbulent field" is that the dynamic properties arise not only from the interactions between the organization and the other players in the field but also from the field itself.

Another conceptual difference in regard to the time variable merits attention. In the Middle Ages, and even currently in cultures such as that of Native Americans, time was viewed as unified; one did not separate past, present, and future. This may be attributed to the fact that the world was experienced as stable and there was no reason to make these distinctions. The contrast between that conception of a unity of time and our concept of time as highly demarcated is dramatic. Not only do we refer to our historical past to understand present realities, but we are simultaneously concerned with the present and its impact on the future. For example, what about the status of the Social Security Trust Fund in the year 2050? And what about the consequences of the depletion of the earth's resources and the "greenhouse effect"? And yet, in what appears to be a contradiction, many executives focus only on the present situation within their organizations and pay little attention to the organizations' historical past or relevant future. Macarov (1992) challenges social service executives to become future oriented in spite of the pressures of current problems.

Space is the second conceptual variable used in this discussion. Until recent times, executives of nonprofit organizations could focus on the immediate locales in which their organizations were located, and the impact to be dealt with was a confined one. Attention to vertical relationships, in addition to horizontal ones (Warren, 1966), was the exception and not the rule, affecting primarily federated systems such as Planned Parenthood (Rein and Morris, 1965). By contrast, today there is no aspect of contemporary life that is not affected by the globalization of national economies and all the attendant social concerns. Thus, the impact of loss of jobs, mass immigration, new diseases, and other indications of social instability directly related to the globalization process affect the core of nonprofit organizations in the human services.

Clearly, the pace of social, political, and economic change has become so intense in recent decades that commentators have difficulty finding language that adequately describes these dizzying phenomena. Emery and Trist's description is still the most acute: "The 'ground' is in motion. . . . For organizations, these trends mean a gross increase in their area of *relevant uncertainty*. The consequences which flow from their actions lead off in ways that become increasingly unpredictable: they do not necessarily fall off with distance, but may at any point be amplified beyond all expectation; similarly, lines of action that are strongly pursued may find themselves attenuated by emergent field forces" (1965, p. 26; italics in original).

Our concepts of time and space are part of the "ground" that is in motion and that creates a turbulent field. It is this turbulence that necessitates organizational transformation to ensure the relevance of the system with regard to current realities. All nonprofit organizations—in the arts, in health care, or in the social services—are affected by today's turbulent field. In the human services a number of trends challenge agency executives to rethink their core structure and service profile within the context of their agency mission. Since the 1930s, nonprofit social service organizations have concentrated on providing quality professional services to a limited number of clients through agencies that are organized along collegial, rather than bureaucratic, lines. Major developments in society pose challenges to these organizations in all aspects of their structural cores or domains.

An interesting distinction can be drawn between the concept of social problem and social issue. Traditionally, social agencies were stimulated to develop services to meet social problems. However, McWhinney (1992, p. 62) argues that the term *problem* can only be used "when we have the requisite resources to solve it." According to McWhinney, sending a spaceship to the moon is an example of a problem, albeit a formidable and complex one. Homelessness, by contrast, is not a problem but an "issue," because it consists of "an unbounded, ill-defined, overwhelming complex of problems. . . . [T]he word *issue* itself expresses a sense of outflowing, uncontainable at a point in time and space. To dam it in one place is to invite overflow into another. . . . Eliminating [homelessness] . . . requires dissolving an immense psycho-socio-political knot and resolving issues at every level of human existence" (McWhinney, 1992, pp. 63–64; italics in original).

This is a critical point since the changing clientele of social agencies today indeed represent issues, and not just problems. These issues are layered, and they interconnect social, psychological, legal, medical, and economic aspects of society, as is illustrated by an increasing number of clients with AIDS, unmarried pregnant teenagers, chronically mentally ill, the frail and poor elderly, and immigrant populations (Hasenfeld, 1989). "Clearly, there are few effective interventions for clients that are so highly and historically marginalized" (Fabricant and Burghardt, 1992, p. 136). Furthermore, these issues challenge executives to broaden their repertoire of responses by initiating collaboration with other professions and other institutions.

In addition to these complex issues confronting the human services, the changing posture of the public sector adds to the turbulence of the ground, in Emery and Trist's terms. Government, at all levels, is "privatizing" the provision of services, a process Bendick (1989) has termed "load shedding." As a result, nonprofit organizations are engaging in profit-making activity, a process that has resulted in some major organizational transformations. In fact, this has led Perlmutter and Adams (1990) to suggest that we may be witnessing the transformation of the voluntary social service sector as a whole, as the agencies in that sector become market driven rather than mission driven.

It is evident that the world is indeed complex and that the issues that must be addressed require the involvement of a broad array of organizational actors in a broad array of settings. It is not surprising that the appropriate response for executives is to recognize the importance of, and to invest resources in, strategic planning for organizational transformation.

Types of Organizational Transformation

Organizational transformation must be major in scope, a catapulting event that reflects dramatically changing circumstances in the environment. The following list is designed to begin a discussion of what constitutes fundamental change so that executives can recognize the importance of what is transpiring and not view it as a routine event.

Change in legitimacy occurs when an organization shifts from an informal group, such as a self-help group, or an informal group concerned with a particular social problem, to one legitimized by a formal relationship with the state. For example, Gummer (1988) examined the organizational and managerial challenges that face hospices as they change from informally organized volunteer groups to formally organized agencies with paid staff. The major challenge that hospices face as they develop formal structures is how to retain their unique features, such as an emphasis on process rather than product, power sharing, and broad-based participation in all aspects of program operations.

Change in sector occurs when an organization shifts from one sector to the other, such as from the nonprofit to the profit-making sector, or from the nonprofit to the public sector. The shift from the nonprofit to the profit sector, which is becoming more and more frequent, is illustrated by a long-standing, revered, but struggling nonprofit psychiatric hospital that was taken over by a for-profit hospital chain. The change from profit to nonprofit is illustrated by the case of Pierce College, a profit-making family business, which became a nonprofit organization after the Pierce family died out and the trustees decided to continue to run the institution. Shifts from the public to the private sector are relatively infrequent. An example is a psychiatric research hospital, run by the Pennsylvania Department of Mental Health, which was folded into a nonprofit health organization when the state ran into budgetary problems and had to cut many of its programs. While it is true that a change in sector is not a frequently encountered transformation, nevertheless it must be noted, as it too requires careful proactive planning and implementation.

Change in professionalism occurs when an organization shifts its use of personnel, be it from one professional base to another, such as from psychological counseling to vocational counseling, or from the use of paraprofessionals or volunteers to the use of professionals. For example, Community Mental Health Centers in the 1960s used community organizers and nonclinical social workers in the Consultation and Education Service, a service mandated to provide prevention programs to the community catchment areas. When psychiatrists and clinical professionals moved into this area, the prevention mandate was eroded and a more clinical thrust emerged (Perlmutter and Silverman, 1973). In this case, volunteers and paraprofessionals served the organization's mission more effectively than the professionals did.

Change in technology is becoming an increasingly important cause of organizational transformation. In the 1950s, the introduction of psychotropic drugs, such as Thorazine, for the treatment of the mentally ill set the stage for the deinstitutionalization movement of the 1970s, and the development of the polio vaccine stimulated the National Foundation for Infantile Paralysis to undergo a fundamental transformation (Sills, 1957). More recently, the development of computers has created transformations in many organizations, affecting not only their record keeping but also their personnel utilization (Cnaan and Parsloe, 1989).

Change in mission, when carefully planned, is a relatively rare phenomenon that involves all the critical actors on the policy level, and requires extensive analysis and painful choices. While some organizations, like the National Foundation for Infantile Paralysis, are forced to find a new mission, others deliberately choose to refocus their raison d'être. A case in point is the Community Service Society of New York City, which shifted from an agency that provided counseling to individuals and families to one that served the community through social action and advocacy (Goldberg, 1980).

Change in structure occurs when an organization is redesigned to accommodate new community realities. One example is the redesign of one entire agency as it merges with another, an event that is occurring with greater frequency in these days of austerity (Buono, Bowditch, and Lewis, 1985; Taylor, Austin, and Caputo, 1992). A second example is the decentralization of internal working relationships, either to allow for more participatory involvement of the work force or to create a different supervisory chain (Perlmutter, 1988). Structural changes are likely to increase as more participatory management models — such as Total Quality Management — gain wider acceptance in human service organizations (Martin, 1993).

Change in funding occurs when there is a shift in the resource base of an organization (Perlmutter and Adams, 1990; Perlmutter and Adams, 1992). This can happen in several ways: (1) an organization that was responsible for raising its own money becomes part of a federated fund, such as United Way or Women's Way; (2) an organization that had diverse funding streams becomes completely dependent on its contracts with the public sector, thus losing its flexibility; (3) an organization loses its traditional funding from foundations and must seek new sources; (4) an organization, in contracting with industry, loses its capacity to define the terms of the professional services it offers, as the contractor specifies what it will purchase; (5) an organization with membership fees, or fees for services, loses its traditional middle-class clientele and serves a new population that has no capacity to meet these costs.

Change in charismatic leadership occurs most frequently when the founding leader leaves and there is no other developed leadership in the system. While this frequently leads to the death of the organization, it occasionally serves to challenge the members to fight for survival (personal communication, Stephen Blades, November 1992).

Change in societal values is an important impetus for organizational transformation. The Women's Christian Temperance Union did not recognize the necessity to adapt to changing societal values and consequently moved from a mainstream group to a peripheral organization (Gusfield, 1955–1956). By contrast, many women's health centers recognized that, in order to survive during the conservative administrations of the 1980s, they needed to broaden their mission to include preventive care (personal communication, Jean Hunt, July 1992).

Each type of transformation must be understood in terms of the context within which it occurs. Each type of transformation must be analyzed in order to understand the specific elements to be addressed and the specific actors to be involved.

Dilemmas Attending Organizational Transformation

Organizational change is never achieved smoothly; organizational transformation is a major challenge. It is essential to uncover some of the dilemmas that attend the process in order to make possible clearer analysis of the problem. Perhaps most salient is the fact that conflicting values in our society pose dilemmas for nonprofit agency executives. While some values are secure—such as the work ethic, the integrity of the family, the sanctity of the individual, and the right to self-determination—many values that underpin the nonprofit social services are, in fact, precarious and less firmly grounded (Clark, 1956). In fact, a major source of turbulence in American society is that every four years the national elections yield a new set of circumstances that sometimes reflect sharply contrasting values, as illustrated in the views of former President Bush and those of President Clinton on issues such as legalized abortion, educational vouchers, and public employment strategies. As a result, many social agencies that survive and manage to maintain resources are like "butterflies that flit from political flower to political flower" (Salancik, 1981, p. 146).

Although the value conflicts affect all nonprofit organizations, social welfare programs appear to be most vulnerable because they deal with the most fragile members of our society and are involved in matters that the general public is deeply ambivalent about, such as providing income to the poor, caring for children born out of wedlock, and rehabilitating criminals. And human service executives' views often conflict. For example, a nationally respected executive of a prestigious nonprofit social agency convinced his board of directors to shift the agency's priorities from serving all service-eligible clients, including Medicaid patients, to serving middle- and upper-class insured populations who could generate third-party payments. Many executives would see this decision as abandoning the values of the social work field. When asked what would happen to the poor who needed the agency's services, the executive's response was: "I can't carry them on my back." The dilemma was clear. The agency was struggling with fiscal shortfall, and the temptation, which was great, was to allow mission to be replaced by market. In addition to the need to generate income by changing the client mix, another dilemma is created by funds often being nonrestrictive, which allows the executive flexibility and discretion so essential to executive decision making (Adams and Perlmutter, 1992). Consequently, the pressure is to take this route in spite of the responsibility of serving all people who need the agency's aid.

Moreover, this executive's actions are by no means isolated. In a study of 128 nonprofit social service agencies in the Chicago metropolitan area, Gronbjerg (1990) found that nonprofit organizations are not as responsive to the poor as the general public might think, "probably because they have enough to do without focusing on the poor and their difficult problems. Nonprofit organizations see their own problems as lack of resources, not misdirected efforts. . . . These features encourage nonprofit organizations to limit their outreach . . . and help explain why relatively few of the poor have access to and make use of nonprofit service providers" (pp. 228–229).

Further questions arise when a nonprofit has multiple goals or mandates, not all compatible with each other. This is illustrated by the history of Community Mental Health Centers (CMHCs), in which the regulations that accompanied the Mental Retardation and Community Mental Health Construction Act of 1963 specified that while four mandated services would be treatment oriented, the fifth would focus on the prevention of mental illness. This led to tensions within the centers between the psychiatrists, who were treatment oriented, and the community workers, who were prevention oriented. Given limited resources, the executives were confronted with real dilemmas regarding the allocation of funds and the setting of program priorities (Perlmutter and Vayda, 1978), with the ultimate result of transforming the CMHC program into a delimited clinical service.

Complications frequently flow from the strong inertial forces inherent in organizational life. These include investment in physical plant and specialized personnel, limits on the information available to decision makers, internal political constraints supportive of vested interests, organizational history that justifies past action and prevents consideration of alternative strategies, and legal and economic barriers to new areas of activity (Brockner, Tyler, and Cooper-Schneider, 1986; Gummer, 1990; Hannan and Freeman, 1984). In addition, when change does occur, it reactivates the "liability-of-newness" clock. That is, organizations often must abandon areas in which their service delivery skills and resources were high, and move into new areas where it will take them some time to develop the same level of competence. This can render the organization's performance less reliable and possibly hurt its survival chances (Stinchcombe, 1965).

Related to inertia is a quandary associated with changing technology. An executive bind is created when new techniques are demanded as a result of rapid external change, but the implementation does not keep up with the technology (Perlmutter, 1980). For example, a number of social agencies rushed to computerize the work environment even when doing so may have caused dysfunction in their particular situations. Thus, in the initial interview in a welfare department, a process which requires strong interpersonal skills and sensitivity to each client's particular needs, the installation of a computer to record the data served as a barrier in the interaction because it required the interviewer to focus on the computer and not the client.

This discussion suggests a few of the many dilemmas inherent in the change process. An attempt to identify and understand such difficulties helps in the development of strategies appropriate for a particular organizational transformation.

Managing Organizational Transformations

The assumptions that underpin this discussion, as stated earlier, are that the chief executive bears the practical responsibility for organizational decisions and outcomes, and that especially effective executives involve and work with their boards in deciding on and implementing courses of action. We will suggest an array of strategies that we hope will serve to stimulate executives to broaden their repertoire of responses as they work with their boards, staffs, and volunteers in fulfilling this mandate. The material that follows is organized into four broad categories: political, organizational, professional, and personal. In reality, the different strategies may be applied simultaneously, but it is useful to deal with them separately for the purpose of analysis. Furthermore, it is important that the strategies be viewed as suggestions, not prescriptions. Again, they are designed to stimulate executive analysis and decision making.

Political Strategies

Political strategies apply to all situations and contexts: "People will readily admit that governments are organizations. The converse—that organizations are governments—is equally true but rarely considered" (Long, 1962, p. 110). There are a number of reasons why managers are reluctant to think about organizations in political terms and are loath to develop the skills necessary to effectively manage organizational politics. These range from a belief in rational-technical expertise as the only legitimate basis for professional management practice, to the ambivalence, or even disdain, that many Americans show toward the acquisition and use of power as a means of getting things done (Gummer, 1990; Pfeffer, 1992). Often these people make the assumption that by ignoring the social and organizational realities of power and influence they can make them go away, a practice that might be called "ostrich management." The reality, however, is that politics are involved in innovation and change and "unless and until we are willing to come to terms with organizational power and influence, and admit that the skills of getting things done are as important as the skills of figuring out what to do, our organizations will fall further and further behind" (Pfeffer, 1992, p. 32).

As a consequence of the tendencies described above, basic political strategy for the change-oriented manager includes recognizing that politics exist inside and outside the organization and that one must develop political skills in order to deal with them. Recognizing the existence of organizational politics starts with accepting the fact that organizations are many things, and not just rationally designed instruments for the accomplishment of goals. Organizations are also social settings in which people interact and seek social satisfaction from each other. They are also political arenas in which different groups with different interests compete with each other over control of organizational resources and the direction of organizational programs. This reality is best summed up in the bureaucratic adage, "Where you stand depends on where you sit."

Besides recognizing the existence of organizational politics, the change-oriented manager must go one step further and accept the legitimacy of organizational politics. There are two dimensions to politics in general and to organizational politics in particular. The first has to do with the acquisition and exercise of power. It is when we limit our understanding to this dimension that we are likely to see politics as "dirty" and associate it exclusively with the efforts of ambitious people to accrue power by any means in order to promote their selfish interests.

There is a second dimension to politics, though, and that is the use of the power that one has acquired in order to accomplish the goals to which one is committed. In this respect, power is simply the capacity to bring about certain intended consequences in the behavior of others. "To say a leader is preoccupied with power is like saying that a tennis player is preoccupied with making shots his opponent cannot return. Of course leaders are preoccupied with power! The significant questions are: What means do they use to gain it? How do they exercise it? To what ends do they exercise it?" (Gardner, 1990).

Managers must use power and engage in organizational politics because all organizations—and social service organizations especially—are rife with conflicts created by the competing values, goals, and interests of the different units and individuals that constitute those organizations. All human service organizations pursue some conception of social health that they seek to help their clients attain. But, as Donnison (1955, p. 350) points out, "There is no generally understood state of 'social health' toward which all people strive; our disagreements on this question form the subject matter of politics the world over." Because of the prevalence of disagreements in all organizations, human service organizations as well as most nonprofit and public-sector organizations, the manager must be able to structure them to "enable faction to counteract faction by providing political representation to a comprehensive variety of the organized political, economic, and social interests that are found in the society at large" (Rosenbloom, 1983, p. 219) and that are reflected within the organization.

Given this political perspective, executives have several specific directions in which they can go. First, attention must be paid to the policies that affect their organizations, be they external social policies enacted by Congress or by state or local legislatures, or internal governing policies enacted by the board of directors. In either case, executives must, first, serve a *watchdog* function to assure that the needs of the organization's consumers are being met. Second, executives must be ready to serve as *advocates* for their organization in order to assure that policies reflect changing need (Orfield, 1991; Richan, 1980). And third in this process, executives must be proactive in *networking* in order to involve key interest groups and influential members of the community in the process. Weiner (1984) describes a successful political process through which executive directors in addictions programs developed coalitions to fight the state's cutbacks in methadone services. He suggests an array of escalating strategies that move from traditional social action to the use of nontraditional approaches, including involving the media and the legal system.

Betak, a hospice for terminally ill AIDS patients, also serves to illustrate the political strategies necessary to accomplish organizational transformation. The hospice was a new service, to be sponsored by a sectarian social service agency and housed in the facilities of a former nursing home, which was located in a middle-class urban neighborhood of large homes, built at the turn of the century. While the neighbors prided themselves on their social conscience, on living in an integrated community, and on being political activists, all were surprised at the wrath and resistance that were generated in response to the proposed hospice. It took years of political activity, within the social service organization itself, within the local community, and ultimately within the county and the state (through a bond issue) before the hospice was finally opened. But the political issues remain critical to the continuance of the agency in order to prevent its transformation back to its earlier form.

Organizational Strategies

Organizational strategies address attributes of the system that must be considered in planning for organizational transformation. First is the need to assure that the requirements of the changing context can be appropriately responded to within the unique mission, or niche, of the organization. Thus, for example, the Jewish Employment Vocational Service, an organization established both to serve Jewish refugees fleeing Germany in 1939 and to deal with anti-Semitism in American industry, made a critical decision to accept non-Jewish war veterans as clients after the Second World War. This paved the way for an extensive program with the public sector. However, the agency demonstrated a clarity regarding its mission as it affirmed its sectarian identity in two ways: first, by not being open on Saturdays, and second, by retaining the Jewish designation in its name (Perlmutter, 1969, 1972).

The second issue within the rubric of organizational strategies concerns structure. The issue of centralization versus decentralization must be addressed as it facilitates or impedes the process of transformation. Under the banners of "empowerment," "delayering," and "leaner and flatter," many organizational leaders in the for-profit, public, and nonprofit sectors are moving away from the traditional hierarchical, centralized, command-and-control model of organizational design and management practice. They are replacing this with an organizational design that has fewer hierarchical levels, and with an empowered work force that is more self-directed, self-managed, and self-controlled (Kanter, 1989). In these newly designed organizations, "managers have only themselves to count on for success. They must learn to operate without the crutch of hierarchy. . . . Success depends increasingly on tapping into sources of good ideas, on figuring out whose collaboration is needed to act on those ideas, on working both to produce results" (Kanter, 1989, p. 88).

Argyris (1991) uses the concept of "double loop" to refer to an individual's willingness to learn from past actions, particularly past failures. Researchers have noted that when organizational decision makers are confronted with negative consequences of their decisions, they tend to become defensive and protective of the original decision (Argyris, 1991; Brockner, Tyler, and Cooper-Schneider, 1986). Rather than reviewing the original decision to see what went wrong and how the situation can be improved, they are likely to become more committed to the original bad decision and redouble their efforts to make it work. This process has been called "entrapment," the "sunk-cost" effect, the "knee-deep-in-the-big-muddy" effect, and the "too much invested to quit" effect (Brockner, Tyler, and Cooper-Schneider, 1986, pp. 109–110).

To get staff to be more reflective and less defensive, an organization's educational efforts have to concentrate on changing the cognitive rules of reasoning that members use to design and implement their actions. Argyris (1991) gives an example of how this can be accomplished. An executive of a large organization was preoccupied with the problems caused by the intense competition among the four managers who reported directly to him. He was asked to describe, in a paragraph or so, a meeting he intended to have with these managers to address the problem. But instead of holding the meeting, the executive analyzed this scenario *with* his four subordinates. This became the catalyst for a discussion in which the executive learned several things about the way he acted with his management team. He discovered that his four subordinates often perceived his conversations as counterproductive. He also discovered that many of the tacit evaluations and attributions he had listed turned out to be wrong. "Since he had never expressed these assumptions, he had never found out just how wrong they were" (p. 107).

A third, and relatively recent structural phenomenon, concerns the strategy of mergers, as organizations, especially in the human services arena, are facing threats to their very survival, given stringent fiscal realities. The literature suggests stages of development in the merger process, beginning with the planning phase and progressing through postmerger phases, which include not only physical and legal elements, but psychological ones as well (Buono, Bowditch, and Lewis, 1985). It is interesting to note that mergers in the nonprofit sector are similar to those in the profit sector. In a study of mergers in sixteen human services agencies, Taylor, Austin, and Caputo (1992) found that matters of finance, governance, organization, public relations, and management systems presented fewer difficulties than service delivery and staff matters. "The agencies did not see finance as problematic, although the large agencies did view merging of budgets and the integration of personnel policies as difficult. Governance was not considered troublesome although . . . it was more difficult to integrate the multipurposes of the agencies in the larger mergers into a conceptually neat statement of organizational mission. . . . On board organization, the agencies took a noncontroversial course of action, preferring to achieve unity by combining existing boards of directors. For the most part, public relations was not seen as a problem, although larger mergers found it more difficult to interpret the merger to both the general community and the social work community" (p. 48).

Professional Strategies

Professional strategies involve three elements: conceptual understanding, ideological orientations, and technical expertise. In considering the possibility of organizational transformation it is essential that a thorough understanding of the situation be obtained, such as the policy context, the financial resources, and the service needs. In addition, it is important to clarify whether the values that underlie the current professional practices would apply if the proposed change is effected and whether the professional technical competencies would remain appropriate.

Thus, for example, professionals working in Community Mental Health Centers in Philadelphia in the 1990s are finding themselves at risk for several reasons. When they were originally hired, they saw a broad range of clients and treated them with traditional psychological and psychiatric modalities. With the recent closing of the state's psychiatric inpatient facilities, currently only seriously mentally ill patients can enter the community-based service system, and the services provided have shifted from counseling modalities to concrete services that deal with housing, employment, and other reality problems. This was an organizational transformation created by a policy shift that was not under the control of the executive. The challenge was responded to in a reactive as opposed to proactive manner, and the transformation had to be managed after the fact.

Professional strategies have been effectively utilized by the executive director of the Jewish Children's and Family Agency in Philadelphia. The professional staff had always used individualized counseling as the primary service modality, and the agency hired only professionally trained social workers with master's degrees in social work. With sharp budget cuts, increased service demands, and low salary scales, the agency could no longer attract staff in a competitive market. The executive director hired a consultant who helped reconceptualize the professional services to be provided and who helped design and implement a staff training program so that new modalities could be tried without the traditional resistance created by long-term patterns of practice. Conceptual understanding, ideological orientations, and technical expertise were all involved. This has been a successful professional transformation, perhaps most evident in the amicable contract negotiations between management and labor.

Individual Strategies

Individual strategies are the final ones to be addressed. The successful manager of organizational change will have to be a person who understands the importance of initiative, innovation, and risk taking. In addition to being able to plan for and implement new policies and practices, the manager must be able to critically assess these policies and consider alternatives.

In a study of twenty-five middle managers who successfully introduced information technology innovations into large organizations, Howell and Higgins (1990) identified the personal characteristics that distinguished these managers from others. Extremely high self-confidence, persistence, energy, and risk taking are the hallmark personality characteristics of these change-oriented managers. They have a strong belief in, and enthusiasm for, their mission and what it can do for the organization. Moreover, they have the capacity "to cling tenaciously to their ideas and to persist in promoting them despite frequent obstacles and seemingly imminent failures" (p. 41).

These characteristics are remarkably similar to the characteristics of change-oriented social work managers identified by Gowdy and Rapp (1989). These are managers with "a healthy disrespect for the impossible" and a perception of self that is as powerful and responsible as the situation at hand, flexibility and invention based on a clear focus on people's needs, highly developed problem-solving skills, the ability to blend agendas of seemingly disparate interests, and persistence.

The importance of individual strategies is highlighted in the case of women's alternative health organizations, which are vulnerable organizations that often fail for a number of reasons. While fiscal and political stressors are critical in these systems, an added complexity is their strong ideological commitment to participatory management, something that can often retard or impede essential decision making. Alternative organizations such as these often have a conflict between process and product (Crow, 1978; Miller and Philipp, 1983). Allyson Schwartz, the executive director of the Blackwell Health Center for Women, and now a state senator in Pennsylvania, not only understood the importance of innovation and risk taking but also recognized that even in a "flat" organization like Blackwell, which was committed to participatory management, there had to be a more efficient decision-making apparatus. Ms. Schwartz had the tenacity essential to change-oriented managers and was able to blend disparate agendas into effective organizational processes. The change that she managed in the governance apparatus was a transformation that saved the organization from dissolution. It was stimulated by a change in leadership: the charismatic qualities of the organization's founder were not sufficient to guide the organization (Schwartz, Gottesman, and Perlmutter, 1988).

Summary

Several issues must be highlighted with regard to the management of organizational transformation. It is a process that requires fancy footwork on the part of the executive, footwork that is well practiced in the steps required to utilize the political, organizational, professional, and personal dimensions of the system. This process ultimately requires flexibility and a readiness to engage in new kinds of thinking.

These new kinds of thinking, moreover, often entail unlearning old kinds of thinking. Pfeffer (1992) argues that change-oriented managers must unlearn two lessons that were inculcated in them at school. The first is that there are right and wrong answers to every question. "We are taught . . . that there is a right answer, or at least one approach that is more correct than another. . . . In the world in which we all live, things are seldom clearcut or obvious. . . . [T]he problems we face often have multiple dimensions — which yield multiple methods of evaluation" (p. 36). Change-oriented managers will have to give up any notions of managerial omniscience that they may have held. Managers will have to be open to trying things out to see how they go, and, as unexpected results crop up, they must be able to adjust or even abandon their earlier strategies.

The conventional managerial response to the unexpected is "it should not have happened" (Drucker, 1985), a response that effectively suppresses the recognition of new opportunities. The change-oriented manager needs to see the unexpected as something to be explored rather than hidden. For example, during the 1950s, executives of family service agencies that specialized in long-term counseling were dismayed to see research that showed a decline in the average number of interviews per case. But for practitioners and researchers who were then experimenting with brief treatment methods, these findings provided additional incentives to proceed with their work. Brief-treatment approaches have since created a major transformation in social work practice.

The purpose of this chapter is to help the nonprofit executive become an effective leader in these complex and rapidly changing times. The discussion of dilemmas, types, and strategies related to organizational transformation attempts to delineate a broad context containing many potential courses for action. And since the executive is not a lone star, the material should be relevant to both boards and staff who are critical actors and decision makers in the change process. Which brings us to Pfeffer's second lesson to be unlearned, namely, that life is a matter of individual effort, ability, and achievement. "In the classroom setting, interdependence is minimized. It is you versus the material. . . . Such is not the case in organizations. If you know your organization's strategy but your colleagues do not, you will have difficulty accomplishing anything" (1992, p. 36).

Managers are becoming increasingly aware that if an organizational transformation is to be effective, it must be a *total* organizational effort. Employees at all levels contribute to program success (or failure) in ways that are seamlessly interwoven. The "great man" theory of organizational success is an idea whose time has past (Gummer, 1986). Organizations in all sectors, if they are to weather the changes in our society and the world, will have to create truly collaborative workplaces. "This will happen over the next decade," Reich (1981, p. 30) argues, "because we have no choice but to make it happen if we are to sustain our economic base. The transformation will not be couched in ideological terms, but will be viewed simply as a means of increasing productivity. Our workplaces will become more equitable, secure, and democratic."

To meet the challenges created by both the changing environment and their particular organizational setting, executives in nonprofit organizations must have both the conceptual understanding and the organizational skills to be effective leaders. Their major, multifaceted challenge involves recognizing the need for change, understanding the particular setting and its potentialities, and proactively and effectively managing the change process. If these tasks are successfully accomplished, the transformation that takes place can, in fact, carry the organization to higher levels of effectiveness and efficiency.

References

Adams, C. T., and Perlmutter, F. D. "Commercial Venturing and the Transformation of America's Social Welfare Agencies." *Nonprofit and Voluntary Sector Quarterly,* 1992, *20*(1), 25–38.

Argyris, C. "Teaching Smart People How to Learn." *Harvard Business Review,* 1991, *69*(3), 99–109.

Bendick, M. "Privatizing the Delivery of Social Welfare Services: An Idea to Be Taken Seriously." In S. Kamerman and A. Kahn (eds.), *Privatization and the Welfare State.* Princeton, N.J.: Princeton University Press, 1989.

Brockner, J., Tyler, T. R., and Cooper-Schneider, R. "Escalation of Commitment to an Ineffective Course of Action: The Effect of Feedback Having Negative Implications for Self-Identity." *Administrative Science Quarterly,* 1986, *31*(1), 109–126.

Buono, F., Bowditch, J. L., and Lewis, J. W. "When Cultures Collide: The Anatomy of a Merger." *Journal of Human Relations,* 1985, *38*(5), 477–500.

Clark, B. R. "Organizational Adaptation and Precarious Values: A Case Study." *American Sociological Review,* 1956, *21*(3), 327–336.

Cnaan, R. A., and Parsloe, P. (eds.). *Computers in Human Services,* 1989, *5*(1/2).

Crow, G. "The Process/Product Split." *Quest,* 1978, *4*(4), 15–22.

Donnison, D. V. "Observations on University Training for Social Workers in Great Britain and North America." *Social Service Review,* 1955, *29*(4), 341–350.

Drucker, P. F. "The Discipline of Innovation." *Harvard Business Review,* 1985, *63*(3), 67–72.

Emery, F. E., and Trist, E. L. "The Causal Texture of Organizational Environments." *Human Relations,* 1965, *18*(1), 21–32.

Fabricant, M. B., and Burghardt, S. *The Welfare State Crisis and the Transformation of Social Service Work.* Armonk, N.Y.: M. E. Sharpe, 1992.

Gardner, J. W. *On Leadership.* New York: Free Press, 1990.

Goldberg, G. S. "New Directions for the Community Service Society of New York: A Study of Organizational Change." *Social Service Review,* 1980, *54*(2), 184–219.

Gowdy, E., and Rapp, C. A. "Managerial Behavior: The Common Denominator of Effective Community-Based Programs." *Psycho-social Rehabilitation Journal,* 1989, *13*(2), 31–51.

Gronbjerg, K. A. "Poverty and Nonprofit Organizational Behavior." *Social Service Review,* 1990, *64*(2), 208–243.

Gummer, B. "Lieders for Leaders: Current Perspectives on the Functions of the Executive." *Administration in Social Work,* 1986, *10*(3), 99–111.

Gummer, B. "The Hospice in Transition: Organizational and Administrative Perspectives." *Administration in Social Work,* 1988, *12*(2), 31–43.

Gummer, B. *The Politics of Social Administration: Managing Organizational Politics in Social Agencies.* Englewood Cliffs, N.J.: Prentice-Hall, 1990.

Gusfield, J. R. "Social Structure and Moral Reform: A Study of the Women's Christian Temperance Union." *American Journal of Sociology,* 1955–1956, *61,* 221–232.

Hannan, M. T., and Freeman, J. "Structural Inertia and Organizational Change." *American Sociological Review,* 1984, *49,* 149–164.

Hasenfeld, Y. "The Challenge to Administrative Leadership in the Social Services: A Prefatory Essay." *Administration in Social Work,* 1989, *13*(3/4), 1–11.

Haveman, H. A. "Between a Rock and a Hard Place: Organizational Change and Performance Under Conditions of Fundamental Environmental Transformation." *Administrative Science Quarterly,* 1992, *37*(1), 48–75.

Heimovics, R., and Herman, R. "Responsibility for Critical Events in Non-profit Organizations." *Nonprofit and Voluntary Sector Quarterly,* 1990, *19*(1), 59–72.

Howell, J. M., and Higgins, C. A. "Champions of Change: Identifying, Understanding, and Supporting Champions of Technological Change." *Organizational Dynamics,* 1990, *19*(1), 40–55.

Kanter, R. M. "The New Managerial Work." *Harvard Business Review,* 1989, *67*(6), 85–92.

Kuhn, T. S. *The Structure of Scientific Revolution.* Chicago: University of Chicago Press, 1962.

Levine, C. H. "The Federal Government in the Year 2000: Administrative Legacies of the Reagan Years." *Public Administration Review,* 1986, *46*(3), 195–206.

Long, N. "The Administrative Organization as a Political System." In S. Mailick and E. H. Van Ness (eds.), *Concepts and Issues in Administrative Behavior.* Englewood Cliffs, N.J.: Prentice-Hall, 1962.

Macarov, D. *The Future of Social Work.* Silver Springs, Md.: National Association of Social Workers Press, 1992.

McWhinney, W. *Paths of Change: Strategic Choices for Organizations and Society.* Newbury Park, Calif.: Sage, 1992.

Martin, L. L. "Total Quality Management: The New Managerial Wave." *Administration in Social Work,* 1993, *17*(2), 1–16.

Miller, H., and Philipp, C. "The Alternative Service Agency." In A. Rosenblatt and D. Waldfogel (eds.), *Handbook of Clinical Social Work.* San Francisco: Jossey-Bass, 1983.

Orfield, G. "Cutback Policies, Declining Opportunities, and the Role of Social Service Providers." *Social Service Review,* 1991, *65*(4), 516–530.

Perlmutter, F. D. "A Theoretical Model of Social Agency Development." *Social Casework,* 1969, *50,* 467–473.

Perlmutter, F. D. "Public Funds and Private Agencies." *Child Welfare,* 1971, *50,* 264–270.

Perlmutter, F. D. "System Theory and Organizational Change: A Case Study." *Sociological Inquiry,* 1972, *42,* 109–122.

Perlmutter, F. D. "The Executive Bind: Constraints Upon Leadership." In F. D. Perlmutter and S. Slavin (eds.), *Leadership in Social Administration: Perspectives for the 1980s.* Philadelphia: Temple University Press, 1980.

Perlmutter, F. D. (ed.). *Alternative Social Agencies: Administrative Strategies.* New York: Haworth Press, 1988.

Perlmutter, F. D., and Adams, C. "The Voluntary Sector and For-Profit Ventures: The Transformation of American Social Welfare?" *Administration in Social Work,* 1990, *14*(1), 1–13.

Perlmutter, F. D., and Adams, C. "Leadership in an Embattled Sector." Paper presented at the Association for Research on Nonprofit Organizations and Voluntary Action Conference, New Haven, Conn., Oct. 31, 1992.

Perlmutter, F. D. and Silverman, H. A. "Conflict in Consultation-Education." *Community Mental Health Journal,* 1973, *9,* 116–122.

Perlmutter, F. D., and Vayda, A. "Barriers to Prevention Programs in Community Mental Health Centers." *Administration in Mental Health,* 1978, *5*(2), 140–153.

Pfeffer, J. "Understanding Power in Organizations." *California Management Review,* 1992, *34*(2), 29–50.

Reich, R. B. "The Profession of Management." *The New Republic,* June 27, 1981, pp. 27–32.

Rein, M., and Morris, R. "Goals, Structures, and Strategies for Community Change." In M. Zald (ed.), *Social Welfare Institutions.* New York: Wiley, 1965.

Richan, W. C. "The Administrator as Advocate." In F. D. Perlmutter and S. Slavin (eds.), *Leadership in Social Administration: Perspectives for the 1980s.* Philadelphia: Temple University Press, 1980.

Rosenbloom, D. H. "Public Administration Theory and the Separation of Powers." *Public Administration Review,* 1983, *43*(3), 219–227.

Salancik, G. R. "The Effectiveness of Ineffective Social Service Systems." In H. D. Stein (ed.), *Organization and the Human Services: Cross-Disciplinary Reflections.* Philadelphia: Temple University Press, 1981.

Schwartz, A. Y., Gottesman, E. W., and Perlmutter, F. D. "Blackwell: A Case Study in Feminist Administration." In F. D. Perlmutter (ed.), *Alternative Social Agencies: Administrative Strategies.* New York: Haworth Press, 1988.

Selznick, P. *Leadership in Administration: A Sociological Interpretation.* New York: HarperCollins, 1957.

Sills, D. L. *The Volunteers: Means and Ends in a National Organization.* Glencoe, Ill.: Free Press, 1957.

Stinchcombe, A. L. "Social Structure and Organization." In J. G. March (ed.), *Handbook of Organizations.* Skokie, Ill.: Rand McNally, 1965.

Taylor, J., Austin, M. J., and Caputo, R. K. "Managing Mergers of Human Service Agencies: People, Programs, and Procedures." *Child Welfare,* 1992, *71*(1), 37–52.

Warren, R. L. "Toward a Reformulation of Community Theory." In R. L. Warren (ed.), *Perspectives on the American Community.* Skokie, Ill.: Rand McNally, 1966.

Weiner, H. "Survival Through Coalition: The Case of Addictions Programs." In F. D. Perlmutter (ed.), *Human Services at Risk: Administrative Strategies for Survival.* Lexington, Mass.: Lexington Books, 1984.

PART THREE

&

MANAGING OPERATIONS

In developing programs and activities to achieve their missions nonprofit leaders must organize exchanges with others, including (usually) volunteers, donors, clients or customers, and government officials. This range of exchanges represents the basic marketing relationships in which most nonprofit organizations engage. Following a chapter that describes the progress of the marketing orientation and the uses of marketing theories and skills in nonprofit organizations, two other chapters consider details of the relationships with parties important to many nonprofit organizations. The chapter on volunteer programs examines the issues and choices nonprofit managers face in designing and carrying out volunteer service programs. The chapter on government contracting analyzes the outcomes of government contracting and describes ways in which nonprofit managers can more effectively manage these exchanges.

As various parties that engage in exchanges with nonprofit organizations have become more concerned with accountability and evidence of performance, nonprofit organizations have been challenged to develop better ways to analyze program and organizational effectiveness. Though program and organizational effectiveness are probably related, we think of them as fairly distinct issues. Program assessment involves efforts to measure the outputs and impact of specific programs, such as, for example, a literacy program or a summer jobs for youth program. One chapter in this part describes program evaluation tools that can be used to assess and improve programs.

247

Organizational effectiveness involves judgments about the overall functioning of an organization. While such judgments include program effectiveness, they also involve considerations of financial performance, community involvement, and other factors. The chapter on organizational effectiveness reviews the difficulties of evaluating overall effectiveness and presents an innovative approach to monitoring and evaluating nonprofit organization effectiveness.

12

Marketing
for Nonprofit Managers

Mel S. Moyer

Historically, the scholarly literature on marketing has been substantially skewed. It has tended to focus on the problems of managers who deal in goods, who work in larger enterprises, who market from the manufacturing level, and who operate in a corporate setting. Relatively neglected have been the marketing activities of organizations that sell services (as do universities), of enterprises that tend to be small (as in the professions), of firms operating downstream in trade channels (such as retailers), and of undertakings that are not corporations (like governments). Predictably, the enterprises whose marketing operations have been studied least are those that combine all of these features, namely nonprofit and voluntary organizations.

This skewedness in the marketing literature has been mirrored in a lag in marketing practice. Nonprofit managers have been slower than business executives to embrace and apply marketing ideas. Thus marketing activities, like marketing writings, have tended to be most advanced in corporations and least developed in nonprofits.

This lag in thinking and practice is also seen within the third sector itself. There, most marketing success stories have to do with social marketing campaigns by governments, fundraising campaigns by large health organizations, ticket-vending efforts by major arts enterprises, or commercial operations that are auxiliary to the nonprofit's main mission. Less common are applications involving smaller nonprofits, elements of marketing other than promotion, and offerings where the organization is not exposed to the spur of a conventional open market. In short, the nonprofits that are most fully dedicated to marketing are those that are most like corporations.

However, both in thinking and in action, the gap between corporate marketing and nonprofit marketing has been narrowing (Lovelock and Weinberg, 1978). This has been reflected in the evolution of the marketing literature on nonprofits. In the 1960s, marketing texts began to recognize organizations beyond the private sector by opening with assertions that marketing had relevance to nonbusiness "products" such as organizations, persons, places, and ideas. However, having staked that claim in the nonprofit sector, conventional texts usually went on to concentrate on the for-profit sector. That cursory treatment of nonbusiness settings was consistent with the firmly held but largely untested belief that marketing ideas were universal enough to fit both fields.

By the late 1960s, however, some marketing writers had begun to turn more explicitly and more thoughtfully to "broadening the concept of marketing" (Kotler and Levy, 1969). That led to marketing texts addressed specifically to nonprofit managers. Consistent with thinking at the time, the first opened with the statement that "nonprofit organizations face a host of problems that would be analyzed as straightforward marketing problems if found in the profit sector" (Kotler, 1975, p. ix), and it was primarily an effort to demonstrate, with little modification to the corporate vocabulary, how commercially proven approaches could be profitably borrowed by nonprofit marketers.

In the late 1970s, several writers began to highlight how nonprofits had to modify conventional corporate planning techniques (Newman and Wallender, 1978; Wortman, 1979, 1981).

In the 1980s, there followed two quite personalistic texts (Rados, 1981; Lauffer, 1984), which challenged the alleged universality of the conventional marketing wisdom. They did so implicitly by departing from the organization structure of established texts, and explicitly by questioning the transferability of some accepted marketing thinking.

The evolution continued with the publication of a "second generation" nonprofit text whose preface said: "Instead of merely trying to see what can be learned from business marketing and then applying that knowledge in new contexts, we emphasize the state of the art in marketing practice and theory for public and nonprofit organizations" (Lovelock and Weinberg, 1984, p. vii).

The rest of this chapter aims to continue that healthy process by showing how managers in the third sector can understand, apply, and profit from marketing.

What Is Marketing?

One of the reasons for marketing's relatively slow adoption in third-sector organizations is that it has been misperceived by nonprofit managers. In those enterprises, a common view is that marketing amounts to advertising, public relations, and fundraising—and little more. That perception leads to the conclusion that marketing is inherently aggressive and potentially manipulative—not a congenial belief in a field where nurturing, educating, healing, and civilizing are cherished values.

A more appropriate definition is that marketing is the facilitation of exchange (Bagozzi, 1975). In this construction, marketing is a vital life process that links an organization—corporate or nonprofit—with key elements in its environment. Important exchange partners include donors, governments, media, service collaborators, allies in advocacy, and—of special interest—clients.

This conception of marketing has powerful implications for nonprofit managers. First, it makes marketing a crucial management function, since success in accomplishing these exchanges determines whether an organization will thrive or die. Second, it means that marketing in nonprofits is not optional; it may be conducted implicitly or explicitly, amateurishly or professionally, witlessly or well, but it will occur. Third, it underlines that marketing is much more than promotion, since mutually advantageous exchanges require that the parties do a good deal more than communicate with one another. For the nonprofit manager, then, this more embracing conceptualization of marketing can be both liberating and daunting.

The Marketing Mix

The full impact of that more generic definition can be seen when one translates it into managerial action over a range of situations. Depending on the organization, its "customers" may be called buyers, shoppers, consumers, users, owners, attendees, members, participants, clients, patients, students, believers, supporters, sufferers, and so on. Moreover, to facilitate mutually beneficial exchanges with these other parties, an enterprise must do more than promote itself; it must also tailor its products and services, adjust its prices (both monetary and nonmonetary), and shape its service delivery systems in ways that truly serve the end user. That in turn requires an insightful understanding of the organization's clients, including their demographics, motivations, attitudes, needs, wants, and behavior. In a complex world, such insights are less likely to come from casual observation than from trenchant, marketing-oriented research.

From this it can be seen that to create a fully professional marketing process, one conceived as the facilitation of exchange in all its dimensions, the nonprofit manager must develop a solid knowledge of the organization's external environment and internal capabilities and goals, and must then blend its products, prices, promotions, and service delivery systems into a "marketing mix" that meets the needs of both the organization and its target markets. (In what may be an excessive devotion to alliteration, marketers refer to "the four P's of the marketing mix" as "product, price, promotion, and place.")

Analyzing the Organization's Portfolio

Especially when marketing is accorded this larger domain, marketing strategy verges closely on organizational strategy. To guide marketing strategy, then, management should establish the relative priorities to be given to the organization's main programs. That ranking will probably not be a straightforward exercise. Many nonprofits, especially the larger ones that are most likely to engage in formal marketing planning, are an assemblage of enterprises. A social service agency may run a self-help group for the children of divorce, a social center for isolated senior citizens, a counseling program for substance abusers, a mothercraft program for pregnant teens, and an ongoing campaign to enhance the legal protections for battered wives. Similarly, a municipal art gallery may offer major exhibitions, art workshops, a public lecture series, a gift shop, and a restaurant. Such organizations are, in effect, charitable conglomerates. Accordingly, they confront decisions not unlike those of a corporation that must determine which product lines to push, maintain, or drop.

To settle these inescapable issues, an enterprise needs a process for prioritizing its programs, and for alloting limited resources among them. Especially in a nonprofit organization, with its disparate stakeholders, competing values and ambiguous bottom line, that process can be divisive, even destructive.

To bring order and balance to ordering their priorities, nonprofit managers have begun to borrow from business executives an approach called portfolio analysis. Essentially, portfolio analysis identifies the main programs in the organization's family of enterprises, establishes a set of criteria for judging the relative importance of these "strategic management units" (SMUs), evaluates each SMU against those criteria, places each program in a summary classification in the organization's overall portfolio, and derives a general strategy appropriate to programs that fall into each class.

Several frameworks are available for conducting a portfolio analysis in a nonprofit setting. In them, individual criteria are clustered to produce a summary evaluation of each SMU on two or three key dimensions. For example, after being weighed on a number of subfactors, each faculty in a college may be placed in an overall classification according to its quality and reputation, the size and growth of its market, and its centrality to the mission of the college (Kotler and Andreason, 1991). Similarly, each program in a social service agency may be classified according to its public benefits on the one hand, and its financial results on the other.

These summary appraisals are usually pulled together in a grid in which each SMU is placed in its strategic space. The resulting portfolio matrix is a convenient visual representation of management's best judgment as to the status, place, and prospects of the various members of the organization's family of programs.

One of the richest portfolio frameworks developed for nonprofits is MacMillan's (1983), illustrated in Table 12.1.

Table 12.1. A Strategic Planning Grid for Nonprofit Organizations.

	Program Attractiveness			
	High		Low	
	Alternative Coverage		Alternative Coverage	
Competitive Position	High	Low	High	Low
Strong	I	II	V	VI
Weak	III	IV	VII	VIII

Source: MacMillan, 1983. Used by permission.

By filling in this grid, a nonprofit manager will have taken several important steps toward building marketing strategies. First, the portfolio analysis will have signaled whether, in general, the enterprise is strong or weak, well positioned or in danger. For example, if most of its SMUs are in areas that are unattractive, that have strong alternative coverage, and where their competitive positions are weak (cell VII), then the enterprise's overall health is frail and its future life is perilous. A boys' club competing with the Red Cross in the field of water safety might find itself in that position.

How its programs cluster in the matrix will indicate in turn whether the enterprise's marketing goals should be expansion or retrenchment, whether its marketing strategies should continue past actions or invoke new ones, and whether its marketing animus can be reasonably daring or must be risk averse. Where a program is in a strong competitive position in an area of high attractiveness and low alternative coverage (cell II), management could endorse growth so to secure the field from future entrants. On the other hand, a repertory theatre reviewing a season in which most of its offerings were artistic and financial failures might find most of its offerings in cell III and feel bound to shift its portfolio away from leading-edge plays by local amateurs toward familiar classics by established playwrights.

Or, if most of the portfolio shows SMUs clustered in areas of great attractiveness but dense alternative coverage (cell I), it may signal that management has fallen into the habit of seeking easy funding wherever it may lie—a seductive strategy of drift. Such a diagnosis would indicate that, at the very least, the board should reaffirm or revise the mission of the enterprise. A weak portfolio tends to narrow the organization's options, while a healthy one gives management a wider choice of marketing strategies.

The portfolio analysis also aids the marketing manager by suggesting what strategies are appropriate for individual SMUs. For example, if a program falls in a cell representing an attractive field, but one that fits poorly with the organization's mission and that is served by more capable alternative suppliers, a logical initiative might be to market the program to those agencies better positioned to deliver it. Alternatively, a public library serving a catchment area with a growing number of large single-parent families might see this as a cell IV situation, leading it to add study areas, extend its hours, and target youngsters needing a suitable place to do homework. The same branch, hedged about by new video rental outlets, might judge this to be a cell V setting and prune its own video program accordingly. Thus portfolio analysis gives the nonprofit manager a strategic framework within which to design fitting marketing mixes.

Managing Marketing Research

If marketing is to begin with the end user, its plans must be grounded in a thorough understanding of the organization's intended clienteles. Therefore the manager must usually preface the crafting of a marketing mix by undertaking some form of marketing research.

Yet formal market investigations in nonprofit enterprises are quite rare. The reasons are several. One is management's belief that it already has an informed relationship with those it serves. This conviction is nourished by the fact that, compared to corporations, nonprofits often do seem to be closer to their customers. For example, they tend to operate on a small scale in local markets (community centers, municipal transit systems, crisis counseling units), they frequently deal directly with end users rather than through intermediaries (vocational guidance programs, museums, religious organizations), and the interaction that results may furnish the service provider with substantial personal detail about the client (children's camps, marriage counseling, higher education). In these circumstances, marketing research may seem unnecessary.

And, in other third-sector settings, market studies may appear unwarranted because the service deliverer seems to be in a better position than the user to specify the appropriate product. Thus, when the "customer" is an emotionally disturbed child entering therapy, a recently released convict consigned to a halfway house, or a freshman confronting a curriculum, the service deliverer may see it as a right, even a duty, to prescribe what the other party should receive. Added to these deterrents is another: the perception in the charitable sector that marketing research is an esoteric and expensive tool of big business.

While these views are understandable, they are too flawed to allow professional nonprofit managers to bypass an earnest and open-minded exploration of their markets (Andreason, 1982). A perception that clients are unqualified to have opinions on the treatment they should receive can lead professionals to be inattentive to the legitimate wishes of those they intend to serve. Moreover, when clients are ill-served, their remedies may be few and frail. Compared to shoppers in open markets, the customers of nonprofit organizations are more likely to be disadvantaged and vulnerable, with correspondingly little opportunity to complain or to switch to other offerings. Therefore, despite their apparent closeness to their customers, many nonprofits are sufficiently insulated from and unresponsive to their clienteles as to need an open window on the market.

Moreover, market investigations need not be unsupportable in a charitable enterprise. Quite simple probes can produce highly profitable insights for nonprofit managers. In addition, such investigations can be made more economical by enlisting the expertise of a marketing research firm or a college marketing research class, either as a donation or on an out-of-pocket-cost basis. For a nonprofit manager, then, the marketing mix should be informed and focused through astute, if frugal, market intelligence.

When undertaken in a third-sector setting, a marketing research project may vary in emphasis from its corporate counterpart (Moyer, 1989). For example, nonprofits may find it more possible or more necessary to rely on publicly available secondary information, perhaps from the United Way or a municipality, in lieu of primary data from the proprietary in-house surveys that companies buy. Similarly, the study is more likely to be a joint undertaking by organizations with a common interest—say, in how to reduce vandalism or how to attract tourists to a city's arts festival. Indeed, the investigation may be a public exercise involving shared authority among diverse stakeholders, as in the case of a needs assessment focusing on the problems of a community's recent immigrants, unemployed youth, or handicapped people. Such undertakings call for political and public relations skills beyond those usually required in a company's study.

Despite these differences, the nonprofit manager will find that a third-sector marketing research project should be driven by the same animus, and should follow the same basic steps, as one in the private sector. These procedures are well described in both "corporate" and "nonprofit" writings (Andreason, 1985; Lovelock and Weinberg, 1989).

Choosing Target Markets

Guided by market intelligence, the focus for the marketing mix should be the organization's chosen clienteles. That requires target marketing. It is achieved by first identifying the main population groups that might be addressed by the enterprise, then selecting those market segments that best fit the organization's objectives and abilities, and finally, by tailoring marketing programs to each chosen segment.

To the corporate manager, segmentation is a way of approaching the market that is central if not essential; to the nonprofit manager it may be a process that is often questionable, if not unacceptable. The reason is that choosing some segments means not choosing others—which is to say that serving some people means not serving some others. In a field in which turning no one away is often a cherished norm, neglecting some possible clients as a matter of policy can seem to degrade fundamental organizational values.

Yet in many nonprofits, the case for target marketing is both strong and responsible. In an environment in which human needs are huge and escalating, while resources are constrained and shrinking, no organization can serve all comers. The question then is not whether the enterprise will constrain its domain, but how. Market segmentation can help nonprofit managements to address that question in an orderly and defensible way.

Segmentation carries with it many benefits. It helps an organization to focus its resources on the clienteles that best fit its mission, capabilities, and aspirations. If a venture is launched with a mission of saving homeless adolescents from a destructive life, but begins with little experience and money, it might opt at the outset to target the most readily redeemable in that population. That subset might translate into a market segment defined as youth who had not been on the street long enough to have a pimp, who were not yet addicted to hard drugs, who retained some nontoxic family connections, and who were prepared to work toward achievable vocational goals.

Clearly defined segments also serve to target the marketing mix, thereby improving the likelihood that the enterprise will address chosen publics with programs fitted to their wants and needs, with channels of distribution that reach them effectively, with prices that respond to their ability and willingness to pay, and with promotions that reflect their motivations and media habits. Thus a public agency mandated to aid "disadvantaged consumers" might adopt as its "product" the mediation of customer complaints, might take as its marketing channel a chain of storefront offices on the main streets of economically depressed towns, might set its prices close to zero, and might use unpretentious media and interpersonal networks to advertise itself as local, readily accessible, and user-friendly.

The first step in segmentation is to divide the total market into meaningful groups. There are many possible lines along which the manager may sort out clusters of potential clients. Therefore the partition requires both care and creativity. The most conventional divisions are demographic, geographic, and socioeconomic. These include age, sex, marital status, education, and income. Because available data are most often arrayed along these lines, marketers frequently define their target clienteles in these terms. Thus college recruiters will seek out people in defined areas, age brackets, and educational levels, while the director of a YWCA life skills program will invoke dimensions such as sex, marital status, and income.

Against the operational convenience of segments bounded by demographics, the marketer must weigh the conceptual richness of segments defined by psychographics. Psychographic descriptors include life-styles, values, attitudes, opinions, and personalities. Political parties often seek out supporters according to their attitudes toward government involvement in public life, advocacy bodies search for sympathizers on the basis of the position on key issues, and arts organizations may estimate the market potential in a catchment area disaggregated into the "home-centered," the "sports followers," and the "culture seekers." In effect they are targeting psychographic segments.

One may also consider assigning marketing effort to different groups segmented according to the benefits they seek. Some prospective volunteers for a seniors center may wish to exercise their skills in crafts, while others may need to earn credits toward a certificate, and still others may find reward in befriending lonely people. Benefit segmentation is attractive because it indicates to the marketer the types of products and appeals that will find favor with the other party. Put another way, benefit segmentation is efficacious because, being rooted in the fundamental notion of exchange, it not only identifies homogeneous client clusters, it is suggestive of the most relevant offer for each.

Populations can also be segmented according to how they behave with respect to the product or service being offered. Those who are heavy users can be especially propitious targets. Thus, longtime subscribers to the ballet, excessive consumers of alcohol, frequent donors of blood, extravagant users of energy, or generous supporters of a church may justify specially designed marketing programs.

Finally, because marketing aims ultimately to consummate exchanges, the marketer may find it logical and advantageous to cluster consumers by how they respond to marketing variables. If younger college graduates are more budget minded but more bonded to their alma mater than are older ones, the alumni officer must ask whether they should not be approached as different segments in terms of product and price. Similarly, if some potential donors are moved by sympathy for those who suffer from a given disease, while others react to a warning that they may contract it, then the fund raiser should consider whether it is feasible to mount separate appeals.

As one might expect, pragmatic managers, seeking workable fits between their organizations and their environments, commonly find themselves combining several kinds of segmentation. A political candidate could begin with a geographic delineation (a voting district), then give particular attention to certain demographic sets (suburbanites of voting age), then narrow down to people in particular psychographic groups (disaffected conservatives or loyal liberals), and target those who seek particular benefits (tougher law enforcement or easier abortions). Target marketing presents the manager with many choices and a demanding professional task.

In choosing target markets, the manager may apply several criteria. Logically, the first is whether a candidate segment fits the mission of the enterprise. Because nonprofits must be mindful of many constituencies whose aims and values will not fully mesh, accommodating this criterion may be challenging. A church considering ministering to gays, a college planning to go coeducational, or an agency aiming to discontinue a camp for diabetic youngsters will need to enter into the exercise with care, patience, and sensitivity.

A second test is whether the segment aligns with the organization's capabilities, present or potential. Here too, discerning judgment can be called for. Human service organizations seek to build elan and combat burnout by celebrating the dedication and professionalism of their people. Conversely, they tend to downplay the capabilities, and even the existence, of alternative service providers. Both of these tendencies, while understandable, can be detrimental to clear-eyed organizational stock taking. This means that in appraising their goodness of fit with potential target markets, nonprofit managements must take care not to overvalue the capabilities of colleagues and underestimate the strengths of competitors.

A third criterion is whether the segment is sufficiently large to justify a special marketing treatment. Again, arriving at an answer can be less straightforward than in a business firm. In a commercial undertaking, projected return on investment is likely to be the dominant (though not the only) arbiter of acceptable segment size; in a charitable enterprise, unprofitably small segments are more likely to be taken as target markets because the organization or its founders decide to override financial considerations. This is seen when a transit system mounts a special program for the handicapped or a symphony orchestra undertakes an educational tour to small, remote centers.

A segment is also an attractive choice to the extent that it can be measured and accessed. People with sexually transmitted diseases, seniors with suicidal tendencies, or fathers with incestuous habits are groups whose size is difficult to estimate and whose members are hard to reach. In addressing such targets, marketing-minded managements face several challenges. One is to measure the scope of the chosen segment, this being necessary for an informed budgeting of marketing effort. Another is to find promotional appeals that are powerful enough, nonmonetary prices that are low enough, and service delivery systems that are nonthreatening enough to bring the agency and the client together so that a beneficial transaction can occur. Sometimes, with inventiveness, this can be accomplished by a rifle approach in which only the specified clients are reached, but often it is necessary, and more economical, to use a shotgun campaign, leaving it to members of the target population to "come into the market" through a process of self-selection. Thus, battered women, school dropouts, and obese citizens are urged to seek remedies through a marketing mix of low prices, empathetic services, and mass advertising by widely deployed information centers.

Shaping Products and Services

Having chosen target markets by means of thoughtful segmentation, management is in a position to begin formulating the marketing mix. Among the four P's, the program is usually shaped first because the choice of "product" tends to set the bounds for decisions on place, price, and promotion.

It should be noted that more often than not the product under consideration will be substantially intangible. Some nonprofits do deal in physical goods, of course: an aquarium may have a gift shop, a social service agency a second-hand clothing store, symphony orchestra sets of compact discs, and an environmental group a line of posters. Generally, though, the third sector offers services, its vehicles being concerts, courses, exhibitions, memberships, legislation, and so on. Beyond that, many nonprofits deal in what have come to be called "social behaviors," as when a citizens' group calls for compulsory helmets for cyclists, a corporate volunteer council urges companies to offer employees time off for volunteer activities, and a city council mounts a campaign against littering.

For marketers, these differences are significant. Services and social behaviors have characteristics that call for different treatments than conventional products (Lovelock and Weinberg, 1989). In general, these differences tend to complicate management's task. For example, services usually cannot be created in advance of consumption, mass produced, packaged, stored, evaluated before the purchase, or returned after the purchase. For the marketer, these abstract sounding features of the "product" translate into quite concrete problems. To illustrate, in marketing nonproducts, one cannot as readily routinize production processes, ensure quality control, avoid oversupply and stockouts, and appraise consumer satisfaction.

Social behaviors are products that bring additional marketing challenges (Kotler and Roberto, 1990; Bloom and Novelli, 1981). Some are controversial (birth control information for teens, the ordination of women, the banning of "obscene" art). Others are deeply embedded in individuals' lives (speeding, overeating, discriminating against visible minorities). Others involve target markets that are entire populations (the ownership of handguns, the use of nonmetric measures, the uncontrolled breeding of household pets).

Moreover, the successful marketing of new social behaviors may require changing pleasurable personal habits, even addictions, in favor of a larger and more remote public good. Examples of such behaviors are converting to energy-saving appliances, adopting weight-loss regimens, and giving blood. All of this means that the nonprofit manager who would change social behaviors can expect a formidable task. Among other things, the successful marketer must usually find compelling incentives for individuals to "buy into" what is proposed, mobilize allied organizations to facilitate or even enforce the advocated ways of acting, and counter forceful opposition from determined adversaries. The acrimonious struggles over abortion, handguns, and school prayer are among the most vivid illustrations.

To add to these, management will face other challenges in shaping its product lines. Because the pressure from rivals seems weak, third-sector enterprises frequently have difficulty freeing up resources to scan the environment for new market opportunities. They may also lack the funds, or believe they do, to probe the wants and needs of potential clients and to develop prototypes of new offerings, as commercial firms routinely do. Additionally, where a case can be made for upgrading or downgrading a program, management's deliberations can be complicated by the dedication of some directors, funders, professionals, staff, and volunteers to particular priorities. On occasion, that dedication can approach fanaticism. Underlying all of these obstacles to timely and rational product-line planning is the absence of a market mechanism to arbitrate disagreements as to the adding and dropping of nonprofit programs.

To cope with these complexities, management should have in place an orderly process for developing new products and services. At least conceptually, the steps prescribed for business enterprises are appropriate. They begin with the generation of new ideas. These may be stimulated internally or they may come from external sources such as competitors, clients, conferences, or journals. At this stage, care should be taken not to abort fresh ideas through an unhealthy preference for internal sources, an undue reliance on past experience, and a premature intolerance for unconventional proposals.

When sufficient candidate ideas have been generated, they should be winnowed down to a manageable number by the application of screening criteria. Such considerations would include the size and urgency of the need to be served, the degree of competition to be met, the costs and risks involved in the launch, and the availability of funds to build the program. To illustrate, if an agency began with an idea for a special weapons and tactics (SWAT) team to intercede in violent domestic disputes, it would then have to work through how it would mesh with the police and allied social agencies, what neighborhoods it would cover, and whether it would be on call at all times or only during the most dangerous hours of the weekend.

In a search for the best prototype, several models might be developed for further testing. These alternative concepts can sometimes be tested by asking intended users to respond to verbal descriptions, as in the case of commercial products. When teachers are quizzed as to the best configuration for class tours of a heritage village, or when symphony goers are asked to react to the notion of a mixed sampler subscription with the ballet and the opera, then in effect the prospective user participates in the unfolding design of the product.

With a promising concept now outlined, management can proceed to trace through the associated costs and revenues. To develop such estimates, it will be necessary to take a provisional position on key marketing variables, including distribution costs and promotional outlays. Similarly, the calculation of break-even volumes will require an estimate of the prices that might be charged. At this business analysis stage, then, the marketing manager is called on to sharpen the projections by outlining a marketing strategy to accompany the product.

The final stages in the product development process are to test the offer in the market and to move toward a full launch. Often the two tend to merge: a dance company may offer a summer program-in-the-park unless and until it is found that voluntary donations will not cover the costs, and a college's on-campus day for graduating high school students may be adopted subject to a review of its effect on applications.

As in the conventional commercial marketplace, the offerings of nonprofits are subject to changing circumstances: a tilt in the balance of competition with the entry of a new substitute service, a shift in the market with the emergence of an unserved population, or a revision of the organization's position with the loss of a funding source. Once launched, then, a program should be reappraised over its life, and opening marketing strategies should be revised as required.

To assist in this process, the nonprofit manager can borrow and bend a tool that has been useful to the business executive: the concept of a product life cycle (PLC), or in this case, the offer life cycle (Wasson, 1978). The life cycle is a widely observed phenomenon. Indeed, some marketing writers have commented on the similarity of the marketplace to an ecological environment, while others have compared the competition among products to the struggle among organisms, and others have likened the emergence of winning brands to the survival of nature's fittest. The analogy is not perfect, and in particular cases the relevant life cycle may not be easy to define and apply, but the open-minded nonprofit manager should consider the usefulness of the concept.

Most verbal models of the PLC divide the product's evolution into stages of introduction, growth, maturity, and decline. These stages are defined and differentiated by the changing level of "sales" for the brand or the product category. In a nonprofit setting this could be, for example, the value of ticket subscriptions sold, the number of voters registered, or the percentage of the population affected.

Each phase in the PLC is described in terms of the consumer behavior and competitive actions that one tends to see at that point. These generalizations serve as suggestions for the manager wanting to anticipate future stages and aiming to adapt the marketing program to each. Inconveniently, these moving pictures are most detailed where the theory describes product life cycles for commercial products, especially consumer packaged goods. That means that to profit from the PLC concept, the nonprofit marketer must undertake some careful transpositions to a different marketplace.

In guiding products through their life cycles, marketers can also take advantage of what is known about how innovations are adopted. Scholars in several fields have been interested in how new ways of thinking and acting are accepted. What explains the pattern whereby farmers move to new strains of seeds, physicians accept new kinds of drugs, and women adopt new styles of dress? The relevance for marketers is plain: by better understanding the diffusion of innovations they can better manage the marketing of new products.

Such insights can also aid third-sector enterprises. An explanation of why some forms of birth control are more acceptable than others in developing countries can have action implications for a nongovernmental organization (NGO); a profile of the kinds of people who lead in accepting environmentally friendly consumption habits can provide an opening target for conservation groups; and knowledge of the interpersonal connections through which crack is sanctioned, accepted, and spread can assist governments, police, and social workers who aim to shut those networks down.

These examples suggest some of the aspects of diffusion that can be especially useful to nonprofit marketers. One is the nature of those who, within the life of innovations, play the roles of early adopters, the early majority, the late majority, and the laggards. Special interest is likely to attach to those who are active and influential at the outset of the life cycle. Rogers (1962) has generalized that, compared to those who come along later, early adopters in a social system tend to be younger, of higher social status, financially better off, more plugged into impersonal and cosmopolitan information sources, and in closer contact with the origins of new ideas. This portrait could be suggestive for the targeting of recruiting efforts by an organization espousing world government, for example, and might frame a more focused probe to detail its most likely advocates.

By applying diffusion theory, the third-sector marketer can be assisted in two other product management tasks: estimating how quickly the organization's newly launched offer will be accepted, and accelerating that process. Six characteristics have been found to speed or impede the diffusion of an innovation. The first is its relative advantage: for example, is this new teen phone-in service less likely to alert one's parents than a walk-in center? The second is its compatibility with existing values and past experiences: will this parking-lot church service meet the traditional expectations of immobile seniors? Another is the innovation's complexity: how difficult is it for householders to sort out recyclable garbage from the regular stuff? In addition, the marketer should ask about its trialability or divisibility: if applicants fail this admission test, does this graduate school make it a permanent part of their record? A further consideration is the innovation's observability or communicability: if one makes the substantial personal investment to take and pass the docent course for the art gallery, will this accomplishment be celebrated in ways that are important to the prospective volunteer? Finally the marketer must consider the risk as seen by the user: if one joins this new kind of protest movement, what are the odds of public embarrassment or physical harm?

Formulating Pricing Policies

Too often in nonprofit organizations, prices are set in casual and arbitrary ways. The result may well be unnecessary loss of revenue to the enterprise and/or a diminution of available benefits to customers. The professionally minded manager should enter into price making in an orderly and analytical manner.

Reduce Nonfinancial Costs

The first step should be to aggressively and creatively search out ways in which the organization might reduce the nonfinancial costs of making its product or service available to those who need it. There are, potentially, a significant number of subtle but substantial barriers to patronage in many nonprofit offerings including, for example, symphony concerts, nursing homes, and sanitary water systems (Kotler and Andreason, 1991). These consumer deterrents are, in effect, product costs. Reviewing them may lead the nonprofit manager, as part of the pricing exercise, to revisit the design of the offer.

As an illustration, in deciding whether to use the "free" services of a small claims court, a citizen may weigh the considerable number of very real costs: the awkwardness of asking for time off from work, the expense of parking, lost wages, the embarrassment of airing a messy personal dispute in a public forum, the fear of cross-examination, the uncertainty as to how to conduct oneself under legal procedures, the boredom of waiting, the fear of losing, the frustration that will follow if the case does not come up during the designated day, and the trouble of actually collecting whatever the court may award. A marketing perspective would argue that before putting resources into promoting the use of such a service, especially to those in the lower socioeconomic groups that will be a key target market, one should search out opportunities to reduce each of these costs.

Establish Pricing Objectives

The next step is to establish the pricing objectives. In pricing tickets for a fundraiser or gifts in a hospital shop, profit maximization may be a dominant goal; in establishing membership fees for a save-the-wetlands group or the tariff for a college reunion, expanding the base of supporters could override other aims; in setting the charges to housebound convalescents for friendly visits or the price per seedling in a tree-planting program, cost recovery may have the first claim; and in establishing a fee scale for a legal aid office or a day camp for handicapped children, social equity might be the first pricing objective.

However, it will be observed that in each case other desirable aims will lay some claim. The hospital gift shop will not want to appear to gouge people who are distressed; the wetlands group will want to generate a surplus to pay for lobbying; the tree-planting program should want to avoid charges of unfair competition from private nurseries; and the legal aid office will want to discourage frivolous consultations. At the outset, then, the marketing manager will have to find an acceptable balance among pricing objectives that are multiple and conflicting.

Having established pricing goals and their priorities, management must fashion a strategy for achieving them. In doing so, it should take account of three key considerations: *costs, demand, and competition.* Of these three, the least problematical may be costs. To calculate the cost per child for a day-care center or the cost per unit for a proselytizing video will not be a difficult exercise. However, when an organization produces a number of services out of a common facility, as conglomerate nonprofits often do, management must make judgments as to the allocation of joint costs. To determine how much to charge a learned society for the use of summertime conference space, a university will have to decide how to apportion the year-round costs of operating its facilities. The same kind of decision will arise in pricing a church wedding, a visit to a hospital emergency ward, or a fee-for-service contract. As when diverse products come out of a single factory, management must arrive at a basis for allocating charges—by the percentage of total space used or total time taken, for example—that seems rational under the circumstances (see Young's management accounting chapter in this book for details about cost allocation methods).

Pricing policies should be informed by break-even analysis. In settling on a price for a product or a program, a manager will want to take into consideration how many units would have to be sold at a given price in order to cover all costs. To determine this, one begins by separating expenses that vary with the number of participants from those that are fixed regardless of patronage. For example, the handout materials in a board management workshop cost, say, $50, versus the instructor's stipend, say, of $1,000. The difference between the intended fee or revenue per unit (say, $75) and the variable cost per unit (the $50 for handouts) is called the "contribution per unit." That is because it is the amount ($25) that each sale contributes to covering the fixed costs. The number of units (registrations) necessary to break even, then, is the number of enrollments that will just cover all the fixed and variable costs. The calculation would be as follows:

$$\text{Break-even volume} = \frac{\text{fixed costs}}{\text{contribution per unit}}$$

$$= \frac{\text{fixed costs}}{\text{price} - \text{variable cost per unit}}$$

$$= \frac{\text{instructor's stipend}}{\text{fee} - \text{cost of handouts per participant}}$$

$$= \frac{\$1,000}{\$75 - \$50}$$

$$= 40 \text{ registrants}$$

If 40 registrants seemed more than could be expected, then the workshop planners might ask, "With 25 participants, what fee would allow us to break even?" The calculation would be as follows:

$$\text{Break-even fee} = \frac{\text{total cost}}{\text{number of participants}}$$

$$= \frac{\text{fixed costs} + \text{variable costs}}{\text{number of participants}}$$

$$= \frac{\$1,000 + (25 \times \$50)}{25}$$

$$= \$90$$

The question then would be whether $90 is a price that the intended participants would pay. If that seemed unlikely, then the break-even analysis would help the workshop planners to calculate their options for subsidizing the event.

It will be noted that the marketer began with costs to calculate the break-even price but was soon led to ask how prospective buyers might respond to that price. The example thereby illustrates another point about price making: cost analysis is linked to demand analysis.

In analyzing demand, a useful concept is that of elasticity. Essentially, price elasticity is the responsiveness of demand to changes in price. When a large change in the price of an offering causes a relatively small change in its sale, then demand for it is called "price inelastic." When small changes in price (up or down) have a relatively large effect on sales, then its demand curve is elastic at that point. In general, an inelastic demand suggests that the marketer can increase total revenue and perhaps net profits by raising the price, while an elastic demand tends to encourage management to avoid price increases and to expand patronage by lowering prices. Clearly, knowledge of the elasticity of demand can be helpful in deciding on user fees — in a day when more and more charitable enterprises are moving to them.

In some situations, elasticity of demand varies significantly across market segments. That variability invites different prices in various segments. The differential pricing of various seat locations in an opera house, the offering of lower-priced student memberships by a political party, and the subsidizing of some children in a YMCA computer camp all represent pricing schemes that recognize and respond to differing demand elasticities in component segments of a market.

It should be noted that demand-oriented pricing requires that the seller estimate the value of the offer as perceived by the buyer. That has import for nonprofit administrators. Executives who are insulated from their markets may substitute their own appraisals of the worth of their offers. In doing so, they risk inventing inaccurate pricing data. To illustrate, a social service agency aiming to offer employee counseling services in competition with private firms, and assuming that "nonprofit" would be equated with "second rate," opted for low prices and lean margins. Subsequent inquiries with corporate customers showed that the agency's long history, high profile, and nonprofit status invested it with a reputation for professionalism, dedication, and quality. That finding translated into an unforeseen opportunity for the manager of the employee assistance program to justify high prices. With that, the program became a cash cow that subsidized the expansion of counseling services to low-income individuals. Astute pricing rests on accurate market inputs.

Of course differential pricing involves ethical as well as economic issues, which nonprofit leaders must resolve and defend.

Along with costs and demand, the price maker should analyze competition. Pressed to keep up with the demand for their services, some nonprofit managers are inclined to dismiss competition as irrelevant to their own decisions. Yet the intended clienteles of most nonprofit enterprises do have alternatives to their patronage. A family considering joining an art gallery may see for itself a large number of acceptable suppliers—those ranging across the arts, education, recreation, and entertainment fields. As well, a couple with marital problems can look in many directions for help: to religious organizations, legal firms, family service agencies, self-help groups, phone-in shows, author-gurus, family, and friends. End users often define relevant competitors as those enterprises that offer equivalent benefits, rather than just similar-looking products; using this perspective, managers of nonprofit organizations, even ones that appear to be semimonopolies, may find that they do in fact have generic competition.

Appraising competition—the third element of pricing—can be useful in several ways. First, it will help to identify the ceiling—the highest price the marketer can charge. Studying competitors' prices, monetary and nonmonetary, can also reveal ways in which service deliverers can offer better products at lower prices. Competitive analysis is thus an essential part of the pricing process.

Designing Marketing Channels

In the process of designing, pricing, and market testing a proposed new offering, management will have had to think about how best to distribute it. Now, though, it will become necessary to give explicit attention to the design of suitable marketing channels.

These decisions can have a major effect on the fortunes of the offering itself. As in the private sector, a worthy and attractively priced product that is not effectively deployed may well fail. Thus, when an ombudsman for low socioeconomic groups requires that complaints be registered in writing and in English, the service becomes, for practical purposes, inaccessible to many of its intended users. Conversely, a part-time master's program in business administration might successfully connect with young professionals by locating its classrooms on commuter trains.

In some respects, the choice of channels can be more critical in the third sector than in the private sector. When the product is a service, it is often consumed at the same time and place that it is manufactured, thereby putting the nonprofit manager in direct contact with end users. Religious, psychological, and educational services tend to be of that sort. That buyer-seller contact may be inherently sensitive and intrusive, making the quality of the product/channel offering unusually crucial to a satisfactory outcome. Such is the case with marriage counseling and correctional services. Under such circumstances, the nonprofit marketer must be a consumer-oriented channel manager.

It follows from this that the first step in channel design should be to analyze the requirements of the end user. How promptly must a police car arrive at the scene of a robbery in order to foil it? How far can a recreation center be from seniors and still attract them? How crowded can a subway become before the system loses regular users? In building a marketing channel, then, a basic building block is the user's specification of acceptable performance. That will require market knowledge.

In designing service facilities, management may find it useful to invoke a concept common in retailing: that of convenience, shopping, and specialty goods. Convenience products are those that the shopper will not exert much effort to investigate, access, and buy. At the other extreme, specialty products will call forth considerable effort by the buyer. Shopping goods lie between. These consumer-imposed definitions have implications for marketing logistics: convenience goods must be readily accessible, usually through broadcast distribution, while specialty goods can be successfully marketed through fewer and more remote outlets.

Where alternative suppliers are absent, suppliers are inclined to design distribution systems that suit their convenience more than the end user's. Governments provide the most notorious examples. Still, the marketer does have to balance the customer's desire for buying convenience with the service deliverer's need for operating efficiency. Secondhand goods outlets, concert halls, and licensing bureaus demand minimum sizes if economies of scale and acceptable levels of service are to be enjoyed by both users and operators. This trade-off should be management's next consideration.

Organizations have found several ways to manage the trade-off (Lovelock and Weinberg, 1989). One is to decentralize the customer contact function while centralizing the technical operations, as when the Red Cross collects blood via bloodmobiles and processes it at a headquarters location. Another is to offer more limited services at branches than at the main site — a channel compromise commonly struck by post offices, hospitals, and libraries. Another is to join with providers of compatible products and services to form a larger meaningful assortment at a local site. Community information booths in shopping centers are, in effect, retailers of a broad line of complementary products distributed to them by governments and charitable organizations. Ticket agencies play the same kind of brokerage role for consortiums of live theaters.

Related to the issue of a site's accessibility is the question of the kind and quality of the experience it will deliver. Conventional retailers have come to pay systematic attention to what are called atmospherics, namely the total gestalt delivered by the outlet (Kotler, 1974). Especially in the past, the ambience of libraries, hospitals, and museums has attracted critical comment. In contrast, an agency serving the insecure sons of single mothers enhanced its service delivery by relocating from an aging and intimidating mansion in an out-of-the-way neighborhood to an economical loft, walled in wood, furnished with junior-sized furniture, brightened by children's paintings, and located near a subway stop. Those who distribute their services through immigration centers, courtrooms, employment offices, and other nonprofit sites might find innovative channel ideas by shopping their own systems and then by studying merchants' applications of atmospherics.

While many third-sector organizations market their programs directly to end users, and while there are substantial advantages in the short, controlled channels that result, some nonprofit managers, like some commercial marketers, find it necessary or advisable to take an indirect approach by using channel intermediaries. Channels handled by others may be cheaper, more quickly activated, more expert, and more accessible to end users. The government of India, committed to the mass distribution of condoms, engaged the vast distribution system of Lever Brothers of India, thereby reaching out to health clinics, barbers, rural stores, and vending machines (Demerath, 1967). The Canadian Post Office vends stamps and basic postal services out of booths in drug stores. The Girl Guides and Boy Scouts build their channels around churches and schools.

Enterprises that seek changes in social behavior are usually active in promotion but not the other three P's. Therefore, in order to complete the "sale," they may be drawn into collaboration with other players. To illustrate, advocacy alone may persuade some smokers that they should quit, but their behavior may not change unless it is validated by medical judgments, mandated by laws, and supported by workplace regulations. Clearly, no organization acting alone can deliver all of those components. Out of such imperatives come marketing partnerships among hospitals, cancer societies, medical associations, school boards, industry associations, and government departments of health.

The classic example of a behavior-change product that failed to "sell" because of failure to prearrange the cooperation of needed channel intermediaries, in this case reluctant retail merchants, was the Jefferson $2 bill.

One device for meshing the efforts of channel partners is to administer the task in terms of its functions. Within a distribution network the total marketing job can be broken into its constituent activities. Most academics' categorizations of the marketing functions that must be performed somewhere in the system include such activities as storage, promotion, financing, and market research, but the nonprofit manager may find a custom-made list more serviceable. From such a list, one can assign portions of each function to the most appropriate channel functionaries. Table 12.2 shows such an analysis for a network of organizations addressing the need for an adequate consumer complaint-handling capability in a large marketing system. A matrix of this kind can be the basis for rough work specifications for each channel participant. As in a conventional plant or office setting, these job descriptions can help in clarifying expectations, coordinating efforts, and appraising performance where the accomplishment of an overall task demands effective teamwork.

Table 12.2. Functions Within a Service Delivery System: Handling Complaints.

Functions in the Overall Complaint-Handling System	Organizations Handling Complaints							
	A	B	C	D	E	F	G	H
Handling present complaints		xx	x			x	x	
Seeing unmet needs	xx	x	x	x	x	x	x	
Serving unmet needs	xx	x	x			x	x	
Setting legislative priorities	xx							x
Developing basic standards	xx			xx	xx			xx
Developing cost/benefit approaches to complaint handling	xx			xx	x			
Generating new ideas for handling complaints	xx	x	x	x	xx	x	x	xx
Establishing an institute of complaint-handling organizations	xx		x		x	x		
Training complaint handlers	xx				xx			xx
Publicizing complaint-handling services	xx				x			xx
Sharing useful complaint-handling ideas						x		xx
Training arbitrators								xx
Auditing complaint-handling schemes								xx
Certifying complaint handlers and complaint-handling schemes								xx

x = Participation in that function
xx = Leadership and/or major responsibility for the performance of that function
Organizations:
A = Governments
B = Individual companies
C = Better Business Bureau
D = Universities
E = Society of consumer affairs professionals
F = Consumers associations
G = Voluntary community organizations
H = An institute of complaint-handling organization

The experienced nonprofit manager will know that interinstitutional cooperation is anything but automatic. Even enterprises that want to collaborate will bring to the table not just potentially complementary competencies but also potentially competing values, goals, perceptions, and priorities. For this reason, the literature on distribution systems takes it as given that some channel conflict is inevitable, even useful, and that the management task is to keep it to levels that are workable rather than pathological. As a consequence, marketing writers have explored how various kinds of power can be used to bring harmony to the roles of channel members (Stern, El-Ansary, and Brown, 1989; Hardy and Magrath, 1988). Because charitable enterprises are highly value driven, imprinted with founders' visions, protective of their turf, and in competition with one another for scarce funds, they are probably just as liable as business firms to interorganizational conflict. Therefore the third-sector administrator should be as assiduous as the private-sector executive in consulting marketing writings for promising strategies for forging channel partnerships that work to the advantage of the distribution system as a whole, including the end user (Andreason, 1985).

Managing Advertising Programs

It was observed earlier that third-sector managers tend to equate marketing with advertising. Regrettably, those managers are then inclined to define all marketing challenges as "communications" problems; to rush to judgment about mounting promotional efforts; to overlook opportunities for improved products, prices, and channels; and, as a consequence, to burden advertising with an unrealistically heavy part of the total marketing task.

To avoid charging advertising with more than it can accomplish, management should remember that the market is a clamorous place and that people develop built-in defenses against its noise. These filters include selective perception (an affluent alum may not open mail from his fraternity or a pregnant drinker may gloss over the article citing the effects that alcohol can have on the fetus) and selective retention (a driver who does not buckle up may remember particularly well those accounts of traffic accidents in which those killed were wearing seat belts). These common human coping mechanisms combine to present the nonprofit manager, like the business executive, with powerful barriers to successful communication.

So do the complexities of the communications process itself. How messages are encoded, transmitted, screened, decoded, stored, retrieved, and acted on can be modeled in the abstract, but they may be unfathomable in a particular situation. To open that black box may require market research. It will probably reveal that the promotional process is more complicated and less persuasive than the advertiser would have wished.

The advertising program must flow logically from, and fit consistently with, the other parts of the overall marketing strategy. To accomplish that overall effect, management should begin with the embracing objectives of the total marketing effort. In an institute for the blind, the product, price, and place elements of the marketing program will be shaped in one way if the goal is to introduce a friendly visiting service to partially blind seniors and in quite another way if the aim is to warn schoolchildren against unprotected observation of a coming eclipse—and the role of advertising will then vary accordingly. Here one sees how reliant the promotional planner is on the goals and guidelines drawn from the mission, portfolio, and priorities of the enterprise as a whole.

To give further focus to the promotional effort, there should be a subset of targets for the advertising program in particular. A key question will be What is the target audience? The answer should flow from earlier decisions as to the organization's target markets, as when a museum offers its curators as guest lecturers in nearby college courses, when a young people's theater concentrates its phone solicitation on upscale young families, and when an engineering faculty targets promising high school women.

However, within the organizations' natural client group, further choices will remain. A smoking cessation program with a wide mandate may target teenage girls because they are taking up the habit at a particularly high rate or long-time smokers because they are especially at risk, and a hospital bequest program may focus on nearby seniors because they are likely customers or on recent patients because they may want to express their gratitude.

An often relevant way to define target groups for promotional purposes is according to their "readiness to buy." The notion is that on the way to a purchase an audience moves through unawareness, awareness, knowledge, liking, preference, conviction, and action. People in one or more of these states may then be targeted by the advertiser. Subdividing the market in this way helps to sharpen advertising's goals, clarify its tasks, and shape its strategy. For example, the preliminary research for a public fitness campaign in Australia revealed that the population could be classified as those who were unwilling to engage in exercise ("the tuned out"), those who understood the arguments for it but were unconvinced ("the drifters"), and those who were already physically active ("the tuned in"). The role of the first phase of the promotional program became to target the drifters—to use a gentle, humorous approach on this antiauthoritarian segment—and to achieve among them a 50 percent awareness of specified, undemanding fitness activities within eighteen months (Lovelock and Weinberg, 1989).

These kinds of communications objectives set the stage for the next step, which is setting the promotional budget. Without clearly stated goals, management may simply imitate what others spend or may allocate an arbitrary percentage of the organization's revenue. Both approaches are essentially mindless.

The most appropriate method is to work back from the promotional goals to the level of spending that would seem to be necessary to their accomplishment. Operationally, this approach will not be easy. Forecasting audience response to various advertising outlays will be daunting, especially if there is no track record to consult. And, when the necessary spending has been estimated, it may be unaffordable, in which case the original objectives have to be revised. Conceptually, however, the objective-and-task method is the right one, and it should be followed (Colley, 1961).

There follows the question What essential message is to be conveyed? The answer will be suggested in the prior choice of target audiences and in the statement of communications objectives, but now the central themes and copy platforms must be articulated with more precision. Are prospective foster parents to be appealed to on the basis of compassion or compensation? How should a navy recruitment program weight the appeals of adventure, education, fellowship, and patriotism? In designing a program to raise money to allay birth defects, the March of Dimes tested twenty different advertising themes (Mindak and Bybee, 1971).

Related to the advertising's themes is its style and tone. A political candidate can make the same point by invoking revered symbols in a respectful way, by enumerating proposed policies in a businesslike way, by attacking opponents in a dismissive way, or by citing the record in a proud way. A range of stylistic choices will also be available to persuade inner-city youngsters to stay in school, to urge construction workers to follow safety rules, and to sign up neighborhood people for a walkathon.

Each promotional medium has its own capabilities and limitations. Direct mail can deliver personalized messages but may be lost in the daily shuffle; television can demonstrate through action but leaves no record for later reference; billboards can command attention but only momentarily; personal representations can deal with objections but are expensive; and so on. Low cost is a strong inducement to use public service announcements, but one should remember that the advertiser has little control over when—and if—they will be aired.

Evaluating the results of advertising is a worthy but tricky undertaking. One reason is that the final transaction is brought about by the combined action of all four elements of the marketing mix, plus the intervention of external variables such as competition, legislation, and the economy. Even where the results are strongly governed by promotion alone, as in the case of lobbying, there remains the problem of disentangling the effects of speeches, position papers, petitions, media campaigns, and personal solicitations. Moreover, the advertiser must try to take account of the time lag between the stimulus and the response: taking action to become a Big Brother, enter a detox center, or switch churches normally follows a protracted period of persuasion and deliberation.

Despite these difficulties, a number of techniques are available for testing alternative messages, media, and spending levels. They range from the simple to the sophisticated. Part of effectively managing promotional programs is being aware of the means for evaluating advertising's impact and determining which tests are justified under the circumstances (Kotler and Andreason, 1991).

Marketing Marketing in Nonprofit Organizations

Marketing originated in corporations, and the private sector remains its heartland. Indeed, some leading firms define themselves as "marketing companies." In the nonprofit field, it is not so. There marketing-oriented cultures, proactive marketing thinking, identifiable marketing managers, explicit marketing budgets, and formal marketing plans are all less common. Few nonprofit organizations describe themselves as market driven (Reilly and McCullough, 1982; Walker, 1983).

If marketing is to be serviceable to nonprofits and their clients, then that gap must be addressed (Etgar and Ratchford, 1974). More specifically, the nonprofit manager who would take full advantage of marketing ideas on the job has a concomitant task: to market marketing to key fellow workers (Moyer, 1988).

The sensible way to begin is to identify the causes for the gap. Because of its roots in economics, marketing has been comfortable with the construct of commercial Darwinism and has celebrated the value of competition. In fact, how to be competitive in a borderless world is a current preoc-cupation in business forums. But these themes are somewhat at odds with the experiences of nonprofit workers. To begin with, the catchment areas of nonprofits are mostly local rather than global. More important, their well-being often turns on effective collaboration with allied enterprises as much as on successful competition with rival agencies (Lauffer, 1984).

Beyond that, the play of market forces seems more muted. In the mar-kets for the inputs they seek, notably for funds and volunteers, charities feel escalating competition and are prepared to accept the relevance of market-ing, at least as a regrettable necessity. But in the markets for the services they offer, their experience is more mixed. Managers in large mainline cul-tural organizations (the opera, the ballet, the symphony) typically moil in markets that are open to consumer preferences and competitive thrusts. Ac-cordingly, they see themselves as arts marketeers (Mokwa, Dawson, and Priere, 1980), and their operations, outlooks, and attitudes are not far re-moved from those of executives in business firms. On the other hand, leaders in less popular enterprises (modern dance groups, fringe theater companies, unconventional artists) are more dependent on financial grants and are less reliant on revenues from sales. Consequently, they are more dedicated to the Muse and less driven by the market.

In nonprofits that deal in social services, the influence of the market may be even less evident. "In philanthropy . . . the market is often far larger than the services available. The number of aged, poor, youth, whales, birds, and rivers to be protected is almost unlimited" (Selby, 1978, p. 95). When rationing is construed to be the central management task, marketing can seem a patently gratuitous exercise.

These deterrents to marketing, largely external, lead to others that are essentially internal. To be fully effective, a marketing mix must be in-tegrated. That is most readily accomplished when the marketing executive, like a product manager in a consumer packaged-goods company, has sub-stantial authority over all of the four P's (product, price, promotion, and place). In a nonprofit organization, that felicitous situation seldom exists. Typically, workers in nonprofits are found to be willing to share responsi-bility, and therefore authority, for one of the four P's, namely promotion. Thus one finds public relations specialists in social service agencies, publi-cists in arts organizations, and development directors in universities. Fund raisers and volunteer administrators, both widely used specialists, are also consigned major responsibilities for promoting charitable organizations to publics that must be wooed. Pricing policies may also be open to discussion across several jurisdictions in a nonprofit enterprise.

The same is not true for decisions about product and place. In a stage company, the playbill is largely chosen by the artistic director; in a family service agency the programs to be mounted are primarily determined by professional social workers; in a university the curriculum is mostly shaped by faculty; in a dance company the repertoire is essentially the province of the choreographer; in a public art gallery decisions about acquisitions lie primarily with curators; and in a hospital the specialties to be emphasized are primarily governed by physicians. These customary organizational arrangements are highly significant for anyone who would champion marketing within a nonprofit organization. They testify to the fact that in many parts of the nonprofit field, key decisions about the most pivotal parts of the marketing mix are not made by what could be called marketing professionals but by workers who, by training and experience, have little exposure to, curiosity about, or regard for, marketing.

To address these obstacles is not a trivial task. One must begin by establishing the fact that all human organizations, like all biological organisms, live by interacting successfully with their environments. More particularly, they thrive or die according to their ability to arrange mutually advantageous exchanges with key elements of their environments.

Then it must be shown that marketing's fundamental purpose is the facilitation of those exchanges. Indeed, marketing focuses on some of the most critical of those exchanges, namely with the clients that the organization seeks to serve. And, to help accomplish a finished transaction, marketing must do more than shape demand; it must also help fit the organization's total offer, including its product, its channels, and its prices, as well as its communications, to potential users.

Further, this role is no less valuable in a nonprofit enterprise. Healthy organizations are fully responsive to their environments. Lacking unambiguous feedback from a conventional market mechanism, nonprofits must find other ways to ensure that they respond effectively to clients' wants and needs. Without such measures, nonprofit managers, like business executives, risk working hard in wrong directions. Marketing can help avoid that. How? By sharing in monitoring the organization's environment, by contributing to SWOT (strengths, weaknesses, opportunities, threats) analyses, by participating in portfolio analyses, by undertaking insightful marketing research, by suggesting suitable target markets, by participating in the mounting of the organization's offer, and by appraising client satisfaction with the result. Each of these actions contributes to a healthy relationship between a nonprofit enterprise and its most significant others.

And, just as nonprofit organizations have a particular need to be responsive, they have a special duty to be responsible. The third sector deals in products and services that affect not only our standard of living but our quality of life. And it must be remembered that not all of the resources they expend are won through voluntary payments by satisfied clients; some are given in trust by intermediaries that serve as surrogates for the public (corporations, foundations, United Way, governments). Moreover, nonprofits often deal with publics that are dependent and vulnerable, which is to say that their clients may be, to some degree, captive customers. Each of these features of nonprofit organizations adds to the obligation of their leaders to manage at least as responsibly as their corporate counterparts, and to explore how marketing might contribute to that important end.

While the case for an organization-wide marketing orientation and a specific marketing responsibility is strong, the adoption of both may be gradual (Lovelock and Weinberg, 1990). It can be useful, then, to think of a series of phases through which a nonprofit enterprise may pass as it moves toward the full potential of marketing. In the early stages, management may tap marketing expertise on a trial basis by having business school students do a marketing project, by bringing marketing experts onto the board of directors, or by sending key staff to marketing seminars. A more fulsome but still limited commitment would be represented by a full-time marketing position with staff authority. Then, with growing confidence in marketing's contribution, an organization would logically move toward a more senior marketing appointment with line authority; with responsibility for coordinating such activities as public relations, advocacy, and development; and with a staff as required (Kotler, 1979; George and Compton, 1985).

Especially in the opening phases, it is critical to find demonstration projects whereby doubters and detractors can sense the scope and test the value of marketing. It has been suggested that early marketing undertakings should be ones that can be evaluated by explicit performance measures, that can be completed within a short to medium time period, that use limited portions of available resources, that are neither peripheral nor central to the enterprise, and that are visible to key decision makers within the organization (Lovelock and Weinberg, 1989). It can be added that they should address problems or issues of recognized significance to the enterprise, that they should have a substantial chance of success, and that they should translate into productive action without delay.

One such project is straightforward marketing research, which challenges conventional ways of thinking and points to heretofore unseen opportunities to manage better. An example was a simple study that demonstrated to a complacent board that its agency was much less productive than others in raising its own funds and was therefore much more reliant on United Way for its survival, but that in each of the prior five years it had received a declining share of the annual United Way allocation, with the result that, in terms of real dollars, their enterprise was shrinking. Those insights led to a more informed relationship with United Way and a more realistic strategy for financing the agency. From a similarly productive study, a repertory theater learned that price discounts were not a major benefit that its subscribers sought, so that it was able to discontinue its standard "seven-for-six" offer without any decrease in its renewal rate (Ryans and Weinberg, 1978). One can imagine the effect on the theater's financial ability to meet its artistic mandate. Projects of this sort should not be seen as serendipitous incidents: to successfully market marketing in a nonprofit organization, one must present an overarching rationale, to be sure, but equally important, one must deliver "profitable" results.

Summary

Marketing has been most advanced in corporations and least developed in nonprofits. However, that gap is narrowing as voluntary sector managers come to see marketing as all of those activities that facilitate exchange between the organization and its clients.

That generic conception of marketing is both liberating and daunting. It means that, as in the private sector, the enterprise must do more than promote itself; it must tailor its products and services to chosen population segments, adjust its prices (both monetary and nonmonetary) to those target clienteles, and shape its service delivery systems in ways that serve the end user. To add to the task, nonprofit managers must adapt each of these elements of the marketing mix to the special features of the voluntary sector setting. Finally, if the process is to be truly useful to the nonprofit organization and its clients, its leaders must, with sensitivity and respect, market marketing to those colleagues who are to act it out.

References

Andreason, A. R. "Nonprofits: Check Your Attention to Customers." *Harvard Business Review,* 1982, *60,* 105–110.

Andreason, A. R. "'Backward' Marketing Research." *Harvard Business Review,* 1985, *63,* 176–182.

Bagozzi, R. P. "Marketing as Exchange." *Journal of Marketing,* 1975, *39,* 32–39.

Bloom, P., and Novelli, W. D. "Problems and Challenges in Social Marketing." *Journal of Marketing,* 1981, *45,* 79–88.

Colley, R. H. *Defining Advertising Goals for Measured Advertising Results.* New York: Association of National Advertisers, 1961.

Demerath, N. J. "Organization and Management Needs of a National Family Planning Program: The Case of India." *Journal of Social Issues,* 1967, *4,* 179–193.

Etgar, M., and Ratchford, B. T. "Marketing Management and Marketing Concept: Their Conflict in Nonprofit Organizations." In *Proceedings.* Chicago: American Marketing Association, 1974.

George, W. R., and Compton, F. "How to Initiate a Marketing Perspective in a Health Services Organization." *Journal of Health Care Marketing,* 1985, *5,* 29–37.

Hardy, K. G., and Magrath, A. J. *Marketing Channel Management.* Glenview, Ill.: Scott, Foresman & Company, 1988.

Kotler, P. "Atmospherics as a Marketing Tool." *Journal of Retailing,* 1974, *50,* 48–64.

Kotler, P. *Marketing for Nonprofit Organizations.* Englewood Cliffs, N.J.: Prentice-Hall, 1975.

Kotler, P. "Strategies for Introducing Marketing into Nonprofit Organizations." *Journal of Marketing,* 1979, *43,* 37–44.

Kotler, P., and Andreason, A. R. *Strategic Marketing for Nonprofit Organizations.* Englewood Cliffs, N.J.: Prentice-Hall, 1991.

Kotler, P., and Levy, S. J. "Broadening the Concept of Marketing." *Journal of Marketing,* 1969, *33,* 10–15.

Kotler, P., and Roberto, E. L. *Social Marketing.* New York: Free Press, 1990.

Lauffer, A. *Strategic Marketing for Not-for-Profit Organizations.* New York: Free Press, 1984.

Lovelock, C. H., and Weinberg, C. B. "Public and Nonprofit Marketing Comes of Age." In G. Zaltman and T. O. Banoma (eds.), *Review of Marketing.* Chicago: American Marketing Association, 1978.

Lovelock, C. H., and Weinberg, C. B. *Marketing for Public and Nonprofit Managers.* New York: Wiley, 1984.

Lovelock, C. H., and Weinberg, C. B. *Public and Nonprofit Marketing.* Redwood City, Calif.: Scientific Press, 1989.

Lovelock, C. H., and Weinberg, C. B. "Public and Nonprofit Marketing: Themes and Issues for the 1990s." In C. H. Lovelock and C. B. Weinberg, *Public and Nonprofit Marketing: Readings and Cases.* Redwood City, Calif.: Scientific Press, 1990.

MacMillan, I. C. "Competitive Strategies for Not-for-Profit Agencies." *Advances in Strategic Management,* 1983, *1,* 61–68.

Mindak, W. A., and Bybee, H. M. "Marketing's Application to Fundraising." *Journal of Marketing,* 1971, *35,* 13–18.

Mokwa, M. P., Dawson, W. D., and Priere, E. A. (eds.). *Marketing the Arts.* New York: Praeger, 1980.

Moyer, M. S. "Marketing in Nonprofit Organizations: A Problem in the Diffusion of Innovation." In *Proceedings.* Brussels: European Marketing Academy, 1988.

Moyer, M. S. "Marketing Research in Nonprofit Organizations: Some Suggested Revisions." In *Proceedings.* University of Glasgow: Marketing Education Group, 1989.

Newman, W. H., and Wallender, H. W. "Managing Not-for-Profit Enterprises." *Academy of Management Review,* 1978, *3,* 24–31.

Rados, D. L. *Marketing for Non-Profit Organizations.* Boston: Auburn House, 1981.

Reilly, M., and McCullough, J. "A Survey of Marketing Activity in Nonprofit Organizations." In F. K. Shuptrine and P. Reingen (eds.), *Nonprofit Marketing: Conceptual and Empirical Research.* Tempe, Ariz.: Bureau of Business and Economic Research, College of Business Administration, Arizona State University, 1982.

Rogers, E. M. *Diffusion of Innovation.* New York: Free Press, 1962.

Ryans, A. B., and Weinberg, C. B. "Consumer Dynamics in Nonprofit Organizations." *Journal of Consumer Research,* 1978, *5,* 89–95.

Selby, C. C. "Better Performance from Nonprofits." *Harvard Business Review,* 1978, *56,* 92–98.

Stern, L. W., El-Ansary, A. I., and Brown, J. R. *Management in Marketing Channels.* Englewood Cliffs, N.J.: Prentice-Hall, 1989.

Walker, J. M. "Limits of Strategic Management in Voluntary Organizations." *Journal of Voluntary Action Research,* 1983, *12,* 39–55.

Wasson, C. R. *Dynamic Competitive Strategy and Product Life Cycles.* Austin, Tex.: Austin Press, 1978.

Wortman, M. S., Jr. "Strategic Management: Not-for-Profit Organizations." In D. E. Schendel and C. W. Hofer (eds.), *Strategic Management.* Boston: Little, Brown, 1979.

Wortman, M. S., Jr. "A Radical Shift from Bureaucracy to Strategic Management in Voluntary Organizations." *Journal of Voluntary Action Research,* 1981, *10,* 62–81.

13

❧

Designing and Managing Volunteer Programs

Jeffrey L. Brudney

One of the most distinctive features of the nonprofit sector is its ability to harness the productive labor of literally millions of citizens in service to organizational goals, without benefit of remuneration. This remarkable achievement does not just happen spontaneously as a consequence of compelling agency missions, although, certainly, the desire to help people by donating time to a worthwhile cause is a powerful motivation for most volunteers. The credit belongs, instead, to the volunteer program, which allows citizens to realize the helping impulse, as well as a variety of other motives, through work activities designed by the organization to meet its needs and objectives.

An organized volunteer program provides a structure for meeting certain requisites: volunteers must be recruited; they must be screened and given orientation to the agency; they must be assigned to positions and afforded training as necessary; they must be supervised, motivated, and accorded appropriate recognition; they should be evaluated to assess the efficacy of their placement for themselves as well as for the organization. This inventory focuses too narrowly on the volunteer, however, and overlooks the groundwork the organization must first lay for an effective program. The agency must determine its reasons for enlisting voluntary assistance and formulate clear plans for involving and integrating citizen participants. Based on that philosophy, it must develop job descriptions for volunteer positions and arrange for orientation and training for employees who are expected to work with nonpaid staff. The agency should make clear the importance of collaborating with volunteers and hold these employees accountable for doing so.

279

The volunteer program is a vehicle for facilitating and coordinating the work efforts of volunteers and paid staff toward the attainment of organizational goals. The core program functions that make this achievement possible can be grouped as follows:

- Establishing the rationale for volunteer involvement
- Involving paid staff in volunteer program design
- Integrating the volunteer program into the organization
- Creating positions of program leadership
- Preparing job descriptions for volunteer positions
- Meeting the needs of volunteers
- Managing volunteers
- Evaluating and recognizing the volunteer effort

This chapter elaborates the essential components of the volunteer program and offers suggestions for increasing their effectiveness. Two caveats with respect to coverage are in order. First, "volunteer recruitment" would ordinarily merit inclusion in any listing of program functions. Because recruitment is the subject of another chapter in this handbook, however, it is treated only in passing here (see Chapter Twenty-Two).

Second, this chapter concentrates on "service" volunteers—individuals who donate their time to help other people directly—rather than on "policy" volunteers, who assume the equally vital role of sitting on boards of directors or advisory boards of nonprofit organizations. Although the demands of managing the performance and incorporating the benefits into the agency of these two types of volunteer activity are quite distinct, some overlap does exist. Service volunteers can bring a wealth of practical experience and knowledge that might prove a great asset to an advisory board; similarly, experience in direct service might usefully shape or sharpen the observations and insights of board members. Yet, service volunteers may not always possess the breadth of perspective and background important to effective policy-making, or an interest in this pursuit, while board members may lack the immediate skills or motivation to perform well in a service capacity. As a result of such trade-offs, a great variety of practices governs the relationship between service and policy volunteering across the nonprofit sector. Some organizations encourage service volunteers to become board members, others permit the interchange, and still others prohibit it. The term "volunteer program" conventionally refers to the organization and management of service volunteers for best results—the topic of the present chapter.

Establishing the Rationale for Volunteer Involvement

No agency, no matter how overburdened with work, constrained in human and financial resources, eager for fresh input and innovation, and enthusiastic about the potential contribution of citizens, should begin the effort to incorporate volunteers with recruitment. The agency must resist the temptation to "call in the volunteers" until the groundwork for their sustained involvement has been put in place. Unfortunately, well-intentioned but premature calls for (undifferentiated) "help" can breed apprehension among paid staff and frustration among volunteers, and can exacerbate the very problems volunteerism was intended to solve. Because this scenario would reinforce negative stereotypes about volunteers and undermine their credibility as a vital service resource, it must be avoided.

The foundation for an effective volunteer program rests, instead, on a serious consideration by the agency of the rationale for citizen involvement, and the development of a philosophy or policy to guide this effort. The initial question must be For what reasons are volunteers sought?

Especially in times of fiscal exigency, top organizational officials will often express "cost savings" as the primary reason for enlisting volunteers. Yet, the claim is misleading. While the labor of volunteers may be "free" or donated, a volunteer program requires expenditures, for example, for orientation, training, reimbursement, promotion, materials, and so forth. Consequently, for volunteers to finance cost savings (rather than extend agency resources), cutbacks must be exacted somewhere in the agency budget. If cutbacks are to be visited on paid staff, officials risk the kind of resentments and antagonisms that have scuttled many a volunteer program.

A more accurate description of the economic benefits that volunteers can bring to an agency is "cost-effectiveness." For example, a volunteer program that has been designed to supplement or complement the work of paid staff can help an agency to hold costs down in achieving a given level of service, or can increase services for a fixed level of expenditure (Brudney, 1990; Karn, 1983, 1982–83; Moore, 1978). From the perspective of organizational efficiency, volunteers offer the capacity to make more productive application of existing funds and person-power. With a relatively small investment of resources, volunteers have the potential to increase the level and quality of services that an agency can deliver to the public. While costs are not spared in this situation, to the degree that volunteers improve the return on expenditures, they extend the resources yet available to an agency to meet pressing needs for assistance and services.

Additional or different purposes may drive a volunteer program. The leadership of a nonprofit organization may decide to enlist volunteers to interject a more vibrant dimension of commitment and caring into its relationships with clients. Or, the goal may be to learn more about the community, nurture closer ties to citizens, and strengthen public awareness and support. Volunteers may be needed to reach clients inaccessible through normal organizational channels, that is, to engage in "outreach" activities (for example, May, McLaughlin, and Penner, 1991; Dorwaldt, Solomon, and Worden, 1988; Young, Goughler, and Larson, 1986). They may be called upon to provide professional skills, such as computer programming, legal counsel, or accounting expertise, not readily available to an agency. The purpose may be to staff an experimental program otherwise doomed to fiscal austerity. Enhancing responsiveness to client groups may offer still another rationale.

Volunteers also make excellent fund raisers. Because the public tends to perceive them as neutral participants who will not directly benefit from monetary donations to an agency, organizations frequently enlist volunteers in this capacity. In fact, a 1989 national survey reported that nearly half (48 percent) of volunteers had had assignments in fundraising (Hodgkinson, Weitzman, Toppe, and Noga, 1992, p. 46).

That the list of possible purposes for establishing a volunteer program is lengthy attests to the vitality of the approach. Before seeking volunteers, agency leaders should settle on the ends their organization hopes to achieve through a volunteer program. An explicit statement of goals advances several important facets of program design and functioning. First, it begins to define the types of volunteer positions that will be needed and the number of individuals required to fill these roles. Such information is at the core of eventual recruitment and training of volunteers. Second, it aids in delineating concrete objectives against which the program might be evaluated, once in operation. Evaluation results are instrumental to strengthening and improving the program.

Finally, a statement of the philosophy underlying volunteer involvement and the specific ends sought through this form of participation can help to alleviate possible apprehensions of paid staff that the new participants may intrude on professional prerogatives or threaten job security. Clarifying the goals for voluntary assistance can dampen idle, typically negative speculation and begin to build a sense of program ownership on the part of employees — especially if they are included in planning for the volunteer program.

Involving Paid Staff in Volunteer Program Design

While the support of top level organizational officials is crucial to the establishment and vitality of a volunteer program (for example, Ellis, 1986; Valente, 1985; Farr, 1983; Scheier, 1981), they are not the only ones who should be involved in defining the mission, philosophy, and procedures of this effort. Paid staff and prospective volunteers, if they are already known to the agency or can be identified, should also be included in these meetings and discussions. Their involvement will add to the knowledge base for crafting policy and inculcate a sense of ownership and commitment that can prove very beneficial to the acceptance of the program. Because the incorporation of volunteers into an agency can impose dramatic changes in work life, the participation of paid staff is especially important (Graff, 1984, p. 17). The sharing of needs, perspectives, and information among agency leadership, employees, and prospective volunteers during the planning process plays a pivotal role in the design, organization, and management of a program that can attain agency goals. At the same time, the process helps to alleviate any concerns of paid staff regarding volunteer involvement and its implications for the workplace.

A primary purpose of the planning meetings is to develop policies and procedures that will govern volunteer involvement and that will be endorsed by all parties. Steve McCurley and Rick Lynch (1989, p. 22) advise that agency guidelines should address the following aspects of volunteer participation:

- Attendance and absenteeism
- Performance review procedures
- Benefits, such as insurance, parking, and continuing education
- Grievance procedures
- Reimbursement policies
- Use of agency equipment and facilities
- Confidentiality requirements
- Probationary acceptance period
- Suspension and termination
- Record-keeping requirements

In all areas, these policies should be as comparable as possible to pertinent guidelines for employees.

Although some may lament the formality of conduct codes for volunteers as somehow inimical to the spirit of help freely given, this device is associated with positive results. By formulating explicit policies for volunteers, an agency demonstrates that it takes their participation seriously and values their contribution to goal attainment. By setting standards as high for volunteers as for paid staff, an agency builds trust and credibility, increased respect — and requests — for volunteers from employees, a healthy work environment, and, perhaps most important, high-quality services (for example, McCurley and Lynch, 1989; Goetter, 1987; Deitch and Thompson, 1985; Wilson, 1984). A seasoned volunteer administrator advises, "One should not have different qualifications for staff than one has for volunteers doing the same work" (Thornburg, 1992, p. 18). These guidelines and expectations greatly facilitate organizing the volunteer program, handling problem situations, protecting rights, and managing for consistent results.

In addition, explicit policies for the volunteer program help to solidify the "psychological contract" linking volunteers to the agency and, thus, may reduce turnover. In one study, Jone L. Pearce (1978, pp. 276–277) found that those organizations most successful in clarifying the volunteer-agency relationship suffered the lowest rates of turnover. These agencies distributed notebooks with all written policies, formal job descriptions, and training manuals to citizen participants. By contrast, the organization with the highest turnover in Pearce's sample provided none of this information to volunteers.

Although volunteers may not be involved in initial discussions concerning program planning and design, once this effort is launched and in operation, they should definitely have input into major decisions affecting the program. Just as for paid employees, citizens are more likely to invest in and commit to organizational policies, and provide useful information for this purpose, if they enjoy ready access to the decision-making process.

Participation in decision making is a key element of the "empowerment" movement in volunteer administration. The term has not been defined precisely, but in general it connotes a genuine sharing of control over the volunteer program with citizen participants, more attentive listening to volunteer ideas and preferences, and greater recognition of the time, skills, and value provided to organizations through this approach. Empowerment is thought to result in increased ownership of the volunteer program by participants and, hence, greater commitment and effectiveness (for a full discussion, see Scheier, 1988–89, 1988a, 1988b; Naylor, 1985).

Integrating the Volunteer Program into the Organization

As these comments suggest, the volunteer program must be organized to respond to the motivations and requirements of volunteers and employees. With respect to volunteers, the program should have mechanisms for determining people's preferences for types of work and ways of meeting those preferences, and for engendering an organizational climate in which volunteers can pursue their goals, with the acceptance, if not always the avid endorsement, of paid personnel. From the perspective of staff, the program must have structures and procedures in place to assume the task of volunteer administration, and to generate a pool of capable citizens matched to the tasks of participating offices and departments.

To accomplish these goals, the volunteer program must be linked to the structure of the nonprofit organization. A small nonprofit may accommodate volunteers with a minimum of structural adaptations, but larger agencies need to consider alternative structural configurations for integrating volunteers into their operations (Valente and Manchester, 1984, pp. 56–57). In order of increasing comprehensiveness, these arrangements consist of ad hoc volunteer efforts, volunteer recruitment by an outside organization with the agency otherwise responsible for management, decentralization of the program to operating departments, and a centralized approach. Each option presents a distinctive menu of advantages and disadvantages.

Volunteer efforts may arise spontaneously in an ad hoc fashion to meet an organization's needs as they arise, especially on a short-term basis. Normally, citizens motivated to share their background, training, skills, and interests with organizations that could profit by them are the catalyst. Fiscal stress, leaving an agency few options, may quicken the helping impulse. The Service Corps of Retired Executives (SCORE), an association primarily of retired business persons who donate their time and skills to assist clients of the U.S. Small Business Administration (SBA), began in this manner in the early 1960s; retired business executives approached the SBA to offer assistance with its huge constituency (Brudney, 1986). The alacrity with which an ad hoc effort can be launched and operating is inspiring: within six months of its inception, SCORE supplied two thousand volunteers to the SBA. Crisis and emergency situations can provoke an even more spectacular response, mobilizing huge numbers of volunteers in a remarkably short time.

Spontaneous help from citizens can infuse vitality (and labor) into an agency and alert officials to the possibilities of volunteerism. Offsetting these advantages, however, is the fact that only selected parts or members of the organization may be aware of an ad hoc citizen effort and thus be able to avail themselves of it. In addition, because energy levels and zeal wane as emergencies are tamed or fade from the limelight, the ad hoc model of volunteer involvement is vulnerable to the passage of time. A volunteer program requires not only a different type of ongoing, rather than sporadic, commitment from citizens, but also an organizational structure to sustain their contributions and make them accessible to all employees. Unless the agency takes steps to institutionalize participation, it risks squandering the long-term benefits of the approach. Almost from the start, the SBA and the SCORE volunteers worked to develop an appropriate structure. In 1989, they celebrated the twenty-fifth anniversary of a partnership that has brought a continuous stream of volunteers to the agency and assistance to over a million small businesses.

A second option sometimes open to nonprofit agencies is to rely on the expertise and reputation of an established organization, such as United Way and its affiliates, or a volunteer center or clearing house, to assist in the recruitment of volunteers, but to retain all other managerial responsibilities internally. Since recruitment is the most fundamental program function and, arguably, the most problematical, regular professional assistance with this task can be highly beneficial, particularly for an agency just starting a volunteer program. Some private business firms seeking to develop volunteer programs for their employees have extended this model; they find it advantageous to contract with local volunteer centers not only for help with recruitment but also other main program functions, such as volunteer placement and evaluation (Haran, Kenney, and Vermilion, 1993).

When outside assistance is used, caution is necessary with regard to quality control, just as with the delegation of any organizational function. Recruiters must be familiar with the nonprofit agency's needs for voluntary assistance, lest volunteers be referred whose backgrounds, skills, and interests do not meet the desired profile. A recruiter may also deal with multiple client organizations, so that the priority attached to the requests of any one of them is unclear. More important, trusting recruitment to outsiders is a deterrent to developing the necessary capacity in-house, which is an essential aspect of a successful volunteer program. By all means, organizations should nurture positive relationships with agencies in the community to attract volunteers and for other purposes. But they must avoid total dependence on external sources and endeavor to implement recruitment mechanisms of their own.

The volunteer program can also be decentralized in individual departments within a larger nonprofit organization. The primary advantage offered by this approach is the flexibility to tailor programs to the needs of specific organizational units and to introduce volunteers where support for them is greatest. Yet, duplication of efforts across several departments, difficulties in locating sufficient expertise in volunteer management to afford multiple programs, and problems in coordination—particularly restrictions on the ability to shift volunteers to more suitable positions or to offer them opportunities for job enrichment across the organization—are significant liabilities.

In the public sector, the selective approach can unwittingly generate disincentives for managers to introduce volunteers (Brudney, 1989, p. 117). Top agency officials may mistakenly equate nonpaid work with "unimportant" activities, to the detriment of a department's (and a manager's) standing in the organization, or they may seize upon the willingness to enlist volunteers as an excuse to deny a unit essential increases in budget and paid personnel. Such misunderstandings must be ameliorated prior to the introduction of volunteers.

Despite the limitations, the decentralized approach may serve an agency quite well in starting a pilot or experimental program, the results of which might guide the organization in moving toward more extensive volunteer involvement. Alternatively, a lack of tasks appropriate for volunteers in some parts of the agency, or, perhaps, strong opposition from various quarters, may confine voluntary assistance to selected departments.

The final structural arrangement is a centralized volunteer program serving the entire agency. With this approach, a single office or department is responsible for management and coordination of the program, while volunteers are actually deployed and supervised in line departments of the organization. The office provides guidelines, technical assistance, screening, training, and all other administration for volunteer activity throughout the agency. The advantages of centralization for averting duplication of effort, assigning volunteers so as to meet their needs as well as those of the organization, and producing efficient and effective voluntary services are considerable. However, the program demands broad support across the organization, especially at the top, to overcome issues that may be raised by departmental staff and any limitation in resources. When such backing is not forthcoming, the other structural arrangements may serve the nonprofit agency well.

Creating Positions of Program Leadership

Regardless of the structural arrangement by which the volunteer program is integrated into agency operations, the program requires a visible, recognized leader. All program functions, including those discussed above (developing a rationale for the volunteer effort, involving paid staff in program planning and design, and housing the volunteer program), benefit from the establishment and staffing of a position bearing overall responsibility for management and representation of the volunteers. The position goes by a variety of names (for example, "Volunteer Coordinator"); in this context it is called "Director of Volunteer Services" (DVS) to signify the importance of the role.

The manner by which the office is staffed sends a forceful message to employees regarding the significance of the volunteer program to the agency and its leadership. Organizations have experimented with an assortment of staffing options for the post, including volunteers, personnel with existing duties, and employee committees. None so manifestly demonstrates a sense of organizational commitment and priorities as does a paid DVS position. Establishing the office as close to the apex of the agency's formal hierarchy as feasible conveys a similar message of resolve and purposefulness. Unfortunately, the evidence suggests that agencies do not always attend to supports for the position (for a review, see Brudney, 1992, pp. 272–273).

The DVS should enjoy prerogatives and responsibilities commensurate with positions at the same level in the organization, including participation in relevant decision making and policy-making, and access to superiors. In this manner, the incumbent can represent the volunteers before the relevant department(s) or the organization as a whole, promote their interests, and help to prevent officials from taking their contributions for granted. A part-time or full-time (as necessary) paid position lodges accountability for the program squarely with the DVS, presents a focal point for contact with the volunteer operation for those inside as well as outside the organization, implements a core structure for program administration, and rewards the office holder in relation to the success of the volunteers.

In addition to these roles, the DVS has important duties that further substantiate the need for a dedicated position (Ellis, 1986, pp. 45–49). The DVS is responsible for volunteer recruitment and publicity, a critical function requiring active outreach in the community and highly flexible working hours. The incumbent must communicate with department and organizational officials to ascertain workloads and requirements for voluntary assistance. Assessing agency needs for volunteers, enlarging areas for their involvement, and educating staff to the approach should be seen not as a one-time exercise, but as an ongoing responsibility of the DVS. The DVS interviews and screens all applicants for volunteer positions, maintains appropriate records, places volunteers in job assignments, provides liaison supervision, and monitors performance. The office must coordinate the bewildering variety of schedules and backgrounds brought by volunteers to the agency. The DVS also bears overall responsibility for orientation and training, as well as evaluation and recognition, of volunteers. Since employees may be unfamiliar with the approach, training may be appropriate for them, as well; the DVS is the in-house source of expertise on all facets of volunteer involvement and management. Finally, as the chief advocate of the program, the DVS endeavors not only to express the volunteer perspective but also to allay any apprehensions of paid staff and to facilitate collaboration.

As volunteer programs increase in size, the DVS will likely have to share leadership duties with volunteers and/or paid staff, but the functions must be performed. Given the scope of the job tasks, secretarial support for the position is advisable.

Preparing Job Descriptions for Volunteer Positions

The essential building block of a successful volunteer program is the job description. Paradoxically, no intrinsic basis exists to create (or classify) a position as "paid" or "volunteer." Even among agencies that have the same purpose or mission, or that work in the same substantive or policy domain, a given position can be classified differently (for example, business counselor, computer programmer, day-care provider, receptionist, ombudsperson, and so on). Within an agency, moreover, job definitions are dynamic, so that volunteers can give way to paid service professionals in some areas (for example, see Ellis and Noyes, 1990; Park, 1983; Schwartz, 1977; Becker, 1964) and gain responsibility from them in others (for example, see Brudney, 1986).

Without an intrinsic basis for designating a task or position as "volunteer" or "paid," the *process* by which work responsibilities are allocated assumes paramount importance. As elaborated above, the most enduring foundation for an effective volunteer program is one worked out by top agency officials and employees (and if possible, volunteers) in advance of program implementation. Among these parties, explicit understandings are needed regarding the rationale for the involvement of volunteers, the nature of the jobs they are to perform, and the boundaries of their work (Ellis, 1986; Graff, 1984; Brown, 1981; Wilson, 1976). This agreement should designate (or provide the foundation for distinguishing) the jobs assigned to volunteers and those held by paid staff.

The second critical step in the job design process is a survey of employees, or perhaps personal interviews with them, to ascertain key factors about their jobs and to make them aware of the potential contributions of volunteers. At a minimum, a survey should seek to identify those aspects of the job that employees most enjoy performing, those that they dislike, and those for which they lack sufficient time or expertise. Since employees may lack background information regarding the assistance that volunteers might lend to them and to the agency, the survey or interview, or alternatively in-service training, should provide resource material regarding volunteers, such as a listing of the jobs or functions that unpaid staff are already performing in their agency or in similar organizations (compare McCurley and Lynch, 1989, pp. 27–28).

Popular stereotypes to the contrary, not all volunteer positions need be in roles supportive to employee endeavors. In some Maryland counties, for instance, paid staff facilitate and support the activities of volunteers in delivering recreation services, rather than the reverse (Marando, 1986). Many organizations rely on donated labor for highly technical professional services, such as accounting, economic development, and computer applications, not provided by employees and which they otherwise could not obtain. More important is that the delegation of tasks take into account the unique capabilities that staff and volunteers might bring toward meeting organizational needs.

To allocate work responsibilities among employees and volunteers, Susan J. Ellis (1986, pp. 89–90) recommends that an agency reassess the job descriptions of the entire staff. Tasks that are prime candidates for delegation to volunteers have the following characteristics:

- They are performed periodically, such as once a week, rather than on a daily or inflexible basis.
- They do not require the specialized training or expertise of paid personnel.
- They might be done more effectively by someone with special training in that skill.
- They are being performed by people who feel unprepared or uncomfortable doing them.
- They require expertise not to be found within the agency.

The product of the task analysis should be new sets of job descriptions — for employees and for volunteers — that are sensitive to prevailing organizational conditions. Staff "are primarily now assigned to the most important daily functions," while volunteers "handle work that can be done on a once-a-week basis or that makes use of special talents for which the volunteers have been recruited" (Ellis, 1986, p. 90). The intent is to achieve the most effective deployment of both paid and nonpaid personnel, their respective tasks codified in formal job descriptions, with the stipulation that neither group will occupy the positions reserved for the other.

A pioneer in the field, Harriet H. Naylor, insisted that "most of the universally recognized principles of administration for employed personnel are even more valid for volunteer workers, who *give* their talents and time" (1973, p. 173, emphasis in original). Naylor's insight into the parallels between the administration of paid and volunteer positions is especially pertinent with respect to job specifications, placement, and orientation. Studies undertaken by the International City/County Management Association on volunteer programs in local governments indicate that "volunteer job descriptions are really no different than job descriptions for paid personnel. A volunteer will need the same information a paid employee would need to determine whether the position is of interest" (Manchester and Bogart, 1988, p. 59). Specifications for volunteer positions should include:

- Job title and purpose
- Benefits to occupant
- Qualifications for position

- Time requirement (for example, hours per week)
- Proposed starting date (and ending date, if applicable)
- Job responsibilities and activities
- Authority invested in the position
- Reporting relationships and supervision

The parallels to paid administration noted by Naylor (1973) and others continue beyond the job description to other key functions of the volunteer program. Applicants for volunteer positions should be *screened* for relevant competencies and interests, as well as pertinent background and qualifications. They should be *interviewed* by officials from the volunteer program and/or the agency to ensure a suitable fit of individual and organizational needs. Like new employees, new volunteers will require an *orientation* to the agency and its volunteer component. Among the topics that orientation activities should address are the overall mission and specific objectives of the organization, its traditions and philosophy, its operating rules and procedures, the rationale and policies of the volunteer program, and the roles and interface of paid and nonpaid staff members. Finally, as needed, *training* should be provided to volunteers to assume the organizational tasks assigned to them. (Chapter Twenty-Two in this book treats these important elements of an effective volunteer program in the depth and richness they deserve.)

Meeting the Needs of Volunteers

To this point, the analysis has focused primarily on the demands of the nonprofit organization for attracting, structuring, and managing volunteer labor. Agency needs constitute only half of the equation for a successful volunteer program, however. The other half consists of meeting the needs of volunteers. An effective volunteer program marries organizational demands for productive labor with the disparate motivations that volunteers bring for contributing their time.

The theme of voluntary action gives to the study of nonprofit institutions much of its characteristic identity. Most nonprofit organizations are vitally dependent on volunteers to carry out missions and objectives. Accordingly, voluminous research has been concerned, directly or indirectly, with the motivations that spur volunteers. A basic conclusion emanating from this research is that volunteers' motivations are complex and multifaceted, and that they may serve a variety of functions for the individual volunteer, including values; the realization of the development of understanding; the meeting of career, social, and esteem needs; and the fulfillment of protective dimensions (Clary, Snyder, and Ridge, 1992).

Although the reasons for volunteering are rich and diverse, several large national surveys extending back more than a quarter of a century reveal a markedly consistent (and interpretable) pattern of professed motivations. Table 13.1 displays the reasons for involvement in volunteer work

Table 13.1. Motivations for Involvement in Volunteer Work
by Year, 1965–1991 (in percentages).

Motivation	1965	1974	1981	1985	1987	1989	1991
Help people	37	53	45	52	—	—	70
Do something useful	—	—	—	—	56	62	61
Enjoy doing volunteer work	31	36	29	32	35	34	39
Interest in activity or work	—	—	35	36	—	—	—
Sense of duty	33	32	—	—	—	—	—
Religious concerns	—	—	21	27	22	26	31
Could not refuse request	7	15	—	—	—	—	—
Friend or relative received service[a]	—	22	23	26	27	29	29
Volunteer received service	—	—	—	—	10	9	17
Learning experience[b]	—	3	11	10	9	8	16
Nothing else to do, free time	—	4	6	10	9	10	8
Thought work would keep taxes down	—	—	5	3	—	—	—

Note: The percentages do not add up to 100 because respondents were permitted multiple responses. In the 1965 and 1974 surveys, volunteers were asked about the reason for doing their first "nonreligious" volunteer work. In the 1981, 1985, 1987, 1989, and 1991 surveys, the motivations also pertain to "informal" volunteer work, that is, work that does not involve a private-sector association or formal organization.

[a]In 1974, this category referred exclusively to respondents' children; in 1989, this category stated that a family member or friend would benefit.

[b]In the 1974 study, this category referred to the idea that volunteer work can lead to a paid job.

Source: Many of these data appear in Chambré (1989). The data are adapted from U.S. Department of Labor (1969); ACTION (1974); Gallup Organization (1981); and Hodgkinson and Weitzman (1986, 1988, 1990, 1992).

expressed by representative samples of Americans in seven surveys, the earliest taken in 1965 and the most recent in 1991.

According to the data presented, the most common stimulus for volunteering is the desire to "do something useful to help others" (or to "help people"), manifested by nearly a majority (and often substantially more than a majority) of the respondents in each survey. Approximately one in four mentions "religious concerns." About 10 percent of volunteers, rising to 17 percent in 1991, state as a motivation that they had previously benefited from the activity; perhaps their volunteer work is motivated by a desire to "give something back" for the services or attention they had earlier received.

While such altruistic motivations appear to drive a great amount of volunteering, more instrumental motivations are common as well. For example, in the survey findings summarized in Table 13.1, approximately 30 to 40 percent of the volunteers gave as reasons that they "enjoy doing volunteer work" or that they "had an interest in the activity or work." A substantial number of volunteers (22 to 29 percent) said that they have a friend or relative who either is involved in the activity in which they volunteer or would benefit from it.

In the surveys conducted in the 1980s, another 8 to 11 percent of respondents identified volunteering as a "learning experience" (16 percent in the 1991 survey). The educational or training benefits afforded by this opportunity are especially important to individuals who seek entry or reentry into the job market but lack requisite competencies or experience. According to one volunteer coordinator and consultant, "*Any* marketable skills can be strengthened and brought up to date in a well-structured volunteer setting" (O'Donald, 1989, p. 22; emphasis in original).

The data in Table 13.1 suggest that many people seem simultaneously to hold both other-directed and self-directed motivations for volunteering. In order to capture some of the richness of these motivations, the national surveys allowed multiple responses, and in each survey the cumulative percentages surpass 100 percent. Volunteering, then, appears to spring from a mixture of altruistic and instrumental motivations. Volunteers can — and most likely do — pursue both types of rewards simultaneously: one can certainly help others, derive strong interest and satisfaction in the work, learn and grow from the experience, and enjoy the company of friends and co-workers in the process. These rewards emanate from the quality and meaning of the volunteer experience. As Jon Van Til (1988, p. 8) observes, volunteering is helping behavior deemed beneficial by participants, even though this action "may contribute to individual goals of career exploration and development, sociability, and other forms of personal enhancement."

It is also worth noting in Table 13.1 what the volunteering impulse is not: apparently very few citizens engage in this activity with the motivation to spare organizational funds or because they believe that their "work would keep taxes down" (only 3 to 5 percent of volunteers).

How might these motivations evolve as individuals join organizations and engage in volunteer work? Strong altruistic or service motivations could reasonably lead individuals to seek productive outlets for donating their time. As might be expected, however, once they have begun to assist an organization, the immediate rewards of the work experience — such as the social aspects of volunteering and the characteristics of the job they are asked to perform — tend to rise in salience.

For example, based on a study of diverse work settings, Pearce (1983) discovered that volunteers stated that they joined the organization for predominantly service reasons, but that friendships and social interaction became more influential in their decision to remain with it. While the long-range rewards of helping others, supporting organizational goals, and making a contribution decreased in importance to them (albeit the scores remained at high levels), the rewards of meeting people and enjoying the company of friends and co-workers increased. Similarly, in a study of volunteers to local government, the importance attached by participants to doing something useful or benefiting a family member or friend diminished over time, but interest in or enjoyment of the work grew as a motivation (Sundeen, 1989).

Pearce concludes, "The rewards individuals expected from volunteering are often not the rewards most salient to them once they have become volunteers" (1983, p. 148). If not anticipated and addressed, this shift can result in rapid and ruinous turnover of volunteers. The volunteer program must be designed to counteract this possibility; fortunately, many options are open.

To reinforce volunteers' initial emphasis on service motivations, they might be placed in positions where they can contribute directly to organizational goals, for example, through contact with clients or participation in policy activities. Agencies should offer entry-level counseling and careful placement to assist volunteers in reaching their personal goals, and in addition, should attempt to foster a work environment conducive to their efforts. Training programs and orientation sessions should present an accurate picture of the rewards of volunteering, so that citizens — and the organizations they serve — do not fall prey to unrealistic expectations of the experience.

Agencies also need to respond to changes in the motivations of volunteers. While an organization may have a standard set of activities designed to recruit volunteers, retaining them is a dynamic process of reviewing — with each volunteer — performance, growth, and aspirations, and modifying work assignments accordingly. In addition to the methods discussed above, volunteers' continued involvement can be encouraged through a variety of inducements, depending upon individual circumstances. These can include a series of steps toward greater responsibilities, participation in problem solving and decision making, opportunities for training, supportive feedback and evaluation, and letters of recommendation documenting work performed.

Managing Volunteers

Managing volunteers is different from managing employees. Volunteers are much less dependent on the organization to which they donate their time than are paid staff members, who must earn their livelihood from it. Volunteers can usually leave the organization and find comparable opportunities for their labor with far less effort and inconvenience than can employees. As a result, nonprofit managers and supervisors do not have as much control over volunteer workers.

These differences in control help to explain some oft-noted characteristics of volunteers in the workplace. Volunteers can afford to be quite selective in accepting job assignments. They may insist on substantial flexibility in work hours. They may not be as faithful in observance of agency rules and regulations as regular employees, particularly rules they deem burdensome or "red tape." Such attitudes may stem in part from the fact that nearly all who volunteer do so on a part-time basis and, thus, cannot be expected to have full information about organizational policy and procedures. Too, many regard the more rigid aspects of the job and agency as inimical to the spirit and practice of help freely given and so may choose to evade or even ignore them. Social interaction is part of the fun and spark of volunteering, and participants may place high value on this feature of the experience.

Given the relative autonomy of volunteers, a heavy-handed approach to supervision can be expected to elicit antagonism and turnover rather than productivity and compliance. Standard organizational inducements for paid employees, such as pay, promotion, and perquisites, are not operative for volunteers. Conventional organizational sanctions are likely to prove unavailing. For example, referring a problem to hierarchical superiors for resolution or disciplinary action (or threatening to do so) is far less apt to sway volunteers than employees.

These considerations may leave the impression that volunteers cannot be "managed," but that conclusion is unfounded. Instead, the message is decidedly more positive: the foundation for effective management of volunteers rests on applying different techniques and incentives than commonly used for paid employees to motivate and direct work behaviors toward agency goals. Managerial investment in building trust, cooperation, teamwork, challenge, growth, achievement, values, excitement, and commitment are much more effectual strategies for this purpose than are the conventional methods. Moreover, as Thomas J. Peters and Richard H. Waterman (1982) discuss in their highly influential study, *In Search of Excellence*, "America's best-run companies" use the same approach for paid employees — with enviable results.

Based on a careful examination of a volunteer program servicing a large, urban public library system, Virginia Walter found that administrators who embraced this style of "management-by-partnership" enjoyed greater success in dealing with volunteers and meeting objectives than did those officials intent on control (1987, p. 31). In a major study of the volunteer Service Corps of Retired Executives sponsored by the U.S. Small Business Administration, Brudney (1990, pp. 112–114) arrives at a similar conclusion. The volunteer business counselors who assisted the SBA sometimes fit the stereotypes attributed to volunteer workers. For example, they displayed low tolerance for necessary government paperwork and "bureaucracy," uneven knowledge of SBA rules and procedures, and keen interest in deciding what cases they would accept (or reject) for counseling. Yet, SBA staff rated the performance of the volunteers as comparable to their own on signal dimensions, including quality and timeliness of services to clients and dependability in work commitments. Like Walter (1987), Brudney (1990) attributes these beneficial results to the partnership approach to managing the volunteer program practiced by the SBA and SCORE.

A successful volunteer program must do more than advance changes in managerial style. It must also institute a framework to facilitate the task of volunteer supervision. To channel volunteer talents and energies productively, agencies must elucidate the behaviors expected from nonpaid staff. The procedures discussed earlier in this chapter offer a viable means to elaborate and promote mutual understanding of the volunteer-agency relationship. Developing a coherent philosophy for volunteer involvement, preparing guidelines for the volunteer program, creating formal positions for volunteers, preparing the relevant job descriptions, interviewing applicants and placing them in mutually satisfactory work assignments, and presenting orientation and training are potent means to define what volunteer service means to the agency and to citizens, and to coordinate the needs and motives of both parties. Probably no factor aids more in supervising volunteers (and paid staff) than placing them in positions where they can put their strongest motivations and best skills to work.

In short, effective management of volunteers calls for more than changes in managerial style, although these adjustments are certainly important. The volunteer program must also provide a structure to impart a shared conception of volunteer service. Absent such a framework, managerial adaptations in themselves are likely to prove insufficient.

Evaluating and Recognizing the Volunteer Effort

Researchers contend that the evaluation function is carried out less often and less well than the other central elements of a volunteer program (Allen, 1987; Utterback and Heyman, 1984). For example, in a study of 534 cities whose populations numbered over 4,500 that enlisted volunteers in the delivery of services, Sydney Duncombe (1985, p. 363) found that just a handful (62, or 11.6 percent) had made an evaluation study. Understandably, organizations that rely on the assistance of volunteers may be reluctant to appear to question through evaluation the worth or impact of well-intentioned helping efforts. In addition, officials may be apprehensive about the effects of an evaluation policy on volunteer recruitment and retention, and on public relations. Nevertheless, for individual volunteers and the paid staff who work with them, as well as for the volunteer operation as a whole, evaluation and recognition activities are essential program functions.

Evaluation of Volunteers and Employees

The fears of organizational leadership notwithstanding, volunteers have cogent reasons to view personnel assessment in a favorable light. A powerful motivation for volunteering is to achieve worthwhile and visible results; evaluation of performance can guide volunteers toward improvement on this dimension. No citizen contributes his or her time to have the labor wasted in misdirected activity or to repeat easily remedied mistakes and misjudgments. That an organization might take one's work so lightly as to allow such inappropriate behavior to continue is an insult to the volunteer and an affront to standards of professional conduct underlying effectiveness on the job.

Evaluation of performance, moreover, is actually a form of compliment to the volunteer (Ellis, 1986, pp. 81–82). A sincere effort at appraisal indicates that the work merits review, and that the individual has the capability and will to do a better job. For many who contribute their time, volunteering offers an opportunity to acquire or hone desirable job skills, and/or to build an attractive résumé for purposes of paid employment. To deny constructive feedback to those who give their time for organizational purposes, and who could benefit from this knowledge and hope to do so, is a disservice to the volunteer.

Open to nonprofit organizations are an assortment of procedures for carrying out evaluation of volunteer performance. Often, the employee to whom the volunteer reports will prepare the appraisal. Or, the responsibility may rest with the director of volunteer services or with the personnel department in larger organizations. A combination of these officials might also handle the task. To complement this agency-based perspective, volunteers might evaluate their own accomplishment and experience in the agency, as suggested by some authorities (for example, Manchester and Bogart, 1988; McHenry, 1988). The assessment should tap volunteer satisfaction with important facets of the work assignment, including job duties, schedule, support, training, opportunities for personal growth, and so on. The self-assessment is also a valuable tool to obtain feedback on the management and supervision of volunteers; employees should learn from the process as well. Regardless of the type of evaluation, the goal ought to be to ascertain the degree to which the needs and expectations of the volunteer and the agency are met, so that job assignments can be continued, amended, or redefined as necessary.

Agency officials might recognize and show their appreciation to volunteers through a great variety of activities: award or social events, such as luncheons, banquets, ceremonies; media attention in newsletters or newspapers; certificates for tenure or special achievement; expansion of opportunities for learning, training, or management; and, especially, personal expressions of gratitude from employees or clients. A heartfelt "thank you" can be all the acknowledgment many volunteers want or need. Others require more formal recognition. The director of volunteer services should make letters of recommendation available to all volunteers who request them. Recognition is a highly variable activity that, optimally, should be tailored to the wants and needs of individual volunteers.

Some agencies choose to recognize volunteers who evince especially strong potential, and who seek employment with the agency, by considering them for paid positions when openings occur (for example, police auxiliaries). One volunteer administrator refers to this process as a "try before you buy" opportunity for paid staff (Thornburg, 1992, p. 20). The advantages offered by this procedure notwithstanding, volunteering should not be seen as a necessary credential or requirement for paid employment with a nonprofit organization.

In general, volunteer-based services require the participation of both volunteers and paid staff. If organizational officials are committed to having employees and volunteers work as partners, program functions of evaluation and recognition should apply to both members of the team. Though frequently neglected in job analysis, employees who are expected to work with volunteers should have pertinent responsibilities written into their formal job descriptions. Equally important, performance appraisal for the designated positions must assess requisite skills in volunteer management. Just as demonstrated talent in this domain should be encouraged and rewarded, an employee's resistance to volunteers, or poor work record with them, should not be overlooked and thus implicitly condoned in the review. As necessary, the organization should support training activities for paid staff to develop competencies in volunteer administration.

Similarly, recognition activities for volunteer programs normally focus on citizen participants, rather than on both members of the team. Employees value recognition as well, especially when awards ceremonies, social events, media coverage, agency publications, and the like bring their efforts and accomplishments with volunteers to the attention of organizational leadership. Similarly, feedback on employee achievement from volunteers and the director of volunteer services belongs in agency personnel files. By giving serious attention to the evaluation and recognition of paid staff with regard to their collaboration with volunteers, nonprofit officials provide incentives for an effective partnership.

Evaluation of the Volunteer Program

The overriding goal of a volunteer program ought to be to exert a positive effect on the external environment, and/or to better the life circumstances of agency clients. Periodically, agencies that mobilize volunteers for such purposes should undergo evaluation of the impact or progress they have registered in ameliorating the conditions or problems identified in their mission statements. Too often, what passes for "evaluation" of the volunteer program is a compilation of the number of volunteers who have assisted the organization, the hours they have contributed, and the amount of client contacts or visits they have made. Some agencies go a step further and calculate the "equivalent dollar value" of the services donated by volunteers, based on the market price for labor the organization would otherwise have to pay to employed personnel to accomplish the same tasks (for a complete discussion of the requisite methodology, see Karn, 1983, 1982–83).

Impressive and significant though these data may be—normally documenting tremendous levels of contributed effort and monetary value across nonprofit and public institutions—they tap the inputs to or resources of a volunteer program, rather than the results or accomplishments of such a program. Some researchers complain, too, that this approach slights the expenses associated with volunteer programs, for example, for paid staff supervision, reimbursement for expenditures, and use of organizational resources and facilities (Utterback and Heyman, 1984, p. 229).

Nonprofit organizations should consider additional forms of evaluation for volunteer programs. Much as they might be expected to do for any other operational unit, at regular intervals agency officials should assess the outcomes of the volunteer program against its stated goals or mission. Volunteer activity is other-directed; it should do more than gratify citizen participants and accommodate employees. Officials need to review the aggregate performance of the volunteers in assisting clients, addressing community problems, expediting agency operations, and meeting further objectives. Not only does the assessment yield information that can improve functioning of the program, but also it reinforces for all concerned — citizens, paid staff, and agency clients alike — the importance attached by the organization to the volunteer component.

A second type of evaluation, also recommended, pertains to assessing the processes of a volunteer program. Officials should determine that procedures to meet essential program functions discussed in this chapter are in place, and that they are operating effectively. Additionally, the evaluation should attempt to gauge the satisfaction of volunteers and paid staff members with the program, as well as their perceptions concerning its impact on clients and the external environment. Continuing struggles with, for example, recruiting suitable volunteers, arresting high rates of volunteer burnout and turnover, relieving staff antagonisms, reaching mutually agreeable placements, and so forth, point to flaws in program design that must be addressed. By diagnosing such difficulties, a process evaluation can enhance progress toward achievement of program objectives.

Summary

According to the *Nonprofit Almanac, 1992–1993,* in 1989, an estimated 98.4 million Americans — 54.4 percent of adults eighteen years of age or older — volunteered an average of 4 hours per week (Hodgkinson, Weitzman, Toppe, and Noga, 1992, pp. 46–47). They gave a total of 20.5 billion hours, of which 15.7 billion hours comprised formal volunteering, that is, specific time commitments to organizations. (The remaining 4.8 billion hours consisted of informal volunteering, such as helping neighbors or friends.) The 15.7 billion hours of formal volunteering represented an equivalent of 9.2 million full-time employees; if recipient organizations had to purchase this labor, the estimated dollar value would have reached $170 million. Nearly 70 percent of the total full-time equivalent volunteer time went to the nonprofit sector in 1989, and this contribution represented at least 41 percent of total employment in the sector (Hodgkinson, Weitzman, Toppe, Noga, 1992, pp. 7–8).

The key to integrating this staggering volume of talent and energy into nonprofit organizations is the volunteer program. This chapter has elaborated the central elements of a successful organizationally based volunteer effort:

- The program should begin with the establishment of a rationale or policy to guide volunteer involvement.

- Paid staff must have a central role in designing the volunteer program and creating guidelines governing its operation.
- The volunteer program must be integrated structurally into the nonprofit organization.
- The program must have designated leadership positions to provide direction and accountability.
- The agency must prepare job descriptions for the positions to be held by volunteers, as well as see to the related functions of screening, orientation, placement, and training.
- The volunteer program must attend to the motivations that inspire volunteers and attempt to respond to them, with the goal of meeting both the individuals' needs and those of the organization.
- Managing volunteers for best results typically requires adaptations of more traditional hierarchical approaches toward teamwork and collaboration.
- All components of the volunteer effort — citizens, employees, and the program itself — benefit from evaluation and recognition activities.

The listing is ambitious, but well within the reach of the nonprofit organization. So, too, are the advantages to be derived from an effective volunteer program.

References

ACTION. *Americans Volunteer, 1974.* Washington, D.C.: ACTION, 1974.

Allen, N. J. "The Role of Social and Organizational Factors in the Evaluation of Volunteer Programs." *Evaluation and Program Planning,* 1987, *10*(3), 257–262.

Becker, D. G. "Exit Lady Bountiful: The Volunteer and the Professional Social Worker." *Social Service Review,* 1964, *38*(1), 57–72.

Brown, K. "What Goes Wrong and What Can We Do About It?" *Voluntary Action Leadership,* Spring 1981, pp. 22–23.

Brudney, J. L. "The SBA and SCORE: Coproducing Management Assistance Services." *Public Productivity Review,* Winter 1986, pp. 57–67.

Brudney, J. L. "The Use of Volunteers by Local Governments as an Approach to Fiscal Stress." In T. N. Clark, W. Lyons, and M. R. Fitzgerald (eds.), *Research in Urban Policy.* Vol. 3. Greenwich, Conn.: JAI Press, 1989.

Brudney, J. L. *Fostering Volunteer Programs in the Public Sector: Planning, Initiating, and Managing Voluntary Activities.* San Francisco, Calif.: Jossey-Bass, 1990.

Brudney, J. L. "Administrators of Volunteer Services: Their Needs for Training and Research." *Nonprofit Management and Leadership,* 1992, *2,* 271–282.

Chambré, S. M. "Kindling Points of Light: Volunteering as Public Policy." *Nonprofit and Voluntary Sector Quarterly,* 1989, *18*(3), 249–268.

Clary, E. G., Snyder, M., and Ridge, R. "Volunteers' Motivations: A Functional Strategy for the Recruitment, Placement, and Retention of Volunteers." *Nonprofit Management and Leadership,* 1992, *2*(4), 333–350.

Deitch, L. I., and Thompson, L. N. "The Reserve Police Officer: One Alternative to the Need for Manpower." *Police Chief,* 1985, *52*(5), 59–61.

Dorwaldt, A. L., Solomon, L. J., and Worden, J. K. "Why Volunteers Helped to Promote a Community Breast Self-Exam Program." *Journal of Volunteer Administration,* 1988, *6*(4), 23–30.

Duncombe, S. "Volunteers in City Government: Advantages, Disadvantages and Uses." *National Civic Review,* 1985, *74*(9), 356–364.

Ellis, S. J. *From the Top Down: The Executive Role in Volunteer Program Success.* Philadelphia, Pa.: Energize, 1986.

Ellis, S. J., and Noyes, K. H. *By the People: A History of Americans as Volunteers.* (Rev. ed.) San Francisco, Calif.: Jossey-Bass, 1990.

Farr, C. A. *Volunteers: Managing Volunteer Personnel in Local Government.* Washington, D.C.: International City Management Association, 1983.

Gallup, Inc. *Americans Volunteer, 1981.* Princeton, N.J.: Gallup Organization, 1981.

Goetter, W.G.J. "When You Create Ideal Conditions, Your Fledgling Volunteer Program Will Fly." *American School Board Journal,* 1987, *194*(6), 34–37.

Graff, L. L. "Considering the Many Facets of Volunteer/Union Relations." *Voluntary Action Leadership,* Summer 1984, pp. 16–20.

Haran, L., Kenney, S., and Vermilion, M. "Contract Volunteer Services: A Model for Successful Partnership." *Leadership,* Jan.-Mar. 1993, pp. 28–30.

Hodgkinson, V., and Weitzman, M. *The Charitable Behavior of Americans: A National Survey.* Washington, D.C.: Independent Sector, 1986.

Hodgkinson, V., and Weitzman, M. *Giving and Volunteering in the United States.* Washington, D.C.: Independent Sector, 1988.

Hodgkinson, V., and Weitzman, M. *Giving and Volunteering in the United States.* Washington, D.C.: Independent Sector, 1990.

Hodgkinson, V., and Weitzman, M. *Giving and Volunteering in the United States.* Washington, D.C.: Independent Sector, 1992.

Hodgkinson, V., Weitzman, M., Toppe, C. M., and Noga, S. M. *Nonprofit Almanac, 1992–1993: Dimensions of the Independent Sector.* San Francisco: Jossey-Bass, 1992.

Karn, G. N. "Money Talks: A Guide to Establishing the *True* Dollar Value of Volunteer Time, Part I." *Journal of Volunteer Administration,* 1982–83, *1,* 1–17.

Karn, G. N. "Money Talks: A Guide to Establishing the *True* Dollar Value of Volunteer Time, Part II." *Journal of Volunteer Administration,* 1983, *1,* 1–19.

McCurley, S., and Lynch, R. *Essential Volunteer Management.* Downers Grove, Ill.: VMSystems and Heritage Arts Publishing, 1989.

McHenry, C. A. "Library Volunteers: Recruiting, Motivating, Keeping Them." *School Library Journal,* 1988, *35*(8), 44–47.

Manchester, L. D., and Bogart, G. S. *Contracting and Volunteerism in Local Government: A Self-Help Guide.* Washington, D.C.: International City Management Association, 1988.

Marando, V. L. "Local Service Delivery: Volunteers and Recreation Councils." *Journal of Volunteer Administration,* 1986, *4*(4), 16–24.

May, K. M., McLaughlin, R., and Penner, M. "Preventing Low Birth Weight: Marketing and Volunteer Outreach." *Public Health Nursing,* 1991, *8*(2), 97–104.

Moore, N. A. "The Application of Cost-Benefit Analysis to Volunteer Programs." *Volunteer Administration,* 1978, *11*(1), 13–22.

Naylor, H. H. *Volunteers Today—Finding, Training and Working with Them.* Dryden, N.Y.: Dryden Associates, 1973.

Naylor, H. H. "Beyond Managing Volunteers." *Journal of Voluntary Action Research,* 1985, *14*(2/3), 25–30.

O'Donald, E. "Re-Entry Through Volunteering: The Best Jobs That Money Can't Buy." *Voluntary Action Leadership,* Fall 1989, pp. 22–27.

Park, J. M. *Meaning Well Is Not Enough: Perspectives on Volunteering.* South Plainfield, N.J.: Groupwork Today, 1983.

Pearce, J. L. "Participation in Voluntary Associations: How Membership in a Formal Organization Changes the Rewards of Participation." In D. H. Smith and J. Van Til (eds.), *International Perspectives on Voluntary Action Research.* Washington, D.C.: University Press of America, 1983.

Pearce, J. L. "Something for Nothing: An Empirical Examination of the Structures and Norms of Volunteer Organizations." Doctoral dissertation, Yale University, 1978.

Peters, T. J., and Waterman, R. H., Jr. *In Search of Excellence: Lessons from America's Best-Run Companies.* New York: HarperCollins, 1982.

Scheier, I. H. "Positive Staff Attitude Can Ease Volunteer Recruiting Pinch." *Hospitals,* 1981, *55*(3), 61–63.

Scheier, I. H. "Empowering a Profession: What's in Our Name?" *Journal of Volunteer Administration,* 1988a, *6*(4), 31–36.

Scheier, I. H. "Empowering a Profession: Seeing Ourselves as More than Subsidiary." *Journal of Volunteer Administration,* 1988b, *7*(1), 29–34.

Scheier, I. H. "Empowering a Profession: Leverage Points and Process." *Journal of Volunteer Administration,* 1988–89, *7*(2), 50–57.

Schwartz, F. S. "The Professional Staff and the Direct Service Volunteer: Issues and Problems." *Journal of Jewish Communal Service,* 1977, *54*(2), 147–154.

Sundeen, R. A. "Citizens Serving Government: Volunteer Participation in Local Public Agencies." In *Working Papers for the Spring Research Forum.* Washington, D.C.: Independent Sector, 1989.

Thornburg, L. "What Makes an Effective Volunteer Administrator? Viewpoints from Several Practitioners." *Voluntary Action Leadership,* Summer 1992, pp. 18–21.

U.S. Department of Labor. *Americans Volunteer.* Washington, D.C.: Department of Labor, Manpower Administration, 1969.

Utterback, J., and Heyman, S. R. "An Examination of Methods in the Evaluation of Volunteer Programs." *Evaluation and Program Planning,* 1984, *7*(3), 229–235.

Valente, C. F., and Manchester, L. D. "Rethinking Local Services: Examining Alternative Delivery Approaches." Information Service Special Report no. 12. Washington, D.C.: International City Management Association, 1984.

Valente, M. G. "Volunteers Help Stretch Local Budgets." *Rural Development Perspectives,* 1985, *2*(1), 30–34.

Van Til, J. *Mapping the Third Sector: Voluntarism in a Changing Social Economy.* New York: Foundation Center, 1988.

Walter, V. "Volunteers and Bureaucrats: Clarifying Roles and Creating Meaning." *Journal of Voluntary Action Research,* 1987, *16*(3), 22–32.

Wilson, M. *The Effective Management of Volunteer Programs.* Boulder, Colo.: Johnson, 1976.

Wilson, M. "The New Frontier: Volunteer Management Training." *Training and Development Journal,* 1984, *38*(7), 50–52.

Young, C. L., Goughler, D. H., and Larson, P. J. "Organizational Volunteers for the Rural Frail Elderly: Outreach, Casefinding, and Service Delivery." *Gerontologist,* 1986, *26*(4), 342–344.

14

Evaluating the Effectiveness of Nonprofit Organizations

Vic Murray
Bill Tassie

The end of the twentieth century marks a critical period for nonprofit organizations. It is not only that they are facing funding shortages. Not having enough money is a chronic condition that has always plagued this sector. Now, however, growing pressures are compounding the problem created by budget concerns:

- For many, the *demand* for services is increasing as funds decline (or at least fail to increase at the same rate as demand).
- Funders are no longer willing to allocate funds simply on the basis of showing the *need* for the services an agency supplies. Now they want some kind of "proof" that the money they donate is actually having an impact on the causes it is supposed to be aiding. The watchwords of the day are "accountability," "impact," "outcome effectiveness," "quality service," and the like.
- Funders are not the only ones using these watchwords. The *recipients* of services—clients, patients, members, patrons—are no longer willing to accept what is provided if they are not satisfied. They, too, are organizing to demand client satisfaction as the ultimate test for nonprofit managers.

These points boil down to nonprofit organizations having to focus as never before on the process of evaluating organizational effectiveness. But what *is* organizational effectiveness? How can it be measured? What happens if there are several definitions and measurements of effectiveness?

This chapter presents an overview of what is known about the evaluation process and the implications of this knowledge for management. Our objective in offering this information is to help executives of nonprofit organizations improve their ability to manage the process of evaluating their organizations' effectiveness. We begin by reviewing the generic concept of organizational effectiveness evaluation (henceforth abbreviated OEE), surveying the dimensions of OEE, and considering how these can be combined into OEE models.

Organizational Effectiveness Evaluation: Dimensions and Models

Current pressures for more measures of program effectiveness and outcome accountability often sound somewhat simplistic. Understanding the complexity of the idea of organizational effectiveness and how to evaluate it requires the identification of the basic dimensions of the concept. Five questions address the dimensions of the organizational effectiveness concept, and, answered together, provide a coherent picture of models of OEE. As we will see, various writers have proposed different models over the years, each of which has underlying problems.

The Dimensions of OEE

Answers to the following five questions are key to making explicit an understanding of organizational effectiveness:

1. Why evaluate organizational effectiveness? The answer to this question seems self-evident: in order to improve the organization's performance. The measurement of performance is part of the decision-making rationality of organizations depicted by March and Simon (1959). These points detail the logic underlying OEE:

    - Organizations have one or more formal goals (aims, objectives, missions).
    - Those who decide what the organization will do choose activities aimed at achieving these goals, and they take steps to measure the effectiveness of these activities.
    - When these measurements indicate that progress toward goal achievement is unsatisfactory, "problems" are defined for decision makers.
    - Decision makers can follow rational procedures to solve these problems: gather information on causes, identify alternative solutions, estimate the relative costs and benefits of the alternatives, choose the optimum alternative, and evaluate the impact of its implementation.

In theory this is simple. However, as management writers have been pointing out since the late 1950s, the ideally logical model for decision making rarely operates as it should (see Burrell and Morgan, 1979, for a summary of this critique). For one thing, the people doing the evaluating are not necessarily those who defined the goals or those who caused the problems. So the various parties involved in the decision-making process may have different answers to the question "why evaluate?"

In addition, there are those who study the evaluation process for its own sake. For them, the question "Why evaluate?" is irrelevant. They are the academics who are less interested in the consequences of evaluation for the effectiveness of the organization than in the processes by which evaluation results are obtained.

2. What is an effective organization? To evaluate the effectiveness of an organization, it is necessary to have a clear idea of (1) the ultimate goals of the organization, (2) the means being used to achieve these goals, and (3) the causal links between means and ends. For example, "spending another million dollars on advertising will decrease substance abuse in this city by 2 percent."

The problem is that it is difficult to be clear on these three points. Organizational goals are often numerous, vague, and even potentially contradictory (for example, long-term growth versus short-term financial results). Furthermore, the various groups that can influence the very survival of an organization may not emphasize the same goals. The means used to achieve goals (sometimes called strategies) can have long causal chains. For example, the goal of profitability for a business may be achieved based on a marketing strategy, a research and development strategy, a joint venture strategy, and so on. Each of these strategies can be expressed as a set of objectives that, in turn, are achieved by various means that can act as sub-goals for yet further means. Unfortunately, it may be very difficult to prove that performing well at the level of means will necessarily be reflected at the level of ends. For example, an organization may measure its efficiency (cost per unit of goods or service produced) on the assumption that efficiency leads to good financial results. But what if the service is obsolete? Measuring efficiency as an indicator of organizational effectiveness would then be worse than useless; it might be damaging if the organization emphasized efficiency but not other indicators of goal attainment, such as service innovation.

As we will see, some theories of evaluation have concentrated on measuring *goal attainment*. Others have concentrated on various *means*, taking for granted their eventual impact on the desired ends. Particularly in the nonprofit sector, some organizations measure neither the ends nor the means, but only the acquisition of the "raw material," or *inputs*, the organization uses to produce services — inputs such as money raised or new clients attracted. Evaluating inputs does not consider whether or not the additional funds are used effectively, or the new clients are helped.

3. How is organizational effectiveness evaluated? As we will see, much of the existing evaluation literature takes the answers to the first two evaluation questions for granted. It focuses on finding valid methods for answering a clear question such as "Are our clients satisfied?" or "How effective and efficient is our employee records system?" However, even here, methods can range from highly precise quantitative measures to very subjective, "unscientific" impressions. But are objective quantitative measures more valid than qualitative impressions? Not necessarily. It depends on how well the measures accurately reflect the selected effectiveness indicators.

4. Who is OEE for? Early theories of evaluation assumed that there would be universal agreement on what an effective organization would be in terms of goals and the means to achieve them. Hence the answer to the question was "everyone." However, the implicit evaluation perspective was that of the organization's leaders, who defined what "effective" would look like. Now it is recognized that different stakeholders could well have differing ideas on what effectiveness indicators should be.

5. When is it best to evaluate? This is a subset of the "what" question, highlighting the time dimension. Is it enough that an organization be effective over a short period of time, such as a quarter or a year, or should the time period be longer? For example, a frequent criticism of American business is that it demands that profit levels be as high as possible every year, whereas Japanese firms evaluate effectiveness over a much longer time period, and some short-term losses are not necessarily considered to be indicators of ineffectiveness.

Some Common Existing Models of OEE

The period from the late 1970s to the mid-1980s saw several excellent attempts to review the literature on evaluating organizational effectiveness (Cameron and Whetten, 1983; Goodman and Pennings, 1980; Quinn and Rohrbaugh, 1983; Spray, 1976). So many definitions of organizational effectiveness were noted and so many ways of measuring it were suggested that a few writers (for example, Goodman, Atkin, and Schoorman, 1983; and Quinn, 1988) suggested a moratorium on effectiveness research. We will not discuss all the points of view at length here, but by drawing on the previous reviews, we present a brief summary of the main schools of thought on OEE, in terms of three models. Table 14.1 highlights these viewpoints. Note that many of these views addressed private-sector organizations and so need to be interpreted in the context of the nonprofit sector.

Goal Achievement Model.
In a sense, the goal achievement model is the original "common sense" evluation model long used by organizations to see how

Table 14.1. Models of Organizational Effectiveness Evaluation.

Dimension of OEE	Goal Achievement Model	Means Achievement Model	Human Resources Model	Political Model
Why evaluate	Indicate degree of goal achievement	Indicate effectiveness of means for achieving goals	Indicate effectiveness of human resources in shaping OEE	To understand how stakeholders determine nature and use of OEE
What to evaluate	Main organizational goals, such as profit, growth, membership growth	Main indicators of internal performance, such as productivity, cost efficiency	Employee motivation, job performance	Choice of criteria depends on power of stakeholders
How to evaluate	Objective output measures, such as income, costs	Objective throughput measures, such as budget, time, and motion standards	Objective and subjective measures of employee performance, such as absenteeism, job satisfaction	Measures of stakeholder influence and their agenda priorities, such as negotiating skills
Who evaluation is for	Implicitly for owners or shareholders	Implicitly top management view	Implicitly top management view, but sold by HR specialists and union leaders	Tries to be neutral; all stakeholders benefit from understanding process
When to evaluate	Short-term intervals	Short-term intervals	Not discussed	Continuous

well they were doing. As we will show shortly, there can be intense disagreement over what the ultimate objectives of an organization should be. However, the naive view came from the business world and was that an organization's main objective was to earn a profit (Cyert and March, 1963). The main organizational evaluations, therefore, were those of the accounting and financial experts who devised rules for keeping track of the various forms of revenue and expenditures so as to precisely measure profit and loss. In the nonprofit world, the "pure bottom line" of profit is more difficult to find, but one or more goals *can* be defined. Measures of growth in revenues or numbers of clients are commonly included in this kind of evaluation. As Table 14.1 shows, this approach has emphasized quantitative financial measures, and was aimed at owners and investors by showing the value of the firm.

Means Achievement Model. From the viewpoint of those responsible for managing organizations and achieving financial success, having only the final score of the game was never sufficient. They needed to know which of their many decisions contributed to financial success. This results in a "means" focus. Keeping costs low is an important ingredient in producing desired financial results. So is productivity, quality, and the speed with which program changes are made to meet changing user demands. These and other determinants of surplus/deficit can serve as a set of secondary goals. Then another set of processes can be identified that are the means to achieve these goals.

Management can systematically create the chain of means-ends connections with processes such as strategic planning and management by objectives. Full implementation of these processes can result in every member of the organization having a set of goals or objectives. These goals provide the means by which the next level in the organization will achieve its goals, and so on down the hierarchy. If each level achieves its goals, the organization will achieve its ultimate goals. In theory, each level in the hierarchy can be evaluated for effectiveness.

Professional organizational effectiveness evaluators tend to focus on means evaluation. The taken-for-granted links between means and ends constitute a basic assumption for the means achievement school of OEE.

Human Resource Effectiveness Model. A number of years ago a separate school of thought arose within the means achievement school, taking the position that focusing on indicators such as productivity and efficiency diverts attention from the key determinant of organizational success — people. They argued that the emphasis must be on the organization hiring the best people, training them the right way, and motivating them to work hard, cooperate with one another, and be open to new ideas. Here effectiveness measurement focuses on employee attitudes, beliefs, and performance, as well as on how well various policies and practices shape these (such as training programs and employee empowerment programs). Top managers are not the only ones who subscribe to this point of view. Human resource management specialists and some union representatives advocate it strongly (although they may not agree on what the specific effectiveness criteria should be).

Political Model. The approaches to evaluation discussed so far implicitly take the view that either an organization is effective or it is not. There may be technical problems in measuring effectiveness, but once these are solved, the final judgment is absolute. The other assumption in these models is that the universally accepted indicators of effectiveness are those of the organization's key stakeholders and/or its top leader(s). In brief, the "why," "what," and "who" dimensions of OEE are taken as given, and discussion centers on the "how" and "when" dimensions.

The political model, however, focuses on understanding "what really goes on" when people are purporting to evaluate an organization's performance. It assumes that there are various organizational stakeholders whose influence can help make or break the organization. They may have very different ideas about what indicates effectiveness. Some will emphasize different ends and/or different means. Those with the most power will impose their beliefs about what ends and means are important and how they should be measured. But others will continue to push their own agendas to the extent they can. Finally, these stakeholders choose the extent to which they will consider effectiveness in making decisions related to the organization. Those advocating this view of OEE like to feel that they are not taking sides, but are merely describing the political processes at work, and trying to understand these processes and their outcomes.

The foregoing discussion of models is only one of many ways to categorize the OEE literature. Other ways tend to be more oriented to the interests of academic organizational theorists; hence they may not be as useful to readers who are unfamiliar with these theories (institutional theory, resource dependence theory, population ecology, contingency theory, and so on). Since this chapter is aimed at practitioners, not academics, we chose not to follow an academic approach.

OEE in Nonprofit Organizations: A Special Case

As we have seen, OEE is a process that is full of problems at the best of times. Yet in spite of this, increasing numbers of internal and external stakeholders demand some kind of evaluation and at least claim that evaluation results will affect their decisions about the organization. Managers must know how to respond to these demands. To do this they need to assess the five basic dimensions of OEE as they apply to their own situation.

In this section we will first look at how the special characteristics of the nonprofit sector create an OEE pattern that differs significantly from that of the business sector. Next we will consider variations in the patterns that can occur between segments within the nonprofit sector.

Nonprofits Versus Businesses: Different Contexts, Different OEE Patterns

As Bozeman (1987) has pointed out, the line between private for-profit and public not-for-profit organizations is not a clear one. There is a continuum along two dimensions: the extent to which the organization provides its services in a competitive market, and the extent to which it must respond to the political forces of stakeholders with agendas that go beyond the basic "value-for-money" concern of the typical consumer. Here we will look at the two extremes of Bozeman's continuum of "publicness": the market-driven business whose survival depends primarily on making profits in a highly competitive environment, and the politically driven not-for-profit agency whose survival depends on satisfying a number of powerful stakeholders with varying interests in the organization. Table 14.2 summarizes the essential differences between the task of evaluating organizational effectiveness in business and in nonprofit organizations.

Table 14.2. Differences in OEE Patterns in Business and Nonprofit Organizations.

Dimensions of OEE	Business Sector	Nonprofit Sector
What	"Bottom line" (profits)	Many, varied, and mutually contradictory criteria
Who	Mainly investors, customers	Mainly varied client and funding groups
Why	To improve profitability	To further the agendas of varied stakeholder groups
How	Agreed-to indicators of profitability	Subjective indicators not clearly understood or agreed to
When	Regular measures, at least annually	Variable time lines

Typically in *for-profit businesses,* OEE criteria relate to the famous "bottom line" — return on investment, market share, and so on, (the "what" of the organization). The stakeholders the business needs to satisfy most (the "who" dimension) are customers and investors. Usually, getting and keeping more customers will keep everyone happy. The purpose of measuring organizational effectiveness (the "why" dimension) is primarily to provide a scorecard that indicates the company's profitability. The most common way to carry out the evaluation (the "how" dimension) is to apply standardized numerical measures of items such as income, expenditures, or market share, as provided by accountants and other professionals using standardized tools. Finally, it is generally agreed that the evaluations should be made regularly at short intervals, such as quarterly.

(Admittedly this is an overly simplified picture of how business organizations are evaluated. There is a political dimension in most businesses that can complicate matters. Some stakeholders, such as government regulators or consumer groups may not see profitability as the main objective. Various groups can differ over how much profit is desirable over what period of time. Groups inside the organization may choose not to emphasize output goals over throughput, and may disagree over acceptable indicators of efficiency, motivation, innovativeness, and the like. And, of course, as the number of business bankruptcies attests, looking good in terms of whatever effectiveness indicators are used is not easy. All of this notwithstanding, we would argue that the market forces of the business world generally make OEE relatively more straightforward than in the nonprofit world.)

For the typical *nonprofit* organization, there is no single "bottom line"; rather, there are several. The criteria for defining an effective organization (the "what" dimension) can be multiple and contradictory. Because most nonprofits' income does not derive directly from the sale of services to clients, there are usually at least two very different stakeholders — those who supply the funds and those who use the services (the "who" dimension). Clients may want more and better services and, because they do not pay for them, they may not be concerned with costs. Funders may have many reasons for giving, only one of which may relate to the quantity or quality of services delivered. Corporate donors may be seeking publicity, governments may be trying to avoid political problems, and United Ways may be concerned with balancing competing demands for funds.

Even among clients, and among staff and volunteers within the organization, there may be groups with conflicting demands on the organization. For example, in charities organized to help victims of specific health problems, such as cancer or Alzheimer's disease, there are those who would say that the main indicator of the organization's success is how much it gives to medical research into the disease, while others would emphasize the quality and quantity of educational programs aimed at prevention; or services provided for existing victims.

Whereas in business the main reason for OEE is to improve profitability, the multiple stakeholders for a nonprofit, with their multiple effectiveness criteria, means that there are also multiple reasons for evaluation (the "why" dimension). In fact, mapping the agendas of the most powerful stakeholders becomes one of the key skills in managing the evaluation process in most nonprofits.

The "how" dimension is also characteristically fraught with problems. Agreed-to indicators of profit and loss, sales, market share, and so on, are rarely available. How is one to measure the quality of artistic expression produced by a theater organization? How is one to ascertain how much an environmental organization has contributed to reducing pollution? How can one conclusively show the effect of family therapy on reducing the incidence of spouse abuse? The list goes on. The point is that it is often very difficult to measure the outcome of nonprofit organizations' actions, and even when they are measured, it can be just as difficult to get agreement on what the standards for acceptable performance should be.

Finally, the existence of multiple stakeholders with multiple evaluation criteria also means that the time dimension for evaluation can be highly variable. While audited annual financial statements can measure the basic financial status of the nonprofit organization, the attainment of many of the nonfinancial organizational goals may entail measurement over much longer time intervals, if at all. (Again it should be mentioned that the foregoing discussion is simplified to capture an extreme, although common enough, situation. As we will see later, some consultants and evaluators would argue that there is nothing inevitable about the problems of evaluating nonprofits. All the complicating factors discussed here, they would suggest, could be overcome if only evaluations were done "properly." This point is addressed at the end of this chapter.)

Some Common Variations in OEE Patterns Within the Nonprofit Sector

The discussion so far contrasts the approaches to evaluation in the "typical" business setting as opposed to the "typical" nonprofit setting. This serves to highlight the main differences. But it is obvious that there is a great range of variation within the nonprofit sector (as there is within the business sector). The political model of OEE discussed in the previous section turns out to be the one best suited for understanding these within-sector differences.

The main factors that distinguish between OEE patterns in nonprofits are (1) the extent to which various stakeholders consider evaluation to be important (evaluation emphasis), (2) the degree of divergence between powerful stakeholders over what the effectiveness indicators should be (criteria conflict), and (3) the degree of difficulty in measuring and interpreting effectiveness indicators (ambiguity).

Low levels of evaluation emphasis occur when neither the stakeholders nor the management group care how well the organization is doing. This occurs in times of crisis and emergency when the demand for services is high and insistent. At such times, *anything* the organization does is "good enough"; no one has the time to care about "how good." Low evaluation emphasis also occurs when resources are plentiful and various stakeholders treat the nonprofit organization more as a symbol than an instrument to achieve objectives. The important thing in such cases is that the organization simply exist. For example, in more affluent times, governments have been known to sponsor the creation of nonprofit organizations for purposes such as fostering the arts, teaching "life skills" to the poor, and so on. They give every sign that their main concern is that such organizations be seen to exist under their sponsorship, but they show little interest in what the organization actually does. In such situations the organization's leaders, particularly if untrained in management skills, often find it all too easy to go along with the status quo, never questioning how well they are achieving the organization's objectives. In these days of government budget cuts, however, this is less and less common.

Once evaluation does become a concern, four common evaluation patterns can be discerned, depending on the configuration of the criteria-conflict and the ambiguity dimensions for an organization. Figure 14.1 illustrates these patterns.

Maximum complexity OEE is the first pattern. In this situation OEE is emphasized but there is disagreement between stakeholders on effectiveness indicators. This usually reflects differences in the relative priority given to various organizational objectives. There is also disagreement on how to measure any given criterion, and how to interpret the results of such measurement. For example, consider science museums. Certain funders may want to see such a museum heavily utilized by tourists and the general population as a leisure attraction. Internal curators of exhibits and outside scholars may want to emphasize the museum's research function. Schools and internal education specialists may want to emphasize the museum's use as an educational tool for school children.

Assuming that all parties agree that a certain amount of emphasis should be placed on using the museum for educating school children, there

Figure 14.1. Four Common Patterns of OEE in Nonprofit Organizations.

Measurement Ambiguity

		Low	High
Criteria Conflict	High	Negotiation-dependent OEE: problems of politics and conflict of criteria	Maximum complexity OEE: problems of negotiation and measurement
	Low	Low-profile OEE: OEE not emphasized or implemented routinely	Measurement-dependent OEE: problems of ambiguity and interpretation of results

remains the problem of evaluating how well it does so. Some stakeholders may emphasize simple "numbers of school visits" as an indicator. Some may emphasize "student satisfaction" with these visits. Others may stress students' absorption and retention of scientific knowledge following a museum program as compared to the "typical" classroom coverage of the same subject. Given that measurement of one or more of these indicators is carried out, the problem of interpreting what the results mean remains. How many students is enough? How satisfied do students need to be? How much better than the typical classroom should the museum-based learning be? Putting costs into the equation just complicates the judgment of effectiveness; what should be the appropriate ratio of costs to benefits in order to decide how effective the "schools program" is?

Negotiation-dependent OEE is the second pattern. In this situation there are also high levels of conflict over what the effectiveness indicators should be, but not as much confusion over what to measure. For example, in a community services center, the heads of the various programs may believe that "their" program deserves the greatest support (a program for seniors, for example, or for recent immigrants, street kids, or single parents). The program heads deem the organization to be effective to the extent that it directs its resources to one area more than to another. However, the measurement of each stakeholder's concern is relatively simple: dollars or percentage of budget allocated to each area. Therefore the main OEE emphasis is on negotiating with stakeholders the relative priority of objectives.

Measurement-dependent OEE is the third pattern. This is the opposite of the pattern that emphasizes the negotiation of evaluation criteria. In this situation stakeholders generally concur as to what effectiveness should look like but have great difficulty coming up with unambiguous measures of it. Everyone involved with an agency for helping victims of spouse abuse to rebuild their security and self-esteem may agree on the objectives and their priority. But how is one to measure these concepts? And how much improvement is enough? Almost any indicator that cannot be expressed in numerical terms will be seen as ambiguous, which is why so many stakeholders prefer input and internal efficiency measures of various kinds, such as funds allocated or numbers of clients treated per budget dollar. Even with numerical measures, however, the problems remain of interpreting the meaning of numbers and deciding what adequate standards are.

Low-profile OEE is the fourth pattern. In this situation there are relatively low levels of criteria conflict, and there is little measurement ambiguity. This situation occurs either because OEE is not a concern of powerful stakeholders or because it is a simple, straightforward exercise. For example, this could occur in a small mutual-benefit or self-help organization run entirely by volunteers for members like themselves, such as a hobby group or a group of unemployed single parents. All that really matters is that the members feel satisfied with their membership in the organization. There is little need to measure the effectiveness of the organization as such, and members indicate their satisfaction by renewing their memberships. (Organizational effectiveness problems can still remain, however; for example, how should the group interpret the meaning of a decline in membership.)

Political Games People Play: Looking at the Evaluation Process

By far the most common pattern in OEE in nonprofit organizations is the "maximum complexity" pattern. With this pattern, the cry "Show us the impact of what you do" comes from various sources. The criteria that would indicate effectiveness vary from one source to another, as do acceptable standards for performance. As well, there are few unambiguous measures to signal the level of effectiveness attained. Finally, it is rarely clear how much OEE actually enters into decisions made about the future, such as funding levels or new program initiatives. Sometimes evaluation is a major influence on such decisions, but often the talk about the importance of OEE is mere rhetoric. When this pattern is dominant, and when the pattern is "negotiation dependent," evaluation is primarily a political process. The parties involved play a variety of games as they try to influence one another to make the organization adhere to their agendas. Let us look at some of these political games from the points of view of various evaluators and of those being evaluated — the evaluatees.

Evaluator Games

Two common evaluator games emerge from observations of OEE processes. One is based on emphasizing the countable, and the other on selective impressions.

Emphasize the countable is the first game. People who are serious about OEE generally want to be "objective." They want the "real truth" about what is going on. In modern Western societies it is often believed that countability indicates truth. Dollars spent or raised, numbers served, hours of service provided per client, client-staff ratios, degree of budget variance, and so on, are all numbers that can be stated precisely, graphed, put into tables, and compared over time or between agencies. Hence the first, and most common, evaluation game is to insist that evaluatees "say it with numbers." This has two major effects.

1.   Those matters that cannot be measured numerically are ignored. In most cases the easiest things to count are "inputs" and some "means" activities. Favorite input measures include client waiting lists or dollars raised from donors. Examples of common means activities are dollars spent on general administration as a percentage of direct program delivery costs, and units of service provided per dollar spent. It is in the area of goal attainment that numerical measures are most difficult to obtain. How is one to quantify the quality of the artistic expression of a dance company, the extent to which a seniors' organization enhances the quality of life of its clients, or the pleasure that children get from a community recreational program? We are not saying that it is impossible to express these outcomes quantitatively, just that it is difficult. Hence the tendency is to downplay subjective qualitative estimates in favor of "hard data." Unfortunately, in the nonprofit world, the hard data are not always the most important data, so it is possible for a nonprofit to "look good" in terms of its numbers while it is becoming increasingly irrelevant to those it is attempting to serve. The converse is also common: an agency may have a high impact yet be subject to criticism because of poor, but irrelevant, numbers.

2.   The other effect of measuring the countable is that those whose work is being measured come to believe that the most important thing to do is to "make the numbers." Sociologists Peter Blau (1955) and Robert Merton (1940) noted this years ago. Merton called it the "displacement of goals" of phenomenon. Blau noted that when supervisors used statistical controls to judge the performance of subordinates and emphasized these judgments when rewarding or punishing them, subordinates would go to any length to "make the numbers," including distorting the figures and withholding cooperation from co-workers. Meanwhile, since the numbers did not reflect the real goals, the real goals received no attention.

Evaluation on the basis of *selective impressions* is the second game. The opposite of the evaluator who goes by the numbers, no matter what they stand for, is the one who forms opinions about the agency and finds "proof" for these conclusions in randomly gathered impressions. An example is the funding agency representative who is already convinced that the organization being evaluated is not doing enough to "reach out" to visible minorities in the community. As proof of this conclusion, the evaluator offers a conversation with one member of a visible minority group who had no knowledge of the evaluated organization. Even among those with no prior bias, experiences of this kind can be sufficient to "prove" the validity of a conclusion if no countervailing evidence is provided. However, in the nonprofit sector, where belief in rightness of a cause is a dominant motive for becoming involved in a given organization, the tendency is particularly strong to selectively emphasize evidence that supports one's preexisting ideological position.

Evaluatee Games

According to the political model of evaluation, the main aim of those being evaluated is to "look good," or, if something is deemed to be faulty, to shift the blame elsewhere. Two of the tactics available for this game are equating need with effectiveness and controlling the agenda.

One tactic is to argue that *need equals effectiveness*. Here it is common for evaluatees to deflect attention from evaluation altogether, and direct it toward need. The existence of growth in the problem areas with which the organization deals is offered as "proof" that the organization is doing an important job and ought to receive increased funding. Not considered is whether the services provided help solve the problems. Measures of demand and the importance of the issue in the eyes of the community replace organizational and program performance.

The second tactic is to *control the agenda*. When performance is to be measured, the most common way for you, as an evaluatee, to deal with evaluators is to persuade them to judge you on the basis of criteria *you* identify as the most important. Not surprisingly, these criteria usually coincide with those on which it is possible to show positive results. For example, a funder might want to emphasize the results of cost control programs (without mention of possible negative effects on clients being served). For a client group making the evaluation judgment, controlling the agenda may mean showing a positive trend in numbers served (without mention of costs or client satisfaction). For a professional association, an evaluation might emphasize a positive trend in the qualifications of staff hired or money spent on employee training (again, without mention of costs or effects on clients).

In most of these game-playing situations, what is really going on is a complex process of illusion making and negotiation, designed to keep the "other side" from imposing its will. But must this always be the case? Can OEE ever be an honest, shared attempt to find out what can be done to improve the organization's effectiveness? We will argue that, though difficult, it is not impossible. The final section of this chapter discusses how this might be achieved.

Toward a More Effective OEE Process

The previous section showed various ways in which OEE could "fail" by causing more harm than good or by simply contributing nothing that would make the organization more successful. We saw how the rhetoric of OEE could be a substitute for real efforts at improving organizational effectiveness. We saw how fixation on input and throughput indicators of effectiveness could deflect attention from actual outputs or impacts. And we saw the distortions that can arise from faulty measurement methods derived from ideological bias. It was the recognition of how common these pitfalls were that led writers in the late 1970s and early 1980s to suggest that OEE might be a waste of time and might as well be abandoned as a subject for study (Goodman, Atkin, and Schoorman, 1983; Quinn, 1988).

Yet in spite of the problems and pitfalls we have noted, managers and other stakeholder groups continue to evaluate the effectiveness of organizations, formally or informally. The conclusions they reach influence such matters as funding, regulation, and cooperation. While organizational evaluation can never be an exact science and, indeed, there is no such thing as one objective reality in the measurement of success, we can avoid the worst pitfalls of the process and obtain at least an incremental gain in perceived effectiveness. We will first sketch what the ideal OEE world would look like, then discuss ways to try to reach it.

An Ideal OEE Process

A successful OEE process depends on a shared understanding between all of the significant evaluators and evaluatees as to what is desirable in terms of the five dimensions discussed in this chapter: the who, why, what, how, and when of evaluation. To be more specific, here are guidelines for constructive OEE:

1. Know who the key internal and external stakeholders are. Be sure they know about each other.

2. Try to understand how all parties involved feel about why OEE is to be undertaken, and how the evaluation results are to be used.

3. Build consensus around the principle that all evaluation is undertaken to reveal improvement opportunities. Make it clear that once these opportunities are revealed, help will be available, if needed, for those responsible for acting on the opportunities. (The idea is *not* to point the finger of blame, and then to leave the accused to fix the problems.)

4. Build consensus among the stakeholders that evaluation must be an integrated, multilevel process. There must be a shared understanding of what actions cause what results in the organization. For example, the concerned stakeholders of an agency helping disadvantaged youth must agree that activities or policies such as a new staff training program or a new client intake system will contribute to the organization's mission of keeping their clients from dropping out of school. In other words, the layers of ends and means to be evaluated, and the connections between them, should be spelled out for all to see and agree on.

5.   Not everything can be evaluated. A key part of successful OEE is finding out the basis on which each stakeholder *currently* evaluates the organization. It can take time to ensure that what they say they are evaluating is what they actually are evaluating, as the rhetoric of evaluation may differ from practice. But it needs to be done. The resulting "evaluation map" likely will be a mix of goals, means, and inputs.

6.   Show each evaluator-stakeholder the evaluation map and obtain consensus on a limited set of criteria for evaluation. Those most critical to organizational survival should receive the greatest relative priority.

7.   Obtain consensus on the *evaluation process, standards,* and *time perspective* to be applied in judging degrees of effectiveness. For example, there needs to be agreement among stakeholders on whether to use qualitative and/or quantitative methods to gather data; on what score on a questionnaire given to clients represents "acceptable" client satisfaction; and on the time period the evaluation should cover.

8.   Assuming that it is possible to reach the desired consensus on the why, what, how, and when of OEE, it is folly to believe that this consensus will be maintained. People and times change. Thus an effective OEE system should contain a mechanism to *check* and *renegotiate* consensus as needed. This does not mean having ways to bring "deviants" back into line when their views on OEE start to change. It may well mean recognizing that the present system is no longer working and that some stakeholder has discovered this, signaling a need for large-scale change.

Getting There from Here

A reader might be permitted a slightly cynical smile after reading the above guidelines to better OEE because of the references to the need for evaluators and stakeholders to share a common understanding of the process. The reaction may well be, "They don't even know of one another's existence, or if they do, they rarely talk to each other, so how can we get consensus?" Is this chapter another completely unrealistic "recipe for success"? We know we are not providing the only recipe, but we do have suggestions. We conclude this chapter with recommendations for evaluatees and evaluators on how to implement the guidelines.

1.   The most important single step to improved evaluation is to adopt the principle that "the best evaluation is self-evaluation." If you are the CEO being evaluated, this simply means subjecting your organization to the evaluation process. State outcome objectives, and think how progress toward them can be measured. Many external evaluators wish only to see an effort being made to measure effectiveness and will happily adopt the criteria and measurement methods already in place. If there are differences of opinion, at least you are in a position to argue persuasively for an alternative, rather than merely voicing opposition to the evaluator's agenda.

It is important to note that there are many specific technical methods for carrying out a variety of forms of "internal evaluation," although this chapter cannot go into detail. Managers uncertain about how to evaluate their organizations should consider specific books on evaluation (see Love, 1991), and/or seek the advice of specialized consultants.

2.   The best way to institutionalize organizational self-evaluation is to make it part of the planning process. Doing so ensures that whenever changes are made, ways to evaluate their outcomes will be determined along with the changes themselves. The evaluation part of the plan must then be carried out. Unfortunately, in the nonprofit sector, good intentions to evaluate programs often remain just that—intentions. Chronic shortages of time, money, and technical expertise often conspire to stop the implementation of evaluation processes until external stakeholders demand an impact analysis on *their* terms.

3.   Good evaluation is *continuous* evaluation. This means that the information on which evaluation is to be based needs to be gathered regularly over time. It is important to devote attention to designing information systems that regularly measure key indicators of success. For example, surveys to determine client satisfaction with services are more likely to cause controversy when done sporadically in response to funder pressures for proof that the agency is meeting client needs. A regular process of client interviews that routinely gathers and analyzes client opinions is much more likely to gain acceptance. The conclusions of the ongoing evaluation and actions planned can then become part of the reports directed to interested stakeholders.

4.   It is best to negotiate the "what" and "how" of evaluation when relationships with stakeholders are sound. The least effective kinds of OEE occur when there is no mutual trust or respect between the evaluators and the evaluatee. Illusion-making game playing will result if an agency's leaders believe that an important external stakeholder (like the government) is pushing for more evaluation simply for "political" reasons, or if they believe that the emphasis on evaluation is only rhetoric that will not be used in decision making. For this reason nonprofit CEOs should proactively initiate talks with key stakeholder groups to map expectations and negotiate a common understanding of them before a crisis arises.

5.   In spite of the best of intentions, disagreement between evaluators and evaluatees can become destructive conflicts if the parties are unable to communicate and resolve their differences effectively. Therefore it is important to provide training in negotiation and conflict management skills. The OEE process gets derailed when evaluators are unclear about the criteria they are using or fail to make their standards clear. Training is available in presentation skills, listening skills, the negotiation of differences, and the avoidance of destructive forms of conflict.

6.   Even people with strong interpersonal skills can get into difficulty when the stakes of an evaluation are high. In these situations, it can be bene-

ficial to use a professional facilitator as well as professional evaluators. Whenever emotional tension is likely to be high, professionally trained consultants with experience in facilitating negotiation and resolving conflict can be useful. Professional evaluators are skilled in the design of evaluation studies as well as in the techniques of measurement and interpretation.

Taken together, these recommendations represent an approach to the creation of a positive, externally oriented OEE culture in an organization. The incorporation of evaluation into planning, improved information systems, continuous measurement, and the use of specialized training, when implemented, would all contribute to the formation of a set of organizational values that welcomes evaluation and treats it as a way of seizing opportunities for improvement, rather than casting blame.

A Special Case of OEE: Total Quality Management in the Nonprofit Sector

No discussion on how to improve OEE would be complete without reference to the most renowned effectiveness recipe of the 1990s — Total Quality Management (TQM). TQM has reached a stage that can be called a "movement" in business circles, particularly in the manufacturing sector. The TQM approach developed from issues related to improving profitability, return on investment, market share, and chances for business survival. Its basic tenets are simple. Organizations succeed by satisfying customers, and customers want the best possible value for money. Those who serve "customers" must ensure the maintenance of the highest possible standards of customer service. People who serve customers directly rely on others in the organization to support them, and they become the "customers" of those providing this support. Thus everyone in the organization has "customers." TQM is a system in which every segment of an organization is involved in providing the best value for money to its "customers."

There are various versions of the guiding principles of TQM and how to implement it (for example, Crosby, 1978; Deming, 1986; Ishikawa, 1985; Juran, 1986; Townsend, 1990). Although details might differ, most would espouse the following TQM principles:

- It must be customer driven.
- There must be total organizational commitment to the system.
- The emphasis must be on problem prevention, not problem detection.
- Emphasis on quality improvement must be continuous, consistent, and persistent.
- The focus must be on discrete areas of activity or process that, taken together, make a significant contribution to the production of the ultimate goods or services the organization was created to provide.
- Quality improvement must be measurable.

- There must be an emphasis on continuously increasing the ability of all organizational members to monitor and improve the quality of their work by means of better training, tools, and information.

To achieve a "TQM culture" throughout the organization, a number of steps must be followed:

- Start creating change at the top, with top management internalizing TQM's values and principles.
- Inculcate these values and principles in every element of the organization by means of symbolic events and artifacts, such as posters, slogans, speeches, and celebrations.
- Build the system around teams that are made up of those responsible for a more or less distinct area of activity, such as order taking, shipping, final assembly, and product promotion.
- Change the role of people in middle- and lower-management levels from overseer and monitor to coach, facilitator, trainer, and coordinator.
- Devote substantial resources to TQM training.
- Build new information systems around the areas of activity that TQM teams will be working on; this will produce accurate and timely measurement of the results of the teams' actions.
- Implement reward systems that reinforce TQM values and actions while discouraging "old" values and actions.

The picture TQM gurus present is bright and positive. When it works it seems to be an extraordinarily successful way to improve organizational effectiveness. Unfortunately, there are indications that business is "souring" on TQM because it is difficult to implement successfully and more difficult to maintain (Mathews and Katel, 1992). What is its potential for the nonprofit sector?

The manufacturing origins of TQM render it difficult to translate into a nonprofit environment. Features of the nonprofit sector that make OEE difficult create formidable barriers for TQM: the lack of a market mechanism to drive the need to improve; the emphasis on needs over results; multiple, vague, and often contradictory stakeholder expectations; client difficulties in articulating expectations for quality; the conditioning of professionals to believe that they know what is best for the client whatever the client may say or do. Further, demand for nonprofits' services typically far exceeds their ability to supply those services, and rather than facing inadequate consumption of what they produce, their problems usually lie in obtaining enough resources to continue providing it.

A further issue derives from the nature of nonprofit service-producing activities, where there is often a simultaneous production and consumption of services, and clients often participate actively in this production (Bowen and Schneider, 1988). Training employees, an important aspect of traditional TQM approaches (see Curtis, 1989), addresses only a portion of service production resources, and the nonprofit may have little control over client participation in production activities. In other words, when the "raw material" on which the staff of a service organization works is an individual person rather than a thing, it is much more difficult to use TQM methods. Humans are not as predictable or controllable as metal or plastic. To date the TQM literature devotes little attention to the service sector in general, and less to nonprofits.

Just as earlier "one right way" approaches (such as scientific management, MBO, quality circles, and so on) have been shown not to apply equally well in all circumstances, so too may TQM not be equally useful to all organizations. This does not mean that nonprofits should ignore the TQM movement. However, nonprofits should approach TQM fully aware of the special characteristics of their sector. In terms of this chapter, this means developing awareness of the political nature of organizations and the need to negotiate consensus every step of the way.

Summary

The concept of OEE has evoked considerable debate in academic literature in recent years, debate that peaked in the late 1970s and early 1980s. At that time writers were noting the conceptual disarray and contradictions of organizational effectiveness, with some suggesting a moratorium on research into the topic. Yet managers still must manage, and various stakeholders still make judgments on whether specific organizations are effective. Executives concerned with the effectiveness of their organizations require an understanding of the why, what, how, who, and when of OEE.

OEE processes can be categorized as goals achievement, means achievement, human relations, and political models. In the nonprofit sector, different patterns of OEE emerge: the maximum complexity, negotiation-dependence, measurement-dependence, and low-profile patterns. The most common pattern is maximum complexity, and the political model is the most useful for understanding this pattern. The political model can help reveal evaluator and evaluatee games. Examples of these games are emphasizing the countable, justifying selective impressions, equating needs with effectiveness, and controlling the agenda.

These games can be destructive for OEE. Constructive OEE entails identifying stakeholders, understanding the reasons for OEE, focusing OEE on identifying improvement opportunities, and building and maintaining consensus on the OEE process. This approach entails emphasizing self-evaluation, building evaluation into the planning process, making OEE a continuous process, establishing processes when stakeholder relationships are good, building negotiation and conflict management skills, and using professional facilitators when necessary. The ideal OEE process may be difficult to achieve, but managers in nonprofits can be proactive in striving for the best process possible. It is in everyone's interests to do so.

References

Blau, P. M. *The Dynamics of Bureaucracy.* Chicago: University of Chicago Press, 1955.

Bowen, D. E., and Schneider, B. "Services Marketing and Management: Implications for Organizational Behavior." In L. L. Cummings and B. M. Staw (eds.), *Research in Organizational Behavior.* Greenwich, Conn.: JAI Press, 1988.

Bozeman, B. *All Organizations Are Public: Bridging Public and Private Organizational Theories.* San Francisco: Jossey-Bass, 1987.

Burrell, G., and Morgan, G. *Sociological Paradigms and Organizational Analysis.* Portsmouth, N.H.: Heinemann, 1979.

Cameron, K. S., and Whetten, D. A. "Organizational Effectiveness: One Model or Several." In K. S. Cameron and D. A. Whetten (eds.), *Organizational Effectiveness: A Comparison of Multiple Models.* New York: Academic Press, 1983.

Crosby, P. B. *Quality Is Free: The Art of Making Quality Certain.* New York: McGraw-Hill, 1978.

Curtis, B. "The Quality Partnership: Responsibility and Involvement." In J. S. Oakland (ed.), *Total Quality Management.* Oxford: Cotswold Press, 1989.

Cyert, R. M., and March, J. G. *A Behavioral Theory of the Firm.* Englewood Cliffs, N.J.: Prentice-Hall, 1963.

Deming, W. E. *Out of the Crisis.* Cambridge, Mass.: M.I.T. Press, 1986.

Goodman, P. S., Atkin, R. S., and Schoorman, F. D. "On the Demise of Organizational Effectiveness Studies." In K. S. Cameron and D. A. Whetten (eds.), *Organizational Effectiveness: A Comparison of Multiple Models.* New York: Academic Press, 1983.

Goodman, P. S., and Pennings, J. M. "Critical Issues in Assessing Organizational Effectiveness." In E. E. Lawler, D. A. Nadler, and G. Camman (eds.), *Organizational Assessment: Perspectives on the Measurement of Organizational Behavior and the Quality of Work Life.* New York: Wiley, 1980.

Ishikawa, K. *What Is Total Quality Control? The Japanese Way.* Englewood Cliffs, N.J.: Prentice-Hall, 1985.

Juran, J. M. *Juran on Leadership for Quality: An Executive Handbook.* New York: Free Press, 1986.

Love, A. J. *Internal Evaluations: Building Organizations from Within.* Newbury Park, Calif.: Sage, 1991.

March, J. G., and Simon, H. A. *Organizations.* New York: Wiley, 1959.

Mathews, J., and Katel, P. "The Cost of Quality: Faced with Hard Times, Business Sours on 'Total Quality Management.'" *Newsweek,* Sept. 7, 1992, pp. 48–49.

Merton, R. K. "Bureaucratic Structure and Personality." *Social Forces,* 1940, *18,* 560–568.

Quinn, R. E. *Beyond Rational Management: Mastering the Paradoxes and Competing Demands of High Performance.* San Francisco: Jossey-Bass, 1988.

Quinn, R. E., and Rohrbaugh, J. "A Spatial Model of Effectiveness Criteria: Toward a Competing Values Approach to Organizational Analysis." *Management Science,* 1983, *29*(3), 363–377.

Spray, S. E. "Organizational Effectiveness: The Problem of Relevance." In S. L. Spray (ed.), *Organizational Effectiveness: Theory-Research-Utilization.* Kent, Ohio: Kent State University, 1976.

Townsend, P. L. *Commit to Quality.* New York: Wiley, 1990.

15

Managing the Challenges of Government Contracts

Steven Rathgeb Smith

In the last thirty years, a major restructuring of the provision of public services has occurred; increasingly, public services are provided by nonprofit service agencies through government contracts. Consequently, nonprofit managers are on the front lines in government's response to major social problems, including AIDS, homelessness, chronic mental illness, and drug and alcohol abuse. Nonprofit managers are now faced with meeting the demands and expectations not only of their own boards of trustees and supporters but also of public contract managers, the legislature, the governor, and even social policy advocacy groups. Contracting exposes nonprofit agencies to government budgetary politics and complex funding issues, such as rate setting and cost-reimbursement contracts. Funding delays, political interference in contract negotiations, and uncertainty about future agency revenues are only a few of the many new concerns for nonprofit managers due to the growth of contracting.

Contracting also tends to precipitate internal changes within the organization, including greater formalization and professionalization. New internal accountability structures need to be created, and the board's role in agency oversight tends to become more focused on long-term strategic issues

Note: The author would like to acknowledge the support of the Center for the Study of Philanthropy and Voluntarism at the Sanford Institute of Public Policy, Duke University. Helpful comments on early drafts of this chapter were provided by Charles T. Clotfelter. Portions of this chapter were adapted from Smith and Lipsky, 1993.

rather than operational concerns. The efficient allocation of resources becomes a much more pressing concern as the extent and duration of contracting increases.

The central focus of this chapter is an examination of the dilemmas posed by contracting for nonprofit management and the implications of contracting for the future role of nonprofit managers and boards of directors. The chapter is based on extensive research on the impact of government contracting on nonprofit health and social welfare organizations. While this chapter concentrates on nonprofit service organizations, the effects of contracting and the management recommendations are applicable to other types of nonprofit organizations receiving public contract funds, such as arts and cultural organizations.

The Rise of the Contracting Regime

Prior to the 1960s, nonprofit service agencies were overwhelmingly dependent on private funds, primarily endowment income, client fees, and charitable contributions. However, many nonprofit and public organizations faced mounting criticism in the late 1950s and early 1960s for their failure to adequately serve the poor and disenfranchised. In response, the federal government sharply increased its role in addressing social problems. New federal initiatives included neighborhood health centers, community mental health centers, community action agencies, and greatly increased discretionary spending on social services.

This new federal role was reflected in the rapid rise in federal spending on social services. Federal expenditures for social welfare services almost tripled between 1965 and 1970, from $812 million to $2.2 billion. Federal funding continued to expand throughout the 1970s. By the 1980s, federal funds comprised 65 percent of total government spending at all levels on social welfare services, compared to 37 percent in 1960. Total federal spending (in current dollars) rose from $1.1 billion in 1960 to $13.5 billion in 1980. Per capita spending (in constant 1988 dollars) rose from $22.72 in 1970 to $84.36 in 1980 (Bixby, 1991, pp. 6, 9, 12). A large percentage of the increase in public funding of social services was channeled through nonprofit agencies in the form of government contracts. In 1977, twenty-five states used half or more of their state human service expenditures for contracts with nonprofit agencies (Kettner and Martin, 1985, p. 8). In Massachusetts, the Department of Welfare increased its contracting with nonprofit agencies from $36 million (380 contracts) to $84 million (over 1,000 contracts) between 1977 and 1980 (Gurin, Friedman, Ammarell, and Sureau, 1980, p. 137). Many state agencies relied almost exclusively on nonprofit agencies to provide services, especially new and innovative services such as community residential programs, respite care, and day treatment.

The Reagan administration came to power in 1981 with a commitment to reduce federal spending. During his first year in office, President Reagan successfully achieved the enactment of the Omnibus Budget Reconciliation Act (OBRA), which radically changed the role of the federal government in social policy. Key features of the legislation included an approximate 20 percent reduction in federal spending on social services, the consolidation of many different categorical federal social programs into block grants, and the decentralization of the administrative responsibility for the expenditure of federal funds to state and local governments (Gutowski and Koshel, 1982).

The impact of these Reagan administration policy changes on public social expenditures is evident in the shifts in federal and state funding. Total federal spending on social welfare services through a variety of block grant and categorical spending programs declined from $8.8 billion in 1980 to $8.5 billion in 1987. During this period, state and local spending rose from $4.8 billion to $6.8 billion. Federal expenditures as a percentage of total social welfare spending declined from 64.6 percent in 1980 to 52.4 percent in 1988 (Bixby, 1991, p. 13).

The actual effects of federal cutbacks and the changed federal role since 1981 vary depending on the service category. Family planning services, job training, legal services, social policy advocacy, and many counseling programs have been particularly hard hit. Yet, programs for drug and alcohol addicts, the developmentally disabled, chronically mentally ill, and child protective services have received significant funding increases, primarily from greater state appropriations and specially earmarked federal legislation.

Despite the funding increases in selected social services, the overall funding climate is very tight and competitive. The recent slump in state economies limits the ability of state governments to substitute state funds for reduced federal funds. United Way chapters have relatively little money to fund new agencies whose federal or state grants or contracts have been reduced. And private foundations typically provide only modest short-term grants for very specific purposes.

Partly due to this austere funding climate, the extent of contracting for services continued to grow throughout the 1980s. State and local governments, eager to save money, view contracting as a less costly way of providing needed public services. Indeed, the major public policy response to the emergent problems of homelessness, hunger, AIDS, child abuse, and domestic violence has been through government contracting with nonprofit organizations. Moreover, the percentage contribution of government revenues to many nonprofit organizations remains high. For some organizations, such as residential programs for developmentally disabled adults or emotionally disturbed children, government revenues can comprise almost all of an organization's revenues.

The Emergence of the Contracting Regime

The growth of contracting has created patterned relationships and expectations between government and nonprofit agencies that can be characterized as a "contracting regime." A regime is a "set of principles, norms, rules, and decision-making procedures around which actor expectations converge in a given issue area" (Krasner, 1982, p. 185). This concept has been most fully developed by analysts in international relations, who used the regime concept to characterize the relatively stable relationships that appear to exist between countries, despite the absence of a single entity to act with authority in managing the relationship. Thus, countries can develop certain formal and informal rules and expectations about the interaction between countries, even though the countries may not be bound by legal agreements.

The nonprofit-government contracting relationship is similar to the regime in the following respects. First, regimes tend to have accepted means of resolving disputes and addressing particular problems. This is evident in the tendency today to utilize nonprofit organizations funded by government to address current social problems and in the accepted norms governing the interaction between nonprofit organizations and government. Second, the regime concept is helpful in illuminating the regularized patterns of interaction between government and nonprofit agencies, even when these nonprofit organizations are opposed or resistant to government regulations and mandates. Third, participants in regimes are mutually dependent and marked by continuity. And, if participants depart from the regime norms, they are sanctioned, either by the dominant party or by third parties. Fourth, regimes are usually sustained and dominated by a powerful party. In international relations, this role is performed by a country whose policies and norms are accepted by other countries in the regime. The government-nonprofit relationship is similar because despite the mutual dependence of government and nonprofit organizations, government tends to be the more powerful in the relationship. Thus, nonprofit organizations often are in the position of accepting or following the norms and policies of government.

The implications of the contracting regime for nonprofit management are profound. Managers of nonprofit agencies receiving government contracts are not free agents but are linked in an ongoing relationship with government, which at once constrains their behavior and provides certain incentives for managerial action. The dilemma for nonprofit managers is that the process of government contracting may undermine a nonprofit's financial stability while at the same time encouraging nonprofit organizations to move away from their own distinctive mission and reflect more closely the priorities and goals of government administrators. The following sections address in more detail these specific problems posed for nonprofit managers.

The Uncertainties of Contracting: The Problem of Managing Nonprofit Service Organizations

Public attention to contracting has often focused on the lack of accountability that exists for the expenditure of government funds by nonprofit agencies. This is certainly an important policy concern. However, much less focus has been given to the many ways in which government may undermine nonprofit contract organizations, creating serious and enduring management problems for nonprofit organizations.

The Cash Flow Crisis

Nonprofit service organizations tend to be always short of cash to pay their bills. The roots of this problem reflect the unique role played by nonprofit organizations in social service delivery. Nonprofit agencies, especially grass-roots community agencies, such as battered women's shelters, poverty agencies, and youth organizations, emerge through the collective efforts of like-minded individuals interested in addressing a particular social problem. Typically, these organizations are dependent upon a mix of small cash and in-kind donations. They are also woefully undercapitalized. Many leaders of these organizations are inattentive to the need for adequate capitalization. Foundations and United Way chapters generally do not provide money for capitalization. Many nonprofit organizations rent rather than own their buildings, so they are unable to secure credit lines or borrow money from banks.

The constraints on building an adequate capital base make it difficult to weather disruptions in cash flow. When nonprofit organizations are young and small, a cash flow interruption may represent a minor problem. The sole paid staff member skips a pay check. Or a board member steps in to make up the difference. Or a creditor agrees to forgive a bad debt.

But, when a nonprofit becomes involved in a contractual arrangement with government, the implications of cash flow disruptions become more serious since contracting means more resources for the agency—hence much greater cash flow demands. Perhaps one of the best examples of how agencies can change is provided by many associations of retarded citizens (ARCs) across the country. These ARCs typically started very small and often existed for many years without a full-time executive. The revenue demands were very small. Over time, ARCs began to provide contracted services. During the 1980s, state governments looked to ARCs to provide community-based services to deinstitutionalized persons with developmental disabilities through the Intermediate Care Facilities for the Mentally Retarded program funded through Medicaid (Bradley, 1981; Braddock, 1990). This program is very costly, often requiring ARCs to generate tens and sometimes hundreds of thousands of dollars every month to pay the bills of participants in the programs. Shortfalls in client censuses, management miscues, payment delays, or unexpected expenses can often prove fatal for an organization with such high revenue needs. The same problems affect smaller organizations whose programs are less costly. The cash flow problem is exacerbated by a common characteristic of the contracting regime: the inability of the contract to cover all an agency's costs under the contract requirements. This serious problem can be due to several factors. The nonprofit manager may underestimate the costs of implementing the contract. Through no fault of the manager, agency expenses may rise when unexpected increases in the cost of doing business occur in such areas as insurance, utilities, and staff salaries. The contract amount, although adequate at the start of the contract, may over the years lose ground to inflation and state budget cutting. In these situations, the nonprofit manager is often put in the position of either giving up the contract, with its implications for staff layoffs and shrinkage of the agency, or continuing with the contract, albeit an underfunded one. Since nonprofit executives are rarely rewarded for staff layoffs and the accompanying organizational turmoil, most nonprofit executives keep the contract and try to make the best of a difficult situation.

In short, the cash flow problem is not an idiosyncratic occurrence or primarily due to mismanagement; instead it is built in to the very structure of the contracting regime. Cash flow problems are to be expected. Nonprofit managers are in the position of coping with chronic cash flow concerns. Managers respond with a variety of strategies. They may delay their payments to their vendors, ask their bankers for easier terms on their loans, request that staff take unpaid leave or vacation time, temporarily lay off employees or freeze hiring, even in cases of staff members leaving. In particularly serious cases, agency executives may forego some of their salary or decide to suspend payment of the agency's payroll taxes.

Nonprofit executives faced with these difficult management decisions often try to obtain additional revenues for the agency. They may try to obtain a line of credit or increase their credit line. Or they may seek private donations from individuals and companies or tap into the principal of their endowments. These strategies, however, are not feasible for most nonprofit agencies. Banks are generally reluctant to extend credit to nonprofit service agencies unless they are larger agencies with substantial collateral or long-standing roots in the community. Foundations rarely provide funding for operating expenses, preferring to give money for capital expenditures or short-term projects. Only the very largest nonprofit organizations have endowments. United Way funds are only available to a relatively small number of member agencies; becoming a member entails a long application and review period, thus these funds are not an option for agencies in cash flow binds.

The difficulty of raising or gaining access to alternative funds to make up for revenue shortfalls is one reason that government administrators often prefer to contract with large agencies. Only the large agencies have the credit lines, the endowments, or the fundraising capacity to compensate for the inevitable cash flow problems experienced by nonprofit agencies.

Contract Renewal

The ongoing and enduring cash flow problems of nonprofit agencies are often intensified by the uncertainties that accompany contract renewal. When government contracts with a nonprofit agency, it has a vested interest in the sound and smooth operation of the agency. Nonetheless, it frequently undermines the operations of the agency through debilitating delays and un-predictability in naming and providing contract renewal awards — circum-stances that make it extremely difficult for nonprofit contract agencies to adequately plan and manage their affairs.

Delays in contract renewal occur for many reasons. The state legisla-ture may be deadlocked, requiring that the state agencies suspend final ac-tion on contract renewals since the potential amount available for contracts is unknown. Key administrators at the state office contracting with nonprofit agencies may have left or been replaced. An election may be under way, generating uncertainty among state administrators as to their futures and having a ripple effect on the contracting process.

Other reasons for delay may be more strategic from the standpoint of the government contract administrators. State administrators may want to delay the process of contract renewal in order to gain greater compliance by nonprofit agencies to contract terms and expectations. For example, a contract administrator may have found the nonprofit agency resistant to ac-cepting certain government client referrals. Delaying renewal may, in the eyes of the state administrator, make it more likely that the agency will soften its position on these problematical client referrals.

Alternatively, state contract administrators may use their ability to expedite the contract renewal process, to at least some degree, as a way of currying favor with contract agencies. This debt may then be useful in fu-ture negotiations between government and contract agencies.

The renewal process is fraught with uncertainties despite the high rate of contract renewal. Most contracts are renewed. A battered women's shelter awarded a contract in 1982 is likely to still have the contract in 1992, bar-ring any major shocks to the provider system. But the high rate of renewals masks the regular dilemmas faced by nonprofit agencies during the contract renewal process.

Nonprofit managers may be unclear as to the exact amount of the new contract. Given cutbacks in state governments, a renewed contract might well be for a lower amount than the previous one. Also, the state may de-cide to rewrite the contract upon renewal. A child welfare agency might have a contract for several years to provide counseling services to children. But a change in political priorities might lead state administrators to use con-tract renewal as an opportunity to restructure the agreement so that the child welfare agency, if it wants to keep the contract, would be required to pro-vide intervention services to abused and neglected children. Other exam-ples of substantive changes in contracts by state officials include requiring nonprofit agencies to serve a larger geographic area, giving part of a con-tract to another agency, reducing the administrative costs allowed on a con-tract, and restricting agency referrals to state personnel as opposed to al-lowing a nonprofit agency to accept referrals directly from other public and private organizations.

Nonprofit managers, at least theoretically, have the option of refusing to rewrite the terms of the contract or to abide the long delays often accompanying contract renewal. Yet these, too, are impractical strategies for many nonprofit agencies. First, the last twenty-five years have witnessed an explosion in the number of nonprofit agencies. In the past, many nonprofit agencies enjoyed a monopoly position in their geographic area, giving them substantial leverage with state administrators in a contract situation. Most agencies, except for very specialized services, have lost this status. Now, nonprofit managers know that if they resist the renegotiation of a contract, many agencies are waiting in line to take the contract on the terms stipulated by the state.

Second, competition is fierce for private charitable funds, which might serve as alternatives to contract funds. Moreover, most foundation grants are unable to replace lost contract funds because they tend to be short-term and for much smaller amounts than contract funds. As noted, United Way moneys are very difficult to obtain. And raising private funds with appeals to individuals is a long-term project that cannot substitute for lost contract funds. Agencies that have lost contracts are rarely able to approach the level of contract funding using private donations. As a result, these agencies often merge with other agencies or shrink drastically. In extreme cases, agencies will go out of business.

Third, nonprofit agencies often find that the only way they can fulfill their mission to address a particular problem, such as juvenile delinquency or child abuse, is through government funding. Private funding is either unavailable or inadequate to the agency's needs.

Strategic Management in the Age of Contracting

The cash flow crisis and the uncertainties of contract renewal create unprecedented challenges for nonprofit managers. Responding to these challenges is complicated when contracting precipitates changes within the organization. Strategies exist, however, that can help nonprofit executives and board members adequately manage their agencies through difficult times. The following pages detail these changes and outline specific initiatives that may help staff and board cope with contracting.

A New Role for the Board of Directors

In their ideal type, nonprofit organizations are governed by a volunteer board of directors who serve as the connecting link between the organization and the local community. Alexis de Tocqueville ([1835–1840] 1956) and, more recently, Robert N. Bellah and others (1985, 1991) and Benjamin R. Barber (1984, 1992) have been attracted to this very quality of nonprofit organizations. To them, nonprofit organizations can serve as vehicles for promoting, safeguarding, and invigorating democracy.

But contracting poses serious problems for many boards. Most board members tend to be unfamiliar with contracting and the intricacies of the contracting process. It is often difficult for board members to exercise oversight over contracts and the management of contracts by executives. Further, the executive is usually the person within the organization knowledgeable about contracting opportunities and potential sources of new revenues for the agency.

Also, contracting requires the agency to develop new systems of accountability to track expenditures and clients. Inevitably, these new systems require greater staff specialization and a more formal organization of the agency. A full-time bookkeeper may be hired. New program managers may be necessary. Additional secretarial support may be needed to process new forms and requests for information about clients and agency spending. As the paid staff expands and the demands on the agency's resources grow, the board may find itself less capable of "setting the agenda" for the agency, especially if the agency is highly dependent on contract revenues. The board may be relegated to a position of supporting the executive's initiatives rather than the executive implementing the board's directives and policies.

The danger for the organization inherent in this kind of shift is that the board may encounter some unpleasant surprises. The executive, in the pursuit of contract revenues, may obligate the agency to contracts that are underfunded or ill-advised. Board involvement in the agency may wither as board members find that they are severely limited in terms of the type of input sought by the executive. As board involvement declines, management mistakes or morale problems may go undetected until a crisis develops.

Other types of management problems may develop due to conflicts over agency mission. For example, the board may be made up of the founding members of the organization, who have a commitment to a specific mission. They may feel that the executive is trying to take the organization in a direction that violates its spirit, as originally defined by the board. The result may be protracted negotiations between the board and staff about the agency's future. Sometimes, the outcome is the resignation of some board members or the ouster of the executive as the board and staff try to define the agency's mission.

The executive may have the key role in agency governance until a crisis develops, such as inadequate cash flow, staff discontent, or lost contracts. In response, the board may exert greater control and oversight over agency operations. Yet, the board often withdraws to its previous role as the crisis eases. In other cases, the board may simply be unable to find an appropriate executive director, so the board retains an important role in day-to-day agency management and the overall agenda-setting for the organization.

The shift in power from the board to the executive director and his or her staff is a general tendency among nonprofits, although the extent of this change will differ depending on organizations' individual circumstances. This kind of change — and the organizational problems created by this new staff role — are most visible in new community-based organizations that emerge out of the informal helping system of community members, neighbors, and social movements. For them, professional management often represents values and policies antithetical to the original purposes of the organization (see Wilson, 1973, for a full discussion).

To a certain extent, the enhanced role of the executive is part of the process of organizational growth and development (see, specifically, Wilson, 1973, Chapter Ten). The board and the organization as a whole, however, can take steps to minimize the extent to which the board's role in agency oversight is unduly altered. First, the board can recruit individuals with knowledge of contracting for board membership. Second, the board can institute procedures that require the executive director and his or her staff to submit timely reports on various programmatic and fiscal aspects of the agency. Third, the board should tour agency facilities and programs on a regular basis, to learn in detail about agency activities and consumers. Fourth, depending on the agency, the board should include consumer or community representatives. These individuals can supply useful feedback to the rest of the board on agency performance and provide very valuable advice and input on agency mission and goals.

Finding the Right Executive

When contract funding was rising rapidly during the late 1960s and 1970s, the executives' management mistakes were often overlooked by board members or masked by new contracts. Many nonprofit agencies were essentially kept afloat by forgiving contract managers eager to spend escalating federal dollars and develop new services. But in the current era, contracting is quite different. Contract managers and board members can no longer tolerate management miscues. Even a relatively small management mistake can create a fiscal crisis for the agency.

Ideally, agency executives should have facility with government contracting procedures and financial management as well as a sensitivity to the agency's mission. The process of selecting the executive may lay bare some of the underlying cleavages within the organization as to the agency's future. And, many agencies find themselves mired in controversy as a newly hired executive takes the agency in a direction perceived to be contrary to its original mission. This is a particularly common problem in the current contracting environment because many individuals with the credentials necessary to cope with the management complexities of contracting may not be well attuned to the subtleties of the agency's approach to its surrounding community or consumers. Relatedly, the fiscal problems of nonprofit agencies lead many boards of directors to hire individuals who would operate the agency as a business, prompting internal feuds over agency mission and direction.

Thus the ideal type of executive for a nonprofit service agency cannot be determined without reference to the particular characteristics and needs of the organization. And, while it may no longer be sufficient to have a respected clinician with relatively little management training or experience as an executive, it is equally true that a board of directors would be in error if they simply sought an executive whose primary qualification was a management background in another agency or organization. While individuals with a business background may bring a new focus on efficiency to an agency, over the long run costs may be very high in terms of staff turnover, morale, and client dissatisfaction. An agency needs to strike a balance between the concern for the efficient utilization of resources, due in part to the demands of the contracting regime, and the commitment to agency mission that exists outside market-driven imperatives.

Enlarging the Agency Constituency

Nonprofit agencies, as noted, often represent at their founding the efforts of like-minded people to address a particular problem. Often, these organizations are not representative of their community as a whole; many agencies are directed by people from a particular political, ideological, ethnic, or income group in a community. Indeed, nonprofit organizations are valued, in part, because of their ability to represent specialized or minority constituencies (see Weisbrod, 1988). This narrowness can become a handicap as an agency develops and becomes involved in a contracting relationship with government. Cash flow problems and the uncertainties of the contract process are part of contracting. But, they may be addressed or alleviated through the support or intervention of community notables, politicians, consumers, and board members. Consequently, a crucial part of nonprofit management today is the diversification or enlargement of the organization's constituency.

Several strategies to achieve this goal are possible. First, an agency may create an affiliate organization that can help with fundraising, community support, and program visibility. Typically, these organizations are directed by the paid staff of the parent organization but are run and operated primarily by volunteers. Second, the organization may alter the composition of its board in order to bring interested supporters directly into an oversight and governance role for the organization. Third, the agency might join community organizations, such as the Chamber of Commerce. The regular presence of a nonprofit contract agency at Chamber meetings can go a long way to creating a role for the agency as a vital and important member of the community.

Fourth, the agency may alter its rules for membership. Many nonprofit organizations were established by a relatively small number of people who formed the core of the initial board of directors; no official membership in the organization apart from the board and staff may have existed. In such agencies, the board of directors was frequently self-perpetuating rather than elected by the membership. Later, however, an agency can change the rules to allow interested community supporters or financial contributors to be eligible for membership. This may give important friends of the organization a stake in it that would be very useful for purposes of political and financial support. It may also give the organization greater leverage in its relations with government contract administrators.

Enlarging the agency's constituency is, however, fraught with risks. New members or supporters may try to change the agency's mission and lead it in new directions. An agency may trade dependence on state contract administrators for dependence on a powerful donor or group of donors. More community members may make the organization more risk averse. For example, a community residence program for the developmentally disabled might shy away from developing an innovative apartment program if it knew that substantial community opposition might develop. Consequently, clarity about an organization's mission and the role of new constituency groups is absolutely critical if an agency is to avoid organizational instability.

Strengthening Political Advocacy and Associational Activity

Prior to the advent of widespread contracting, nonprofit management existed relatively separate from the political process. Dependent primarily on private revenues, management decisions and the fate of the organization were relatively disconnected from decisions made by state and local legislatures, the federal government, or governors and mayors. Contracting has changed this situation. Nonprofit management is now inextricably connected to the political process. Important political decisions, legislation, and administrative rulings can have a profound impact on the success of nonprofit managers. If the legislature refuses to allocate sufficient funds for a contract rate increase, the nonprofit executive may be forced to lay off personnel, with the accompanying implications for morale and program diminution. Accountability requirements instituted by the legislature may have a major impact on how a nonprofit executive spends his or her time. Funding cutbacks may require agencies to merge with each other or go out of business entirely. Cash flow problems and the contract renewal process can create severe management difficulties for nonprofit agencies. The success of nonprofit managers now hinges, at least in part, on decisions made in the political arena. This changed relationship between nonprofits and the political world requires nonprofit executives to adopt new strategies in order to manage their organizations effectively.

Enhancing the Agency's Political Presence

Nonprofit executives need to increase their agency's political visibility and support. The executive should strive to enlist the support of local political figures, including municipal leaders and state legislators. This goal can be accomplished, in part, by enlisting key politicians or friends of politicians as agency board members. Also, a nonprofit executive can significantly help the agency's image by making local leaders aware of agency activities through mailings, articles in the local newspaper, and letters. Over time, these sometimes minor efforts can create a positive public image of the agency and garner favorable political support in the community.

This enhanced local political presence is especially important given the numerous local issues confronted by nonprofit service agencies. Many nonprofits need special zoning permits in order to house their facilities. Other nonprofits receive various cash and in-kind subsidies from municipalities. Nonprofit programs for children often send participants to local public schools. And many nonprofit clients and consumers use local public transportation. Consequently, if an agency does not have good relations with its surrounding community and its political leaders, it may be very difficult to successfully implement its programs.

A major problem for the agency occurs when it disagrees with a major decision of its state or local contracting authority. The state contract administrators may want to refer different types of clients to the agency. Or the state may want to restrict or curtail certain contract expenditures. Or the state may want to end the contract altogether and award it to another agency. Personal appeals by the executive, letters from the board of directors, or intervention by community political supporters may produce a reversal of unfavorable rulings. But many nonprofit agencies, especially smaller or newer agencies, lack the political clout to overturn these decisions. Further, many nonprofits, even the large ones, are averse to aggressive political action out of concern that such efforts may alienate government contract officials and lead to retribution against the agency at a later date. For this reason, it is also crucial for nonprofit executives to try to work together through nonprofit associations to create a strong political base. This may not ensure that unfavorable rulings will be overturned, but it may make it more difficult for government administrators to implement arbitrary or ill-advised policies.

Nonprofit Associations and the Contracting Regime

Associations can perform a number of valuable functions for nonprofit managers, in addition to providing a means for collective influence with government. Many nonprofit agencies have participated in associations for decades. The Child Welfare League of America and Family Service America are just two of the many national associations of nonprofit organizations engaged in political advocacy for their members. However, these organizations have not generally been involved in issues of contracting. More recently, though, many nonprofit associations have been founded at the state level. These organizations have tended to be more directly involved in state policies pertaining to contracting.

The new associations tend to be of two types. First, service-specific associations exist, such as the North Carolina Association of Home Care Agencies and the Massachusetts Association of Community Mental Health Centers. Second, statewide associations of different types of nonprofit agencies have been established. Good examples include the California Association of Nonprofits and the Massachusetts Council of Human Service Providers.

Both types of organizations can be helpful to nonprofit managers on key policy issues relating to agency contracts, including rates, funding levels, service priorities, and contracting procedures. At times, these associations may also be helpful in advocating for agencies in specific disputes between the state and individual organizations.

The second type of nonprofit association can also be very helpful in a number of other areas of interest to nonprofit managers. These statewide associations are able to call attention to the organizational difficulties faced by nonprofits in general. This may be helpful as state policy makers deliberate on issues pertaining to nonprofits. These associations can also assist member agencies with more practical concerns. Many contract agencies are squeezed financially because of declining state funding. Statewide associations can facilitate bulk purchasing of supplies and equipment to help the nonprofit save money.

Many nonprofit associations must contend with internal issues that constrain their advocacy role on behalf of nonprofit contract agencies. Some associations are forced to be very cautious in their advocacy work because of their members' concerns about alienating government policy makers. Other associations are divided on such issues as appropriate funding levels, contract requirements, and rates. As a result, the associations are tentative or vague in their policy proposals. Some associations have such diverse memberships that they are only capable of forcefully engaging nonprofit issues that concern every nonprofit, such as the treatment of fundraising costs by the state. Thus, these associations may not be a big help to nonprofit executives trying to cope with the organizational concerns posed by contracting.

Contracting Reform and Nonprofit Management

The management dilemmas of contracting are beginning to get the attention of government policy makers who worry about the long-term stability of many nonprofit agencies on which they depend. One indication is efforts by government officials and nonprofit executives to enact systemwide reform in contract financing and procedures. Some of these reforms offer the hope of significant and lasting improvement in the ability of nonprofit managers to effectively do their job. Many of these reforms require nonprofit contract agencies to work with concerned legislators and the political parties to gain the necessary legislative support.

One line of attack in contract reform is fundamental change in reimbursement policies. For example, in 1984 New York State enacted "prompt payment" legislation to address the cash flow problems of nonprofit contract agencies. Under this legislation, the state is required to pay interest on any overdue payments to vendors. While this law helped ease the cash flow problem somewhat, nonprofit agencies still complained of cash flow difficulties related to delays in contract renewal and approval. In response, new legislation was passed in 1991 called the Prompt Contracting Law, which contains a number of innovative provisions including time targets for the renewal of continuing contracts as well as new or one-time contracts, and a legislation appropriation, to be managed by the Office of State Comptroller, for interest-free loans to contract agencies experiencing cash flow problems (Grossman, 1992). This legislation appears to have had a positive effect on the cash flow situation, although the severe fiscal crisis of New York's state government has forced systemwide cutbacks among contract agencies.

Another strategy for addressing payment problems of nonprofits is component pricing. This is a method of payment that departs from the common, time-consuming practice of setting contract rates by determining each agency's historical costs. The component pricing system establishes uniform costs for various "components" of nonprofit agency operation, such as social workers' and psychologists' fees, space rental, and reporting costs. A cost range is determined for all providers of these components. Negotiated contracts then contain these cost ranges, allowing greater discretion on the part of nonprofit managers to move money from one category to another, depending on agency needs. This greater management latitude may ease the cash flow problem for nonprofit managers (Koch and Boehm, 1992, p. 45).

Despite these potential management advantages for nonprofits, component pricing is resisted by many legislators and contract administrators. The fiscal crises of state and local government have made many policy makers even more insistent on accountability for the expenditure of public funds. Component pricing can be perceived as undermining accountability since it permits nonprofit executives greater management discretion; thus some policy makers are reluctant to jettison the old system of setting rates without very firm assurances of agency accountability.

Another set of contract reform strives to address the undercapitalization of many nonprofits. Many states provide loans and grants to nonprofit agencies to renovate their buildings, purchase new facilities, and buy needed equipment. Massachusetts offers many nonprofit contract agencies access to bond money traditionally reserved for large educational facilities.

Many state and local governments are simplifying the contracting process, permitting nonprofit managers to devote their scarce resources to other agency activities and expediting the contracting renewal and application process. This simplification may help with cash flow and improve program equality.

Summary

The rise of widespread government contracting has remade nonprofit management. It has allowed many nonprofit agencies and managers to expand their services, client bases, and geographical jurisdictions. But organizational stability has been very elusive in the contracting regime due to cash flow and contract renewal problems. Moreover, contracting has altered the balance of power within nonprofit agencies. With the goals of many service contracts set outside the agency, the role of the board in agency governance tends to shift to fundraising, supporting the executive, and long-range planning. By politicizing nonprofit management, contracting propels nonprofit agencies into the world of lobbying, political associations, legislative politicking, and appeals to the mayor and governor.

Nonprofit agencies receiving government contracts are now part of the nation's public service system. As a result, the management of nonprofit agencies is more diffuse, with more constituencies and with important linkages to political leaders, groups, and the political process in general. The task of defining a nonprofit agency's mission and its future direction is more complicated because the fate of the agency is at least in part determined by political decisions made outside the agency. While such decisions may be influenced by nonprofit political advocacy, they are necessarily influenced by the imperatives faced by government agencies and legislatures. The mission of a nonprofit contract agency is no longer strictly "private," but includes a substantial "public" dimension. As nonprofit executives and board members try to navigate the difficult and challenging fiscal and political environment of the 1990s, they will have to carefully balance their public and private responsibilities if they are to preserve the vital role of nonprofits as alternatives to government agencies while at the same time maintaining the fiscal and programmatic health of their agencies.

References

Barber, B. R. *Strong Democracy*. New York: HarperCollins, 1984.

Barber, B. R. *An Aristocracy of Everyone: The Politics of Education and the Future of America*. New York: Ballantine Books, 1992.

Bellah, R. N., and others. *Habits of the Heart: Individualism and Commitment in American Life*. New York: HarperCollins, 1985.

Bellah, R. N., and others. *The Good Society*. New York: Knopf, 1991.

Bixby, A. K. "Public Social Welfare Expenditures, Fiscal Year 1988." *Social Security Bulletin*, 1991, *54*, 2–16.

Braddock, D., and others. *The State of the States in Developmental Disabilities: An Exploratory Analysis*. Baltimore, Md.: Paul Brookes, 1990.

Bradley, V. "Mental Disabilities Services: Maintenance of Public Accountability in a Privately Operated System." In J. J. Bevilacqua (ed.), *Changing Government Policies for the Mentally Disabled*. Cambridge, Mass.: Ballinger, 1981.

Grossman, D. A. *Paying Nonprofits: Streamlining the New York State System*. Albany, N.Y.: Nelson A. Rockefeller Institute of Government, 1992.

Gurin, A., Friedman, B., Ammarell, N., and Sureau, C. *Contracting for Services as a Mechanism for the Delivery of Human Services: A Study of Contracting*

Practices in Three Human Service Agencies in Massachusetts. Waltham, Mass.: Florence Heller School of Advanced Studies in Social Welfare, 1980.

Gutowski, M. F., and Koshel, J. J. "Social Services." In J. L. Palmer and I. V. Sawhill (eds.), *The Reagan Experiment.* Washington, D.C.: Urban Institute, 1982.

Kettner, P. M., and Martin, L. L. "Purchase of Service Contracting and the Declining Influence of Social Work." *Urban and Social Change Review,* 1985, *18,* 8–11.

Koch, D., and Boehm, S. *The Nonprofit Policy Agenda: Recommendations for State and Local Action.* Washington, D.C.: Union Institute, 1992.

Krasner, S. D. "Structural Causes and Regime Consequences: Regimes as Intervening Variables." *International Organization,* 1982, *36,* 185–205.

Smith, S. R., and Lipsky, M. *Nonprofits for Hire: The Welfare State in the Age of Contracting.* Cambridge, Mass.: Harvard University Press, 1993.

Tocqueville, A. de. *Democracy in America.* Edited by R. D. Heffner. New York: New American Library, 1956. (Originally published 1835–1840.)

Weisbrod, B. *The Nonprofit Economy.* Cambridge, Mass.: Harvard University Press, 1988.

Wilson, J. Q. *Political Organizations.* New York: Basic Books, 1973.

16

Program Evaluation and Program Development

John Clayton Thomas

Nonprofit organizations need to know how effectively they are performing their jobs. Are their programs achieving the desired results? How could programs be modified to improve those results? Because the goals of nonprofit programs are often subjective and not readily observable, the answers to these questions may be far from obvious.

To get the answers, nonprofit executives may want to employ the techniques of program evaluation. Program evaluation provides information on the effects of public and nonprofit activities. That information is useful in deciding whether and how programs should be continued in the future. Used appropriately, the tools of evaluation can help with a wide range of decisions about program development.

This chapter introduces the techniques of program evaluation as they might be employed by nonprofit organizations in evaluating their activities. These techniques are not designed for more general evaluations of organizational effectiveness (but see Chapter Fourteen in this volume). The emphasis here is on how these tools can be useful to organization executives by providing information that speaks to decisions those executives must make. To make that case, we will consider two contrasting approaches to evaluation before turning to a step-by-step description of how to conduct an evaluation.

Two Approaches to Program Evaluation

Program evaluation can seem a frightening prospect. For many, it raises the specter of outside experts "invading" the organization, seeking information in a sometimes mysterious and furtive manner, and ultimately producing a report that may contain unexpected criticisms. Organization executives may understandably balk at employing a technique that carries so much risk, with, at best, an unclear potential for gain.

Such fears are not ungrounded. The traditional approach to program evaluation, here termed the "objective scientist" approach, often proceeds much as described above. Borrowed from the natural sciences, this approach can bring more cost than benefit to the programs being evaluated.

The rationale underlying the objective scientist approach contains several elements. To begin with, objectivity is valued above all else; the evaluator must remain detached from partisan opinions about the program being evaluated. To achieve that objectivity, the evaluator should maintain critical distance from the programs and organizations being evaluated. By getting close to the program, the evaluator risks being influenced by program staff who are biased in favor of the program. The objective scientist also strongly prefers quantitative data, viewing qualitative data as subjective by nature — the very antithesis of an objective approach. Finally, the usual purpose of an evaluation by an objective scientist is to determine whether or to what extent the program has achieved its goals. Is the program sufficiently effective to be continued, or should it be terminated? The objective scientist takes little interest in how a program's internal mechanics are functioning.

The popularity of this approach is understandable given the origins of program evaluation. When evaluations first became popular in the United States in the late 1960s and early 1970s, the social sciences in general were modeling themselves after the natural sciences by trying to be "objective." Evaluators simply followed the lead of other social scientists.

Two decades of experience have shown that this approach does not work well, either for evaluation specifically or for the social sciences generally. Evaluators who insist on keeping their distance miss the special insights staff often have into their programs. Disdaining qualitative data further limits the evaluator's ability to assess a program because the goals of most public and nonprofit programs are too subjective to be measured only by quantitative techniques. Finally, the insistence on critical distance combined with the exclusive focus on program outcomes can result in evaluations that fail to answer the questions decision makers have about programs. Decision makers learn nothing, for example, about how to improve programs.

Recognition of these problems led to the development of an alternative approach, what Michael Quinn Patton (1986) has termed *utilization-focused evaluation.* As Patton has explained, this approach begins with a goal of balance rather than objectivity (pp. 195–198). Where objectivity implies taking an accurate and unbiased view of a program by observing from a distance, balance implies making the effort to view the operation from up close as well as from afar. Viewing from afar may not reveal important details discernible only from up close. Achieving balance also requires the use of qualitative as well as quantitative data because the latter are unlikely to capture all that is important about programs whose goals are subjective. Evaluators should seek the balanced assessment that is only possible through multiple perspectives.

The balanced approach also rejects outcome assessment — did the program work? — as the only purpose of an evaluation. Recognizing that most programs, even if negatively evaluated, are *not* terminated, the utilization-focused approach also seeks information for use in modifying programs. Getting close to the program helps here by putting the evaluator in contact with the program administrators who have questions about how programs should be modified as well as the authority to make changes.

The balanced approach is not appropriate for every program, every evaluator, or every nonprofit executive. In getting close to a program, the evaluator risks being "captured" by the program — that is, of becoming only a "mouthpiece" for those who are vested in the program. For that reason, some evaluators prefer to maintain distance — and thereby objectivity. Nonprofit executives who have serious questions about the quality of a program or the competence of its staff may also prefer an evaluation made from the critical distance of the objective scientist, especially if program staff are not trusted.

For the most part, however, nonprofit executives will find that the utilization-focused evaluation approach promises both a more balanced assessment and information more likely to be useful in subsequent program development. As a consequence, this chapter concentrates on evaluations as they would be undertaken from a utilization-focused approach.

Who Does the Evaluation?

A first question, when planning a program evaluation, is who should conduct the evaluation. Here the principal options are (a) an internal evaluation performed entirely by the organization's staff, (b) an external evaluation performed by outside consultants, and (c) an externally directed evaluation with extensive internal staff assistance.

An internal evaluation is possible only if the organization has one or more staff members who have extensive training and experience in program evaluation. Evaluation is too technical a task to attempt without that expertise. An internal evaluation also requires that the nonprofit executive give essentially a free rein to the evaluation staff. Inside evaluators can face strong pressures to conform their findings to the predispositions of program staff. Standing up to those pressures is possible only if the nonprofit executive has made an unequivocal commitment to producing an unbiased evaluation.

As a practical matter, most nonprofit organizations will not have sufficient in-house expertise to perform internal evaluations. They need to find outside assistance from private-sector consulting firms, management assistance agencies for the nonprofit sector, or university faculty, usually in public administration, education, or psychology departments.

Hiring an outside consultant carries its own risks. Perhaps the greatest risk is that the evaluation may be conducted with insufficient concern for the organization's needs. Where internal evaluators can get too close to a program, external evaluators, many of whom were trained in the objective scientist tradition, may not get close enough. Their preference for critical distance may blind them to the questions and insights the nonprofit organization's staff have about the program.

To minimize this risk, the nonprofit executive should discuss at length with the prospective evaluator(s) how the evaluation should be conducted. Assuming an interest in more closeness than the objective scientist approach provides, the executive should consider whether prospective evaluators are capable of taking a utilization-focused approach. It may be wise to negotiate a contract that specifies in detail how the nonprofit organization is to be involved in the evaluation (that is, how close the evaluator should get to the subject).

Perhaps the best means for conducting an evaluation is through a combination of outside consultants and internal staff. With this approach, the outside consultants provide technical expertise plus some independence from internal organizational pressures. Internal staff perform much of the legwork and collaborate with the consultants in developing the research design, collecting data, and interpreting findings.

The advantages of this approach are several. First, it provides the necessary technical expertise without sacrificing closeness to the program. Second, greater staff involvement should produce more staff commitment to the findings, increasing the likelihood that the findings will be utilized. Third, the evaluation can be used to provide training to enable staff to serve a greater role in future evaluations. Finally, having staff do much of the legwork should reduce the out-of-pocket costs for the outside consultants. This reduction is possible, however, only with a careful effort to ensure that working with the staff does not itself require too much of the consultants' time.

One way to minimize that time commitment is by creating a small evaluation advisory committee to provide oversight to the evaluation. This committee should include the outside evaluator(s), the nonprofit executive (or the executive's personal representative), and two or three other staff members in the nonprofit organization. The committee thus constitutes a central mechanism to which the evaluatee reports, thus reducing the time necessary for working with program staff. Keeping its size small, in the range of four to eight members, facilitates the committee's providing clear and prompt feedback to the evaluation process. A committee of this kind probably should be developed for wholly internal or external evaluations, too.

Finally, the nonprofit executive should plan to be personally involved in the evaluation. This involvement is the only way to assure that the manager's concerns are addressed. In addition, as the literature on organizational change attests, programmatic change is unlikely to occur through an evaluation unless the chief executive is involved and committed to the process (see, for example, Rodgers and Hunter, 1992, pp. 33–34). Optimally, the executive should be a member of the evaluation advisory committee. Alternatively, the executive should have a representative on the committee who reports back regularly on its deliberations.

The goal of this involvement is not to ensure that the "right" answers — answers that conform to the executive's biases — are obtained, but to ensure that the right *questions* — the questions crucial to the program's future — are asked. The chief executive should emphasize this distinction to the evaluator(s), whether internal or external, and then check to be sure the distinction is preserved as the evaluation proceeds.

Determining the Purpose of the Evaluation

The evaluator's first task is to define the purpose of the evaluation. That is, what sort of information is desired and why? How will the information be used? Answers to these questions will be crucial in determining all of the other elements of the evaluation.

Discussion of evaluation purposes often begins with a dichotomy between summative and formative purposes (Scriven, 1967, pp. 40–43). A *summative* purpose implies a principal interest in program outcomes, in "summing up" a program's overall achievements. A *formative* purpose, by contrast, means that the principal interest is in forming or "re-forming" the program by focusing the evaluation on how well the program's internal mechanics are operating.

In reality, the purposes of evaluations are much more complex than a dichotomy can convey. Saying an evaluation has a formative purpose, for example, does not indicate which of the program's internal mechanisms are of interest. For example, are we concerned with the quality of services clients receive, with how decisions are made as to which clients receive services, or with some other issue?

The purpose of an evaluation should reflect the concerns key stakeholders have about the program. The process of defining this purpose thus should begin with the nonprofit organization's executive: What questions does he or she have about how the program is working? What kinds of information might be useful for future decision making about the program? The opinions of other stakeholders should also be solicited. Funders obviously should be asked if continued funding is in question. Program staff ordinarily should be asked, too, since they may see issues about the program not evident to anyone outside the program.

In the end, any of a wide variety of purposes is possible, depending on the perceptions of stakeholders and the specific program. An evaluation performed primarily for funders often will have a summative purpose because funders usually want to know if a program is having the desired impact. However, if a program has only recently been implemented, it is likely to be a poor candidate for a summative evaluation because most programs require time to produce an observable impact. New programs are better candidates for *implementation* assessments—evaluations of how a program has been put into operation. Evaluation designed mainly for program staff are likely to have principally formative purposes to help staff in modifying the program.

The importance of defining the evaluation purpose cannot be exaggerated. Because this purpose will guide decisions at all subsequent steps in the evaluation, a mistake here can flaw the entire effort. The nonprofit executive should consequently review this purpose, making certain that it reflects his or her concerns as well as the concerns of other key stakeholders.

Even when great care has been taken to define the purpose of an evaluation, the need may arise to revise it. Indeed, the purpose often emerges more clearly as an evaluation progresses. Stakeholders may be able to articulate their questions about programs only as they consider program goals and measures. Evaluators should be open to this possibility.

Evaluators and nonprofit executives must also be alert to the possibility of so-called *covert purposes,* unvoiced hidden purposes for an evaluation (Weiss, 1972, pp. 11–12). Program managers, for example, sometimes have an unspoken goal of "whitewashing" a program by producing a favorable evaluation. An evaluation with such a purpose can be performed ethically only if the covert purpose is made overt. That is, the evaluation must be explicitly conducted and reported as an effort to make the best case for the program (see Foster, 1980). In most cases, however, the executive should reject such an evaluation as incapable of producing useful information.

It is at the stage of defining the purpose that the evaluator and the organization's executive should also consider whether the evaluation is worth doing. The revelation of a dominant covert purpose would provide one reason to bow out. Or, it may be impossible to complete an evaluation in time to inform an approaching decision about the program. Program evaluation consumes too many resources to be justified unless the results can be meaningful and useful.

Defining Program Goals

Program evaluation is a goals-based process; that is, programs are to be assessed against the goals they were designed to achieve. Defining those goals can be a difficult task. The evaluator must define and differentiate several types of goals, while at the same time navigating the often difficult politics of goal definition. This section first explains the several goal types and then discusses how to define them in a political context.

Types of Goals

A first type of goal refers to the ultimate desired program impact. *Outcome goals* are the final intended consequences of a program for its clients and/or society. An outcome goal has public value of itself, not as a means to some other end, and is usually people oriented because most public and nonprofit programs are designed ultimately to help people.

Activity goals, by contrast, refer to the internal mechanics of a program, the desired substance and level of activities within the program. This specifies the actual work of the program, such as the number of clients a program hopes to serve. How the staff of a program spend their time—or are supposed to spend their time—is the stuff of activity goals.

The distinction between outcome and activity goals can be illustrated through a hypothetical employment counseling program. An activity goal for this program might be "to provide regular employment counseling to clients," with an outcome goal being "to increase independence of clients from public assistance." The activity goal refers to the work of the program, the outcome goal to what that work is designed to achieve. As this example also suggests, outcome goals tend to be more abstract, conceptual, and long term; activity goals more concrete, operational, and immediate.

Understanding the distinction is crucial if the evaluator is to resist pressures to evaluate program success in terms of activity rather than outcome goals. Program staff often push in the direction of activity goals for several reasons. First, activity goals are easier for them to see: they can more readily see their day-to-day work than what that work is designed to achieve sometime in the future. Second, activity goals tend to be more measurable; it is easier to measure the "regularity" of counseling than "independence from welfare." Finally, activity goals are also usually easier to achieve. Police working in a crime prevention program, for example, can be much more confident of achieving an activity goal of "increasing patrols" than an outcome goal of "reducing crime."

Evaluators often can sidestep pressures of this kind by including both types of goals in the goal definition. As a practical matter, both outcome and activity goals are important in most evaluations. Although a summative purpose implies more interest in outcome goals, and a formative purpose more interest in activity goals, most evaluations have mixed formative and summative purposes, as when the question is how different parts of the program process affect the achievement of program outcomes. The evaluator may thus be able to satisfy program staff by examining activity as well as outcome goals.

Falling between activity and outcome goals are *bridging goals,* so named because they supposedly connect activities to outcomes (Weiss, 1972, pp. 48–49). Bridging goals, like outcome goals, relate to intended consequences of a program for society, but bridging goals are supposed to result in a route to the final intended consequences, rather than be final ends themselves. In an advertising campaign designed to reduce smoking, for example, a bridging goal between advertising (activity) and reduced smoking (outcome) might be "increased awareness of the risks of smoking." That increased awareness would be one consequence of the program for society, but instead of being the final intended consequence, it is only a bridge from activity to outcome.

Bridging goals can be important in evaluations for a variety of reasons. For one thing, because they are often essential linkages in a program's theory, their achievement may have to be demonstrated to show that engaging in program activities has produced the desired outcomes. To be sure that a program works, an evaluator may need to establish that the bridging goal is achieved before the outcome goal. For another, bridging goals sometimes provide a means to obtain an early reading on whether a program is working. Evaluators may be able to observe a program impact on a bridging goal even though it is still too early to see any final outcome.

Evaluations will also occasionally have an interest in side effects. Side effects, like outcome and bridging goals, are also consequences of a program for society, but *unintended* consequences. They represent possible results other than the program's goals. An effective neighborhood crime prevention program may displace crime to an adjacent neighborhood, producing the side effect of increased crime in the latter neighborhood. A side effect can also be positive, as when a neighborhood street cleanup program induces residents to spruce up their yards and homes, too.

An evaluation should focus on side effects only if they are viewed as part of the evaluation purpose. Is there an interest in examining a possible negative side effect, perhaps with an eye to changing the program so as to reduce or eliminate that result? The organization's executive and other stakeholders must make that judgment based on how they want the evaluation to be used. In most cases, given a principal interest in activity and outcome goals, the executive will probably not want to spare any of the limited evaluation resources to assess side effects. On occasion, however, possible side effects may loom so important that they must be addressed.

Goal definitions, whatever the type of goal, must satisfy these other criteria: (1) Each goal should contain only one idea. A goal statement that contains two ideas (for example, "increase independence from welfare through employment counseling"), should be broken into two separate ones, each idea expressed as a distinct goal. (2) Each goal should be distinct from every other goal. If goals overlap, they may express the same idea, and so should be differentiated. (3) Goals should employ action verbs (for example, increase, improve, reduce).

Goal definitions can be derived from two principal sources. One source is the program documentation, including initial policy statements, program descriptions, and the like. The other is the personnel of the program, including program staff, the organization's executive, and possibly other stakeholders.

The Politics of Goals Definition

Understanding the different types of goals and where to find them may be the easy part of goal definition. The difficult part can be articulating that definition in a manner satisfactory to all of the important stakeholders. To do that may require overcoming the difficulties inherent in the politics of goal definition.

As a first difficulty, many programs begin without clearly defined goals. Program formulation may have focused on where money should be spent but neglected what the expenditures should be designed to achieve. Second, as programs adapt to their environments, their goals may change, perhaps departing from the program's original intent. "Policy drift" can result in programs moving away from that original intent and in goals becoming fuzzy or inconsistent (Kress, Springer, and Koehler, 1980).

More difficulties can arise at the time of evaluator intervention. The common perception of an evaluation as threatening may lead program staff, when they are asked, to be evasive about goals. Or, staff or other stakeholders at different places inside and outside the program may simply have different perspectives, and thus may express conflicting opinions about a program's goals.

Evaluators have available a variety of techniques to cope with these problems, while still respecting the goals criteria defined above. Fuzzy or inconsistent goals may be accommodated by including all of the different possible goals in a comprehensive goals statement. If some perspectives are too contradictory to fit in the same statement, the evaluator might propose a goals clarification process (Kress, Springer, and Koehler, 1980) prior to any substantive evaluation. Helping staff and stakeholders to clarify the goals of a program could be the most important contribution an evaluation can make to a program, building a cohesiveness previously lacking.

Disagreement over goals can also sometimes be sidestepped as irrelevant to the evaluation. Patton (1986, pp. 90–92) recommends asking stakeholders what they see as the important *issues* or questions about the program. These issues, because they represent areas where information might be used, should be the focus of the evaluation anyway. And, there may be more agreement about issues than about goals. The evaluator may then be able to express these issues in terms of the types of goals outlined earlier.

The organization's chief executive can — and should — help in the goal definition process in several ways. First, the executive should oversee the goal definition process to ensure the necessary cooperation. The executive's endorsement may be necessary to obtain staff participation. Second, the executive should review proposed goals as they are defined, at a minimum to ensure their relevance to evaluation purpose. Finally, if conflicts over goals arise, the executive may need to intervene to assure resolution.

The Impact Model

The organization's executive may also want to ask the evaluator to combine the various goals in a visual impact model — an abstracted model of how the goals are expected to link to produce the desired outcomes (see Rossi and Freeman, 1989, pp. 72–75). This model should have several characteristics.

First, it should be an abstraction, removed from reality but representing reality. Second, it should simplify, reducing substantially the detail of reality. Third, the model should make explicit significant relationships among its elements, showing, for example, how activity goals are expected to progress to outcome goals. Fourth, the model may involve formulation of hypotheses — the suggestion of possible relationships not explicitly stated in program documents or by program actors. This last element can be the most valuable part of a model: its development may prompt program stakeholders to articulate hypotheses they had not previously recognized.

To illustrate, Exhibit 16.1 shows an impact model for a training program for executives of local branches of a national nonprofit organization.

Exhibit 16.1. An Impact Model for a Training Program for Executives of Local Branches of a National Nonprofit.

1. Determine developmental needs of local executives (AG).
2. Develop training materials to address these needs (AG).
3. Screen and select executives for training (AG).
4. Conduct training of executives (AG).
5. Executives formulate individualized plans for development of their organizations (BG).
6. Executives attend follow-up training (AG).
7. Local organizations increase volunteer membership (OG).
8. Local organizations increase volunteer giving (OG).

Key: AG = activity goal
     BG = bridging goal
     OG = outcome goal

The model links the various goals from the initial activity goals through bridging goals to the ultimate outcome goal. As the model illustrates, bridging goals sometimes fall between two activity goals, but still serve as links in the chain from activity goals to outcome goals. This model is perhaps atypical in that the goals follow a single line of expected causality. More often, a model will fork at one or more points (as, for example, if different types of executives were placed in different kinds of training).

Development of an impact model can help staff and stakeholders to clarify how they expect a program to work and what questions they have about that operation, thereby better defining the evaluation purpose. Should staff and/or stakeholders disagree about the likely impact model, the evaluator must determine whether the disagreement is sufficiently important to require resolution before the evaluation can proceed.

Measuring Goals

Once the goals have been defined, the evaluator must decide how to measure them. These decisions are best made cooperatively by the evaluator(s) with the program staff, including the organization's executive. The evaluator can bring to this effort knowledge of the techniques of measurement.

Program representatives can bring a special program knowledge important in determining the feasibility of possible measures.

For staff to assist in this process, they need to understand some basic measurement concepts and the various possible types of measures. These topics are discussed below, with the roles staff can play explained in that context.

Concepts of Measurement

Measurement is an inexact process, as suggested by the fact that many social scientists speak of "indicators" rather than measures. As the term implies, measurement instruments indicate something about a concept (that is, about a goal), rather than provide perfect reflections of it. For example, crimes reported to police as a measure constitutes only a fraction of actual crime; and scores on paper-and-pencil aptitude tests reflect the test anxiety and/or cultural backgrounds of test takers as well as their aptitudes.

The concepts of *measurement validity* and *measurement reliability* come from a recognition of the inexactness of measurement. "Measurement validity" refers to whether or to what extent a measure taps what it purports to measure. More valid measures capture more of what they purport to measure. "Measurement reliability" refers to the measure's consistency from one application to another. Reliability is higher if a measure produces the same reading when applied to the same phenomenon at two different times (or when applied by different observers to the same phenomenon at the same time). Obviously, evaluators prefer measures that are relatively more valid and reliable.

If outside evaluators are involved, the executives and staff of the nonprofit organization need not know a great deal about how to assess the validity and reliability of measures, but two points merit mention. First, given the fallibility of any particular measure, evaluators will want to have multiple measures — two or more indicators — for any important goal. Any major outcome goal, in particular, is likely to call for multiple measures. (By contrast, many activity goals may require only one measure.) The different measures can then be compared to see if they appear to be tapping the same concept. Second, if there are concerns about reliability, taking multiple observations is recommended. Any important measure should, if possible, be applied at a number of time points to see how the indicator fluctuates across time. (Multiple observations are also useful for other aspects of research design, as explained below.)

Evaluations must also consider "face validity," that is, whether measures appear valid to key stakeholders. Evaluation experts sometimes discount the importance of face validity, arguing that many measures that appear valid really are not. But the appearance of validity can be crucial to the acceptance of the findings of an evaluation and thus to the evaluation's eventual usefulness. As a consequence, evaluators can fairly be asked to respond to concerns about face validity. It is reasonable, at a minimum, to ask evaluators to explain why measures that appear valid in fact are not.

Professional evaluators have no monopoly on the ability to assess measurement validity. Program staff, by virtue of their experience with the program, often have unique insights into the merits of specific measures, insights that outside evaluators could not otherwise obtain. Staff can play an important role by advising evaluators as to whether specific measures are likely to get at what the program is about.

Types of Measures

Evaluators can choose from several types of measures, and to achieve the benefit of multiple measures, will utilize two or more of these types in most evaluations. The different types are briefly introduced here in terms of what nonprofit executives and staff may need to know about each one.

1. Program records and statistics: The obvious source for data is the program itself. Records can be kept and statistics maintained by program staff for a variety of measures. Almost every evaluation will make use of at least some measures recorded within the program itself.

These measures must be chosen and used with caution, however. For one thing, program staff ordinarily should be asked to record only relatively objective data, such as the gender and age of clients, dates and times services are delivered, and the like. Staff can usually record these more objective data with little difficulty and high reliability. By contrast, staff cannot be expected, without special training, to record subjective data, such as client attitudes, client progress toward goals, and so on.

In a similar vein, program records should be used only sparingly as outcome measures and probably never as the *sole* outcome measures. Program staff are placed in an untenable position if they are asked to provide the principal measures of their own effectiveness, especially when those measures include subjective elements. Program records are better employed as measures of relatively objective activity goals.

The staff who would be asked to record measures should be involved in decision making about the measures. In addition to whatever insights they may have about measurement validity, staff can speak to whether the demands of the proposed record keeping have been kept reasonable. The requirements of record keeping should not be so great that staff must choose between the evaluation and the program. If that happens, either the evaluation will interfere with the program because staff give too much time to record keeping, or the measures will produce poor data because staff slight record keeping in order to devote more time to the program. This dilemma may be avoided by giving staff an opportunity to comment on the proposed measures in advance.

2. Client questionnaire surveys: Programs that have subjective goals for special client populations, including most nonprofit programs, can seldom be evaluated without obtaining client perceptions and attitudes. Clients must be asked about their feelings, and a questionnaire survey is a useful means of doing this. There are several forms of surveys, and each has its own advantages and disadvantages (see Rea and Parker, 1992).

Phone surveys can produce good response rates (that is, responses from a high proportion of the sample), assuming respondents are contacted at good times (usually in the evening) and interviewed for no more than ten to fifteen minutes. These surveys can be expensive, however, due to interviewers' costs. In addition to the actual interview time, interviewers will need to make several contacts before reaching many respondents.

The desire for a lower-cost procedure often leads to consideration of *mail surveys,* which involve mailing questionnaires to respondents, who are asked to complete them and return them by mail. In spite of their costliness, the principal trade-off with phone surveys is the high response rate, which can be low for mail surveys of most population groupings. Questions on mail surveys must also be structured more simply since no interviewer is available to guide the respondent through the questionnaire. A mail survey is thus unlikely to work with a nonreading or language-impaired client population. The technique may produce a high number of usable responses only when sent to groups that are not only highly motivated to respond but willing and able to work through written questions independently. Even then, obtaining a high response rate usually requires sending one or two follow-up mailings to nonrespondents.

The best choice for many program evaluations will be the so-called *convenience survey,* a survey of respondents who are available in some convenient setting. For example, client samples are often available for a possible convenience survey when they receive program services. An evaluator can capitalize on that availability by asking clients to complete and return a brief questionnaire at that time. As with mail surveys, the questionnaires must be kept simple and brief to permit easy and rapid completion. To reassure respondents about the confidentiality of their responses, ballot-box-like receptacles might be provided for returning the completed questionnaires. A well-planned convenience survey can produce a good response rate, almost certainly better than that of a mail survey, often at a cost lower than that of any of the alternatives.

Construction of any kind of questionnaire survey requires some expertise. Executives wishing to economize here might propose to share the construction process with an outside evaluator. The nonprofit organization's staff might draft initial questions, which the evaluator could then critique. Staff could then revise the questions before the evaluator polishes them to final form. This collaborative procedure can both reduce the organization's costs and provide training in questionnaire construction to program staff.

3. Formal testing instruments: With many programs, the outcomes desired for clients — self-confidence, sense of personal satisfaction — are sufficiently common that experts elsewhere have already developed appropriate measurement instruments. Some of these formal testing instruments are available free in the public domain; others may be available at a modest per-unit cost. In either case, it may be wiser to obtain these instruments than to develop new measures. Program staff can often help here since, by virtue of their exposure to similar programs elsewhere, they may know of appropriate instruments that are new to evaluators.

4. Governmental statistical series: Governments maintain a variety of statistics (for example, population, income, crime, and unemployment statistics), which can be useful in evaluations. These statistics usually have the advantages of (a) low cost, (b) longitudinal scope (beginning well before the program began and continuing after its conclusion), and (c) lack of any systematic program-related bias. As a principal disadvantage, these data can be difficult to fit to the specific goals and clients of the program being evaluated. As a consequence, these statistics often are most useful for assessing secular trends relevant to the program. In evaluating a job-training program, for example, governmental economic statistics might provide indicators of general economic trends that could affect an outcome goal of trainee employment success.

5. Qualitative measures: Evaluation research has made increasing use in recent years of so-called qualitative measures, measures designed to capture nonnumerical in-depth description and understanding of program operations. After long disdaining these measures as too subjective to be trusted, most evaluators now recognize that programs with subjective goals cannot be evaluated without qualitative data.

Qualitative measures can be obtained through two principal techniques, observation and in-depth interviews. Observation can provide a sense of how a process is operating, as, for example, in evaluating how well group counseling sessions have functioned. By observing and describing group interaction, an evaluator could gain a sense of process unavailable from quantitative measures (for example, measures of psychological health).

In-depth interviews have a similar value. In contrast to questionnaire surveys, these relatively unstructured interviews are composed principally of open-ended questions. The questions are designed to permit respondents to report feelings about programs unconstrained by the predefined multiple-response choices of structured questionnaires. This approach can be extremely useful, for example, in assessing the success of individualized client treatment plans.

Qualitative measures—and quantitative measures, for that matter— should be used with caution. Nonprofit executives are best advised to avoid either too much or too little reliance on qualitative measures. Evaluation of most nonprofit programs calls for multiple measures, including both quantitative and qualitative measures. The executive should work with the evaluators to ensure that both perspectives are obtained.

Finally, nonprofit executives should be prepared for the possibility that the discussion of measures may rekindle debate about goals. It may not be that staff paid too little attention to the earlier goal definition (although that can happen). Instead, just as thinking about goals can prompt rethinking the evaluation purpose, so thinking about measures can prompt staff to see goals differently. Executives can play an important role here by seeing that, where appropriate, this new thinking is incorporated into the formulation of goals.

Outcome Evaluation Designs

Most program evaluations will be concerned to some extent with assessing program impact — with determining whether or to what extent instituting a program has resulted in the desired outcomes. To achieve that end, evaluators can draw on a number of outcome evaluation designs. Nonprofit executives and staff usually will neither need nor desire to become expert on these designs, but they should understand their basic structure and underlying principles to be able to participate intelligently in the evaluation process. This section will first explain those principles, and then briefly survey the most important of the designs. (For a detailed recent discussion, see Mohr, 1988).

Causality

The goal of any outcome evaluation design is to demonstrate causality; that is, whether a program has caused the desired changes. To do that, a design must satisfy three conditions:

1. Covariation: Changes in the program must covary with changes in the outcome(s). Changes in outcome measures should occur in tandem with changes in program effort.
2. Time order: Since cause must come before effect, changes in the program must *precede* changes in the outcome measures.
3. Nonspuriousness: The evaluator must be able to rule out alternative explanations of the relationship between program and outcome. The evaluator must show that the relationship is not spurious; that is, that it is not the result of a joint relationship between the program, the outcome, and some third variable.

An evaluation design has *internal validity* to the extent that it satisfies these three conditions. Internal validity, in other words, refers to how accurately a design describes what the program actually achieved or caused.

Evaluation designs can also be judged for their *external validity:* how much the design's findings can be generalized to contexts beyond that of the program being evaluated. Ordinarily, however, nonprofit organizations will have little or no concern for external validity. One reason is that internal validity must have first priority; we must be sure that findings are accurate before considering at all how they might be generalized. In addition, with most programs, nonprofit executives are interested only in how their program works, not with how the program might work elsewhere. External validity becomes a major concern only if, for example, a program is being run as a pilot to test its value for possible broader implementation.

Threats to Internal Validity

The difficulties of satisfying the three conditions for causality can be shown by examining three so-called preexperimental designs:

1. One-shot case study: X 01
2. Posttest only with comparison group: X 01
                                                           02
3. One-group pretest/posttest: 01 X 02

In each case, X refers to treatment, 01 to a first observation, and 02 to a second observation (on the experimental group in item 2, on a comparison group in item 3).

The one-shot case study can satisfy none of the conditions of causality. As the most rudimentary design, it provides no mechanism for showing whether outcomes and program covary, much less for demonstrating either time order or nonspuriousness.

The posttest only with comparison group design can establish covariation. The comparison of a program group to a nonprogram group will show whether outcomes and program covary. However, this design can tell us nothing about time order; we cannot tell whether outcome differences occurred *after* the program's inception or were already in place beforehand.

The one-group pretest/posttest design can satisfy the first two conditions for causality. Taking observations before and after the program tests for both covariation and time order. The weakness of this design—and it is a glaring weakness—lies in its inability to establish nonspuriousness.

Take, for purposes of illustration, a rehabilitation program for substance abusers as evaluated by a one-group pretest/posttest design. This design can establish covariation (whether substance abuse decreases with program involvement) and it can establish time order, since substance abuse is measured both before and after the program intervention. But it does not control for such threats to nonspuriousness as the following:

1. Maturation: Decreased substance abuse could have resulted from the maturing of participants during the time of the program, a development that occurs independent of the program.
2. Regression: Extreme scores tend to "regress toward the mean" rather than become more extreme. Since program participants may have been selected on the basis of their extreme scores (that is, high levels of substance abuse), decreased abuse could be a function of statistical regression rather than an effect of the program.

3.   History: Events concurrent with but unrelated to the program can affect program outcomes. For example, a rise in the street price of illegal drugs could produce a decline in substance abuse, which might otherwise be attributed to the program.

These flaws make the preexperimental designs undesirable as the principal outcome designs in most evaluations. Stronger designs are necessary to provide reasonable tests of the conditions of causality.

Experiments

Experimental designs promise the strongest internal validity. The classic experimental design takes this form:

$$R\ 01\ X\ 02$$
$$R\ 03\ \ \ \ 04$$

R refers to *randomization,* meaning that subjects are assigned by chance — for example, by lot or by drawing numbers from a hat — to the experimental or control group in advance of the experiment.

Randomization is a crucial defining element of experimental designs. With the intergroup and across-time components of this design testing for covariation and time order, randomization controls for the final condition of causality, nonspuriousness, by making the experimental and control groups essentially equivalent. As a consequence of that equivalence, the control group provides a test of "change across time" — the changes due to maturation, regression, history, and so forth, which could affect program outcomes. Comparing the experimental and control groups can thus separate program effects from other changes across time, as this simple subtraction illustrates:

Program effects + change over time $(02 - 01)$
– Change over time $(04 - 03)$
––––––––––––––––––––––––––––––––
= Program effects

Unfortunately, many practical problems work against the use of experimental outcome evaluation designs. In particular, randomization poses a number of difficulties. First, it must be done prior to the beginning of an intervention; participants must be randomly assigned before they receive treatment. Second, randomization often prompts ethical or political objections. Ethical objections may be raised to depriving some subjects of a treatment that other subjects receive. Political objections may be raised to providing treatment on anything other than a "first come, first served" basis.

On the one hand, experiments entail problems. They can be costly, given the need to establish, maintain, and monitor distinct experimental and control groups. They also require maintenance of the same program structure throughout the length of the experiment. Many programs are still changing as they begin operation, and so lack the rigid structure an experiment demands.

On the other hand, these difficulties can be exaggerated. The need for prior planning sometimes can be surmounted by running an experiment not on the first cohort group of subjects, but on a second or later cohort group (for example, a second treatment group of substance abusers). Ethical and political objections often can be overcome by giving the control group a traditional treatment rather than no treatment. That choice may make more sense for the purpose of the evaluation since the ultimate choice may be between the new treatment and the old treatment, not between the new treatment and no treatment. In short, experiments should not be too quickly eliminated as possible evaluation designs. They often represent the best choice.

Quasi Experiments

If for any reason an experimental design cannot be used, the evaluator should consider one of the so-called quasi-experimental designs. These designs are so named because they attempt, through a variety of means, to approximate the controls that experiments achieve through randomization. The strongest of these designs come close to achieving the rigor of an experiment.

A first quasi-experimental design is the *nonequivalent control group:*

$$01 \ X \ 02$$
$$03 \quad 04$$

Here, in lieu of randomization, a comparison group is matched to the experimental group in the hope that the pre-post comparison of the two groups will furnish an indication of program impact.

This design is as strong as the quality of the match. The goal of matching is to create a comparison group that is as similar as possible to the experimental group, except that it does not participate in the program. A good match can be difficult to achieve because the available comparison groups often differ in crucial respects from the experimental group.

Take, for example, a hypothetical job-training program for the unemployed that takes participants on a first come, first served basis. The obvious candidates for a comparison group are would-be participants who volunteer *after* the program has filled all of the available slots. The evaluator might select from those late volunteers a group similar to the experimental group in terms of race, sex, education, previous employment history, and the like — similar, in other words, on the extraneous variables that could affect the desired outcome of employment success.

The difficulty lies in matching on all of the key variables at once. Creating a comparison group similar to the experimental on two of those variables —

say, race and gender—may be possible, but the two groups are unlikely then also to have equivalent education levels, previous employment histories, and other characteristics. In addition, the two groups may differ on some other unrecorded or intangible variable. Perhaps the early volunteers were more motivated than late volunteers. If that difference in motivation were not measured and incorporated in the analysis, the program could erroneously be credited with employment gains that actually stemmed from the difference in motivation. In cases such as this, no match, no comparison group, is preferable to a bad match that distorts the assessment of program impact.

When a nonequivalent control group design is considered, outside evaluators should take principal responsibility for ensuring the quality of the match. It cannot hurt, however, for organizational executives and program staff to be aware of the difficulties of matching. Knowledgeable program staff might recognize a crucial difference between the experimental and comparison groups that the evaluator does not see.

A second kind of quasi-experimental design is the *interrupted time series design*, diagramed as follows:

$$01\ 02\ 03\ X\ 04\ 05\ 06$$

The defining elements of this design are three or more observations recorded both before *and* after the program intervention. These multiple observations are important because they provide a reading on trends, thereby controlling for most of the changes over time (maturation, regression, and so on), which randomization controls for in an experimental design. Those controls give this design relatively good internal validity.

"History" is the principal weakness of this design, with respect to internal validity. The design contains no control for any events that, by virtue of occurring at the same time as the program, could affect program impact. A program to improve the situation of the homeless could be affected, for example, by an economic upturn (or downturn) that began at about the same time as the program.

Obtaining the necessary multiple observations can also prove difficult. On the front end, preprogram observations may be unavailable if measurement of key outcome indicators began only when the program itself began. On the back end, stakeholders may demand evidence of program impact before several postprogram observations can be obtained.

The strongest of the quasi-experimental designs is the *multiple interrupted time series,* which looks like this:

$$01\ 02\ 03\ X\ 04\ 05\ 06$$
$$07\ 08\ 09\ \quad 010\ 011\ 012$$

The strength of this design results from combining the key features of the interrupted time series and the nonequivalent control group design. The time series dimension controls for most changes across time; the nonequivalent control group dimension controls for the threat of history.

The potential problems with this design are the weaknesses of its component parts. A bad match can provide a misleading comparison; the lack of longitudinal data can preclude use of this design at all.

Other Designs and Controls

The realities of many programs preclude the use of either experimental or quasi-experimental designs. Perhaps no one planned for an evaluation until the program was well under way, thereby ruling out randomization and providing no preprogram observations. Finding a comparison group may also prove too difficult or too costly.

Under such conditions, the evaluator may be forced to rely on one or more of the preexperimental designs as the principal outcome evaluation design, leaving the evaluation susceptible to many threats to internal validity. Fortunately, there are means available by which the evaluator can compensate for these design weaknesses.

A first possibility is to use *statistical controls*. If their numbers and variability are sufficient, the subjects of a program can be divided for comparison and control. For example, a one-group pretest/posttest might be subdivided into those receiving a little of the program (x), and those receiving a lot (X). The resulting design becomes more like the stronger nonequivalent control group design:

$$01 \; X \; 02$$
$$03 \; X \; 04$$

There remains the question of whether the two groups are comparable in all respects except for the varying program involvement. If that comparability can be shown, the design can provide a reading on whether more program involvement produces more impact, substituting for the unavailable comparison of program versus no program. Preexperimental designs can be strengthened by other kinds of statistical controls, too. Subjects might be divided on the basis of race or gender, for example, to see how those variables affect program impact.

The option to strengthen designs through statistical controls is not restricted to preexperimental designs. These controls can also be useful with quasi-experimental or even experimental designs. When a nonequivalent control group design is used, the evaluator may want to subdivide and compare subjects on variables on which the matching was flawed. If the two groups were matched on race and gender but not on education, the evaluator might compare the experimental and control groups while statistically controlling for education. Or, where a time series design is employed, the evaluator might seek additional data to control for threats of history. In a study of how the 55-mile-per-hour speed limit affected traffic fatalities, researchers examined data on total miles traveled to test the alternative explanation that fatalities declined as a consequence of reduced travel (amid the 1974–75 energy crisis), not as a consequence of reduced speed (Meier and Morgan, 1981, pp. 670–671). The data added to the evidence that reduced speed was the cause.

The combination of several different outcome evaluation designs can also add to the strength of the overall design. Many evaluations will employ multiple designs, each used for a different measure. Often in those circumstances, the weaker designs necessary for some measures can be supplemented by stronger designs on other measures.

If an outside evaluator is involved, these design decisions will be made principally by that person, not by the nonprofit organization's agency executives and/or staff. Still, to the extent that executives and staff understand these basic principles of evaluation design, they may be able to advise evaluators on important design refinements.

The nonprofit executive can perform an even more important role by monitoring the design planning to assure its fit to the purposes of the evaluation. The most rigorous experimental design will be of no use unless it speaks to the issues of concern to the organization's executive and/or other stakeholders. The highly technical nature of outcome designs can sometimes obscure that fact. It is up to the executive to ensure that the evaluation is relevant and appropriate to the organization's needs.

Process Evaluation

With most program evaluations, nonprofit executives will want to evaluate the program process as well as its ultimate impact. Outcome evaluation designs usually indicate only whether a program is working, not why. Process evaluation may be able to discern what steps in a program's process are not working as intended, thus perhaps pointing to how a program might be changed to increase its effectiveness. These suggestions will often prove the most useful to nonprofit executives.

The techniques of process evaluation are both simpler and less systematic than those for outcome evaluations (see also Thomas, 1980). As the prerequisite, the evaluator must have defined the program's principal activity goals and their expected sequencing. Attention can then be focused on which activity goals to measure and how.

Seldom will an evaluator want to measure all of the activity goals. Many programs have so many activity goals that measuring all of them would require more of the evaluator's time than is affordable. Measuring all of those goals could also demand too much of program staff, perhaps interfering with the program itself. Perhaps most important, nonprofit executives usually have questions only about some of the activity goals; they may already feel adequately informed about performance as it pertains to many activity goals. Process evaluation should focus on the goals for which they still have questions.

As a consequence, the evaluator should plan to measure activity goals only at key junctures in the program; that is, only at the major points in the program sequence where information is wanted. In addition, the measures at those points should be kept simple enough that program staff, assuming they are given the task, can record the data validly, reliably, and efficiently.

The executives and staff of nonprofit organizations have important roles to play in this effort. First, they should review the evaluation plan to ensure that the questions they have about program process can be answered with the proposed measures of activity goals. Second, they should apply their own criteria of validity and reliability. Staff who are intimately familiar with a program often can see shortcomings of measures not evident to outside evaluators. Third, they must consider whether the task of measurement will interfere with the operation of the program.

The basics of a process evaluation can be illustrated by the case of an affirmative action program designed to increase the hiring of minority firefighters by a municipal government. The activity goals of interest in this evaluation included the following:

1. Increase the number of minority applicants.
2. Increase the success rate of minority applicants on the written examination.
3. Increase the success rate of minority applicants on the physical examination.

These activity goals are designed to lead to this outcome goal (among others):

4. Increase the proportion of minority firefighters in the fire department.

The several activity goals fit the suggested standards: they are relatively few in number; they focus on key junctures in the program; they are relatively easy to record; and they appear likely to be both valid and reliable. They also illustrate how a process evaluation can be useful. Data on these various activities could indicate where, if at all, the program might be failing. Are too few minorities applying? Or, are minorities applying only to be eliminated disproportionately by written or physical exams? Answering these questions could help a program administrator to decide whether, how, and where to change the program.

A high-quality process evaluation can provide other benefits, too. First, it can serve as the basis for a regularized performance monitoring system for ongoing use by program staff and administrators. Regular collection and analysis of the affirmative action hiring data, for example, could give program staff regular feedback on the efficiency of the program's internal operation, and perhaps provide warning signs of problems in that operation. Institutionalization of such a system is possible, however, only if staff have been so involved in its development that they support its continuation.

Second, a good process evaluation can also compensate for weaknesses in the outcome evaluation designs. As explained above, the difficulty of controlling for all threats to internal validity in outcome evaluation designs can leave unanswered questions about the linkage of program to outcomes. A process evaluation provides an additional test of this linkage by indicating whether program activities have occurred in a manner consistent with the observed outcomes. If, for example, an impact evaluation shows significant gains on the outcome measures *and* the process evaluation shows high levels of program activities, the evaluator can argue more convincingly that the impact was caused by the program. By contrast, evidence of low activity levels in the same scenario would raise doubts about whether the program could be responsible for outcome gains.

In any event, most program evaluations should contain some form of process evaluation. Though less systematic than outcome designs, process evaluation techniques will often provide the more useful information for nonprofit executives.

Data Development, Report Writing, and Follow-Up

Once the designs have been selected, the actual evaluation can begin. Data must be collected and interpreted, reports must be written, and plans need to be made for following up on the evaluation. As with the earlier steps, these last steps, too, are best accomplished collaboratively by the evaluators and program staff. Costs can be minimized, for example, if staff can be assigned much of the work of data collection.

Nonprofit executives should also plan to extensively involve themselves and the program staff in the analysis of data and the writing of reports. As in the evaluation planning, this involvement is necessary first for accuracy: staff review of data and reports minimizes the risk of outside evaluators making and reporting inaccurate interpretations. Staff involvement is important to maximize utilization: staff are more likely to believe findings and implement recommendations if they were involved in their development.

Nonprofit executives must plan carefully for this involvement to ensure that the evaluators do not feel their integrity compromised. Perhaps the best approach is to ask evaluators for the opportunity to review and comment on interpretations and reports, while at the same indicating that the evaluators retain final authority on the substance of reports. Most evaluators will welcome this arrangement as protecting them and the program; no evaluator wants to go public with conclusions that are subsequently shown to be in error.

Staff involvement in data interpretation can be achieved through a variety of means (see Patton, 1986, pp. 245–280). When data printouts are received, for example, staff might be invited to meet with the evaluators to review them. The evaluators can, as necessary, explain to the staff the format of the data, with staff and evaluators then working in tandem to interpet the data.

Before those interpretations can be put in written form, the executive must decide what final written product(s) to request. A comprehensive evaluation report is usually desirable, both for the historical record and as a reference if questions arise about the evaluation. These reports can be lengthy, however, limiting their readership. As a consequence, the executive may also want a brief executive summary, of one to three pages in length, for broader distribution and readership. Other reports may also be desirable for particular clienteles inside and outside the program.

The expense of preparing reports can be reduced by sharing the task between the evaluators and the nonprofit organization's staff. Staff—probably not the program staff, given their stake in the program—might draft reports for the evaluators, program staff, and the executive to review. The evaluators might then revise the reports into final form to reflect the questions and comments provided by the reviewers of the draft.

The job of the outside evaluator customarily concludes at this point. For the nonprofit organization's executive and program staff, however, much work may remain. The evaluation may give program administrators new agendas for where and how the program should be changed. Failure to recognize and act on these agendas can squander much of the worth of the evaluation.

To avoid this pitfall, executives should arrange to discuss the evaluation findings and reports with program staff. Where appropriate, plans of action should be developed, including a schedule of what changes are to be made and when, as well as how they are to be monitored. Only through such planning can the nonprofit organization gain the full value of a program evaluation.

This planning should also consider whether and how the evaluation mechanisms will be institutionalized in a performance-monitoring system. Program evaluations can offer a unique opportunity to regularize a measurement and reporting system to facilitate easier, faster, and cheaper periodic program reviews in the future.

Summary

Program evaluation in its formative years developed an unsavory reputation, which persists in many quarters today. Evaluations designed more to meet "scientific" standards than organizational needs led many program administrators to see the technique as more threatening than promising for program development.

Program evaluation has changed for the positive since those early years; evaluation now constitutes an invaluable tool for program development in the nonprofit and governmental sectors. Used appropriately, program evaluation can provide nonprofit executives with essential information unavailable through any other means.

But the techniques must be used appropriately. For one thing, program evaluations must be planned to meet the needs of stakeholders, usually including the nonprofit executive, program staff, funders, and perhaps others.

Evaluations should not be academic exercises designed primarily to meet the technical standards of evaluators. Furthermore, program staff must be involved in the evaluation process. This involvement is essential to ensure both that the staff's information needs are addressed and that the evaluators hear about the program from the people who know it most intimately. Needless to say, that involvement can also build staff support for implementing any recommendations the evaluation might produce.

It is the responsibility of the nonprofit executive to see that these conditions are met. The executive is the one person capable of (a) negotiating an evaluation plan that will meet agency needs, (b) insisting on involvement of program staff in that evaluation, and (c) providing the leadership for implementing evaluation recommendations. Without this top-level management support, program evaluation — or any other organizational innovation — is unlikely to produce real change. *With* this support, program evaluation can give the executives and staff of nonprofit organizations the knowledge necessary to improve the effectiveness of their programs.

References

Foster, J. L. "An Advocate Role for Policy Analysis." *Policy Studies Journal,* 1980, *8,* 958–964.

Kress, G., Springer, J. F., and Koehler, G. "Policy Drift: An Evaluation of the California Business Enterprise Program." *Policy Studies Journal,* 1980, *8,* 1101–1108.

Meier, K. J., and Morgan, D. P. "Speed Kills: A Longitudinal Analysis of Traffic Fatalities and the 55 MPH Speed Limit." *Policy Studies Review,* 1981, *1,* 157–167.

Mohr, L. B. *Impact Analysis for Program Evaluation.* Chicago: Dorsey Press, 1988.

Patton, M. Q. *Utilization-Focused Evaluation.* (2nd ed.) Newbury Park, Calif.: Sage, 1986.

Rea, L. M., and Parker, R. A. *Designing and Conducting Survey Research: A Comprehensive Guide.* San Francisco: Jossey-Bass, 1992.

Rodgers, R., and Hunter, J. E. "A Foundation of Good Management Practice in Government: Management by Objectives." *Public Administration Review,* 1992, *52,* 27–39.

Rossi, P. H., and Freeman, H. E. *Evaluation: A Systematic Approach.* (4th ed.) Newbury Park, Calif.: Sage, 1989.

Scriven, M. "The Methodology of Evaluation." In R. W. Tyler, R. Gagne, and M. Scriven (eds.), *Perspectives of Curriculum Evaluation.* American Educational Research Association Monograph Series on Curriculum Evaluation, no. 1. Skokie, Ill.: Rand McNally, 1967.

Thomas, J. C. "'Patching Up' Evaluation Designs: The Case for Process Evaluation." *Policy Studies Journal,* 1980, *8,* 1145–1151.

Weiss, C. H. *Evaluation Research: Methods of Assessing Program Effectiveness.* Englewood Cliffs, N.J.: Prentice-Hall, 1972.

PART FOUR

∽

DEVELOPING AND MANAGING FINANCIAL RESOURCES

Much too commonly, nonprofit management is seen mainly as a matter of fundraising. No doubt fundraising is a major leadership and management task, and fundraising is becoming more competitive and sophisticated. Nonetheless, nonprofit organizations don't (or shouldn't) exist to raise money. They do (or should) exist to pursue a mission or cause that benefits some part of the public. The first chapter in this part of the book rightly emphasizes how to develop the fundraising effort so that it fits with and flows from the mission and culture of the organization. Those seeking details on the techniques of fundraising will find the suggestions for further reading at the end of that chapter helpful. The extent to which nonprofit organizations rely on donations varies substantially. For many nonprofit organizations, earned income has become at least as important a source of revenues as donations. Chapter Eighteen, the second in this part, shows how nonprofit organizations can make better decisions about enhancing various types of earned income, including unrelated business income.

While fundraising techniques are sometimes overemphasized as the essence of nonprofit management, the principles, practices, and uses of accounting are often underemphasized. In light of their significance for effective nonprofit management, this part of this handbook includes two extensive chapters on accounting and control. The financial accounting chapter describes how nonprofit managers and others can use various financial ratios to improve financial and program management. The management accounting chapter shows various managerial uses of cost accounting data. The final chapter in this part provides thorough, easy-to-understand guidance for improving risk management in nonprofit organizations.

17

Designing and Managing the Fundraising Program

Robert E. Fogal

Fundraising is increasingly important in the life of charitable organizations. Regardless of the consideration that boards and senior management now give to resource development and income generation, more attention will be required in the future. This chapter addresses ways to *integrate fundraising into an organization's life*. These emphasized words are central to the perspective called "philanthropic fundraising," understood as the philosophy and practice that fosters voluntary giving to achieve public good. This author supports the view that philanthropic fundraising will substantially assure the future of nonprofit organizations and the good work that they aim to accomplish. Three themes will amplify this view: fundraising as a management function, fundraising as a management process, and issues in fundraising management.

Fundraising as a Management Function

Fundraising is important to nonprofit leaders for many reasons. The first, which is most obvious and most practical, is that fundraising generates essential income for charitable organizations. The 1992 *Nonprofit Almanac* reported the following illuminating facts: "In 1989, private contributions . . . accounted for 27.2 percent of total annual funds for the independent sector, up from 26.2 percent in 1982. These private contributions represented 5.5 percent of total annual funds in health services (down from 9.7 percent in 1977); 14.6 percent in education and research (about the same as in 1977);

33.9 percent in social and legal services (up from 31.9 percent in 1977); 30.9 percent in civic, social, and fraternal organizations (up from 28.6 percent in 1977); and 62.5 percent in arts and cultural organizations (down from 65.7 percent in 1977)" (Hodgkinson, Weitzman, Toppe, and Noga, 1992, p. 9).

An equally important (but typically less obvious) reason for fundraising to be a priority for nonprofit leaders is that fundraising success measures the degree to which an organization's purpose is affirmed. Donors' support for a particular organization or institution reflects their perception of that entity as an effective vehicle in meeting a community or human need. The responsibility of a nonprofit's board and senior managers to clearly articulate their organization's mission and document its effectiveness in fulfilling that mission — that is, to provide a strong case for support — is critical to successful fundraising. Through their contributions, donors show their acceptance of an organization's mission and respect for the organization's leadership. Low response to fundraising appeals can suggest that an organization and its mission are little known or poorly understood; that its prospective donor constituencies have not accepted the nonprofit's purposes.

This perspective competes with other views about fundraising among nonprofit leaders. Henry A. Rosso, the founding director of the Fund Raising School (which is now a program at the Indiana University Center on Philanthropy), developed a succint grid that characterizes different organizational attitudes toward fundraising (see Table 17.1). Rosso titled this grid "Three Stages of Fundraising Development" because it represents the steps through which nonprofits often progress in developing their fundraising programs. The idea is that most begin at the formative stage, when fundraising is a new activity, and potentially, they reach the integrative stage, when fundraising is a fully developed component of an organization's life and work.

At the formative stage, fundraising is viewed as an appendage to organizational life — something we do because we have to, a "necessary evil." It is characterized by an emphasis on fundraising techniques that generate needed income, such as the mass appeals through direct mail and telephone

Table 17.1. Three Stages of Fundraising Development.

	Stage 1: Formative	Stage 2: Normative	Stage 3: Integrative
Who	Vendor	Facilitator	Strategist
What	Product	Relationships	Growth partnerships
Skills	Sales	Soliciting	Building and maintaining relationships
Result	Making a continued sale	Maintaining relationships	Assured organizational growth

Note: The text of this table is based on verbal communication from H. A. Rosso; the language used in the graphic representation of the model is the author's. Used by permission.

solicitation. Fundraising in the formative stage is motivated primarily by the nonprofit's need to have more money. The objective is to "sell" the organization and what it does (the products) to donors who want to "purchase" the idea or service that the nonprofit represents. Success is measured by how often gift solicitation results in "taking an order" or "closing the sale." In this stage, fundraising is commonly carried out by personnel who are hired to perform as a sales staff, with their primary role being to interact with prospective donors and persuade them to contribute to the nonprofit. If volunteers participate in this style of fundraising, they also view their work as sales activity.

At the normative stage, fundraising is understood in terms of family, applying fundraising techniques largely to prospective donors whose connections to the nonprofit have been established through some other relationship, such as that of a student, a concertgoer, or a volunteer worker. Good relationships among those who are already in "the family" are important, so that their continued financial support can be sustained. In the normative stage, leaders and managers typically concentrate on the internal operation of the institution, with members of the "family" being defined mostly in terms of how they used to or continue to relate to the institution's primary operations or services. Fundraising in this style is commonly staff-centered also, with a small number of others, usually the chief executive and a handful of volunteers, occasionally participating in the process of cultivating a prospect's interest and asking for a contribution.

At the integrative stage, philanthropy is at the center of who we are and what we do—that is, it is central to the building of a human community that achieves a common good. Donors are regarded as thoughtful participants in the organization's life and work, filling a role that is appropriate to them and essential to the well-being of the nonprofit. In the integrative stage, volunteer leaders are vocal advocates of the nonprofit and its work, and they participate fully in the entire process of building constituencies who can financially support the organization.

In addition, senior staff, board members, and other volunteer leaders work at sustaining healthy relationships with those who have made philanthropic investments in the organization, responding to donors' needs and interests that relate to the nonprofit and its activity. There is a high level of communication between the nonprofit and those who make "leadership" gifts. These donors know the organization well. They consider their gifts to be investments in values that are important to them. Furthermore, their views are valued by others, and they can be articulate advocates of the organization. In this stage, organizational leaders are capable of looking at their agency from the perspective of those who live primarily outside it, and can thus bring important levels of objectivity to their views.

The three stages are not mutually exclusive. Fundraising technique is important to all three. But how the techniques are used reflects the organization's style of management and institutional philosophy. Philanthropic fundraising strives to achieve the integrative stage of fundraising practice, which incorporates voluntary giving as one of the nonprofit's core values.

Fundraising as a Management Process

Classic management practice consists of five activities: analysis, planning, execution, control, and evaluation. Fundraising as a management process utilizes all these activities. The most effective fundraising staff are managers who assure that discipline based on the five activities is applied to the fundraising process.

Through *analysis,* a nonprofit assesses whether or not it is ready for fundraising. Analysis is guided by questions like these: What is the history of past fundraising? How many donors contributed at what levels? Are constituencies and gift markets well defined and responsive? Are internal resources adequate to meet the costs of fundraising? Is the case for support valid and compelling? Analysis is the basis for problem solving and provides information for decision making.

Planning grows out of analysis. Too little planning impedes success; too much planning leads to inaction. Good planning encourages prudent risk taking and helps nonprofits respond to opportunities that will advance their purposes. Answers to the following questions will facilitate good planning: How many gifts in what amounts are needed from whom? How should donor prospects be solicited? By whom? When should the gift be solicited? How should the case for support be articulated? What training is required for volunteers to carry out successful prospect cultivation and gift solicitation? How much money should be invested to accomplish fundraising objectives?

Effective planning involves a nonprofit's leadership; the planning process is as valuable as the plan. Plans can be changed, and should be, to take advantage of giving opportunities when they occur.

An essential tool in both fundraising analysis and planning is the gift range chart, a device that focuses the attention of staff and volunteers by outlining the number and size of gifts needed to reach fundraising goals. Gift range charts were used historically only for capital campaigns, but their use is increasingly accepted in annual campaigns for funds as well. Table 17.2 is an example of a gift range chart for a well-established organization's annual fundraising goal of $160,000.

The gift range chart, when compared with current patterns of voluntary contributions, helps nonprofit leaders understand the potential of the donor base by comparing "what is" with "what needs to be achieved." As part of planning, the chart makes clear the kind of giving that is needed to reach a goal, and provides a tool for identifying how prospective donors might participate in the nonprofit's philanthropic support.

Execution means carrying out the plan. Tasks are assigned and responsibilities are accepted, individuals are trained and empowered, time lines are established and respected, and that tasks are completed is ensured by

Table 17.2. Gift Range Chart for $160,000 Annual Fundraising Goal.

Level of Gifts ($)	No. of Gifts	No. of Prospects	Subtotals ($)	Totals ($)
8,000	2	8	16,000	—
4,000	5	20	20,000	—
2,000	10	30	20,000	—
1,000	20	60	20,000	—
500	40	80	20,000	96,000[a]
250	80	160	20,000	—
100	200	400	20,000	40,000[b]
Less than 100	Many	Many	24,000	24,000
			Grand Total	160,000

Note: This arithmetic for an annual fundraising gift chart is commonly accepted by experienced fund raisers. For a full explanation of the arithmetic of gift range charts, see Rosso (1991), pp. 54–57 for annual funds and pp. 82–85 for capital campaigns.

[a]Sixty percent of the goal, derived from major or "leadership" gifts, which represent about 10 percent of the total number of donors.

[b]Twenty-five percent of the goal, commonly obtained from donors who have been upgraded from the broad base of contributors.

follow-up efforts. Fundraising staff are guided by the question "What should we do to ensure that all who are involved in our fundraising are successful on behalf of our nonprofit?" Fundraising managers have the challenge of directing the energy and activity of people to whom they are responsible (senior staff, board members, and other volunteers) in their fundraising tasks. This requires a high level of mutual respect and a firm commitment on everyone's part to their common effort and success. Planning provides the framework within which effective execution is accomplished.

Control depends on information systems that enable fundraising staff to manage the fundraising process. Fundraising encompasses a multitude of details and tasks that must be monitored and coordinated. Gift processing must be timely, gift records must be accurate, and gifts must be acknowledged. Reports must be generated. Volunteer and staff time must be used effectively. Time lines should be honored. Budgets have to be well utilized.

Evaluation enables a nonprofit, its leaders, and its staff to grow and become more effective. By reflecting on its fundraising practices, as well as all its management and programs, a nonprofit's leadership determines whether or not resources are maximized, constituents' needs are served, and the mission is fulfilled. Good evaluation depends on a spirit of cooperation and a sense of common purpose. It combines objectivity and sensitivity. It fosters organizational integrity and leads to a more productive future. As a result, voluntary giving in support of the nonprofit's mission will be enhanced.

Nonprofits that are successful in philanthropic fundraising apply all these activities to their fundraising management in the three dimensions of institutional life: at the department level, throughout the organization, and in its interaction with the environment that surrounds it. In each dimension, specific management fundraising activities are required. Table 17.3 shows how the tasks of fundraising pertain in all three dimensions.

Within the fundraising office or department, fund raisers implement several technical tasks for which they are solely responsible. Alongside these are several organizational tasks that fundraising staff may foster and coordinate but that involve other staff and board leadership and may require some compromise to accomplish. Finally, a number of activities are directed beyond the nonprofit and require that fundraising managers exercise considerable judgment and negotiation in their realization. The responsibilities and tasks listed in the table are not mutually exclusive. Nor does the table list all possibilities. It does indicate, however, how the five management activities in fundraising intersect with the various dimensions of a nonprofit's life.

Table 17.3. Fundraising Management Grid.

Fundraising Management Tasks	Dimensions of the Institution		
	Departmental	Organizational	External
Analysis	Fundraising history Vehicle productivity Data systems Office space Staff resources	Case resources	Market/social needs Constituencies Gift markets Volunteer resources Feasibility study

Planning	Budget
	Gift range chart
	Gift market
	  identification
	Vehicle selection
	Time lines
		Fundraising goals
		Internal case statement
		Vehicles and markets
		Case expressions
		Public information
			Leadership training
			Solicitation: to whom/
			  by whom/how much/
			  when
			Gift incentives

Execution	Communication:
	  letters/phone
	Staff relationships/tasks
		Marketing fundraising
		  internally
		Cultivation/solicitation
		Staff relationships
			Cultivation/solicitation
			Case expressions
			Volunteer/donor
			  relationships
			Public information

Control	Gift processing Gift acknowledgment Gift records Gift reports Fundraising costs	Gift reports	Volunteer recognition Donor recognition Time lines Prospect system

Evaluation	Vehicles
	Budget
	Markets
	Staff performance
		Effectiveness of
		  programs being
		  supported
			Markets
			Volunteer leaders
			Case expressions

Professional stance	Integrity of judgment
	  about techniques
	  and vehicles to be
	  used, information
	  to be reported
		Integrity of leadership
		  among program
		  and other adminis-
		  trative colleagues to
		  achieve institutional
		  commitment
			Integrity of mission in
			  achieving public
			  good

Issues in Fundraising Management

Volunteer Leadership and Giving

The three stages of fundraising development suggest several issues that are central to philanthropic fundraising. The first focuses on the various roles that board members, other volunteers, and staff play in fundraising. Fundraising will be most successful, and the "integrative stage" most readily attained, when leadership for fundraising is shared among many people. At the minimum, the board chair, the chair of the development committee, the chief staff officer, and the fundraising manager need to work together to develop fundraising policies. Their leadership sets the tone for the entire organization and its commitment to building effective partnerships with "investors" whose gifts (as illustrated in the gift chart) are major contributions.

The involvement of board members and other key volunteers reinforces the philanthropic character of nonprofit organizations. Their voluntary service demonstrates their commitment to the cause that the nonprofit serves, providing an example and setting the standard for others' participation as volunteers and as donors. If board members, who are the volunteers most closely related to the organization, do not support it financially, it is unrealistic to expect others to contribute to the nonprofit's mission and work. When board members are recruited to serve, expectations regarding their financial support should be made clear. One of the most effective statements of standards for board giving is the following: "After your contributions to your religious community, we expect that our organization will be among your charitable priorities." This allows for people of different financial ability to demonstrate their commitment in the manner most appropriate for them, while still emphasizing that their giving is an essential responsibility of being a board member. This standard also encourages broad diversity on a board, along with the philanthropic commitments of time, service, and money.

Volunteer service has a direct bearing on contributions. Research carried out by INDEPENDENT SECTOR has clearly documented that people who volunteer are more generous in their giving. In a 1991 survey, respondents who gave but did not volunteer represented 26 percent of all households in the United States. Their contributions averaged $477, or 1.4 percent of household income. In contrast, the 46 percent of all households who both volunteered and gave had average contributions of $1155, or 2.6 percent of income (Hodgkinson and Weitzman, 1992, p. 2). It is also worth noting that the most recent study found that those who both volunteer and give have an average household income that exceeds $44,400 annually, while those who give and do not volunteer average about $34,000 in annual income.

Organizational Readiness

As noted above, nonprofits too often pursue fundraising solely on the basis of their need for additional revenue. When this occurs, fundraising is characterized by the use of techniques designed to acquire as much money as possible in the shortest time possible. To succeed in the long-term development of philanthropic support, nonprofits must be prepared for fundraising. Leaders and managers must fully understand and be able to articulate the *case for support*. A compelling statement of the case will draw prospective donors to an organization's effective mission and efforts by answering these questions, posed by H. R. Rosso (1991, p. 9):

1. What is the problem or societal need that is central to the organization's concern? Why does the organization exist?
2. What special services or programs does the organization offer to respond to that need?
3. Who should support the program?
4. Why should any individual, corporation, or foundation contribute to a specific organization?
5. What benefits will accrue to the contributor who makes such gifts?

The answers to Rosso's questions should clarify the value of an organization to the community it aims to serve. They should explain how community life will be enhanced because the nonprofit meets community needs; what specific goals, objectives, and programs the nonprofit plans to implement in response to the needs it identifies; and what constituencies will be served by those who help to support the organization. A nonprofit cannot exist in isolation from its environment. Its programs and activities must be valued, not only by the clients it serves but also by potential donors who view the nonprofit as contributing to the quality of community life. Fundraising success will depend on how well a nonprofit responds to its environment, adapts to changing conditions in the environment, and builds constituencies who believe in its value. An effective case is the basis for building philanthropic support.

Stewardship and Investment

The cost of raising money and the effectiveness of fundraising programs are critical issues for nonprofit leaders. Donors have the right to know that the nonprofits in which they invest are credible. Nonprofits that merit philanthropic support are able to justify fundraising costs. Standards of fundraising costs are not widely established, although experienced fund raisers increasingly accept certain guidelines as reasonable (see Exhibit 17.1). These guidelines are best understood in the context of a nonprofit's own giving history.

A well-established program will likely have costs that are lower than a new fundraising program. Introducing a new component of fundraising will be more expensive than maintaining a program component. The guide-

Exhibit 17.1. Suggested Guidelines for Fundraising Costs.

	Cost per $ Raised
New donor acquisition	Up to $1.50
Special events	Up to $0.50
Donor renewal up to $100 to $250	Up to $0.25
Major gifts and capital campaigns	Up to $0.15
Planned giving	Up to $0.15[a]
Corporate and foundation grant seeking	Up to $0.20

[a]After four to seven years of initial investment.
Source: Adapted from the Fund Raising School, 1992, p. III-39.

lines listed in Exhibit 17.1 demonstrate that different fundraising strategies require different levels of investment. The more expensive forms of fundraising reflect the need to constantly renew the donor base with large numbers of smaller gifts. The less expensive strategies involve smaller numbers of larger gifts, commonly received from donors who have long giving histories with an organization. These people—whose donations are variously identified as "major gifts," "leadership gifts," and "strategic gifts"—provide important credibility for an organization through the example they set for others.

Another important consideration in budgeting for fundraising is efficiency (the cost per dollar raised) versus effectiveness (the net total amount raised). One nonprofit, for example, might raise an annual fund of $400,000 with a budget of $100,000. The entire program would net $300,000 by spending $0.25 for each dollar raised. Another nonprofit might raise $600,000 with a fundraising budget of $200,000, netting $400,000 at a cost of $0.33 per dollar raised. The first organization would be considered more efficient because it spent less money per dollar raised, but the second would be considered more effective because it raised more money. The balance between fundraising efficiency and effectiveness is an issue that nonprofit boards must consider when setting their organizational budgets. Occasionally boards must decide to increase their fundraising investment so that their organizations can move to qualitatively improved levels of voluntary support. Fundraising managers are responsible for showing how such investment can yield new levels of contributions.

Stewardship, which can be defined as how we exercise ethical accountability in the use of resources, applies equally to an organization's fundraising and its general success in fulfilling its mission. Nonprofit boards carry ultimate responsibility for the fiduciary well-being of their organizations. This includes assuring that all resources are used both efficiently and effectively. Volunteer leaders have the right to be fully informed by staff about how resources are being used. Program evaluation is an essential part of this process. Fundraising managers have a key role to play in helping volunteer leaders meet their stewardship responsibilities.

Ethics in Fundraising

In the daily activity of fundraising, evaluation is too often based on the precept that "what works is what is right." As indicated at the beginning of this chapter, fundraising can be seen only as a strategy for obtaining needed support. In fact, how a nonprofit raises funds is a powerful index of the degree to which its leaders grasp the moral dimensions of the nonprofit's purposes. We all live according to the customs, traditions, and values that have been handed down to us, and we apply this heritage to the decisions we make each day. The advances of technology and the challenges of a changing world, however, increasingly cause people to reflect on their purposes and think about how they should conduct their lives. Nonprofit leaders who think about philanthropic fundraising, the integrative stage of fundraising, organizational readiness, the case for support, and efficiency and effectiveness in fundraising, will very likely find themselves reflecting on ethical matters on behalf of their organizations.

One of the most comprehensive statements on ethics in fundraising is to be found in the National Society of Fund Raising Executives' "Code of Ethical Principles and Standards of Professional Practice." Members of the society agree to abide by these standards, and nonprofits who hire the society's members should expect to support the standards as well. Nonprofits whose fundraising staff do not belong to the society will do well to apply these principles as guidelines for professional performance. The complete text of the society's standards follows:

National Society of Fund Raising Executives
Code of Ethical Principles
and Standards of Professional Practice

Statements of Ethical Principles
Adopted November 1991

The National Society of Fund Raising Executives exists to foster the development and growth of fund-raising professionals and the profession, to preserve and enhance philanthropy and volunteerism, and to promote high ethical standards in the fundraising profession.

To these ends, this code declares the ethical values and standards of professional practice which NSFRE members embrace and which they strive to uphold in their responsibilities for generating philanthropic support.

Members of the National Society of Fund Raising Executives are motivated by an inner drive to improve the quality of life through the causes they serve. They seek to inspire others through their own sense of dedication and high purpose. They are committed to the improvement of their professional knowledge and skills in order that their performance will better serve others. They recognize their stewardship responsibility to ensure that needed resources are vigorously and ethically sought and that the intent of the donor is honestly fulfilled. Such individuals practice their profession with integrity, honesty, truthfulness, and adherence to the absolute obligation to safeguard the public trust.

Furthermore, NSFRE members

- Serve the ideal of philanthropy, are committed to the preservation and enhancement of volunteerism, and hold stewardship of these concepts as the overriding principle of professional life;
- Put charitable mission above personal gain, accepting compensation by salary or set fee only;
- Foster cultural diversity and pluralistic values and treat all people with dignity and respect;
- Affirm, through personal giving, a commitment to philanthropy and its role in society;
- Adhere to the spirit as well as the letter of all applicable laws and regulations;
- Bring credit to the fund-raising profession by their public demeanor;
- Recognize their individual boundaries of competence and are forthcoming about their professional qualifications and credentials;
- Value the privacy, freedom of choice, and interests of all those affected by their actions;
- Disclose all relationships which might constitute, or appear to constitute, conflicts of interest;
- Actively encourage all their colleagues to embrace and practice these ethical principles;
- Adhere to the following standards of professional practice in their responsibilities for generating philanthropic support.

Standards of Professional Practice
Adopted and incorporated into the NSFRE Code of Ethical Principles November 1992

1. Members shall act according to the highest standards and visions of their institution, profession, and conscience.
2. Members shall comply with all applicable local, state, provincial and federal civil and criminal laws. Members should avoid the appearance of any criminal offense or professional misconduct.
3. Members shall be responsible for advocating, within their organizations, adherence to all applicable laws and regulations.
4. Members shall work for a salary or fee, not percentage-based compensation or a commission.
5. Members may accept performance-based compensation such as bonuses provided that such bonuses are in accord with prevailing practices within the members' own organization and are not based on a percentage of philanthropic funds raised.
6. Members shall neither seek nor accept finder's fees and shall, to the best of their ability, discourage their organization from paying such fees.
7. Members shall disclose all conflicts of interest; such disclosure does not preclude or imply ethical impropriety.
8. Members shall accurately state their professional experience, qualifications, and expertise.
9. Members shall adhere to the principle that all donor and prospect information created by, or on behalf of, an institution is the property of that institution and shall not be transferred or removed.
10. Members shall, on a scheduled basis, give donors the opportunity to have their names removed from lists which are sold to, rented to, or exchanged with other organizations.
11. Members shall not disclose privileged information to unauthorized parties.
12. Members shall keep constituent information confidential.
13. Members shall take care to ensure that all solicitation materials are accurate and correctly reflect the organization's mission and use of solicited funds.
14. Members shall, to the best of their ability, ensure that contributions are used in accordance with donors' intentions.

15. Members shall ensure, to the best of their ability, proper stewardship of charitable contributions, including: careful investment of funds; timely reports on the use and management of funds; and explicit consent by the donor before altering the conditions of a gift.
16. Members shall ensure, to the best of their ability, that donors receive informed and ethical advice about the value and tax implications of potential gifts.

The sixteen statements address five areas of fundraising practice:

Good conscience standards	Statements 1, 2, and 3
Compensation of fundraising personnel	Statements 4, 5, and 6
Professional qualifications	Statements 7 and 8
Technology and donor privacy	Statements 9, 10, 11, and 12
Donor relations	Statements 13, 14, 15, and 16

The statements imply that fundraising staff bring to their responsibilities the technical and managerial competency appropriate to these standards. Such competence, and the commitment to continually strengthen that competence, is an ethical condition of fundraising that is an integral part of staff professionalism. Successful nonprofit organizations will serve as vehicles for fundraising that is ethical and professional.

Summary

"Fund raising is an essential part of American philanthropy; in turn, philanthropy—as voluntary action for the public good—is essential to American democracy" (Payton, Rosso, and Tempel, 1991, p. 4). This observation affirms the reality that fundraising cannot be an isolated activity in a successful nonprofit organization. Fundraising practices reflect what we are as organizations. The values, style, and commitment that undergird fundraising will likely be the same as those that characterize the rest of an organization's work.

Philanthropic fundraising is mission driven. That is, funds are sought to enable a nonprofit to serve the community good the organization addresses. Philanthropic fundraising is also volunteer centered. Over the long term, the involvement of volunteers in governance, advocacy, and giving is essential to healthy nonprofits.

Successful fundraising is also the result of disciplined management. When fundraising professionals provide leadership to other staff and to volunteers, a productive collective effort results. Just as disciplined fundraising management is important to obtaining resources, it is also important in exercising accountability for resources. Nonprofits must ensure that they use contributed income for the purposes for which it was sought. Although they are privately controlled, mission-driven nonprofits will want to be publicly accountable.

The public good that fundraising supports is essential to the well-being of our communities and our nation. Weaving philanthropic fundraising into the fabric of their existence is integral to the moral purpose of ethical nonprofits.

References

Fund Raising School. *Principles, Techniques of Fund Raising.* Indianapolis: Fund Raising School, 1992.

Hodgkinson, V., and Weitzman, M. *Giving and Volunteering in the United States.* Washington, D.C.: INDEPENDENT SECTOR, 1992.

Hodgkinson, V., Weitzman, M., Toppe, C. M., and Noga, S. M. *Nonprofit Almanac 1992–1993: Dimensions of the Independent Sector.* San Francisco: Jossey-Bass, 1992.

Payton, R. L., Rosso, H. A., and Tempel, E. R. "Toward a Philosophy of Fund Raising." In D. F. Burlingame and L. J. Hulse (eds.), *Taking Fund Raising Seriously: Advancing the Profession and Practice of Raising Money.* San Francisco: Jossey-Bass, 1991.

Rosso, H. A. *Achieving Excellence in Fund Raising: A Comprehensive Guide to Principles, Strategies, and Methods.* San Francisco: Jossey-Bass, 1991.

Additional Readings

Burlingame, D. F., and Hulse, L. J. (eds.). *Taking Fund Raising Seriously: Advancing the Profession and Practice of Raising Money.* San Francisco: Jossey-Bass, 1991.

Greenfield, J. M. *Fund-Raising: Evaluating and Managing the Fund Development Process.* New York: Wiley, 1991.

Howe, F. *The Board Member's Guide to Fund Raising.* San Francisco: Jossey-Bass, 1989.

Mixer, J. R. *Principles of Professional Fundraising.* San Francisco: Jossey-Bass, 1993.

National Fund Raiser. Roseville, Calif.: Barnes Associates. (Month-by-month guidance for effective fundraising management and resource development.)

New, A. L. *Raise More Money for Your Nonprofit Organization: A Guide to Evaluating and Improving Your Fund Raising.* New York: Foundation Center, 1991.

18

Enterprise Strategies for Generating Revenue

Cynthia W. Massarsky

Everyone was milling around the conference room in an anxious state. Brad Miller, the executive director of the North Street Settlement House, had called a meeting of his key staff. No one knew exactly what he planned to discuss in this "emergency" session, but several staff could offer some good guesses.

Susan Fine, North Street's director of finance, had spent the last month preparing organizational budgets and trying to get things to "balance out." It wasn't working. North Street's work was critical to the neighborhood, but she felt that the budget for staff was top-heavy and that program expenditures were increasing beyond their means. Susan was in favor of making some serious cuts—not a move that others would welcome.

Maria Sanchez, North Street's director of program services, was preparing her case once again. Staff are the backbone of the organization—they are the ones who make it happen, she thought. She couldn't imagine running North Street's current program without every one of them. In fact, she was about to request an increase in her budget to hire two additional social workers for the new counseling program for seniors. There was no way that she could cut her program budget either. She wouldn't do it—things were lean enough already.

The director of development, Sam Golding, was "burning out." He had been with North Street for the last eleven years, having seen it grow from a small activity center with a $200,000 budget to a full-service settlement house with a $3 million budget. Sam felt he had squeezed every dollar available from local foundations, corporations, and government sources. He had created all the "campaigns"—general support, endowment, special projects, and corporate memberships. North Street offered a host of special events, too. Whether the others wanted to acknowledge it or not, the fact was that it was taking more time and money to secure each new grant dollar and hold on to each old one than it was worth. As usual, everyone would look to him to raise more money to cover program expenses. Sam knew it could not be done.

Brad walked in and called the meeting to order. "You all must know why we're here. We've got a serious problem. We have just heard from two of our major supporters. They've decided to turn their grantmaking in new directions and have notified us that this year's grants are to be considered 'exit' grants and will be our last. We can't be too hopeful about receiving much public funding next year, either, with federal and state budget cuts the way they are. As I see it, we have about one year to make some serious alterations in the way we do our work or we might not make it. Sad to say, we need to find some creative short- and long-term solutions and implement them quickly if we want to celebrate North Street's fifteenth anniversary."

Sound familiar? This is a scene that is played in most nonprofit organizations, at one time or another if not year after year. The numbers may change, but the story remains the same. Nonprofit organizations want to, and must, continue their important work. Yet their survival is in the hands of funders—foundations, corporate giving offices, government agencies, and individual givers. The typical nonprofit creates a host of programs in concert with its mission and then seeks grant monies to support them. When programs are fresh and innovative, the fundraising task is easier. But as programs become more commonplace, regardless of their need and importance, the task gets more difficult.

The environment for receiving special project grants is getting more and more competitive every day. General support grants are even more difficult to come by. Privatization is growing. Government retrenchment continues. Corporate monies are available, but in shorter supply, and an increasing number of mergers and acquisitions means that there are fewer entities to tap. Many individual givers, usually reached via direct mail campaigns, are finding it more difficult to repeat donations made in previous years. Yet nonprofits must balance their budgets. Foundation and public funding agencies do not appreciate deficit spending. So what is a nonprofit organization to do?

One solution is to explore the potential for generating earned income. With an earned-income venture, a nonprofit creates a business — sells a product or service or both — and, if successful, provides its organization with another stream of revenue or support. Earned-income ventures are sexy. They are in vogue. But they are serious endeavors that require a significant amount of research and planning. And they usually require a change or shift in attitude among board and staff, as well.

During the last decade, the distinction between nonprofit and private sector practices has blurred. Nonprofit organizations are becoming more business and marketing oriented as they learn the rewards of selling, as opposed to giving away, their much desired products and services. It is not unusual to observe the business community discovering new market opportunities, as well, in areas that were once the near exclusive domain of nonprofits. And from within these two new roles, a third scenario has surfaced — the corporate-nonprofit co-venture. The nonprofit and business communities are now working together in a variety of innovative ways, each to accomplish its own goals and often those of its partner, as well.

Types of Enterprise Strategies

Business Ventures for Nonprofit Organizations

The most common approach for generating new streams of income for nonprofits is through the creation of business ventures. Business ventures exist in many forms, from traditional fee-for-service charges to full-scale commercial activities.

Business ventures are best categorized according to the product or service being sold in the commercial arena. *Program-related products* are those that are closely identified with the organization and promote the organization's mission, as well as earn money. One of the best known examples is Girl Scout cookies. In 1992–93, the Girl Scouts of the United States sold nearly 172 million boxes of cookies and netted approximately $218 million (phone interview with Bonnie McEwen, Girl Scouts of the USA). *Program-related services* — ancillary services provided to members, friends, and alumni, as well as to the general public — can enhance the tax exempt mission of the organization. Museum gift shops, parking lots, and food sales through vending machines and cafeterias are typical examples.

Staff and client resources are a third area. Here, nonprofit organizations provide the expertise of their staff members and clients, such as the New York Public Broadcasting Service (PBS) television affiliate WNET-13 that provides production and postproduction services to corporate and nonprofit clients, or Family Service America, a social service agency that provides drug and alcohol counseling to corporate employee assistance programs. The sale, lease, development, and rental of land and buildings — referred to as "hard property" — are ways of making use of an organization's downtime. Colleges and universities, for example, often rent excess dormitory, cafeteria, gymnasium, and field space during slack summer months to such groups as professional sports teams and summer camps. Lastly, "soft property" encompasses income-earning assets that include copyrights, patents, trademarks, art and artifacts, and even mailing and membership lists.

Cause-Related Marketing

Another way that nonprofits are generating new streams of income is through cause-related marketing. Cause-related marketing, or joint venture marketing, links a for-profit organization with a nonprofit organization for their mutual benefit. For nonprofits, cause-related marketing offers new sources of financial support and increased public exposure. For corporate partners, cause-related marketing provides an opportunity to increase product sales, gain public recognition, and, at the same time, support the causes they care about.

Since American Express helped launch the Statue of Liberty–Ellis Island campaign in 1981, the use of this strategy has proliferated. As part of the campaign, American Express made a donation to the Statue of Liberty–Ellis Island Foundation every time one of its customers used its credit card. In 1983, American Express helped raise $1.7 million for the foundation and claimed a dramatic 28 percent increase in card usage for itself (Josephson, 1984).

Other collaborations have taken the cause-related marketing effort a step further. Easter Seals, for example, works with a number of companies to extend the partnership beyond their quarterly promotions. In some instances, corporate employees become involved as volunteers. In others, corporations initiate programs to hire people with disabilities. In 1980, Easter Seals' corporate sponsors contributed $3 million. By 1990, corporate support totaled more than $13 million from such companies as Century 21 International, Safeway Stores, Amway, and Enesco Corporation (Garrison, 1990).

Clearly, the push for companies to demonstrate that they are politically and socially "correct" is coming from all angles—employees, consumers, stockholders, and social and political organizations. Cause-related marketing has offered business an ideal vehicle for achieving a healthier bottom line and a better public image. Borden, Inc., sponsored the Beach Boys' 1991 summer concert tour, donating a portion of the proceeds to the Better Homes Foundation for homeless families. The campaign promoted more than fifteen of Borden's brands and resulted in incremental sales gains, better display space, and improved trade and sales force relations (Rigney and Steenhuysen, 1991).

Licensing

"Licensing" is the term commonly used for the legal agreement of one party to allow a second party to use its name, logo, characters, or products. In the case of corporations and their nonprofit partners, it is typically the corporation that licenses rights from the nonprofit, paying the nonprofit a royalty based on sales. When licensing arrangements are well targeted, both the licenser and licensee benefit financially, as well as in increased publicity.

Perhaps one of the best-known examples of licensing is between Children's Television Workshop (CTW), the nonprofit organization that originated "Sesame Street," and many toy, video, book, record, and clothing manufacturers, such as Hasbro, Playskool, Western Publishing, and JC Penney. In 1991, CTW grossed $22 million from its agreements (phone interview with Ken Graber of CTW).

Other nonprofit organizations permit the use of their names (such as the National Audubon Society) and still others license the rights for reproduction of collections of art, artifacts, and furniture (such as Winterthur and the Museum of the City of New York). The Metropolitan Museum of Art has earned substantial income by licensing artistic designs from its collections to textile companies. The Sierra Club licenses the rights to its name and photographs to companies that manufacture greeting cards and calendars.

Working with a Corporation to Market Its Products and Services

The most recent type of corporate-nonprofit co-venture to have evolved is one in which the nonprofit organization helps market the products or services of the corporation in return for a donation or a percentage of sales. Corporations view this supplemental sales force or distribution arm as another vehicle to enhance their marketing efforts. As with cause-related marketing and licensing, this approach also helps to increase a corporation's brand image and awareness. Nonprofit organizations view this approach as a way to increase and diversify their revenue, as well as to enhance the ways in which they are viewed by potential contributors and other important groups.

This type of co-venture is still in its infancy stage; there are a limited number of examples of a nonprofit helping to market a corporation's products or services. Perhaps the most common instance involves a corporation providing a nonprofit organization's member-related services; for example, travel or insurance. Here, the nonprofit organization makes various plans available to its members and receives a commission from the corporation in return for sales to members. For example, the Smithsonian Institution and the Music Center of Los Angeles offer their members travel excursions through Cunard Cruise Lines. A nonprofit "umbrella" organization that serves other nonprofits in the state of New Jersey offers its member organizations group liability insurance for directors and officers through Colonial Insurance, health insurance through General American, disability insurance through Equitable, a 403(b) pension plan through the Calvert Fund, errors and omission insurance through Chubb, and an unemployment trust through Marsh & McClennan.

Another example of a member-related service is through American Telephone & Telegraph (AT&T). To gain new accounts AT&T offers nonprofit organizations a reduction in members' telephone rates. The nonprofit organization promotes AT&T to its members, encouraging them to sign on to its long-distance program. Members receive slightly discounted telephone bills, and the nonprofit organization receives a percentage of the total billings. So AT&T secures new business, the nonprofit organization generates revenue, and its members save money while helping the nonprofit at the same time.

A third example of a member-related service is through supermarket chains such as the Grand Union Company. Here, a nonprofit organization purchases "Grand Union scrip" in block amounts and at a discount and resells it to its members. Members then use the scrip when purchasing groceries at Grand Union. As a result of this program, Grand Union is able to make advance bulk sales and potentially reach new customers, the nonprofit organization keeps the difference between the purchase and resale amount (usually 5 to 10 percent), and its members purchase in the way they normally do while helping the nonprofit at the same time.

A final model of corporate-nonprofit collaboration, with the nonprofit helping to market the corporation's products and services, is in the financial services area, with the use of "affinity" cards. A growing number of nonprofits work with credit card companies to issue their own cards to their constituents. Most of these cards feature a logo or some symbol of the nonprofit group. The Nature Conservancy, for example, has an affinity card and receives 0.2 percent of all charges, $7 for each new cardholder, and $4 of each annual fee (phone interview with Amy Longsworth of the Nature Conservancy). Some banks pay a fee per transaction rather than a percentage of charges incurred.

Affinity cards provide an effortless way for people to contribute to a favorite charity or organization. Typical of the nonprofit organizations that provide these cards are colleges and universities and such groups as the International Association of Junior Leagues, the Sierra Club, the American Automobile Club Association, and the Association for Retarded Citizens. Visa, MasterCard, Fleet Bank (formerly Norstar), Working Assets, Banc One, and others offer affinity card programs to nonprofit groups.

Questions Nonprofits Typically Ask About Business Venturing

During the last ten years I have helped a number of nonprofit organizations investigate potential income-generating ventures. Initially, the same questions arise:

> We need money quickly. What's a good business to go into that will net us enough money in six months to cover our deficit and then some?
> Is this really legal? We're a nonprofit. Doesn't that mean that we aren't allowed to earn money?
> Might we lose our tax-exempt status if we are successful?
> Why don't we just try out an idea and see if it works?

Although these are good questions, they are not the heart of the issue. If a nonprofit organization looks for a quick fix, it will surely be disappointed. Just as it takes time to mount a fundraising campaign, so does it take time to explore whether earning income is an appropriate way to "make ends meet." Finding a business that meets the needs of the organization and returns significant revenue to it is not like looking over the latest fashions and purchasing one. The investigation process and business planning, the decision making that occurs every step of the way—not to mention the typical business start-up that doesn't break even for eighteen months—can take well over two years to accomplish. Moving ahead without proper analysis—that is, trying out an idea to see if it works—can frustrate staff, anger members, confuse supporters, and put a nonprofit in debt.

Initially, however, time is not well spent in being overly concerned about legalities and tax issues. By law, nonprofit organizations are permitted to earn income—to operate business and generate profits. What they cannot do is pass along profits to equity owners. In this regard, an organization's tax-exempt status is not jeopardized as long as net earnings are not turned to the advantage of persons in their private capacities.

One legal and tax issue that does concern nonprofits is whether the business is related to the mission of the organization and, consequently, whether the nonprofit will incur unrelated income tax. To put this in the simplest terms, if a business is deemed unrelated to the mission of the organization (a determination made by various rules and "tests"), it probably will incur a tax. Many nonprofit organizations pay unrelated business income tax. Nonetheless, tax liability should not be the determining factor in deciding to engage in business venturing. If the business is viable, it should have the capacity to support a tax. However, it is generally held that organizations receiving in excess of 20 percent of their revenue from unrelated activities might receive continuing scrutiny as to their tax-exempt status, to ensure that they are organized and operated primarily for exempt purposes.

A second legal and tax issue that concerns nonprofits is whether the business should become a part of the nonprofit entity or be "spun off" as another profit or as a for-profit subsidiary. Because the interpretation of IRS rules depends on what the organization intends to do and how it intends to do it, legal and tax counsel cannot adequately assess these two issues until the decisions have been made. With a feasibility study and a decision to proceed in hand, a nonprofit should seek the counsel of legal and tax specialists whose business it is to advise on structuring nonprofit business ventures, even if the organization already retains other counsel for its regular operations.

Questions Nonprofits Should Ask About Business Venturing

The important questions that nonprofits should ask are the ones that require taking a long, hard look at the organization—its mission, strengths and weaknesses, and financial wherewithal. Answers to such questions as these will help a nonprofit determine whether it is ready to undertake such an activity:

> What is our current and projected financial status and how will earned income help us?
>
> Are we feeling desperate?
>
> Is business venturing compatible with our mission? Do we feel comfortable with the idea of selling a product or service?
>
> Will business venturing distract us from what we were founded to do? What are the potential risks and returns in terms of our finances, organization, and reputation?
>
> If we create an earned-income venture, will we have the support of our staff, board, funders, members, and others?
>
> How will an earned-income venture fit into the overall structure of our organization? What priority will it have among staff? Among senior management?
>
> Are we prepared to allocate the staff to investigate possible ventures and get one up and running, or to hire someone to do it for us? Do we have a "champion" among us who will take responsibility for the work and who has the influence and authority to move forward?
>
> Are we prepared to allocate the time necessary to proper analysis, planning, and start-up to meet the demands of the marketplace?
>
> Do we have financial resources to put toward the process of identifying a business venture and starting it up? Do we have access to other sources of capital?
>
> Do we really have a product or a service that people would be willing to pay for?

How Nonprofits Can Find Answers to Their Questions

To obtain full, useful answers to the questions listed above, nonprofit organizations are advised to proceed through a series of steps, making a go/no-go decision after each one.

Step 1: Designate a Team to Explore the Issues

The team can include staff, board members, close friends, and others who would offer both a current and historical perspective. Some nonprofits have found it helpful to bring in a consultant to keep the discussion on track and to provide an unbiased opinion.

Perhaps the most difficult questions are those involving ethical considerations. It is critical that the nonprofit and its key constituents feel comfortable with the notion of business venturing. To some people the idea may sound quite exciting. They may envision creative ways to incorporate a business and see how it enhances the mission of the organization. Others may see it as mercenary and contrary to what nonprofits are all about.

Oftentimes, venturing requires that staff and board redirect their thinking or alter their attitudes about what they do and how they do it. They need to move

From being	*To being*
Reactive	Proactive
Reliant	Self-reliant
Traditional	Entrepreneurial
Conservative	Innovative
Risk averse	Risk taking
Mission driven	Market driven

If these ideas present significant obstacles that cannot be overcome, it is probably best not to proceed.

Step 2: Conduct an Organizational Audit

As is true with several other steps in the process, when a nonprofit conducts an organizational audit, it benefits from exploring not only how its assets might be useful in business venturing but also how healthy the organization is as a whole, what its strengths and weaknesses are, and where it might want to make some improvements. Further, the discipline involved in "writing it down" forces careful thought, clarity of purpose, and communication and coordination among all the relevant players — staff, management, board of directors, members, and others. These are important ingredients for any well-run organization. They are critical ingredients for the nonprofit that intends to create and sustain an earned-income venture.

An organizational audit is a systematic examination and accounting of the assets of the nonprofit — from the expertise and skills of its staff to the scope and quality of its programs, from the nature of its physical plant to the status of its financial portfolio. Equally important, an organizational audit tallies responses to the issues discussed in Step 1, such as staff commitment and board or trustee support.

Although it can be a difficult task, the nonprofit should conduct an honest review of its organizational weaknesses, as well. Some might significantly affect the success of a business venture, but if they are recognized early on, they can be reversed or ameliorated. If, for example, the organization is particularly weak at record keeping, it might contract with an outside firm to maintain data on its customers. Or, if the weakness is one that the nonprofit cannot contract for and the new business cannot do without, it might eliminate that type of enterprise from its list of possibilities.

Oftentimes, nonprofits find it difficult to begin the process. They are not used to describing or even thinking about strengths and weaknesses, but tend rather to relate lists of particular programs and activities they offer. To be effective, participants in an organizational audit should try to characterize the *quality* of what their organization has, is, and does, in addition to making straightforward lists. They should look at the number and types of current constituents (clients, members/subscribers, supporters, and others) to see not only *what* they do for them but also *how well* they serve them.

One way to begin is to proceed through the outline of questions that follows:

Organization, Management, and Personnel

Where is our organizational expertise? (What is our specialty? What do we know how to do? How well do we do it?)

What particular talents does our staff have? (What is our breadth of knowledge and experience about specific subjects? What is our ability to communicate with various audiences? How well do we communicate internally with one another? Are we "team players"? How interested are we in exploring and implementing new ideas? Do we have a sense of business?)

What level of support do we have for business venturing? (How comfortable with the idea are our clients, staff, board of directors, members, funders, and other constituents? How does each of us feel about our exempt goals?)

Program

What specific activities and products do we offer?

Who wants to use our products and services? (Why do they want them? What needs would we meet? Do the users pay for what we offer?)

How do we make our products and services known to others? (Do we publish any material? Do we conduct public relations and/or direct mail campaigns?)

Finances

What is our financial status? (How has our budget grown or declined over the last five years? Are we "desperate" for operating capital?)

Are our sources of revenue diversified? (What percentage of our monies do we get from grants from government, foundations, corporations, individuals? From membership fees, program fees, earned income, investments? From other sources?)

Are we likely to gain or lose support in any of these areas over the next five years?

Do we have capital or access to capital for earned income venturing? (If so, how much? How difficult would it be to obtain it? Do we have credit and/or borrowing power? Do we have monies for start-up as well as working capital?)

Equipment and Facilities

What type of equipment do we own or rent, and what is its state of repair? (What do we have in the way of furniture, specialized equipment or machinery, kitchen equipment, computers, software, a telephone system, a library?)

Do we have a management information system (MIS) in place? (Is it manual? Computerized?)

What characterizes our building/offices and grounds? (How many square feet do we have? How many offices do we have? On what floors are we located? Do we have elevators, air conditioning, storage space? What is our outdoor space like? Do we rent or own? Do we have excess capacity?)

Where are we located? (In the building? In the neigborhood? Is storefront space available?)

Are we close to public transportation? Are there parking facilities? Are there loading docks?

How attractive are our facilities? In what state of repair are they?

Other Assets

What is our reputation? (Who has opinions about us? How solid are those opinions? Are we considered an authority?)

Do we have a following? (Among whom? How stable is it?)

Do we have a network of contacts on whom we can rely? (Who are they? How might they be used?)

Do we own a trademark or copyright?

Do we have a mailing list? (Who is on it? Are there duplicates?)

Do we have an 800 number?

Step 3: Brainstorm Ideas

In Step 3, the nonprofit moves from determining whether it is ready for an earned-income venture and listing its organizational assets to brainstorming ideas. Here, the task is to find connections between what the nonprofit "brings to the table" and potential businesses with which it feels comfortable. In brainstorming to list potential businesses, the organization should think about its interests and capabilities, the degree to which it desires a business that is related to its mission, the size and scale of business it can handle, and its desired geographical outreach. It should consider the monies it wishes to earn, how labor intensive it wishes the business to be, and its ability to capitalize the costs of various start-up and ongoing operations.

The best way to do this brainstorming is to call a meeting of the team and any others who have an entrepreneurial spirit. They can include staff, board members, friends of the nonprofit, current clients and constituents, and even trusted outsiders who just have great ideas. Before the session begins, it is important to lay down some ground rules. The ones I like to set are the following:

1. Participants will sit facing each other. Everyone will have an opportunity to speak. Participants should feel free and comfortable to suggest any ideas they may have.
2. Group leaders will act as facilitators and will refrain from offering suggestions or opinions. They will guide the discussion, help determine speaking order, and take notes.
3. There will be three rounds of brainstorming:
    *   Idea generation—including brief descriptions of what each product/service might be and how it would work (no playing "devil's advocate" allowed here).
    *   Pros and cons discussion—including a review of the suggestions made and group feedback on the advantages and disadvantages of each.
    *   Narrowing of the list and priority setting—including a general consensus of the areas most worthy of further investigation.

Typically, participants find it helpful to concentrate on the enterprise categories discussed earlier (products, services, staff and client resources, hard and soft property), thinking in terms of the enterprise's current and potential customers, who they are, and what they are willing to pay for. The following questions are helpful in defining these factors:

> What do we give away to our current constituents that we might sell to them instead?
> What do we give away to our current constituents that we might sell to a new group of customers?
> What new product or service might we develop and market to our current constituents?
> What new product or service might we develop and market to new customers?
> Which nonprofit organizations or private-sector corporations might we partner with to market a new or current product or service?

In addition, it is useful to set some parameters by asking questions such as:

> Which industries should we consider (high-tech, garment, food, recycling, real estate, others)? What are the "good" businesses to get into and which ones should we avoid?
> Should the venture be located within our current facility or should it be off site?

Should the venture operate as a wholesaler or retailer of its product
or service?

Should we start our venture in a market where there is a lot of competition (possible benefit that it is a known quantity) or where there
is very little (possible drawback that there are barriers to entry and/or
potential for others to copy)?

Where should the product/service be in terms of its product life cycle?

Should we look for a business venture that is labor intensive? That
relies on large inventories? That relies on strict quality control? That
is a margin versus a volume business? That is credit oriented? That
requires limited capitalization?

Step 4: Conduct One or More Feasibility Studies

Step 4 begins with the list of potential businesses that resulted from the brainstorming session: select two or three businesses on which to conduct feasibility studies, and designate a project leader or champion to shepherd the
process. A feasibility study is a formal and systematic analysis that explores
a number of issues critical to the success of the business and determines
whether it can succeed at the level required by the principals. Because a
feasibility study is the tool that is used most often to make the final go/no-go
decision about a particular business venture, nonprofits are advised to be
exacting. Those conducting a feasibility study should ask all the questions
they would want answered if this were someone else's business proposal and
they were conducting a serious evaluation of it, or if they were considering
whether to invest a significant amount of their *own* money in this new venture. One of the best ways to do this is to take an adversarial position. That
is, to ask the question, "What is wrong with this idea," and to find honest
and acceptable answers.

It is important to note here, however, that the purpose of a feasibility
study is to explore, in detail, whether or not an idea for a business is really
viable. Although it is very exciting to get a positive result from a feasibility
study, nonprofits must be prepared to learn that, oftentimes, the result indicates that the nonprofit should not proceed. This is not an indication of
failure, it is an indication that you have done a good job at investigating
all aspects of the business and that you have the good sense to look in other
directions.

A feasibility study usually involves a significant amount of market research, but many nonprofit organizations assume that they know all there
is to know without conducting any. A typical statement, for example, says
that "this is a perfect business for us to go into because we *know* there is a
need for a service that renovates apartment buildings and makes them suitable for the handicapped." But, in the commercial world, there is a fundamental difference between a *need* and a *demand* for a particular product or service. It is not enough, or even relevant, to say that a need exists because
this service is important to the health and safety of disabled people. Although

this may be true, a successful business cannot be based on need alone. People must demand the service in sufficient quantity and be willing to pay for it at a price that will generate net income for the business. If these conditions are not met, the project will just be another program for which the nonprofit must go out and raise funds.

In order to demonstrate demand, it is usually necessary to conduct consumer-oriented market research. In simple terms, this means investigating what consumers want and are willing to pay for, not what you want to do and are willing to provide. It means analyzing the *marketplace* in terms of the following:

- The size and status of the market (economic, social, technological, political, and business environments; dollar and volume sales over time; growing, declining, or stable industry; seasonality; future projections; barriers to entry)
- Typical consumers and their buying habits (demographics, affiliations, purchasing motivation, willingness to pay)
- The competition (who they are, their size of operation and geographical outreach, products/services offered, pricing, general competitive advantage, experience of those who are no longer in business)
- Product/service attributes and production and delivery process (product/service description, typical pricing strategies, typical and/or innovative manufacturing/service delivery systems, retailing versus wholesaling, distribution channels)

It also means developing a general *marketing strategy* by specifying the following factors and tasks:

- Product/service creation and positioning
- Market segmentation and target marketing (relevant buyer groups, buyers versus end users)
- Product/service pricing
- Promotion (including personal selling, print advertising, direct mail, newsletters, collaborations with related associations and organizations, mail stuffers or inserts, conferences, workshops and special meetings, special projects, and public relations)
- Evaluation, tracking, and monitoring (management information system)

The *operating plan,* another essential tool, involves the clear delineation of the following:

- Requirements for daily operations (major tasks and responsibilities)
- Management and personnel
- The business location and physical features of the facility
- The type, quality, and quantity of inventory required
- Capital equipment requirements

The nonprofit must also set up a *financial plan and legal structure* that cover the following aspects of doing business:

- Estimated revenues and expenses
- Capitalization requirements
- Options for legal structure (nonprofit program, for-profit subsidiary)

This vast amount of information must be gathered over a period of usually three to six months. Some nonprofits choose to collect it themselves, while others contract with consultants who specialize in conducting feasibility studies and putting the results in a format that is most useful to nonprofits and potential funders.

Regardless of who performs the task, it is best to see first what information already exists. This can be accomplished by compiling and analyzing in-house data, conducting library searches for books and articles on the subject, contacting relevant associations and industry groups for any studies or reports that have been generated, and performing a competitor analysis by making blind telephone calls or actually purchasing various products or services.

There are many sources for this information, including the nonprofit's organizational records, lists, and surveys; federal, state, and local government agencies; the library; the telephone book; corporate annual reports; associations; suppliers and vendors; bankers; real estate offices; colleagues; and the competition. Researchers should pay attention to how dated information sources are, however; political, social, and technological events within just one year can change the picture dramatically.

To supplement information that already exists, researchers can design mail, telephone, and/or face-to-face surveys. They can conduct personal interviews and focus groups. They can begin to track telephone inquiries or solicit specific information when people call or visit. Some may want to actually create the product or service and test market it with a limited, representative sample of people.

Step 5: Secure an Organizational Commitment

In Step 5, the nonprofit reviews the results of the feasibility studies, selects the one it wishes to pursue, and secures an organizational commitment. Although this sounds like a relatively simple step, it is not as simple as it seems. At this point, the nonprofit has yet another opportunity to make its go/no-go decision, but this time it has much more information at hand. Because each feasibility study details the exact nature of the business venture and the risk-return trade-offs associated with it, the nonprofit can reevaluate its position, asking questions such as these:

Are staff, management, and board still as committed to the idea of earning income as they were when discussions began? Why or why not?

Is this particular earned-income venture worth the investment of time and money that is required? Will it actually serve the purposes for which it would be created?

Does this particular business venture show significant market potential? Do we have a competitive advantage? Do we have the skills to produce and market the product or service, or can we purchase them? Can we capitalize the business through our own sources or do we have sufficient access to others?

Are there any lingering conflicts between this business and the mission of our organization? Does it fit our style and values?

Should other ideas be investigated?

If the answers to these questions and others particular to the organization can be given to the satisfaction of those involved in the decision-making process, then the nonprofit should obtain a formal organizational commitment and move forward to the business planning stage.

Step 6: Develop the Business Plan

Step 6 involves writing a business plan that describes what the business will do, how it is going to do it, and why. The business plan is one of the most important tools for developing a business. It forces careful thinking, encourages discipline, forges internal communication, and enhances coordination and clarity of purpose among managers and investors. Because it is the written document that outlines the venture and the amount of capital required, it is an ideal vehicle for securing any financial support that may be required. Once the business is operating, the plan provides management with a yardstick against which to define and measure progress.

A business plan differs from a feasibility study in its degree of detail. Where a feasibility study examines the key business categories in a broad sense, a business plan delves into the very specifics of each category. For example, the section on promotion in a feasibility study would investigate and list various types of promotional activities that the business *might* undertake, whereas a business plan would provide specific details about each activity it *will* undertake — the target market, time and event schedule, schedule of tasks, staff responsibility, anticipated expenses, and projected results.

It can be the responsibility of one person to research and write the business plan, or several can participate in a team effort. In determining who should write the business plan, the three most important considerations are who has the requisite skills, the available time, and a clear understanding of the relationship and interplay between the business and the exempt mission of the organization. When a business venture involves different kinds of expertise in separate areas, it is not unusual to find various sections of a plan delegated to several people, each with a particular area of expertise. For example, it is common to find a financial manager writing the financial plan, a marketing manager writing the marketing plan, and an operations specialist writing the operating plan. This can work very well, provided those involved in the process communicate with one another, make few assumptions, and ask questions in sufficient detail so that all aspects of the business are considered. It is critical that all members of the research and writing team realize that their areas are interconnected and that most of what they decide will have a direct impact on the plans of the others.

There are numerous books available that provide guidance to the novice in writing business plans. Although the sequence and details may differ, most provide outlines for covering the same general categories. Writers need not conform to any one particular format, so long as the plan is comprehensive. The selection of a format should only depend on the specific business involved and the most useful way in which to present it. For the nonprofit, however, there are several sections that are not typically found in traditional business plans (see Massarsky, 1988). They include a description of the mission of the nonprofit, its purpose and goals in business venturing, and the operational, financial, and legal relationships between the nonprofit and the new business venture. A table of contents for a nonprofit-business co-venture might look something like this:

I.   Executive Summary
II.   Mission Statement
III.   Description of the Business
IV.   Industry Overview
V.   Customers
VI.   Competition
VII.   Description of Business Operations
VIII.   Management and Personnel
IX.   Marketing Plan
X.   Financial Plan
XI.   Legal Structure and Relationship to the Nonprofit
XII.   Supporting Documents

Step 7: Seek Capitalization

In Step 7, the nonprofit seeks any capitalization required for its new venture. It is rare to find a nonprofit organization that does not need some financial assistance in capitalizing its business, although depending on the extent of the need, some may be fortunate enough to have some of their own monies available. There are a number of sources of capital for nonprofit business venturing, although the appropriateness of each source depends, in part, on the legal structure of the business. If the business is to remain a part of the nonprofit organization, that is, within the nonprofit, it can solicit funds from outside sources in the form of grants, gifts, and donations, and it can also borrow funds from banks and others. If the business is spun off as a for-profit subsidiary, it has access to loans, as well, and can also raise funds through the sale of equity in its business. It is rare for a for-profit subsidiary to receive grant monies, and it is illegal for a nonprofit to offer an equity position. Both types of legal arrangements, however, have access to venture capital, bank or insurance company loans, loans from social lenders, joint venture financing (nonequity for the nonprofit), loans or credit from suppliers or vendors, and program-related investments (PRIs), which are low-interest loans made by foundations for social-purpose ventures.

Depending on need, nonprofits can try to secure funding at various times during the life cycle of their business. The typical stages are the conceptual stage, the development stage, the growth stage, and the mature stage. Obviously, the type of capital that might be needed differs with each stage, as does the source. At the *conceptual stage,* it is difficult to obtain either debt or equity capital. At this point, most nonprofits subsidize their business venturing themselves or seek foundation, corporate, or government grants to conduct feasibility studies. At the *development stage,* equity capital is easier to obtain, but a significant amount of ownership might have to be given up. Debt is harder to secure at this stage, unless the borrower is willing to pay high rates and relinquish some management control. As in the conceptual stage, grant monies are still available here. At the *growth stage,* it is easiest to obtain both equity and debt capital, provided there is strong evidence that growth will continue. Grant monies are harder to come by. At the *mature stage,* the business is less attractive to equity investors and grantors, but most attractive to lenders.

One of the first questions that a lender or investor will ask is what type of financing is needed. From their point of view, the purpose of the loan, the availability of collateral, the probability of repayment, and the amount of time it will take to recover the loan or investment are of primary concern. In structuring a capitalization plan, a nonprofit must determine the answers to these questions, regardless of whether it seeks seed capital (to conduct a feasibility study or provide for start-up expenses); cash flow financing (to cover expenses in anticipation of revenues); bridge financing (usually in the form of a loan); mortgage of permanent financing (usually long term and for real property); construction or equipment financing; or working capital financing (such as through a line of credit).

Having a good understanding of capital sources and the logic of lenders and investors can make the difference between capitalizing a business and not. It is critical that the nonprofit understand that, unlike some grant-making organizations, investors and lenders will not provide assistance simply on the virtues of an organization or cause. In fact, they may be more scrupulous in their analysis *because* the request comes from a nonprofit organization. Nothing takes the place of (1) a well-researched, well-written business plan that takes every contingency into account, and (2) the presence of an articulate and well-informed negotiating team. Although it is certainly advisable to leverage any financial commitment it might receive, nonprofits are advised not to proceed with business operations or commit the business in any way until funds are in hand.

Lessons Learned by Those Who Have Succeeded and Those Who Have Not

Many nonprofit organizations have succeeded in creating and sustaining earned-income ventures, particularly the ones that have carried out the proper market research and proceeded in a serious, formal, and calculated way. The lessons they have learned include the following:

- Operate from your strength and experience, viewing your work with an "entrepreneurial eye."
- Make certain that you have the support and formal commitment of your key constituents—staff, board, and funders.
- Develop a market-driven strategy that responds to what customers want and are willing to pay for—not what you think they need and are willing to provide.
- Develop a full cost-pricing strategy: don't price your product or service the way you price your programs.
- Create contingency plans.
- Hire management and personnel who have the knowledge and experience to run the business. Look for people who have a sensitivity to the work your nonprofit does, and be prepared to pay them market rates, even if their salaries are higher than those of staff at your nonprofit.
- Create a sufficient time line to cover the various stages of concept, development, and start-up. Rushing to begin before key components are in place can lead to failure.
- Don't begin business operations if you are not fully capitalized. Try to cover feasibility studies, business planning, and start-up activities with grants and contributions.
- Think about ways to work with corporate sponsors and to exploit the opportunities for public/private/nonprofit ventures.
- Whenever possible, presell and sell wholesale, as opposed to retail.
- Cross-market your products or services, using every opportunity to market your wares; for example, put notices about your new business in your organization's newsletter and brochures in your direct-mail fundraising appeals.

A good example of a nonprofit following these pointers is the Rockland Family Shelter, which created the Company of Women. The Company of Women is a national, socially aware mail-order company offering products designed to inspire women to respond positively to their changing roles in society today. The majority stockholder of this for-profit company is the Rockland Family Shelter, a nonprofit shelter for victims of domestic violence and sexual abuse. The Rockland Family Shelter has an annual budget of $1 million.

The Company of Women was initially capitalized with $40,000 from two Midwestern religious orders and $25,000 in seed capital from a New York state agency. In 1988, the Company of Women mailed 25,000 copies of its first eight-page catalog offering do-it-yourself and personal security items for women. Sales were $10,000 from 175 customers.

Today, the Company of Women continues as a source of unrestricted funds and an earned-income venture for the Rockland Family Shelter, as well as a vehicle for providing information about family violence to a wide audience. In addition, the company advocates economic justice for women by marketing products that promote women as strong and able and by acting as a distribution channel for emerging women-owned cooperatives, women-focused nonprofits, and women entrepreneurs worldwide. The Company of Women's product line has grown to include decorative items, clothing, self-help books, and children's merchandise. The business mails its twenty-four-page catalog twice yearly to a list of 1.75 million women and men. Gross revenues were approximately $1 million in 1992, and projected 1993 revenues were $2.3 million.

Summary

During the last decade, nonprofit organizations have begun to view business venturing as a viable way to obtain revenue to support program budgets. Many have experimented and succeeded in creating businesses that offer various products and services to the public, and co-ventured with the private sector in cause-related marketing campaigns, licensing agreements, and marketing products in return for a percentage of sales.

Although many nonprofits are eager to plunge into earning income, they should not do so without exploring thoroughly the risks and returns associated with business venturing. Creating successful enterprise is hard work. It is not for everyone and it is not a quick fix.

Before beginning to think about specific businesses, nonprofits are advised to take a critical look at whether business venturing is compatible with their organization's culture and mission. They need to explore how earning income will fit into the overall structure of their organization. They need to secure the support of staff and other key constituents.

When these issues and answers are resolved satisfactorily, nonprofits can move on to conducting an organizational audit—that is, to examining and accounting for all the assets of the organization in order to understand and make explicit its strengths and weaknesses. Once it has determined that it is ready for earned-income venturing and has listed its assets, the nonprofit can begin to brainstorm ideas—to find connections between what it has to offer and potential businesses with which it feels comfortable.

Next, the nonprofit takes the list of potential businesses created from the brainstorming session, selects two or three on which to conduct feasibility studies, and designates a project leader or champion to shepherd the process. The extensive investigation and analysis explores the marketplace and develops a marketing strategy, operating plan, financial plan, and legal structure for each business contemplated. With the selection of the most promising venture and an organizational commitment secured once again, the nonprofit is able to develop its business plan and seek the capitalization required for start-up and ongoing operations.

References

Garrison, J. R. "A New Twist to Cause Marketing." *Fund Raising Management,* 1990, *20,* (12), 40–44.

Josephson, N. "American Express Raises Corporate Giving to Marketing Act." *Advertising Age,* 1984, *55,* (4), 10–11.

Massarsky, C. "Business Planning for Nonprofit Enterprise." In E. Skloot (ed.), *The Nonprofit Entrepreneur.* New York: Foundation Center, 1988.

Rigney, M., and Steenhuysen, J. "BusinessTrack: Conscience Raising." *Advertising Age,* 1991, *62*(55), 19.

19

Accounting and Financial Management

Robert N. Anthony
David W. Young

Accounting information falls into two general categories: financial accounting and management accounting. The main purpose of financial accounting is to provide information to outside parties; management accounting provides information to an organization's managers. Financial accounting information is governed by a variety of principles and rules that are subject to audit by an outside party, generally a certified public accountant. All organizations must follow these principles and rules if they are to obtain a satisfactory *auditor's opinion* on their financial statements.

By contrast, information provided by the management accounting system varies considerably according to senior management's perception of the organization's needs. There are, however, some principles and concepts that most organizations tend to follow in the preparation of their management accounting information.

In this chapter, we discuss financial accounting and financial management. Our discussion is divided into three broad sections. In the first, we review financial accounting principles. In the second, we discuss the technical aspects of financial statement analysis. In the third, we discuss the strategic aspects of financial statement analysis. Management accounting is covered in the next chapter.

Note: Much of the content of the financial accounting principles section of this chapter was taken from Anthony and Young (1994). Much of the content of the two sections on financial statement analysis was taken from Young (1994).

Nature of Financial Accounting Principles

All nonprofit organizations periodically report their financial status as of a certain date and their financial performance for the accounting period (usually a year) ending on that date. Although the principles governing the preparation of these financial statements are largely the same for both for-profit and nonprofit organizations, this chapter focuses on principles applicable primarily to nonprofit organizations. Our discussion assumes that the reader is familiar with the basic principles of accounting. (Those who have not had a course in accounting or who want a refresher should see Anthony and Young, 1994, appendix to Chapter Three. An even more basic introduction to financial accounting can be found in Anthony, 1993.)

In some cases, an outside party can prescribe the principles used to prepare the financial accounting reports; these are called *special-purpose reports*. Nonprofit organizations, for example, must furnish information annually to the Internal Revenue Service in a specific format, using a report called Form 990. In other cases, the outside party does not prescribe the content or format of the report; these reports are called *general-purpose financial statements*. Reports to lending agencies and the general public are examples of general-purpose financial statements. Because these reports must conform to a common set of principles, the information provided by various organizations is comparable. General-purpose financial statements are prepared according to generally accepted accounting principles (GAAP).

Source of Principles

Generally accepted accounting principles followed by nonprofit organizations are prescribed by the Financial Accounting Standards Board (FASB), a private-sector body comprised of seven full-time members supported by a large staff. The FASB has an annual budget of about $12 million, contributed by accounting organizations, accounting firms, and related businesses. Many FASB principles (which it calls standards) apply to both for-profit and nonprofit organizations. Its specific principles on nonprofit organizations are contained in Statements 93, on depreciation (published in 1987); 116, on contributions (1993); and 117, on financial statements (1993). All three principles are highly controversial, especially 116 and 117, which require radical changes in accounting practices. As this chapter is being written, Statements 116 and 117 have just emerged, and we have no way of knowing how, or whether, their requirements will be implemented. We therefore describe accounting systems that are used currently, recognizing that some parts of these systems may change over the next few years.

Accounting standards for state and municipal organizations are set by the Governmental Accounting Standards Board (GASB), which is located in the same building as the FASB but has a much smaller staff. This board has five members, three of whom are part-time. Although in operation only since 1983, the GASB has made considerable progress in writing a complete set of standards.

By law, standards for federal agencies are set by the Comptroller General of the United States. Implementation of these standards is the responsibility of the Department of the Treasury and the Office of Management and Budget. Despite the law, many agencies have accounting systems that are inconsistent with these standards. Partially because of this, in 1990 the Congress created a new advisory body to develop standards for federal government accounting.

Although generally accepted accounting principles are required only for the preparation of general-purpose financial accounting reports, they also influence many aspects of management accounting. If this were not the case, an organization would have to keep two sets of books, incurring an additional bookkeeping cost and, more important, possibly causing confusion by reporting the same event in different ways.

Financial Statements

An organization for which accounts are kept is called an *accounting entity,* and the time period for preparing reports is the *accounting period.* In all organizations, the official reporting period, known as the *fiscal year,* is one year. The fiscal year need not end on December 31; in fact many organizations end their fiscal years on June 30, September 30, or some other date. Usually the entity prepares interim reports for shorter periods, such as months or quarters. In this description we shall assume the preparation of annual financial statements.

Balance Sheet. Nonprofit and for-profit organizations report assets and liabilities in essentially the same way. Equity reporting differs, however, because of differences in the nature of equity transactions in each type of organization.

In a for-profit entity, *equity* reflects the amount of capital obtained from two main sources: (1) investors and (2) the profitable operation of the entity. In a corporation, investors are known as shareholders or stockholders. They supply capital, called *paid-in capital,* in exchange for the entity's stock. The entity generates additional equity by operating profitably. The amount of profit in a period is the entity's net income or earnings. Some of this income may be paid to shareholders as dividends, so the *net* amount of equity obtained from operations is the difference between earnings and dividends. The amount reported on the balance sheet is called *retained earnings* (or, sometimes, *operating capital*). It is the total earnings since the corporation first began to operate, less the total dividends paid during that time.

A nonprofit entity has no investors; therefore its balance sheet has no item for paid-in capital. It does, however, generate earnings from its operations. Since it is legally prohibited from paying dividends, the full amount of earnings it has generated increases its equity. Nonprofit organizations do not use the term "retained earnings." Instead they label this amount as *net assets* or *fund balance*. Whatever the label, the amount is conceptually the same as retained earnings in a for-profit corporation.

Some nonprofit entities obtain capital from contributions. Capital contributed as money or its equivalent is called *endowment,* and the contribution of other assets is known as *contributed plant*. If a nonprofit is to abide by GAAP, its contributed capital must be kept separate from its operating capital. This is done by preparing separate financial statements for capital contributions. (We will describe these statements later in the chapter.)

Operating Statement. Like a for-profit organization, a nonprofit organization prepares an operating statement (or income statement) that explains the change in operating equity between two balance sheets. The operating statement reports the revenues and expenses of the period.

A primary goal of a for-profit entity is to earn income, and its net income (often referred to as "the bottom line") is an indication of how the entity has performed in attaining this goal. As a general rule, the larger an entity's net income in relation to its invested capital, the better it has performed.

Statement of Cash Flows. Revenues and expenses are measured by what is called the *accrual concept*. According to this concept, revenue is recorded when it is earned, and expenses are recorded when they are incurred. These are not necessarily the same as the amount of cash received or paid out. Because of this, entities prepare a third statement — the statement of cash flows (SCF) — that explains the reasons for cash changes. The SCF classifies cash changes into three categories: operations, financing, and investing.

Features of Nonprofit Accounting

In many respects, the principles of accounting in nonprofit organizations are the same as those in for-profit ones. The Financial Accounting Standards Board has stated that, unless another treatment is specifically required, nonprofit entities should account for transactions according to standards that apply to all organizations. Some special aspects of nonprofit accounting are discussed in this section. With the exception of the standard on depreciation, they all pertain to transactions that do not occur in for-profit entities, rather than to different ways of treating the same types of transactions.

Revenues. Revenues in nonprofit organizations are recognized in accordance with the same principles used in for-profit ones. (The term *income* is sometimes used instead of *revenue,* as in "patient care income," "interest income," and so on. This usage is incorrect and potentially confusing. *Income* always refers to a difference. Income is the difference between revenues and expenses — not the revenues, themselves.) Matters relating to the application of these principles are described below.

Sales revenues. Amounts generated through the sale of goods and services in a period are revenues of that period. Patient charges in a community health center are revenues of the period in which the patient received the center's services, for example, even though this is not necessarily the same period in which the patient (or a third-party payer) was billed or in which payment actually was received. The amount of revenue recognized is the amount that is highly likely to be received. If some patients are unlikely to pay their bills, the recognized revenues are the amounts billed less an allowance for possible bad debts. Similarly, if third party payers disallow certain items on a bill, the amount of revenue recognized is limited to the amount billed less these "contractual allowances."

Membership fees. Some nonprofit organizations, such as associations, have members who pay fees. These membership fees are revenues of the membership period, whether they are collected prior to (as is often the case), during, or after the period. If fees are not collected until after the period, the asset *membership fees receivable* must be adjusted downward at the end of the period to allow for the amount that may not be received. If the collection of fees is fairly uncertain (as in an organization with high membership turnover), an exception to the general principle may be made, and fees may be recorded as revenues when cash is received.

Life membership fees present a special problem. Conceptually, a part of the total should be recorded as revenue in each year of the member's expected life. As a practical matter, this calculation is complicated and requires considerable record keeping. Many organizations therefore take the simple solution of recording life membership fees as revenues in the year received.

Pledges. In accordance with the basic revenue concept, pledges of future financial support of operating activities are revenues in the year to which the pledged contributions apply, even if the cash is not received in that year. Unpaid pledges are adjusted downward to allow for estimated uncollectible amounts, just as is done with other accounts receivable. Some people argue that the basic revenue concept should not apply to pledges because, unlike accounts receivable, they are not legally enforceable claims. Others maintain that the difficulty of estimating the amount of uncollectible pledges is so great that a revenue amount incorporating such an estimate is unreliable. Neither of these groups would count unpaid pledges as revenues.

Operating contributions. A fundamental concept in accounting is the matching concept. According to the matching concept, when a given event has both a revenue aspect and an expense aspect, both should be reported in the same accounting period; that is, they should be "matched." If, for example, a museum gift shop purchases an item of merchandise for $60 in July and sells it for $100 in August, both the $100 revenue and the $60 cost are reported on the operating statement for August. The $60 is held in the asset account *merchandise inventory* at the end of July.

In both for-profit and nonprofit organizations, a problem with matching arises with respect to advance payments. These are payments that are received in one period for a purpose that will cause expenses to be incurred in some other period. Suppose, for example, a foundation made a $30,000 contribution to a university in year X on the condition that the university hold a conference in year $X + 1$. The conference is held in year $X + 1$, and $30,000 is spent on it. Clearly, there was an expense of $30,000 in year $X + 1$. The matching concept requires that the $30,000 contribution be reported as revenue in year $X + 1$, not in year X, when it was received. The $30,000 cash received in year X is a liability as of the end of year X, representing the university's obligation to incur expenses for the conference in year $X + 1$. It is reported as a liability on the balance sheet, with a title such as *precollected* or *unearned revenue.*

If the expenses of the conference were less than $30,000, and if the foundation did not require that the difference be returned, the university had income in year $X + 1$. If the difference had to be returned, the revenue would be reduced by this amount, in which case the revenue would equal the expense. If the expense were more than $30,000, there would be a loss in year $X + 1$.

Some nonprofit organizations do not apply the matching concept to such transactions. They report operating grants and contributions as revenues in the period in which they were received. This practice can lead to misleading operating statements during both the year when the grant is received and the year when the associated expenses are incurred.

Endowment earnings. Some nonprofit organizations have endowment funds. The donors who provide these funds usually intend that the principal of the fund be held intact permanently, or at least for a long time, and that the earnings on the investment of this principal be used for current operating purposes.

Earnings on invested endowment principal are called *endowment revenues.* Traditionally, endowment revenues for a year were the sum of dividends, interest, rents, and other earnings of the endowment fund during that year. Although this is still the practice in some organizations, many organizations now calculate the amount of endowment revenues on a *spending-rate* basis. To do this, they apply a percentage, in most cases about 5 percent, to the average market value of the endowment fund. The 5 percent is the amount of endowment earnings recognized as revenue for operating purposes. The remaining earnings from the investment of the endowment fund are retained in the endowment fund.

There are three related reasons for using the spending-rate method. First, dividends on common stock typically do not reflect the real earnings on that stock. In most instances, the investor expects the stock to increase in value, and this increase is not reflected if the return is calculated on the basis of dividends alone. Second, if 100 percent of endowment earnings were used for operating purposes, the purchasing power of the endowment would decrease because of inflation. The use of a spending rate of 5 percent assumes that, if there were no inflation, invested funds would earn 5 percent. Earnings in excess of 5 percent are therefore expected to approximate the rate of inflation. They are retained in the principal of the endowment so as to maintain its purchasing power. Third, the 5 percent approach provides senior management with a more predictable flow of operating revenues than does the use of dividends and interest, which can vary widely from year to year, depending on the organization's investment policies.

Expenses. Nonprofit organizations report most expenses according to the principle that applies to all organizations. To understand this principle, we distinguish among the various possibilities for recognizing decreases in equity: obligation, expenditure, expense, and disbursement (see Exhibit 19.1).

**Exhibit 19.1 Distinction Among Certain
Operational Activities and the Associated Accounting Terms.**

Month:	*September*	*October*	*November*	*Anytime*
Activity:	Order is placed.	Resources are received.	Resources are consumed.	Cash is paid.
Accounting Term:	*Obligation or Encumbrance*	*Expenditure*	*Expense*	*Disbursement*
Accounts Affected:	None	Inventory is increased.	Inventory is decreased.	Cash is decreased.
		Accounts payable is increased.	Equity is decreased.	Accounts payable is decreased.

Source: Adapted from Anthony and Young (1994), p. 101.

When an entity places an order for goods or services, it incurs an *obligation* or an *encumbrance.* If an entity places an order for $1,000 worth of fuel oil in September, it incurs an obligation of $1,000 in September. At one time, many entities reported obligations as decreases in equity, but this practice is now rare, except in the federal government. Instead of reporting obligations in the accounts, entities may keep separate records of them outside the formal accounting system.

An *expenditure* occurs when an organization receives either goods or services. The expenditure occurs regardless of whether the organization pays cash or incurs a liability (such as an account payable). Thus, if the fuel oil is received in October, the organization has an expenditure of $1,000 in October. The organization's fuel oil inventory account is increased by $1,000, even if the $1,000 has not been paid in cash.

An *expense* occurs when resources are consumed—that is, used up. If $400 of the fuel oil is used up in November, this is an expense of $400 in November, and the fuel oil inventory account is decreased by $400. If the remaining fuel oil is used up in December, this is an expense of $600 in December, and the fuel oil inventory account is reduced to zero.

For personnel costs, the expenditure and the expense usually occur at the same time — either when the employee works or when the services are performed. If an organization's automobile is repaired in October, for example, the organization incurs both an expenditure and an expense in October. Both the expenditure and the expense are incurred regardless of whether or not the bill is paid in that month.

Some entities report expenditures as decreases in net income (and hence in equity), but technically this is incorrect. Ordinarily, for items added to inventory and for long-lived assets (such as equipment), the expenditure occurs prior to the expense.

When cash is paid out, a *disbursement* occurs. This can happen at the same time as the expenditure is made, as in the case of a cash purchase, or it can happen in a later period, such as when a purchase is made on credit or when personnel are paid after the period in which they performed work. Disbursements can also occur earlier than the expenditure; this happens with advance payments, such as insurance premiums. Similarly, a disbursement can be made in the same period, an earlier one, or in a later period than an expense occurs.

Some small entities have cash-based accounting systems; they decrease net income (and equity) when disbursements are made. This is not in accordance with GAAP, but in organizations that have mostly cash transactions, the difference may not be great.

Inventory. Some entities record inventory items as expenses in the period in which goods are received, rather than when they are consumed. Most entities do this for minor supplies on the grounds that the extra record keeping required to trace consumption is not worthwhile. Some do it for all items; they argue that if additions to inventory in a period are approximately equal to consumption from inventory, the results would be the same, and that in any event this practice records expenses earlier than the alternative of waiting until the item has been consumed, which is a more conservative reporting practice.

Long-lived assets and depreciation. Long-lived assets, by definition, provide service for several periods after the entity has made the expenditure to acquire them. If in year X a truck is acquired at a cost of $30,000, there was an expenditure of $30,000 in year X. If the truck was estimated to provide transportation services for the next five years, $6,000 in depreciation expense is incurred in each of these years (assuming the usual straight-line method of depreciation and a zero salvage value). GAAP requires that this depreciation expense be recognized in each of the five years.

If an entity does not use the depreciation mechanism, and instead records an expense when the asset is purchased, it will not measure net income correctly. In the year of purchase, net income will be understated; in the succeeding years, net income will be overstated. Nevertheless, some nonprofit entities do not depreciate their long-lived assets. As is the case with inventory, some people argue that this practice is conservative. Others use the principal repayments on loans made to acquire long-lived assets as a substitute for depreciation, arguing that the effect on equity will be approximately the same. This possibility is discussed next.

Debt service. Many entities acquire major long-lived assets, such as buildings, trucks, and other "big ticket" equipment items, by borrowing an amount approximately equal to the purchase price. Often, the terms of a bond issue or other form of borrowing require that annual payments be made to retire the issue over the useful life of the asset acquired. The annual payments are called *debt service.* A debt service payment has two components: interest on the amount of the loan outstanding and repayment of a portion of the principal. Interest is properly an expense of the period. Under GAAP, a principal repayment is not an expense.

If, however, the loan is for the full cost of an asset, and the term of the loan and the economic life of the asset are about equal, the principal payment will approximate the annual amount of depreciation that otherwise would have been charged as an expense. Under these circumstances, treating debt service as if it were an expense may have approximately the same effect on net income as recording depreciation and the related interest amount separately. The validity of such treatment depends, of course, on how closely the principal component of debt service comes to the amount that would have been charged as depreciation.

For example, assume that we finance the above $30,000 truck with a five-year loan of $30,000. The principal payments on the loan would be identical to the amount of depreciation, that is, $6,000 per year ($30,000 ÷ 5 years). If, on the other hand, we financed the truck with, say, a three-year loan, the depreciation expense and principal payments would differ. The depreciation would still be $6,000 per year ($30,000 ÷ 5 years), but the principal payments would be $10,000 ($30,000 ÷ 3 years).

This process works well for many state and local governments, since all their fixed assets are acquired with debt and the debt usually has a term that approximates the service lives of the assets it finances. It would not work well for an organization that uses contributions or retained earnings as a source of fixed-asset financing. With these sources, there is no debt service and hence no substitute for depreciation.

Contributed services. In many nonprofit organizations, volunteers donate their services to the organization. Although these services are valuable, they are not ordinarily counted as either revenues or expenses. If management can control the activities of the volunteers in the same way they control the work of paid employees, the services are measured at the going wage rate and are counted as expenses. This is sometimes referred to as the "rule of reprimand." If volunteers can be reprimanded in the same fashion as employees (for example, for tardiness or absences), the value of their services is recognized. If these services are counted as expenses, an equal amount is reported as revenue, so there is no effect on net income.

In organizations operated by a religious order, the members of the order—be they teachers, nurses, physicians, clergy, or clerical workers—may be paid less than the going rate for their services. When this happens, the difference between the actual compensation and the going rate for similar services is considered to be a contribution. Although this was customary practice some years ago, most religious orders now bill the organization where these persons work at the going rate, and this amount is clearly an expense. In this case, however, there is no revenue.

Fringe benefits. The costs to an entity for its employees' services include not only salaries but also the pension, health care, leave pay, holiday pay, and various other benefits to which the employees become entitled by virtue of having worked. The total cost of these services is an expense of the period when the work was done. The same amount is an expenditure of the period when the work was done. This is because the organization has incurred a liability to pay for the total cost, including benefits, at the time the services were acquired. This is true even in the case of pensions and other postemployment benefits, where the actual cash disbursement may not be made until many years in the future.

Failure to record pension costs in the year in which they are incurred is one of the most serious weaknesses in many accounting systems. This omission understates the costs of current operations and also puts the burden of providing for the pensions on future generations, rather than on the current one, even though the current generation received the benefit of the labor services. In New York City, for example, the present value of the amount that had been earned by employees but not yet charged as an expense was approximately $3 billion in 1985.

The principles for measuring the current cost of payments that will be paid to employees when they retire are complicated, but well worked out for all organizations except government. They are set forth in FASB Statement 87 for pensions and Statement 106 for other postemployment benefits, such as health care, provided after the employee retires. The Governmental Accounting Standards Board is developing a standard on the same topic.

Significance of Net Income

Net income is an extremely important measure of the performance of a for-profit entity; it measures both the effectiveness and efficiency of an organization's operations. In a nonprofit organization, its meaning is slightly different.

Since the goal of a nonprofit organization is to provide service, rather than to earn income, the importance of its operating statement may not be obvious. Nevertheless, the operating statement does convey important information about financial performance. If revenues do not at least equal expenses—that is, if the organization does not at least break even—there is a danger signal. If this situation persists, the organization eventually will go bankrupt. Conversely, if revenues exceed expenses by too wide a margin, the organization probably is not providing as much service as it should with the funds available to it.

Operating Capital Maintenance. If, in a given year, an entity's revenues at least equal its expenses, it is said to have maintained its operating capital. Some entities try to maintain their operating capital each year; others do not. Fiscal policy in many governmental units specifies that spending should equal revenue. Many states require such a policy, and rates of taxation are set so that this relationship will occur. If a governmental unit operates at a loss, those responsible for its management have, in effect, drawn on either past resources or future resources (supplied by future taxes or grants) to finance current operations.

In many other nonprofit organizations, the amount of revenue available in a given year is essentially fixed, and the policy is to limit expenses to this amount, or in other words, to break even. This is the case in many membership organizations, universities, and health care organizations.

Other nonprofit organizations may decide to have some net income in a given year to recoup the loss of a prior year, to provide funds for expansion, to provide a reserve for contingencies, or for a variety of other reasons. An organization may also decide to operate at a deficit in a given year to use accumulated equity, to meet an unusual need, or for other reasons. If the organization is financially well managed, net income reflects the results of these policies.

Many nonprofit organizations have a policy of doing somewhat better than breaking even. They attempt to generate net income (or a surplus) every year, reasoning that additional equity is needed for three purposes: (1) to acquire new fixed assets, (2) to replace worn out fixed assets in periods of inflation, and (3) to finance the working capital needed to support a growth in services. Many nonprofits are unable or unwilling to issue bonds or incur other forms of debt for 100 percent of these requirements. Since they cannot obtain equity capital from investors, the only sources of equity are contributions and their own operating activities. When contributions are insufficient, net income is the only other possibility.

Generational Equity. The capital maintenance idea is often described as *generational* or *interperiod equity.* The principle is that each generation affected by an entity should provide enough revenue to meet the expenses of the services it uses from that entity. If a social service agency operates at a loss in a given year, for example, this indicates that clients, third party payers, or donors have not provided enough revenues to meet that year's expenses. Thus, future generations must make up the loss or the entity will go bankrupt. The idea, then, is that each generation should pay its own way, or more specifically, in each year the entity should meet its expenses. Anthony (1989–90) discusses interperiod equity and its relation to operating and capital budgets in government. The principles outlined in that article are applicable to many nonprofit organizations.

Classifying Expenses and Revenues by Program and by Element

Expenses on the operating statement may be classified either by elements (such as salaries, fringe benefits, supplies, depreciation) or by programs. A program is a set of activities the entity undertakes to achieve its objectives. The American Institute of Certified Public Accountants' *Audits of Voluntary Health and Welfare Organizations* explains that a supplemental financial statement should be used to report expenses by program category. If a program reporting structure is used, it usually is desirable to report the entity's administration costs as a separate program item. Also, if the entity incurs significant expenses for fundraising, it should report them separately.

Classification of expenses by program is generally more informative than classification by element. Some organizations report a main classification by program and report expenses by element under each principal program. They may report only two elements: "employee compensation" and "all other"; this is because employee compensation is a large fraction of total expenses. If expenses are incurred jointly for two or more programs, the accounting staff attempts to allocate an equitable share of such joint or common expenses to each program.

If revenues can readily be identified with programs, they too may be classified by program. Another common basis for classifying revenues is by source. Examples of revenue sources in a hospital include third party reimbursement, patient reimbursement, contributions from private parties, government grants, and endowment earnings.

Contributed Capital and Fund Accounting

Financial accounting focuses mainly on the *operating* performance of the entity. Many nonprofit entities have financial transactions that are not associated with operating performance per se. These transactions are not reported among the assets, liabilities, and equity associated with operations. Instead they are reported in separate funds. The result is a need for an accounting and financial reporting process called *fund accounting*. (The main class of nonoperating activity in nonprofit organizations is *contributed capital*. The discussion here touches on the nature of, and the accounting for, contributed capital and also describes fund accounting briefly. More thorough treatments can be found in the Additional Readings at the end of the chapter.)

Contributions for operating purposes are revenues; they add to the resources available for use in operations and hence to the organization's operating equity. Capital contributions are not revenues; they are direct additions to an organization's equity. There are two general types of capital contributions: contributions for endowment and contributions for plant. When a donor contributes to an entity's endowment, the entity invests the amount received, and only the earnings on that amount are available for operating purposes. (This restriction is a matter of law; the entity has a fiduciary duty not to use the principal of donor-restricted endowment funds for operations.) Similarly, when a donor contributes money to acquire a building or other item of plant, this contribution must be used for the specified purpose; it is not available to finance operating activities. Both types of contributions add to equity—they make the entity better off—but neither is associated with operating activities.

Because it is not associated with operating activities, a capital contribution does not affect the measurement of net income as reported on the operating statement. Nor do capital contributions affect the balance sheet items associated with operating activities because the cash or other assets received are not available to pay operating bills. To insulate operating activities from the effect of these capital contributions, the accounting system has separate funds for endowment and plant. Each of these funds is a separate accounting entity, with its own balance sheet and its own way of reporting increases and decreases in equity. Each is governed by the fundamental accounting equation:

$$\text{Assets} = \text{Liabilities} + \text{Equity}$$

Financial Statement Presentation. The balance sheet for each fund reports the fund's assets, liabilities, and equity. For reporting purposes, each fund usually is contained in a separate column on a page that shows the balance sheet items for all the entity's funds. Some entities also report the total amounts for all funds on the balance sheet, but these totals have little meaning. The total of the entity's cash, for example, might imply that the cash in any fund can be used to pay any bill, but this is not the case. Only cash in the operating fund can be used to pay operating bills. Sometimes an entity will borrow from a nonoperating fund to obtain cash for its operating fund, but this can only be done on a temporary basis. Like any other loan, it must be repaid.

The most informative presentation is a full balance sheet for each separate fund, as shown in Exhibit 19.2. Transactions related to operating activities are reported in a section labeled "operating fund" (often called "general fund" or "current fund"). Note that each section of Exhibit 19.2 is a self-balancing set of accounts, with total assets equal to total liabilities plus equity. Note also that each section has a cash item. The cash in one fund should not be mingled with the cash in the others. The equity in each fund is usually clearly labeled with the name of its fund, although on some balance sheets it is simply called "fund balance."

By definition, the terms *revenues, expenses,* and *net income* are associated with operating activities, so there is no operating statement as such for the endowment or plant funds. To summarize the transactions that occurred in the year, however, the accountants prepare a flow statement for each fund. This statement shows the amounts that flowed into the fund during the period and the uses made of the fund's resources. It is often titled "statement of

Exhibit 19.2. Sample Organizational Balance Sheet
for End of Fiscal Year (in thousands).

Assets		Liabilities and Equity	
		Operating Fund	
Cash . . . .$	200	Accounts payable . . . .$	400
Accounts receivable	300	Precollected revenue	600
Inventory	400	Bonds payable	1,200
Investments	800	Total liabilities	2,200
Buildings and equipment	1,400	Operating equity	900
Total Assets . . . .$	3,100	Total Liabilities and Equity . . . . .$	3,100
		Endowment Fund	
Cash . . . .$	10	Legal endowment . . . .$	7,000
Bonds	9,100	Board-designated endowment	13,010
Stock	10,900		
Total Assets . . . .$	20,010	Endowment equity . . . . $	20,010
		Plant Fund	
Cash . . . .$	20	Accounts payable . . . .$	30
Investments	400	Plant equity	11,590
Buildings and equipment	11,200		
Total Assets . . . .$	11,620	Total Liabilities and Equity . . . . .$	11,620

Source: Adapted from Anthony and Young, 1994, p. 108.

changes in equity" or "statement of changes in fund balance." Such a statement for the endowment fund would report contributions to endowment and earnings from dividends, interest, and rent as additions. The amount of earnings recognized as revenue and transferred to the operating fund would be reported as reductions.

Endowment Fund. Donors may specify that their contributions are for the organization's endowment; that is, only the earnings are to be used for operating purposes. Alternatively, even if a donor does not make a legally binding restriction, the circumstances may clearly indicate that the contribution is for endowment purposes. If, for example, a university receives a million-dollar bequest, the size of the gift makes it obvious that it was not intended for use in the year in which the entity received the money. Such a contribution is called *board-designated endowment.*

By contrast, a legally binding contribution to endowment is called *legal endowment.* The difference is that the principal amount of legal endowment can never be used for operating purposes, whereas the governing board could vote to use a portion of board-designated endowment for operating purposes. It normally would do so only in the event of a financial emergency, however.

Assets of the endowment fund consist principally of investments in stocks, bonds, and real estate. The assets are for the endowment fund as a whole. They are not separated according to individual donors, or even according to whether they derive from legal endowment or board-designated endowment.

A donor may specify that the income from his or her contribution to the endowment may be used only for a particular purpose — to provide financial aid for low-income students in a university, for example, or even for students from the donor's hometown. For internal management purposes, records of these restrictions must be maintained. These records do not appear in the general-purpose financial statements, however.

Plant Fund. Contributions made for the purchase of buildings, equipment, and the like (or the contribution of a building, piece of equipment, or the like itself) are often reported in a separate plant fund. Donated assets such as these are recorded at their fair market value at the time they were received, even if their cost to the entity was zero. Because accounting usually does not recognize increases in market value, a subsequent increase in market value is not reflected in the accounts.

FASB Statement 93 requires that contributed buildings, equipment, and other depreciable assets be depreciated. Some organizations object to this requirement. They argue that because a building was donated, the entity did not — and never will — require the use of revenues to finance it. Therefore, the inclusion of a depreciation component as an expense item on the operating statement would result in understating the amount of income earned through operating activities. FASB Statement 93 is based on the premise that the buildings are used for operating purposes and that omission of depreciation would understate the real expenses of operating the organization.

A recently proposed solution to this dilemma is to report depreciation on contributed plant as an expense, and to report an equal amount as revenue of the period. The revenue component represents the donor's contribution to the operations of the period, while the expense component reports the cost of using the facilities. Since the two amounts are equal, there is no effect on income. Although recommended by an international accounting standards group, this practice so far has not been adopted in the United States.

Other Fund Types. Although operating funds, endowment funds, and plant funds usually are the largest funds in nonprofit entities, many organizations have other types of funds. Some of these also exist in for-profit organizations, although texts on accounting in such organizations may not describe them.

Restricted operating funds. Some entities set up a separate fund to account for operating contributions whose use is restricted to a specified purpose or to a specified period. This happens, for example, in the case of a grant or contract. Since such contributions are associated with operations, there is no strong reason for creating separate categories for them. As noted earlier, such contributions are essentially advance payments, and they can be accounted for in the way such payments are usually noted: by recording a liability when the contribution is received. The liability is eliminated and revenue is recognized when the organization incurs the expenses for the specified purpose or in the specified time period.

Other nonoperating funds. An entity may have a loan fund that makes loans to employees or clients, a pension fund that is used to pay pensions, a sinking fund used to guarantee payments due on bond issues, or other resources that must not be mixed with operating resources or included in reports on operating activities. Some nonprofits create separate funds for these purposes and report them as part of their general-purpose financial statements. Others follow the practice of for-profit organizations and treat them as separate entities, excluded from the organization's annual financial report. For pension funds, such a separation is required by law.

Transfers. When an entity has several funds, its transactions usually involve transferring amounts from one fund to another. The transfer of earnings from the endowment fund to the operating fund is an example. Such a transfer results, quite properly, in an item of revenue on the operating statement. Other types of transfers may or may not represent legitimate items of revenues or expense. For example, an entity that has earned a large income in a given year may transfer funds to its plant account to be used for the construction of new buildings. If the transfer is reported as a deduction from revenue on the operating statement, the amount of income reported would be lower than the actual amount earned.

Transfers from the operating fund to the plant fund actually reflect decisions as to how the surplus earned in the period should be used. The transfer of an amount of cash equivalent to the depreciation expense is an example. This is called "funding depreciation" and entails making a transfer of cash from the operating fund to the plant fund. Organizations that fund depreciation claim that the transfers provide a pool of cash that can be used to pay for the replacement of assets. Because of this, many people believe that the funding of depreciation enforces a degree of fiscal discipline on nonprofit organizations. (Since such a pool could be maintained in the operating fund just as easily, however, the funding of depreciation is purely a disciplinary matter; it serves no other purpose.)

Some transfers are mandatory; that is, they are required by contract. An example is the condition imposed by bondholders to pay a specified amount to a debt service fund. Depending on their nature, these transfers may or may not represent expenses. As pointed out above, the amount of debt service may be an approximation of interest and depreciation expense on long-lived assets. In some health care organizations, the funding of depreciation is required by third party payers. In these cases, the transfer is mandatory.

Variations in Practice

Unless the FASB has issued a standard to govern accounting practices in nonprofit organizations, the practice is influenced by the *Audit Guides* produced by the American Institute of Certified Public Accountants (AICPA) and other pronouncements for several types of organizations. Strictly speaking, entities are not required to follow these *Audit Guides*. However, the FASB states that if an entity changes an accounting practice, the change must be to a practice prescribed by the appropriate *Audit Guide*.

The *Audit Guides* for health care, voluntary health and welfare organizations, and other nonprofit organizations recommend practices that generally are similar to the descriptions given above. The *Audits of Colleges and Universities* is different in several respects, however. Indeed, this *Audit Guide* states that the report that is closest to an operating statement "does not purport to present the results of operations or the net income or loss for the period"; we have emphasized, however, such information is the central focus of financial accounting.

Government Accounting. The accounting details for state and local governments can be found in Douglas (1991), Hay and Wilson (1992), Henke (1992), and Government Accounting Standards Board. Federal agencies are affected by essentially three types of accounting systems: (1) appropriation accounting, (2) accounting systems required by the General Accounting Office, and (3) systems they develop themselves for their own purposes. Details can be found in the above references as well as the Comptroller General of the United States (1972).

Problems with Inconsistent Practices. Some people are interested only in the financial statements of a specific type of organization, such as a hospital. Those individuals learn the peculiarities of the accounting practices in that type of organization. People who are interested in several types of organizations must understand the different practices employed in each type. The problem is especially complicated when a single entity operates several types of organizations. A medical center could have a hospital subject to the health care *Audit Guide,* a medical school subject to the college and university *Audit Guide,* and a physician's clinic subject to business accounting principles. Such a medical center would have difficulty in developing a meaningful set of financial statements for the whole entity.

Terminology presents still another problem. Even if they use the same basic principles, different entities tend to use different names for identical procedures or concepts. Because of this, readers will need to look beyond labels and headings to function and use in order to determine a report's meaning.

Summary

Most revenues and expenses should be measured the same way in both for-profit and nonprofit organizations. Revenues increase operating equity, and expenses decrease it. Both should be reported in the accounting period to which they relate, in accordance with the realization and matching concepts.

Contributed capital, such as contributions to the organization's plant or endowment, is added directly to equity and is accounted for separately from operating transactions. Such a separation leads to individual funds for nonoperating items and the related practice of fund accounting, which has no counterpart in a business.

Despite the similarity of most transactions in all organizations, actual accounting practices vary greatly among various types of nonprofit organizations. These variations reflect primarily the different treatments suggested in the *Audit Guides* that apply to these organizations. The Financial Accounting Standards Board and the Governmental Accounting Standards Board are now responsible for developing accounting standards for nonprofit organizations. In due time, they will eliminate, or at least greatly reduce, these variations.

Financial Statement Analysis: Technical Aspects

A set of financial statements conveys a great deal of information about an organization's financial strengths and weaknesses. Financial statement analysis usually focuses on four separate but related matters: profitability, liquidity, asset management, and long-term solvency. This section defines and examines these terms.

Purpose of Financial Statement Analysis

The purpose of financial statement analysis is not to determine how well or poorly an organization has followed GAAP, although this occasionally will be a necessary ingredient in such an analysis. Rather, the purpose is to determine the overall quality of an organization's financial management. As we discuss in this section, there are several facets to such an analysis.

The asset side of the balance sheet contains those items that an organization owns or has claim to, whereas the liability and equity side shows how the assets have been financed. Since the balance sheet is the result of all of an organization's historical financial activities viewed at a given point in time, it provides a "long-run" view of the organization's asset acquisition and financing decisions.

The long-run view can be supplemented by an analysis of both the operating statement and the statement of cash flows, which show management's specific financing choices and activities over the course of a given accounting period, usually a year.

As we discussed above, the operating statement shows an organization's *profitability*—that is, its excess of revenues over expenses—during a given accounting period. The SCF, by contrast, shows how the organization has managed its *cash* over the same time period. The SCF gives specific information about the sources of funds during a year and the uses to which those funds were put. By using the SCF, a reader of financial statements can determine the extent to which an organization acquired more fixed assets or current assets during a year, and how those new assets were financed (operations, short-term debt, long-term debt, additional capital contributions, or donations). Consequently, the balance sheet, the operating statement, and the SCF together provide some indication of the financing decisions made by an organization's management, both over time and during the course of the most recent accounting period.

Ratio Analysis

One technique used to assess the quality of an organization's financial management is ratio analysis. By dividing the sum of one or more elements on the statements by the sum of one or more others, a mathematical comparison — a ratio analysis — can be made. In particular, ratios involving both the operating statement and the balance sheet can assist analysts to assess relationships among surplus (or net income), assets, and liabilities. For example, ratio analysis facilitates assessments of the relationship between net income (or surplus) and equity, or between current assets and current liabilities. Each is important for different reasons. By permitting the analyst to move beyond the absolute magnitude of the numbers on the financial statements to *a set of relationships between and among the numbers,* ratios can assist greatly in the analysis of a set of financial statements.

The principal purpose of ratio analysis is to facilitate comparisons, either for a single organization over a period of several years or among several similar organizations for a given year or other time period. It allows an analyst to look closely at profitability, liquidity, asset management, and long-term solvency.

Many ratios can be calculated under each heading, and, in some instances, alternative elements can be included in the calculation of a given ratio. The discussion that follows covers the most common ratios and the elements that frequently are included in their calculation.

Profitability Ratios. Profitability ratios attempt to measure the ability of an organization to generate sufficient funds from its operations to both sustain itself and provide an acceptable return to its owners. Both aspects are important. Over the long term, an entity must generate enough funds from operations to allow it to (1) replace fixed assets as they wear out, (2) purchase new fixed assets as revenues grow, (3) service its debt, and (4) provide for the cash needs associated with growth. Of course, investors in a for-profit entity also expect that the profits will be used to provide them with a reasonable return on their investment. Profitability ratios provide some evidence of how well an organization is satisfying these requirements.

An organization's profitability can be examined along two dimensions: size and validity. The following are specific questions an analyst might want to ask:

- How large was net income (or surplus) relative to revenue? Is this amount about right or too small?

- To what extent is the net income figure valid? That is, was it based on estimates? For example, was there an estimate of bad debts and contractual allowances, and, if so, is any information available on its accuracy? Does the depreciation expense appear to be a reasonably accurate representation of the using up of the associated assets?
- What was the organization's return on assets? Is this about right or too low?

The first profitability measure is *profit margin:*

$$\text{Profit margin} = \frac{\text{Net income}}{\text{Revenue}}$$

This ratio effectively measures how much of each dollar in revenue received by the organization ultimately becomes net income. Profit margins tend to vary widely from one type of nonprofit organization to the next. For example, a nonprofit with commoditylike product or service, such as a day care center or a publisher of newsletters, will tend to have a relatively low profit margin; its profitability is largely a result of a high volume of sales. By contrast, a highly capital-intensive nonprofit, such as a port authority or a hospital, will need a larger profit margin. We will examine this matter more fully in the next section.

A second profitability ratio is *return on assets:*

$$\text{Return on assets} = \frac{\text{Net income}}{\text{Total assets}}$$

Depreciation recognizes the expense associated with the using up of an asset. It also provides for the recovery of the cash expenditures associated with an asset's acquisition. Since it is based on the historical cost of the asset, it does not compensate for the effects of inflation. Moreover, there are a variety of other factors to consider with respect to the replacement of assets. Nevertheless, the return-on-asset ratio provides at least a rudimentary indication of whether an organization is earning a sufficiently large income to maintain itself in a steady state. Accordingly, an appropriate return-on-asset ratio would be at least as high as the rate of inflation in an organization's service area. This issue also will be explored in the next section.

The final profitability ratio is *return on equity:*

$$\text{Return on equity} = \frac{\text{Net income}}{\text{Total equity (or Fund Balance)}}$$

This ratio, generally abbreviated as ROE (or sometimes ROI, for "return on investment"), is one of the most commonly used indicators of profitability. It allows an investor or potential investor to compare the earnings on an investment in one organization with a variety of other uses of those funds (such as savings certificates, treasury notes, and the like). Because it is of primary interest to investors, the return-on-equity ratio tends to be less important in nonprofit organizations than in for-profit ones.

Liquidity Ratios. Liquidity ratios help to measure an organization's ability to convert its noncash assets into cash — that is, to "liquidate" its assets. Liquidity ratios generally are computed with some portion of an organization's current assets, occasionally comparing them with its current liabilities. Current assets are those that will be, or have a reasonable expectation to be, converted into cash within a year; current liabilities are those obligations that must be paid in cash within a year.

   In sum, the question of liquidity is essentially one of cash availability and use. Among the questions an analyst might ask are the following:

- How well is the organization using its cash? Does it have enough cash to meet current obligations? Does it have too much cash sitting idle?
- How well is the organization managing its accounts receivable? Are collection periods too long? Are they lengthening?
- How well is the organization managing its inventory? Does it have too much, thereby tying up cash in an otherwise unproductive asset, or does it have too little inventory?

The most commonly used liquidity ratio is the *current ratio:*

$$\text{Current ratio} = \frac{\text{Current assets}}{\text{Current liabilities}}$$

Many considerations govern the appropriate size of this ratio for any given entity, and there tend to be wide variations across industries (even *within* some industries, such as health care, where, say, HMOs and hospitals would have quite different current ratios). Despite these differences, a figure of 2.0 often is used as an appropriate level. That is, current assets should be roughly twice as large as current liabilities.

   A variety of other liquidity ratios can be computed in order to measure some portion of the current ratio. The most frequently used is the *quick ratio* (sometimes called the *acid-test ratio):*

$$\text{Quick ratio} = \frac{\text{Cash} + \text{Marketable securities} + \text{Net accounts receivable}}{\text{Current liabilities}}$$

The purpose of the quick ratio is to eliminate those current assets that, for one reason or another, may *not* be readily or fully convertible into cash, principally inventory and prepaid expenses. A quick ratio of less than 1.0 suggests that the organization may encounter some difficulties in meeting its current liabilities when they come due.

Although included in both the current and quick ratios, accounts receivable frequently can be a somewhat questionable asset. Both ratios attempt to compensate for this uncertainty by using a *net* accounts receivable figure (that is, gross accounts receivable less the allowance for doubtful accounts). Nevertheless, more detail on accounts receivable frequently is helpful. A third liquidity ratio, *average days receivable,* allows an analyst to make an assessment of how quickly an organization is collecting its accounts receivable.

$$\text{Average days receivable} = \frac{\text{Net accounts receivable}}{\text{Revenue} \div 365}$$

The denominator of this ratio is average revenue earned per day (ideally using credit sales only, which, for many nonprofit organizations, is a high percent of total sales). When this figure is divided into net accounts receivable, the result is the average number of days of revenue that are included in the net accounts receivable figure. This provides a rough estimate of the average number of days needed to collect an account receivable. This figure, compared with the entity's payment policies, indicates how well clients, on average, are abiding by the entity's expectations.

A final liquidity ratio is one that is comparable to the average days receivable ratio: *average days inventory:*

$$\text{Average days inventory} = \frac{\text{Inventory}}{\text{Cost of goods sold} \div 365}$$

Cost of goods sold, when divided by 365, gives the average cost of goods sold per day. When this is divided into inventory, the result is the average number of days that inventory remains on hand before being sold.

With few exceptions, nonprofit organizations do not sell their inventory. Rather, they use up a supply income (such as medical supplies) in the course of operations; in these cases, there is no cost of goods sold. When this happens, total expenses (or, better, total expenses less salaries and depreciation) can substitute for cost of goods sold. Although some precision is lost, the ratio, when used comparatively over several years, may help to reveal potential weaknesses in inventory management.

Asset Management Ratios. The average days receivable and average days inventory ratios lie at the intersection of liquidity and asset management, since they contain aspects of both. Asset management ratios help to assess how effectively an organization is using its assets (which include accounts receivable and inventory).

Assessment of an organization's assets requires the examination of both current and noncurrent components. Current assets were considered under the heading of liquidity. With regard to noncurrent (or fixed) assets, several questions must be answered:

- What is the nature of the fixed assets? Are they appropriate to the organization's strategy?
- How well are assets being utilized? How much revenue is being generated, for example, for every dollar of assets?
- How old are the fixed assets? Are they in need of replacement? If so, are funds available to replace them?

A commonly used asset management ratio is *asset turnover:*

$$\text{Asset turnover} = \frac{\text{Revenue}}{\text{Total assets}}$$

This ratio shows how much revenue an organization has earned for each dollar it has invested in assets. Organizations that have an asset base consisting largely of accounts receivable and inventory usually have a relatively high asset turnover; that is, each item in the asset base is used up and replaced many times a year, and revenue is earned in the course of doing so. By contrast, organizations with a high proportion of fixed assets, such as plant and equipment, generally have a low asset turnover, since it takes several years for a fixed asset to be used up (via depreciation) and replaced. Universities, hospitals, and port authorities would fall into this latter category.

If an organization is fairly capital intensive, a modified ratio may shed more light on the quality of its asset management; this is the *fixed-asset turnover ratio:*

$$\text{Fixed-asset turnover} = \frac{\text{Revenue}}{\text{Net fixed assets}}$$

This ratio assesses the relative productivity of new plant and equipment, compared to plant and equipment assets that are highly depreciated. One would expect that, as assets depreciated (and, hence, *net* fixed assets fell), the ability of those assets to earn revenue also would fall. The magnitude of this fall can be assessed with this ratio. A comparison might be made to the organization's past performance (when the assets were newer), for example, or to other organizations with relatively new assets.

Long-Term Solvency Ratios. Long-term solvency ratios indicate how an organization has financed its assets over the long term (that is, for a period extending beyond one year). Generally, two issues are of concern here. First is the balance between debt and equity financing. The former consists of loans, mortgages, bonds, and other similar debt instruments; the latter consists of contributed capital and retained earnings. Second is the ability of the organization to meet its debt obligations.

To determine if the organization has made good financing decisions, thereby providing for its solvency over the long term, analysts can look at both the operating statement and the liabilities on the balance sheet. They attempt to answer the following sorts of questions:

- What is the nature of the organization's liabilities? Are they truly obligations that must be repaid or are they the result of higher than appropriate estimates? Have some liabilities, such as pensions, been underestimated, such that there may be unanticipated drains on cash in the future?
- How much long-term debt is there relative to the amount of equity? Is this about right? Is there too much debt given the inherent riskiness of the organization's operations? Could the organization take on more debt without jeopardizing its ability to repay both the new and existing debt?

In looking at the balance between debt and equity, the most commonly used ratio is the *debt/equity ratio:*

$$\text{Debt/Equity} = \frac{\text{Total liabilities}}{\text{Equity (or Fund Balance)}}$$

The higher this ratio, the greater the entity's "leverage"; that is, the greater the extent to which it has utilized external funds (debt) to supplement internal funds (equity).

Several other measures of leverage exist also. One of the most common is obtained by dividing total assets by equity.

$$\text{Leverage} = \frac{\text{Total assets}}{\text{Equity (or Fund Balance)}}$$

Effectively, this ratio is the same as debt/equity plus one. (This is true by virtue of the fundamental accounting identity: Assets = Liabilities + Equity. If $A = L + E$, then $A/E = L/E + E/E$, or $A/E = L/E + 1$, or assets/equity equals debt/equity plus one.)

Because of the need to make both short- and long-term assessments, analysts frequently distinguish between short- and long-term debt (that is, between current and long-term liabilities). This gives rise to a modified— and more frequently used—version of the debt/equity ratio, the *long-term debt/equity ratio:*

$$\text{Long-term debt/equity} = \frac{\text{Noncurrent liabilities}}{\text{Equity (or Fund Balance)}}$$

Looked at over time, this ratio can reveal the extent to which an organization is relying increasingly (or decreasingly) on long-term debt to finance asset acquisition.

As indicated above, debt—either long- or short-term—gives rise to a debt service obligation—the payment of principal and interest. An organization's ability to meet its debt service obligation can be measured by a ratio called *debt service coverage:*

$$\text{Debt service coverage} = \frac{\text{Net income} + \text{Depreciation} + \text{Interest payments}}{\text{Principal payments} + \text{Interest payments}}$$

The numerator is a rough estimate of the cash available to meet debt service obligations; the denominator is the debt service obligation itself. Depreciation is included in the numerator because it is a noncash expense. Interest payments are included because we want to know the funds available to meet principal *and* interest payments, and net income measures the funds left *after* interest payments; therefore we must add back interest payments. Thus, the ratio provides an indication of the extent to which the debt service obligation is "covered" by available cash.

Variations on the Theme. As indicated previously, there are many other ratios that could be calculated. The interested reader can find more information on ratio calculations and ratio analysis in Young (1984), Anthony (1993), and Young (1994).

Using Ratios for Financial Statement Analysis

Ratio calculations are an important aspect of financial statement analysis because they facilitate an assessment of the relationship among various parts of a single statement (such as the balance sheet) or between elements on two different statements (generally the operating statement and the balance sheet). The current ratio—which examines the relationship between current assets and current liabilities—is an example of the former; the return on assets ratio—where net income (from the income statement) is compared with assets (from the balance sheet)—is an example of the latter.

Although ratios can assist in the analysis of a set of financial statements, they do not in themselves provide all the answers. One important question that emerges in the use of ratios is the standard to which a ratio should be compared. For example, as indicated above, the current ratio provides some indication of an organization's liquidity, and therefore can assist an analyst in assessing the way an organization is managing its current assets.

Although a figure of 2.0 was suggested as about right, there may be acceptable variations. A current ratio of 1.5, for example, may be perfectly acceptable under certain circumstances. Indeed, it is possible that under some circumstances 1.5 might be too high. To make these judgments, analysts seek some standards for comparison. In general, three such standards exist: industry, historical, and managerial.

Industry Standards. Industry standards are popular and can form an easy basis for assessing the quality of an organization's financial ratios. However, industry standards can also be misleading. There are several concerns with industry standards. The first is whether the organization being analyzed is truly a member of the "industry" for which the standards have been developed. For example, there has been considerable work developing industry norms for hospitals, and yet within this so-called industry there may be a number of subindustries that are more relevant for analysis. There are teaching hospitals and community hospitals, rural hospitals and urban hospitals, large hospitals and small hospitals, investor-owned hospitals and nonprofit hospitals, hospitals in the Southwest and hospitals in the Northeast.

For a variety of reasons, such as regulatory requirements, regional payment patterns by insurance companies, and so on, a hospital in a particular region of the country may, by necessity, have a ratio that diverges from the so-called norm. Certainly, the financial ratios for a large, nonprofit teaching hospital in an urban setting in the Northeast will be somewhat, if not considerably, different from those of a small, investor-owned, rural community hospital in the Southwest.

Second, industry norms generally have been derived from published data, and it is important to ascertain that the ratios for both the organization under analysis and the industry have been calculated in the same (or approximately the same) way. For some ratios, there is only one method of calculation. However, there may be several legitimate ways to calculate other ratios, each of which will produce slightly different results. Moreover, despite the presence of generally accepted accounting principles, there is a lack of a uniform chart of accounts or uniform reporting in most nonprofit industries. This means that some ratio comparisons may not be valid even if it appears that the same elements are being included.

Finally, the ratios must be for roughly the same time period. This is particularly important if there have been changes in the organization's environment and strategy. For example, assume that the industry norm for an accounts receivable collection ratio for a mental health agency being reimbursed by a state government for Medicaid patients had been calculated during a period when the state's resources were plentiful and payments were being made in a timely way. It would be quite misleading to compare that ratio with one calculated when the state's fiscal resources were less plentiful and its payments less timely. As many organizations have learned quite painfully, changes of this sort frequently do not happen gradually, but rather quite dramatically, so that a comparison of ratios to an industry norm developed only one year previously could be quite misleading.

Apart from regional variations and calculation differences, an "industry norm" is not necessarily the right level for a ratio. Some studies attempting to develop industry norms, for example, have looked at organizations that ultimately went bankrupt—hardly a standard to aspire to. Moreover, philanthropy has been diminishing rapidly in recent years, causing many nonprofits to take on increasing amounts of debt. Thus, what was a norm five or ten years ago may no longer be appropriate. In short, industry norms must be viewed with considerable skepticism.

Historical Standards. Although they involve similar problems with regard to norms as those described above, historical standards also avoid many other problems associated with industry standards. For example, since they consist of ratios calculated over time for the same organization, there is no question that the industry is the same (unless the organization has had a major strategic shift and moved into a new industry). It is also quite easy to avoid the problem of calculating the ratios in different ways.

Potential problems with historical comparisons arise with changes in accounting practices. For example, prior to 1991, universities and several other types of nonprofit organizations were not required to include depreciation on their income statements. The 1991 change in accounting policy led to dramatic changes in some ratios, as compared to prior years. Moreover, in 1991, there also was a one-time inclusion of depreciation for all prior years on the balance sheet. Thus, ratios for 1991 are particularly suspect, and comparisons between, say, 1992 and any prior year are misleading unless the depreciation effect is included in the analysis.

Apart from problems deriving from accounting changes, the weakness of historical ratios is the absence of external validation. For example, an organization's accounts receivable collection period may have remained at sixty days for several years, but management may be unaware of a technique used by similar organizations in the same industry to accelerate collections to, say, thirty days. Without some external validation, management may continue to think that a sixty-day collection period is appropriate.

Managerial Standards. Industry ratios are not the only way an organization's management learns of practices in its industry. For example, managers generally engage in a variety of activities that make them aware of how other organizations in their industry are being managed.

Because of the availability of external information and because different organizations have different strategic objectives, an organization's senior management may establish certain standards that deviate from historical patterns. These standards may, however, be consistent with the organization's chosen strategic directions and with management's sense of how the organization's balance sheet needs to be handled.

It is also possible that where industry norms are available, management will decide to deviate from them. Management may wish, for example, to tolerate longer collection periods for its accounts receivable than other organizations in its industry because it knows that many of its clients have difficulty making timely payments. Rather than insist on timely payments (which might result in a loss of clients), it may choose instead to accept a longer collection period. Indeed, this may be how it gains market share in a very competitive environment. Without knowing this kind of information, an external analyst has difficulty being critical of an organization's financial management practices.

The Need for Judgment. In summary, the use of ratio analysis to make comparisons between an organization and its "peers"—or among several similar organizations—must be done with great care. Not all organizations, even those in the same industry, prepare their financial statements in the same way or incorporate the same information into accounts with similar names. Thus, when ratios are used to compare two or more organizations, even if the ratios included in the comparison utilize very specific accounts on the financial statements, the results should be viewed with skepticism. In general, then, while comparisons among organizations *can* be made, or the ratios of a given organization *can* be related to an industry norm, the most valid comparisons usually are those made over time for a single organization.

Even when ratios are calculated historically for the same organization, however, changes in the organization's environment, strategy, or managerial tactics may invalidate the comparisons. In short, it seems quite clear that an external analyst must exercise considerable caution in interpreting an organization's ratios. About all the analyst can do is raise questions about the organization's profitability, liquidity, asset management, or long-term solvency decisions, but it is quite difficult to be critical or judgmental without some understanding of the organization's environment, strategy, and overall management. These matters are discussed in the next section.

A Disclaimer. There is no general agreement that the four categories of ratios discussed above are the most appropriate ones. In addition, some writers and analysts would assign some ratios to different categories. Still others would calculate the ratios themselves somewhat differently. They would use different numerators or denominators, for example, or they would use averages rather than ending amounts for balance sheet items.

These differences lose significance in light of the fundamental thrust of ratio analysis. Its purpose is not to arrive at the "right" ratio or the "right" classification. Rather, its purpose is to assist in the analysis of a set of financial statements, and to help understand an organization's financial management tactics. In this regard, the goal is to see what "story" a *set* of ratios tells about the entity. In general, greater precision in calculating certain ratios, or a reclassification of some of the ratios into different categories will not change that story much, if at all. Nevertheless, many analysts fall into the trap of worrying about the precision of specific ratio calculations and classifications rather than the overall story.

Summary

This section, which has looked at the role of ratio analysis, has begun the discussion of *financial analysis.* Financial analysis assesses the quality of an organization's financial statements—and thus its overall financial performance. It does so using ratio analysis, the statement of cash flows (SCF), and other related information. The next section focuses on the SCF and other kinds of information that might be used to analyze a set of financial statements. It also discusses a variety of financing considerations, including the concept of leverage and the role of surplus.

Financial Statement Analysis: Strategic Aspects

As the previous section indicated, ratio analysis can reveal a great deal of information about an organization's financial strengths and weaknesses, its operations, and its financial management activities. However, the value of ratio analysis depends to a great extent on the quality of the data that are used to construct the numerator and denominator of the calculations. In this section we examine the issue of data quality and build on ratio analysis by considering some additional aspects to analyzing a set of financial statements. Although there is no one "right" set of financial statements for an organization, certain techniques can be employed to determine whether and where potential problems exist.

Process of Financial Statement Analysis

As the discussion in the previous section pointed out, the purpose of financial statement analysis is not to determine whether an organization has followed generally accepted accounting principles. Nevertheless, prior to undertaking a financial analysis, we first must identify any accounting issues that would affect the conclusions of the analysis.

The distinction between *accounting* and *financial management issues,* although frequently ignored, is extremely important. There is little use in calculating a current ratio in the normal fashion, for example, if there is evidence to suggest that the organization has misclassified some of its current assets or current liabilities. Similarly, calculating a normal profit margin is of little value if the organization has some significant estimated expenses wherein the estimates may have been either unduly high or low—in either case, the profit margin will be misleading. Similar problems can exist for other ratios as well.

Accounting Issues. An important step in the process of financial statement analysis is to identify those accounts on the balance sheet and income statement that might have misleading numbers. In general (but not always), these will be accounts whose totals are derived through estimates. Some of the accounts that are candidates for having misleading numbers are the following:

- Bad debts, contractual allowances, and the allowance for doubtful accounts (accounts that rely on estimates and that will affect the profit margin and net accounts receivable figures)

- Inventory (where obsolescence, spoilage, or other forms of shrinkage may mean that the usable inventory is much less than the reported figure, or where the choice of an accounting system [LIFO (last in; first out) versus FIFO (first in; first out)] provides misleading information about the inventory's market value)
- Accumulated depreciation (which is affected by choices about economic lives and residual values of an entity's fixed assets)
- Any asset where amortization is involved and where the amortization schedule can result in a book value for the asset that diverges considerably from the asset's market value
- Any asset or liability where estimates affect both income on the income statement and the size of the asset or liability on the balance sheet

The *notes to the financial statements* are an important source of information concerning accounting estimates and their effect on the associated accounts. The notes are used by the organization's management to describe some of the underlying detail in the financial statements, disclose important accounting policies, and identify any special or unusual accounting practices followed in preparing the financial statements.

The notes should be read with care. They identify many of the accounting issues the organization faces and show how those issues affect the financial statements. For example, in the case of accounts receivable, the notes might contain a description of the organization's different types of clients, and the expectations for payment for each group. Frequently, the notes also provide a fair amount of information about the organization's debt structure, which can facilitate an analysis of long-term solvency.

The notes also explain the reasons for any "extraordinary items." Extraordinary items are highly unusual and nonrecurring financial events. Typically, they occur outside an organization's normal course of operations. They are identified separately, listed below the income from operations, and discussed in the notes.

Once significant accounting issues have been identified, an analyst can take one of three actions: (1) ignore them, (2) adjust the accounts to obtain more appropriate totals, or (3) keep them in mind in drawing conclusions. It would be appropriate to ignore relatively minor accounting issues or issues affecting accounts that were relatively unimportant to the rest of the analysis.

Adjusting accounts is difficult since it is rarely possible to obtain enough information to make appropriate emendations. Even if it were possible to obtain the information, in comparing the resulting account totals to totals from prior years or other organizations, the analyst would need to be sure that similar adjustments had been made in all accounts being compared. Because such adjustments are difficult to make, the third option probably is the most reasonable. That is, when ratios are calculated, the analyst would need to keep in mind that a more accurate accounting effort would result in slightly (or significantly) different ratio results.

Financial Management Issues. Having identified the significant accounting issues, and having made any necessary adjustments to the financial statements, the analyst can undertake an assessment of the financial management issues. This distinction between accounting and financial management issues is critical: accounting issues relate to the *validity (or accuracy)* of the figures on the financial statements, whereas financial management issues focus on the *meaning* of those figures. That is, in looking at financial management issues, analysts are attempting to assess an organization's profitability, liquidity, asset management, and long-term solvency. In so doing, they either assume that the figures on the financial statements are accurate or make appropriate modifications. The modifications can be either to the figures themselves prior to undertaking the financial analysis or to the conclusions, based on concerns with the accuracy of the accounting process.

Analyzing financial management issues requires three separate but related activities: calculating ratios, using the SCF, and relying on whatever other information is available.

Calculating ratios. Ratios are calculated in the manner shown in the prior section. These can lead to a variety of conclusions about the organization's financial management, especially when related to some standards. Analysts usually employ industry, historical, and other standards in this effort.

Using the SCF. Apart from ratios, the statement of cash flows can be a very powerful tool for understanding the kinds of financing decisions management has made during an accounting period, as well as management's ability to make effective and efficient use of the organization's assets. For example, the SCF can be used to determine whether an organization is financing itself appropriately (for example, using short-term debt to finance its seasonal and other short-term needs, and long-term debt and equity to finance its fixed assets).

Compiling other descriptive information. Most organizations publish annual reports or other literature that provide descriptive information about their operations. This can help an analyst determine the nature of the organization's activities, its environment, its strategy, and other matters relevant to the quality of its financial statements. Of course, if the analyst has an opportunity to interview the organization's management, he or she may be able to identify other factors that bear upon financial management decisions and their underlying rationale. All of these factors are important ingredients in a thorough analysis of an organization's financial statements. Taken together, they give some indication of the organization's financial management goals and constraints, and therefore some basis for identifying and analyzing the quality of management's performance in achieving the goals.

Beyond the use of ratios and a reliance on supplemental information, such as the SCF and the notes to the financial statements, an analyst also must have an understanding of some of the fundamental financing issues faced by almost all organizations. Two of these stand out as particularly significant: leverage and the role of a surplus (or profit). They relate to two questions addressed in any good analysis of fiscal management: (1) How much debt is appropriate for this organization? and (2) How large should this organization's surplus be?

Leverage

Leverage is a subject of great concern to managers of many organizations. In the previous section, it was defined as:

$$\frac{\text{Assets}}{\text{Equity (or Fund Balance)}}$$

If an organization had no debt whatsoever, its assets and equity would be equal, and its leverage ratio, therefore, would be one. As an organization begins to rely on debt to finance its assets, however, the ratio increases. In effect, leverage allows an organization to finance more assets than would be possible if it relied only on its own equity. This, in turn, allows it to deliver more services than otherwise would be possible, and therefore to earn more revenue.

Leverage has some drawbacks, however. Funds borrowed must be repaid, generally with interest. Organizations that rely heavily on borrowed funds spend considerable effort predicting and managing their cash flows to assure themselves of sufficient cash on hand to meet their debt service obligations.

Leverage can be assessed in terms of the *financial risk* it creates, compared with the organization's overall *business risk*. Financial risk and leverage are synonymous. That is, other things equal, high leverage means a high debt service obligation, which increases the risk that the entity will be unable to meet this obligation. Under these circumstances, it has high financial risk.

Business risk, by contrast, refers to the certainty of annual cash flows. Organizations that have high business risk have a high degree of uncertainty about their cash flows. A good example of an organization with a high business risk is a farming cooperative, where product availability and cost are greatly influenced by unpredictable climatic conditions. A good example of an organization with a low business risk is a day-care center located in a wealthy neighborhood with many dual-career couples. The farming cooperative quite likely would face a great deal of uncertainty about its annual cash flows, whereas the day-care center would be almost completely certain of its.

The combined effect of financial and business risk is illustrated in Figure 19.1. As it suggests, other things equal, an organization with low business risk can have a fairly high financial risk. Assuming management does not take on more debt service obligations than cash flow can support, the relative certainty of annual cash flows gives some reasonable assurance that debt service obligations can be met. By contrast, an organization with a high business risk generally would find it unwise to have high financial

Figure 19.1. Business Risk Versus Financial Risk.

Financial Risk

	Low	High
Low	Very safe	Possible
High	Necessary	Danger zone

Business Risk

Source: Young, 1994, p. 313. Used with permission.

risk. Since debt service obligations remain constant each year, the management could find itself in a situation where, because of events beyond its control, cash flows were insufficient to meet these obligations. The result could be detrimental to the organization's continued existence as a financially viable entity.

The Role of an Operating Surplus

Economists frequently cite profit as the fundamental characteristic of capitalism. According to them it motivates, measures success, and rewards. Indeed, economists see an adequate profit as a legitimate cost of operating an organization. It is excess profits (those greater than "normal") that give new organizations an impetus to enter a market. In the purely competitive model, excess profits entice new organizations to enter a market and increase the supply of goods and services. This continues until prices fall to a level where all organizations earn a normal profit. At that point, the market is in "equilibrium."

Accountants and managers view profit somewhat differently than economists. In the first place, as indicated in the first section of this chapter, profit (or net income) is simply the numerical difference between revenues and expenses. Second, in addition to providing a return to the owners of an organization, one of profit's principal purposes is to finance asset acquisitions. A basic financial management principle is that an organization should finance its fixed assets with some combination of long-term debt and equity. Contributions by donors and retained earnings from operations are the sources of equity. Also, as indicated earlier, not all contributions are available for any purpose management chooses. Because of this, earnings retained from operations — profit or surplus — become an important source of financing.

The financing role of a nonprofit's surplus is important. Universities that must add to plant capacity, purchase new and more sophisticated equipment, and the like have large fixed-asset bases; financing these assets entirely with debt could create debt service obligations that are difficult to meet. Moreover, even small nonprofit organizations—which must add office equipment, microcomputers, and the like as they develop and grow—have financing needs. Indeed, any organization that wishes to remain in a steady state must provide for the replacement of assets, since inflation, however slight, effectively serves to erode its asset base.

While it is true that organizations could avoid the need for a surplus by relying exclusively on long-term debt, this is not an adequate approach. For many organizations, there comes a point when debt has increased to the maximum prudent level; this is the point where annual cash flows are about equal to debt service obligations. At that point, equity is the only additional source of funds.

Surplus and Growth. Independent of its need for fixed assets, an organization experiencing growth in its revenues also requires increasing amounts of cash. For example, because of the time lag in collecting accounts receivable, an organization that is both growing and extending credit to its clients has increasing amounts of cash tied up in accounts receivable. This is the case for many nonprofits that sell services to a state government, for example. Moreover, organizations with sizable inventories need cash to finance the time that passes between acquiring inventory and either selling or using it.

In short, the cash outflows that take place between the acquisition of inventory and the collection of accounts receivable must be financed. If managers of growing organizations use debt to finance the increases in inventory and receivables, the organization's indebtedness will continue to expand until growth slows or stops.

While a variety of financing or strategic options other than debt exist for a rapidly growing organization, the five that have the greatest impact are (1) slowing growth, (2) shortening the collection period for accounts receivable, (3) shortening the inventory holding period, (4) extending the period for paying accounts payable, and (5) generating equity either through surplus or donor contributions. Reliance on debt—either long- or short-term—instead of one or more of the other options ordinarily will not suffice, since the debt will not be repayable until management invokes one of the five options.

How Much Surplus Is Needed? Because these two uses of surplus—fixed asset replacement and current asset growth—are so different, managers need to take different approaches to assess the surplus needed for each. The first is related to the financing of fixed assets; the second concerns providing the cash needs for growth.

Financing fixed assets. Most for-profit entities need to retain some of their earnings; they therefore need to establish selling prices to provide for both dividends plus the desired amount of retained earnings. Price, then, becomes one element of the profit formula, a formula that includes both volume and cost. Further, the required profit level generally is related to the organization's desired return on equity.

As emphasized in the section on calculating ratios, ROE is closely related to another figure of concern to managers: return on assets, or ROA. Indeed, as indicated in the discussion of ROA, if an organization — for-profit or nonprofit — does not obtain a sufficiently high return on assets, it will be unable to sustain itself over the long term (see the heading "Profitability Ratios," earlier in this chapter). This is because, as fixed assets wear out or become technologically obsolete, management must replace them and, because of inflation, doing so requires more funds than depreciation provides.

One way of analyzing this problem is with a combination of several ratios discussed in the prior section. The ratios in Exhibit 19.3 demonstrate some important relationships and highlight some key managerial concerns. In particular, two important questions emerge from a careful analysis of the distinction between ROA and ROE: (1) Which is the preferable measure? and (2) How much is enough? The first question is not trivial. By using leverage, an organization can transform a low ROA into a high ROE. A high ROE is no guarantee that assets can be replaced as they wear out, however. Indeed, if managers wish to replace assets without a decline in ROE, they must maintain their organization's leverage at the initial level, but often managers of highly leveraged organizations can neither obtain more debt nor refinance existing debt. As a result, they may not be able to replace their assets.

Exhibit 19.3. A System of Ratios.

$$\frac{\text{Net Income}}{\text{Revenue}} \times \frac{\text{Revenue}}{\text{Assets}} = \frac{\text{Net Income}}{\text{Assets}}$$

$$Profit\ margin \times Asset\ turnover = ROA$$

$$\frac{\text{Net Income}}{\text{Assets}} \times \frac{\text{Assets}}{\text{Equity}} = \frac{\text{Net Income}}{\text{Equity}}$$

$$ROA \times Leverage = ROE$$

Source: Young, 1994. Used with permission.

The second question can be answered by recognizing that, other things equal, an ROA equivalent to the rate of inflation is necessary to replace assets as they wear out. Therefore, the desired ROA figure needs to be at least as high as the rate of inflation, and higher if the organization is expanding its asset base.

Once a desired ROA figure has been selected, it can be attained by using a variety of combinations of margin and asset turnover. In general, the easiest approach to take is to determine a reasonable asset turnover level — based on, say, past performance — and to use it, in conjunction with the desired ROA figure, to calculate the necessary profit margin percentage. This, in turn, can be used to set *desired* prices at an appropriate level above expenses. While market forces and third party payers clearly will affect the prices an organization actually is able to charge, such an approach nevertheless provides a starting point. Moreover, it allows managers to determine which services and products are priced below desired levels, so that they can manage more effectively the cross-subsidization from other services and products.

Providing cash to support growth. The need for cash arises from a combination of three factors: profit margin, changes in current assets (especially accounts receivable and inventory), and changes in current liabilities (especially accounts payable). Exhibit 19.4 illustrates why organizations need additional cash. The exhibit looks at the effect of growth on cash that arises *only* out of the time lag in collecting accounts receivable, and when there is no surplus. Although additional cash requirements will result from the difference between the growth rate of remaining current assets and that of current liabilities, the most significant factor in many growing organizations generally is accounts receivable.

As this exhibit indicates, under these circumstances there is a constant need for cash. As a result, if managers use debt to finance their cash needs, they will not be able to repay the debt unless the growth rate slows or

Exhibit 19.4. Cash Needs Associated with Growth.

Assumptions:

1. Growth in revenue and expenses of approximately 2 percent a month.
2. Accounts receivable collection lag of two months.
3. Accounts payable paid immediately.
4. Inventory, prepaid expenses, and other current assets grow at same rate as revenue.
5. Current liabilities (other than payables) grow at same rate as inventory, prepaid expenses, and other current assets.

	Month					
	1	*2*	*3*	*4*	*5*	*6*
Operating statement:						
Revenue	100	102	104	106	108	110
Expenses	100	102	104	106	108	110
Surplus	0	0	0	0	0	0
Cash flow:						
Cash collections[a]	96	98	100	102	104	106
Cash payments[b]	100	102	104	106	108	110
Change in cash	(4)	(4)	(4)	(4)	(4)	(4)
Cumulative change	(4)	(8)	(12)	(16)	(20)	(24)

[a]From revenue earned two months ago that went into accounts receivable.
[b]Same as expenses due to assumptions 3, 4, and 5.
Source: Young, 1984, p. 316. Used with permission.

they take measures to lessen their need for cash (such as accelerating the collection of accounts receivable or delaying the payment of expenses). Therefore, under these circumstances, managers generally consider debt to be an undesirable alternative, and once again, a surplus is called for. In the simplified example in Exhibit 19.4, a surplus figure equivalent to the "change in cash" line would be satisfactory.

The Analytical Process

Most people will develop their own process for analyzing a set of financial statements. Some will begin by immediately calculating some ratios, others with a careful reading of the notes to the financial statements. Regardless of the sequence of steps taken, there are three activities that need to take place: strategic assessment, determination of accounting issues, and analysis of financial management issues.

Strategic Assessment. To put a set of financial statements into a context, it is helpful to try to gain an understanding of an organization's overall strategy. Doing so includes assessing the organization's environment, including identification of the relevant competitive and regulatory forces, the nature of the organization's clients, possible changes in client needs in the future, and so forth. In conducting this analysis, one attempts to answer two very basic sets of questions:

- What are this organization's critical success factors? That is, what must the organization do well to succeed? How, if at all, will these factors show up on the financial statements?
- What are the important (and tricky) accounting issues for this organization? Does it, for example, have volatile accounts receivable, so that the bad debt expense estimate is difficult to make?

Accounting Issues. In assessing the accounting issues that the organization faces, an analyst needs to spend some time reading the notes to the financial statements and attempting to answer the following questions: What accounting issues do the notes mention? How important are they?

To assess the importance of an accounting issue, one fairly easy technique is to identify the relatively large numbers on the financial statements and to ask whether a change in accounting policies would affect any of these numbers in a significant way. For example, if inventories constitute only 5 percent of the organization's total assets, the inventory accounting choice is probably relatively unimportant. On the other hand, if accounts receivable constitute 50 percent of assets, the analyst no doubt will want to learn about the process for estimating bad debts.

Clearly there are gray areas; thus it is not possible to say with total certainty how one determines significance. In general, however, the steps are as follows:

- Read the notes to the financial statements. What accounting issues do they suggest are present?
- Look for the large numbers on the financial statements. Are any influenced by estimates? What do the notes say about the estimates?
- Are any of the assets influenced by a distinction between book value and market value? What do the notes say about this distinction? What does intuition say? If, for example, the organization purchased a building in 1960 in a wealthy and growing neighborhood, the chances are good that the market value exceeds the book value.

Financial Management Issues. In assessing the significant financial management issues, many analysts proceed along the lines of the ratios discussed earlier, using the SCF and other information to support their analyses. A set of questions for each of the four ratio areas was given in the section on ratios. Some further considerations are given below:

Profitability. Once a set of ratios has been calculated, the analyst can ask the following questions:

- How does this organization generate a profit? Selling many units of a relatively low-margin item, or selling a few units of a relatively high-margin one?
- How do the ratios compare to conclusions from the strategic analysis?
- Is the organization earning a sufficiently high return on assets to counteract the forces of inflation? If not, what steps has it taken to correct for the deficiencies? What else might be done?

Liquidity. Here, the analysis can begin with a review of the statement of cash flows and with the computation of some of the liquidity ratios. Then the following questions can be addressed:

- Is this organization generating cash from operations? If not, why not?
- What are the organization's other sources of cash? Are these likely to continue into the future? How have they been managed over time?
- Given the strategic assessment, what is the "business risk" of this organization? That is, are its cash flows fairly predictable and certain from year to year (low business risk), or is there considerable uncertainty (high business risk)?

Asset management. The analysis here can begin with a review of the investing portion of the statement of cash flows, and with the calculation of the two asset management ratios, as well as the accounts receivable and inventory turnover ratios. The following questions can then be asked:

- How does the asset turnover compare to the expectations for this organization, given its industry? For example, is this an industry with low profit margins where high asset turnover is key to success? If so, how is this organization doing?

- How is the organization managing its current assets, particularly accounts receivable and inventory? Have these turnover rates been improving or worsening over the time period for which financial statements are available? Why?

Long-term solvency. The analysis here can begin with a review of the financing portion of the statement of cash flows, and the calculation of some of the long-term solvency ratios. Then the following questions can be asked:

- How has this organization structured its debt? Has it done a good job of matching the term of its debt to the life of its assets?
- How much leverage does this organization have? Does it have too much financial risk compared to its business risk (that is, is it in the "danger zone" on Figure 19.1)?
- What kind of debt service coverage does the organization have? Is there a reasonable margin for safety given its business risk?
- What does the environmental assessment indicate about the future for this organization? Are any of the circumstances surrounding its business risk likely to change? If so, how will the changes affect its business risk? What does this suggest for its debt?

Summary

This section and the previous one have provided an overview of some important aspects of financial analysis. Essentially, financial analysis consists of assessing the quality of an organization's financial statements — and thus its overall financial performance — through the use of ratio analysis, the statement of cash flows, and other related information. The SCF in particular provides some valuable insight into an organization's financial management activities over the course of the most recent accounting period.

Financing considerations inevitably result in the need to pay some attention to the issue of leverage. Indeed, one of the most important aspects of financial management is the management of debt, or leverage. Further, however, managers must be aware of the need to earn a sufficiently large surplus to provide for both asset replacement and the cash needs associated with growth, since to incur debt for these activities is to flirt with serious financial difficulties.

References

American Institute of Certified Public Accountants. *Audits of Colleges and Universities.* New York: AICPA, 1973.

Anthony, R. N. "Observations on Government Financial Accounting Research." *Government Accountants Journal,* 1989–90, *38*(4), 33–37.

Anthony, R. N. *Essentials of Accounting.* (5th ed.) Reading, Mass.: Addison-Wesley, 1993.

Anthony, R. N., and Young, D. W. *Management Control in Nonprofit Organizations.* (5th ed.) Homewood, Ill.: Richard D. Irwin, 1994.

Young, D. W. *Financial Control in Health Care.* Homewood, Ill.: Dow Jones–Irwin, 1984.

Young, D. W. *Introduction to Financial and Management Accounting: A User Perspective.* Cincinnati, Ohio: South-Western, 1994.

Additional Readings

General

Anthony, R. N. *Essentials of Accounting.* (5th ed.) Reading, Mass.: Addison-Wesley, 1993.

Douglas, P. P. *Governmental and Nonprofit Accounting: Theory and Practice.* Orlando, Fla.: Harcourt Brace Jovanovich, 1991.

Hay, L. E., and Wilson, E. R. *Accounting for Governmental and Nonprofit Entities.* Homewood, Ill.: Richard D. Irwin, 1992.

Henke, E. O. *Introduction to Nonprofit Organization Accounting.* (4th ed.) Cincinnati, Ohio: South-Western, 1992.

Lynn, E. S., and Freeman, R. J. *Fund Accounting Theory and Practice.* (2nd ed.) Englewood Cliffs, N.J.: Prentice-Hall, 1983.

Pahler, A. J., and Mori, J. E. *Advanced Accounting: Concepts and Practice.* (3rd ed.) New York: Harcourt Brace Jovanovich, 1988.

United Way of America. *Accounting and Financial Reporting: A Guide for United Ways and Not-for-Profit Human Service Organizations.* Alexandria, Va.: United Way of America, 1974.

Federal Government

Comptroller General of the United States (General Accounting Office). *Accounting Principles and Standards for Federal Agencies.* Washington, D.C.: Government Printing Office, 1972.

Health Care

American Institute of Certified Public Accountants. *Audits of Voluntary Health and Welfare Organizations.* New York: AICPA, 1974.

American Institute of Certified Public Accountants. *Healthcare Accounting and Audit Guide.* New York: AICPA, 1990.

Seawell, L. V. *Introduction to Hospital Accounting.* Dubuque, Ia.: Kendall/Hunt, 1992.

U.S. Department of Health, Education and Welfare. *A Guide for Non-Profit Institutions: Cost Principles and Procedures for Establishing Indirect Cost Rates for Grants and Contracts with the Department of Health, Education and Welfare.*

DHEW Publication No. (OS)72-28. Washington, D.C.: Government Printing Office, 1970.

State and Local Government

Governmental Accounting Standards Board. *Codification of Governmental Accounting and Financial Reporting Standards.* Norwalk, Conn.: GASB, annual publication.

20

Management Accounting

David W. Young

As the introductory paragraph in Chapter Nineteen indicated, management accounting is concerned with the information needs of individuals within an organization, principally its managers, planners, and staff analysts. Much of the material in management accounting is concerned with costs and cost behavior. However, costs can be seen through a variety of lenses. With *full cost accounting,* the main focus is on determining each service's or each program's fair share of the organization's costs. By contrast, *differential cost accounting* focuses on how costs change as circumstances change (such as when a program or a service is eliminated). With *management control systems,* the analysis of costs is made from the perspective of the individuals in an organization who control the various cost elements. These three types of costs are shown schematically in Exhibit 20.1.

Because of these different approaches, the central theme of this chapter is *different costs are used for different purposes.* There is nothing illegal or unethical about looking at costs differently for different purposes. Rather, as managers' decision-making needs change so do the costs that are relevant for a particular decision (Kaplan, 1988; Cooper and Kaplan, 1988). Moreover, there is considerable room for judgment in management accounting, and managers frequently need to consider a variety of nonquantitative factors before arriving at a decision.

Note: Much of the content of this chapter has been adapted from Anthony and Young (1994), Young (1994), and Young and Pearlman (1993).

Exhibit 20.1. Different Costs for Different Purposes.

	Type of Management Accounting		
	Full Cost Accounting	*Differential Cost Accounting*	*Management Control Systems*
Costs Used	Direct and indirect	Fixed and variable	Controllable and noncontrollable
Activities Performed	Assignment to cost centers	Analysis of cost behavior	Programming
	Choice of allocation bases	Break-even analysis	Budgeting
	Allocation of service center costs to revenue centers	Contribution analysis	Measurement and variance analysis
			Reporting and evaluation
Management Uses/Decisions	Pricing	Add or discontinue a program or service	Program additions and modifications
	Some cost control	Contract out	Cost control
		Offer a special price	Performance measurement
		Sell an obsolete asset	

Source: Young, 1994, p. 359. Used with permission.

The discussion of management accounting is divided into four broad sections. The first examines full cost accounting. The second discusses differential cost accounting. The third discusses management control systems (sometimes called "responsibility accounting"). The final section looks at some of the management control issues that arise under Total Quality Management (TQM), or what is called here the design of *administrative systems*.

Full Cost Accounting

An answer to the question What did it cost? is perhaps one of the most slippery in both for-profit and nonprofit organizations. The question is rather easily answered if one is discussing the purchase of inputs (supplies, labor, and so on) for the production or service delivery process. Even calculating a total cost of a unit produced—be it a widget or fifty minutes of psychotherapy—is relatively easy as long as the organization is producing goods or services that are completely homogeneous. Complications arise, however, when an organization produces multiple goods and services, particularly when it uses different kinds and amounts of resources to manufacture the goods or provide the services. This section addresses some of the key decisions that are made in a cost accounting context, focusing on how those decisions can influence the answer to the question What did it cost?

Issues to Consider in Calculating Full Costs

An assessment of costs is inherently complex in any large organization. Nevertheless, selecting a methodology is important, not only to help assure accurate cost measurement, but especially if one wishes to undertake cost *comparisons* between or among sites, as is the case for many managers, third party payers, and policy makers (Young, 1988).

Comparable cost data are especially difficult to obtain in many nonprofit organizations because of the effects on costs of such variables as client mix, service mix and intensity, standby capacity, seasonal program utilization patterns, overlapping programs, the use by clients of ancillary or collateral services, managerial efficiency, and geographical differences in wages and supply prices. Thus, before discussing a cost accounting methodology, we must first address the more conceptual question of the factors that influence costs.

Resource Usage: A Conceptual Framework

The fundamental issue that cost accounting attempts to address is the *use of resources*. Accordingly, an appropriate question to ask is What are these resources and how might they be defined and measured?

At the most fundamental level, the resources used in any production effort — nonprofit or otherwise — are the classic ones of the economist: land, labor, and capital. As Figure 20.1 indicates, the most complex resources are labor and capital.

The Labor Resource. Labor can be classified as either professional or administrative. Professional labor is done by individuals such as physicians, nurses, social workers, curators, mental health counselors, teachers, and so forth. Administrative labor can be subdivided into professional support and general support.

Professional support labor is done by individuals who perform the administrative activities within any given professional department (for example, scheduling visits in an ambulatory care center or providing secretarial support for a research project). General support can be divided between program services and general administration. The former includes those administrative functions that provide direct support to the organization's programs, such as housekeeping or laundry in a hospital. General administration consists of staff in the organization's central office, who perform activities that typically are unrelated to specific programs or services, such as computer operations, legal work, and billing.

The Capital Resource. Capital can be classified as either program or administrative. The former includes all capital resources needed to provide direct support to the service delivery activity, and can be further categorized as short-lived (used up in one year or less) or long-lived (used up over several years). Short-lived capital consists principally of client- or program-related supplies, such as syringes in a hospital, or classroom materials in a high school. Long-lived capital includes equipment and facilities used in client-related activities. Computer facilities, beds, laboratory equipment, and sports equipment are all examples of long-lived program capital.

Administrative capital is also either short-lived or long-lived, and consists of those items that provide general support rather than support to a specific program or service delivery. Supplies used in the president's office of a university are an example of short-lived administrative capital. Similarly, equipment such as photocopying machines, fax machines, and an administrative computing center would be considered long-lived administrative capital.

Units of Measure. Land is usually rather easily measured in terms of rent per unit of time (such as a month). The cost of labor is measured by wages — either per unit of time or per unit of activity (for example, a procedure, a visit, or a class session). Short-lived capital — either program or administrative — usually is measured in terms of the factor price per unit — what the organization paid to obtain the item. Long-lived capital typically is measured in terms of depreciation per unit of time.

The Cost Accounting Methodology

Relating resources to costs puts cost accounting into its broader economic context. Specifically, the principal goal of cost accounting is to measure as accurately as possible the consumption of resources associated with producing a particular good or delivering a particular service. In some instances, the measurement process is quite easy. For example, an organization that produces a single good or delivers a single service has little difficulty calculating the cost of each unit. All costs associated with the organization, and hence the good or service, can be added together and divided by the number of units produced or delivered during a particular accounting period to arrive at a unit cost.

Organizations that produce a variety of goods or deliver multiple services — each requiring different amounts of land, labor, and capital — have a much more difficult time determining unit costs. This more complex process requires managers to make several decisions: these are (1) defining a cost object, (2) determining cost centers, (3) distinguishing between direct and indirect costs, (4) choosing bases for allocating overhead costs, (5) selecting a "step-down" sequence, and (6) choosing between process and job order accounting. Together these six determinations constitute the cost accounting methodology. Each is discussed briefly below.

1. Defining the Cost Object. The cost object is the unit of good or service for which we wish to know the cost. Generally, as the cost object becomes

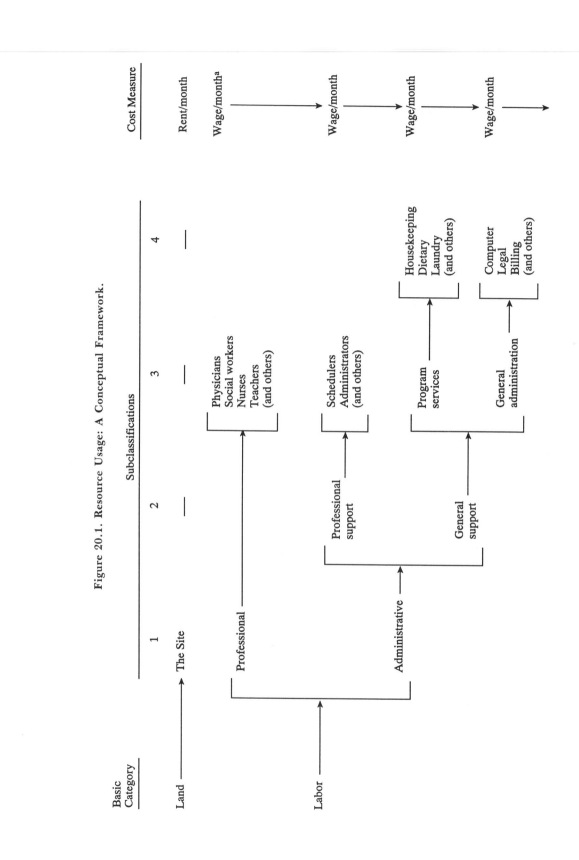

Figure 20.1. Resource Usage: A Conceptual Framework.

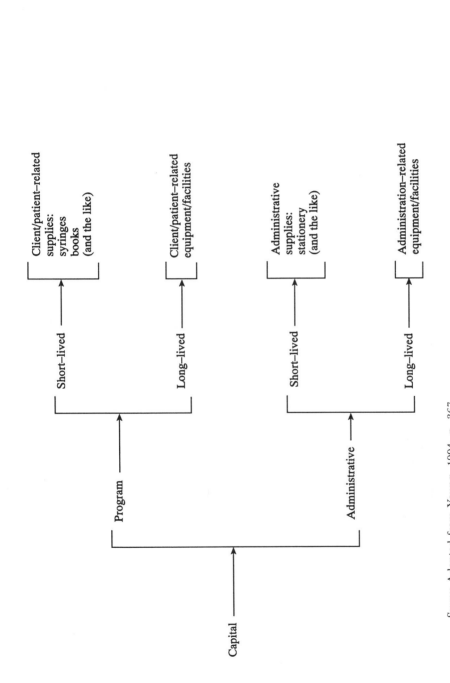

Source: Adapted from Young, 1994, p. 367.

more specific, the methodology necessary to account for the associated costs becomes more complex. In some acute care hospitals, for example, the cost object is a day of care. Sometimes the day is "all inclusive"; that is, it includes surgical procedures, laboratory tests, radiology exams, pharmaceutical dispensation, and so on. When this is the case, determining the cost of a day of care is relatively simple.

In most hospitals, the cost object is more specific than an all-inclusive day of care. In some instances, for example, the day of care is for "routine" activities only (room, dietary, nursing, and similar costs), and separate cost objects exist for other activities, such as laboratory tests.

It is also possible to consider a cost object that is totally different from a day of care—an admission, for example, or an episode of illness. If an admission is the cost object, we would include all costs associated with the patient's entire stay in the hospital (that is, for all days of care, rather than just an average single day). If we chose an episode of illness as our cost object, we would then include costs for *all admissions* associated with a particular illness for a given patient. Similar choices must be made in other nonprofit settings. For example, in a college, one cost object might be cost per course; another might be cost per student. If the latter, the choice might be further narrowed between cost per graduate student and cost per undergraduate student, or cost per science student and cost per humanities student.

2. Determining Cost Centers. The choice of cost centers affects the way cost data are accumulated. In effect, cost centers are categories used to collect cost information. To understand how they work, consider again an organization that delivers a single service. The organization may treat itself as a single cost center, thereby creating a relatively simple cost accounting system. In this case, the category used to collect cost information would be the organization itself.

Alternatively, the organization may subdivide itself into several cost centers—such as direct care delivery, administration, housekeeping, and the like—for purposes of the cost accounting effort. If this is done, the cost of a particular cost object will be the sum of the costs attributed to it in each of the cost centers.

The value that derives from the extra effort associated with separating an organization into multiple cost centers depends largely on management's intended uses of the information. For example, a multiple cost center structure may help management compare its costs with those of other organizations, which may assist it with cost control. A comparison between a museum's administrative costs and those of other similar museums, for example, could reveal areas of potential inefficiency, thereby assisting management in its efforts to improve the museum's administrative operations. Of course, in undertaking an analysis of this sort, there are many comparability problems similar to those that relate to ratios, discussed in Chapter Nineteen.

Another potential use of the multi-cost-center structure is pricing, either for clients or for reimbursement from third parties. If each program (or service) offered by an organization were represented by a cost center, then the costs of that center could be used as the basis for setting the appropriate rates.

In a multi-cost-center structure, an organization's cost centers generally are divided into two broad categories: *revenue centers* and *service centers*. Revenue centers, as the name implies, are those that charge for (or are reimbursed for) their activities. They sometimes are called "mission centers" since they are considered to represent the organization's mission.

Service centers, by contrast, accumulate the costs of those activities the organization carries out to support its revenue centers. In a university, maintenance and administration would be considered service centers, while the school of social work or a university-wide program would be a revenue center. A service center does not need to be a physical location. For example, in most organizations, institution-wide (as opposed to department-specific) depreciation, personnel services, plant maintenance, and the like generally are service centers.

Since service center costs are allocated to revenue centers, the cost for a given cost object depends upon (a) the revenue center or centers in which a client receives services, (b) the number of units of service received in each center, and (c) the cost per unit of service. This latter element not only depends on the costs in the revenue center itself but also the costs of the institution's service centers that are allocated to the revenue center. In general, the full cost accounting system attempts to allocate each revenue center its "fair share" of the organization's service center costs.

3. Distinguishing Between Direct and Indirect Costs.

A third distinction made in a cost accounting system is between direct and indirect costs. *Direct costs* are unambiguously associated with, or physically traceable to, a specific cost center. *Indirect costs* apply to more than one cost center, and thus must be distributed among the cost centers that use them.

Again, under the simplest of circumstances, where an organization produced one product or service in one cost center, there would be no indirect costs; it would not be possible to have costs that applied to more than one cost center. The creation of multiple cost centers means that some costs become indirect, thereby necessitating their distribution or *assignment*.

4. Choosing Allocation Bases for Service Center Costs.

The fourth step in the cost accounting process is the allocation of service center (or *overhead*) costs to revenue centers. In doing so, the accountants must determine an *allocation basis* for each service center that accurately measures its use by the remaining cost centers (both other service centers as well as revenue centers). Examples of allocation bases are square feet and salary dollars. In effect, *allocation,* as it is defined here, is the process of distributing service center costs to revenue centers to determine the full cost of each revenue center.

(Accountants are not always consistent in their use of this terminology. For example, an allocation is sometimes called an "apportionment" and vice versa. The context usually will clarify the meaning.)

Precision of allocation bases. In the context of deciding on allocation bases, it should be noted that increased precision generally requires greater effort and hence higher accounting costs. For example, housekeeping costs are frequently allocated on the basis of square feet. Alternatively, and more accurately, housekeeping costs could be allocated on the basis of hours of service. Clearly, although hours of service is a more accurate base, and would give us a more accurate full cost figure, its use requires a possibly costly compilation of the necessary data.

The choice of using the more accurate basis depends to a great extent on the uses management might make of the information. In some instances, the information can improve pricing decisions; in others, it will have an effect on the institution's reimbursement from third party payers; in still others, it may influence the motivation of people responsible for managing the cost centers. These and other similar considerations will determine whether a more accurate — and generally more costly — allocation basis should be used.

In sum, the more precise the assignment and allocation processes, the more accurately one can capture true resource consumption. Exact measurement of resource consumption can be a time-consuming and complicated process, however, and thus less accurate measurement procedures often are adopted in response to time, staffing, and technical constraints.

To allocate service center costs, then, we must (1) determine the direct costs of each cost center, (2) assign indirect costs to the appropriate cost centers, (3) choose an allocation basis for each service center, and (4) use the allocation basis to allocate service center costs to revenue centers.

5. The Stepdown Method. Several methods of varying complexity and accuracy can be used to allocate service center costs to revenue centers; the *stepdown* method is the most common. Its use is based on its relative ease of application. In health care, since it traditionally has been the method preferred by the American Hospital Association, it is required by many third party payers.

The stepdown procedure is a method of sequentially "trickling down" service center costs into revenue centers. This process is shown schematically in Exhibit 20.2. It begins with the first service center in the sequence, and spreads that center's costs over the remaining service centers as well as revenue centers. The distribution is based on the use of the service centers by other cost centers as determined by the chosen allocation basis. This process is followed for all remaining service centers.

In Exhibit 20.2, the total direct plus assigned costs — $10,000, shown in the row labeled "housekeeping" — are *allocated* to the remaining cost centers; the allocation is shown in the *column* labeled "housekeeping (square feet)." The term "square feet" indicates that that measure is the basis for the alloca-

Exhibit 20.2. The Stepdown Method Illustrated.

	Cost Centers	Direct Plus Assigned Costs	Housekeeping (square feet)	Administration[c] (Salary $)	Total Costs
Service Centers	Housekeeping	10,000			
	Administration	54,425	4,375[a]		
Revenue Centers	Client Services	109,575	4,375[a]	47,040[d]	160,990
	Client Education	26,000	1,250[b]	11,760[e]	39,010
	Total Costs	200,000	10,000	58,800	200,000

Note: All numbers are hypothetical, for illustrative purposes only.

[a]$1.25 per square foot x 3,500 square feet = $4,375.
[b]$1.25 per square foot x 1,000 square feet = $1,250.
[c]Administration costs = $58,800 ($54,425 + $4,375); see line labeled "Administration." Salary dollars in Client Services and Client Education = $105,000 ($84,000 + $21,000). Therefore, Administration costs per salary dollar = $56 ($58,800 + $105,000).
[d]$.56 per salary dollar x $84,000 salary dollars = $47,040.
[e]$.56 per salary dollar x $21,000 salary dollars = $11,760.

Source: Adapted from Young, 1994.

tion. The row amount ($10,000) has a heavy black outline; the allocations are shown in the shaded box, with a total at the bottom.

With the allocation of the housekeeping costs, the administration service center now has a total of $58,800 to be allocated. This is the sum of its $54,425 of direct plus assigned costs, *plus* the $4,375 of housekeeping costs allocated to it. The amount to be allocated is shown in the heavily outlined box in the row labeled "administration" (the sum of the two amounts is not shown). Administration costs are allocated using salary dollars (shown in parentheses in the column labeled "administration"), and the shaded box shows how the $58,800 was allocated to the remaining cost centers — the two revenue centers, in this case. The total amount allocated is shown at the bottom of the column. The result is that the total costs in this organization's revenue center are their direct and assigned costs plus those costs allocated to them from the service centers.

Determining the sequence. The sequence followed in allocating the service centers can affect the costs in each revenue center (although not total costs, which will remain the same — $200,000 in the above example — under all sequences). Occasionally, the sequence decision will have a significant effect on a particular revenue center, however.

In general, service centers are allocated in order of their use by other service centers. That is, the service center that uses other service centers' resources the *least* is allocated *first,* and the service center that uses other service centers' resources the *most* is allocated *last.* Clearly, judgment is involved in determining this sequence.

Important features of the stepdown method. There are several important features of the stepdown method.

1. Only service center costs are allocated. Revenue center costs are not. Revenue centers receive costs from service centers, but once a cost has been allocated to a revenue center it stays there.
2. The "basis of allocation" for each service center represents an attempt to measure the use of that center's resources by the remaining cost centers — both other service centers and revenue centers. For example, "pounds of laundry" is frequently used as the basis for allocating the costs of a laundry service center. When this is the case, each cost center receives a portion of the institution's laundry costs based on the total pounds of laundry it sends to be processed. If a particular cost center sends no laundry, it would not receive any allocation of the laundry center's costs.
3. The amount of a given service center's costs allocated to a particular revenue center will depend, in part, on whether that service center is allocated early or late in the sequence. If it is allocated late in the sequence, it will be "loaded" with some costs from service centers allocated earlier in the sequence. If it is allocated early, it will not.
4. Total costs do not change. All that changes with different allocation bases and stepdown sequences is the distribution of total costs among the various cost centers.

6. *Choosing Between Process and Job Order Cost Systems*. A final decision in a full cost accounting system concerns the way revenue center costs are distributed to an organization's cost objects. Although there is a range of choices, we will look only at the two ends of the spectrum. At one end is the *process method,* which typically is used when all units of output are roughly identical. The production of chairs, plastic cups, and so on — often performed by a production line — usually calls for a process method. All production-related costs for a given accounting period are calculated and divided by the total number of units produced to give an average cost per unit.

At the other end of the spectrum is the *job order method,* which typically is used when the units of output are quite different. A good example is an automobile repair garage, where adding all costs for a given accounting period, such as a day, and dividing by the number of cars repaired to determine an average cost per repaired car, almost certainly would provide quite misleading information to management. Instead, the cost accounting system uses a job ticket to record the time and parts associated with each repair effort; these are then costed out by means of hourly wage rates and unit prices.

In choosing between a process and a job order method, managers frequently are weighing the expense associated with the increased reporting and processing effort of the job order method with the managerial benefits (such as competitive pricing needs and the management control potential) that such a system provides. As with many other managerial activities, the choice between the two methods — or among a variety of intermediate methods possessing some characteristics of both job order and process — rarely is a completely clear one.

Summary of Cost Accounting Choices. As the above discussion has indicated, the choices involved in developing a cost accounting system frequently are quite difficult. Moreover, they are highly interdependent. For example, the choice of cost centers will influence the distinction between direct and indirect costs. The choice of a particular cost object frequently will require the use of certain kinds of cost centers. And the allocation of service center costs will be determined, in part, by the choice of the service centers themselves and by the assignment process that is used.

In this context, it is important to reiterate that any changes in the total of one cost center are always accompanied by changes in another direction to the totals in one or more other cost centers. That is, once incurred, *total costs* will be the same on any given cost report. Thus, the effect of any change in methodology is solely one of making shifts among cost centers. Sometimes these cost shifts can be quite significant, however.

Full Cost Accounting and Third Party Reimbursement

In most for-profit organizations, full cost accounting is a management accounting activity; that is, full cost data are rarely if ever presented to outsiders. This is not the case in some nonprofit organizations. For example, to receive reimbursement from third party payers (such as Medicare, Medicaid, and many Blue Cross plans), health care organizations must comply with a variety of requirements related to the full cost accounting process. These reimbursement requirements include distinctions between direct and indirect costs, as well as methods for allocating service center costs to revenue centers. Further, most third party payers require that organizations reimbursed by them prepare cost reports on a regular basis.

As a result of this constrained decision-making ability in the full cost accounting process, the cost reports that are prepared for third party payers frequently do not represent the "full cost" of a particular activity as accurately as might be desired for internal purposes. Indeed, some would argue that when third party reimbursement is involved, the purpose of a cost report is not to measure the costs of programs, but to maximize reimbursement. A focus on reimbursement maximization means that similar cost centers delivering similar services quite likely will have different costs from one organization to the next. These differences are not due to variations in actual resource consumption, however, but to variations in cost accounting methodologies. Consequently, attempts to use third party cost reports to make cost center comparisons among organizations should be viewed with some skepticism.

In sum, the principal purpose of full cost accounting is to help management measure the resources devoted to a particular cost object, and to use that information internally for pricing, profitability analysis, or control. This is not the case in nonprofit organizations that receive third party reimbursement, however. As a consequence, the cost reports prepared for third party payers are not particularly valuable as management tools.

Differential Cost Accounting

As mentioned in the introduction to this chapter, one of the most significant aspects of cost accounting is the notion that "different costs are used for different purposes." The full cost accounting principles discussed in the previous section, while valuable for activities such as pricing and reimbursement, have some important limitations. Specifically, they are not appropriate for several types of alternative choice decisions that must be made frequently by nonprofit organization managers. These decisions include whether to (1) continue or eliminate a program or service, (2) make or buy (that is, do the work yourself or contract out for services), (3) accept or reject a special request (such as to sell a service below full cost to use a certain amount of otherwise unused capacity), or (4) sell obsolete supplies or equipment. For these types of decisions, the appropriate information is *differential costs*.

The key question asked in the context of the above decision situations is, How will costs (and revenues) change under the new set of circumstances? If a program or service is discontinued, for example, some costs will be eliminated, but so, usually, will some revenues. Similarly, adding a program ordinarily will add both revenues and costs. In a decision to make or buy, in contrast, certain costs will be eliminated but other costs will be incurred. In the decision to accept a special request or to sell obsolete assets, certain revenues will be received, but costs will not change in accordance with the indications of a full cost analysis.

As this section explains, full cost information can be misleading in analyzing the financial consequences of alternative choice decisions. Indeed, to use full cost information as a basis for deciding which costs will change or how costs will change under alternative sets of circumstances, can lead to managerial decisions that are financially detrimental to the organization.

The process of differential cost analysis in nonprofit organizations will vary depending on the type of organization where the analysis is taking place. Organizations that are paid according to their fees or that operate with an essentially fixed budget (such as health maintenance organizations, some membership organizations, and many government agencies) typically will undertake the same sort of differential cost analysis as a for-profit organization.

Nonprofit organizations that derive a portion of their revenue from cost-based reimbursement will find it necessary to undertake a different form of differential cost analysis. To illustrate the differences as clearly as possible, this section first addresses the nature of costs and then discusses the process of differential cost analysis as performed in for-profit organizations; included are illustrations of the concepts of *contribution* and *sunk costs*. Once terms and concepts have been defined, the subject of break-even analysis, a special form of differential cost analysis, can be addressed. Finally, the somewhat more complex process of differential cost analysis under cost-based reimbursement can be discussed.

The Nature of Costs

Fundamental to any analysis of differential costs is the question of cost behavior. Cost behavior can best be considered by distinguishing between fixed and variable costs, including the refinements of semivariable and step-function costs. These distinctions let an analyst see how a change in the volume of activity of a given cost center will affect the center's costs. A discussion of each cost type follows. (Some forms of differential analysis do not look at cost behavior in relation to changes in volume. Since these situations are infrequent, the following discussion focuses exclusively on cost-volume relationships.)

Fixed Costs. Fixed costs are costs that remain at the same level regardless of the number of units of service delivered. While no costs are fixed if the time period is long enough, the *relevant range* for fixed costs (that is, the span of units over which they remain unchanged), or the time period within which they are considered, generally is quite large. A good example of a fixed cost in most organizations is rent. Ordinarily, regardless of the number of clients seen, the amount of rent the organization pays remains the same.

Step-Function Costs. Step-function costs are similar to fixed costs, except they have a much narrower relevant range; as such, they increase in a "steplike" fashion. An example of a step-function cost in most organizations is supervision. As the number of nurses, social workers, or other professionals increases, the organization must add supervisory personnel. Since most organizations find it difficult to add part-time supervisors, supervisory costs will tend to behave in a step-function fashion.

Variable Costs. Variable costs change in a roughly linear fashion with volume changes. That is, as volume changes, total variable costs change in some constant proportion. The result is a straight line, the slope of which is determined by the amount of variable costs associated with each unit of output. An example of a variable cost in a nonprofit organization is membership (or client-related) supplies, which will change in almost direct proportion to changes in the number of members or clients. Some organizations will have relatively high variable costs per unit, while others will have variable costs that are relatively low for each unit of output.

Semivariable Costs. Semivariable costs share features of both fixed and variable costs. There is a minimum level of costs that is fixed, but the cost line then increases with increases in volume. The result is a line that begins at some level above zero, and slopes upward in a linear fashion. A good example of a semivariable cost is electricity. Typically, there is some base cost each month for electrical service that an organization must incur even if it uses none at all. Costs then increase in a linear fashion with the number of kilowatt-hours used. Similar cost patterns exist for other utilities as well, such as telephone, gas, and water.

Cost Behavior in Organizational Settings. The four different cost types are shown schematically in Figure 20.2. Classifying an organization's costs into these categories requires analyzing the actual or expected behavior of each cost item, and attempting to determine how costs will change with changes in the volume of activity.

The Differential Cost Concept

An understanding of cost behavior according to the fixed, step-function, variable, or semivariable nature of costs facilitates a differential cost analysis. Effectively, the analyst attempts to identify the behavior of an organization's costs under different sets of assumptions so that cost behavior can be related to the type of decision being made. There are several principles that must be kept in mind in undertaking such an analysis.

Principle 1. Full Cost Information Can Be Misleading. The kind of information available from most full cost accounting systems can produce misleading results if it is used in differential cost analyses. This is due mainly

Figure 20.2. Types of Costs.

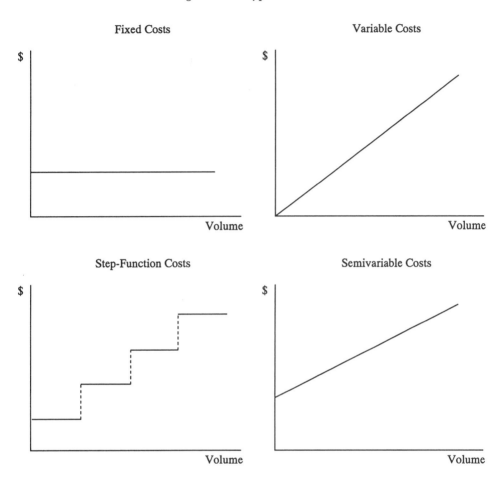

Source: Young, 1994. Used with permission.

to the *apparent* behavior of overhead costs when allocated as contrasted with their true behavior.

Principle 2. Differential Costs Can Include Both Fixed and Variable Costs.
Although it may seem paradoxical, differential costs can include both fixed and variable costs. A program manager's salary, for example, ordinarily would be considered a fixed cost. Yet, the elimination of the program would completely eliminate the cost. The key point is that as long as we operate the program, we have the fixed cost of the manager's salary; it does not fluctuate in accordance with the number of clients (within the relevant range). But when we eliminate the program, we also eliminate the entire cost; thus, it is differential in terms of a decision to eliminate or retain the program.

Principle 3. Assumptions Are Needed. Differential cost analysis invariably requires assumptions. All differential analyses focus on what will happen in the future, thereby requiring assumptions about many factors, from unit prices to staff efficiency. In addition, inflation will affect an organization's costs, and it may be possible for the organization to raise its own prices. Moreover, the general state of the economy along with a wide variety of other matters will affect volume. Of course, managers make many decisions where they do not have perfect knowledge of the future. An alternative choice decision involving cost behavior thus is one of many decisions requiring assumptions.

Because assumptions play such a crucial role in a differential analysis, the analyst needs to identify and document them as completely as possible. Furthermore, the analyst needs to explore how changes in the assumptions would affect the conclusions of the analysis. This latter activity generally is called sensitivity analysis.

Principle 4. Information Must Be Structured Appropriately for Decision-Making Purposes. Information for differential cost analyses is structured differently than it is for full-cost analyses. In particular, a key question in differential cost analysis is the behavior of overhead (or service center) costs. Ordinarily, an analysis of differential costs is most easily performed when the fixed and variable costs of the particular activity itself are analyzed separately from the organization's overhead costs.

An analysis that separates costs in this way, usually is structured in terms of the *contribution* of the particular program, product, or service to the organization's overhead costs. Contribution is the amount that each program or service in the organization has left after its program-specific costs (variable, semivariable, fixed, and step-function) have been deducted from its revenue. This is the amount that it contributes to the recovery of the organization's overhead costs.

If a particular program or service is losing money on a full cost basis but is contributing to the coverage of the organization's overhead costs, management generally would not want to eliminate it in the short run. In effect, eliminating it would reduce the total contribution to overhead costs and thus would either reduce the organization's surplus or increase its deficit. (Over the longer run, of course, management has a more strategic choice to make as to whether it wishes to carry a program that does not cover its full costs.)

Principle 5. Ignore Sunk Costs. One of the most difficult aspects of differential cost analysis concerns the concept of sunk costs. Since an alternative choice decision always looks toward the future rather than the past, full cost analyses, which typically rely on historical data, are inappropriate for these kinds of decisions. Nevertheless, even when their efforts are focused on the future, analysts frequently are plagued by history, particularly when it presents itself in the form of sunk costs.

The term *sunk cost* is used to refer to an expenditure that was made in the past, that appears on a full cost report, but that, because it already has been incurred and the decision cannot be changed, is inappropriate for future considerations. Thus, it should not be incorporated into a differential cost analysis (which is concerned only with the future). The classic example of a sunk cost is depreciation. Although depreciation appears on a full cost report, its inclusion in a differential cost analysis is inappropriate since it will not change regardless of the alternative chosen.

For most people, the notion of sunk costs is difficult to accept. Since sunk costs are present in many alternative choice decisions, however, analysts should make the effort to become comfortable in dealing with them.

Break-Even Analysis

One important technique used in differential cost situations is break-even analysis. The intent of break-even analysis is to determine the volume of activity at which the total revenue for an organization (or a program in an organization) equals its total costs. A break-even analysis thus begins with the fundamental equation:

$$\text{Total revenue (TR)} = \text{Total costs (TC)}$$

Total revenue for many activities is quite easy to calculate. If we assume that an organization's charge per unit (or price) is represented by the letter p and its volume by the letter x, then total revenue is equal to price times volume:

$$\text{TR} = px$$

Total costs are somewhat more complicated. Break-even analysis requires a recognition of the previously discussed types of cost behavior in an organization: fixed, step-function, variable, and semivariable. In a situation where there were no step-function or semivariable costs, the formula would be quite simple:

$$\text{Total costs} = \text{Fixed costs} + \text{Variable costs}$$

Fixed costs generally are represented by the letter a, and variable costs *per unit* by the letter b. Thus, total variable costs can be represented by the term bx, where, as before, x represents volume. The resulting cost equation is as follows:

$$\text{TC} = a + bx$$

This means that the fundamental break-even equation can be shown as:

$$px = a + bx$$

Thus, if we know price, fixed costs, and variable costs per unit, we can solve the formula algebraically for *x*, which would be the break-even volume. Similarly, if we know any three of the four items in the equation, we can solve for the fourth.

Unit Contribution Margin. An important aspect of break-even analysis is the concept of unit contribution margin. This is the contribution to fixed costs that comes about as a result of each additional unit sold. In effect, the unit contribution margin is the difference between price and unit variable cost, or *p – b*. Thus, by rearranging the terms of the break-even formula, we can arrive at the conclusion that break-even volume is simply fixed costs divided by unit contribution margin, as follows:

$$px = a + bx$$

$$px - bx = a$$

$$x\,(p - b) = a$$

$$x = \frac{a}{(p - b)}$$

In effect, price minus unit variable cost tells us how much each unit sold contributes the recovery of fixed costs. Thus, when we divide this amount into fixed costs, we arrive at the volume (number of units of activity) needed to recover all our fixed costs. This is our break-even volume.

Special Considerations in Break-Even Analysis. There are a number of special considerations that can complicate a break-even analysis. Two of the most significant are the presence of semivariable and/or step function costs, and the existence of more than one product.

　　Break-even with semivariable and/or step-function costs. Incorporating semivariable costs into a break-even analysis is relatively easy. Since semivariable costs have a fixed component and a variable component, an analyst simply needs to add the fixed component to the fixed cost total, and add the unit variable cost amount to the existing unit cost amount.

　　The introduction of step-function costs is conceptually more difficult than it might first appear. Ideally, we would like to assume that, for any given relevant range, we could simply add together the step-function costs and the fixed costs to give us the total applicable fixed costs. We then could use the formula as described above. Unfortunately, the process is not quite that simple. In many instances, the break-even volume will be invalid for the relevant range of the step-function costs, and a new break-even analysis will need to be conducted until a valid solution is found. In short, incorporation of step-function costs in the break-even formula requires a trial-and-error process to reach the break-even volume.

　　Break-even with multiple products or services. Thus far, the discussion about break-even calculations has involved only one product or service. When there are two or more products or services involved in the calculation, the analysis can become considerably more complicated, mainly because of the impact of the mix of products or services on the break-even number. That is, since some products or services ordinarily will have a higher contribution margin than others, a break-even volume with multiple products or services is very unstable—as the product or service mix changes, so will the break-even volume. It is important to bear in mind, however, that an unstable break-even figure only exists when the individual contribution margins are quite different. If they are roughly similar, changes in mix, even if they are large, will have relatively little impact on the break-even number.

Differential Cost Analysis Under Cost-Based Reimbursement

Recognizing that differential costs are the proper costs to use for alternative choice decisions is sufficient to provide a focus for the analytical efforts involved in such decisions, but it by no means simplifies either the decisions themselves or the analyses that underlie them. Indeed, there generally are a variety of strategic aspects to these decisions that go beyond the financial analysis and create highly complex situations. Adding to this complexity in many nonprofit organizations is the presence of cost-based reimbursement.

Cost-based reimbursement is used by third-party payers in some nonprofit settings. Rather than paying an organization's charges, these payers reimburse its costs. In these instances, any projected savings from contracting out or dropping a product or service must be reduced by the percentage of cost-based payers; the resulting amount is the savings to the organization itself. Alternatively, the organization's *real* savings equal the *projected* savings multiplied by the percentage of its payers who pay charges.

Of course, many people (especially taxpayers) would argue that this is completely justifiable. Cost-based payers reimburse increases in costs, and therefore should be allowed to enjoy the fruits of cost reductions. Nevertheless, an organization's incentive to engage in cost-reducing efforts is lessened considerably by a system in which its reimbursement falls by the amount it saves. This is why many third party payers in health care and elsewhere are moving away from cost-based reimbursement and into more fixed-price approaches to paying for the services they receive.

Differential Cost Analysis and Allocated Overhead

Additional complexities are introduced into the differential cost analysis when overhead costs are associated with the decision. The principal complexity relates to the allocation bases that are used. Specifically, if the costs of a particular revenue center are reduced, some of the service center costs allocated to that center usually will fall. But, due to the presence of fixed costs in the service centers, the service center costs themselves will not fall by as much as the reduced allocation. As a result, the service center's fixed costs will be reallocated to other cost centers.

A good example of this phenomenon is administration and general (A&G). A reduction of staff in a given revenue center will lead to a reduction in total salaries in the center. If A&G costs are allocated according to salary dollars, there will be a reduction in the amount of A&G allocated to that revenue center. It is highly unlikely, however, that there will be any reduction in the staff or in other costs associated with the A&G service cost center. Thus, rather than being reduced, A&G costs simply will be reallocated to other cost centers.

By contrast, it is possible that a service center's costs may be reduced, but that the costs allocated from it to a given revenue center may not fall by a like amount. For example, a reduction in the level of, or change in the nature of, activity in a given revenue center may reduce the center's need for housekeeping services, which may lead to a reduction in the costs of the housekeeping service center. Yet, if the cost report allocates housekeeping in a square-footage basis, it will not indicate this reduction unless the space utilized by the revenue center also is decreased. While the costs allocated to the revenue center will decline slightly as a result of the lower amount of housekeeping costs overall, the fall will be much less than the actual reduction that took place in the housekeeping department.

Recognizing these complexities and others, and incorporating them into analytical efforts, is one of the most challenging aspects of differential cost accounting in both for-profit and nonprofit organizations. Determining which costs are indeed differential, how they behave, and the impact of cost-based reimbursement on an institution's revenue are all extremely difficult, particularly when a stepdown cost report is the principal source of information.

The Future

In the next five to ten years, many nonprofit organizations can be expected to improve upon both their full cost and differential cost accounting systems. For example, many hospitals have not yet developed full cost accounting systems that respond to the need to identify "winners and losers" under diagnosis-related groups (DRGs). Their full cost systems worked well when senior management's goal was revenue maximization under cost-based reimbursement, but they are inappropriate to the demands of Medicare's fixed-price (DRG) reimbursement. Other nonprofit organizations facing similar financing difficulties can be expected to undertake improvements in their cost accounting systems as well.

Some organizations that have developed good full cost accounting systems have not distinguished between fixed and variable costs. Yet, information on cost behavior is essential when an organization must bid competitively. Moreover, without a separation of fixed and variable costs, a nonprofit organization has difficulty determining whether it makes sense financially to subcontract for some services. Because of these demands, many nonprofits are modifying their cost accounting systems to include fixed and variable cost breakdowns in each cost center.

Management Control Systems

Good full cost and differential cost information is not especially useful for a nonprofit organization that wishes to encourage its professionals and managers to engage in cost management. To move from improved cost *measurement* to improved cost *management,* an organization needs to think of its costs in terms of the individuals who control them. It also must structure its departments and programs to provide appropriate incentives to these individuals to engage in cost control. These matters are the subject of the management control system.

Management Control Systems Defined

The goal of a management control system is to help assure the effective and efficient use of an organization's resources. In practice, one finds a wide variety of management control systems in nonprofit organizations. Sometimes they function well and sometimes not. Sometimes the control system consists of highly formal procedures and regularly scheduled activities, and sometimes it is quite informal and sporadic. Sometimes the system involves a great deal of time on the part of senior management, and sometimes senior managers are only marginally involved. Sometimes a great deal of decision-making autonomy is delegated to divisional, departmental, or program managers, and sometimes these middle managers have almost no authority or responsibility in decisions concerning the use of resources.

In large part, these differences arise because there is no easy way to specify the precise characteristics of a management control system. As is the case with many principles of management, management control principles are incomplete and occasionally contradictory. Moreover, because they are concerned with the behavior of people, the motivation of managers and professionals, and the role of information, the principles do not easily lend themselves to experiment or "proof." Nevertheless, they provide a way of thinking about some important management problems. Indeed, managers of both for-profit and nonprofit organizations have found management control principles useful for both planning and controlling resources.

As these comments suggest, while there are principles, there is no single correct way to design a management control system. Many successful for-profit organizations operating in the same industry, and competing for business from the same customers, have very different management control systems. The same is true for nonprofit organizations. Some organizations, for example, use a very formal reporting process; they provide managers at all levels with information pertaining to their activities, and expect close adherence to the financial objectives established in the equally formal budget formulation process. Other organizations will use the budget only as a rough guide, and will look only at a manager's performance at year's end to see if it is satisfactory. There are many variations.

The idea that there is no "right" management control system is relatively new—perhaps fifteen to twenty years old. It came about both as a result of direct observation by management researchers of the activities of successful organizations, and as part of a new way of thinking about organizational design in general, called "contingency theory." Contingency theory holds that there is no "right" way to organize, but rather that the most suitable organizational form will be one that provides a "fit" with (a) the environment in which the organization operates, (b) the organization's general strategic thrust, and (c) the values and motivations of key personnel (Lawrence and Lorsch, 1969). A similar fit must be attained for the organization's management control system (Young, 1979).

In its broadest sense, then, a management control system is concerned with the *control* rather than the *measurement of resources*. Clearly measurement is imporatant to control, so the two cannot be completely divorced. Nevertheless, the focus of this section is on controlling resources. To sharpen the focus, we must consider the *structure* of an organization's management control system as well as the *process* followed in its use. Structure is what the system *is;* process is what it *does*. In studying the system of the human body, for example, students learn about anatomy (its structure) and physiology (its process). Similarly, a management control system can be thought of having an anatomy and a physiology.

The Management Control Structure

The structure of a management control system can be assessed in terms of groups of individuals working together toward some common purpose. Each group is called a "responsibility center" and is led by a manager who has overall responsibility for its performance. Responsibility centers can take a wide variety of forms. The development office of a university is a responsibility center. So is a museum's curatorial department. A laboratory in a hospital is also a responsibility center. An alcohol detoxification program in a community center is a responsibility center. And so on.

Organizational units with some sort of responsibility exist in almost all organizations. Therefore, the central question is not whether responsibility centers exist but rather whether their design facilitates the organization's ability to achieve its goals in an efficient fashion. Examples abound of organizations where (a) responsibility centers have overlapping goals and objectives that frequently come into conflict, or (b) some of the important goals and objectives of the organization have not been assigned to any particular responsibility center, or (c) managers of particular responsibility centers are not given appropriate incentives to achieve the center's objectives. As a result, the decision about the most appropriate type of responsibility center for a given organizational unit is an extremely important one.

Types of Responsibility Centers. There are five main types of responsibility centers: revenue centers, standard expense centers, discretionary expense centers, profit centers, and investment centers. The principal factor guiding the selection of one type over another is the kind of resources controlled by the responsibility center manager (see Exhibit 20.3).

Exhibit 20.3. Types of Responsibility Centers.

Type of Responsibility Center:	*Responsible for:*
Revenue center	Revenue earned by the center
Standard expense center	Expenses *per unit of outcome,* but not total expenses, incurred by the center
Discretionary expense center	Total expenses incurred by the center
Profit center	Total revenues and expenses of the center
Investment center	Total revenues and expenses of the center, computed as a percentage of the assets used by the center; this is the center's return on assets

Source: Young, 1994, p. 330. Used with permission.

If the manager of a department has a great deal of control over the organization's revenue, such as is ordinarily the case in a development office, the manager's department usually would be considered a *revenue center.* This is true even though that department incurs some expenses. The salient point is that the manager's *performance* is evaluated in terms of the *revenue generated* by his or her department. On the other hand, if a manager has a great deal of control over his or her department's expenses, but no ability to generate revenue, the department ordinarily would be an expense center.

There are two types of expense centers: standard and discretionary. A *standard expense center* exists when a manager can control the expense *per unit* of output but not the *number of units* of output. The radiology department of a hospital, for example, might be a standard expense center. The chief of radiology would be responsible for the expense per procedure — for example, per chest X ray (the department's output) — but not for the total expenses of the department. This is because total expenses depend on the number of procedures ordered, which is not under the chief's control.

A *discretionary expense center,* by contrast, has *no easily measurable unit of output.* This is the case in, say, a legal or accounting department. Under these circumstances, the department would simply receive a fixed budget, negotiated with senior management, but not tied to any units of output. The manager would be expected to adhere to this budget during the budgetary period (usually a year).

If the manager has control of both revenue and expense, the center ordinarily would be a *profit center* (a term used in both nonprofit and for-profit organization). Increasingly, over the past several years, many large, and even some small, nonprofit organizations have instituted profit centers as a way to give their managers incentives to both control expenses and worry about the generation of additional revenues.

Finally, it is possible that a manager also exerts some control over the acquisition and management of certain assets, such as machines, other equipment, accounts receivable, or inventory. If this is the case, the manager could reasonably be expected to have control over the productivity of those assets in addition to the center's revenue and expenses. This would imply designation as an *investment center*. In an investment center, the manager is responsible for his or her center's return on assets, that is, surplus, the center's surplus as a percent of its assets.

Large organizations frequently have a complicated hierarchy of responsibility centers, such as units, sections, departments, branches, and divisions. Except for those activities at the lowest levels of the organization, each responsibility center generally consists of aggregations of smaller responsibility centers. A significant managerial activity for senior management in any organization, regardless of its size, is to design, coordinate, and control the work of all of these responsibility centers.

Design of Responsibility Centers. From the perspective of the structure of a management control system, everyone in an organization is responsible for something. Moreover, since employees typically work in groups, each group can be thought of as a responsibility center. As a result, the issue of importance for designing the structure of a management control system is capsulized in the question, For what resources is the group responsible? Senior management's objective is to design the organization's responsibility centers in such a way that *individuals are held responsible for those financial results over which they exercise a reasonable amount of control*. This simple-sounding task frequently is quite complicated in practice.

In considering the design of responsibility centers, senior managers must begin with the fundamental premise that their organization is an investment center. This is true for nonprofit organizations as well as for-profit ones. Indeed, as discussed in the chapter on financial accounting, a nonprofit organization must obtain a sufficiently high return on assets (ROA) to allow it to replace its assets as they wear out and to provide the working capital needed to finance growth. This means that a fundamental structural design question for a management control system is how to decentralize that investment responsibility among the various organizational units.

In determining how to best decentralize responsibility, we can turn to the basic elements of ROA and assess who controls each. In any organization, ROA is determined by a combination of factors: price, volume (the number of units sold), variable costs per unit (such as supplies and some labor costs), fixed costs (such as the managers' salaries and rental of facilities), the depreciation on plant and equipment, and asset levels.

This framework can be used to assess which elements of the ROA formula a given manager controls. That information can then help determine what kind of responsibility can most appropriately be assigned to that manager's organizational unit (responsibility center). In some instances, the ability of the manager to control certain elements of ROA is quite clear, and in others there is considerable ambiguity. When ambiguity is present, senior management must be extremely careful to select types of responsibility centers that correspond to the control and decision-making authority of middle managers. If this is not the case, middle managers quite likely will feel that they are being held responsible for resources they cannot control. This can lead to considerable stress within the organization.

Responsibility for program results. In a nonprofit organization, responsibility center design issues extend beyond the question of which *financial* resources a manager controls, to include *program* results as well. Indeed, in most nonprofit organizations, financial objectives frequently are viewed as constraints on a manager's ability to achieve a desired set of program results. In essence, then, program results must be measured separately from financial ones, and attained, if possible, in the context of the limited financial resources available.

While the above argument would appear to call for a responsibility center structure in which each of an organization's programs was defined as some sort of responsibility center, this is not always the case. Frequently, a given center will have responsibility for several programs, and, by contrast, some responsibility centers may serve several programs. For example, in many health care organizations, medical records is a responsibility center that serves all the organization's programs; but it generally is not thought of as a "program." Similarly, nursing is an example of an activity that might either stand alone as a responsibility center, serving a variety of programs or departments in a hospital, or be viewed as an activity that can be divided among the organization's programs in such a way that each program manager's responsibility extends to the supervision and management of several nurses.

The contingency view. As the above discussion suggests, there is no one "right" answer to the problem of responsibility center design. Each organization is unique in terms of its strategy, management philosophy, programs, and a wide variety of other characteristics. The guiding principle is that of aligning responsibility and control, but no clear-cut prescription can be given. As a result, senior management in many organizations spend considerable time debating the most appropriate responsibility center structure for a given strategy and organizational structure. Moreover, when either strategy or organizational structure shifts, as they frequently do, senior management must reconsider its responsibility center structure.

The Management Control Structure and Motivation. A management control structure can provide a powerful motivating force for middle- and lower-level managers in an organization, as well as for the organization's professionals. It is therefore extremely important for senior management to consider the incentives the structure provides to the affected individuals. Indeed, in designing a management control system, senior management must ask a very fundamental question: *Does the responsibility center structure that is in place motivate managers and professionals to take actions that are in the best interest of both their individual responsibility centers and the organization as a whole?* If the answer is yes, *goal congruence* has been achieved, and an appropriate responsibility center structure most likely exists. If the answer is no, there is an absence of goal congruence, and a redesign effort is necessary. Goal congruence can be defined as a situation in which the goals of individual managers and professionals, based on senior management's expectations for their responsibility centers, are consistent with the overall goals of the organization.

Transfer prices. A lack of goal congruence frequently arises in situations where several responsibility centers in a large organization buy and sell products and services from each other. When this happens, the main question concerns the prices at which these transactions should take place. Indeed, if an organization contains a number of responsibility centers that are not completely independent of each other, they almost certainly will engage in "buying and selling" transactions among themselves. As a result, the prices at which these transactions take place — the transfer prices — become important elements of the management control structure.

Resolving transfer pricing problems is one of the most complicated aspects of designing a management control structure. In part, this is because transfer pricing rules convey senior management's views concerning the amount of autonomy it wishes to give to responsibility center managers. Will senior management, for example, allow managers of "selling centers" to set their own prices without intervention, or will senior management intervene to set negotiated prices? If it chooses the former course, it must be prepared to have some "buying centers" purchase services from entities outside the organization rather than intraorganizationally. Other things equal, these transactions will cause the organization's surplus to fall. Senior management must believe, therefore, that increased autonomy will give managers of responsibility centers the motivation to increase their surpluses, and that the resulting increases will more than offset the declines in surplus caused by the use of outside purchases.

If senior management chooses to intervene, it must be prepared to engage in many detailed price-setting activities, and to assist in the resolution of the frequent conflicts that will arise between responsibility center managers. Both courses of action have advantages and disadvantages, and successful organizations can be found that have chosen each course.

Role of Full Cost Information. It would be useful if the system for accumulating full cost information were also the system for accumulating responsibility center information. Unfortunately, this is rarely the case. Consider, for example, the cost of a day of inpatient care in a hospital. From a full cost accounting perspective, we would wish to add together the various resources that went into that day: room, board, nursing care, medications, and so on.

By contrast, from a management control perspective, we are concerned with the individuals who control those resources. For example, physicians carry a major responsibility for the use of resources: they decide on the level of nursing care; order tests, procedures, and medications; and determine a discharge date. A nursing director or supervisor, who determines the staffing and efficiency of nurses, carries some additional responsibility. A director of housekeeping, who is responsible for the efficiency and quality of the cleaning effort, also has some responsibility. And so on.

Effect on Strategy. In a hospital, decisions about responsibility centers require senior management to determine whether it wishes to set up its clinical departments (such as the department of surgery) as profit centers, standard expense centers, or some other type of responsibility center. This determination will affect far more than costs. Indeed, the responsibility center decision can affect the hospital's entire strategic posture, including its mix of diagnoses, its mix of third party payers (and hence the socioeconomic levels of its patients), its programs, and its quality of patient care. The same is true in other large nonprofit organizations, such as colleges and universities, museums, community agencies, and governmental agencies.

The Management Control Process

As the above discussion has suggested, the design of the management control structure must be carried out in the context of the organization's overall strategic directions. Similarly, the management control process must begin with the organization's strategy, and, as with the management control structure, it must be *contingent* upon it.

Much of the management control process is informal. Meetings, ad hoc memoranda, and hallway and lunchtime conversations, all can serve to influence the ways managers make decisions about the use of resources. Nevertheless, in most organizations there also is a more formal process. This formal process usually consists of a regularly scheduled set of activities in which decisions are made about the kinds and quantities of outputs the organization expects during an upcoming accounting period (such as a fiscal year), and the kinds and amounts of resources it will use to generate those outputs. During the accounting period, records usually are kept on actual results (outputs and inputs). Most organizations use this information to prepare regular reports on these results that senior and middle managers can use as a basis for determining whether corrective action of some sort is needed.

In most nonprofit organizations, the above activities constitute the formal management control process. They can be classified into four separate phases:

1. Programming
2. Budget formulation
3. Operating and measurement
4. Reporting and evaluation

These phases recur in a regular cycle and build upon each other, as indicated in Figure 20.3. Thus, by describing each phase, we can gain an appreciation for the nature of the formal aspects of the management control process.

Programming. In the programming phase of the cycle, managers make a variety of decisions of a long-term nature. These decisions concern both the kinds of programs the organization will engage in and the kinds and amounts of resources it will devote to each. In general, as Figure 20.3 illustrates, these decisions are made within the context of the organization's overall strategy, coupled with whatever information is available concerning new opportunities, increased competition, new or pending legislation that might affect the organization's efforts, and other external inputs.

Because programming decisions are long-range, the programming phase of the management control process frequently looks ahead by as much as five or ten years. The program planning document in a large nonprofit organization frequently is lengthy, describing each proposal in detail, estimating the resources necessary to accomplish the program, and calculating the expected social and financial returns from the effort. Nevertheless, there generally are many benefits that are difficult to quantify and that complicate the decision.

Because many of the benefits of new program proposals are difficult to quantify, and because profit center managers will tend to be quite optimistic about their program proposals, there frequently is a *new program bias* involved in the programming phase. Senior management will tend to counteract this bias by using its own staff to analyze proposals submitted by profit center managers, and, as might be imagined, there occasionally is friction between the planning staff and line managers, not to mention a political undercurrent to the entire process. Managing this friction and the political element so that the final result is a tough but realistic analysis is perhaps one of the most challenging tasks senior management faces in the programming process.

Budget Formulation. As contrasted with the programming phase, which looks ahead several years, the budget formulation phase generally looks ahead only one year. It accepts programs as given and attempts to determine the amount of revenues and expenses that will be associated with each. In many organizations, programs fall neatly into responsibility centers, so that each responsibility center manager can be charged with preparing a budget for each of his or her programs. Sometimes a program and a responsibility center are identical. In many organizations, the fit between programs and responsibility centers is not so neat, and a more complicated budgeting process will be necessary. This frequently happens when programs cut across several responsibility centers.

Because of differing kinds and levels of complexity, each organization

Figure 20.3. Phases of the Management Control Process.

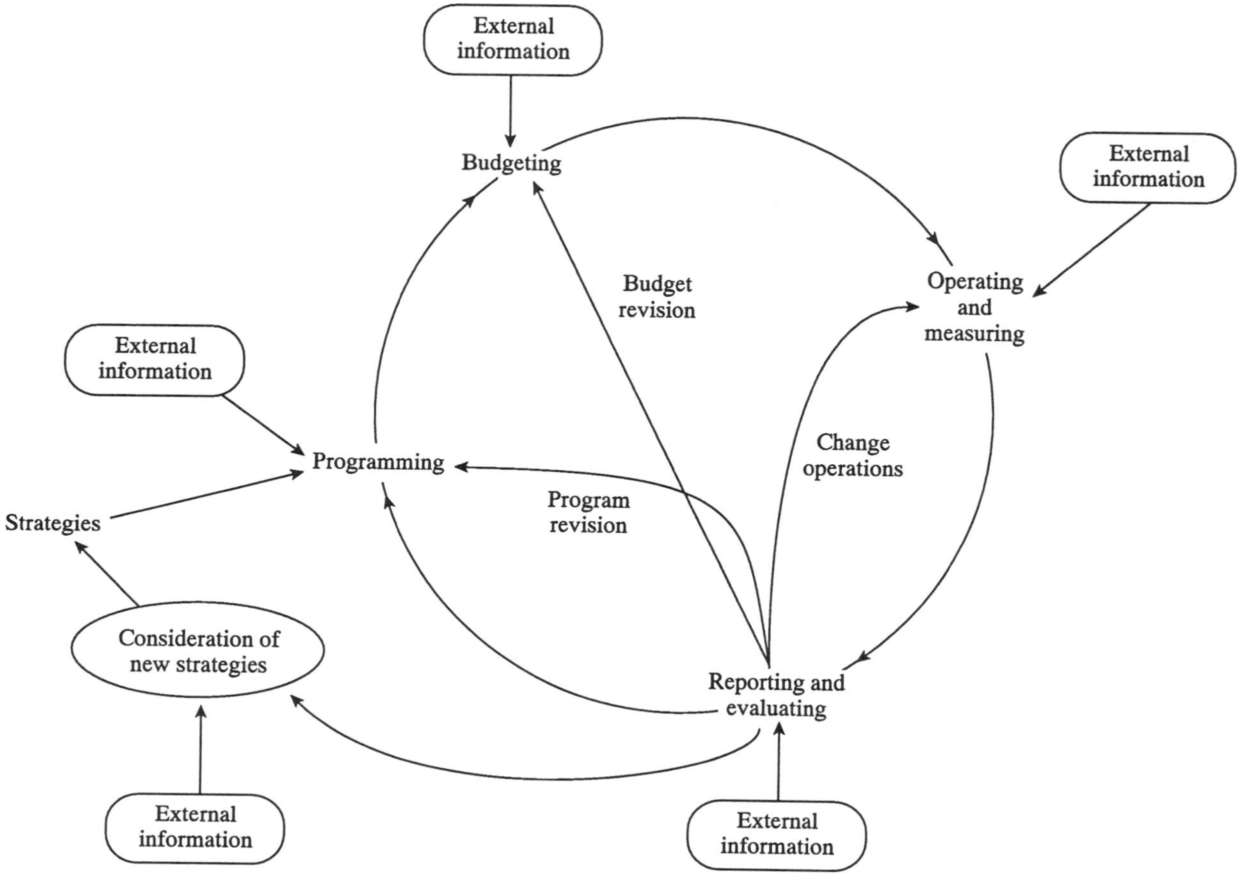

Source: Adapted from Anthony and Young, 1994, p. 19.

must develop a budget formulation process that meets its own individual needs. In general, however, a good budget formulation process has several key elements:

- A set of guidelines that are developed by senior management and communicated to line managers. Generally this is the first step in the annual process. It usually is done in writing, and sets forth a timetable for the rest of the process.
- A participatory element in which managers at the lowest levels have an opportunity to prepare budgets for their responsibility centers and discuss them with their superiors.
- A central staff (usually in the controller's office) responsible for coordinating the activities, carrying out many of the technical aspects of the process, and occasionally providing analyses that serve as checks and balances against projections by responsibility center managers.
- A hierarchy of information, beginning with the smallest responsibility center and accumulating budget information by successively larger responsibility centers, eliminating excessive detail at each step.
- A negotiation phase in which, if necessary, each responsibility center manager can defend his or her budget against anticipated reductions, or otherwise argue why it should be retained as originally prepared.
- A final approval and sign-off by senior management authorizing responsibility center managers at each level to carry out the budget as agreed upon in the preparation and negotiation phases.

In general, this final approval constitutes a commitment between each responsibility center manager and his or her superior that the budget will be adhered to unless there are "compelling reasons" to change it. Compelling reasons include large and unanticipated changes in volume, a lengthy strike, fuel shortages and resulting large price increases, a fire in the main building, or other similarly significant or catastrophic events.

As anyone who has participated in a budget preparation effort knows, the process frequently has a certain "gamelike" quality to it. This, in part, is the reason senior management uses staff analyses in addition to the information submitted by responsibility center managers. The principal intent of this effort is to eliminate any "slack" in the budget, so that the final budget estimates the future as realistically as possible. Ultimately, the budget for each responsibility center should be relatively difficult to attain, but attainable nevertheless.

Operating and Measurement. Once programs have been established and a budget has been agreed upon, the organization commences operating during the budget year. This is, of course, an oversimplification, since all organizations except newly established ones operate continually. However, if some new programs have been approved, or if new funds have been made available for existing programs, it is quite likely that a variety of new or different types of operations will commence at the beginning of a new budget year.

From a management control perspective, new or different types of operations have important implications. Specifically, if the budget is to be adhered to, managers must receive information concerning their responsibility center's performance compared to budgeted objectives. Consequently, new as well as ongoing activities must be measured. More specifically, data must be collected about both financial and nonfinancial activities, and this information must be incorporated into the management control system. The operating and measurement phase of the process, then, is one of putting plans into effect and measuring the relevant inputs and outputs.

Role of the accounting system. If the measurement aspect of this phase of the management control process is to be effective, the organization must have a well-developed accounting system. The accounting system must be designed so that it can both keep records of revenues and expenses, and permit the information to be used for several related purposes:

1. To prepare financial statements, such as the balance sheet and operating statement. These must be prepared in accordance with the rules and guidelines of outside agencies (such as the Financial Accounting Standards Board or the American Institute of Certified Public Accountants). As discussed in Chapter Nineteen, these rules govern how the information is to be organized and presented.
2. To prepare full cost analyses, in which overhead is allocated to products and services for purposes of analyzing costs and establishing prices or reimbursement rates.
3. To distinguish between fixed and variable costs where necessary.
4. To classify both revenues and expenses by programs and responsibility centers. The information on programs is used as a basis for evaluating the programs themselves and for future programming decisions. The information on responsibility centers is used to measure the performance of the managers of these centers; that is, to compare actual performance to budgeted objectives.

Need for integrated information. Although the information has multiple uses, it must be *integrated.* That is, although data collected for one purpose may differ from those collected for another, or certain data elements may sometimes be reported in a detailed fashion and sometimes in summaries, in all instances the data should be reconcilable from one report to another. This requires careful and thoughtful design of the information coding structure at the outset, and a cautious, systematic process for including new data elements when the system must be modified.

In designing and modifying the accounting system, the organization's accounting staff must be carefully managed to ensure that they consider the information's potential multiple uses. In addition, the system ordinarily is built on a financial base (that is, amounts are stated in monetary units), since these generally are the easiest to collect, maintain, and integrate. Nevertheless, managers frequently wish to see a variety of nonmonetary measures, such as minutes per visit, number of clients, percentages, client outcomes, and so forth. These nonmonetary items also are part of the *measurement system,* which is thus somewhat broader than the accounting system.

Changing information needs of managers. The role of the measurement phase of the management control system is to determine and gather the appropriate information to meet the decision-making needs of responsibility center and program managers. This role is complicated by two factors: (a) different managers in an organization make different kinds of decisions, and (b) all managers make a variety of decisions depending on the particular circumstances they face at various times in the operating year. These factors require the measurement phase of the management control process to be flexible and dynamic: in any growing or evolving organization, the information needed by senior and middle managers not only will differ from one responsibility center or program to the next, but will be changing constantly.

Reporting and Evaluation. The final phase of the management control process is the presentation of information to program and responsibility center managers. The information collected in the measurement phase of the cycle is thus classified, analyzed, sorted, merged, totaled, and finally reported to these managers. The resulting reports generally compare planned outputs and inputs with actual ones, and thereby allow both operating managers and their superiors to evaluate performance during the period. This information, along with a variety of other information (from conversations, informal sources, industry analyses, and the like), generally leads to one of three possible courses of behavior, as indicated in Figure 20.3.

Change in operations. If the operating manager or his or her supervisor is not satisfied with the results shown on the reports, action of some sort may be necessary to correct the situation. Action can include activities such as examining sources of supply to attempt to obtain lower material prices, asking supervisors about the use of overtime, speaking with the agency's professionals (such as social workers, curators, teachers, physicians, and nurses) about client satisfaction or dissatisfaction with the organization's services, and so forth. Action also can include praise for a job well done, constructive criticism, reassignment, or, in extreme cases, termination.

Revision of budget. In some instances, certain aspects of a responsibility center are not under control of the center's manager. For example, if the volume of activity in a laboratory is determined exclusively by the test orders submitted by physicians, the laboratory manager has little ability to control that volume. If supply prices are the responsibility of the purchasing department, or if wage rates are determined by senior management in its negotiations with labor unions, managers of the affected responsibility centers generally will have little control over variations from the budget.

Moreover, the effect of a strike or a natural disaster may mean that it is all but impossible for a responsibility center manager to meet the budget. In these instances some organizations will make revisions in the budget.

Revision of program. The reports also can be used as a basis for program evaluation and revision. For any of a number of reasons, an organization's programming decisions may not be optimum. The anticipated demand for the product or service may not exist; competition may be stronger than was thought; technological improvements may have made the product or service obsolete; the organization may not be able to develop the skills necessary to run the program well. In extreme situations, the reports may indicate a need not only to revise or discontinue one or more of the organization's programs but to change the organization's overall strategy as well.

Because the reporting and evaluation phase has this feedback characteristic, Figure 20.3 shows a closed loop. As a consequence, the process tends to be rhythmic — it follows a pattern which, although variations may exist, is about the same every year. Managers learn this pattern and adjust their activities to it.

Recent Approaches to Management Control in Nonprofit Organizations

Recently, many nonprofit organizations have begun to recognize the importance of improving their management control systems. Many have approached the redesign effort by thinking about cost management in terms of a series of *cost-influencing factors* or *cost drivers,* coupled with the individual or individuals who control them. Cost drivers thus have some important management control implications.

Cost Drivers Defined

When cost drivers are used in the management control effort, management's focus moves beyond responsibility centers to include the factors that influence the kinds and amounts of resources a client or a program consumes. These factors often are called "cost drivers" (Cooper, 1989, 1990).

A cost driver is an activity that can be directly linked to an increase in costs (Miller and Vollmann, 1985). As such, the number and nature of cost drivers will differ from one organization to the next. Certain costs in a social service agency, for example, arise from the number of client visits. Others arise from the number and complexity of clients' presenting problems. Similarly, in a university, certain costs are a result of the number of students, while others arise from the number and complexity of programs available to students. In a hospital, the principal cost drivers are the number and mix of cases, and the resources used to treat a given type of case.

Regardless of the number or nature of cost drivers, the key thrust of the approach is to shift managers' thinking away from the traditional responsibility center structure of the management control system to a listing and classification of the *activities that cause the existence of costs*. Frequently, some of these activities transcend traditional responsibility center boundaries. Indeed, the concept of cost drivers allows us to bridge the gap between the broad overview of costs given in Figure 20.1 and potential managerial actions to influence and control costs, which is the concern of a management control system.

Cost Drivers and Management Control Systems. To move the cost driver idea into the realm of management control, senior management must identify the forces that control each cost driver. This allows the alignment of responsibility with control, a key aspect of the management control structure. Finally, cost drivers can be linked to a budget by the use of *target costing,* an approach that has proven successful in many manufacturing firms (Hiromoto, 1988). In these companies, target costing focuses attention on the design phase of a product, which is well in advance of the actual manufacturing process. By engaging in target costing, managers can identify potential manufacturing problems and can avoid them with a redesign effort (Sakurai, 1989). Similarly, in some hospitals, physicians have used target costing to develop clinical treatment protocols (Young and Saltman, 1985). In this way, they can identify the resources typically needed for each case type or diagnosis.

In a hospital, efficiency in resource delivery is based on the costs generated by the actual production of ancillary and support services — principally the provision of physician-ordered services. As a result, this area also can benefit from target costing. That is, target costing can be used to manage the efficiency with which professional care mission centers (such as operating rooms, radiology departments, pharmacies, and laboratories) provide the services ordered by attending physicians. To do so, hospitals have developed administrative efficiency protocols (Young and Pearlman, 1993). Indeed, many hospitals have realized that they do not need to confine target costing to clinical areas. For example, Massachusetts General Hospital studied the transportation of inpatients. The hospital's staff focused on the tasks involved in the transportation process and identified the causes of several problems. They not only improved the quality of the transport process but gained a heightened awareness of the cost drivers in the transport area (Sullivan and Frentzel, 1992).

In general, nonprofit organizations that have begun to develop improved management control systems have recognized that responsibility center managers and professionals control different resources. Managing operating costs requires each set of actors to take responsibility for the resources it controls. This shift in thinking about costs is particularly significant from the perspective of the distinction between cost measurement and cost management.

Organizations that have incorporated cost drivers into their management control systems have shifted their focus from responsibility centers to clients. Those making this sort of move have found that they can control costs more effectively than before. Indeed, because their old control systems had focused on responsibility centers rather than clients, many nonprofits had not fully understood a crucial distinction: they must manage the number and kind of resources used for a given client differently from the way they manage the cost of providing each of those resources. Making this distinction allows them to use professional protocols to address *resources per client,* and administrative protocols to address the *efficiency of resource provision.* Hospitals have taken the lead in these sorts of activities, but other nonprofit organizations have begun to engage in them as well.

Changes to Budget Preparation. By focusing on cost drivers, many nonprofit organizations have been able to revise the way they calculate their budgets. When cost drivers and their controlling agents have been identified, an organization can ask each controlling agent to prepare estimates for the cost drivers that he or she controls. Moreover, by using a model where members of each controlling group estimate their own cost drivers, many organizations have found that they can simulate program plans and budgets under different strategic alternatives, such as with different product lines or different client mixes within a product line. Doing so allows them to apply the principles of target costing to reduce resource consumption while maintaining client services at acceptable levels.

Designing Administrative Systems

The shift toward a focus on cost drivers does not mean eliminating responsibility centers. Rather, it asks responsibility center managers to consider the factors that influence costs (and sometimes revenues) in their centers. Although this shift is an important step in cost control, many nonprofits are finding it is not sufficient.

One of the main characteristics of a management control system based on cost drivers is its emphasis on administrative efficiency. However, many responsibility center managers have limited opportunities to improve efficiency. In a hospital's radiology department, for example, the manager can try to get technicians to work faster, thereby increasing the number of films processed per hour. Or he or she can rethink the mix of technicians, perhaps shifting toward those who command lower wages. Or there may be some minor savings in material usage. But that is about all.

An administrative systems focus, by contrast, shifts the decision-making perspective to the entire set of activities that takes place from the time an attending physician in, say, the pediatrics department, orders an X ray until that physician has the results of the procedure (including the radiologist's report) in hand. Figure 20.4 shows, in simplified form, the contrast between a departmental and an administrative systems approach.

As Figure 20.4 suggests, under an administrative systems approach,

Figure 20.4. The Administrative Systems Perspective.

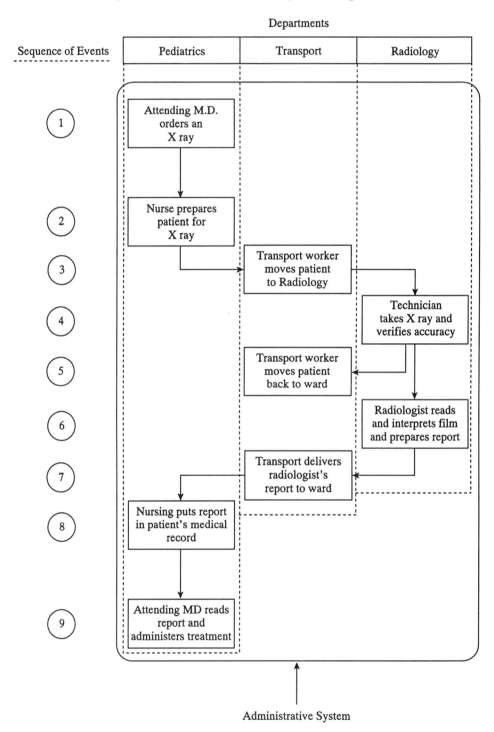

Source: Adapted from Young and Pearlman, 1993, p. 78.

senior management considers each department to be part of a larger whole. It assesses a given department's contribution to an administrative system (such as the X-ray system) by juxtaposing its activities with those of the other departments involved in that system. The result is a reorganization of the entire hospital—away from departments and into administrative systems. This sort of view typically characterizes a Total Quality Management (TQM) approach to performance improvement.

In adopting an administrative systems approach, some nonprofits have found it necessary to expand the measurement aspect of their management control systems. The expanded system frequently includes some *nonfinancial indicators* that monitor the activities of each administrative system. In the example shown in Figure 20.4, the expanded information might include waiting times at various intervals, transport time, number of films taken (as opposed to a standard), number of retakes needed, and others. Some of these will not have easily calculable cost figures, yet each is a surrogate for costs. Improvements in each can result in lower total costs in the future.

In effect, under an administrative systems approach, costs are controlled by managing the processes that take place rather than focusing on units of activity. To control costs in this way, organizations have shifted their thinking away from individual departments and responsibility centers. They have begun to define, analyze, and manage the administrative systems carried out within and across those departments and centers. Many observers see this approach as the next wave in the quest for cost control in both for-profit and nonprofit organizations.

Summary

While good full cost accounting, differential cost accounting, and management control systems are critical to survival in the 1990s and beyond, nonprofit organizations nevertheless need to distinguish between (a) full cost and differential cost accounting (where the accounting staff improves the existing system) and (b) management control systems, including an administrative systems approach (where senior management changes the entire focus of the system). These different systems and their characteristics are summarized in Exhibit 20.4.

Many nonprofits attempting to improve their management control systems have begun to focus on cost drivers, thereby requiring responsibility center managers to focus on their cost control efforts on groups of clients with similar characteristics. Moreover, by changing their management control systems to focus on cost drivers and the individuals who control them, many nonprofits have found that they can assign and monitor responsibility for cost changes. As a result, they have a much greater ability to control their costs. In particular, the use of target costing can lead to a set of clinical treatment and administrative efficiency protocols that give organizations an opportunity to think about costs at the design stage, thereby linking cost drivers to budgets.

Exhibit 20.4. Nonprofit Management Accounting: A Summary.

Type/Goal Primary Responsibility	Information Used	Key Activities Performed	Managerial Uses
Full Cost Accounting	Direct and indirect costs	Choice of cost object	Product line profitability
Improving the Full Cost System		Assignment of costs to cost centers Choice of allocation bases	Strategic decisions (programs, facilities, personnel needed to support chosen product lines)
Accounting Staff		Allocation of service center costs to revenue centers	
Differential Cost Accounting	Fixed and variable	Analyses of costs	Offer a special price
Assessing Cost Behavior		Contribution analyses	Contract out for services Retain or discontinue an unprofitable program
Accounting Staff			
Management Control Systems	Client and responsibility center costs	Determine cost drivers	Cost control Motivation
Controlling Costs		Budget using cost drivers	Performance measurement
Senior Management		Determine responsibility centers	Professionals' involvement in cost management
		Assign responsibility to controlling agents	
Administrative Systems	Process-related costs	Define administrative systems	Measuring performance across traditional functional boundaries
Designing Administrative Systems	Nonfinancial measures of performance	Calculate costs by administrative system	Shifting measurement focus from individual or department to a cross-functional group
Senior Management		Develop nonfinancial measures of performance	

Source: Adapted from Young and Pearlman, 1993, p. 60.

Beyond these changes, many nonprofits are finding that negative financial results may be caused by problems in a broader set of activities. As a result, senior management has begun to define and manage the organization's administrative systems.

Relatively few nonprofit organizations have moved to an administrative systems approach. Yet, a move of this sort is essential if an organization is to *control* rather than just *measure* its costs. Reconceptualizing an organization as a series of administrative systems is a difficult step. Yet, such an approach can be a powerful tool for nonprofit managers concerned about rapidly escalating costs in a era of shrinking public and private revenues.

References

Anthony, R. N., and Young, D. W. *Management Control in Nonprofit Organizations.* Homewood, Ill.: Richard D. Irwin, 1994.

Cooper, R. "The Rise of Activity-Based Costing — Part Three: How Many Cost Drivers Do You Need, and How Do You Select Them?" *Journal of Cost Management,* Winter 1989, pp. 34–46.

Cooper, R. "Cost Classification in Unit-Based and Activity-Based Manufacturing Cost Systems." *Journal of Cost Management,* Fall 1990, pp. 33–39.

Cooper, R., and Kaplan, R. S. "Measure Costs Right: Make the Right Decisions." *Harvard Business Review,* 1988, *88*(5), 96–103.

Hiromoto, T. "Another Hidden Edge — Japanese Management Accounting." *Harvard Business Review,* 1988, *88*(4), 22–26.

Kaplan, R. S. "One Cost System Isn't Enough." *Harvard Business Review,* 1988, *88*(1), 61–66.

Lawrence, P., and Lorsch, J. W. *Organization and Environment.* Boston: Division of Research, Harvard Business School, 1969.

Miller, J. G., and Vollmann, T. E. "The Hidden Factory." *Harvard Business Review,* 1985, *85*(5), 142–150.

Sakurai, M. "Target Costing and How to Use It." *Journal of Cost Management,* Summer 1989, pp. 4–14.

Sullivan, N., and Frentzel, K. U. "A Patient Transport Pilot Quality Improvement Team." *Quality Review Bulletin,* July 1992, pp. 215–221.

Young, D. W. "Administrative Theory and Administrative Systems: A Synthesis Among Diverging Fields of Inquiry." *Accounting, Organizations and Society,* 1979, *4,* 235–244.

Young, D. W. "Cost Accounting and Cost Comparisons: Methodological Issues and Their Policy and Management Implications." *Accounting Horizons,* 1988, *2*(1), 67–76.

Young, D. W. *Introduction to Financial and Management Accounting: A User Perspective.* Cincinnati, Ohio: South-Western, 1994.

Young, D. W., and Pearlman, L. K. "Managing the Stages of Hospital Cost Accounting." *Healthcare Financial Management,* Apr. 1993, pp. 55–80.

Young, D. W., and Saltman, R. B. "Preventive Medicine for Hospital Costs." *Harvard Business Review,* 1983, *61*(1), 126–133.

Young, D. W., and Saltman, R. B. *The Hospital Power Equilibrium: Physician Behavior and Cost Control.* Baltimore, Md.: Johns Hopkins University Press, 1985.

21

Risk Management

Charles Tremper

In the wake of Hurricane Andrew, thousands of volunteers pitched in to clean up the wreckage. They all wanted to help, but not all were trained or supervised adequately to prevent accidents. A well-meaning but inexperienced volunteer with a chain saw is armed and dangerous! Tragically, avoidable accidents involving chain saws and other equipment added to Andrew's toll.

In dramatic form, this example presents the central dilemma of risk management for nonprofit organizations: is it better to do as much as possible and accept the inevitable losses, or scale back efforts to a level that can be conducted safely? Prodded by the threat of legal liability and increasing recognition that good intentions can produce horrendous results, nonprofits are increasingly embracing risk management principles to improve the quality of their services and prevent negative outcomes that can range from petty annoyances to full-blown tragedies.

In the case of disaster relief, the move to risk management is perhaps best exemplified by the American Red Cross. The Red Cross goes to great lengths to train volunteers before they participate in a relief operation. The national office of the Red Cross includes a department devoted to risk control. That department serves as a resource center for the chapters and also prods them to remain vigilant.

How committed is the Red Cross to risk management? Chief executive Elizabeth Dole addressed the 1992 convention of the Risk and Insurance Management Society. Several other nonprofits share the risk management commitment of the Red Cross, but experts in the field conjecture that most nonprofits lag behind the business and government sectors.

Benefits of Risk Management

Nonprofit organization managers sometimes resist rather than embrace risk management because they fear that it will divert resources from ordinary operations. Insurance costs money and almost all precautions diminish momentum. Moreover, the losses being prevented are contingent, whereas the costs of implementing risk management are immediate and tangible. Nonetheless, the benefits of risk management amply justify the attendant burden.

Most important, risk management helps a nonprofit to avoid causing harm, and causing harm is antithetical to any organization's mission. At the same time, risk management reduces the likelihood of a lawsuit and improves the organization's position if it is sued. Because the consequences of legal liability fall directly on the organization and its personnel, this may be the strongest motivator. With that in mind, the next section explains the rudiments of legal liability for nonprofit organizations and lays the foundation for the subsequent discussions of insurance and risk-reduction strategies.

Liability Exposures

General Principles

We all know that people can fall and hurt themselves. If they fall while engaged in an organization's activities, they can probably sue the organization. They may also be able to sue a volunteer or employee involved in the activity. Under some circumstances, they might even be able to sue the executive director and perhaps the board. If they win, the financial consequences can be devastating. Regardless of the outcome, the cost of hiring an attorney to defend against the suit may be more than an organization can afford.

The variety of suits that can be filed against nonprofits and volunteers is almost limitless. Some of the most common legal actions against nonprofit organizations are briefly described here.

1. Accidents provide the basis for the largest number of lawsuits. In the legal system, causing an automobile accident or creating a dangerous condition that results in injury is a "tort." Under tort law, liability ordinarily is based on negligence. Liability may result if the person causing harm did not exercise the degree of care that a reasonable person would have exercised in the same situation.

2. Most accidents result directly from a negligent act, as with a volun-

teer driver who runs a red light. Alternatively, the negligence may be an indirect cause of an accident. For example, an organization may be held liable for a drowning that occurred while a lifeguard who had not received adequate training was on duty. Even more remotely, the organization may be liable if it did not adequately screen its lifeguard applicants. Literally hundreds of child abuse claims against nonprofits have alleged failure to adequately screen or monitor staff.

3. Claims based on board negligence in adopting policies are also possible. Patients who were given AIDS-infected blood have received million-dollar awards from blood banks that did not implement AIDS screening procedures at the first sign of the threat.

4. Employment practices are another fertile source of litigation. Employees may recover for discrimination, wrongful dismissal, sexual harassment, and other employment-related wrongs that the law did not recognize a few decades ago.

5. The financial liability of an organization and its directors extends beyond the risk of being sued by another party who alleges injury: the government, too, may file suit or assess fines and penalties. Directors are subject to numerous administrative requirements, including detailed rules of the Internal Revenue Code. The Internal Revenue Service may seek to recover from directors personally for failure to file tax forms for the organization or breaching certain other rules.

Board Liability

As one of the preceding examples illustrates, boards of directors may incur liability and commit acts that cause liability for their organizations. Because board members tend to be very sensitive about their exposure to personal liability, this topic often receives special attention. Every primer on board responsibilities emphasizes three principal legal duties of board service: care, loyalty, and obedience (which is sometimes included as part of the duty of care). Failure to satisfy these duties can lead to a lawsuit if the error causes harm and an injured person is able to sue. In addition to these duties, boards are subject to a variety of responsibilities imposed by statute and other sources of law (American Bar Association, 1993).

Although the accompanying list may suggest that boards are besieged by a wide variety of lawsuits, in fact the number of suits is relatively small and the vast majority of claims derive from just one source: employment law. The most common claims against nonprofits' boards are for wrongful dismissal, discrimination, or other labor law violations. Typically they are filed against the organization, an administrator, and/or an officer, rather than against individual directors. Thus, the quality of an organization's employment practices strongly affects the likelihood that a claim will be filed against its board and, if it is so filed, whether it will be successful.

Legal Bases for Claims Against Nonprofits' Boards

Common law duties: care, loyalty, obedience
Employment law
Tax
Civil rights
Employee Retirement Income Security Act (ERISA)
Regulatory actions
Solicitation of funds
Bankruptcy
Antitrust
Breach of contract
Criminal Acts

Charitable Immunity

Across most of the country, nonprofit organizations are liable for harm they cause to the same extent as for-profit businesses. At least for charitable organizations, this legal vulnerability contrasts sharply to the protected status they enjoyed at one time.

Until the last few decades, the doctrine of charitable immunity protected many nonprofits from any liability. Even if suits were legally permitted, claims against charitable organizations and volunteers were extremely rare. Since the 1940s, though, the traditional doctrine of charitable immunity has disappeared in every state except Arkansas, where its continuing validity is questionable.

In place of charitable immunity, the following states have enacted various types of limitations on the liability of charitable organizations: Alabama, Colorado, Georgia, Maine, Maryland, Massachusetts, New Jersey, South Carolina, Tennessee, Texas, Utah, Virginia, and Wyoming. Some of these laws cap the dollar amount of organizations' liability, others limit certain types of claims, and some tie liability limitations to insurance coverage (Nonprofit Risk Management Center, 1992).

Volunteer Protection

Every state now has legislation pertaining specifically to the legal liability of at least some types of volunteers. All of this legislation has contributed to a false impression that volunteers nationwide are immune from suit. To the contrary, many volunteers remain fully liable for any harm they cause and all volunteers remain liable for some actions. Only about half of the states protect volunteers other than directors and officers. Legislatures came to the aid of board members because, of all volunteers, they faced the worst insurance problems when most of the volunteer protection statutes were enacted. The resulting anomaly is greater protection for the volunteers who make policy than for the ones who carry it out.

Moreover, every volunteer protection statute has exceptions. The most common and understandable are exclusions for claims based on a volunteer's willful or wanton misconduct. Several laws also exclude gross negligence or some other category of error above negligence. A few laws even permit suits based on negligence, which nullifies the protection they purport to offer. In addition to the listed exceptions are actions based on federal law. The Supremacy Clause of the United States Constitution prevents states from cutting off federal claims. Thus, the Internal Revenue Service can sue a volunteer director for failure to comply with tax withholding rules and wronged employees can sue for civil rights or employment violations. Congress alone can reduce the federal threat to volunteers' personal assets, but Congress has not acted.

Aside from using different liability standards, volunteer protection laws also differ in the scope of their application and the conditions they impose. Most apply to volunteers of any nonprofit organization, but some are limited to volunteers of charitable or social welfare organizations. Other laws require that the organization itself be insured, and some limit recovery to the amount of insurance the volunteer has.

In addition to the various exclusions are gaps that result from ambiguity in much of the legislation. Some of these laws are confusingly worded, exceptionally complicated, designed for profit-making corporations, or otherwise problematical. Even the very best laws require careful analysis to determine which volunteers they cover and what exceptions they contain (Nonprofit Risk Management Center, 1992.)

The diversity of the laws reflects varying conclusions of state legislatures that weighed the competing equities inherent in volunteer protection. Reasonable people can differ over the choice of protecting a volunteer from personal liability or providing compensation to the innocent victim of the volunteer's negligence. Some statutes address this conflict by immunizing volunteers only if the agencies they serve are insured. Beyond that requirement, the laws do not attempt a comprehensive response to the broad issue of how individuals who suffer harm from volunteer activity should be compensated. A fully adequate response would entail reconsideration of liability and damages standards for both volunteers and their sponsoring agencies. Although that undertaking is beyond the scope of the present effort, this assessment of the state of the law may serve as a step toward creating a more fully satisfactory arrangement.

The Risk Management Process

The risk management process provides a systematic method of responding to the dangers of an organization's operations. It is designed to protect the financial resources of the organization and staff as well as to protect the community from harm that the organization might cause. The surest strategy to avoid being sued is to avoid causing harm. Because nearly every action entails some risk of harm, precaution may not be entirely successful, but it can do a great deal to reduce the likelihood of an accident or improper action.

The following steps form the basis for risk management in any organization.

Step 1. Identify risks.
Step 2. Evaluate risks.
Step 3. Reduce risks to an acceptable level.
Step 4. Obtain insurance or make other financial arrangements as needed.
Step 5. Monitor activities, the environment, and risk-control activities, and revise as necessary.

In most respects, the process is similar to any other management procedure. The simple structure leads through recognition of risks to an assessment of their magnitude, and implementation of appropriate measures to manage them. The process is never finished, however. As the environment and the organization change, arrangements must be periodically reassessed and modified as necessary.

Although having a designated risk manager to supervise this process is an advantage, it is hardly essential. Any organization can designate a staff member, paid or volunteer, to spearhead its risk management efforts. Adding that responsibility to someone's job description may make excellent use of a person whose talents for spotting the dangers in every plan had previously gone unappreciated!

Identifying Risks

The first step of the whole risk management process is to acknowledge the reality of risk. Denial is a common tactic that substitutes deliberate ignorance for thoughtful planning. Once the mind is ready to entertain the possibility of risk, the risk identification step can proceed.

Anyone can begin the risk identification process merely by taking out a piece of paper and writing down the risks that come to mind. That simple exercise is a good first step. The following list offers ideas for identifying risks that are not immediately obvious:

• Consult with other individuals in the organization to learn about the risks they perceive.
• Review your procedures manuals for legal compliance, dangers, and feasibility of required procedures. The last of these is as important as the first two. Setting impossible standards invites litigation when you do not live up to them.
• Use checklists available from some insurers or printed in risk management manuals for nonprofit organizations.

- Review safety records, such as those provided by the Occupational Safety and Health Administration (OSHA) and workers' compensation providers.
- Consider the responsibilities of employees and volunteers with respect to their ability to perform the tasks they are assigned. Take into account not only their skills but also their judgment.
- Walk the premises where you conduct your operations with an eye to hazards. Try to visualize the setting in an emergency situation and from the perspectives of individuals who are differently abled.
- Invite each of the following, as appropriate, to join you in your risk audit: your insurance agent, a lawyer, a building safety engineer, a risk manager from a local business or government, the director of a similar organization (you might offer to return the favor in exchange).

Any list will necessarily be incomplete. Part of the challenge of risk management is to be aware of changing circumstances that require a change of strategy. Being sensitive to the risk element of the ever-changing legal, physical, and interpersonal environments is the essential predicate to effective evaluation and action.

Evaluating Risks

Risk assessment is an inherently subjective task with no meaningful absolutes. For example, in establishing safety regulations, federal agencies have estimated the dollar value of a human life from as little as $70,000 to as much as $132 million.

Many nonprofit organizations, by their charter or raison d'être, undertake tasks that thoughtful risk managers in the for-profit sector would avoid at any cost. Based on its mission, each organization has its own set of risks and its own level of risk aversion. These factors shape the risk evaluation process.

The best way to start evaluating risks is by reviewing each of the risks that were uncovered in the risk identification process; assess the probable frequency with which each risk will occur and the potential severity of the loss should the risk occur. Sophisticated risk management programs may attempt to estimate the likelihood and severity of each known risk to facilitate comparisons and concentrate resources on the most serious dangers. Most organizations can proceed without such a rigorous analysis by weighing the risks in a more ad hoc fashion. An organization that transports food to soup kitchens faces a high-frequency/low-severity risk of minor damage to its vehicle fleet. This same organization has a low-frequency/high-severity risk that a driver will cause a fatal accident.

The purpose of evaluating risks in this fashion is to make conscious decisions about which risks can be tolerated by the organization, which require the purchase of insurance, which can be reduced or controlled without sacrificing the benefit of the program, and which are simply too great to bear. High-exposure activities that may be peripheral to the organizational mission are best forgone, like bungee jumping at a fundraiser.

Nonprofit organizations must keep in mind that a risk assessment must extend beyond the financial costs of an incident. Ford Motor Company made a financial decision when it decided not to recall Pintos with defective gas tanks. The tragic results were preventable deaths and a flood of negative publicity that badly tarnished Ford's reputation. Nonprofits need to be especially sensitive to the loss of goodwill (and potential fundraising and volunteer resources) they may suffer if they cause a serious accident or become embroiled in a high-profile legal battle.

Controlling Risks

Once an organization has acknowledged risks, it can prudently choose how to respond. Four options are available:

1. Avoidance: prohibit the activity
2. Modification: change the activity so that the likelihood and severity of the risk are acceptable
3. Retention: accept the risk either intentionally or because no alternative exists
4. Transfer: shift at least the financial aspect of the risk through contract or insurance

The second technique, modification, can be used in tandem with all of the other techniques. The better an organization can conduct its activities to control risk, the less it will have to retain, the better record it can show its insurance companies to receive a more favorable insurance rating, and the less the likelihood that popular programs will not have to be discontinued. Various forms of modification receive the most attention here. Because the most popular method of transferring risk is through insurance, that topic is covered in a separate section later in this chapter.

Avoidance

Using the frequency/severity assessment described earlier can clarify which risks are unacceptable. The first category of unacceptable risk includes activities that cannot be performed safely because personnel lack expertise, training, equipment, or practice. Activities generally to be avoided include performing surgery, operating a backhoe, and lifting heavy objects. Any of these activities can be performed safely, however, with the appropriate resources.

The second type of activities to forgo are those that can be conducted safely but that could result in accidents for which the organization is not protected through insurance or contract. Examples of these types of activities include giving financial advice and driving a client's car.

Modification

Few risks need to be avoided if an organization takes proper precautions. Because organizations engage in such a wide variety of activities, no guide can offer complete advice on how to reduce losses. Some of the most common strategies are described below.

    1.   *Use written guidelines.* Developing and documenting an organization's policies and procedures provides guidance to board members, employees, and volunteers as to what is and is not expected of them. Policies for reporting an emergency, speaking to the press, and retaining records, for example, can help an organization perform its tasks more efficiently and defend against a challenge in court.

    Beware the organization that ignores its own written policies. This group is opening the door for increased liability. Regular monitoring and enforcement of the policies and procedures is an integral part of establishing them.

    2.   *Provide training for the job.* Whether the job is lifting heavy boxes or interviewing potential job candidates, proper training is an important loss-control technique. Well-trained, informed employees and volunteers are less likely to make mistakes that could turn into losses or lawsuits.

    The caveat regarding written policies also applies to training. Simply transferring information without follow-up to ensure appropriate behavioral changes provides ammunition for a lawsuit. Design and test training and orientations to accomplish specific objectives. Be sure that training programs are regularly reviewed and monitored.

    3.   *Conduct safety programs.* For a safety program to be effective requires commitment from the top. Employees must see a commitment to safety from the CEO to effect a safe environment. A written safety policy signed by the CEO is a good start. A safety program starts with the physical environment, including buildings, worksites, offices, and facilities. Regular inspections and appropriate follow-up are important aspects of a successful safety program. If staff work in the field, the safety of their activities warrants separate analysis.

    Organizations have an obligation to correct problems within a reasonable time after receiving notice of them. Failure to do so can create an additional liability. A citizen's group in New York was frustrated by potholes in the streets that caused tire damage. The city's policy was to pay claims only for damage caused by known potholes that were not repaired within a specified time frame. The protesters organized and in one day documented virtually every pothole in Manhattan. After putting the city on notice, the group began filing tire damage claims en masse. This forced the city to quickly repair the streets or pay many more claims.

    Training is another element of risk reduction. Safety training for employees and volunteers can include employing proper lifting techniques, using the proper equipment to perform specific tasks (such as stepladders or surgical gloves), recognizing dangerous behavior patterns, and reporting potential hazards.

4. *Ensure legal compliance.* Nonprofits are obligated to follow a bewildering array of rules promulgated by every form of government including the Internal Revenue Service (IRS); state and federal occupational safety and health agencies (OSHA); the Environmental Protection Agency (EPA); federal laws regarding employment, pensions, and benefits; and local health regulations for food preparation, to name a few. Monitoring and complying with these rules and regulations is the responsibility of the organization. A simple property acquisition could become a nightmare if the recipient is not aware of laws requiring it to pay for cleanup of hazardous waste stored on the site.

Nonprofit administrators should consult with their attorneys and professional associations to keep abreast of laws and regulations that may affect their organizations. Most enforcement agencies do not consider ignorance of the law an acceptable defense.

Whatever risks an organization has, it can develop strategies for controlling them, often simply by following standard procedures for good management. In this sense, the entirety of this book is about risk management. Management savvy, combined with common sense and a little extra creativity, can produce ideas for controlling the risks of almost any activity.

The city of Santa Monica's response to problems with its Independence Day festivities provides an instructive example. Santa Monica's problem was that its fireworks display had become too successful. Although the hazard of the fireworks was minimized by shooting them over the Pacific, the risks of rowdy crowds were not so easily controlled. Disorderly out-of-towners were souring the community spirit that the celebration was designed to foster. Along with the uninvited guests came a rising tide of injuries from firecrackers, fistfights, and traffic accidents. The simple solution was to cancel the fireworks. No crowds. No risk. No fun either. To keep the celebration but eliminate the troublemakers, the city took an unusual approach. It rescheduled the fireworks display from nightfall to sunrise, a time that doesn't draw large crowds from out of town. The result is "Dawn's Early Light," a special event with more of a family orientation than ever before.

Responding to a Potential Liability Incident

Despite the best precautions, things can still go wrong. When they do, taking appropriate action can reduce the likelihood that an incident will culminate in a lawsuit. The appropriate response can also reduce misery and negative publicity. Because an incident can become a claim, however, proper steps should always be taken to preserve a legal defense and activate insurance coverage. The following responses can help prevent or mitigate a claim.

Express concern for the injured person. Aid the person to obtain necessary treatment; provide care if you are able, without admitting or implying liability. People are more likely to sue if they are not treated well after the incident. Note that your insurance company may not pay expenses incurred prior to the formal filing of a claim. Moreover, an offer of assistance may be construed as an admission of liability. Thus, you should confer with your insurer before any incident occurs to develop a plan for responding if a problem does occur and to ensure that you will be covered if you offer to pay an injured person's expenses.

Repeat: do not admit liability. As obvious as liability may seem in the situation, the rules of law could produce unexpected results. Try not to say anything about why you think the incident occurred. After an auto collision, do not pay a ticket or fine without consulting your attorney. Unless immediate changes are necessary to protect public safety, do not modify conditions that caused the incident until you have conferred with counsel.

Write down the names of any witnesses and any other necessary information.

If possible, *take photographs* of the scene.

Immediately notify your insurer, attorney, and sponsor. Delay can jeopardize your ability to defend against a claim and your right to insurance coverage. Do not assume that some other party will be liable and you need not report the incident.

- Insurer: Notify both your agent and the carrier named on the insurance policy. If in doubt about which policy covers an incident, notify all possible sources of coverage.
- Attorney: Involving legal counsel early can be vital to your defense. Discuss this matter with your insurer immediately to determine who will choose counsel.
- Sponsor: If you operate under the auspices of or in collaboration with another entity, notify that entity in accord with its requirements. Follow special procedures the sponsor has established for reporting incidents, such as bypassing normal channels to make sure upper echelons are aware of the situation.

As soon as possible, *record your recollection* of the incident and encourage others involved in the incident to do the same. Memories fade quickly. To capture your thoughts while they are fresh, you might talk into a tape recorder. Be sure to answer the questions who, what, where, when, and how. Limit your statements to what you personally know: *do not assume anything.* If you record anything based on what someone else told you, be sure to indicate the source of that information.

Do not talk about the incident without consulting counsel. Anyone you talk to may be subpoenaed.

Support the people involved in the incident. The distress of staff members involved in an incident is often made worse by ostracism. Extra support may be needed to maintain morale.

Prior to any incident, an organization should *develop a response plan* and train staff in its procedures. The prospect of a shaken volunteer appearing on the nightly news muttering, "I always knew this would happen," should be sufficient motivation.

Working with Other Entities

Risk management becomes a bit more complex when two or more organizations are involved in an activity. To limit liability in such situations, organizations may make arrangements that allocate responsibility for obtaining insurance or otherwise providing for potential losses. In the absence of any agreement, each organization may be financially responsible for a claim. The following discussion uses collaborating organizations as an example, but the same principles are applicable to arrangements involving contractors.

Obtaining a certificate of insurance from a collaborating organization provides assurance that the organization is covered in the event of a claim. The certificate should provide for a thirty-day notice in the event of cancellation or nonrenewal of the policy. If existence of the coverage is critical, a policy requiring merely that the agent "endeavor to" notify you of cancellation should be altered to require actual notification. Absent special circumstances, limits for the coverage should be at least as high as the limit for your own general liability insurance policy. Obtaining a certificate of insurance reduces the likelihood that an injured party will look to you as the deep pocket. By itself, though, a certificate of insurance does not prevent lawsuits against your organization or increase your insurance coverage.

Requiring the sponsoring organization to list you as an additional insured party on its liability insurance policy gives you extra insurance protection. To obtain this protection, the sponsoring organization must ask its carrier to add your organization to its liability policy's coverage, either for a specific event or for all purposes. If later a suit is brought against your organization arising from an event that is within the scope of the policy, you will be entitled to protection under the sponsor's insurance policy. To verify the arrangement, you should obtain a certificate of insurance that specifies the extent of the coverage and its applicability to claims against your organization.

A "hold harmless" agreement signed by the sponsoring organization obligates the sponsor to indemnify you if anybody sues. Because a hold harmless agreement is a contract, its terms can be tailored to meet specific needs. The agreement functions by requiring the sponsoring party to pay on your behalf; it does not grant you immunity from being sued. Thus, it is useful only if the organization has substantial assets or adequate insurance. In most instances, a hold harmless agreement should be combined with a certificate of insurance that verifies the adequacy of coverage and the applicability of the policy to liability assumed under contract.

For assistance in making these arrangements, you may need to work with your attorney and/or your insurance agent or broker. Agents and brokers are generally willing to assist with these matters because of their own financial interest in getting the job done right.

Insurance and Indemnification

Risk reduction alone is not enough. No amount of prudence can totally eliminate the possibility of a loss. If a loss occurs, an organization needs to have a financial reserve readily available or face extinction. Because few organizations are well enough financed to rely entirely on their own assets, some form of insurance is likely to be necessary.

Given all the difficulties and frustrations of obtaining insurance, an organization might be tempted to skip the whole process and "go bare." To organizations with few assets, this option may appear appealing, but it has its own drawbacks.

Without insurance, an organization places the personal assets of its employees and volunteers at greater risk. An organization cannot act except through some person. Absent a law to the contrary, an injured party is free to seek a judgment against the individual who caused the harm as well as against the organization. As a practical matter, injured parties have no incentive to sue individuals if the organization is insured or has sufficient assets. If suing a volunteer or employee is the injured party's only recourse, however, such an action is much more likely.

The need for organizations to carry adequate coverage is heightened because individuals cannot easily make up for an organization's lack of insurance by relying on their personal policies (other than professional malpractice). Most homeowner's policies and even personal "umbrella" policies will not cover many forms of liability an individual may incur as a volunteer, particularly as a board member. (Umbrella policies are explained later in this chapter.)

In addition, insurance may be necessary to qualify for contracts with government agencies or foundations, or as a condition of licensure. Some states require an organization to be insured in order for volunteers to be protected from suit. Whether an organization wants to or not, it may have no choice but to insure.

Whether insurance is a good buy is a separate question that receives different answers depending in part on conditions in the insurance industry. During a "hard" insurance market — when premiums are high and coverage is hard to find — the attractiveness of insurance diminishes. The insurance market is cyclical, though, and "soft" markets with ample availability and lower prices have always followed hard markets. During a soft market, the task for nonprofits shifts from finding coverage at any price to obtaining appropriate coverage that is likely to remain relatively stable when the market turns again.

The following discussion describes the most common forms of liability insurance for nonprofit organizations and then suggests strategies for obtaining satisfactory coverage.

General Liability Insurance

The general liability policy, often in the form of a "package policy" that includes property insurance, is the most common and the most inclusive type of insurance. Undoubtedly the most common type of liability insurance is the general liability policy that covers most bodily injury and property damage claims. Although virtually essential, the general liability policy is not comprehensive. The exclusions to coverage generally constitute a very long list. Of principal concern are claims resulting from board action, use of a vehicle, rendering "professional" services, and types of harm that do not come under insurers' headings of "bodily injury" or "property damage." Excluded as "professional" may be the services of nurses, social workers, and counselors. Other exclusions may include civil rights and employment claims.

Separate policies must be obtained for those excluded elements. Like individuals, organizations also may obtain umbrella policies that can provide protection against claims that are outside the scope of specific policies or that exceed the monetary limits of other policies.

Directors and Officers Insurance

Directors and officers (D&O) insurance policies are designed for a variety of claims alleging harm attributable to the governance or management of an organization. The terms of any particular policy may make its coverage both broader and narrower than claims against boards. Policies may be broader by covering claims against the organization itself as well as staff and volunteers other than board members. (Such policies may be referred to as "Association Professional Liability Insurance.") Policies are narrower because they do not cover all types of claims against boards. Most significantly, D&O insurance does not cover bodily injury or property damage claims, even if a board member caused the harm.

This coverage is easily confused with a general liability policy because a single incident may result in claims under both policies. For example, a swimming accident will be covered under the general liability policy because it involves bodily injury, even if a board member is named in the suit. If a lawsuit is filed to stop the board from operating a swimming pool, the D&O policy would respond.

This case illustrates both the truth and the limitation of the statement that directors and officers are covered by a general liability policy. Although the general liability policy may cover board members, the scope of coverage does not include the kinds of claims ordinarily filed against boards.

One of the most striking differences between D&O policies and general liability policies is the methods they use for determining whether claims fall within the time period the policy covers. Directors and officers policies are almost universally written on a "claims-made" form that limits insurers' long-term obligation to pay claims.

The essence of the "claims-made" rule is that the claim, rather than the incident, must occur within the time period the policy covers.

The nature of claims-made coverage necessitates extra care to avoid a coverage gap. One strategy is to remain forever with the same insurer. Staying with the same carrier automatically extends coverage from one policy period to the next. The claims-made feature does not prevent changing insurers, however, especially if no incidents likely to lead to claims have occurred. The prudent strategy is to choose a policy that includes coverage for wrongful acts that occurred while the previous policy was in effect or, better still, regardless of when a wrongful act occurred.

Almost all D&O policies also differ from standard insurance policies in that they do not obligate the insurance company to defend a claim. Instead, the policy requires only that the reinsurer reimburse costs after they are incurred. The timeliness of that reimbursement can be critical to a cash-strapped organization. A related difference is that *legal defense costs are within the policy limits of most D&O policies.* Rather than paying legal expenses in addition to claims up to the policy limit, the D&O policy subtracts legal expenses from the policy limit. Thus, a one-million-dollar limit does not provide adequate protection for a one-million-dollar claim. Legal defense costs can exhaust the entire policy limit, leaving no coverage for a settlement or judgment.

Although few nonprofit organizations carried D&O insurance twenty years ago, the practice is becoming increasingly common. Among large organizations, the question of whether to purchase D&O insurance differs little from the decision to purchase general liability insurance. The risk of a lawsuit is higher for a large organization and that risk places the substantial assets of the organization in jeopardy. The issues listed here need to be considered by any nonprofit making the decision to purchase or forgo D&O insurance:

- Board members' (and others') willingness to risk personal liability
- The organization's ability to indemnify individuals
- The organization's financial resources to mount an effective defense and, if necessary, pay a settlement or judgment
- The extent to which the organization can reduce the likelihood of a claim through effective risk management
- The anticipated likelihood and expense of a claim
- The cost of coverage

For smaller organizations that lack assets to pay a claim, the personal liability of individual board members takes on greater importance. Their willingness to accept the risk of an unlikely but financially disastrous claim must be considered. Some may believe that the state's volunteer protection statute adequately shields them, despite the limitations of those laws, or that their own insurance is adequate. Others may be unconcerned about personal liability, either because they have no assets or because they would rather take the risk than spend the organization's money.

Volunteers

Insurance for volunteers may need to cover two types of situations: injuries to a volunteer and harm caused by a volunteer. For the latter, coverage is ordinarily desirable for claims against the organization and against the volunteer personally. An organization's general liability policy usually covers any claim by a third party against the organization because of something a volunteer did. Even if the policy does not explicitly mention volunteers, the coverage is present as long as the organization is legally responsible for the volunteer's conduct.

For claims against a volunteer personally, coverage may come from the volunteer's own insurance, a general liability policy that specifically includes volunteers, or a special volunteer liability policy. To determine whether volunteers are covered under the general liability policy, check the definition of "insured" to see whether it lists "volunteers." If it does not, check the endorsements at the back of the policy to see if one of them adds volunteers. As an option to covering volunteers under the general liability policy, some organizations purchase a special volunteer liability policy. This coverage may be even better than inclusion in the organization's general liability policy because it provides independent protection and it may have broader terms.

Injuries to volunteers often fall through gaps in coverage. In most states, volunteers are not included in the workers' compensation system. Thus, they cannot recover under a workers' compensation policy nor are they bound by the system's limitations on suing an "employer" for work-related injuries. In a few states, organizations can elect to cover their volunteers under workers' compensation, but even in those states that option is rarely optimal. Instead, an organization may have the medical payments portion of its general liability policy expanded to cover volunteers' injuries or obtain an accident and injury policy especially for volunteers.

Motor Vehicle Coverage

The need for automobile insurance is obvious, but not easily met. Particularly if volunteers or employees drive their own vehicles on behalf of the organization, the coverage may be hard to find and expensive. Insurers prefer to exclude autos not owned by the organization (non-owned autos) to reduce uncertainty about a driver's purpose at the time of an accident. Was the driver on his or her way to transport a client or merely going out for groceries?

To minimize the cost of non-owned auto coverage, an organization may require its drivers to carry insurance up to a specified amount, with the organization insuring only for damages in excess of that amount. While this technique will reduce the organization's insurance, it has the unavoidable effect of shifting the primary responsibility for insurance to drivers. At a minimum, those drivers should verify that their insurance will cover accidents occurring in the course of service to the organization. Conversely, the organization should verify that all its drivers are insured.

Financial responsibility for motor vehicle accidents lies primarily with the owner of the vehicle. In furtherance of this general rule, states generally require every vehicle owner to carry liability insurance of at least some minimum amount. If you are involved in a collision while driving your own vehicle, most nonprofit organizations will expect you to rely on your own coverage up to the policy limits.

Even if you have a personal auto policy, coverage under a separate policy by the organization may be desirable. Personal auto policies may exclude the commercial operation of a van or bus, especially if you must have a special driver's license to operate the vehicle. Also, the organization may purchase a non-owned auto policy or excess insurance to increase the limits over your personal auto insurance.

Coverage Gaps

One of the most distressing aspects of obtaining insurance is that purchasing all of these specialized coverages may not offer complete protection. Some matters, such as intentional wrongdoing, may not be insurable. Moreover, claims may exceed policy limits or a particular claim may fall into a gap in the coverage. A defamatory statement appearing in a child-care center's newsletter may be excluded under a general liability policy because it did not cause either bodily injury or property damage. The center's professional liability policy may not pay the claim because staff members' professional activities do not ordinarily include composing a newsletter.

Failure to understand policy provisions may result in an unexpected coverage deficiency. One critical difference among policies that may go unnoticed concerns the duty to defend. Ordinarily, general liability policies obligate the insurer to defend against claims by providing legal counsel as needed once a claim is filed. The insurer must pay these defense costs in addition to any judgment or settlement up to the amount of the policy limit. Under this standard arrangement, a $500,000 policy may obligate an insurer to provide unlimited legal services and still pay a settlement or judgment up to $500,000 if the defense is not successful.

Not all policies have these features, however. With some policies, the policyholder may be required to pay the defense costs initially and seek subsequent reimbursement from the insurer. Moreover, defense costs may be within policy limits. Under this type of $500,000 policy, once the insurer had paid $500,000 in defense costs, the policy would be exhausted and wholly unavailable for use in paying any amount toward a judgment or settlement. These features are common in directors and officers insurance and professional liability insurance. They also tend to appear in policies sold during a hard insurance market.

Gaps also may occur if an organization obtains coverage under a "claims-made" policy rather than an "occurrence" policy, which has been the industry standard. With occurrence policies, an insurer's obligation to defend against claims and pay any resulting settlements or judgments depends on whether the injury occurs during the policy period. Determining the insurer's obligations under a claims-made form is not so straightforward. Unless the claim itself is filed within the policy period, the coverage may not apply. Avoiding a coverage gap when changing insurers becomes very difficult.

To reduce coverage gaps, an organization may purchase yet another policy: an *umbrella*. For claims covered by other policies, an umbrella policy increases the total dollar value of protection. For example, umbrella coverage (or an *excess* policy) might pay claims up to $1 million rather than the $250,000 of the primary policy. Its value in protecting against gaps is that it contains fewer exclusions; thus it may pay claims that no other policy covers. Even an umbrella policy is not comprehensive, however, and the policyholder should be aware of what it does not cover.

Another strategy for reducing coverage gaps is to obtain all policies from a single insurer and stay with that insurer over time. That sensible approach may not be possible to implement, however. Insurers specialize and may offer only a few of the coverages an organization needs. Combining coverage from several insurers is a complicated undertaking that is best performed by someone with considerable expertise. A good agent or broker may help, but may not be willing to devote the necessary time to a small account. Alternatively, nonprofits working through an association or other group program may be able to coordinate coverage efficiently on behalf of association or group members.

The Insurance Market

Many nonprofit organizations were stunned when their liability insurance premiums rose suddenly in the mid-1980s and have been nearly as surprised, although much less disturbed, when premiums subsequently went down. Despite the novelty of this experience for most organizations, though, such fluctuations are not unusual in the insurance industry. Commercial insurance markets are inherently unstable.

Pricing. Insurance pricing is based primarily on two factors: (1) average claims for large numbers of organizations, and (2) insurers' expectations about future claims. Taking these two factors together, insurers are most concerned about future average claims. As difficult as this prediction may be, it is much easier than trying to predict claims for a single organization. In any given year, claims for some organizations are likely to be higher than the average and others lower, but no one knows in advance how to tell which will be which.

Without being able to foresee which organizations will end the year with high claims and which will have none, insurers work with the averages. Roughly similar organizations tend to be treated the same. Thus, if an insurer anticipates greater than average claims, an organization's premiums may rise sharply, even though it has never been sued.

This strategy of charging premiums based on expected average claims is especially necessary for types of insurance with low incidence rates. For example, many organizations have never filed a claim under their directors and officers insurance policies. Among those that have filed, however, some of the claims have been very costly. A small increase in the number of such claims, or fear that such claims will increase, may lead insurers to increase premiums substantially for all directors and officers policies.

Group Insurance. Because insurers have not offered true stability on their own initiative, nonprofits need to work together to have their needs met. Through group purchasing, nonprofits may be able to increase their bargaining power sufficiently to interest an insurer in offering stable coverage in return for the groups' continuing patronage. For this purpose, nonprofits may form purchasing groups under the federal Liability Risk Retention Act, or participate in insurance programs sponsored by state and national associations. Insurance programs that are negotiated by representatives of the nonprofit sector can offer significant advantages. At the national level, the Partnership Umbrella, which United Way helped to create, coordinates insurance programs from its Alexandria, Virginia, offices.

Collective insurance purchasing alone does not guarantee stability, however. Unless an insurer provides assurances that go beyond marketing claims, the dynamics of the insurance market may still result in sharply higher premiums, coverage reductions, and even policy cancellations. In 1985, a group of over a thousand nurse-midwives lost their insurance. Finding a new insurer at that point was extremely difficult.

Some organizations that have tired of the roller coaster ride have followed the lead of many businesses and governmental units by leaving the commercial insurance market. To meet their insurance needs, they have formed risk pools and other financial risk-sharing arrangements. These arrangements perform the function of an insurance company, but differ in several respects. The principal differences are that they serve *only* nonprofit organizations and they are not as tightly regulated as ordinary insurance companies.

Not being owned by private investors who have an overriding economic interest in increasing their profits gives risk pools greater flexibility in satisfying their members' needs. In this regard, the experience of government entities that have joined risk pools is illuminating. In response to a survey conducted for the Public Risk Management Association, 92.1 percent of the government risk managers polled agreed with the following statement: "Pools have, on the whole, done a much better job of underwriting and managing risks than private insurers" (Young, 1988, p. 2).

Along with their advantages, these alternative insurance arrangements also have several drawbacks. Because they are not fully regulated as insurance companies and are unable to use state insurance guarantee funds, they may be riskier than commercial insurers, although the pools can be structured to protect their integrity. For purposes of meeting state financial responsibility laws, coverage from a risk pool or risk-retention group may not be considered insurance. Moreover, nonprofits' pools are not exempt from the economic forces that lead commercial insurers to raise rates during hard markets. Consequently, they cannot offer complete stability. Regardless of these and other limitations, however, risk pooling for nonprofits has worked well where it has been tried.

Nontraditional risk-pooling mechanisms function under special laws that provide exemptions from some insurance regulations. The first such law passed over a decade ago in Illinois, which is now home to several of the country's largest and most established risk pools for nonprofits. As a result of the last hard insurance market, a number of other states modified their laws and additional pools have formed to serve nonprofits in those states. In addition, some national associations now operate insurance mechanisms for their members.

How to Approach Insurers

By understanding insurance from an insurer's perspective, an organization can substantially improve its insurance prospects. The first thing to realize is that insurers have tremendous discretion in deciding which organizations to insure and how to charge. To make these decisions, insurers rely in part on statistics about insurance claims filed against similar organizations. Statistical analysis is not the only factor in the underwriting process, however. According to a former insurance regulator, as "much as the conscientious actuary would like to otherwise provide, his decisions are often overruled either explicitly by management or subversively by the underwriting process in order to accommodate to the vicissitudes of the market place" (National Association of Insurance Commissioners, 1974, pp. 3–4).

If nonprofit organization administrators put the same effort into completing insurance applications that they put into writing grant proposals, far fewer organizations would be denied coverage. As in writing a grant proposal, portraying the organization in the most favorable light is essential. Applicants should accompany unfavorable information with a positive explanation, if possible. The organization has only $1,000 in its bank account? Be sure to explain, if you can, that diligent fundraising has kept the organization afloat for years, despite low reserves. If the future looks brighter than the past, offer your optimistic projections supported by verifiable facts.

In particular, emphasize anything the organization does that reduces the likelihood of claims. Are volunteers trained before they perform services? Is the organization accredited by a national standard-setting body? If so, append a list of the accrediting standards to the application. Accreditation and risk management standards are not identical, but they usually overlap.

No organization is risk free and every applicant has an obligation to reveal known risks. At the same time, be careful of words that may alarm an insurer. "Operating a halfway house for drug addicts" is scarier than "providing assisted living arrangements for substance abusers." *Keep in mind that the application is for insurance and not for funding.* For insurance purposes, an underwriter really does not care whether the organization does good deeds. What matters is the riskiness of the organization's activities and the extent of its precautions.

At an absolute minimum, an insurance application must be accurate and complete. Neglecting to inform an insurer of a hazard may invalidate the policy. Failing to attach requested audit reports or other documents may result in a summary rejection of an application, which in turn makes obtaining insurance from another company more difficult.

Finally, everything you want an insurer to know should be communicated in writing. Saying something to an insurance agent may have no effect because agents ordinarily do not decide whether to issue a policy. That decision is made by another person who probably will see only the papers you submit.

To avoid surprises, insurers prefer to stick with familiar types of clients. This preference for the familiar presents a challenge to nonprofits because many insurers do not know much about nonprofit organizations. Moreover, what insurers know or think they know about nonprofits may increase rather than reduce their apprehension. The unfamiliarity is owing largely to the relatively small amount of insurance nonprofits purchase. According to a recent estimate, nonprofit human service organizations spent approximately $500 million for property and liability insurance in 1988. Although this is a substantial amount in the nonprofit world, it represents less than one percent of total commercial insurance premiums.

Fortunately, these generalizations about insurers are not universally true. A few agents and brokers around the country specialize in serving nonprofits and several insurance companies offer programs specifically for nonprofits. In some states, nonprofits have formed risk pools or other risk-sharing arrangements dedicated exclusively to meeting their insurance needs.

Dealing with any of these specialists in insurance for nonprofits can reduce the common barriers to obtaining adequate coverage. Still, an organization that appears to be excessively risky may not be able to obtain coverage from any insurer. To obtain the most coverage at the lowest cost, an organization must convince an insurer that it is a good risk.

Liability Insurance Mistakes to Avoid

- Purchasing a "premises policy" that limits coverage to incidents that occur at the office. (Such policies are inadequate for organizations that send staff into the field.)
- Failing to obtain coverage for personal injury claims. (An increasing number of lawsuits allege defamation and other types of harm that are not covered by a general liability policy limited to bodily injury and property damage.)
- Relying on a traditional directors and officers liability insurance policy to protect the organization from claims involving board or administrative actions. (Coverage for the organization, rather than for directors and officers individually, may be added by endorsement or obtained with a broader policy, such as an Association Professional Liability Insurance policy.)
- Overlooking liability coverage for volunteers. (Standard insurance policies cover the insured entity and its employees. Volunteers usually need to be added by endorsement.)
- Having no coverage for claims by injured volunteers. (Volunteers usually are not covered by workers' compensation and generally cannot collect against the general liability policy. An accident policy or adequate medical payments provision in a general liability policy may suffice.)
- Thinking that a general liability policy covers employment disputes. (The bodily injury or property damage coverage of general liability insurance rarely applies to employment claims; a directors and officers policy covers most employment-related claims—unless specifically excluded.)
- Switching carriers each year to save a few dollars. (A stable, long-term relationship has many advantages when the market changes or the organization files a claim.)
- Ignoring non-owned auto liability. (Accidents caused by staff using their own vehicles—or other vehicles the organization does not own—can lead to claims against an organization.)
- Choosing a policy limit for a D&O policy without recognizing that defense costs are within policy limits. (Although the policy limit for general liability policies is generally in addition to costs of defending against a claim, defense costs are subtracted from the limit of a D&O policy.)
- Having no coverage for finished products. (Organizations that produce or sell materials may need this coverage.)
- Purchasing a D&O policy that excludes nonmonetary claims. (Such policies do not apply to lawsuits brought to force a change in the organization's operations rather than to recover money.)

Indemnification

Nonprofit organizations' bylaws typically include provisions that require indemnification of the directors if they are named in a lawsuit. *Indemnification* is simply an undertaking by the organization to pay legal costs and any settlement or judgment in certain circumstances. Adequate protection may require both indemnification and insurance because of limitations on each, including the reality that indemnification without money to back it up is a hollow promise.

State laws for nonprofits generally require indemnification in some situations, permit it in most, and forbid it in a few. Most states require indemnification for volunteer board members who successfully defend against a claim. Prohibitions against indemnification are generally designed to prevent a volunteer from profiting at the organization's expense. To make full use of indemnification, an organization may need to state in its charter or bylaws that it will indemnify its volunteers in specified situations or to the maximum extent permitted by law.

Summary

Many nonprofit organization managers comment that risk management is "a good idea if we had the time." Many are coming to realize, though, that they must take the time because failure to do so can leave all their other plans open to devastation. Nonprofits, as well as their staffs and boards, are capable of causing harm and are subject to lawsuits if they do. Some states afford a measure of protection from liability, but the rules vary widely and none provide complete immunity.

The risk management process is a systematic method of responding to the dangers inherent in any organization's operations. Five steps are involved in risk management:

Step 1. Identify risks: recognize what risks the organization faces and acknowledge risks when making decisions.

Step 2. Evaluate risks: use a frequency/severity model that directs appropriate risk treatment.

Step 3. Reduce risks to an acceptable level: eliminate those risks that are too costly, using loss control techniques to limit the impact of the risks that the organization chooses to accept, and transferring as much risk as possible to other organizations.

Step 4. Obtain insurance or make other financial arrangements as needed: purchase appropriate insurance policies and budget to accept small losses.

Step 5. Monitor and revise: know that risk management is not an event but an ongoing process; see the potential hazards in every endeavor, and revise risk management strategies in light of changing circumstances.

Navigating the insurance maze is an important part of risk management. Organizations may choose to purchase insurance for a variety of reasons: to protect their boards and volunteers, to protect against catastrophic loss to property, or to protect their assets against a lawsuit. In addition, some government, foundation, and agency funding sources require that grantees or contractors have appropriate insurance coverage.

Organizations armed with a basic knowledge of available insurance policies, their coverages and exclusions, and the most effective ways to complete insurance applications can better ensure that they are and will remain covered. Most important, risk management cannot be the sole responsibility of one individual or department. Effective risk management occurs when top administrators support risk management so that everyone in the organization applies its principles to their everyday tasks.

Assistance with all aspects of risk management is available from the Nonprofit Risk Management Center, 1828 L St., NW, Suite 505, Washington, D.C. 20036, phone (202) 785-3891. Many of the publications listed in the References for this chapter can be ordered from the center. The center can help to find and evaluate insurance coverage, but it does not sell insurance nor endorse specific insurance providers.

References

American Bar Association. *Guidebook for Directors of Nonprofit Organizations.* Chicago: American Bar Association, 1993.

Kurtz, D. *Board Liability: Guide for Nonprofit Directors.* Mt. Kisco, N.Y.: Moyer Bell, 1988.

Lai, M., Chapman, T., and Steinbock, T. *Am I Covered for . . . ?: A Guide to Insurance for Non-Profits.* (2nd ed.) San Jose, Calif.: Consortium for Human Services, 1992.

National Association of Insurance Commissioners. *Monitoring Competition: A Means of Regulating the Property and Liability Insurance Business.* Kansas City: National Association of Insurance Commissioners, 1974.

Nonprofit Risk Management Center. *D&O — Yes or No?: Insurance for the Volunteer Board.* Washington, D.C.: Nonprofit Risk Management Center, 1991.

Nonprofit Risk Management Center. *State Liability Laws for Charitable Organizations and Volunteers.* Washington, D.C.: Nonprofit Risk Management Center, 1992.

Tremper, C. "Compensation for Harm from Charitable Activity." *Cornell Law Review,* 1990, *76,* 401–475.

Tremper, C. *Reconsidering Legal Liability and Insurance for Nonprofit Organizations.* Lincoln, Neb.: Law College Education Services, 1989.

Tremper, C., and Kostin, K. *No Surprises: Controlling Risks in Volunteer Programs.* Washington, D.C.: Nonprofit Risk Management Center, 1993.

Young, P. *Risk Pooling: Scope and Practices 1987–88.* Washington, D.C.: Public Risk Management Association, 1988.

PART FIVE

∞

MANAGING PEOPLE

The final part of this book addresses any nonprofit organization's most important asset—the employees and volunteers who carry out the organization's mission through day-to-day work. One chapter in this part describes how to recruit and retain effective service volunteers, while another chapter describes recruiting and hiring the right employees. Both chapters give careful attention to the legal issues involved in working with volunteers and in recruiting and selecting employees, while keeping the mission in the forefront. The third chapter provides detailed information on designing and managing employee compensation and benefits, an increasingly difficult task in today's changing labor market. The final chapter in this part examines the principles and practices for designing and carrying out appropriate training and development efforts for volunteers and for paid staff.

The book's concluding chapter assesses the forces toward cooperation and the forces toward competition within the nonprofit sector. Rather than summarizing all the prior chapters, this final chapter argues that the future of nonprofit management will be very different, depending on whether relations among nonprofit organizations become more cooperative or more competitive, and makes a case for the desirability of building a more cooperative community of nonprofit organizations.

22

Recruiting and Retaining Volunteers

Stephen McCurley

Nonprofit agencies have always relied on the assistance of unpaid volunteers in delivering their services. In 1991, these volunteers provided the equivalent of nine million full-time employees to the nonprofit work force (Hodgkinson and Weitzman, 1992, p. 2). As this unpaid work force has become larger, as volunteer jobs have become more complex, and as competition among agencies for available volunteers has become more common, volunteer management practices have, of necessity, also become more sophisticated (see Silver, 1988; Seita, 1990).

Effective involvement of volunteers involves a planned and organized process similar to that required by any organizational project or effort (Wilson, 1976; McCurley and Lynch, 1989). The basic elements of this volunteer management process are shown in Figure 22.1.

The descending steps on the left side of the figure represent the major elements involved in determining the needs for volunteers within the agency, identifying suitable volunteers, and then creating a motivational structure that will support those volunteers. They are roughly analogous to personnel and supervisory procedures for paid staff. The elements on the right side of the figure represent the other universes that interact with and must support volunteer personnel (the staff with whom volunteers will be in contact, upper management of the organization, and the community at large) and that therefore must be involved in the process of volunteer utilization.

All of these elements are interactive, and as in most creative management processes, rarely proceed in a totally linear fashion. During the existence

Figure 22.1. Volunteer Management Process.

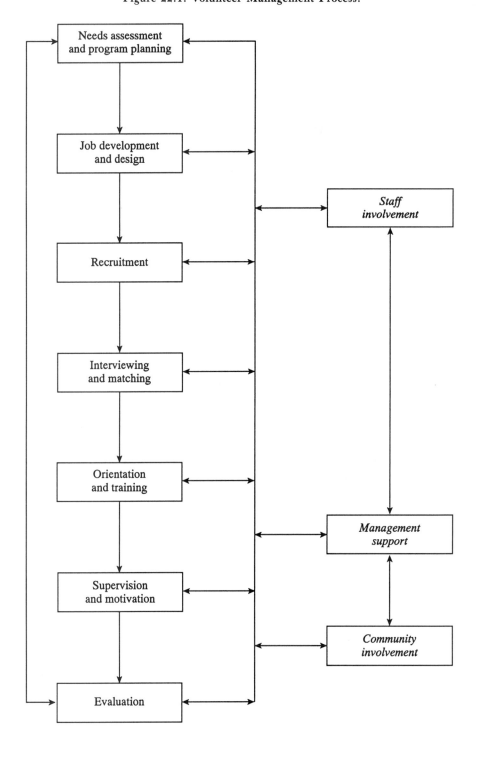

of the overall volunteer program, the elements within this process will tend to recur with the addition of each new area of volunteer utilization (as new projects or areas of usage are created) and with the addition of each new volunteer (as the process is customized to the requirements of the individual). The process will also be reenacted as new staff are added to the agency who must interact with volunteers.

This chapter will deal with the process for recruiting community volunteers and with maintaining motivational levels of those volunteers. It will concentrate on the volunteer recruited at the service provider level, not at the board or advisory committee level, where policy is made. The suggestions in this chapter will be aimed at the mid- to large-size organizational structure in which there is significant paid staff presence, requiring a high degree of interaction and cooperation between paid employees and volunteers recruited from the community. Smaller agencies, or those where the primary service delivery is done by volunteers without interaction with paid staff, can still follow the general principles offered, but will need to adapt them to their less-structured operational environment. (Those groups that operate in all-volunteer environment with no paid staff will find Scheier (1992) of use.)

Needs Assessment and Program Planning

Initial Planning

Program planning and design begins with an assessment of why the agency wishes to utilize volunteers and what the benefits and problems are likely to be in volunteer utilization. Possible benefits to volunteer utilization might include:

- Delivery of services at reduced cost
- Access to additional expertise
- Better contact with the community
- Better assistance to clients

Possible disadvantages might include:

- Lack of control and reliability of volunteers
- Time demands for volunteer supervision
- Potential negative impact on paid jobs
- Difficulties in recruiting enough qualified volunteers

It is essential that the agency and its staff have an overall appreciation that the utilization of volunteers will, on balance, be worth the investment of organizational resources that are required to make the volunteer program operate. This appreciation is vital in explaining the need for volunteers both to staff within the agency (who must make changes in their own work styles to accommodate volunteers) and to the community (which must understand why the agency needs volunteers).

The philosophical determination by the agency to involve volunteers is often written up as an official policy and approved by the agency's policy-setting group. The Juvenile Court of Spokane County, Washington, for example, formulated the following statement in regard to volunteer involvement:

> The Spokane County Juvenile Court is committed to providing the best and most appropriate services possible. To realize this goal, our Department shall make every effort to enlist the cooperation of all available resources. The Department is committed to the development of a public-private partnership which includes volunteers as an important and necessary ingredient in the development and delivery of services.
>
> In addition to the above, our Department plans to actively implement and maintain a responsible program of citizen involvement because:
>
> 1. Our Department will never have sufficient resources to meet all service needs. Even if such resources were available (professional staff, finances, facilities, etc.), the Department would still believe it necessary for the community to become involved in juvenile issues.
> 2. It has been demonstrated repeatedly that volunteers can significantly enhance, expand, and upgrade services. With appropriate recruitment, screening, training, and supervision, volunteers can perform almost any task effectively and responsibly.
> 3. The Department feels it necessary to involve the community in the problems we are trying to alleviate or solve. Efforts to involve the community in agency affairs will help to educate the public about these problems and will create a more enlightened and active citizenry.

Such an official endorsement of the volunteer effort becomes the framework upon which agency decisions regarding a consistent set of procedures for volunteer involvement can be based (Ellis, 1986).

Staff Involvement

Relationships between agency paid staff and volunteers have always played a crucial role in the eventual outcome of the volunteer program (Scheier, 1977; Snyder, 1985; Ellis, 1986; Mausner, 1988). Developing a good working relationship between staff and volunteers has always been one of the major tasks of the director of the volunteer program. In the words of Ilsley (1990, p. 119): "One of the greatest fears among managers of volunteers is tension between volunteers and paid staff. So prevalent is this fear that when asked to name the most difficult aspect of their job, twenty-nine out of thirty managers of volunteers in organizations that have a paid staff responded that it is tension between that staff and volunteers." It is essential that the decision to utilize volunteers be agreed upon by the staff of the agency. If staff are uncomfortable with the decision to utilize volunteers, their resistance or even passive acceptance will serve as an effective barrier to volunteer involvement. Staff who do not support the concept of volunteer involvement will resist the development of creative or significant jobs for volunteers, thus reducing the agency's ability to offer desirable work opportunities to potential volunteers. Nonsupportive staff will also communicate their discomfort to agency volunteers, delivering a clear message that the volunteers are not really "wanted" by the agency despite its public pronouncements.

Nonsupportive staff will also function less effectively as volunteer supervisors. The relationship between volunteers and their immediate staff supervisors will have direct bearing on the job satisfaction of the volunteers (Gidron, 1983; Colomy, Chen, and Andrews, 1987).

In addition to obtaining staff agreement to the utilization of volunteers, it is also important to provide staff with training in how to work effectively with volunteers (Skillingstad, 1989). This training should introduce staff to the operational procedures of the volunteer programs and should enable staff to learn the techniques of effective volunteer supervision. This training is particularly crucial when agency staff do not have much supervisory experience or training because in their work with volunteers they will be both learning and implementing managerial skills. Expecting young and/or inexperienced staff members to acquire supervisory skills without assistance through a process of "try it and see" is probably optimistic; expecting volunteers to enjoy the process of experimentation is delusionary.

Job Development and Design

The next step in involving volunteers is to determine where and how those volunteers can best be engaged. The development of specific jobs or volunteer positions is the most important stage in volunteer recruitment and retention. Before any volunteers are sought, the agency should have a clear picture of what each volunteer will be doing and a clear written description of that work and the supervisory mechanisms and personnel that will surround the work situation. As Wilson (1976, p. 102) puts it: "Recruiting before designing jobs is rather like trying to dance before the music begins. The possibility of ending up out of step is very good indeed."

The importance of a volunteer job description cannot be overstated. The job description is the agency's planning tool to help volunteers understand the results to be accomplished, what tasks are involved, what skills are required, and other important details about the job. A job description provides an organized means of creating continuity in a job from one volunteer to the next. It is also a "living" document that will need to be revised as the program changes, or as the volunteer develops during service with the agency.

Job descriptions are the building blocks of the volunteer program, insofar as all recruiting, interviewing, placing, supervising, and evaluating is based on the information contained in the job description. The key to a good job description is to keep it short, succinct, and clear. The format for the job description is arbitrary, but its final content should be developed in concert with the volunteer who is accepting the position. The job description should provide the volunteer and their supervisor with a clear common conception of the purpose of the volunteer's job and of the expectation of results.

Developing ideas for potential jobs will require creative thought by current staff, who must be able to visualize tasks that might be suitable for volunteers. One way to approach this is to think of categories of potential tasks:

- Direct assistance to an individual client: counseling, visitation, mentoring, and so on
- Administrative office help: information services, filing, delivering messages, and the like
- Direct assistance to staff: research, training, computer assistance
- Outreach to the community: speakers' bureau, fundraising, client marketing, and so forth

Each job design should meet certain requirements:

- The work must be meaningful and significant, both to the agency and to agency clientele. The work must be needed and should be interesting to someone. This means that the volunteer job must have a defined goal or purpose that the volunteer can work to accomplish and can feel good about having achieved.
- The volunteer ought to be able to feel some ownership of and responsibility for the job. Volunteers are not robots, but must feel that they have some input into and control over the work they are asked to do. This will mean including the volunteer in the flow of information and decision-making within the office. It will also mean holding the volunteer responsible for the accomplishment of the job.
- The work must fit a part-time situation. Either the work must be small enough in scope to be productively approached in a few hours a week or it must be designed to be shared among a group of volunteers.
- The work must fit into the overall context of the agency, including strategic goals (relationship to agency mission and clientele), physical logistics (work site, equipment), and management procedures (assignment of a supervisor).

For the agency, this developmental planning will enable the creation of a structure that can effectively support the volunteer. For the volunteer, this planning will create a job situation that can be utilized both in recruitment (the volunteer can be attracted by the prospect of performing meaningful and contributory work) and in retention (the volunteer will experience a more productive and enjoyable work environment) (see Gidron, 1983; Colomy, Chen, and Andrews, 1987).

Recruitment

Identifying Potential Recruitment Appeals

The second stage in volunteer utilization is determining appeals that might motivate potential volunteers to become involved. The possible range of volunteer motivations is very broad (Hodgkinson and Weitzman, 1989), encompassing practically every psychological attribute. This tends to lead agencies to develop very broad motivational appeals, believing that someone among all those potential volunteers will respond to them. It is important, however, to realize that what is needed in the development of the recruitment appeal is a slightly narrower approach, motivating potential volunteers not just to decide, in general, to volunteer, but to volunteer with this particular agency, doing this particular job (Lynch, 1984). To create this more defined appeal, the agency should develop answers to the following questions:

- Why should this job be done at all? What is the need in the community for this work? What bad things will happen if this volunteer job is not done?
- What will the benefit be to the community or to the clientele if the job is done? What will the work accomplish? What changes will it make in people's lives?
- What are some possible fears or objections concerning this job which must be overcome? The type of clients? The subject area? The skills needed to do the work? Geography?
- What will be the personal benefit to the volunteer in doing the job? Skills? Experience? Flexible work schedules? New friends?

The answers to these questions can be utilized in communicating to potential volunteers why the agency and its work are important and why the potential volunteer should contribute to the accomplishment of that work. Different aspects of this message may be emphasized more than others, or may be communicated differently to various populations. An appeal to young persons, for example, may stress job experience possibilities, while an appeal to previous clients of the agency may focus on the effects of the problem and the opportunity to help others obtain the relief that they themselves have experienced.

Creation of this message is much more difficult than it seems, particularly for paid employees. Quite often their own innate knowledge interferes with writing an effective appeal; in a sense they are too familiar with the subject to remember that others lack knowledge of it. They will often forget to include the most basic of facts—numbers of persons in the community who face the problem, harmful effects of the condition—because they assume that others in the community are as familiar with the situation as they are. This means that field-testing of recruitment appeals is quite important, to make sure that the general population receives the appropriate information in a form that they can both understand and relate to.

Designing a Recruitment Campaign

Effective volunteer recruitment consists of doing only as much work as is needed to obtain the quantity and quality of volunteers required by the agency. While this may sound simplistic, failure to heed this advice will subject the agency to one of the hidden dangers of volunteer involvement—the risk of ending up with too many of the "wrong" volunteers. While an oversupply of candidates to choose from is not viewed as problematical when dealing with paid jobs, it can be so when dealing with volunteer positions. Either the agency must "reject" some of the applicants, who may then harbor negative feelings toward the agency, or the agency may accept applicants for whom it does not have available volunteer positions, following which the applicants will develop negative feelings toward the agency for wasting their time. In either case, an oversupply of applicants will consume valuable staff time in interviewing and screening.

Three different approaches to recruitment campaigns can help the agency to obtain the number and types of volunteer applicants that it needs:

- *Warm body recruitment.* The "warm body" recruitment campaign is utilized when the agency needs a relatively large supply of volunteers for tasks that can easily be taught to most people in a short period of time. An ideal warm body recruitment situation might be a weekend event, such as a Special Olympics contest in which volunteer huggers and judges are needed.

A warm body recruitment campaign involves dissemination of information about the agency and its need for volunteers to as wide a segment of the community as possible. Typical mechanisms include distribution of brochures and posters, announcements on television and radio, articles in the newspapers, talks to local groups, and so on.

- *Targeted recruitment.* The targeted recruitment campaign operates in exactly the opposite fashion as the warm body campaign. Targeted recruitment is intentionally designed to limit the number of volunteer applicants by shaping the recruitment message and information dissemination process. Design of the campaign involves working through a series of three questions about the volunteer position being filled:

1. *What are the skills/attitudes needed to do this job?* If we draw a composite picture of the type of person who could do this job well and would *enjoy* doing it, what would it look like? Cover age, sex, motivations, hobbies, possible occupations, related interests, and whatever else fills out the picture.
2. *Based on this picture, where can we find these types of people?* Think about work settings, educational backgrounds, leisure time organizations and activities, publications they might read, parts of town in which they might live, and so on.
3. *What motivations of this type of person can we appeal to in our recruitment effort?* In particular, which of their psychological needs can be met through this job with our agency? Examples might include self-help, job enhancement, socialization, learning new skills, career exploration, leadership testing, giving back to the community, keeping productively involved, and the like.

Answering these planning questions will help limit and target dissemination sites and mechanisms as well as sharpen and focus motivational appeal. This will tend to limit the applicants to those who are more likely to fit the profile of the "ideal" volunteer. Targeted recruitment works best for volunteer jobs that require a particular skill or interest.

- *Concentric circles recruitment.* Concentric circles recruitment is designed to provide the agency with a small but steady flow of volunteer applicants. Concentric circles recruitment works through the application of word of mouth principles. Through its day-to-day operation, the agency is in contact with a variety of populations: staff and their friends, volunteers and their friends, clients and their families, and people in the surrounding neighborhood. These groups are already familiar with the existence of the agency, and some of these people have direct experience with its work or an indirect relationship through a friend who is familiar with the agency.

Concentric circles recruitment works efficiently because it relies on two favorable factors. The first is that it approaches groups whose familiarity with the agency makes them more receptive than people would be who know nothing of the agency or its work. And the second is that it makes use of the "personal appeal" factor—that is, the recruitment message is conveyed by people who are personally acquainted with potential volunteers and who have credibility with that audience. This method of recruitment is almost universal among agencies, with perhaps as many as 94 percent making some use of it (Watts and Edwards, 1983, p. 13). In 1988, over 40.4 percent of those who volunteered reported being recruited by someone they knew, and 27.6 percent were recruited because a family member or friend benefited from the activity; only 5.3 percent saw an advertisement, and 19.2 percent sought the activity on their own (Hodgkinson and Weitzman, 1988, p. 28).

Recruiting for Difficult Situations

Recruiting for a controversial activity, for a job perceived as "dangerous" or recognized as "difficult" is obviously harder than recruiting for easy or attractive jobs. Recruitment can be particularly difficult when the subject area or the job is likely to provoke an initial fear reaction from the potential volunteer. The following are some suggestions for trying to design a recruitment campaign for these types of volunteer positions:

1. Advertise by television, radio, or newspapers, so that thousands of potentially recruitable people see the message. In essence, saturate the community with your recruitment message. Some of the people who see it won't be afraid.
2. Solicit those who are acquainted with the problem area because they already work in it or in an industry related to it. They will not have the same level of fear as the general public. Be sure to remember ancillary and connected industries, such as educators who teach in subject areas that discuss the problem area. Also remember to solicit the families of those who work in the subject area.
3. Appeal to those who once worked with the problem area or who are seeking careers related to the problem area.
4. Solicit former clients, their families, and their friends and relatives. This group is less likely to be afraid of the problem area, more likely to identify with your group because they have received services, and quite likely to be committed to doing something about the problem.
5. Ask current volunteers to help. Emphasize word of mouth communication. Their communication of personal involvement ("I work in this area and I know that it is both safe and rewarding") will often overcome barriers of fear and resistance.
6. Start with recruiting people for a noncontroversial job in your agency. Develop a two-tier recruitment system. First give volunteers safe and easy jobs; then offer them tougher assignments after they've gotten to know your organization better.
7. Create an educational program to combat the fear. Start offering seminars in the community presenting the facts about the situation. Ask some of your more motivated volunteers to talk about their experiences. Recruit from those who attend the seminars.

Recruiting for Volunteer Diversity

The volunteer recruitment process is one way in which the agency can attempt to broaden its base of community involvement. A variety of authors have examined the mechanisms by which agencies can attempt to increase the diversity of their volunteer component (see, in particular, Vineyard and McCurley, 1992, for a look at a variety of populations; Nestor, 1984, 1991;

and Wright, 1992). Chambré (1982) suggests that an agency wishing to recruit black and Hispanic volunteers should engage in efforts such as personalized approaches, establishing collaborative relationships with community groups, and arranging "trigger events" that crystalize individuals' decisions to volunteer. Latting (1990) suggests that black volunteers are more motivated by altruistic impulses than white volunteers, and that recruiting attempts might best be targeted toward blacks who strongly identify with the black community and have strong feelings of social responsibility.

It is possible that agency concerns about the difficulty of minority recruitment are overstated. Carson (1987) offers data that suggest that blacks, for example, contrary to some perceptions, actually volunteer more than is thought, noting "the findings indicate that at every level of income blacks are more likely than whites to volunteer their time" (p. 108). Data from the 1990 Gallup Survey strongly suggest that if there is any problem with minority involvement it lies with the agency rather than the potential volunteer: "Among the 41 percent of respondents who reported they were asked to volunteer in the past year, 87 percent volunteered; among the 57 percent of respondents who reported that they were not asked, only 30 percent volunteered. Those respondents who were least likely to be asked were blacks (26 percent), Hispanics (27 percent), persons 18 to 24 years of age (31 percent), and those with household incomes below $20,000 (26 percent). Among the smaller proportion of these groups who were asked, the proportion who volunteered was more than three times higher than among those who were not asked" (Hodgkinson and Weitzman, 1990, p. 5).

All of those who have examined this issue have concluded that any attempt in this area can only be effective if it is matched with overall adjustment in the agency, including examination of staff recruitment practices, changes in the composition of the agency board, reassessment of agency priorities to reach diverse community populations, and the like.

Interviewing and Matching

One of the most neglected areas of volunteer management training has been that of effective interviewing of volunteers. This is unfortunate, since good interviewing skills are essential to performing that most crucial of all volunteer management tasks, matching potential volunteers with tasks and working environments they will enjoy. Saxon and Sawyer (1984, p. 43) describe this interviewing and matching process as follows: "The selection and assignment of volunteers may be viewed as a process of matching skills and abilities to requirements, and work values to job activities. To maximize utilization and retention of volunteers, the director of volunteer services is attempting to assign volunteers to activities that meet each person's expectations and needs and that produce high levels of satisfaction. If skills and abilities also match the activity assignment, the value of the volunteer to the agency will be enhanced and the contribution to the agency will be maximized."

Even more unfortunate is the fact that much of the management training on interviewing that does exist deals with employment interviewing, which is actually based on a totally inappropriate approach for volunteer interviewing. The main difference is quite easily stated: "Volunteer interviewing consists of evaluating a person for *a* job, not for *the* job" (McCurley, 1991b, p. 8). Effective volunteer interviewing does not so much consist of examining an applicant's suitability for *one* job as it does of evaluating the ability and desire of that applicant to fit productively in *some* position within the agency. Employment interviewing focuses on the question, Who can do this job? while volunteer interviewing should focus on the more creative question, How can this person help us?

Purposes of Volunteer Interviews

Among other things, this difference in approach means that a volunteer interview has to accomplish more than the usual employment interview. There are two basic purposes:

- *Identify "fit."* This includes determining the interests and abilities of potential volunteers, determining their suitability for particular jobs, and assessing their rightness for the organization, its style of operation, and its mission.
- *Recruit.* This includes answering any questions or concerns that potential volunteers may have and selling them on their ability to make contributions to the agency and its clientele, or to derive personal satisfaction from helping.

The Interviewing Site

Since a volunteer interview requires a greater exploration of personal characteristics than an employment interview does, site selection can be critical. Three attributes are critical: accessibility, a friendly atmosphere, and privacy. Remember the old adage: "You never get a second chance to make a first impression." What potential volunteers see and feel during the first interview may shape their attitude toward the agency.

Preparation for the Interview

The following items should be ready before the interview:

- A list of possible jobs with descriptions of required work and qualifications
- A list of questions related to qualifications for each job
- An application form completed by the volunteer, with background information
- A list of open-ended questions to explore the motivations of the volunteer
- Information and materials on the agency and its programs

Opening the Interview

At the beginning of the interview, you should:

- Make the applicant feel welcome. Express appreciation for the person's coming to meet with you. Remember that they are evaluating you while you are evaluating them, and this first introduction will greatly affect their comfort level with the agency.
- Build rapport by explaining what you would like to accomplish and how the applicant might fit into the process. Let the person know that the discussion is intended to help them decide whether volunteering would be suitable. Let the applicant feel "in charge."
- Give the applicant background information about the agency. Ask what questions they have about the agency and its purpose and programs. These questions will both allow you to "sell" your agency to the potential volunteer and to discover their interests and concerns.

Conducting the Interview

During the major portion of the interview, the following issues should be covered:

- Explore the applicant's interests, abilities, and situation. Determine why the applicant is considering volunteering and what types of work environment he or she prefers.
- Discuss various job possibilities. Explain the purpose and setting of jobs and let the applicant consider them. Use this as an opportunity to let the applicant discuss how he or she would approach various jobs, which will tell you more about that person's intentions and level of interest.
- Discuss agency requirements: time commitments, training requirements, paperwork, confidentiality rules, and the like. Let the applicant know what is expected of volunteers. Do not be afraid of telling the volunteer about requirements that are important to the agency because the volunteer will learn about them sooner or later. It is much better to have a volunteer honestly decline a potential job at the beginning than disappear from it later.
- Remember that you are still "recruiting" the volunteer at this stage, so do not forget to explain why each job is important to the interests of the agency and the clientele.
- Look for personality indicators that will help you "match" this person to a situation where they will be happy. These can include such details as whether they smoke, desire individual or group work, like paperwork, and other preferences.

It is vital to delay reaching conclusions during this interview. Do not assume that what a volunteer tells you at first about his or her motivations presents a complete picture of the person's interests. And do not assume that what the applicant is currently doing, for example, in their present job, automatically indicates what the person should do as a volunteer. As Keyton, Wilson, and Geiger (1990, p. 13) explain it: "Although a frequent way to uncover a person's abilities is to ask about work experience, stereotyping a volunteer's ability by vocation can be harmful to the volunteer's relationship with the organization." Remember that you are attempting to determine not just what the volunteer *can* do, but also what he or she will *want* to do. One factor in matching volunteers to jobs is the attempt to give them satisfactions they do not have in their present situation (McCurley, 1991a, p. 11).

Once you have determined a possible job placement for the volunteer, the nature of the interview may change from an openended exploration to the determination of a volunteer's qualifications and fitness for a specific position. Hollwitz and Wilson (1989) suggest the use of a "structured interview" for this task, in which a consistent set of questions based on preidentified volunteer role performance indicators are utilized. This systematic format for interviewing has advantages in situations in which candidates for a position are being compared, and it may also have some benefit in screening out potential volunteers who may be inappropriate.

One of the important skills that an interviewer needs is the ability to perceive an unexpected talent in the volunteer and to begin to construct a possible volunteer role on the spot. This requires a good understanding of the agency and its programs. If you make use of volunteers to conduct interviews (and they often are great at building rapport and seeing things from the viewpoint of the potential volunteer) make sure they have a broad and solid understanding of the agency and its program needs.

Closing the Interview

The interview should conclude with these final steps:

- Make an offer of a possible position to the volunteer, or politely explain that you have no suitable openings at this time.
- Explain what will happen next: background or reference checks, a second interview with staff, a training session, and the like. Explain the process, the time frame, and schedule the necessary meetings.
- Ask for the volunteer's permission to conduct the necessary reference or background checks.

Face-to-Face or over the Telephone?

There are times when in-person interviews are impossible to arrange. An interview by telephone is obviously a less "personal" situation, and it inhibits both the ability of the agency to evaluate the volunteer and of the volunteer to assess the agency. Generally speaking, it is important to conduct face-to-face interviews for situations that have the following attributes:

- The job requires a significant time commitment and thus a high motivational level on the part of the volunteer.
- The job entails great responsibility or requires a capacity or skill above the ordinary.
- The job is a highly sensitive one because of the nature of the work or the relationship with clients.

If you are unable to conduct an in-person interview for a job that involves any of these characteristics, it is highly desirable to schedule a thirty-day review.

Matching Volunteers to Positions

Determining the correct job situation for a volunteer involves analysis of the person's job qualifications and temperament. The volunteer must certainly be capable of doing or learning to do the job for which he or she is selected. But it is equally important that the volunteer "fit" into the work situation. That is, the volunteer must be satisfied with the job that is being offered and view the job as desirable and fulfilling work. It means that the work setting (including the schedule and site of the job) must also be agreeable to the volunteer. And finally it means that the staff with whom the volunteer will be working must also be amenable to working with volunteers in general, and with this volunteer specifically — and vice versa. This last factor will likely be influenced by some relatively personal issues, such as compatibility of personality type, style of work, or even personal habits, such as smoking.

Since it is difficult to make totally accurate decisions about truly complex untested circumstances on the basis of a thirty-minute interview, it is desirable to make sure that all beginning assignments are understood to be on a trial-period basis. Let the volunteer know that the first thirty days of work will be a probationary period for both the volunteer and the agency. At the end of the thirty days, a second interview will be conducted in which both the agency and the volunteer will reevaluate the assignment. During this second interview either party may request a change of assignment, based upon their additional knowledge of the situation.

An initial testing period will make it easier to induce volunteers to try out jobs about which they are uncertain and will also make it more likely that any problems of mismatching will be identified early and corrected quickly.

Liability Issues and Volunteer Screening

In more ways than one, the interviewing process is the point at which an agency attempts to determine the suitability of a volunteer for a job. Some aspects of this part of the process are fraught with legal implications of which agencies should be aware (McCurley, 1991b). On one hand, there are developing legal questions about the extent to which an agency can decide not to accept particular volunteers, particularly if such decisions appear to be levied against classes of individuals and to be based on sex, race, sexual preference, or the like. These questions are slowly being settled by litigation in which greater interpretation is being granted to the word *employee* as it relates to guarantees of employment protection enacted in recent years. (See, for example, *Big Brothers, Inc.* v. *Minneapolis Commission on Civil Rights* [1979] and *Curran* v. *Mount Diablo Council of the Boy Scouts of America* [1984].)

Equally troubling for nonprofit agencies have been findings of legal responsibility in instances where a volunteer engages in conduct such as child abuse and the agency is sued under the doctrine of negligent screening for its failure to ascertain the risk posed by the volunteer and to deny the volunteer a position with the agency. This has been particularly prevalent in agencies where volunteers work one on one with children. In this area, as well, precise legal guidelines are still being developed. An example of the direction in which courts seem to be going is provided in *Big Brother/Big Sister of Metro Atlanta* v. *Terrell,* (1987), in which the court applies a "reasonable effort" test, noting that "there is nothing in the record to suggest that Big Brother, a nongovernmental entity, has access to FBI records. Nor does it appear from the record that a credit check would have revealed anything to affect Big Brother's decision whether to accept Hendrick as a volunteer. As to the other two suggestions [a psychological test and a check of the volunteer's life-style], it appears that Big Brother came as close as is practicable for a volunteer organization to meet those criteria through its application form, family history, and assessment by a case worker (p. 242)." It is crucial that agencies in which volunteers are assigned to work with vulnerable clients attempt to determine the suitability and safety of potential volunteers. This means having procedures to carefully examine volunteer applicants; it also necessitates ensuring that these procedures are followed with each volunteer and that a record is kept of findings and actions during this process (see Potts, 1992, for an example of such procedures in the Boy Scouts of America).

Orientation

Orientation involves giving volunteers adequate background information about the agency, its operation, and its procedures. Orientation is required because each volunteer needs to be made a part of the organizational environment, and this process requires each volunteer to understand what the organization is and how it operates. A good orientation session will provide volunteers with the following types of information:

- Description and history of the organization
- Description of the overall programs and clientele of the organization
- Sketch of the organizational chart of the organization
- Orientation to the facilities and layout of the organization
- Knowledge of general policies and procedures
- Description of the volunteer management system

The purpose of orientation is to provide the volunteer with a context within which to work and a feeling of comfort about the work setting. The better the volunteer understands what the organization is and how it operates, the better the volunteer will be able to fit his or her own actions into proper methods of behavior and to display initiative in developing further ways to be helpful to the organization. The orientation session also provides a formal opportunity to welcome volunteers into the agency and to officially make them members of the "team."

Training

Training is the process of instructing volunteers in the specific job-related skills and behaviors that they will need to perform their particular volunteer jobs. Training should be designed to tell volunteers:

- How to perform their particular jobs
- What they are not supposed to do in their jobs
- What to do if an emergency or unforeseen situation arises

An effective training program operates by identifying the skills, knowledge, and behavior that are essential in good job performance and then designing a training format that instructs volunteers in these. It should be practical, experiential, and tailored to the individual needs of volunteers (George, 1985; Hipp and Davis, 1987).

Training should be followed by a period of on-the-job coaching in which volunteers are given additional assistance and feedback (McCurley and Lynch, 1989, pp. 72–82). This coaching can be provided either by paid staff or by other volunteers.

It is helpful to involve both staff and experienced volunteers in designing and delivering volunteer training. This improves the content of the training and begins to cement the relationship between the volunteer and paid staff of the agency.

Supervision and Motivation

Many studies have examined the effects of volunteer motivation on overall service to the agency, including such factors as organizational commitment, length of service, and other variables. Most studies have discovered the importance of providing job satisfaction to the volunteer. Dailey (1986), in a study of fundraising volunteers, found that job satisfaction was critical in determining level of organizational commitment. Pierucci and Noel (1980), in a study of corrections volunteers, found that a volunteer's satisfaction with the orientation process, staff relationships, and contact with agency clients predicted commitment better than did personality variables. Gidron (1983), in a study of Israeli social service volunteers, found that organizational variables (such as adequate preparation for the task) and attitudinal variables (such as task achievement, relationships with other volunteers, and the nature of the work itself) were the best predictors of volunteer retention. Brown and Zahrly (1990), in a study of crisis intervention volunteers, examined an investment motive for volunteering, in which volunteers acquired skills through performing volunteer jobs that they may later utilize in their careers.

Colomy, Chen, and Andrews (1987), in a study of volunteers at various agencies, perhaps summarize all this work when they cite the importance that volunteers give to what the researchers refer to as "situational facilities," a variety of job-related factors, including suitable workload, clearly defined responsibilities, competence of their supervisor, and a reasonable work schedule. They conclude: "Perhaps the single most important finding reported in this study is the relatively high importance volunteers accord situational facilities. The high ranking and high mean score of situational facilities are evident both for the sample as a whole and for each of the three subgroups of volunteers. In addition to the intrinsic and extrinsic incentives associated with volunteer work, then, it appears that individuals strongly desire conditions and organizational settings that facilitate effective and efficient volunteer work" (1987, p. 23).

Much as paid workers, volunteers are motivated by their ability to perform their work well in compatible surroundings. Unlike paid workers, however, it is somewhat easier for volunteers to decide to leave their positions when they find their ability to perform that work limited or their working conditions unpleasant. Failure to provide a satisfactory work environment may lead to reductions in volunteer retention levels (Morrow-Howell and Mui, 1987). This means that effective supervision of volunteers must provide an environment that enhances overall job satisfaction.

General Aspects of Volunteer Supervision

Supervision of volunteers entails all of the aspects of supervisory practice exercised with paid employees. Heidrich (1990, p. 104) describes this supervisory process as involving three elements:

1. Establishing criteria of success, standards of performance, and program objectives, such as the job description and annual plan of work
2. Measuring actual volunteer performance with respect to these stated criteria of success through observation, conferences, and evaluation
3. Making corrections, as needed, through managerial action

Volunteers need to be "managed" just as paid staff are managed, and, in fact, they need to be treated just as paid staff are treated to avoid giving the indication that there are different "classes" of workers within the agency.

Reporting, record keeping, and evaluation processes for volunteers should mirror processes for paid staff. The agency should also have a developed process for dealing with problem supervisory situations (MacKenzie, 1988) as well as with recognition of volunteer contributions (Vineyard, 1989).

Special Supervisory Issues

While supervision of volunteers is essentially no different in concept or execution than supervision of any other type of staff for an agency, some aspects of supervision need an extra emphasis in the volunteer relationship. These include:

- *Naming the supervisor.* Is supervision to be provided by the volunteer coordinator or by the staff person with whom the volunteer will work most closely? Both systems work, but it is essential to make sure that all parties are in agreement as to where the responsibility for day-to-day supervision and management lies, and who will deal with any problems that arise. In general, it is more desirable to give supervisory responsibility to the staff person who will be working most directly and most often with the volunteer.
- *Using flexible management approaches.* Supervisors need to treat volunteers as individuals, recognizing that their motivations and styles are different. The supervisor must be able to accommodate individual variations as well as deal with situations that do not occur with paid staff; for example, the volunteer may accord a higher priority to circumstances that arise in his or her personal life than to the volunteer position.
- *Allocating time for management.* The pervasive myth that volunteers are "free" is often the bane of good management. Staff who are responsible for volunteers must recognize that they must allocate time for relating to, managing, and dealing with the volunteers. Staff must be available to volunteers and relate to them on both a professional and a personal basis. To encourage this availability, open time can be scheduled in the week during which any volunteer can make an appointment. Specific lunch meetings for groups of volunteers can be regularly scheduled during which open discussions can be held. Supervisors can practice "management by walking around," thereby making themselves accessible to volunteers. The intent is to develop an attitude of open and ready communication and access.
- *Integrating the volunteer into the flow of the organization.* Above all, the supervisor is responsible for maintaining the communication flow between the volunteer and the organization and with ensuring that the volunteer feels informed of and included in decisions that affect the volunteer and his or her ability to perform the work. Since volunteers most often work on a part-time or occasional basis, it is very easy for them to become separated from the general informational systems of the agency. If this sense of separation is allowed to continue, it deepens and results in the volunteer losing a sense of connection with the agency.

Evaluation

Evaluation of the volunteer component should take place on two levels: that of the individual and that of the agency (Vineyard, 1988; Fisher and Cole, 1993). It may also need to take place on the project level to review the operation of a special event operated by a team of volunteers, for example.

At the individual level, volunteer evaluation needs to give both the volunteer and the agency a chance to review progress and suggest improvements for the future. It should not replace day-to-day supervision and management, but rather allow a more relaxed "big picture" examination of the volunteer's relationship with the agency. Much like an evaluation session for paid staff, a volunteer evaluation session should consist of a regularly scheduled meeting with supervisors to review past performance and expectations for the future. Unlike an evaluation session for paid staff, it should also provide an opportunity to review motivational aspects of the volunteer's involvement with the agency. This will allow identification of volunteers who have lost motivation due to burnout or who need a new challenge. In a sense, evaluation should allow for "rematching" the volunteer to the agency, and rebuilding his or her commitment, as appropriate, by saluting accomplishments, identifying new tasks and opportunities to provide service, or transferring the volunteer to an entirely new area of work within the agency.

At the agency level, the volunteer management component should engage in periodic evaluations. Input should be sought from current volunteers, paid staff, and agency clientele on the quality of services being provided by volunteers and on working relationships. Input should also be sought from volunteers who have left the agency, particularly if those individuals voluntarily resigned from volunteer service. These varying perspectives will allow the agency to identify ways to continually improve the volunteer utilization system. It will also allow the agency to determine whether the volunteer program is meeting the objectives identified in the program planning process. One common component of evaluation is whether the work performed by volunteers meets standards of quality and cost (see Henderson, 1988; Utterback and Heyman, 1984; and Brudney and Duncombe, 1992).

Summary

The above description is intended to capture the basic structural components of a volunteer program and to stress the need for planning and attention to defining and developing that program. Successful volunteer involvement does not just happen; it requires the same thought and work of any complex task. Assuming that a volunteer program can operate without good management is to expect too much of good intentions.

To be successful, volunteer programs need an organized plan of development, integrating the needs of the agency with the needs of the volunteers. This requires carefully developing roles for volunteers that can contribute meaningfully to the mission of the agency; consciously seeking, verifying, and training qualified volunteers who can perform those roles; and providing a nurturing atmosphere that will enable those volunteers to feel and be productive.

References

American Bar Association Center on Children and the Law. *Criminal History Record Checks: A Report for Nonprofits.* Washington, D.C.: National Assembly of National Voluntary Health and Social Welfare Organizations, 1991.

Big Brothers, Inc. v. *Minneapolis Commission on Civil Rights,* 248 N.W.2d 823 (1979).

Big Brother/Big Sister of Metro Atlanta v. *Terrell,* 359 S.E.2d 241 (Ga. App. 1987).

Brown, E., and Zahrly, J. "Nonmonetary Rewards for Skilled Volunteer Labor: A Look at Crisis Intervention Volunteers." *Nonprofit and Voluntary Sector Quarterly,* 1989, *18*(2), 167–178.

Brown, E., and Zahrly, J. "Commitment and Tenure of Highly Skilled Volunteers: Management Issues in a Nonprofit Agency." Working paper no. 12, Institute for Nonprofit Organization Management. San Francisco: University of San Francisco, 1990.

Brudney, J. *Fostering Volunteer Programs in the Public Sector: Planning, Initiating, and Managing Voluntary Activities.* San Francisco: Jossey-Bass, 1990.

Brudney, J., and Duncombe, W. "An Economic Evaluation of Paid, Volunteer, and Mixed Staffing Options for Public Services." *Public Administration Review,* 1992, *52*(5), 474–481.

Carson, E. "The Charitable Activities of Black Americans." *Review of Black Political Economy,* 1987, *12,* 100–111.

Chambré, S. M. "Recruiting Black and Hispanic Volunteers: A Qualitative Study of Organizations' Experiences." *Journal of Volunteer Administration,* 1982, *1*(1), 3–10.

Colomy, P., Chen, H., and Andrews, G. "Situational Facilities and Volunteer Work." *Journal of Volunteer Administration,* 1987, *6*(2), 20–25.

Curran v. *Mount Diablo Council of the Boy Scouts of America,* 147 Cal. App. 3d 312, 195 Cal. Rptr. 325 (1983), appeal dismissed, 468 U.S. 1205 (1984).

Dailey, R. "Understanding Organizational Commitment for Volunteers: Empirical and Managerial Implications." *Journal of Voluntary Action Research,* 1986, *15*(1), 19–31.

Ellis, S. *From the Top Down: The Executive Role in Volunteer Program Success.* Philadelphia: Energize, 1986.

Ellis, S., and Noyes, K. *By the People: A History of Americans as Volunteers.* (2nd ed.) San Francisco: Jossey-Bass, 1990.

Fischer, L., and Schaffer, K. *Older Volunteers: A Guide to Research and Practice.* Newbury Park, Calif.: Sage, 1993.

Fisher, J., and Cole, K. *Leadership and Management of Volunteer Programs: A Guide for Volunteer Administrators.* San Francisco: Jossey-Bass, 1993.

George, I. *You Can Teach Others: A Professional Approach to Training Volunteers.* Montgomery: Alabama Office of Voluntary Citizen Participation, 1985.

Geyer, P. "The Determinants of Volunteering at 'Partners.'" *Journal of Volunteer Administration,* 1983–84, *2*(2), 1–14.

Gidron, B. "Sources of Job Satisfaction Among Service Volunteers." *Journal of Voluntary Action Research,* 1983, *12*(1), 7–19.

Heidrich, K. *Working with Volunteers in Employee Services and Recreation Programs.* Champaign, Ill.: Sagamore, 1990.

Henderson, K. "Are Volunteers Worth Their Weight in Gold?" *Parks and Recreation,* 1988, *23*(11), 40–43.

Hipp, L., and Davis, D. "Using Experiential Techniques in Hospice Volunteer Training." *Journal of Volunteer Administration,* 1987, *6*(1), 30–46.

Hodgkinson, V., and Weitzman, M. *Giving and Volunteering in the United States.* Washington, D.C.: Independent Sector, 1988.

Hodgkinson, V., and Weitzman, M. *Dimensions of the Independent Sector: A Statistical Profile.* Washington, D.C.: Independent Sector, 1989.

Hodgkinson, V., and Weitzman, M. *Dimensions of the Independent Sector: A Statistical Profile.* Washington, D.C.: Independent Sector, 1990.

Hodgkinson, V., and Weitzman, M. *Giving and Volunteering in the United States.* Washington, D.C.: Independent Sector, 1992.

Hollwitz, J., and Wilson, C. "New Directions in Volunteer Selection: The Case for Structured Interviewing." In B. Long and J. Long (eds.), *Worn Paths and Unbroken Trails: The Volunteer Movement at the Turning Point.* Walla Walla, Wash.: MBA Publishing, 1989.

Ilsley, P. *Enhancing the Volunteer Experience: New Insights on Strengthening Volunteer Participation, Learning, and Commitment.* San Francisco: Jossey-Bass, 1990.

Keyton, J., Wilson, G., and Geiger, C. "Improving Volunteer Commitment to Organizations." *Journal of Volunteer Administration,* 1990, *8*(4), 7–14.

Lammers, J. "Attitudes, Motives, and Demographical Predictors of Volunteer Commitment and Service Duration." *Journal of Social Service Research,* 1991, *14*(3–4), 125–140.

Latting, J. "Motivational Differences Between Black and White Volunteers." *Nonprofit and Voluntary Sector Quarterly,* 1990, *19*(2), 121–136.

Lucas, W. "Cost Savings from Volunteer Services: A Research Note." *Journal of Offender Counseling Services and Rehabilitation,* 1988, *12*(2), 203–207.

Lynch, R. "Preparing an Effective Recruitment Campaign." *Voluntary Action Leadership,* Winter 1984, pp. 23–27.

Lynch, R. *Precision Management.* Seattle: Abbott Press, 1988.

McCormack, A., and Selvaggio, M. "Screening for Pedophiles in Youth-Oriented Community Agencies." *Social Casework,* 1989, *70*(1), 37–42.

McCurley, S. "How to Fire a Volunteer and Live to Tell About It." *Grapevine,* Jan./Feb. 1993, pp. 8–11.

McCurley, S. *Recruiting Volunteers for Difficult or Long-Term Assignments.* Downers Grove, Ill.: Heritage Arts, 1991a.

McCurley, S. "Liability and Volunteer Management: Screening Volunteers." *Grapevine,* Sept./Oct. 1991b, pp. 8–9.

McCurley, S., and Lynch, R. *Essential Volunteer Management.* Downers Grove, Ill.: Heritage Arts, 1989.

Macduff, N. *Episodic Volunteering: Building the Short-Term Volunteer Program.* Walla Walla, Wash.: MBA Associates, 1991.

MacKenzie, M. *Dealing with Difficult Volunteers.* Downers Grove, Ill.: Heritage Arts, 1988.

Mausner, C. "The Underlying Dynamics of Staff-Volunteer Relationships." *Journal of Volunteer Administration,* 1988, *6*(4), 5–9.

Miller, L. "Understanding the Motivation of Volunteers: An Examination of Personality Differences and Characteristics of Volunteers' Paid Employment." *Journal of Voluntary Action Research,* 1985, *14*(2–3), 112–122.

Miller, L., Powell, G., and Seltzer, J. "Determinants of Turnover Among Volunteers." *Human Relations,* 1990, *43*(9), 901–917.

Morrow-Howell, N., and Mui, A. "Elderly Volunteers: Reasons for Initiating and Terminating Service." *Journal of Gerontological Social Work,* 1987, *13* (3–4), 21–33.

Nestor, L. "Hispanic Volunteers—Tapping a New Volunteer Market." *Voluntary Action Leadership,* Fall 1994, pp. 19–25.

Nestor, L. "Managing Cultural Diversity in Volunteer Organizations." *Voluntary Action Leadership,* Summer 1991, pp. 18–19.

Pierucci, J., and Noel, R. "Duration of Participation of Correctional Volunteers as a Function of Personal and Situational Variables." *Journal of Community Psychology,* 1980, *8,* 646–652.

Potts, L. "The Youth Protection Program of the Boy Scouts of America." *Child Abuse & Neglect,* 1992, *16*(3), 441–445.

Saxon, J., and Sawyer, H. "A Systematic Approach for Volunteer Assignment and Retention." *Journal of Volunteer Administration,* 1984, *2*(4), 39–45.

Scheier, I. "Staff Nonsupport of Volunteers: A New Look at an Old Failure." *Voluntary Action Leadership,* Fall 1977, 32–36.

Scheier, I. *When Everyone's a Volunteer: The Effective Functioning of All-Volunteer Groups.* Philadelphia: Energize, 1992.

Seita, T. *Leadership Skills for the New Age of Nonprofits: Keeping Volunteers Happy in a Changing World.* Downers Grove, Ill.: Heritage Arts, 1990.

Silver, N. *At the Heart: The New Volunteer Challenge to Community Agencies.* Pleasanton, Calif.: Valley Volunteer Center, 1988.

Skillingstad, C. "Training Supervisors of Volunteers." *Journal of Volunteer Administration,* 1989, *8*(2), 29–34.

Snyder, A. "The Dynamic Tension: Professionals and Volunteers." *Journal of Extension,* 1985, *23,* 7–10.

Utterback, J., and Heyman, S. "An Examination of Methods in the Evaluation of Volunteer Programs." *Evaluation and Program Planning,* 1984, *7*(3), 229–235.

Vineyard, S. *Evaluating Volunteers Programs and Events.* Downers Grove, Ill.: Heritage Arts, 1988.

Vineyard, S. *Beyond Banquets, Plaques and Pins: Creative Ways to Recognize Volunteers.* (2nd ed.) Downers Grove, Ill.: Heritage Arts, 1989.

Vineyard, S., and McCurley, S. (eds.). *Managing Volunteer Diversity.* Downers Grove, Ill.: Heritage Arts, 1992.

Watts, A., and Edwards, P. "Recruiting and Retaining Human Service Volunteers: An Empirical Analysis." *Journal of Voluntary Action Research,* 1983, *12*(3), 9–22.

Wilson, M. *The Effective Management of Volunteer Programs.* Boulder, Colo.: Volunteer Management Associates, 1976.

Wright, B. "Some Notes on Recruiting and Retaining Minority Volunteers." *Voluntary Action Leadership,* Winter 1992, p. 20.

23

Finding and Keeping the Right Employees

M. Sue Sturgeon

Recruiting and selecting people for one's organization is arguably the most important function any manager performs, since everything the organization is and does depends on the individuals who embody it. Judicious selection of lieutenants and managers is a key mechanism through which dynamic leaders ensure the day-to-day communication and implementation of their values and vision throughout their organizations. In the private sector, successful corporate leaders often devote significant attention and resources to this aspect of their organizations.

From the perspective at the top of an organization, it is abundantly clear that organizational success depends on melding the energies and talents of many different kinds of people — those who "see the forest," those who "see the trees," those who focus outwardly, those who focus inwardly, "bean counters," and "people persons." Organizations suffer if they do not contain a variety of diverse perspectives: corporate inbreeding and group-think have been the cause of many an organization's downfall (Bolman and Deal, 1991; Boyett and Conn, 1991; DuBrin, 1990).

However, the perspective at the individual level is different. Human beings seem to feel most comfortable when interacting with others most like themselves, and there seems to be a tendency in most people to seek comfortable associations rather than the more stimulating (and stressful) associations with dissimilar others (DuBrin, 1990; Leavitt and Bahrami, 1988). This general tendency is heightened in the workplace, where people must depend on relative strangers in order to meet their work goals (and thereby satisfy deep personal needs for security, satisfaction, and recognition). This is the essence, in fact, of a manager's situation. And managers hire the organization's staff.

As a result, selecting new staff members for an organization usually involves a subtle contest between the needs of the organization for broad diversity and the needs of the hiring manager for conformity or compatibility (usually called "the right chemistry"). Complicating this situation is the experiential truth that any working group can handle only so much variety or dissimilarity among its members before it begins spending the bulk of its time dealing with members' differences—to the detriment of achieving common work goals.

The unique culture, values, and mores of each organization determine how much diversity the staff members of that organization will tolerate, enjoy, or demand within the legal obligations every organization has in the area of nondiscrimination (Leavitt and Bahrami, 1988). Each opportunity to add a person to the staff of an organization is, therefore, an opportunity for its top manager(s) to assess the current mix of the work force as a whole, test the diversity level, and assert whatever leadership is necessary to achieve an appropriate balance and mix (Yate, 1990). The chief executive needs to decide on the best strategic mix for his or her organization and *require* that the recruitment and selection practices do, in fact, achieve that outcome and thereby optimize the organization's human capabilities (Bolman and Deal, 1991; Boyett and Conn, 1991; Morrison, 1992).

This requires that the top person be able and willing to confront managers when they feel they "must" hire someone who the top person perceives will not fulfill the organization's broader needs or the manager's narrower ones (Lynch, 1993). I know of no more critical managerial function of the leader of an organization than this. Poorly staffed organizations are built one person at a time—exactly the same as superbly staffed ones.

First Steps in Recruiting

Whether the position is that of the chief paid staff officer or of a newly budgeted but unspecified "additional resource," before recruiting, it is important to develop as concrete a picture as possible of the job to be done—and to *write it down*. Metaphorically, one draws the outline of a fictional person by detailing the functions, responsibilities, skills, abilities, and behaviors that the organization will expect from the real person who steps into the outline.

Getting as clear an outline as possible—and taking the time to develop consensus about it among the major decision makers in the selection process—will ultimately save recruiting time, help the process stay focused, avoid organizational embarrassments (or worse, litigation), and provide crucial objectivity to assure that the hiring managers do not stumble into illegal discrimination during the selection process.

Employment Systems as an Integrated Part of the Whole

There are a variety of legally valid personnel systems available on which to base the interrelated hiring, performance appraisal, and pay processes of an organization (Bolman and Deal, 1991; Cascio, 1989; Fear and Chiron, 1990). Such systems provide a unified conceptual framework within which to view and analyze the organization's work. These systems usually have names that denote their basic concept; for example, "a behaviorally based system."

Although not legally required, it is generally preferable not to vary the basic orientation of the differing personnel subsystems. That is, if each part of the people-management system reflects the same basic assumptions about the work of the organization, the system will provide strong support for the organization's culture and values. Therefore, keep in mind that there are other options available if a given system or subsystem doesn't seem to work well for your organization.

Functions of the Job Description

Having a set of clear, detailed, system-derived position requirements helps all concerned to focus on the main objective: the job to be done and the kinds of qualifications that are required to do it. This will support the hiring manager's consideration of a broad range of individuals. It will also document a key part of the organization's nondiscriminatory recruitment and hiring practices, which are indispensable should a legal challenge arise. Finally, the job description is necessary to determine an appropriate pay level and is an integral part of most pay sub-systems. (See Chapter Twenty-Four in this handbook for more details on managing compensation systems.)

The first step, then, is to pin down as concretely as possible the major functions of the position in terms of desired results, and to describe the academic, experiential, and behavioral requirements for the successful candidate (Byrne, 1991). This isn't always easy, especially in small organizations where a few people perform many different tasks and each individual's assignments may depend in part of his or her preferences or persuasiveness in negotiating with others on the staff.

Additionally, some managers have a philosophy that overall productivity is enhanced if each job is tailored to fit the occupant (Cascio, 1989); this is an intensification of every manager's real-life experience—that jobs are changed to fit the person to some degree over time. Then too, some managers prefer to keep the outline hazy to better accommodate the candidacy of an outstanding individual who may or may not fit more concrete guidelines, but who will assuredly enhance the organization overall.

Despite these contrary rationales, the need for a well-written and objective job description that sets forth the basic requirements for the job and its holder is compelling, for legal, ethical, and practical management reasons. Not only does it protect the organization legally by assuring that all qualified applicants compete on a level playing field (essential to meet fair employment regulations), but it "metacommunicates" to all applicants that the organization is organized as well as professional and aboveboard in its dealings with its employees.

Applicants form lasting impressions of an organization based on the manner and clarity with which the job is presented to them. Indeed, it is the primary way in which their early needs for information and affiliation are met. One of the worst situations that can occur in recruiting — and it happens more often than you might think — is that a much sought after and badly needed "ideal" applicant appears, only to be confronted by vague information or conflicting descriptions of the job — from which they conclude that the organization is not right for them, and withdraw (Boyle, 1990). Additionally, disillusioned applicants will certainly share their opinions with others. (Everybody knows who the best and worst employers are in their town.) Your organization's ability to attract top-drawer applicants is heavily influenced by the quality of your recruitment practices and systems.

There must be someone somewhere who actually likes to write job descriptions, but most of us hate it. However, the length of such a document doesn't necessarily equate with quality, and the time spent really thinking through the job beforehand will lead to a variety of dividends later.

If, happily, a written job description already exists, then it only needs to be reviewed and updated, but with a critical eye. Please don't just use the description because it exists; make certain that it actually describes the job you want done. Consider, for instance, whether a differently structured job might not allow your unit to operate better.

Either way, a current description of the job, written by the hiring manager, the incumbent, or a personnel specialist, and approved in writing by the next level manager, is the essential first step in the recruitment and hiring process.

Hiring Authority

Along with a written and approved job description, it is important to determine in advance who will be involved in the hiring decision, and who has the final say. One of the chief causes of confusion in hiring comes from a lack of clarity among the hiring participants as to their role and authority — and their unwitting communication of that to the candidates. This can be averted with the use of a one-over-one written approval requirement for both the job description and the final hiring decision, with the manager of the hiring manager serving as the final approver. The higher level manager will have a broader perspective of the organization's needs, which will balance the more personal and focused perspective of the manager to whom the position reports. A better overall hiring decision will result if the hiring manager is required to discuss and defend the decision with his or her own manager.

Interviews

Before any interviews are scheduled, certain matters need to be addressed: Who should be involved? What kind of interview should be conducted? How long should it last? (A minimum of two people should be involved in every hiring decision—but what is the maximum desirable number?) All of these issues involve, to some extent, various characteristics of the organization and the position: Is the organizational culture more egalitarian or hierarchical? With how many different people and/or units within the organization does this position interact? How high up in the organization are the people with whom the position interacts? Egalitarianism, a higher number of interactions, and work at higher organization levels all lead to a higher number of interviewers and affect the nature of the interview.

From time to time, managers raise questions about using "nonstandard" interviewing practices. The two most frequently desired are *peer interviews* and *clerical interviews*. The desire for peer interviews arises especially in situations where close teamwork and/or lots of interaction among differing work units is required, or such specialized job knowledge is required that only peer experts can assess a candidate's depth of knowledge. Using peer interviews in professional and managerial staff selection can work well as long as each interviewer has the training and skills to interview correctly, and as long as each interviewer works from the same written job description.

Clerical interviews of clerical, professional, or managerial candidates are a different matter. I've worked with managers who felt strongly that having their clerical staff involved in assessing clerical, professional, and supervisory level candidates was important to the overall smooth working of their units. However, my experience has been mixed at best. Providing sufficient training in the legal requirements for interviewing is both critical and time-consuming. Input I have seen from clerical interviewers has been strongly subjective and has sometimes resulted in active sponsorship of a preferred candidate, with consequent difficulty in accepting a different decision.

I recommend instead, in cases where it is deemed essential to involve them, that clerical staff have a "get acquainted" time on the interview schedule to meet each final candidate (perhaps over lunch or coffee). This involves them in the process and allows a sense of the various candidates to be formed, but does not require objective selection assessments or formal input. It also keeps the lines of decision responsibility clear for all.

There are several additional benefits from involving nonmanagement staff in the interview process: it provides job enrichment and variety, introduces them to an important managerial responsibility, and signals a confidence that enhances their self-esteem (Redeker, 1991). It has also been known to help educate idealistic nonmanagerial staff to the realities of managerial decision making.

The Length of the Interview

There is no "magic" interview span. Some interviewers only need twenty to thirty minutes; some need ninety minutes or more. This appears to vary more with the individual manager's personal style than with the complexity or type of position.

In order to fit all interviews into a reasonable amount of time, two strategies can be used: (1) group interviews can be arranged, in which a candidate meets with several persons, each from a different unit with which he or she will be working; or (2) selecting one or two representative individuals to interview on behalf of all the different units or functions. Two caveats: in group interviews, it is important that the same people interview all candidates; no substitutions can be allowed along the way. It is better to leave an area unrepresented in the selection than to introduce a new interviewer part-way through who hasn't met the first few candidates. And, in representative situations, it is important that the person(s) selected to interview not only be knowledgeable about the areas or functions they are representing but also be seen as credible by their fellow staff members (Warmke, 1992).

The Interviewing Process

Interviewing is an art, a science—and a legal process. The "don'ts" are very important—you can be sued over them. Interview questions will be unlawful if they require applicants to provide information that can result in illegal discrimination; examples are asking about the number and ages of children, foreign language proficiency if not required by the job, birthplace, age, height and weight, arrest history, marital status, and military service record (Barnadin and Russell, 1993; Fear and Chiron, 1990; Fyock, 1993; Player, 1991; Yate, 1990). A good seminar or book on interviewing will provide the detailed information that is needed to assure that only lawful interview questions are used.

While interviewers must be careful not to make biased judgments for unlawful reasons, research shows that there are a variety of general biases that are likely to affect interviewer ratings (Bernadin and Russell, 1993; Fear and Chiron, 1990). Examples of such biases include attractiveness, speech patterns or pacing, and type of eye contact. In any specific instance such biases may not result in an illegal selection decision, but taken together they can easily prevent interviewers from making the right selection for any job (Morrison, 1992).

The "do's" are also critical to making good selections, and together with the "don'ts" they constitute a process that requires objectivity, careful attention to detail, and skills that, unfortunately, get rusty with disuse. If you take the time to put together a manual that explains your organization's hiring process and that describes proper interviewing techniques and questions in some detail, time, energy, and risk will be minimized each time you are once again sitting in the hiring manager or interviewer chair.

There are a variety of effective interviewing approaches, but they all contain some common basic elements: courtesy, objectivity, legal correctness, open-ended questioning, and astute listening (Freedman, 1992; Sunseri, 1991). My number one suggestion is that you find a good one- or two-day local training course in interviewing (these can run from $100 to $200) and see that all your hiring managers attend it; then put together that hiring manual for ongoing reference purposes. If time and money are too limited for this, buy a book on the interviewing process that fits your organization, make sure every manager digests it—and make up the hiring manual. (The manual makes a great managerial staff development project—and you'll also get a current analysis of your organization's strengths and limitations into the bargain.)

Nondiscrimination (EEO) and Affirmative Action

Nondiscriminatory hiring really stands for two things: commonsense recruiting and employment practices, and a set of federal regulations that require certain employment practices (Cascio, 1989). Affirmative Action calls for certain voluntary actions by participating employers. (Affirmative Action plans are required only for contractors and subcontractors with federal contracts over $50,000.) Everything contained in this chapter is to be understood within the context of adherence to both the spirit and the letter of these regulations.

Equal Employment Opportunity

Common sense first: in a country in which non-Caucasians will constitute a majority of the total population by the year 2000, it simply makes sense that ethnic/racial "minorities" be significantly represented in the work force of every organization—if only to avoid being out of sync with the organization's external environment, which also happens to contain its constituents, members, and markets (Cascio, 1989).

Additionally, every organization has a responsibility to support the society that sustains it. One of the striking features of the United States is the strength of the belief held by people at all levels of society that achieving "the American dream" is really possible for any citizen. It is hypothesized that this belief is a major reason behind America's historic avoidance of overt class warfare: the deeply-held belief by even "have-nots" that anyone in America can "make it" has mitigated against the growth of conflict between rich and poor. However, it follows that to whatever extent Americans come to believe that people cannot better their lot through their own merit and efforts, society stands at risk. Equal employment opportunity is not only simple common sense, it is a responsibility that every organization owes to the society as a whole.

Federal Regulations

The activities, processes, and materials (forms, contracts, and the like) involved in hiring (and firing) employees are subject to a number of federal statutes, including:

Age Discrimination Employment Act, 1967, as amended in 1978 and 1986
Americans with Disabilities Act, 1990
Civil Rights Act (Title VII), as amended in 1991
Equal Employment Opportunity Act, 1972
Equal Pay Act, 1963
Fair Labor Standards Act
Immigration Reform and Control Act, 1985
Rehabilitation Act, 1973
Veterans Reemployment Rights Act

A variety of agencies are involved in administering these regulations: the Equal Employment Opportunity Commission (EEOC) and federal courts; the Department of Labor; the Office of Federal Contract Compliance Program (OFCCP), state Fair Employment Practices Commissions and municipal courts (Barnadin and Russell, 1993; Cascio, 1989; Player, 1991). The application of the statutes in specific situations can necessitate a certain level of technical or professional proficiency and to explain them in depth would require a book in itself.

Assistance in determining the best course of action in specific situations can be obtained through the organization's legal counselor, a personnel consultant, or by purchasing a book on employment regulations and applying the information in it objectively. As with most significant issues involving any organization's values and practices, it is the chief executive officer who must set and enforce the standards for employment processes and outcomes.

Many people see their organization as monolithic and highly resistant to change, but the power of leadership is not to be minimized. I have personally experienced rapid reform of entrenched inappropriate hiring practices in a large organization at the behest of a new CEO. This person not only mandated the change but also made it clear that the issue was not negotiable and that jobs, promotions, and raises, along with the CEO's personal disapproval, were on the line. The consensus among four tiers of managers in the organization—which employed more than two thousand people—was that he meant it, and the inappropriate hiring practices disappeared virtually overnight.

What the Laws Require

Taken as a whole, nondiscrimination laws forbid all employers from making hiring decisions based on criteria that are either irrelevant to the job or inappropriately subjective. For example, the number and ages of an applicant's children are usually irrelevant to that applicant's ability to perform the job; an applicant's religion is usually irrelevant; an applicant's age, race, sex, marital status, and national origin are usually irrelevant, and so on.

Subjectivity to the point that an underqualified person is preferred over a qualified person is not allowed. And finally, with the Americans with Disabilities Act of 1990, employers must make allowances for disabled applicants so that they can compete on more equal terms (Cascio, 1989; Player, 1991).

Affirmative Action

An affirmative action plan is a company's voluntary effort to redress the effects of past unfair hiring practices or to comply with OFCCP regulations (for federal contractors). A formal affirmative action plan is formally undertaken on an annual basis, and consists of two parts. The first part is narrative, and is basically boilerplate language. (The OFCCP provides advice and technical assistance in developing such a plan.) The second, and far more difficult part, contains "the numbers": a statistical analysis, by race and sex, of the organization's staff in up to nine different job categories, plus a similar analysis of its own relevant (and usually unique) labor market in each of the same job categories (Brown, 1993). Preparing the analysis for the first part of the plan is the most difficult, and external consultation may be the most cost-effective and efficient route. Once the formulas for calculating the relevant labor market have been developed and jobs assigned to the appropriate categories, the annual update work can be done by a numbers-oriented staff person. Additionally, software packages are available to automate the statistical analysis and preparation of the annual plan (Meade, 1993).

The CEO should take an interest in the formula development. It requires a broad organizational perspective to make correct formula and job category decisions and to review the assumptions underlying the formulas as well as the statistical outcomes before accepting a plan. When satisfied, the CEO signs the plan, tells the managers where the organization stands in relation to its goals in each job category, and sees to it that the year's hiring goals are met as opportunities arise. Each year's plan becomes part of the organization's official documents and must be retained for seven years.

Establishing a Pay Range

A "hiring pay range"—minimum for any appropriate hire, and maximum possible for the perfect candidate—should be decided on before recruiting begins and agreed to by the hiring manager and the approving manager. (Its upper limit will normally be less than the entire salary range for the position.) Be sure that, as the hiring or approving manager, you take into account not only your knowledge of the current market for the job but also current salaries of your other staff in like jobs or same-pay-grade jobs (especially long-term staff members). Equal pay and internal equity considerations must be balanced against the market. If you have fallen behind in your pay ranges, or if good long-term staff at the same job level are likely to be paid less than the potential new hire, it is important to at least be aware of the situation. Correcting these kinds of compensation imbalances can take time, so it is important to alert the CEO or human resources specialist as soon as the problems are detected.

Unless there is a professional personnel specialist or a universally accepted alternative process in your organization, no one other than the hiring manager and his or her immediate supervisor should be allowed to discuss salary with candidates. Too much confusion and later unhappiness, not to mention possible illegalities, result when people other than the direct managers (or appropriate personnel staff) discuss compensation (salary *and* benefits). It is prudent and helpful to inform candidates early about who will address compensation issues.

Recruitment Alternatives for Different Positions

You have an approved job description, you have set your hiring range, and know whom you want to have interview. It's time to think about where you're going to recruit for your candidates, and that differs according to where your prospective new employee is most likely to be found. Is this a generic accounting clerk position, or an exempt technical job unique to your organization? Do you need someone with a particular professional background or specialized experience? Is it a clerical or other nonexempt position? Geographically, do you expect to hire from within your city or local area? Your region? Nationally?

Think about the various means available to reach your target audience: ads in the local papers (daily, weekly, business, minority, suburban); notices in college, university, and technical school placement centers, state unemployment offices, public and private retraining centers, job clubs (where job seekers meet in support groups—they're springing up all over, often sponsored by churches, clubs, and other organizations); through staff via internal job postings; and through business and personal acquaintances via networking (Fyock, 1993).

Some managers like to find new staff through temporary services; they want to see the person doing the job for a time before making an offer. Many temporary services will negotiate to reduce or eliminate the "separation fee" if you employ the person as a temporary worker through their office for a given number of weeks. Do have an understanding up front, and it is wise to document your understanding in a confirming letter to the agency.

Employment Agencies

You may want to consider using an employment agency. They will (or will promise to) find and screen people for you so that you only have to deal with appropriately credentialed candidates. They may or may not charge you a fee, depending on who they're representing. Some employment agencies represent the job seeker, from whom they collect their fee. Others represent the employer, and the employer pays the fee.

If you know the agency, or know people who have had continued success with them, you may be able to save yourself time and effort. But, check out an agency's reputation carefully with your business acquaintances, do as much as you can to acquaint the representative with your organization and the job, and be sure that you understand the agency's position and policies. If you are paying the fee, you should get a refund if the candidate doesn't work out or doesn't stay beyond six months or a year.

Employment agencies run the gamut from awful to all right — they're a real toss of the dice. You substitute their judgment for yours in the initial selection, and they try to match your job with candidates they either have on tap or can get easily, rather than with your needs. Since they are not paid unless you hire their candidate, you can expect pressure (often a real sales pitch) to accept the person they present. If they are unable to find a quick match with your job, they often lose interest or, worse, try to get you to accept whomever they do have.

One technique my personnel staff sometimes used was to first give a reputable employment agency an "exclusive" for a limited period of time (two to three weeks) to see if they were able to produce a match. If they did, fine; if not, we did our own recruiting by means of ads and other postings. The bottom line is that the position and the organization are yours — so you must be prepared to manage an employment agency's efforts rather than turn the job over to them. Unfortunately, that can take just as much time and effort as doing the recruiting yourself.

Recruiting Regionally

A regional recruiting effort is basically an expanded version of a local effort, with the same set of alternatives. An added complication is the question of relocation costs if you hire someone from outside your city. Most organizations use fifty miles as the point at which their relocation benefits apply.

Generally, nonexempt and clerical positions lend themselves to recruitment through staff references, temporary agencies, local ads, employment agencies, and unemployment offices. Upper level exempt and managerial positions may be recruited locally or regionally through staff references, local classified or display ads, professional societies, job clubs, and networking.

Recruiting Nationally

A national recruitment campaign is very different from local and regional efforts. The most cost-effective do-it-yourself strategy for a national search will probably be your network of business acquaintances plus notices in the journals and newsletters of appropriate professional organizations and associations. There are usually directories of associations available in your local library's reference section. (If not, ask a business acquaintance in the executive search business if he or she has a set and would let you come by and use it. You can explain that the job isn't at the salary level that would excite a search firm or justify a search.)

You may want to advertise in local newspapers in cities where you believe there are concentrations of the type of person you are looking for. (Find out about ad prices first: in major cities, even a classified ad now costs some serious money.) And, if the salary is $50,000 or above, you may want to consider using a search firm to find the person.

Search Firms

An employment search is a personalized and individualized effort — just about the opposite of working with an employment agency (Brown and Martin, 1991). In a search, the recruiter interviews you about your organization and the job in some detail, writes a description of it (which you should approve in writing), and goes out to find people who match it, whether or not they're looking for a job. A search person uses different strategies than an employment agency, usually making inquiries by telephone networking through individuals in similar jobs. They provide a higher level of service — and charge a higher fee (up to 33 percent of the annual salary). Be sure you understand the terms of their contract: some search firms will only guarantee to provide you with three qualified candidates who meet your specifications, whether you hire them or not, called a "retained search"; others will not only search until they find a person you hire (a "contingency" search), but will do a replacement search for free if the person leaves within the first year.

Ask around to find a good local search person. And discuss the fee level. Search fee flexibility varies with the firm's competitiveness, the target market, and how busy they are at the time (Stump, 1991). If there is the possibility of more search business from you (assuming they do a good job), you can probably negotiate the fee downward. It is fair to explain that, as a not-for-profit, you cannot afford as much as private-sector firms. I have negotiated search fees as low as 23 percent of the annual salary. One search firm I worked with had a strict policy never to lower their 33 percent search fee, but they did agree to make a contribution equal to 5 percent of the fee to my organization after the hire.

In some cases, a nonprofit organization can obtain a pro bono search. Usually such a community service requires the active intervention of a member of the board who knows the search firm principals. However, in some cases a search firm may actually look for appropriate nonprofits in order to donate its expertise (Gunsch, 1993).

One caveat to keep in mind with regard to searches is that candidates' salaries need to be within your position's salary range. At $50,000 and up, you are looking for a certain combination of experience, ability, and expertise, and there is no set market price for it. A search person will often find a superb candidate — who happens to be already making what you want to pay, and who therefore requires at least the next step (or two) up in pay in order to be attracted.

It is amazingly easy to get hooked on the advantages that an up-market candidate might bring to your organization and offer the higher salary. Then, as the dust settles, the new person's peers in your organization (who learned the newcomer's salary in a nanosecond out of the thin air) can be found lining up at your (and/or your fellow managers') doors with question marks and dollar signs in their eyes. Whatever follows won't be pretty.

Next Steps in the Recruiting Process

Whether you are doing the recruiting yourself or working with someone else, the next steps are pretty much the same: read the résumés or employment applications, select the most likely (on paper) for initial interviews (either by phone or in person), administer any tests, and narrow your field down to two to five final candidates for second interviews (Fear and Chiron, 1990). (In the personnel world, people are "applicants" until they have gone through the first screening; those who pass it become "candidates.")

It reflects well on your organization if, as you weed out applicants, you send them a "turn-down" letter (Cook, 1989). It's tough to receive one, but even tougher to never hear back at all. If you have not done so before, you should prepare packets of information about the organization that include a summary of benefits, vacation policy, relocation policy, and so forth. Add some informative material about your organization: a newsletter, annual report, or marketing material that describes your organization. Each serious candidate should receive one of these packets.

Applicant Flow Register

For equal employment opportunity or affirmative action purposes, use an applicant register to document the pertinent ethnic and gender information for all applicants to see. (You can get a sample one from your local Equal Employment Opportunity office or from a book of personnel forms.)

Testing

Preemployment testing is a highly regulated area. It has been the source of much discriminatory selection in the past and even today involves a direct conflict between the employer's right to identify less desirable applicants and individual applicants' rights of privacy. Therefore it should be used with care and moderation.

The two most controversial areas are polygraph and drug testing. You should consult an attorney before embarking on either. Intelligence, educational, psychological, and abilities tests must be determined to be reliable (produce consistent results), valid (there are three approaches: construct, content, and criterion-related), and nondiscriminatory. The test(s) must also relate to the specific requirements for the job; for instance, you cannot give a valid, nondiscriminatory, and reliable typing test to applicants for a non-typing position (Cascio, 1989; Fear and Chiron, 1990).

Some testing is undoubtedly beneficial and even necessary to selection (for example, typing tests for typing positions). Be sure that you obtain reliable, valid, standardized skills tests, and that they are administered in a meticulous, objective manner.

Most people dislike taking tests, and some become very anxious (which may or may not be relevant to the job, depending on what kind of stress it involves). It's good practice to do everything possible to put applicants at ease during testing so that they can do their best. Hold the test in a private space, with no distracting noise or activity, and provide well-operating equipment. (And, please, respond affirmatively if an applicant asks to retake a typing or spelling test; the extra effort is worth it in terms of the applicant feeling that he or she has been treated fairly. Repeats with these tests don't significantly alter the outcome; sometimes people do worse!)

For other kinds of positions, actual job samples probably constitute the most effective and most easily validated type of testing (they are content valid). Choose work samples that can be evaluated objectively (for example, preparing minutes from a transcript of a portion of a meeting, proofreading a document, giving a short oral report or presentation from a list of prescribed subjects) or that illustrate what the candidate can do (a sample of a report written or a publication designed, for instance) (Cascio, 1989). Caveats to keep in mind are that every candidate must be given the same test or be asked to produce a like sample; all test samples must be graded or interpreted by the same person (usually the hiring manager); the tests must be given at the same point in the selection process for any given job (for example, as part of the initial selection of candidates, or before or during final interviews); all test results or scores must be kept with the candidates' files.

Candidate Contacts

Candidates are different from applicants because any one of them could become your new employee. You need to know them individually, and you need to ensure that whoever is in contact with them treats them with courtesy and care. This is a "courtship" stage during which sloppy communications, neglecting to communicate with candidates for weeks at a time, giving misinformation, not responding to their questions — all can lead to losing the cream-of-the-crop person your organization needs. Be aware that the candidates are trying to decide who you (the organization and the people) are, what you really want, how they would fit in, and whether they would be happy. And that is exactly what you want to know, too, so help them. At this stage, the more communication and interaction, the better (Fyock, 1991).

Narrowing the Field

Just at the point when candidates are being "winnowed," many a manager suddenly feels the job "must" be redescribed. Successful recruiting comes from matching square, round, and oblong pegs (people) with square, round, or oblong holes (jobs). You are looking for the best objective match: don't resize the hole to make it happen. And if you are the CEO or authorizing manager, resist your hiring manager's attempt to do so; it is a danger sign that subjectivity is getting the upper hand — or out of hand.

If you required the hiring manager to write a job description earlier, there should be far less need to redescribe the position now. (If the manager didn't think the job through earlier, this is a very disadvantageous time to do so since recruiting efforts to date will have been misdirected.)

If you should decide that the job was significantly misdescribed initially and allow it to be respecified, be *sure* that the job description is rewritten and reapproved before you authorize a job offer. You jeopardize the organization legally if you don't. From a practical standpoint, if you let the hiring manager off the hook and allow an employment offer to be made before the rewrite and reauthorization are completed, that work is very unlikely ever to get done. Then you have a new employee without an appropriate job description but with an assigned salary range that probably isn't correct. It's the single best way I know to wreck the internal credibility plus the external (legal) defendability of *both* your pay program and your hiring program. Be a bear about this!

Final Selection

When the final selection is about to be made, whoever else is to interview candidates should complete the process (Fear and Chiron, 1990). Then, in an ideal world, the interviewers would all sit down together and discuss the finalists. (I have only had the opportunity to do this once — in recruiting for a series of overseas assignments. It was amazing how much good additional information the five main interviewers developed as we talked together. And our success rate was outstanding.) Usually however, interviewers will write down their comments and conclusions, or speak individually with the hiring manager. The hiring manager collects and considers all input and reviews it with his or her immediate superior.

Salary should be discussed during the hiring manager's final interview with each candidate (if it hasn't been talked through before). The precise starting pay to be offered to the top candidates acceptable as hires should be determined now.

Discussing Salary Expectations

Whether or not you established each applicant's salary requirement in your initial screening interviews, during your final interview with each top candidate you need to determine for yourself what it will take, in terms of salary and/or additional "perks," to get each of your top candidates. There will be individual differences in what attracts each person. Treat this discussion as an information-gathering session; you do not have to negotiate the salary yet.

You can open the line of inquiry by saying something like, "I hope you know that we're impressed with your potential for this position, and we're moving quickly toward making a final decision. I need to find out now what it would take to get you if you should be the person we select. What's the minimum salary that you would accept to join us?" Be sure you're prepared to cover additional items: the salary amount may be linked to the value of your benefit package, the perceived value of your retirement plan, whether and how much employees contribute to your health plan, the amount of vacation you offer, your relocation package (for out-of-town candidates), or other noncash benefits. Or the person may be willing to substitute less quantifiable items: anticipated job satisfaction, career development possibilities, payment for professional memberships and/or conference attendance, opportunities to consult on the side, flexibility to keep current commitments (paid or unpaid) that will require time away from the job, time for independent research or sabbaticals, company assistance in helping a spouse find a suitable job, and so forth. Your knowledge of each candidate (and the level of the position) will guide you in knowing what to bring up.

Listen carefully, and don't give an absolute no to anything, however farfetched it sounds to you. Demur when necessary by indicating that such-and-such would be a stretch for the organization, or isn't done ordinarily, or has never been done before. Remember that you don't yet really know how much you or the organization want this person. (There is no experience quite like having discouraged a good number-two candidate at this point, losing the top person to some totally unforeseen circumstance, and finding that number two has accepted another offer in the meantime.)

Competing Offers

The final interview is also the time to clarify other offers the candidates may be pursuing and how they may affect your time frame. It is always desirable to ask the candidates to notify you should they receive competing offers—or need to make a decision about an offer—before you've gotten back to them. Don't be too concerned, let alone anxious, if you hear that all sorts of wonderful alternative offers are just about to break or have broken. This is also the candidates' time to make their case for themselves. (I always ask if they can share any information about a reported offer in hand. When I get solid information, I take note; when matters are vague or "too confidential," I take them less seriously.)

You should come out of your final interviews with a sense of how realistic and how flexible on pay each candidate is—and where you can add incentives, if you know you will have some negotiating to do.

Checking References

Once you have the candidates ordered by preference, it is time to check references. Since the advent of privacy laws, reference checking has become more difficult, but it is still very worthwhile: you can obtain critical information about key abilities or skills while allowing the reference-giver to provide an overall positive recommendation (Cook, 1989; Fyock, 1993). As the old saying goes, "The devil is in the details," and it may be past performance details that will ultimately decide the person best fitted for your position.

Try to speak with people who have supervised, been peers of, or worked for the person, depending on your questions and the position. Describe (briefly) the key elements of your job, and ask open-ended questions about the candidate's past demonstration of the required capabilities. Be sure to cover any important areas about which you have (a) doubts, (b) insufficient information, or (c) ambiguous information.

Phrase questions from the standpoint of behaviors or outcomes, not personal attributes. For example, "This position will require very high level report writing skills. What kind and quality of writing did _____ do for you? Any significant problems? What would you see as the next developmental or growth step for _____ in this area?" You may want to ask if the reference person knows anyone else it would be important for you to talk with. An important caveat is that you need to make sure you have the candidate's permission before you contact current supervisors, managers, or even coworkers. You must respect candidates' requests for confidentiality if any reference contacts could jeopardize their current position. However, in even the most difficult circumstances, it is very rare that there isn't someone at the candidate's current place of employment with whom you can talk.

See if the reference results raise any new questions or change your preference ranking among the top candidates. They should give you a broader, more complete picture of each person's past work and future potential.

Employment Arrangements and Categories

As you think about the various strategies to use to get the person you want, you may need to consider a variety of employment arrangements. Perhaps you'll find just the right person, and they'll want something other than a straightforward full-time employment arrangement. Think about creative possibilities: job sharing and flexible scheduling of work time are two of the leading-edge (and highly desired) employment options today. They cater to the needs of today's increasingly diversified work force.

If you begin thinking about an arrangement other than the standard ongoing full-time position, be aware that there are legal considerations and that the IRS will be looking over your shoulder. (They've become very interested in this subject in recent years.) Regular *ongoing* employees (please! *never* say — or write — "permanent" to describe ongoing employees or positions) basically come in two flavors: full-time and part-time. You (the organization) pay employment (payroll) taxes and deduct federal, state, and local income taxes for these people when you pay them.

Another employment category you may use is *temporary* employee: this is a person (either full-time or part-time), who is working for either a specified or unspecified length of time, but whose employment relationship with your organization is not expected to be ongoing. Agency "temps" are one type of temporary employee, but you can also hire temporary employees directly (for example, a specialist hired for the duration of a grant-funded project). Although you don't put agency-provided temporaries on your payroll, you *do* put on the payroll any temporary employees that you hire directly.

And here's where you must be careful: there are a growing number of individuals who want to be paid for a temporary job as if they were an agency temporary or (for higher pay levels) a self-employed consultant. It is easier and cheaper for the organization, which then doesn't pay the payroll portion of Social Security and other employment taxes, may not provide benefits, doesn't have to calculate and deduct income taxes, and can issue a Form 1099 at the end of the year instead of a W-2 form.

The problem is that there is no clear defining line between temporary employee and independent contractor status for purposes of the Fair Labor Standards Act or the Internal Revenue Code. The U.S. Supreme Court has listed six factors to use in separating true independent contractors from temporary employees for purposes of the Fair Labor Standards Act. Section 3121(d) of the Internal Revenue Code defines an employee for purposes of the tax code.

The dividing line in both lies in who has custody and control of the work: generally, if the worker must conform to your work day, perform the work in your offices, use your equipment and tools, be supervised in the execution of the work, and be paid on the basis of time worked, he or she is an employee, and must be paid through your payroll system. If the worker sets his or her own hours, performs some or all of the work away from your premises, is not supervised during its execution but has been given a set of job specifications, can make *or* lose money on the arrangement, and has a contract, the person is an independent contractor and may be paid separately from your payroll, as a vendor. If you hire an independent contractor, be careful that you execute a contract with the person to substantiate the arrangement.

The IRS believes that large numbers of employers and temporary employees are evading the payment of Social Security taxes and the withholding of federal taxes through the subterfuge of independent contracting — so they're checking carefully. The fines are substantial (payment of all back payroll taxes plus 100 percent penalty and interest).

Making the Offer

You are now ready to select the top person to whom you want to make your job offer. It's time to sit down and focus on your information *and* your instincts about each of the candidates. In some cases, the top choice will be clear, but quite often it's not. And even if you know who you want, remember, it's never over 'till it's over. Do *not* turn loose an acceptable runner-up candidate until you've received a firm acceptance from your first choice.

Usually, the hiring manager is the person who makes the actual offer. Before making the call, review the final amount and any contingencies or strategies with the authorizing manager. Be sure you have a clear go-ahead from that manager (it is no fun to try to back out of an unauthorized offer). If you believe there will be some negotiation needed, have your strategies and facts in hand. And, should something unexpected come to light during the call, be prepared to table the offer until you've thought about it; you can talk again in a few hours or the next day. Don't let yourself be stampeded into making a commitment that you're not sure about, from either a policy or a cost standpoint.

Hiring an employee is a little like getting married — if you suddenly feel that what you're getting is not what you thought, it's a whole lot better to back off than to jump in and live for a long time with the consequences. There's a momentum that builds during the hiring process: stay in control of it and manage it. No organization or manager is ever *that* desperate for a pair of hands. The worst hire I ever made came when I was so overburdened by carrying the load of a vacant position that I jumped in rather than backing off when I got a funny feeling as I was making the offer. I had a long time to regret not backing off, and it took an awful lot of time and energy to deal with the consequences of that hire.

Fortunately, most of the time there is a happy ending: the candidate happily accepts the offer, you happily confirm the start date and say that a confirming letter will be put in the mail immediately (Cook, 1989).

Follow-Up to a Successful Offer

While the glow of all those bright possibilities is still with you, take a moment to jot down what is needed to get this person off to a good start: what he or she needs to be well oriented into the organization as well as the job.

Be sure a sign-up and benefits orientation session is scheduled with the personnel or payroll person. Is any formal training needed (for example, on the organization's computer systems or other technical systems)? Who should the person meet with first? Over what period of time? Are there internal meetings you should arrange for the person to attend? Do you need to write a memo to the staff to announce the person's hire? Some managers like to write a quick "thank you" note to the other interviewers so that the people who helped make the selection know before other staff. Will you announce the incoming staff member to the external community through local newspapers or professional organization newsletters? Should announcements be made to your board, volunteer leaders, or general membership? Setting up a first-day schedule with lunch and other meetings prearranged is often an appropriate way to introduce your new employee to the new job and company. Some organizations put together an orientation checklist as an aid to managers (Comer, 1989; Federico, 1991).

The next item on your "to do" list (or to do as soon as you receive the signed offer confirmation letter back), is to tell the unsuccessful final candidate(s). (You can have someone else convey all but the final one or two candidates' rejections.) Many managers shrink from this, handing it off to the personnel person or, frankly, whomever they can find. That's not a good idea for several reasons, one of which is that you are the person who can best represent the organization in this interaction. No one else in the organization has the same understanding of these people — and all the candidates deserve the same level of consideration when they're being rejected as when you thought you might want them to join your team. It is a mark of courtesy and class on your part that will benefit the whole organization's reputation. On a practical note, it has been known to happen that another vacancy arises (or, alas, the same job becomes quickly vacant again) and you want to revive the candidacy of a previously rejected finalist.

The rejection call should not take long: the news will come as a blow, and the person won't want to discuss it at any length. You can do a brief buildup to let them know what's coming, then deliver the news, and exit quickly on a graceful note. For example: "We've come to a decision on the position. I want you to know that you presented yourself very well and offered a number of excellent qualities (or some other sincere praise). It really *was* a hard decision to make, but I'm calling to let you know that we have offered the position to another person. I've enjoyed meeting you and getting to know you, and should another likely job match come up I'd like to keep you in mind. Would that be all right with you?" Let the person answer and give them a chance to ask any burning question — "Was it a matter of money or experience?" for example. With this type of question, you should be vague. For example, "There were a lot of elements to consider and no one thing was decisive in itself." Or, if there was some overwhelming factor, you can mention it, for instance: "We were fortunate to find someone with substantial experience in _____ , and in the end we decided to go with that." They may have a quick business question to ask, such as about reimbursement for interview expenses. Answer or tell them who you'll have get back to them with the answer. Don't linger at this point; give a cordial exit line and ring off.

Summary

Selecting people for one's organization is probably the most important function any manager has. From the perspective at the top of an organization, it is clear that success depends on melding the energies and talents of many different kinds of people. An organization's ability to attract high-quality applicants is heavily influenced by the quality of its recruitment practices and systems. Finding the right person for a position requires objectivity, clarity of thought, application of energy, and—often—steady nerves.

A well-written and objective job description, which sets forth the basic requirements for the job and its holder, is essential for legal, ethical, and practical management reasons. Getting as clear an outline as possible of the job functions will save recruiting time, help the process stay focused, avoid organizational embarrassments (or worse, litigation!), and provide crucial objectivity to ensure that the hiring manager(s) do not inadvertently discriminate during the selection process. The job description is also needed to determine an appropriate pay level.

Hiring authority, whom to involve in the selection, and legal requirements are all important elements of the selection process. Testing, narrowing the field, selecting final interviewees, discussing salary expectations, handling competing offers, checking references, and handling various employment arrangements and categories are accomplished by hiring managers as they move toward offering the position to the right person.

References

Barnadin, H. J., and Russell, J. A. *Human Resource Management: An Experiential Approach.* New York: McGraw-Hill, 1993.

Bolman, L. G., and Deal, T. E. *Reframing Organizations: Artistry, Choice, and Leadership.* San Francisco: Jossey-Bass, 1991.

Boyett, J. H., and Conn, H. P. *Workplace 2000: The Revolution Reshaping American Business.* New York: Plume, 1991.

Boyle, T. J. "Hiring Thoroughbreds: Pitfalls to Avoid and Rules to Follow." *Business Horizons,* 1990, *33*(6), 28–33.

Brown, L. A., and Martin, D. C. "What to Expect from an Executive Search Firm." *HRMagazine,* 1991, *36*(12), 56–58.

Brown, W. A. "How to Write an Affirmative Action Plan." *American Demographics,* 1993, *15*(3), 56–58.

Byrne, N. C. "Successful Hiring Starts with a Complete Job Description." *Human Resources Professional,* 1991, *3*(4), 38–41.

Cascio, W. F. *Managing Human Resources.* New York: McGraw-Hill, 1989.

Comer, D. R. "Peers as Providers." *Personnel Administrator,* 1989, *34*(5), 84–86.

Cook, M. F. *Personnel Manager's Complete Model Letter Book.* Englewood Cliffs, N.J.: Prentice-Hall, 1989.

DuBrin, A. J. *Effective Business Psychology.* Englewood Cliffs, N.J.: Prentice-Hall, 1990.

Fear, R. A., and Chiron, R. J. *The Evaluation Interview.* New York: McGraw-Hill, 1990.

Federico, R. F. "Six Ways to Solve the Orientation Blues." *HRMagazine,* 1991, *36*(5), 69–70.

Freedman, R. D. "Back to the Basics of Interviewing." *HR Focus,* 1992, *69*(1), 10.

Fyock, C. D. "Selling the Position Is as Important as Selecting for It." *Human Resources Professional,* 1991, *4*(1), 26–29.

Fyock, C. D. *Get the Best: How to Recruit the People You Want.* Homewood, Ill.: Business One Irwin, 1993.

Gunsch, D. "Creativity Can Extend Resources." *Personnel Journal,* 1993, *72*(3), 92–94.

Leavitt, H. J., and Bahrami, H. *Managerial Psychology: Managing Behavior in Organizations.* San Francisco: Jossey-Bass, 1988.

Levesque, J. D. *Manual of Personnel Policies, Procedures and Operations.* Englewood Cliffs, N.J.: Prentice-Hall, 1986.

Lynch, R. *Lead! How Public Nonprofit Managers Can Bring Out the Best in Themselves and Their Organizations.* San Francisco: Jossey-Bass, 1993.

Meade, J. "The Complete Affirmative-Action Plan." *HRMagazine,* 1993, *38*(3), 35–38.

Morrison, A. M. *The New Leaders: Guidelines on Leadership Diversity in America.* San Francisco: Jossey-Bass, 1992.

Player, M. A. *Federal Law of Employment Discrimination.* St. Paul, Minn.: West, 1991.

Redeker, J. "When Peter Piper Picks His Peers." *Human Resources Professional,* 1991, *3*(3), 44–46.

Stump, J. S., Jr. "The Recession and Executive Search: No Longer Business as Usual." *Human Resources Professional,* 1991, *4*(1), 37–38.

Sunseri, A. J. "Ten Steps to Better Employee Interviewing." *Healthcare Financial Management,* 1991, *45*(4), 106.

Warmke, D. L. "Success Dispels Myths About Panel Interviewing." *Personnel Journal,* 1992, *71*(4), 120–126.

Yate, M. *Hiring the Best: How to Staff Your Department Right the First Time.* Holbrook, Mass.: Bob Adams, 1990.

24

Designing and Managing Compensation and Benefits Programs

Nancy E. Day

Some organizations, both for-profit and nonprofit, consider the compensation of their employees as an onerous and expensive obligation on which as little time as possible should be spent. Salaries and benefits may be set haphazardly, based on "gut-feelings" about how much certain jobs probably pay on the general market or on the difficulty of attracting qualified people to key positions. These organizations view compensation as extraneous to their overall mission or strategy.

This is unfortunate and unwise, given that wages and benefits average about 65 percent of all organizational expenses (Heneman, Schwab, Fossum, and Dyer, 1989). It is essential that the compensation system attract and reward the best-quality workforce it can afford, since its human resources are indeed its most important resources. Without them, the organization's goals cannot be achieved and its values cannot be enacted. As Louis Mayer, of Metro Goldwyn Mayer, said, "The inventory goes home at night." This is especially true for nonprofits.

Total compensation includes anything of monetary value that the organization provides its employees in exchange for their services and to motivate them to perform well in the future. This definition includes base salary, incentive pay, and benefits, which include health, retirement, paid time off, as well as services or facilities that the organization may furnish for the employees' benefit (common examples are tuition reimbursement, subsidized cafeterias, credit unions, parking, and child-care centers).

For the purposes of this chapter, we will confine most of our discussion to the more basic forms of compensation: salary, incentives, and benefits. Until recently, a book like this would not have mentioned incentives in the context of a nonprofit environment. However, dramatic changes are occurring in the compensation strategies of the for-profit world, brought on by Total Quality Management programs, self-directed work teams, and other participative management strategies. Nonprofit organizations are also involving themselves in these programs, and consequently, nontraditional pay systems will become an integral part of their compensation packages. Additionally, incentive pay is an avenue by which individual pay can be directly related to the "bottom line" or mission of the organization, reducing fixed costs and encouraging top performance because a percentage of an employee's pay is "at risk." In this time of tight budgets, limited development opportunities, and decreased government and private funding, pay programs that decrease fixed costs while increasing both individual and organizational performance deserve more than passing attention from management of nonprofit organizations.

Compensation Strategy and Organizational Mission

All organizations base their actions on goals that are either explicit or implicit. Long-term or strategic planning is done in well-managed organizations to ensure that current resources—financial, material and human—are used in the manner most effective to the organization's raison d'être. Organizations with effective performance appraisal programs will require individual employees to set performance objectives that are based on departmental goals, which in turn are driven by division and organizational goals. This cascading effect allows effective organizations to link broad, often ambitious goals and values with the activities of their individual workers. Thus, individual employees are responsible for carrying out the fundamental mission of the organization. Because of this obvious yet critical fact, it is imperative that compensation systems be part of the nonprofit's strategic mission or long-range plan and be consistent with the goals, culture, and environmental pressures of the organization. Organizations need to decide where they want to go and how they will get there. Compensation is one of the many important cogs in the total organizational performance machine that must be carefully tended, frequently lubricated, and replaced if it no longer functions adequately in contributing to the achievement of top performance.

For example, an organization that is changing its internal structure must ensure that its pay strategy fits the job changes. The most effective pay for self-directed work teams is probably not a traditional salary program; it probably will require careful analysis of the goals of the work teams, the reasons why teams are being implemented, and the pay strategy history of the organization.

It is imperative that workers are paid for what the organization wants to reward. This obvious yet critical fact is illustrated by Steven Kerr's well-known article, "On the Folly of Rewarding A, While Hoping for B" (1975, p. 769), which states,

> Whether dealing with monkeys, rats, or human beings, it is hardly controversial to state that most organisms seek information concerning what activities are rewarded, and then seek to do (or at least pretend to do) those things, often to the virtual exclusion of activities not rewarded. The extent to which this occurs of course will depend on the perceived attractiveness of the rewards offered, but neither operant nor expectancy theorists would quarrel with the essence of this notion.
>
> Nevertheless, numerous examples exist of reward systems that are fouled up in that behaviors which are rewarded are those which the rewarder is trying to *discourage,* while the behavior he desires is not being rewarded at all.

A familiar example of this mistake occurred frequently several years ago (and in some organizations today!) when employees were given regular, annual cost-of-living increases. Although high inflation demanded some salary escalation to keep workers even with living costs, organizations were in effect paying their employees to merely show up at work, whether or not they were performing in the best interests of the organization. A better way to use pay to accomplish organizational goals is to direct the largest increases to those workers who contribute the most and the best, not equally to all employees, regardless of their performance.

The Need for a Salary Policy

Environmental and market demands also have significant impact on compensation systems. Organizations that have employees whose jobs require extremely high levels of technical skill and expertise, such as medical doctors or engineers, must design pay systems that compensate these key positions adequately. The organization needs to ensure that qualified people are attracted and retained, while at the same time carefully balancing pay relationships across jobs within the company to avoid inequitable pay situations.

Edward Lawler (1990, p. 11) recommends that managers should begin to develop an effective pay strategy "with an analysis of the outcomes or results they need from their pay system and then develop a core set of compensation principles and practices to support these directions." Aligning the pay system to the organization's mission and strategic plan as well as its management style is critical. Thus, before a compensation program is seriously considered, the human resource (HR) professionals responsible for designing the compensation program need to evaluate carefully the organization's goals, values, culture, and strategy to ensure that compensation plays a key role in accomplishing organizational goals.

One way that many organizations define their compensation strategy is through the development, communication, and maintenance of a *salary policy*. This is generally a simple, relatively short statement that communicates how the organization plans to pay people, how the system will be designed and maintained, and the philosophy of what compensation is supposed to accomplish. Also included should be a statement expressing the organization's intention to treat everyone fairly and equitably, regardless of race, sex, religion, age, disability, color, or national origin. However brief such a statement may be, much concern and deliberation needs to go into its development, as the organization must make a commitment to adhere staunchly to the precepts included in the policy so that employee trust is not shaken. The compensation policy should then be communicated to employees along with other key organizational policies.

Using Consultants

Before embarking on any major new salary or benefits program, the nonprofit organization should consider the value and cost-effectiveness of contracting with a compensation consultant. Organizations on tight budgets, particularly nonprofits, often fall into the trap of trying to save money by developing major programs in-house. If current human resources (HR) staff have the needed expertise, this may be the appropriate avenue to take. However, even if current staff are equipped with necessary skills, the following points should be considered with regard to using consultants.

First, consultants generally have a wide range of experience across a number of organizations and therefore may know what will work best for your unique organization. Compensation programs, especially benefits, are sophisticated and complex systems, and even HR professionals with basic compensation knowledge may not have the breadth and depth of experience to develop and install programs that are truly a "good fit."

Second, consultants usually have access to a vast amount of salary and benefits survey data, or have easily accessible sources, and will thus be able to assess external competitiveness better than your organization alone can.

Third, consultants are outsiders, and this gives them an extremely valuable commodity: objectivity. Since the consultant's salary will not be part of the new compensation program, unlike the in-house HR professional's, he or she will be in a better position to tell top managers or the board of directors about unpopular or expensive compensation issues (for example, critical positions that are dramatically underpaid relative to the market and whose recommended salary increases may reach epic proportions). Objectivity also is a great asset in explaining to employees why some jobs have been downgraded and topped-out employees will not be receiving salary increases for the next year or so. Additionally, if the consultant is to conduct a specially designed salary or benefits survey, other organizations may be more likely to participate and share their salary information since the consultant provides a greater guarantee of confidentiality than a rival organization.

The major disadvantage of using consultants is, of course, cost. But keep in mind the above-cited estimates of payroll costs: 50 to 70 percent of total budgets. Sometimes several thousand dollars in consulting fees is money extremely well spent if it is able to provide the organization with a compensation system that maximizes the value of the salary/benefit dollar.

To assist in-house compensation program development, HR professionals can gain useful technical knowledge through the certification program of the American Compensation Association. This program consists of seven two-and-a-half-day seminars in each of the key compensation areas, including benefits. Those serious about establishing, installing, and maintaining a state-of-the-art compensation program should consider obtaining this certification.

Let us now turn to the components of developing a sound salary and benefits program. We will begin with base compensation, usually known simply as salary. Executive pay and incentive programs in nonprofit organizations will be discussed before we move into development of benefits packages.

Traditional Base Compensation Principles

Job Analysis

As is true for many personnel practices (recruitment, staffing, performance management, training and development, and others), the foundation of salary systems is current, accurate, and thorough job analysis. Through this process, data on the content of jobs are gathered, evaluated, compiled, and summarized (usually in the form of job descriptions) so that jobs are thoroughly and accurately understood. This somewhat time-consuming process is absolutely necessary for at least two reasons. First, only by understanding jobs can the level of *internal equity* in the organization be assessed and, if necessary, adjusted. Since establishing internal equity requires comparing jobs, it naturally requires that accurate and current job information be available in a usable format. Second, full and accurate job information is critical in establishing *external competitiveness*. This means that job content must be compared across organizations; that is, what the people actually do needs to be looked at, not merely job titles, which may or may not truly describe a position.

Job analysis is conducted using a number of techniques, depending on its final use (job analysis is also often used for designing programs for training, recruitment, job design, and others, as well as for compensation). These techniques include interviews of incumbents or supervisors (either individually or in groups), observations of workers, highly structured questionnaires or checklists (usually completed by the job incumbent), or open-ended questionnaires completed by the incumbent or supervisor. This last method is the one most frequently used by medium to small organizations, since it allows data to be gathered easily and relatively cheaply. Open-ended questionnaires are typically designed by the organization so that the data gathered fit the needs of the job analysis. Often, in analyzing jobs for compensation programs, *compensable factors* that are used in the job evaluation process (discussed below) are assessed through this questionnaire.

Internal Equity

Internal equity refers to the degree of equity between jobs, both similar and dissimilar, in the organization. In other words, jobs that are of similar levels on key compensable factors, such as skill or knowledge required, supervisory responsibilities, accountability for budget and resources, complexity of the job, or working conditions, should be paid at the same general level. For example, in most organizations the job of accounting clerk requires the equivalent of an associate's degree, knowledge of basic accounting principles, no supervisory responsibilities, and little accountability for financial resources. If this job is compared to a beginning computer operator, a job also requiring an associate's degree, basic technical knowledge, no supervisory responsibilities, and little accountability for financial resources, we would conclude that the jobs are essentially worth about the same to the organization. However, a custodian, as compared to the accounting clerk, would probably not be valued as highly, since custodial work requires less technical knowledge. In a system of internal equity, these differences in internal job value would be appropriately reflected in the pay structure; in a system that is not internally equitable, the custodian may be paid the same or more than the clerk or computer operator, or the computer operator may make significantly more or less than the clerk.

Internal equity is usually established using some form of *job evaluation*. This broad term describes a number of methods by which jobs are valued within the organization. Two of the most prevalent in small to medium sized organizations will be discussed here: slotting and point-factor job evaluation.

Job Slotting. The slotting process begins with gathering as much market data (the amounts other organizations pay for jobs) as possible. After these data are tabulated and checked for accuracy and consistency (methods for gathering and analyzing market data are presented below), the jobs are arrayed in order of their market value. Jobs for which no market data were available (jobs that are unique to the organization) are then *slotted* into this hierarchy. The slotting is done by comparing the job to those in the hierarchy and determining, based on the overall value of the job to the organization, where the job fits in the hierarchy. Slotting done in this manner is often referred to as a kind of "whole-job" evaluation system, meaning that compensable factors (skill, education, working conditions, and others) are not systematically determined and compared, but that the job is looked at as a whole. Of course, in practice, the actual cognitive decision processes that human beings naturally use tend to fall back on informally derived compensable factors. However, they are not formally defined or systematically applied.

Slotting may be appropriate for an organization that has one or more of the following characteristics:

- It does not have many jobs.
- Many of its jobs can be found in a number of organizations in the recruiting market.
- It desires to be as responsive to market forces as possible.

One advantage of the slotting method is cost. Since an elaborate point-factor system does not have to be developed and implemented (see below), much expense in terms of time and effort is saved. A second advantage is that the cost of consultants in establishing internal equity may be avoided. Often consultants are used in installing point-factor job evaluation systems, since the technical skill needed is fairly high.

However, slotting has disadvantages as well. The most obvious is that some organizations have many jobs that are not found in the job market, and thus market data may not be available for a large percentage of the organization's jobs. Second, because of the whole-job technique, the system is generally lower in reliability than is a point-factor system; when two people independently slot jobs, they are likely to come up with different solutions. Thus slotting may be more likely to be challenged by employees.

Point-Factor Evaluation. The most widely used type of job evaluation is point-factor evaluation. The well-known Hay system is a sophisticated version of the point-factor method. The basic steps in establishing and implementing this system involve:

- Identifying and weighting a set of factors that uniquely describes those job characteristics for which the organization wants to pay
- Establishing levels within each factor and assigning points to each level
- Carefully comparing each job to the factors and assigning points appropriate to each factor level that describes the job

Organizations have used a variety of compensable factors in their job evaluation systems, including the following:

- Accountability
- Complexity of job
- Consequence of errors
- Customer service responsibility
- Decision making
- Education and training
- Experience
- Independent judgment
- Interpersonal contacts
- Interpersonal skills
- Physical exertion
- Planning responsibility
- Problem solving
- Sales responsibility
- Scope of job
- Supervision
- Technical knowledge
- Working conditions

However, empirical research using factor analysis (a statistical procedure that defines the basic underlying components) has found that these numerous factors can generally be reduced to four basic ones: skill, effort, responsibility, and working conditions.

Compensable factors appropriate for the organization are determined by a number of methods, ranging from sophisticated computer programs to handpicking the factors that "sound right." However, the people who are choosing the factors should nearly always be top management. There are several reasons for this. First, top management, theoretically, is closest to the mission, goals, and strategy of the organization and can thus translate them into the compensable factors. Second, top management has a broad view of the organization's functions and thus understands the scope and content of the jobs. Third, as in any management program, it is imperative that top management "buy in" to the system. In nonprofit organizations, at the least it is wise to gain approval from members of the board of directors, if not include them in the actual factor determination.

One of the simplest and most straightforward methods used to guide top managers in factor choice involves using these steps:

1. The HR professional in charge of developing this program should identify a universe of appropriate compensable factors. This can be done by reviewing a set of factors such as those listed above and extracting any that are not relevant to the organization. For example, sales responsibility or physical exertion are often not relevant to nonprofits and may be removed.

2. After identifying an appropriate universe, the HR professional should carefully explain the overall point-factor evaluation concept as well as the meaning of each factor to the top managers. Pertinent points include:

   - Job evaluation is a method to measure the *relative worth* of jobs to the organization.
   - It does so by identifying factors (characteristics of jobs) that generally exist, to some degree, in all jobs across the organization.
   - Each job is then "measured" using each factor.
   - Each job will be assigned a point value, and the final product will be a hierarchy of jobs, arrayed in order of their value to the organization.
   - Thus, since the factors will measure the relative worth of the jobs, choosing them is a critical task that requires top managers to take an organizational perspective (as opposed to thinking only of their division or unit) and consider the organization's long-term or strategic goals.

3. Top managers then should *individually* rank the factors.

4.   The HR professional compiles those rankings and selects a set of eight to ten factors.
5.   The HR professional presents this set (as well as those not selected) to the top management in a group, asking them to discuss the set and ensure that it describes the job characteristics *for which they are willing to pay.*

    The final set should not include more than ten factors. More than ten is not only unwieldy, but some will probably be redundant. After the final compensable factors are chosen, they should be weighted according to the relative importance of the factors to each other. For example, an association of physicians is probably driven by jobs that are highly dependent on education and technical training, so that factor would be heavily weighted. Working conditions would probably be of significantly less importance, and would be weighted accordingly. An easy method to accomplish this is to ask the top managers individually to divide 100 points among the set of factors. The HR professional can then compile their responses into one set of weightings, which top management as a group can again assess and sign off on.

    After the factors are weighted, they must be divided into *levels*. An easy example is education and training. Typical levels in this factor include:

1.   High school diploma (or equivalent); basic reading skills required
2.   High school diploma (or equivalent) plus ability to operate simple equipment such as typewriters; basic office or technical skills
3.   Some advanced training, typically found in two-year college or certification program (or equivalent experience); ability to operate moderately complex equipment (such as for word processing); intermediate analytical skills
4.   Theoretical understanding of a body of knowledge similar to that acquired in an academic field of study; may include a bachelor's degree, extensive technical training or equivalent experience
5.   Comprehensive understanding of one or several fields, normally gained through extensive study in an academic environment or business; may include a master's degree (or equivalent experience)
6.   Knowledge of a subject to a level that the incumbent is an authority in the field; may include doctoral degree (or equivalent experience)

    Parenthetically, please note that "or equivalent" is used in order to protect the organization from legal liability. Because protected classes may be adversely affected by educational requirements, it is important to show that these levels are *not* hard-and-fast requirements but are generally the levels of education that incumbents *typically* have. Additionally, practically every organization will have individuals who may be formally "over-" or "under-qualified" for their jobs but are performing adequately or better.

    If an outside consultant is not assisting in the project, it would be helpful for the HR professional to consult a compensation consultant or comprehensive textbook listing typical compensable factors. Defining appropriately sensitive factor levels requires a degree of expertise that generally comes only from previous experience. Points must also be assigned to each factor level within each factor, guided by the factor weightings. Table 24.1 illustrates a typical example of the assignment of these values.

Table 24.1. Assigning Points to Factor Levels.

Factors	Weight	Points	1	2	3	4	5	6
Education and training	25%	250	50	75	100	150	200	250
Accountability	20%	200	35	75	100	135	175	200
Independent judgment	15%	150	25	50	75	100	125	150
Supervision	10%	100	15	30	45	60	80	100
Complexity of job	10%	100	15	30	45	60	80	100
Decision making	10%	100	15	30	45	60	80	100
Consequence of errors	5%	50	5	10	20	30	40	50
Problem solving	5%	50	5	10	20	30	40	50
Total	100%	1,000						

The product of our efforts at this point is essentially a measuring device by which all of the organization's jobs can be measured. The next major phase of the point-factor job evaluation process involves using this point-factor "yardstick" to measure jobs. First, "benchmark" jobs must be identified. These are jobs that are well defined and well known across the organization. Ideally, they will be jobs that have multiple incumbents (not always possible in small organizations) in which the incumbents are performing essentially the same sets of tasks at the same levels of responsibility. Additionally, benchmarks should be jobs for which market data are easily found (see below). The benchmarks will be the jobs that will be evaluated first.

Second, the individuals responsible for evaluating the jobs must be chosen. In the best of all possible worlds, a *job evaluation committee* should be used. This committee is made up, again, of top managers. Under the guidance of the HR professional or compensation consultant, this group of five to eight executives spends several uninterrupted hours or even days carefully discussing each job, debating its rating on each factor, and finally reaching consensus on a final rating. The reasons for using a job evaluation committee made up of executives are identical to those for having top managers choose factors: they have a broad, organizational perspective and understand all organizational functions; they are closest to the strategic goals and values of the organization; the committee process encourages top management to "buy in" to the system. After the committee has evaluated benchmark jobs, a subcommittee (often the HR professional and/or consultant and one top manager) usually evaluates the rest of the jobs in the organization in order to save valuable top management time. However, even using this tactic, the committee process can be extremely expensive in terms of executive time and productivity. An alternative that is often used is for the HR professional, in conjunction with the consultant or other HR staff, to evaluate all jobs, create the job hierarchy, and then gain top management approval for the hierarchy.

Whether or not a committee is used, the same process should be followed in evaluating the jobs:

1. Ensure that all evaluators understand all the factors and levels. Take some time to discuss them and how they relate to the organization.
2. Ensure that all evaluators truly understand each job. This is where current and accurate job descriptions are essential. If necessary, consult the job's supervisor to make sure that essential job functions are thoroughly understood.
3. A critical point that evaluators should remember is that they are evaluating *jobs* and not people. It is essential that discussion center around the requirements of the job and not the unusually high (or low) performing job incumbent.
4. Discuss the job in terms of each factor and what specific job tasks or responsibilities relate to the factor.
5. Try to reach a consensus on the job's rating on each factor. If a consensus is not possible, use majority rule, but only as a last option.

After all jobs have been evaluated, the point values should be entered into a spreadsheet (see Table 24.2). This enables the evaluators to "quality control" their results; that is, to ensure that face-valid and sensible relationships between the jobs are maintained.

A final step in job evaluation is reviewing the hierarchy within each department with its top manager. The array of jobs within the department,

Table 24.2. Job Evaluation Spreadsheet.

Job	Education and Training	Accountability	Independent Judgment	Supervision	Complexity of Job	Decision Making	Consequence of Errors	Problem Solving	Total
Account Clerk I	50	35	25	15	15	15	10	20	185
Account Clerk II	75	75	50	15	30	30	20	30	325
Account Clerk III	75	100	75	30	45	30	30	40	425
Secretary I	75	75	75	15	30	15	20	10	315
Secretary II	100	100	100	15	45	30	30	30	450
Executive Secretary	100	135	125	30	60	45	40	40	575
Administrative Assistant	150	135	125	45	60	60	40	40	655
Program Director	200	175	150	80	80	80	50	50	865

listed *without* point values (point values of jobs should be known only by the job evaluation committee and relevant HR staff in order to avoid misunderstandings with others who do not have an overview of the scope or application of the evaluation system), should be presented to the manager. He or she should check to see that this hierarchy "makes sense" in the accepted understanding of the jobs' functions, values, and relationships. Some minimal fine-tuning may be needed. After all departments have reviewed these hierarchies, a spreadsheet illustrating all jobs within departments across the organization can be produced, which may be reviewed by the top managers. This last step is to ensure that job relationships are equitable not only within departments but all across the organization.

The Need to Review Evaluations. Regardless of the type of job evaluation method that is used, a system of regular review should be established so that jobs are analyzed and reevaluated about every three years. Obviously, organizational needs as well as jobs change over time, and a regular system is necessary so that internal equity is maintained. Often, HR departments will systematically review one-third of the jobs each year to eliminate having to deal with a major project every three years. Additionally, supervisors should have a mechanism for appealing job evaluations to HR outside this regular cycle when they can substantiate a legitimate need to do so.

With nontraditional pay systems increasing due to innovative organizational structures such as self-managed work teams, the usefulness of extensive job evaluation programs has been questioned, since many pay systems are emphasizing external competitiveness rather than internal equity. Any organization, especially the nonprofit in which time and money are in extreme demand, needs to decide the balance it wishes to strike between internal and external pressures and design an internal evaluation system that is at least administratively complex. (The point-factor system is definitely not for everyone.)

Indeed, the hassles of creating an internally equitable salary structure are hard to exaggerate. They nearly always pay off in the long run, however. Although most managers believe that inequities with the external market will foster more pay dissatisfaction than inequitable internal relationships, experiences in the private sector with two-tiered pay systems provide a valuable lesson on the impact of internal inequity. These systems were designed to help financially troubled employers reduce costs by paying new hires dramatically less for the same jobs that previously hired incumbents were doing, sometimes as little as one-half of the incumbents' salaries. Research and experience revealed that not only did new employees exhibit high levels of pay dissatisfaction, longer-tenured employees being paid more were also extremely uncomfortable with the inherent inequities. Additionally, internal inequities will be experienced by the employee on a daily, even hourly basis, as he or she continually interacts with other workers. External market inequities, on the other hand, may only be directly experienced as one reads the classified advertisements or has an occasional conversation comparing wages. Thus, every organization should be cognizant of the consequences of internal inequity and install, implement, and maintain a sound job evaluation program, no matter how simple or complex.

External Competitiveness

Compared to the techniques of establishing internal equity, methods for ensuring that pay levels are externally competitive are much more straightforward. Again, the process is directly dependent on current and accurate job analysis and descriptions.

After ensuring that job information is complete and up-to-date, the first question that must be answered is What are the salary markets for the jobs in this organization? In nearly every organization, several salary markets will exist. The key to answering the question is to determine where the organization recruits for each type of job. For example, clerical jobs are recruited locally, probably from all types of organizations, not just other nonprofits. Therefore, a wide local market is generally needed for clerical jobs. While it is true that many nonprofits will be unable to meet the pay levels for clerical workers paid by large private-sector companies, it is still critical to have information about the pay level in the entire relevant market. Some professional jobs that are technically or specialty oriented will most likely be recruited regionally or nationally, and perhaps from other nonprofits with similar missions and goals. Finally, top executive jobs will probably need to be compared to a national nonprofit market, since those key positions require skills specialized to your particular nonprofit organizational needs.

After identifying the relevant markets, benchmark jobs should be identified. These should generally be the same jobs used as benchmarks in the job evaluation process. Not only should these jobs be well-defined and understood *within* the organization, they should be ones that can easily be found in many other organizations in the job markets you have identified. (Every organization has its own unique jobs that do not exist in the rest of the world and for which, therefore, no market data will be available.) Benchmark jobs, additionally, should be stable, represent nearly all levels across the organization, and, as a group, should vary in levels of compensable factors. Typically, it is desirable to choose a group of benchmarks representing 25 to 30 percent of all jobs in the organization. Finally, jobs for which the organization is experiencing particular difficulty recruiting should be included as benchmarks if they meet the previous criteria (Wallace and Fay, 1988).

A critical point in this process is that job *titles* are not determinants of benchmark jobs, job *content* is. Therefore, to avoid confusion an effort should be made to ensure that titles accurately reflect job contents and are not manipulated to reward employees or increase the prestige of the supervisor.

Published Sources of Salary Data. Salary data are generally collected from two broad sources: published salary surveys and surveys that are conducted by the organization or its consultant. Published surveys are undoubtedly the easiest to obtain but have drawbacks. (Exhibit 24.1 lists a variety of published surveys.) First, some are extremely expensive. Those published by national consulting firms can cost from $200 to $1,000 and more. Such cost issues may be counteracted by payroll dollars saved in an effective salary administration program, however, and several organizations may form a consortium to purchase them jointly. These surveys are generally of very high quality, with the data "cut" in many useful ways (for example, by region, by type of industry, by budget size, and others). However, because these surveys are geared to the private sector, they may only have relevant data for a few jobs in a nonprofit organization. But for some high-level technical or specialized jobs, the data found in them may be essential. Luckily, there are many cheaper published sources of salary data available, such as those published by other nonprofits, including professional associations and government entities.

Salary Surveys. Conducting a custom survey is necessary when no published survey exists for key jobs that are found in other organizations. Finding salary data for highly paid professional jobs that exist only in other nonprofits similar to yours may require a special survey. An advantage of custom surveys is that the organization has control over the data that are retrieved. The main disadvantage is that, because surveying is another fairly sophisticated and technical activity, an organization must either have people on its staff with sufficient time and appropriate expertise or hire qualified consultants. Thus, even custom surveys may be as or even more expensive than some purchased surveys.

Determining where salary data will be found will obviously be driven by what the relevant salary markets are. For local clerical markets, several sources are available. First, local human resources groups often publish salary surveys keyed to a general market. Check with the Society for Human Resource Management for the name of the local chapter. Second, the Bureau of Labor Statistics publishes *Area Wage Surveys,* available at very nominal costs for a number of metropolitan areas across the country. Third, municipalities (often through Chambers of Commerce) or states may conduct surveys of local markets, which may be available for small fees.

Regional and national markets for professional and managerial jobs can be researched through appropriate surveys. Nonprofit managers should be particularly aware of those organizations that provide data for nonprofit markets, such as Abbott, Langer and Associates, Cordom Associates, and the American Society of Association Executives, as listed in Exhibit 24.1. Additionally, many professional associations publish data for specific occupations. Finding these sources can take some detective work, but will save time and money in the long run as compared to conducting a custom survey.

Typically, salary surveys report several statistics for each job, usually including the average salary, weighted average, minimum, maximum, median (fiftieth percentile), and perhaps other percentiles. Generally, the most important statistic in the salary survey is the weighted average, since it

Exhibit 24.1. Selected Salary Survey Sources.

U.S. Department of Labor, Bureau of Labor Statistics
    Area Wage Surveys
    National Survey of Professional, Administrative, Technical and Clerical Pay (PATC)
Professional Associations
    Administrative Management Society
        Management Salaries Report
        Office, Professional & Data Processing Salaries Report
    American Society of Association Executives
        Blue Chip Summary of Executive Compensation
        Salary Survey of the Greater Washington Society of Association Executives
Nonprofit Industry Surveys
    Abbott, Langer & Associates
        Compensation in Nonprofit Organizations, Part I and II
    Cordom Associates
        Salary Survey of Nonprofit Organizations
    Peat Marwick
        Management Compensation & Benefits Practices in Not-for-Profit Organizations in
        New York City
    Towers Perin
        Compensation Survey Report of Management Positions in Not-for-Profit Organizations
Consulting Groups
    Executive Compensation Service
        Hospital & Health Care Report
        Middle Management Report
        Office Personnel Report
        Professional and Scientific Personnel Report
        Technical/Skilled Trades Survey
        Top Management Report
        Sales and Marketing Report
        Supervisory Management Report
    William M. Mercer
        Finance, Accounting and Legal Compensation Survey Results
        Human Resource Management Compensation Survey Results
        Hospital Management Compensation Survey Results
        Information Systems Compensation Survey Results
        Micro-Mini Computer Compensation Survey Results

Source: Courtesy of DeFrain Mayer Lee & Burgess Associates. Used by permission.

represents the average salary across all the job incumbents (not just across organizations) in the market. Several points should be reviewed before using data from a salary source:

- How many organizations have participated? Make sure that data are representative of a sufficiently large sample.
- How does the weighted average compare to the average salary? If they are dramatically different, it may mean that one very large organization's data are skewing the results, since weighted averages are weighted by the number of employees within each organization.
- How do the average and weighted average salaries compare with the fiftieth percentile (median)? Again, a large discrepancy could indicate a skewed distribution that may mean it is a nonrepresentative sample.

Using Salary Data Effectively. At least three different sources of salary data should be collected for each benchmark job, more when possible. This ensures that final market data averages are valid. Since survey data are collected at different points in time (high-quality surveys will cite the effective date of the data), data must be aged by a reasonable inflation factor so that all figures are comparable. This factor should be based on the general increase in salaries and salary structures currently occurring in the market (sources for these statistics will be discussed later). Next, the individual data points need to be checked to see that they are within a reasonable range of each other; outliers, either much higher or lower than others, should be removed. Then, data for each job should be averaged, after which the jobs can be arrayed, if desired, in order of market value.

A useful means of evaluating the organization's current standing in the market is through regression analyses. Using job evaluation points as the independent variable, one regression line should be calculated with market average salaries as the dependent. This regression line should be plotted and compared with the regression line for which current salaries serve as the dependent variable. By looking at the disparities between these two lines, the degree to which the organization conforms to the market can be ascertained. For example, such a comparison may show that the organization is paying competitively for upper level jobs, while lower level jobs are being paid under their market rates. Using these graphs to illustrate discrepancies helps explain compensation needs to decision makers, such as boards of directors, who must consider economic impact.

The next steps involve reconciling internal equity with external competitiveness, formulating salary grades and ranges, and creating administrative procedures consistent with compensation policies.

Sound Salary Administration Policies and Procedures

As part of the compensation policy formulation, top managers must decide where they wish to stand relative to their job markets. Most organizations in the private sector attempt to maintain their pay levels at the median of their relevant markets. This does not mean that every employee will be paid the going market rate, but that overall, the salary ranges and grades will reflect the current market rates (more will be said about this later). Some organizations make policy decisions to pay at the seventy-fifth percentile; they believe that by paying premium salaries they will be sure to attract and retain the top performers in the job market. Some organizations may pay significantly under the market median; they may be driven by a pool of low-skill employees performing easily acquired duties. Thus these organizations do not need to attract and retain the best, or even average, performers. Obviously, such a decision is critical to the organization's strategic planning, its long-range goals, and the current environmental challenges it faces.

Salary Grades and Ranges. When this decision has been made, the HR professional or compensation consultant must make several subsequent decisions regarding the *salary structure,* which is merely the set of grades and their accompanying ranges. A *salary grade* involves several simple but key concepts: minimum, maximum, midpoint, and range spread. The minimum is the minimum dollar amount that the organization has determined the job is worth. Generally, newly hired workers with little or no specific job training will be paid the minimum rate. The maximum reflects the most value the organization expects to receive from the job. Even if an incumbent performs the job superbly and has done so for the last fifty years, the job is simply worth no more than the maximum. In most cases, jobs of similar value will be grouped together in a single grade; systems that use only one job per grade are usually unwieldy and inefficient.

The midpoint is a critical concept in base salary administration. It is the point in the salary range that is keyed to the organization's response to the market. For example, if the market rate for beginning accountants is $2,000 per month and the organization's policy is to pay at 110 percent of the market, the midpoint for the beginning accountant grade will be $2,200. New hires will be paid at the minimum of the range, and some longer-tenured accountants may be paid more, but generally the job of beginning accountant, when performed by a full-performing, not newly hired, incumbent, is worth $2,200 to the organization.

The range spread is the difference between the maximum and the minimum, expressed as a percentage of the minimum. Ranges spreads typically run from 35 to 50 percent, with the smaller ranges usually used for lower level jobs. The idea here is that incumbents in lower level jobs will stay in the range for less time than incumbents in higher level jobs, since the lower jobs are less complex, easier to learn, and incumbents will tend to be promoted quickly to higher levels.

Salary grades should group jobs together that are of the same value to the organization. The number of grades in a pay system depends on several issues, among them the number of hierarchical levels, diversity of jobs, and the culture of the organization (American Compensation Association, 1988). A closely related issue is midpoint progression, or the difference between the midpoints of two grades as expressed as a percentage of the lower grade's midpoint. Sometimes organizations will split the structures into exempt (professional, supervisory, and managerial workers, including those exempt from the provisions of the Fair Labor Standards Act, who are not paid overtime) and nonexempt grades (those that are paid overtime), and use a 5 to 7.5 percent progression for nonexempt grades and 10 to 13 percent for exempts (Greene, 1982). The key issue is that job families have sufficient differentials between them to support the value of the jobs in the marketplace and within the organization.

Building Salary Structures. Salary structures are built beginning with the midpoints. Job evaluation points and market data for benchmark jobs are compared and reconciled. Some jobs may be valued more highly by the organization than by the market. The HR professional must weigh any such differences and create a structure that recognizes both forces. Generally speaking, areas at which breaks are found either in the evaluation points or market average hierarchies, are used to create preliminary grades, which are then refined to fit the jobs and the organization appropriately. After a preliminary structure for benchmark jobs is completed, the other nonbenchmark jobs are included to ensure that all jobs fit the structure. At this point, one of the necessities of job evaluation becomes clear: since nonbenchmark jobs will have no market data associated with them, job evaluation points will determine the grades in which they belong.

Upon installing a new salary system, it is inevitable that some employees' current salaries will be over the new maximums ("red circle" employees) or under the new minimums ("green circle" employees). Theoretically, red circle employees are being paid substantially over the market rate for the job. Therefore, it does not make sense to continue to increase their base pay and thus it is typically "frozen" until the structure's maximum catches up and exceeds it. To maintain their level of motivation, however, many organizations will provide these individuals with annual lump-sum bonuses based on performance. This strategy gives the employees additional income but does not add to the fixed costs of their base salaries. Green circle employees' salaries are substantially below the market rates for their jobs, and consequently should be moved at least to the new minimum as quickly as possible. For organizations with limited resources, that may mean giving small periodic increases to boost the salary gradually. Additionally, some long-term employees may be faced with severe inequity if their salaries are at the minimum and new workers are hired to work alongside them at the same pay level. In these cases, the HR professional must recommend the best approach to balance equity with financial resources. Often, a simple formula combining years of service and performance is created to move longer-term employees to a more equitable position in the range.

Maintaining a Competitive Salary Structure. In order to maintain the salary structure, the market must be checked annually to ensure that the organization's ranges remain competitive. This is done through another kind of survey, the prototype of which is the American Compensation Association's annual *Salary Budget Survey* (available at a small fee to nonmembers). This survey presents data regionally, by industry, and by job level for present and anticipated structure increases. These data are presented as percentages and represent the amount the surveyed companies increased their midpoints (minimums and maximums change accordingly) in the year and the amount by which they expect to increase them in the next year. Organizations will typically use this information to adjust their own structures to remain competitive, but usually do not correspondingly increase employees' wages unless an employee's salary is surpassed by the new minimum. Any green circle employees should be moved to meet the new minimum as soon as possible, unless there are extraordinary circumstances, such as unacceptable performance.

Salary administration procedures must be written that coordinate with the goals and plans of the organization. There should be policies covering the salary impact of transfers, promotions, demotions, reclassifications (which happens when a job is reevaluated and placed in a different grade owing to changes in the duties it comprises) and new hirings. It is essential that these be carefully thought out so that the intentions of the compensation plan are not subverted due to haphazard (and often nonmotivational) administrative procedures.

Pay satisfaction is often popularly regarded as the worker's satisfaction with the level of salary and benefits he or she may receive. However, since research shows that pay satisfaction depends on the structure and administration of the program as well as salary and benefits levels and raises, the wise HR professional will ensure that administrative processes are sound and equitable (Heneman and Schwab, 1985; Carraher, 1991).

Merit Versus Seniority Pay

Merit pay generally refers to an annual salary increase based on the employee's supervisory performance appraisal. Nonprofit organizations, government entities, and school districts have typically based salary increases on seniority rather than performance. Within the last ten to fifteen years, however, even these relatively conservative organizations are moving to some kind of pay-for-performance or merit system. This is an interesting trend, given that many private-sector companies are becoming slowly disenchanted with the difficulties of measuring individual performance and administering the motivational aspects of merit pay. Many of these for-profits, while not strictly abandoning merit pay, are moving toward group or individual incentive programs that tie salient salary increases to objective, measurable organizational outcomes.

These more innovative pay systems do not eliminate the need for sound base compensation programs, however. Individuals must still receive a base wage, which will continue to represent a substantial expense to the organization and must be managed carefully. Therefore, the HR professional in charge of compensation in nonprofits must decide which method will be best to move employees through their ranges: merit or seniority.

There are advantages and disadvantages to either method (Heneman, Schwab, Fossum, and Dyer, 1989). Some advantages to merit pay are the following:

- Employees prefer it because it matches the norms and values of the broader culture in which we live.
- It rewards performance, not just membership in the organization. Rewarding only membership encourages poor performers to stay.

- Merit pay distinguishes between high- and low-performing employees.
- Merit pay provides an excellent source of feedback to employees.
- It can function as a mechanism to encourage employee ownership of the organization's mission, long-term strategy, and goals.

Some disadvantages include:

- Accurate performance ratings are difficult to attain.
- Organizations often do not allocate sufficient amounts to the merit pool so that increases are too small to be motivating or to distinguish between average and superior employees.
- Merit pay is administratively difficult and expensive.
- Since employees often overestimate their own performance, merit pay threatens morale because employees will feel underrewarded.
- In some organizations that have traditionally had seniority-based pay, employees may have a hard time accepting merit pay.

Seniority systems also have certain advantages (Lawler, 1990):

- Unlike performance, seniority is a very reliable criterion and thus seniority systems do not depend on subjective measures for the determination of salary increases.
- Seniority systems are administratively cheaper and easier than merit systems.
- Some organizational cultures are better suited to seniority systems, especially those that are relatively stable and not sensitive to rapid technological change.
- Since they reward membership, seniority systems encourage employee retention.
- They encourage employees to think of their job with the organization as a career.

Disadvantages to the seniority system include:

- Paying only for membership regularly increases fixed costs to the organization, perhaps without accompanying performance increases.
- Employees may experience inequity when they perceive that they are working harder or doing more than their co-workers who are receiving identical increases.
- Determining how to pay for experience gained outside the organization when hiring seasoned professionals can be difficult.
- Because turnover may be low in seniority-based organizations, new employees with more current technology or new perspectives may not be added as needed.

Determining the optimum method for the organization obviously depends on a number of factors. Switching from one system to the other requires careful and thoughtful communication with employees so that they understand why the organization is changing to the new system and how it is similar to and different from the old system.

Communicating Salary Plans

The American Compensation Association (1981) recommends that an effective compensation program should communicate six basic areas to employees:

1. The methods by which jobs are analyzed and evaluated
2. The organization's policy in reacting to the market rates for its jobs
3. How performance relates to pay
4. How pay increases are determined and administered
5. Governmental and economic limitations on compensation levels
6. Administrative policies and procedures

Beyond these sensible recommendations, organizations will have to make their own strategic decisions regarding how much information about the plan should be available to employees. Some public organizations—like federal, state and local governments—make data regarding all salary grades and ranges available to employees as well as taxpayers; even individual salary levels can be easily discovered, just by a trip to the library. Other organizations are less open, some making discussion of individual salaries among employees a disciplinary offense. Generally speaking, most organizations make the minimum, midpoint, and maximum of a salary range available to the individuals whose jobs fall within it. Thus, employees are aware of the earning power of their present jobs.

A case can be made for making the entire salary structure available to all employees because of the developmental (and thereby motivational) aspects. If individuals know the earning potentials of prospective jobs to which they may aspire, theoretically they may be motivated to acquire the necessary skills and experiences to get them there. Additionally, the career-tracking characteristics of this scheme should encourage employees to remain with the organization in order to achieve their personal career goals. However, if such career options do not exist for most employees in the organization, and if the culture does not permit such disclosure, it should not be done. Like practically every human resource function, the method of communicating salary plans must be carefully determined based on its impact on and coordination with the culture of the organization.

Incentive Pay in Nonprofits

Recent attempts by American business to become more competitive have given rise to several innovations in pay systems. Although nonprofit organizations are often so financially constrained that incentives may seem an impossible luxury, it is useful for the nonprofit HR professional to be aware of them, since some of these new systems may have direct applicability to nonprofits that have productivity or motivational issues. Two of these innovative incentive programs that may be applicable for nonprofits are discussed below.

Skill-Based Pay

Under this type of program, employees are hired at one rate and receive pay increases based on the number of skills that they acquire. Most plans designate between four and six levels of skills to be attained that are keyed to the organization's strategic or operational goals. This type of program may be useful to nonprofits having a large number of highly technical jobs for which skills are not typically acquired through formal education. Additionally, this type of program encourages retention, since employees are able to identify avenues for future advancement easily. There are both advantages and disadvantages (Wallace and Fay, 1988). Advantages to the system include:

- Employees are encouraged to learn as many relevant skills as possible, allowing for the efficient use of labor and greater flexibility of jobs.
- Employees are viewed as assets, and relatively low-skilled workers can be hired and developed to maximize their effectiveness to the organization.

Disadvantages include:

- When an employee learns all tasks, he or she "tops out" and thus loses salary increase potential (one reason why these programs are usually combined with a more traditional base pay program).
- Significant investments in training are required.
- There may not be enough organizational space for all employees to advance.
- Skill-based pay conflicts with traditional job evaluation plans.
- Skill-based pay may conflict with market rates.

Gainsharing Programs

Gainsharing programs that allow employees to share a pool of money generated by cost savings to the organization (in for-profit companies, the pot may include increased revenues). This type of program may be particularly appropriate for nonprofits that experience unnecessarily high operating costs. The plans include some employee-participation mechanism whereby employee ideas and initiative not only encourage "buy in" to the program but also, in part, determine methods to save costs. Usually, the organization will split the cost savings pool on an equal basis with the employees, and thus the plan benefits both the individual and the organization.

This type of plan makes sense by encouraging workers to save organizational money to maximize their personal reward. The difficulty in a nonprofit is to sell the idea to the board of directors; often, their attitude will be that "if that much money can be saved, it should all be allocated to the worthy cause for which our organization exists, not to the workers, who are just doing their jobs." Thus, management must clearly and carefully explain the advantages and workings of the program to directors. Another problem with this type of program is that it often involves defining a fairly complicated formula by which to measure productivity gains. This also requires administrative policies sensitive to the motivational objectives of the program, which may necessitate hiring sophisticated consultants to assist in the installation of the plan. Consultants often take a percentage of the productivity gains generated as compensation. A final consideration is that the organizational climate must be conducive to such a program: management must be willing to support a highly participative climate, and employees must feel that management is trustworthy (Wallace and Fay, 1988).

Research on the effectiveness of gainsharing is fairly positive. Advantages include increased coordination and teamwork, recognition and satisfaction of social and participation needs, increased acceptance of innovations and efficient management, and a heightened willingness to work more as well as smarter (Lawler, 1988).

Cash Awards

Many for-profit organizations tie performance to cash awards, or bonuses. There are numerous methods to structure such an incentive program, including informal plans whereby managers receive a pool of money that they may distribute at their discretion to carefully planned programs with specific performance measures linked to specific levels of reward. Surprisingly, even with tight budgets, between 25 and 30 percent of nonprofit organizations surveyed offer managers cash compensation awards based on attainment of some performance goal (Hildebrandt, 1991; Rocco, 1991). These can be effective incentives to achieving organizational objectives, if they are carefully planned and thoughtfully coordinated with long-term strategy. A committee composed of members of the board and top management should choose those eligible to participate in the award program. Measures defining the specific performance levels to be attained and their consequent reward levels should be objectively and painstakingly spelled out in advance (Rocco, 1991). Because funds for such a program in a nonprofit may be limited to upper management, careful planning is essential so that equality perceptions between organizational levels are properly maintained.

An alternative may be to design programs that fund themselves through cost savings or financial development. As in all incentive programs, however, this strategy requires that top policy makers (board members and executives) be enthusiastic about the objectives and possibilities of the incentive system and supportive of an atmosphere of trust and open communication. Additionally, only performance that is clearly excellent should be rewarded (Wein, 1989).

Executive Pay in Nonprofits

Although for-profit organizations are under heavy fire by the media for their top management compensation practices, such has not been the case for top management of nonprofit organizations until recently, when salaries reported in the media have been repudiated as out-of-hand without considering the market forces that may make them necessary. It is imperative that top decision makers, including directors and major contributors, understand that superior performance in top management positions is critical and that the best performers are often in very high demand in the marketplace. Since even reasonable levels of pay for their services may seem unconscionably expensive to the uneducated, those involved in determining executive pay should be extremely thorough in their market analyses and decision making as well as meticulous in communicating market pressures for the top jobs to the directors and major contributors.

However, nonprofits generally have less to worry about in terms of executive pay controversies than do for-profits. For-profits are often criticized not for their base salaries, which tend to be relatively modest ("relatively" is a key word here), but for their incentive pay, often in the form of annual bonuses or stock options. Since nonprofit top managers are not likely to have these incentives, their pay seems somewhat less mysterious. In addition, nonprofits are often severely constrained by limited financial resources, making the magnitude of nonprofit executive pay, in comparison to for-profit counterparts, seem quite modest.

Since stock options or ample annual bonuses as incentives are generally unavailable to nonprofits, the pay of nonprofit top managers should be determined in a very similar manner as that addressed above (job evaluation, market data analyses, and sound policies and procedures). However, external competitiveness issues are usually weighted much more heavily for top managers. There are a couple of reasons for this. For one, the location of these positions in the organization (at the top) means that internal equity considerations are limited to those jobs below. Additionally, these are key jobs that are generally quite visible to organizations competing for talent. Thus, external factors are more salient for these positions.

A recent study conducted by Abbott, Langer and Associates (Langer, 1990) discusses some of the factors determining nonprofit CEO pay. It found that income of CEOs is related to length of relevant experience, level of education, level of managerial responsibility, size and type of organization (banking and financial associations' pay levels are highest, and artistic, cultural, and literacy organizations' are lowest). Also, national organizations provide larger CEO income.

It is often desirable, for obvious reasons, to contract with outside consultants to design the salary plan for top management. Not only do they have access to more data, they have the objectivity needed to make recommendations to the board as to pay for these critical jobs.

Benefits

Although salaries are undoubtedly higher in the for-profit world, benefits may be better in nonprofits (McLaughlin, 1990). Careful design and implementation of benefits programs are essential in attracting and retaining a qualified work force. In fact, as employees have become better consumers, and benefits as a compensation tool have grown, job candidates are more closely scrutinizing benefits packages before accepting employment.

The breadth and depth of the topic of benefits could easily fill several volumes, thus, the scope of discussion presented here will be necessarily limited. The field has become highly technical and specialized within the past several years, necessitating the HR professional who is inexperienced in this area to solicit help from outside the organization to ensure that the organization's benefits programs are competitive and appropriate for its employee base. Many consultants are available to assist the nonprofit in this quest, some of whom are also brokers selling the products and some of whom merely analyze organizational needs and make recommendations. Either kind can be of great assistance to the nonprofit HR professional.

The same concepts of internal equity and external competitiveness applied to salary compensation are relevant in designing benefits programs. Organizations desiring to compete successfully for job candidates must design their benefits programs using current and reliable market data on the benefits offered by competitors. Short benefits surveys are often included as adjuncts to some salary surveys, and surveys specific to benefits are also available. Because of the divergence and variety of different packages, conducting a benefits survey from scratch can be an extremely difficult, frustrating, and cumbersome task. So if data are available from a published source, they are nearly always preferable to a survey conducted in-house.

Just as salary programs need to be developed with internal equity in mind, benefits programs should consider factors internal to the organization also. In other words, the program should meet key employee needs as well as satisfy the employer in terms of financial and other policy obligations.

In meeting employee needs, the HR professional should carefully consider what types and levels of benefits the employees want. Demographics of employee groups will undoubtedly have an impact on benefits attractiveness. For example, middle-aged or older employees may be more concerned with retirement and retiree health insurance than younger employees, whose interests may revolve around beginning families. Their desires will probably include health insurance, especially that covering maternity expenses, family leave, and life insurance. Employee surveys, focus groups, or other means of collecting data on the wants and needs of workers are essential. The amount of money spent on benefits is staggering, and it continues to grow; the U.S. Chamber of Commerce found in 1989 that employers on average paid 37 percent of payroll for benefits costs for current employees, not counting retiree benefits (U.S. Chamber of Commerce, 1990).

One way that organizations can satisfy diverse employee groups is through flexible benefits, or "cafeteria plans." These plans, also called "125 plans" from the section in the IRS codes that refers to the regulation, allow employees to choose to have pretax earning deducted from their paychecks and set aside for particular benefits, such as child care or medical, vision, or dental costs. Not only does this option save the employee taxes, it offers flexibility by allowing employees to choose benefits that are particularly attractive to them.

The Need for a Formal Benefits Policy

Just as a salary policy is crucial to administration of the base compensation program, a benefits policy should be developed to reflect the objectives of the benefits program. Internal and external considerations should be included (McCaffery, 1983):

1. The organization's desire to provide employees with meaningful welfare and security benefits
2. The organization's intention to design benefits to fit employee needs
3. The frequency and philosophy by which the program will be audited and evaluated in relation to benefit costs, salary increases, and external factors
4. The organization's desire to use benefits as a means to motivate and achieve desired levels of productivity
5. How the organization plans to fund the benefits; most often organizations require employees to pay at least part of the costs of most benefits
6. The organization's intention to communicate thoroughly and explain changes in benefits programs to employees
7. The content of individualized annual statements regarding the value of benefits, company contributions, and employee costs
8. The market with which benefits will be compared
9. The requirement that trustees and carriers will submit detailed reports annually to management
10. The commitment that benefits plans will be assessed annually to ensure they meet the needs of changing demographics of the employee group

In addition, considerations such as coverage for full-time versus part-time employees, standard versus flexible coverage, the individual in charge of the benefits plan, and the types of benefits offered should be included (McCaffery, 1992).

Health Care

No one reading this book is ignorant of the crisis in health care that our country is currently confronting. The solutions to this complicated problem will probably be painful. The health care crisis involves two major issues: the dramatically rising cost of both health care and insurance and the large percentage of our population that is underinsured or not insured.

Nonprofit organizations must confront both of these issues, one directly, in our own rising health insurance costs, and the other indirectly, by making the difficult decision as to whether health benefits can be offered to part-timers as well as full-timers. Unfortunately, many nonprofits, like many for-profits, simply cannot afford to offer expensive health benefits to part-time employees. However, some are offering benefits to part-time employees prorated according to the number of hours worked.

In order to deal with health insurance cost issues, nearly all organizations, for-profit and nonprofit, are turning to managed care programs. This is a broad term for programs that require significant monitoring and managing of individual health care occurrences. This can include ensuring that individual care activities are prudently chosen as well as confirming that the costs associated with them are reasonable. Some cost-containment strategies related to the concept of managed care include the following (Cascio, 1992):

1. Raising deductibles and co-payments (the percentage of the health care services bill the employee must carry after the deductible). Theoretically, this not only saves the employer money, it encourages employees to be more responsible in their choice of services.
2. Motivating employees to choose reduced medical coverage by using flexible plans that allow them to "trade-off" the types of benefits they most desire.
3. Ensuring that there are no incentives in the health insurance plan that encourage employees to choose hospitalization over out-patient services.
4. Prior to elective surgery, requiring a second opinion that confirms the necessity of the procedure.
5. Setting rules for employees who enter hospitals, such as forbidding them to enter days before the procedure is scheduled and requiring preadmission certification in which the doctor must substantiate that the procedure is necessary.
6. Auditing large hospital bills to ensure services were billed accurately and reasonably.

Preferred Provider Organizations (PPOs) and health maintenance organizations (HMOs) are alternatives to traditional indemnity health insurance plans that assist in cost savings and are popular with small as well as large busi-nesses. HMOs require employees to choose physicians and other health care providers who belong to the network; PPOs reward employees to choose them. In this way, employers can achieve reduced rates for medical services by either paying en masse for services or receiving discounts on certain procedures.

Another option becoming available to small businesses is state orga-nizations that are set up to create a group for which affordable health insur-ance is obtainable. An example is Florida, which has recently set up the Florida Small Business Health Access Corporation, which serves about a thousand businesses (Lucas, 1991).

Retirement Plans

Retirement plans generally have as their objective to provide retirees with between 50 and 70 percent of their preretirement income. This reduced per-centage is considered sufficient because of several factors: work-related ex-penses are no longer accrued, employment deductions no longer occur, tax breaks give retirees a new advantage, and money does not have to be put away for retirement any longer. This level of retirement income is usually achieved through the coordination of benefits; Social Security payments are coordinated with income from retirement plans to reach the 50 to 70 per-cent level (American Compensation Association, 1989). However, some financial consultants now are recommending that future retirees plan for a larger income, up to 80 percent of preretirement pay.

Since Social Security by itself is unlikely to provide any kind of satis-factory retirement income level, most employees look to retirement programs at the workplace to achieve an adequate level. These are generally provided through two broad types of retirement plans: defined benefit and defined contribution. Defined benefit plans have been the norm until a few years ago. These plans define the income that the employee will receive upon re-tirement, usually based on a percentage of the average compensation over all or a number of employment years. They require extensive actuarial sup-port, making assumptions regarding future earning potential, number of years until retirement, and other pertinent factors. The contribution the em-ployer makes is determined through actuarial assessments. Because of the expense of these programs and the requirement of a fairly large employee base, they are relatively rare in all but the largest nonprofit organizations.

Defined contribution plans, on the other hand, define the amount that is put into some kind of investment vehicle. Therefore, the actual retire-ment income the employee will receive depends on the success of the invest-ment and is therefore unknown, but the amount contributed to the plan is defined. Often the investment is contributed by both the employer and em-ployee. These are commonly found in nonprofit organizations in the form of tax sheltered annuity programs (TSAs), or 403(b) plans.

Similar to for-profit 401(k) plans, TSAs allow employees to reduce taxable income by contributing a percentage of their salaries on a pretax basis to a qualifying individual or group annuities and mutual funds (Braden, 1991). In 1992, the amount is limited to 20 percent of income or up to $9,500. Plans can include an employer match along with the salary reduction or salary reduction alone.

Retirement plans for nonprofits, like for-profit plans, are subject to massive IRS and other legislative regulations (especially the Employees' Retirement Income Security Act, or ERISA, and IRS codes) that are well beyond the scope of this chapter. Nonprofit HR professionals designing retirement programs should ensure that these complicated regulations are appropriately complied with.

Given that generally defined contribution plans in the form of TSAs will be the preferred choice of most nonprofit employers, it is important that employees be aware of the financial risks of such plans. While defined benefit plans have the advantage of predetermining the retirement income level, defined contribution plans are determined only by the investment performance of the funds. Therefore, many organizations offering defined contribution plans provide retirement or financial planning seminars to their employees many years before their normal retirement date. This type of training, which is generally fairly inexpensive, can assist employees in feeling comfortable about their retirement prospects and can aid employers by increasing the commitment level of the employee to the organization.

Paid Time Off

Nonprofit organizations can often more easily offer paid time off than salary increases as rewards for performance. In today's business environment, employees view vacations, holidays, and sick leave as employment rights, and thus paid time off has become a standard part of the total compensation package, totaling over 13 percent of payroll (U.S. Chamber of Commerce, 1990). Determining the best mix of paid time off requires application of the same principles used to determine other compensation and benefits components: internal and external competitive considerations.

The demographics of the employee base will affect the particular kind of paid time off employees prefer. Younger workers may prefer sick leave, personal time off, or family leave provisions in order to raise children. As employees age, there also may be more demand for family leave programs that allow middle-aged employees to care for elderly parents. Questions regarding employee preferences in paid time off issues should be included in any surveys or focus groups the organization uses.

Competitive market pressures also must be taken into consideration. For example, one nonprofit organization gives its employees all working days between Christmas and New Year's as holidays because a major for-profit employer a few blocks away has done so. Although this may be an extreme example, it shows the necessity for nonprofits to be aware of the time-off policies of organizations with which they compete for labor. All organizations should carefully evaluate what their particular labor market competitors are offering before setting their own policies.

On average, most American employees receive 9.2 holidays per year. The six most common are New Year's Day, Memorial Day, Independence Day, Labor Day, Thanksgiving Day, and Christmas Day (U.S. Department of Labor, 1990). Additionally, more and more employers are recognizing Martin Luther King's birthday. Some organizations also offer floating holidays, or days that change depending on the calendar and the needs of the organization. For example, if Independence Day falls on a Thursday, the following Friday may be given as a floating holiday to create a four-day weekend.

American employees receive an average of 6.6 days of vacation after six months of employment, 11.1 days after one year, 12.2 days after three years, and 14.9 days after five years. Employees with twenty years of service receive an average of 21.4 days; employees with twenty-five years receive 22.4 days (U.S. Department of Labor, 1990).

Many organizations now offer what is frequently referred to as "personal time off," either in addition to or in lieu of sick leave. Although policies vary dramatically, personal time off offers a limited number of days that the employee may choose to take off for any personal reasons, from sickness to birthdays to "mental health days." However, when personal days are used up, additional time off for sickness must be taken without pay. The theory behind integrating personal time off with sick leave is that workers may then take time off to care for sick children, go to the doctor, or take care of other necessary personal business and not feel compelled to report sickness when they in fact are not ill. Such programs can be useful in improving or maintaining trust in and commitment to the organization, but to be as effective as possible, they need to be carefully designed using historical sick leave data and employee preference information. Some organizations incorporate all paid time off (except for holidays) in a personal time-off program.

Other paid time-off issues must be decided by the organization, including policies regarding jury duty, military leave, and death of a family member. Additionally, careful formulation of plans must be made to ensure that policies deal appropriately with overtime pay, shift differentials, incentive pay, status of paid time-off provisions during probationary periods, accrual of time off not used and other relevant issues.

Tuition Reimbursement

Many nonprofits provide tuition reimbursement for their employees who are pursuing degrees. Most require the student employee to receive satisfactory grades as well as to be working on a degree that is somehow related to his or her current employment. Just as all compensation components need to be integrally linked to the organization's mission and strategic plan, however, tuition reimbursement programs should be carefully geared to some kind of career development philosophy that helps accomplish the organization's human resource needs. In other words, nonprofits with limited resources need to understand what they are purchasing when they financially assist their student employees. It could be simply employee goodwill or a more strategic goal of training workers to fill needed technologies or professions identified in the human resource planning process. As with any expenditure, management should direct its tuition funds consciously.

Communication of Benefits to Employees

Although effective communication is essential in nearly all aspects of human resources, it may be that no other area is so critically dependent upon it as benefits. Although ERISA requires that employees receive an annual summary plan description, this is not sufficient to thoroughly communicate the program. Not only do they need to know what their benefits are in order to effectively utilize them, ensuring that employees understand them is the only way for organizations to truly maximize returns on their investment. After all, organizations, both for-profit and nonprofit, spend an enormous amount of money on benefits. To obtain the optimum level of motivation and commitment from employees requires communicating to them the value of what they are receiving. McCaffery (1992) recommends several essential steps in effective communication:

- Listen to employees: monitor the type of questions they ask; evaluate errors employees make in following procedures or filling out forms; listen to the employee "grapevine"; ensure upward communication channels are in place to monitor employee preferences.
- Create and expand awareness: use "events-centered" communication that is structured around events such as time of hire, promotion, illness, or other relevant events that will make the information more salient, usable, and retainable to employees; provide personalized reports that state clearly what each individual receives and the monetary value of his or her benefits package; incorporate regular reminders of the value of benefits in newsletters, paycheck inserts, posters, and other communication devices.
- Build understanding: ensure literature is readable by evaluating the writing of benefits materials and using graphics and illustrations where appropriate; communicate with employees in person regularly to ensure employees understand their benefits.
- Gain employee trust: train company representatives to communicate effectively; use nonsupervisory employees as benefits communicators so that knowledgeable and nonthreatening people are readily available to answer questions; systematically audit benefits literature to ensure it reflects current programs; install internal complaint procedures that go beyond

the requirements of ERISA; balance themes of benefits messages to counter any bad news with the proactive communication of positive plan features.

- Ensure that the benefits communication budget is adequate: a standard is to budget 2 to 3 percent of the total cost of benefits.

Justifying Compensation and Benefits Costs to Directors

In nonprofit organizations, as in many for-profit organizations, justifying significant increases in salary or benefits programs to boards of directors can be a formidable task. Often faced with severe financial constraints and sometimes with constituent pressures, many directors are loath to approve policies that may have long-lasting and sizeable financial impact. Therefore, the HR professional in charge of formulating and proposing the program should follow some basic guidelines.

First, most of us realize that others will be more likely to accept a program if they are allowed some kind of input into it. Thus, the HR professional should not begin developing any part of the total compensation program without the knowledge and blessing of the directors. He or she should carefully explain the need for the new program, the means by which it will be developed, and the method of installation. Graphs of turnover statistics, current salaries as compared to market data, and other preliminary information justifying the need for a new program should be presented concisely to the board.

Second, directors should be informed throughout the process. Developing and installing a salary program can take anywhere from six weeks to one year, depending on the size of the employee base, the number of jobs, and the culture of the organization. As the project progresses, the board should be given regular updates.

Third, directors should be involved in critical aspects of the project. It is essential, for example, that they approve the final market determination before salary data are gathered. Unless the directors feel comfortable with the specific data sources to which jobs are being compared, any market data, no matter how painstakingly collected, will be virtually useless. Also, if a job evaluation committee is used, make sure that at least some members of the board, preferably those with longer tenure and greater respect, will be included on the committee. Ensure that the board knows that it will approve all final job hierarchies and salary structures. Include directors, where possible, in focus groups that assess employee needs and desires.

When nonprofit operational needs can be so pressing, allocating money for salaries and benefits can be an imposing challenge. However, clear, concise, and thorough justification and explanation of the needs, development process, and final recommendations to directors will allow them to make reasonable and sensible decisions regarding this critical financial issue.

Also critical is to ensure that corporate and foundation funders, as well as other major donors, understand the necessity and process by which the compensation decisions are made. Although their communication and participation can be light, it is important that they believe the systems and processes by which these crucial decisions are made have been conducted knowledgeably, professionally, and conscientiously.

Summary

Organizations, both for-profit and nonprofit, are being challenged to compete effectively. In order to do this, they must have qualified employees who are motivated to accomplish the strategic goals of the organization. Attraction, motivation, and retention of high-caliber employees require that total compensation systems be carefully and thoughtfully designed. Pay strategies must fit the organization's culture and goals; thorough consideration must be given to identifying the behaviors the organization desires and designing reward strategies to ensure that they occur.

To do this, effective organizations must have up-to-date salary and benefits policies and communicate them to their employees. Second, organizations need to design and build effective base compensation programs, considering how external competitiveness and internal equity will be balanced. While job evaluation programs can be effective in communicating management's intentions to pay equitably, it is important that these time-consuming and expensive systems not be overutilized. Third, management must decide how it plans to encourage the key behaviors needed to accomplish strategic goals. This may be done through group or individual incentive programs, merit pay programs, or other plans. Each system has advantages and disadvantages that need to be weighed and evaluated in light of each organization's unique culture and characteristics.

Fourth, it is critical that nonprofit organizations conscientiously evaluate necessary benefits levels. Especially in the area of health care, it is imperative that organizations understand both competitive pressures and employee desires. Finally, organizations need to design administrative policies and procedures that ensure that their salary and benefits programs are consistently, equitably, and effectively delivered to employees.

References

American Compensation Association. *Elements of Sound Base Pay Administration.* Scottsdale, Ariz.: American Compensation Association, 1981.

American Compensation Association. *Pay Structures, Pay Rate Determination, and Program Administration.* Scottsdale, Ariz.: American Compensation Association, 1988.

American Compensation Association. *Fundamentals of Employee Benefits.* Scottsdale, Ariz.: American Compensation Association, 1989.

Braden, G. "Tax Deferred Annuities: The 401(k) Plan for Nonprofit Employers." *Mid-America Insurance,* 1991, *100*(2), 14–18.

Carraher, S. M. "A Validity Study of the Pay Satisfaction Questionnaire." *Educational and Psychological Measurement,* 1991, *51*(2), 491–495.

Cascio, W. F. *Managing Human Resources: Productivity, Quality of Work Life, Profits.* New York: McGraw-Hill, 1992.

Greene, R. J. "Issues in Salary Structure Design." *Compensation Review,* 1982, Second Quarter, pp. 28–33.

Heneman, H. G., and Schwab, D. P. "Pay Satisfaction: Its Multidimensional Nature and Measurement." *International Journal of Psychology,* 1985, *20*(2), 129–141.

Heneman, H. G., Schwab, D. P., Fossum, J. A., and Dyer, L. D. *Personnel/Human Resource Management.* (4th ed.) Homewood, Ill.: Irwin, 1989.

Hildebrandt, D. "Planning Rewards." *Association Management,* 1991, *43*(5), 97–99.

Kerr, S. "On the Folly of Rewarding A, While Hoping for B." *Academy of Management Journal,* 1975, *18*(4), 769–783.

Langer, S. "Who's Being Paid What — And Why." *Nonprofit World,* 1990, *8*(6), 20–22.

Lawler, E. E., III. "Gainsharing Theory and Research: Findings and Future Directions." In W. A. Pasmore and R. Woodman (eds.), *Research in Organizational Change and Development.* Vol. 2. Greenwich, Conn.: JAI Press, 1988.

Lawler, E. E., III. *Strategic Pay: Aligning Organizational Strategies and Pay Systems.* San Francisco, Calif.: Jossey-Bass Publishers, 1990.

Lucas, B. D. "Health Insurance for Small Business." *Business & Health,* 1991, *9*(5), 85–86.

McCaffery, R. M. *Managing the Employee Benefits Program.* Boston, Mass.: PWS-Kent, 1983.

McCaffery, R. M. *Employee Programs: A Total Compensation Perspective.* Boston, Mass.: PWS-Kent, 1992.

McLaughlin, T. A. "How to Stretch Your Fringe Dollar." *Nonprofit World,* 1990, *8*(2), 26–27.

Rocco, J. E. "Making Incentive Plans Work for Nonprofits." *Nonprofit World,* 1991, *9*(4), 13–15.

U.S. Chamber of Commerce. *Employee Benefits.* Washington, D.C.: U.S. Chamber of Commerce, 1990.

U.S. Department of Labor, Bureau of Labor Statistics. *Employee Benefits in Medium and Large Firms.* Washington, D.C.: U.S. Government Printing Office, 1990.

Wallace, M. J., and Fay, C. H. *Compensation Theory and Practice.* Boston, Mass.: PWS-Kent, 1988.

Wein, J. R. "Financial Incentives for Nonprofits." *Fund Raising Management,* 1989, *20*(7), 28–35.

25

Principles of Training for Volunteers and Employees

Nancy Macduff

What is training? The Oxford American Dictionary says that training is to "gain knowledge of or skill in a subject, etc., by study or experience or by being taught." But what is it in the real world of nonprofit organizations? It can be any contact an organization or agency has with a volunteer or paid staff. It can begin with a brief news story on a local television show, a visit to the facility, a brochure picked up at a library, a preassignment training session, orientation, in-service education, a regional or national conference. Adult skill and proficiency begins with the first contact and lasts through the exit interview. This chapter focuses on the more formal training activities organized for staff, paid and unpaid, who work for nonprofit organizations and agencies.

Training can be divided into categories. Laird (1985) offers two ranges of training: micro and macro. Microtraining exists for just one person or a small group of people; macrotraining exists for everyone within the organization, paid and unpaid.

Training has two functions for the nonprofit organization. First, it establishes a minimum level of competency, and second, it is a benefit of being a part of the organization.

Training publicly acknowledges a necessary level of proficiency. It sends a clear message to people that the organization or agency has standards that those in its employ, paid or unpaid, are expected to meet. Expectations of growth and change through guided learning tells the potential volunteer or staff what the organization values.

Training is a benefit of volunteering or working. A benefit of working for IBM or Xerox is the continual and extensive training opportunities available to employees. Volunteers also see a benefit in learning. Widmer, in a study of voluntary boards, found that 87 percent of board members surveyed listed learning as a benefit of membership in the group (Widmer, 1989, p. 14). Nonprofit organizations should publicize how their training can help people on the job or in their personal relationships.

Principles to Guide Adult Learning

"Training designers need some learning theory upon which to base the activities they specify in the learning systems they create," writes Laird (1985, p. 113). There are some central principles that guide informal learning activities. Trainers who follow and apply the central principles have a greater chance of reaching their objectives and helping individuals grow and learn. Various adult education theorists have outlined these principles. The organizing principles mentioned are those for which the most research exists.

Robinson (1979, p. 1) asserts that "the central organizing principles for adult education must be around problems adults face, not subject matter." Children and adults in educational institutions go to school and study subjects. Adults in informal training sessions are interested in solving problems or addressing issues important to their lives. In the case of staff in a nonprofit, paid or unpaid, they want to know how to do the job. A youth organization began its orientation training for new leaders of youth clubs with an hour-long overview of the national, regional, and local structure of the organization. Participant evaluations of the session said things like, "I came here to find out what to do with eight 12-year-old boys next Thursday. You didn't help at all." Most adults have very immediate needs — and the hows usually take precedence over the whys. It is essential to determine those needs and set about organizing learning to meet them. (Needs assessment is discussed further on.)

Adult learners need a sense of ownership over both content and activities in training. They must see and feel a close connection between the topics under discussion and their own role within the organization. By engaging the learner, the trainer achieves two ends: they help the volunteer and/or staff own the final conclusions, or at least know where the rules come from, and they hear the learners' perceptions about the policies and how they affect their jobs. "All modern learning theories stress that adults must have a degree of ownership of the learning process . . . that they want to invest their previous experience in those processes" (Laird, 1985, p. 131).

Robinson (1979) assures us that adult learners are enthusiastic participants. This organizing principle is often interpreted to mean that all adult learning must take place in small groups, but this is not so. A more useful descriptive word is *interactive.* To obtain ownership and address their immediate needs many adults want to participate through such activities as discussion; observation of clients, members, or patrons; role playing; demonstration; writing; and taking tests or using assessment tools. Robinson's point is that sitting and listening to someone else talk is not effective in adult education. Adults only retain about 20 percent of what they hear when there is no other participatory activity (Dale, 1969, p. 129). Laird says that adult learners want to share their previous experience so they can apply it. The adult learner is full of resources, ideas, experiences, and knowledge. The trainer's job is to bring the full force of that experience to bear on the job or task at hand. The trainer is not a "teller" of facts, but an organizer of learning and colearner with the trainees.

In reflecting on these organizing principles one might see the person being trained as supremely confident and organized in the learning environment. The opposite is true. "Adults typically confront educational opportunity and participate in learning with mixed feelings and even fear" (Smith, 1982, p. 44). As you enter a room of learners, imagine them sitting in their chairs with their personal baggage on the floor around them. The baggage contains such things as their previous educational experiences, their perceived success at learning, their knowledge of the topic or organization, their current life situation, and their adult life stage. Mixed feelings and fear can be reduced by a trainer who understands that the majority of volunteers and staff are fearful about the impending experience. The sooner the trainer moves ownership of activities into the hands of the learner and addresses their needs, the more the anxiety level is reduced.

Another principle of learning is that of *praxis*. Praxis provides an "opportunity for interplay between action and reflection for the student" (Brookfield, 1986, p. 50). Brookfield diagrams it as a circular process (see Figure 25.1).

Figure 25.1. Praxis.

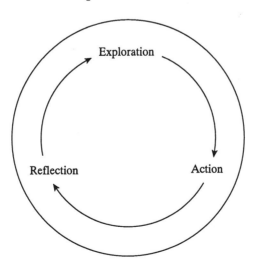

Source: Courtesy of Stephen Brookfield. Used by permission.

Praxis is always present in an adult learning situation. The trainer's responsibility is to help adults bring their previous experience together with new information. It is the struggle between knowing general principles; exploring new concepts, behaviors, or skills; and applying all of these to a situation. For example, most adults think they understand the principles of confidentiality. A volunteer working in a hospice-sponsored AIDS residential center called a radio talk show that was focusing on the AIDS epidemic. He didn't mention names, but provided enough personal information about one client that anyone casually affiliated with the organization could easily identify the person. The director of volunteers contacted the volunteer and found that his understanding of confidentiality did not go far enough. He thought that by omitting the name he was following organizational policies (Murrant and Strathdee, 1992).

Smith (1982) summarizes six conditions that must exist for adult learning to take place. First, *the adult must feel a need to learn* and have some input into the identification of that need. This provides the impetus for the instructional process. Adults resent others orchestrating their lives. They know they have knowledge and experience and want to effect the direction of the instructional activities.

Second, the content of the *training must have a perceived relationship to past experience,* so that what is already known is used as a "resource" for new learning. Adult learners bring a wealth of experience to the training session. By validating that experience, the trainer validates the person and gives encouragement to use their knowledge to reach greater levels of knowledge and skill. For example, imagine teaching a group of volunteers how to use a computerized cash register. Some may have high levels of anxiety and no knowledge. An effective way to begin is to ask if anyone in the group has a pocket calculator or microwave oven. Many people will say yes. These common appliances are computers, and it is easy to begin the transfer of what the adult *already* knows to the skill to be learned.

Third, *learning is related to the individual adult's developmental stage.* Just as children have stages or cycles they go through, so do adults. In 1977, McCoy outlined developmental stages in the adult life: from ages eighteen to twenty-two is "Leaving Home"; twenty-three to twenty-eight is "Becoming Adult"; twenty-nine to thirty-four is "Catch Thirty"; thirty-five to forty-three is "Midlife Reexamination"; forty-four to fifty-five is "Restabilization"; fifty-six to sixty-four is "Preparation for Retirement"; sixty-five and older is "Retirement." McCoy's work has helped identify the need for trainers of adults to consider developmental stage when planning training. Helping a volunteer or staff member see how learning certain skills can help them in their paid employment works for someone at age thirty-five, but has little impact on someone who is seventy. A person who is organizing learning activities must take into account the differences in adult developmental stages. As adults evolve, their sense of self and approach to decision making change. This development occurs with the interrelationship of cognitive style and intellectual tasks (such as perceiving, thinking, and problem solving) with ego development (feelings about self, impulses, aspirations, and relationships with other people) (Knox, 1986).

Knox is emphatic about the trainer's responsibility to accommodate developmental stages. He points out, for example, that "performance in learning tasks such as rote memory, discovering figurative and mathematical relations, and inductive reasoning steadily declines from young adulthood into old age. Consequently, as adults grow older, they tend to substitute wisdom for brilliance when dealing with intellectual tasks" (p. 22).

Smith's fourth condition for learning to take place is that *autonomy in training needs to relate to the autonomy the learner will experience on the job.* If volunteers or paid staff are expected to wait on customers and handle monetary transactions with few or no supervisors to oversee the process, then training should move them to autonomous performance relatively quickly. Conversely if a person's work is going to be closely supervised, the most appropriate training methods might be to work with the person and supervisory personnel together and begin the process of building working teams. If the actual supervisory staff are not available, then surrogates who can replicate the work situation are required.

Fifth, *attention to the learning climate can reduce anxiety and encourage risk taking.* The "climate" includes the physical amenities, the formality or informality of the trainer, and the environment in which the learning takes place. It is the feeling, atmosphere, and attitude present in the learning situation.

Sixth, *diversity of individuals and learning styles needs to be addressed directly by the training activities.* Adult needs are often dictated by life circumstance. Volunteers have very practical needs. They want to be comfortable carrying out the assigned task. This common characteristic crosses ethnic, racial, economic, and educational barriers. It presents a common goal for the trainer. The commonality, however, stops at that point. Learning styles vary from person to person.

"The characteristic and preferred way in which an adult engages in learning activities is termed 'learning style'" (Knox, 1986, p. 20). Learning style inventories developed for adults include the Myers-Briggs Type Inventory, Neurolinguistic Communication Profile, Gregorc Style Delineator, and the Group Embedded Figures Test. These instruments measure such things as cognitive style and the processes adults use to interpret new experiences and the habitual ways in which we conduct learning activities, like goal setting or generating evaluative information (Brookfield, 1990). It is not clear how learning style is related to developmental stages. What is known is that adult learning styles change over time. "Learning ability and style change gradually throughout life. The result is a stable plateau of general learning ability through most of adulthood, but with shifts in what seems important to learn and in how easy it is to master various types of learning tasks" (Knox, 1986, p. 21).

Previous experiences, bad and good, influence the learner. Physical

matters such as eyesight, hearing, and disabilities do, too. Lack of attention
to the specific concerns of an adult audience is risky business. Knox sums
up the application of necessary conditions for the trainer of adults: "Effective teaching depends on being responsive to the learners in the program,
not to adults in general" (1986, p. 38).

Creating a hospitable environment for learning is not the only responsibility of the trainer. An understanding of the motivation of adults to learn
is also important. Just as their physical and cognitive development changes,
adults experience stages in what motivates them to learn. In a model to measure multiple components of motivation, Cross (1981) identifies five steps:
(1) engaging in training; (2) retaining skill or knowledge; (3) applying the
skill or knowledge; (4) gaining material reward; (5) gaining symbolic reward. When adults are paid for training, as when staff attend training during working hours, the motivation to learn is enhanced. Trainers recognize,
however, that pay alone is not sufficient as a motivator.

Monetary rewards are not always possible for volunteers, but other
tangible rewards are. Some trainers of volunteers use donated food coupons,
or restaurant gift certificates as rewards for attending training. In other cases,
promotion is contingent on attendance at certain types of training sessions,
and the promotion is a motivating reward.

Symbolic rewards such as diplomas and certificates can also be effective in recognizing that a person has in fact completed training. The volunteer coordinator at a large performing arts center decided to offer advanced
training for people working at the center's gift shops. Upon completion of
training, volunteers received a symbolic reward—a gold star to attach to
the name plates they are required to wear when working. The coordinator
launched a publicity campaign with the theme "Ask a Gold Star Volunteer."
This had the effect of a material reward: volunteers were stopped by staff
and patrons who needed help solving problems. It also had the effect of allowing the volunteers to apply what they had learned in a real situation.
The trainer designed a program in which all of the motivational steps were
addressed. She followed Laird's admonition: "The ultimate behavior of adult
learners is to apply knowledge over a long range of time, not just to acquire
and retain it for a few days!" (1985, p. 115).

The central principles constitute the foundation of all training for adults.
They guide the tasks of conducting needs assessments, writing training plans,
and evaluating the training. Imagine the central principles as the foundation
of a house; without it, a good wind storm and the house might blow over.

Conducting a Needs Assessment

The first step in planning training is to understand the needs of the potential participants. The adult learning principles tell us that learning is more
apt to take place if the learner sees the information as relating directly to

his or her life. By understanding the discrepancies between what the attendees currently know and what they need to know in order to perform a new job or task, the trainer can make the instruction responsive to learner needs (Knox, 1986). The needs assessment is a process of uncovering information that guides the trainer's planning efforts.

Robinson (1979) identifies three elements that make up a needs assessment. The first is *relevancy*. The content to be discussed and the activities to be undertaken must make sense to the learners attending the training session. For example, a training session for dog walkers at an animal shelter should include contact with the animals. Lectures and pictures are fine, but the learners will be worried about their ability to handle unknown animals of indeterminate size and disposition. The relevant information for the attendees is very practical. It is ideal to ask experienced dog walkers what they needed to know first. It is also useful to check with those who have never done this job about the information they feel they need.

Relationship is the second area to be considered in doing a needs assessment. By "relationship" Robinson means that the trainer must learn something about the learners' previous experience with this topic. An experienced trainer was presenting a workshop on leadership skills at a large national conference for volunteer leaders. She was using the Myers-Briggs Type Inventory, a standard psychological personality test, that is used to understand the differences in how people take in information and process it. During the introductions she asked each participant what they hoped to learn from the workshop. One member of the group said she was an experienced administrator of the Myers-Briggs Type Inventory and was there to get new ideas about using that tool. Throughout the workshop the trainer called upon this individual to share in explaining certain concepts and had her lead one of the exercises. The needs assessment at the beginning of class helped the trainer know the experience level of her learners and strive to relate the concepts and theories to real life.

It is important to remember that starting where the learner is and moving forward will enhance learning. It is hooking relevancy to relationship. That can only happen if the trainer determines learners' needs in advance.

Most learning from early childhood through the teen years place responsibility for organizing and conveying information on the teacher. Children are largely passive participants. Adult learners are aided by the trainer or teacher who helps them take control of their own learning and understand how they learn. The needs assessment process is a means to move control of content and teaching activities into a joint responsibility between the trainer and the learner. Robinson refers to *responsibility* as the third element in needs assessment.

By encouraging learners to take responsibility by participating in the identification of needs, the trainer conveys an interest in moving the responsibility for the actual learning during the training session into the hands of the learners. This is, of course, in addition to giving learners a say in the training course's content and activities.

There are other important processes involved in carrying out a training event. In addition to assessing learners' needs, the trainer will have to prepare a training plan, arrange for the physical facilities and equipment, and present the event. All of this takes time, and time is the first issue in the planning process. How much time is being asked of the volunteer or staff member? The value of a training session can be calculated by taking the hourly wage of staff and multiplying by the length of the session. The same can be done for volunteers, using wages paid to staff for a comparable job. This tells the cost in time, translated to money. There may be other costs as well, for both the trainer and the trainee; these might include such things as parking or transportation fees, child care, lost work time, clothing costs, supplies, and so on. Even volunteering is never free—not for the staff or the volunteers. A needs assessment must determine the actual costs of being trained.

Needs assessments should also consider such things as the energy demanded of the learners and their physical comfort. Training sessions planned for evening hours are best, with a slower pace, but they must be interactive and end at a definite time. Why? The needs assessment might tell you that the evening hours are the most convenient for people with busy daytime schedules, but evening is also the time of the day when most adults' mental energy is sapped. By keeping this in mind, the trainer can organize learning activities that will be active and fun, thus keeping energy levels high just when they might be sinking.

An important consideration for the trainer is physical surroundings. Wheelchair or handicapped access is important. Microphones for head-sets and/or translators are in order for those who might be hearing impaired. Even the comfort of the chairs can affect the number of breaks the group takes during the training session. The trainer must consider these things in advance of the actual event.

Another key consideration in needs assessment is the type of learning activity planned. How much room is needed? Will people be writing during the session? What special equipment will be needed? (A flashy multimedia presentation at a primitive camp site might flop for want of electricity.) The level of audience expectation about training is also an important factor. Is the audience one that expects some amount of formal presentation or one that expects only interactive groups? Those pieces of information gathered through the needs assessment lead directly to an effective training event.

Sometimes it is possible to contact each person who will be attending a training session to learn of their needs ahead of time, but more likely the trainer must employ a variety of needs assessment methods at the first meeting to gather information to guide the next training session. Any of the following can serve this purpose:

Needs Assessment Techniques

Evaluation reports of previous training sessions should be read and the data compiled for future reference. Today's participants in a training session are excellent representatives of those who will attend the next one.

Observation of actual volunteer and staff jobs is another excellent way of determining needs.

Incumbents in the role being trained for are a good source of information about training needs. They can identify the gaps between what they have learned in training to what they needed to know to do on the job.

Past participants (employees or volunteers) are also a useful source of information. They are not so closely connected to the program. Time and distance may have given them perspective on their learning experience.

Performance evaluations are done by many nonprofit organizations for both staff and volunteers. These reports may well be useful in the planning of training sessions.

Experts are a good source of ideas. They generally have the most recent information on a topic and can help the trainer bring learners up to date on the latest developments.

Standard measures or pretests are a good way to determine learners' knowledge of a topic. These can include tests on the use of machines such as copiers, cash registers, and computers, as well as conceptual knowledge.

A very effective way to explore needs is to assemble a surrogate committee to represent those who will be in the training session. The committee should include people with experience in the organization and people who know nothing about either the organization or the job in question. This meeting can be a short, one-time event to get at the issues of relevancy, relationship, and responsibility.

Sometimes if a problem develops with volunteers or staff that is not a performance issue, the person responsible for training may be asked to conduct a session to address the matter. Laird contends that performance problems can occur that are not related to training needs. The way to distinguish between the two is to ask whether training is needed to solve the problem. For example, if volunteers report late to a work unit on a regular basis, the problem is not a training problem. It is an issue to be addressed by the supervisor.

Those who organize training must learn to educate others about what is a training need and what is a performance problem. If paid staff are fearful of addressing performance issues with volunteers, for instance, skill training in effective supervision can help them overcome the fear. At the same time they must be encouraged to solve performance problems immediately. Ignoring such problems is frustrating to staff and to other volunteers, and can even affect clients, members, or patrons.

Staff and Volunteer Training

The principles delineated in this chapter apply equally to volunteers and paid staff. The principles of adult learning do not change when a person is paid to attend a training session. However, a common question with regard to the training of paid staff and volunteers is should they be trained together? What are the advantages and disadvantages? The decision should be made consciously, rather than haphazardly. Thoughtlessly putting volunteers and paid staff together in the same session has the potential for missing the mark on instruction and offending both groups. If staff and volunteers are trained together, teaching and training activities need to be adjusted to accommodate the presence of both groups. By choosing to train volunteer and staff together, you can send a message about teamwork, planning, cooperative relationships, and the values of the organization or agency. Some training lends itself to being done jointly, such as orientation. Many municipal governments train all new hires at the same time. This puts attorneys, secretaries, garbage collectors, and social workers together in the same session.

One of the issues to address when training volunteers and paid staff together is timing. Quite often training must be scheduled for evenings, early mornings, weekends, or lunchtime. Such time slots are designed to accommodate the volunteers—more than 50 percent of whom are employed outside the home. These are often not convenient times for the paid staff. They might also be costly to the organization, if overtime must be paid. So, time of training is a factor in who will attend.

Content is another issue that determines who might attend. If the topic is medical benefits, insurance, and retirement options, it is likely the training session would be held for paid staff. If the content deals with job roles, a joint training session is ideal. Murrant and Strathdee (1992) report on a nurse working full time in a hospital setting who agreed to volunteer at an AIDS residential treatment center. As a volunteer, her role was defined by the nurse or medical professional on duty; she was not a decision maker. In her paid job as a nurse, she was in a leadership position. After a while she became uncomfortable with this role reversal. Her role at the residential center could have been effectively clarified in a joint volunteer and paid staff training session.

If the decision is made to train staff and volunteers separately, the quality and content of the sessions need to be consistent. Trainers for both groups need to work together to ensure that consistency. An excellent way to provide new job challenges to experienced volunteers is to have them lead training sessions. This also provides the person coordinating volunteers some relief from the time needed to plan, organize, and implement training. But volunteers, like anyone providing training, need to be involved in discussions about quality and content.

Many nonprofit organizations provide little or no training for people who supervise volunteers. Supervisory training is usually available, only to those who oversee paid workers. This policy sends a message to staff that supervising volunteers "doesn't really count." Anyone who works with volunteers has management and supervisory responsibilities. They should receive training, accordingly. This is an ideal situation for training volunteers and paid staff together. Often volunteers are in the position of supervising other volunteers, and many paid staff supervise only volunteers. This training must include such topics as the motivation of volunteers, roles and responsibility of the supervisor in relationship to an unpaid work force, formal and informal recognition strategies, and techniques of evaluating volunteer performance.

Formal and Informal Training

"Volunteer managers train on a daily basis. Whenever a volunteer is asked to do something new, or change past behavior, teaching and learning are at work. The volunteer is the learner and the volunteer program manager is the teacher" (Macduff, 1988, p. 38). Most people think of training as what happens in a classroom setting or in an on-the-job "here's how you do it" session. In fact, a nonprofit organization is conveying messages to potential staff and volunteers long before they are hired to work. The first informal contacts come during recruitment and screening. "A key feature of the recruitment process is the imparting of information about a volunteer-based program to rouse people's interest and ultimately persuade them to volunteer" (Ilsley and Niemi, 1981, p. 45).

The first contact with your organization may be through a printed brochure, a radio announcement, or a want-ad listing. The principles of adult learning apply to those early contacts the same as they do to the planning of learning activities. Robinson's tests of relevancy, relationship, and responsibility are good tools to use when evaluating whether the message you think you are sending is the one being received.

Volunteers and paid staff are the biggest recruiters of other volunteers and paid staff. Do you train those people in the appropriate things to say to prospective applicants? Have you developed a brochure for staff and volunteers to use when they are talking to their friends about the positions available in your organization? By doing these things you can exert more control over the first formal training effort your organization offers to the people it recruits.

Minimal information needed by staff and volunteers are the mission statement; information about clients, members, or patrons served; hours; the application process for volunteer or staff jobs; telephone and fax numbers, and address. If the information is written so as to appeal to adults there is a greater chance that the "training" you want to have happen will take place.

Screening of prospective volunteers and paid staff usually includes the completion of an application, an interview, and the signing of some type of work agreement. The interview and work agreement allow the manager to establish the part formal training has in the organization. Training and job expectations are communicated and clarified.

This step is especially important to volunteers. If the organizational message is "You don't need to worry about attending training sessions," then training will have a low priority for the volunteer. Applications should ask questions about availability for training, interviews should include reviews of the different types of training—on-the-job, orientation, and in-service; and the contract should be clear as to expectations related to training. People cannot be expected to attend educational sessions without some "training" on why doing so is important to them and to the organization.

Formal training is a learning event, with objectives, a training plan, and methods of evaluation. A trainer may be part of the presentation, but not necessarily. Volunteers and staff can learn from interactive videos, workbooks, audiocassettes, or other media. These are, however, planned and prepared in exactly the same fashion as a face-to-face training session. "Portable" training sessions that use audiovisual technology is an important growth area for nonprofit organizations. It is especially crucial for organizations whose staff and volunteers are spread over large geographical distances or whose volunteer pool is large.

Some nonprofit organizations use formal training as part of the screening process. A large performing arts center has learned that by requiring preassignment training participation, they weed out people who are not truly interested in the commitment required to be a volunteer. They offer weekday and weekend all-day training sessions for individuals who have completed an application and express an interest in becoming a volunteer. They lose between 25 and 35 percent of the applicants before actual assignments are made. This preassignment formal training session saves both time and money for the staff and for the volunteers.

Most nonprofit organizations provide an orientation for staff and volunteers after they have been hired but before they begin actual work assignments. This is an opportunity to have volunteers and staff in one training session. The material covered in an orientation is usually similar for staff and volunteers. It includes such things as tours of the facility, introductions to key personnel (including supervisory staff), an organizational overview, policies on confidentiality, appropriate attire, parking, security of personal belongings, the relationship between volunteers and paid staff, and methods of recording work hours. The issue of benefits is different for volunteers and paid staff, but most programs offer some "perks" for volunteers.

Part of the orientation is job related. Volunteers and paid staff are anxious to learn about their specific job assignment. This training can be done during the orientation or at a second session. The challenge in the orientation is to provide enough information to give people the confidence to go to their work assignment ready to work, and to help them feel willing to ask questions and listen to the experts who are their supervisors and colleagues.

Formal training does not stop with orientation, nor informal training with an on-the-job explanation of duties by the supervisor. Continuing in-service education is a part of successful nonprofit organizations. Nothing in any organization or agency is static. Societal trends, client needs, membership services, and staffing patterns require constant change and updating. The foundation for active participation in in-service training begins with the first contact with staff, paid and unpaid, and continues as long as the person is affiliated with the organization. In-service education programs are designed to enhance current job skills, build new skills, and train the person for expanded duties. In-service training might also include opportunities for personal development, such as stress management, time management, conflict management, and reduction of burnout.

Another area often missed by nonprofits is training on organizational change. Volunteers are sometimes the last to hear about important structural changes. This sends a powerful message about the importance of volunteers to the mission of the organization or agency. It is much better to arrange for in-service education programs to keep volunteers and staff fully informed about such changes as down sizing, staffing re-structures, or major changes in client, member, or patron services.

Some nonprofit organizations provide clinical type in-service programs for volunteers and paid staff. Hospice is a notable example. Hospice volunteers are expected to attend a monthly meeting where specific problems are discussed and policy and procedural changes are reviewed. The primary focus is to bring staff and volunteers with the most direct client contact together. The sessions usually have an organized formal training component, but the bulk of the time is devoted to talking about the personal impact of the clients on the volunteer or staff member. In doing this, hospice has reduced its loss of volunteers due to burnout. This type of in-service training is especially useful when the emotional toll on the volunteer or staff is high.

Organizing Training Activities for Effectiveness

Planning training activities begins with concern for the teaching-learning climate. Carl Rogers says, "Trainers should be as concerned with their relationship with students as they are about the content of the course" (Laird, 1985). This is not to suggest that teaching or training is in any way a popularity contest. It means that the teacher cares enough about the relationship with the learners to make certain that each person achieves all of the desired learning objectives. In some cases, this requires nudging people away from their comfort zones into uncharted territory.

Climate Setting

Once the needs assessment is complete the trainer must focus on organizing a training plan. The training plan begins with attention to the climate. Climate is made up of five things: responsiveness, respect, reasons, options, and proficiencies (Knox, 1986).

Responsive teachers are those who consider the needs of diverse learners when organizing their training plan. The needs assessment helps them organize the content so that visual, auditory, or kinesthetic learners can absorb it. Responsive teachers factor in physical differences, disabilities, age, previous experience, culture, ethnicity, and developmental life stage into their plan.

Respect means the trainer view his or her role as that of co-learner. Such trainers know that learners have as much or more to offer the learning situation as they do. They support, encourage, and honor learners, but never ignore or ridicule them.

A guiding principle in all adult learning is the importance of making the content relevant to the learners' lives. Adults have a variety of reasons for attending training sessions. The trainer's job is to organize the training plan so learners' needs are met and participants know early on how and when the topics they are concerned about will be covered. It is almost as if the trainer plans around the question, "And when will you get to the issue I came to talk about?"

Lectures, small groups, or demonstrations are different types of teaching techniques. Some learners prefer one over the other. An effective trainer provides options for learners, so that they are different activities during the session (Knox, 1986).

Proficiencies refers not only to ensuring each learner's competence in the skills or concepts being taught, but relates as well to the proficiency of the trainer in terms of both content and process. Learner and teacher must know the skills needed to function on the job. There must be time to practice those skills and evaluate each person's abilities.

Trainers must be well versed in the content they present. Staying current is a must. It is also essential that trainers learn as much as possible about adult education and continually enhance and improve their skills in creating a learning environment.

Writing the Lesson Plan

Bringing the needs assessment, principles of adult education, and content together in a cohesive whole is the training design, and its written format is the training plan. Laird and other authors on adult education call the training plan a "lesson plan."

The lesson plan consists of six elements: the purpose, the learning objective, the time allotted for specific activities, a detailed explanation of the activities designed to accomplish the learning objective, the techniques used to evaluate learner performance (summative and formative), and the resources needed to carry out the training activities. Exhibit 25.1 is an example of a form that can be used to record the lesson plan.

Exhibit 25.1. Training or Lesson Plan.

Purpose of this session:

Learning Objective	Time	Teaching Activity	Evaluation	Resources

The *purpose* is an overview of those things that are to be accomplished by the training session. For example, "The purpose of the orientation training is to acquaint volunteers and paid staff with an overview of this organization and their places in it." The statement of purpose is usually global in scope and does not need to be measurable.

Learning Objectives

Robert Mager (1984) says that instruction is of little use if it doesn't change anyone; it has no effect and no power. The only way to ensure that change has occurred is to begin by identifying behaviors or knowledge that the learner must possess before leaving the training session. The written objective describes that behavior. "An *objective* is a description of a performance you want learners to be able to exhibit before you consider them competent. An objective describes an intended *result* of instruction, rather than the process of instruction itself" (Mager, 1984, p. 3). For example, if the CEO and board president were creating a lesson plan for board orientation, one learning objective might be "The learner will be able to identify the six areas of responsibility of members of the board of directors: legal, financial, personnel, public relations, asset management, and risk management." This learning objective says that the two trainers will have tested the knowledge of the learners before they leave the training session to determine their understanding of the six areas of responsibility. (Mager's book *Preparing Instructional Objectives* is an excellent self-study guide to writing objectives.)

Few people who train volunteers and staff have education courses in their background and thus rarely write learning objectives to guide their training plan. This can lead to a lack of focus and inability to determine the effect of the training session. It can also lead to an incredible waste of time. Writing the learning objectives is the equivalent of zeroing in on precisely the content to be covered, the most effective means of conveying the material, and the best way of evaluating the learners' grasp of the material. It is the single most important step in designing a lesson plan.

Learning objectives are always written from the point of view of the learner; they never describe what the trainer will do. There are no rules for how many learning objectives are needed for a given length of time, but it is reasonable to assume that a four-hour training session would have no more than four learning objectives.

Training Activities

"Training is the subsystem that acquaints people with material and technology. It helps them learn how to use the material in an approved fashion that allows the organization to reach its desired output" (Laird, 1985, p. 6). The basic function of training is to help the volunteer or staff person get control of his or her job. This control comes through activities that are designed to achieve the learning objectives. They define and demonstrate the right way to do the job by means of standards, models, and examples of the job done properly. They should acquaint the learners with the written and unwritten "laws" that govern the jobs they will be doing. Volunteers delivering midday meals to shut-ins, for example, need to know whether they should stop and visit for twenty minutes at each location or move quickly to deliver hot food.

Training activities must also help learners identify the differences in their current level of knowledge and the skills they need to acquire. Training boards and advisory groups is challenging. The learners in these sessions are often community leaders, who feel they have a good understanding of the roles and responsibilities of boards and advisory committees. How can a training plan be organized to help them identify the gap between what they know and what they need to learn?

One trainer divides the members of a board into three small groups. She makes one of the subgroups a nonprofit board, another is a board for a for-profit hospital, and the third is an advisory group to a government agency in the community. Each board is given two problems. In the first problem an individual has fallen in a facility owned or leased by the organization. The person is in the hospital and may die. In the second problem, the organization's money is drying up and significant program cutbacks and paid staff layoffs may be required if something isn't done soon. Each group is told to imagine that they are in emergency session. They are to identify what they need to discuss and their roles and responsibilities as a group. Each "board" discusses its problems separately, and then the trainer stops them to ask some of the following questions: Who had legal responsibilities? Who had personal responsibilities? What and why? Who is responsible for raising actual dollars?

This exercise has several consequences. Board or advisory members who are being trained suddenly realize that they do not share the same roles and responsibilities, that each person has brought different "baggage" to the training session. Individuals' previous experiences are validated by giving everyone the opportunity to discuss their solutions to the problems, but these views are tempered by peers who add their current knowledge. The trainer serves as "devil's advocate" and resource person. The exercise ends with the distribution and discussion of information on appropriate roles and responsibilities for the nonprofit organization in question and an organizational chart.

In this example the teaching activity has helped the learners identify the gaps in their knowledge and begin to see what they can do to close the gap between what they thought they knew and what they need to know in order to function effectively as a board member. This type of activity helps create a receptiveness toward the remaining material.

Adults learn "in layers," and the lesson plan must accommodate that fact. Once adults see the gap in their skill or knowledge, they must be given the material and time to close the gap. Trainers quite often resort to the lecture format because they can cover a great deal of material with it. And that is true: they are covering the material! The learner is not working with the material or processing the information. If there is one irrefutable rule in teaching adults, it is to get them involved as quickly as possible.

Trainers must be reasonable in what they expect adults to retain. They must establish realistic learning objectives given the time, resources, skills, and previous experiences of the learners. Effectively pacing a training plan depends on having clear data from a needs assessment and a realistic approach to what can be accomplished in, say, a two-hour training session.

"One crucial aspect of the teaching/learning transaction is the way you sequence learning activities for progression," writes Knox (1986, p. 9). In the example of board members who were being trained to understand their organizational role, suppose the session began with a lecture by a risk-management expert. It is unlikely that the board members would grasp the connection between their roles and risk-management issues. The most effective way to arrange the sequence of activities is to plan them with the learning objectives. Write them out on small cards and arrange them in a logical progression, from basic information to more complex concepts.

Nonprofit organizations have three basic modes in which they train: individual, small group (less than fifty), and large groups (more than fifty). Different training activities are needed depending on the size of the group. For individual learners, effective techniques and devices include such things as coaching, computer assisted instruction (CAI), correspondence, reading, television, and tutoring. For large groups, some of the most effective techniques and devices include lectures, panels, debates, subgroup discussion, and forums. Small groups are especially responsive to discussions, seminars, case study analysis, simulation, role play, and demonstration (Knox, 1986). There are certainly a wealth of other techniques and devices available. They include, but are not limited to, skits, field trips, programmed instruction, brainstorming, nominal groups, "buzz groups," games, clinics, overhead projections, flip charts, white boards, videotaped programs, audio cassettes, slide shows, puzzles, handouts, and photographs.

Adults generally prefer learning that is interactive. Interactive learning is not necessarily limited to groups, although there seems to be a rush to put all volunteer and staff training into the format of small discussion groups. "Interactive" means the learner interacts with the information or skill to be learned. Knowledge about the history and organizational structure of a nonprofit could be interactively taught to adults through the use of a crossword puzzle and a video. For example, learners would receive a crossword puzzle at the beginning of a training session. The puzzle would be based on a history of the organization and its current structure. In working through the puzzle, the learners laugh, struggle, and are encouraged to share answers with their neighbors. *Fun* is the operative word. Then a video describing the history of the organization and its structure is shown to the group. Afterward, the learners are allowed more time to complete their puzzles. Closure comes with a discussion of the correct answers to the key points (the learning objectives) and any unanswered questions. This is an example of interactive learning, but not necessarily in a small group.

Less experienced trainers need to be wary of using small groups. The interpersonal dynamics unleashed in small groups are fraught with peril, and even the most experienced teachers can have a bad day with them. Small group work is an effective means to learning for the vast majority of adults, but the trainer must be comfortable with all aspects of this teaching technique. "The fundamental criterion in selecting a learning method should be the appropriateness of the method to the learning objective," Laird writes (1985, p. 130). The learning objective should tell the trainer whether a small group is an appropriate technique to use. The trainer must then figure out how to physically move the learners into groups and how to provide instructions as to the assigned task. Then the trainer must consider what to do while the groups are working. Stand still and observe? Walk around and consult? And perhaps the most important issue for the trainer is how to bring the participants out of the small groups and launch into providing validation, new information, closure, and review. "The undoubted value of small group work is lost almost entirely if you rush into this too early in the belief that students will feel insulted by your obvious authoritarianism if you don't," counsels Brookfield (1990, p. 61).

In the process of organizing and sequencing the teaching activities, the trainer should figure out the time required and record it on the written lesson plan. Whether to record the running time for the session or the actual time for each activity is a matter of personal preference.

Evaluating Learner Performance

"Just as needs assessment is viewed as the overture to the program development process, so evaluation becomes its final movement," writes Brookfield (1986, p. 261). Preparing the training lesson plan involves designing formative and summative evaluation techniques. Formative evaluations are done during the training to allow for midcourse corrections. Summative evaluations are done after the training is complete to ensure that the objectives were achieved.

"Evaluative models applied to adult learning tend to be drawn from secondary school or higher education settings and then adapted to the circumstances of adult learners. Rarely are they grounded in or reflective of the concepts, philosophies, and processes of adult learning" (Brookfield, 1986, p. 262). Many adult educators argue for the inclusion of learners in the evaluation process. They argue that the participatory nature of teaching techniques that are most effective in adult learning situations must be used in evaluating the learning. Adults in training sessions must also learn how to evaluate their success. Brookfield (1986) is "compelled by the argument for participatory evaluations," but says, "The educator who abrogates responsibility for setting evaluative criteria to participants is guilty of professional misconduct" (p. 277).

Practicality suggests that teacher and learner need to be engaged in evaluative processes together. Time and activities need to be provided as part of the training plan to allow learners time for reflection, for comparing skill or knowledge acquisition with preestablished standards, to apply the relevant skill or knowledge, and to engage in mutual feedback with the trainer with regard to skills and knowledge covered in the training session. This ongoing process needs to be planned simultaneously with the activities.

Formative Evaluation Techniques

Dick and Carey define formative evaluation as "the process instructors use to obtain data in order to revise their instruction to make it more efficient and effective" (1985, p. 198). They assert that the formative evaluation process is essentially positive, constructive, and nonjudgmental. They suggest several different types of formative evaluation, many of which are included in a needs assessment. They include such things as field tests, small-group evaluation, and one-to-one evaluation. It is also essential that formative evaluation be done during the actual training sessions. The following are a small sample of formative evaluation techniques:

- When planning a discussion group, write out in advance the expected responses. As reports are presented from groups, review the list to ensure that all appropriate topics have been covered.
- Create learning activities wherein learners are evaluating their own and a partner's performance on information or skill to be learned.
- Solicit and record comments or notes made by learners with regard to instructional material, explaining where they encountered difficulties.
- Appoint learner review teams. These groups do periodic reviews to provide midtraining assessments of the material to be learned up to the point of the review.

Summative Evaluation Techniques

"The process of evaluation is essentially the process of determining to what extent the educational objectives are actually being realized . . . since educational objectives are essentially changes in human beings," wrote Tyler in 1949. He went on, "Evaluation is the process for determining the degree to which these changes in behavior are actually taking place" (p. 110). It is the summative evaluation that, in fact, measures quantitatively and qualitatively the learners' progress in meeting the learning objectives. It is the device for determining if the training has been successful and effective. The following are some types of summative evaluation tools:

- Pretest and posttest comparative scores
- Tabulations of such things as units of work per hour, units of work per volunteer or employee, tasks completed, personnel turnover, dollar value per task completed
- Self-reported proficiencies by participants in the training session
- Observations of trainees on the job

Resources and Supplies

The last part of the training lesson plan is the list of resources and supplies essential to the delivery of the training program. This should include such things as equipment, handouts, overheads, flip chart displays, pencils, markers, and the like. By including these details in the lesson plan, the trainer reduces the chances of arriving at the scene of training only to discover that some essential item has been forgotten.

The Cost of Training

A lesson plan must consider the costs of training. A budget for training events must include the cost of equipment rental, resources for learners, trainer fees, room rental, staff time, food and beverages, and supplies. Training is often just another one of the duties delegated to organization staff. Some larger nonprofits have training departments, but they are few. It is rare to see "training" as a line item for in-house costs. Usually that item refers to the expenses of sending paid staff and volunteers to training away from the main office.

Budgets can help in determining whether the current training events and training plans are the wisest use of resources. A large-volume volunteer program offered an orientation to prospective volunteers each month on a Saturday. The cost included room and equipment rental, supplies, beverages, and compensatory time for paid staff. Attendance ranged from twenty-five to thirty-five most Saturdays. A budget analysis revealed the actual and indirect costs were higher than they had appeared. The CEO, the paid staff responsible for training, and volunteers decided to experiment with four sessions per year. A needs assessment was completed and the training plan was redesigned to accommodate more learners. Projected group size was between sixty-five and eighty.

In this case, the organization saved considerable staff time and equipment and supply expenses. Careful monitoring has shown little change in the volunteer program. Even though a person volunteering today may not be placed for two months, the drop-out rate is close to what it was with the one-per-month training schedule. The size of the group presented challenges to paid staff and volunteers who were used to training smaller groups. As they tested and refined the presentation, however, the group of volunteers responsible for training wanted to offer new large-group in-service training sessions. Their experience in the orientation training gave them both the knowledge and courage to try out activities with a larger group. "Decisions about teaching activity are multidimensional. They involve the learning objective, the inventory of the learners, and the norms of the organization, to say nothing of the available budget" (Laird, 1985, p. 130).

An issue for nonprofit organizations is the need for alternatives to face-to-face training. Statistics show a growing need to accommodate volunteers interested in short-term assignments (J. C. Penney's/National Volunteer Center, 1989). Many volunteer groups are serving population segments in geographically and culturally diverse communities. English may not be the language of choice for some volunteers. These issues are prompting many organizations to consider the use of technology in training, especially interactive video and television down-links. The principles of adult education and the techniques needed to create a training plan are no different when a technological delivery system is used. If anything, those responsible for expending training dollars must determine that the training is, in fact, planned in a careful way. An interactive video can cost $20,000 and up. Violating the principles described in this chapter and producing a videotape based on hope could be a costly mistake.

Competencies of the Trainer

"The teacher is not so much a purveyor of knowledge . . . but rather a facilitator, an encourager of another's finding the knowledge for himself" (Robinson, 1979). A trainer cannot make adults learn. Each individual learner controls their own learning. The ability of the trainer lies in creating an environment that encourages discovery. It is forming an environment where it is impossible not to learn. Adult views of training are often rooted in childhood formal educational experiences. As trainers and learners, it is challenging to change that image.

The person who is responsible for training needs to see that role as one of enabler, facilitator, guide, encourager — rarely as teller of facts. Sometimes the most challenging part of training is knowing the "right" answers and waiting while learners grope, when it would be so easy to give them out. It is in discovery that learning takes place — for adults and for trainers. Trainers must know the answers unequivocally and in depth. Then they can help guide the learning struggle in productive ways. This requires competencies beyond "I know this and I will tell it to you." "The competencies vary from understanding of adult learning to computer competency, from questioning skills to presentation skills, from futuring skills to library skills, and from cost-benefit analysis skills to group process skills," writes Laird (1985, p. 14).

Stephen Brookfield, in his book *The Skillful Teacher* (1990, pp. 192–211), offers "truths" about skillful teaching. The following list is adapted to apply to the training prepared and delivered in nonprofit organizations.

- *Be clear about the purpose of your training.* From on-the-job training to an orientation for new volunteers, the individual responsible for the training should have a written purpose for the training session.
- *Reflect on your own learning.* You are a biased trainer. Understand how you like to learn and then work against it. Most trainers teach the way they like to learn. As they plan a training activity they mentally evaluate it based on their own preferences. The audience is diverse and each person has his or her learning style. By understanding your own learning preferences you can broaden the choices you offer learners.
- *Welcome ambiguity.* Despite the best efforts of this chapter to offer a systematic and rational process to address training issues, the actual training is a journey into uncertainty. Trainers often cross the borders of chaos to inhabit zones of ambiguity. Even with a well-designed training plan based on a needs assessment, during the training event the teacher has experiences that confound explanation. The effective trainer needs to welcome those experiences and realize that ambiguity is part of training.
- *Perfection is impossible.* Striving to be better from training session to training session is an admirable trait. Thinking perfection is possible can only frustrate. Adult participants will be different, and that makes each training event new and challenging. Some events will be better than others. The ambiguity of training makes perfection impossible and an unrealistic goal.
- *Know your learners.* This refers to researching the learners' backgrounds, including how they experience learning. In a diverse society this is more important than ever. The more the trainer knows about volunteers, staff, board members, clients, members, or patrons, the better the chance of organizing learning to meet their needs and attain organizational goals.
- *Talk to your colleagues.* Training is carried out in all nonprofit organizations and agencies. Find out what others are doing. It is especially important to talk to people who provide a different type of service. There is much to be learned from those who do not see the world from your perspective.
- *Trust your instincts.* Use all your faculties to assess your progress as a trainer. Listen and observe the learners in the training session and at

work. Touch the things they will touch. Immerse yourself in the learning, and then trust your sense of what works and what doesn't.

- *Create diversity.* Seek a variety of methods and techniques and devices to address the same learning objective. Experiment with different models and encourage your learners to do the same.

- *Take risks.* Model for others in your organization that risk taking is acceptable. Modeling is one of the most powerful training tools.

- *Accept the emotionality of learning.* Learning the simplest task is not a sterile experience. Learners report their experiences using highly emotional terms. Exploration of new territory, being a board president, chairing a committee, serving as a volunteer, staffing a work team, accessing services of a nonprofit organization—all present threats to self-esteem as the individual explores new and difficult knowledge and skills. Acknowledge the emotionality of the experience.

- *Learning satisfaction is not the only evaluation.* Be wary of the evaluations at the end of a training session. Learning is often defined as a change in behavior. Change is painful and is resisted by most adults. Happy learners who have never had their knowledge, skills, values, or beliefs challenged are not necessarily "trained." Likewise, hostile evaluations should not be given any greater weight than positive ones. Remember that learning is emotional, and if the training experience was challenging, the learner may be experiencing pain and anxiety. Sometimes volunteers work for a year or two before valuing the early training they received. This is why needs assessments are an important evaluation tool.

- *Balance supporting and challenging the learner.* This is the most difficult training skill to develop. By trusting your instinct you get better at creating a balance between the support of sometimes fragile egos and the challenge of exploring alternative perspectives. Challenge for challenge's sake rarely teaches anything but hostility. Volunteers are not a captive audience; they can choose to avoid future training sessions.

- *Recognize the significance of your actions in all aspects of your job.* View yourself as a helper of learning.

Summary

Training is a regular activity for nonprofit organizations. Staff and volunteers are a team delivering both formal and informal training to each other, the community clients, members, and patrons. The best training creates a team of staff and volunteers who use adult education principles as a guide. The team of trainers conducts needs assessments, which produce information about potential learners and their individual needs. The assessment draws on issues of diversity, costs, competencies, relevancy, responsibility, and relationship for the learner. Once training needs have been determined, decisions are made to present informal training opportunities or organize formal training events. Organizing the training activities includes determining the purpose, assessing and planning for a nourishing learning climate, writing learning objectives, designing training activities, planning to evaluate learner performance, and arranging for appropriate resources. Those with training responsibilities must be attentive to their style of training and how it fosters a climate of healthy adult learning.

References

Brookfield, S. D. *Understanding and Facilitating Adult Learning: A Comprehensive Analysis of Principles and Effective Practices.* San Francisco, Calif.: Jossey-Bass, 1986.

Brookfield, S. D. *The Skillful Teacher: On Technique, Trust, and Responsiveness in the Classroom.* San Francisco, Calif.: Jossey-Bass, 1990.

Cross, K. P. *Adults as Learners.* San Francisco, Calif.: Jossey-Bass, 1981.

Dale, E. *Audio-Visual Methods in Teaching.* (3rd ed.) New York: Holt, Rinehart & Winston, 1969.

Dick, W., and Carey, L. *The Systematic Design of Instruction.* (2nd ed.) Glenview, Ill.: Scott, Foresman, 1985.

Eicher, J. P., Jones, J. E., and Bearley, W. L. "Neurolinguistic Communication Profile." *The HRD Quarterly,* Code #108, 1990.

Gregorc, A. F. *Gregorc Style Delineator.* Columbia, Conn.: Gregorc Associates, 1982.

Ilsley, P. J., and Niemi, J. A. *Recruiting and Training Volunteers.* New York: McGraw-Hill, 1981.

J. C. Penney's/National Volunteer Center. *Report on Volunteering in America.* Arlington, Va.: National Volunteer Center, 1989.

Kirkpatrick, D. L. *How to Manage Change Effectively: Approaches, Methods, and Case Examples.* San Francisco, Calif.: Jossey-Bass, 1985.

Knowles, M. *Andragogy in Action: Applying Modern Principles of Adult Learning.* San Francisco, Calif.: Jossey-Bass, 1984.

Knox, A. B. *Helping Adults Learn.* San Francisco, Calif.: Jossey-Bass, 1986.

Laird, D. *Approaches to Training and Development.* Reading, Mass.: Addison-Wesley, 1985.

Lowman, J. *Mastering the Techniques of Teaching.* San Francisco, Calif.: Jossey-Bass, 1990.

McCoy, V. R. "Adult Life Cycle Tasks." *Lifelong Learning: The Adult Years.* Washington, D.C.: American Association of Adult and Continuing Educators, 1977.

Macduff, N. "Training Adult Volunteers." *Journal of Volunteer Administration,* 1988, *6*(3), 38–39.

Mager, R. F. *Preparing Instructional Objectives.* Belmont, Calif.: David Lake Publishing, 1984.

Miller, H. L. *Teaching and Learning in Adult Education.* New York: Macmillan, 1967.

Murrant, G., and Strathdee, S. "AIDS, Hospice, and Volunteers: Casey House Volunteer Program." *Journal of Volunteer Administration,* 1992, Summer, pp. 11–17.

Oltman, P. K., Raskin, E., Witkin, H. A. "Group Embedded Figures Test." Palo Alto, Calif.: Consulting Psychologist Press, 1971.

Robinson, R. D. *An Introduction to Helping Adults Learn and Change.* West Bend, Wis.: Omnibook, 1979.

Smith, R. M. *Learning How to Learn.* New York: Cambridge Press, 1982.

Tyler, R. W. *Basic Principles of Curriculum and Instruction.* Chicago: University of Chicago Press, 1949.

Widmer, C. "Why Board Members Participate." *Journal of Voluntary Action Research,* 1985, Oct.–Dec., pp. 8–23.

Conclusion

Preparing for the Future of Nonprofit Management

Robert D. Herman

As I reflect on the wealth of information available in the preceding chapters, I am again reminded of how great a challenge effective nonprofit leadership and management is. It is not, however, a challenge that is unattainable. Many nonprofit organizations, and the people who lead and manage them, are achieving much. This handbook provides principles, insights, and guidelines that can help any organization improve. Even the best organizations are never finished. Continuous improvement is an important and meaningful organizational goal.

The chapters in this book have focused on organizations — on the tasks that must be done, the challenges that must be met, and the skills that individuals who lead and manage organizations must develop and apply if their organizations are to succeed. Such a focus is entirely appropriate. Organizations are the instruments through which work, including the work of philanthropy, gets done in North American societies. While organization-focused management and leadership will long be with us, the future of nonprofit charitable organizations, in the United States and Canada, is likely to be determined less by organizationally focused actions than by the extent to which nonprofit organizations build more cooperative or more competitive sectors. The salient question is, then, will the nonprofit sector be more like a community or more like an industry?

By a *community* of nonprofit organizations, I mean a collectivity of philanthropic organizations (and their leaders) that has a shared identity; that has individually differentiated roles, yet a capacity and mechanisms to integrate actions. Within such a community, nonprofit organizations recognize that each one's resources ultimately derive from the larger community and that their missions are legitimized by their fit with the larger community's needs. The organizations that constitute a nonprofit community understand that they are stewards of the larger community's resources and instruments for meeting the public needs of the larger community. Fulfilling such a role requires that members of the nonprofit community often act in cooperative ways.

By an *industry* of nonprofit organizations, I mean a collectivity of organizations that has a shared identity and a capacity and mechanisms to act jointly to achieve benefits in the self-interest of the organizations that comprise the industry. Just as the U.S. steel industry acts to achieve legislation favorable to all steel makers, so too do nonprofit industries attempt to affect legislation. Both organizational communities and industries are characterized by a mix of interorganizational competition and cooperation. However, cooperation is likely to be greater in a community; and more important, a nonprofit community will act more as a steward and agent of the broader community than will a nonprofit industry, whose emphasis is on the survival and growth of the industry.

What are the forces toward intrasectoral cooperation? What are the forces toward intrasectoral competition? To what extent—and how—can nonprofit leaders and managers make and act on choices about which direction to go? While nonprofit industries can be organized at the metropolitan, state (or province), and national levels, nonprofit communities are most likely (and "natural") at the metropolitan level.

Forces Toward Intrasectoral Cooperation

In considering this issue, it is helpful to distinguish between national and local levels. Much of the cooperation and competition between charitable nonprofit organizations occurs at a local (metropolitan) level. Relations among nonprofit organizations at local levels have long been characterized by both cooperation and competition, though the cooperative elements are much more likely to be emphasized and celebrated. The United Way system has been a strong force toward local cooperation. United Way campaigns have tied member or affiliate agencies to a common funding pool, where all have a stake in increasing the size of the pool. Additionally, many local United Ways have undertaken community needs assessments and devised allocation plans that are intended to promote an integrated approach to meeting the community's health and welfare needs. Of course, United Ways do not eliminate competition. Agencies compete to affect United Way allocation criteria and decisions. United Way members or affiliates also compete outside the United Way for contributions, board members, and sometimes volunteers, staff, and even clients.

It is obvious to all that the United Way system (at local and national levels) is changing. Alternative collective fundraising bodies of many types are making great inroads into the United Way's traditional corporate sources of campaign funds. The donor option or donor-directed mechanisms that United Ways have begun to adopt may mean that United Way affiliation will offer diminishing advantages. As local United Ways change, they seem very likely to be less and less a force for local charitable cooperation and more likely to be "another competitor" in the fundraising marketplace.

While United Ways have been a force for cooperation, they include only a limited part of any community's nonprofit sector. Other subsectors — such as the arts, education, community development, and health care (especially hospitals) — typically have had no equivalent to the local United Way. Local relations among organizations in these subsectors have also been characterized by a mix of cooperation and competition. Arts organizations often cooperate in scheduling concerts or plays while discreetly competing for customers. Competition between hospitals has become much less discreet, if not yet cutthroat.

Forces encouraging cooperation at the local level include many funders (foundations and corporate giving programs), pressing for collaboration on provision of services, and the threats and opportunities offered by legislative or regulatory actions. Some funders have attempted to overcome what they see as unnecessary duplication of services (and administrative overhead expenditures) by making grants contingent on collaboration among charitable organizations. Some have even attempted to induce mergers. We lack good evidence on the extent and consequences of such efforts. No doubt collaborative projects have increased and a few mergers have taken place. Nonetheless the number of nonprofit charitable organizations continues to increase.

The threats and opportunities posed by legislative or regulatory actions have been a stronger force for nonprofit cooperation. A number of issues that have or might have led to legislative or regulatory action have engaged the collective attention of nonprofit leaders in the last decade. Complaints of unfair competition with small businesses, challenges to tax exemption on the basis of insufficient charitable care, difficulties in obtaining, or rapid increases in the cost of, liability insurance, and limits on fundraising expenditures or mandatory disclosure of fundraising expenditures, as well as other issues, have enhanced intrasector cooperation. These sorts of issues are probably largely responsible for the increasing numbers of state associations of nonprofit organizations.

The advantages of cooperative approaches to these issues has also been reflected at national levels. In the United States, INDEPENDENT SECTOR has taken the lead in identifying issues of common concern to nonprofits and in mobilizing cooperative efforts to respond to those issues, while the Canadian Centre for Philanthropy has taken on a fairly similar agenda in Canada. Other national-level organizations, such as the National Center for Nonprofit Boards and the National Center for Community Risk Management and Insurance, have also been created. These and similar but more specialized organizations have not necessarily been established to foster intrasector cooperation, but their services and publications probably function to create a greater sense of sector commonality and identity. The increasing number of university programs in nonprofit management, voluntarism, and philanthropy, as well as the increasing number of journals and other publications (like this book) focusing on the nonprofit sector also contribute to a greater sense of sector commonality and identity.

Forces Toward Intrasector Competition

The rhetoric of the nonprofit sector tends to ignore the reality of competition between nonprofit organizations. Indeed, the very term "nonprofit sector" may help to disguise the differences and competition among the individual agencies that make it up. Nonprofit organizations have a legal and operational reality that the notion of "nonprofit sector" does not. A sector is not incorporated; it has no officers, no policies, and so on. The notion of a sector is a more or less useful abstraction. It can be used to aggregate data on organizations with some similar corporate features. It can also be used, as suggested above, as a way of mobilizing organizations that share these features to cooperative action.

The "nonprofit sector" concept often seems especially airy at the local level. What does a multimillion-dollar hospital have in common with a women's shelter? What does a private university with a billion-dollar endowment have in common with an inner-city neighborhood housing development corporation? In most communities, hospitals and educational institutions interact little, if at all, with other (usually much smaller) nonprofit organizations, except that their fundraising managers probably participate in professional fundraising organizations. Indeed, hospitals are proving to be a troubling "part" of the nonprofit sector.

Whether nonprofit hospitals really operate as charities or whether they behave differently than for-profit hospitals are questions being raised more and more frequently. State laws vary as to what level of charitable care, if any, is required in order for a hospital to be exempt from certain state taxes. In several states, legal suits have been brought seeking to have state tax exemption for hospitals revoked because they provide very little charitable care. In some instances, these cases have been decided against the hospital. Tax exemption for nonprofit hospitals will undoubtedly become more contentious in the years ahead. More and better evidence about the differences, if any, between the conduct of nonprofit and for-profit hospitals will be helpful in addressing this issue.

Several studies have attempted to determine whether and to what extent nonprofit hospitals behave differently than for-profit hospitals. Gray (1991) observes that economic theorists predict that for-profit hospitals are likely to be more efficient than nonprofit hospitals, but notes that studies of expenses per day found that for-profit hospitals were 3 to 10 percent higher than nonprofits (p. 92). Critics of these studies argued that they failed to make adjustments for the higher capital expenses that for-profit hospitals incurred in building or buying hospitals and for the payment of taxes by for-profit hospitals. Some more recent studies, which attempt to make some of the recommended adjustments, find little or no difference in expenses. Gray concludes that there is no support for the efficiency hypothesis.

Studies of differences in quality of care, where economic theorists predict that nonprofit hospitals may do better, have been few and equivocal. Few such studies have been conducted because of the difficulties of properly adjusting for patient mix and severity of illness. Gray (1991) reports that two studies found that hospital ownership type and mortality rates were unrelated, while another study found that for-profit hospitals had higher mortality rates than nonprofit hospitals. Professional training and norms as well as review practices are probably much more important than ownership type in accounting for quality of care outcomes.

The provision of charitable (or uncompensated) care is the issue on which we might expect the most notable difference in the behavior of nonprofit and for-profit hospitals. Early critics of for-profit health care assumed that for-profit hospitals would provide little charitable care and not offer services that were unprofitable, yet the evidence summarized by Gray (1991, pp. 99–107), shows that such hospitals, in the aggregate, do provide uncompensated care and many typically unprofitable services. Comparisons of the levels of uncompensated care offered by the two types of hospitals generally show that nonprofit hospitals provide more such care than for-profit hospitals. In a study of five states where large numbers of both types of hospitals operate, the for-profit hospitals' uncompensated care averaged from nearly 3 to 5 percent of gross patient revenues, while nonprofit hospitals in those states averaged from 3 to 10 percent. A longitudinal study of Florida hospitals found uncompensated care increased from 1980 to 1985 from 5.3 percent to 8.3 percent (a 57 percent increase) for nonprofit hospitals. For-profit Florida hospitals' uncompensated care increased during that period from 4.2 percent to 5.4 percent (a 29 percent increase). In short, the evidence indicates that for-profit hospitals do provide charitable care (perhaps, largely because of uncollectable debts rather than as an intentional policy), but that nonprofit hospitals provide somewhat more charitable care.

Whether nonprofit hospitals will or can continue to provide the amount of uncompensated care they recently have is doubtful. Nonprofit hospitals attract relatively little revenue—less than 1 percent as a percentage of total revenue—from contributions and grants—not nearly enough to cover uncompensated care (Gray, 1991, pp. 66–67). Whatever form the coming U.S. health care financing system takes, as the likelihood increases that cost shifting will be reduced or eliminated, nonprofit (and for-profit) hospitals will be forced to reduce uncompensated care. Based on the changes that have taken place in the health care system, Hansmann (1989) observes that the U.S. nonprofit charitable sector is splitting in two: a donative sector, in which non-profit organizations will continue to depend on contributions for a significant portion of their revenues, and a commercial sector, in which organizations will rely on sale of services for virtually all of their revenues. He suggests that the growing differences between the commercial and donative nonprofit organizations mean that legislators, courts, business competitors of the commercial nonprofits, and consumers will be unwilling to continue to treat the two types as if they were the same. He asks whether donative nonprofits should continue to support tax exemption and tax deductibility for commercial nonprofits, as these will be increasingly difficult to defend.

I have considered the issues of the behavior and future of nonprofit hospitals because such issues offer the clearest illustration of the choices facing leaders of nonprofit charitable organizations. I believe a strong case can be made that nonprofit status for most current nonprofit hospitals constitutes a historical artifact — a status that is no longer justifiable. However, the available evidence does show some (perhaps small, but still significant) differences in the behavior of nonprofit and for-profit hospitals. The changing health care system, however, is likely to reduce or eliminate these differences. If that happens, all of us concerned for the integrity of philanthropy and nonprofit organizations will be required to decide whether nonprofit status — and the advantages that status entails — can be justified because an organization was initially organized that way or whether explicit standards of some level of charitable service are necessary. I see no point in attempting to retain organizations that operate strictly as businesses in the sector (except that doing so makes the sector economically larger than it would otherwise be). Retaining "businesses-in-disguise" not only promises to erode public confidence in nonprofit organizations; it also may enhance intrasector competitiveness.

As Salamon observes in Chapter Four, governments in the United States are increasingly relying on consumer subsidies (vouchers) rather than producer subsidies (contracts with service providers) to deliver various health and social services. Such an arrangement is likely to encourage entry of for-profit providers into more service fields. Consumer subsidies may indeed "empower" consumers. Consumer subsidies are also likely to increase competition and may make fundraising by nonprofit providers much more difficult. A voucher mechanism could, depending on what restrictions might be enacted regarding eligible service providers, lead to similar results in the affected service fields as providing health insurance to consumers has had for hospitals.

This line of reasoning leads to the intriguing question of why for-profit schools have not had more success in the higher education market. Perhaps, as Collins and Hickman (1991) have argued, the philanthropic support of private (nonprofit) universities by the wealthy elite not only legitimizes their (the elite's) social position but also legitimizes and increases the attractiveness of such universities to the general public and to potential students.

Certainly private universities have been able to provide—and are perceived as providing—more charitable care (scholarship aid for students unable to afford the tuition) than hospitals, thus justifying their nonprofit status.

While changes in financing mechanisms have enhanced competition in the health care industry and have very likely increased competition in service fields, other more longstanding forces toward competition continue to influence the nonprofit sector. These include contests for contributions and prestigious board members. Despite the undoubted advances in the art of fundraising, giving in the United States has remained fairly constant, in terms of percentage of gross national product (GNP), for several decades. According to the American Association of Fund-Raising Counsel Trust for Philanthropy's 1990 figures, total yearly giving fluctuates around 2 percent of GNP. The proportion was consistently above 2 percent in the 1960s (with 1961's 2.17 percent the highest of that decade) and mostly slightly below 2 percent in the 1970s through the early 1980s. This pattern suggests that giving grows (in absolute dollars) in tandem with the economy, but that giving has not grown more than the economy. Thus, nonprofit charitable organizations that hope to increase their relative "share" of giving must do so by attracting dollars that would otherwise go to another nonprofit. Competition for contributions is seldom overt. Fundraising practices emphasize why potential donors should give to the appealing organization, not why they should not give to other organizations. However, fundraisers, managers, and board members know their organizations are competing and act accordingly.

Competition for donations is clearly consistent with key philanthropic and democratic values. Potential donors should have the freedom to support causes they espouse. In a pluralistic society, no basis exists for identifying or defining one type of philanthropic undertaking as more deserving than another. Nonetheless, the current implicit competitive system leads to a distribution of donations that seems to some difficult to defend on other grounds (than that it reflects donor preferences). For example, in a commentary in the *Chronicle of Philanthropy* (June 1, 1993) Christy argues that donations to higher education are much too concentrated on the elite, research-oriented universities. He maintains that U.S. society would be better served if educational donations were redirected to those colleges and universities that serve much greater numbers of poor and middle-income students. The same type of argument can be made about redirecting donations from organizations that primarily benefit the middle-class to those that primarily benefit the poor. Indeed, one could extend this logic to argue that philanthropy in the more affluent countries should be redirected to Third World countries. The point I am trying to make here is not that the distribution of philanthropy must be changed (much less that I know how and on what basis it should be changed). Rather, it is that if the nonprofit sector is strictly an industry, then this is a nonissue; if, however, the nonprofit sector is a community, then it is an issue that the community needs to address, particularly at the local level. Might not major donors (that is, foundations and corporate giv-ing programs) and a wide array of service providers develop community forums or other means for considering the match of local needs and local resources?

Making Choices About the Future

The foregoing assessment of forces toward cooperation and toward compe-tition in the nonprofit sector suggests that more competition is coming. That is the conclusion that analysis supports; it is not the conclusion that I per-sonally prefer. While I recognize the virtues of competition (even among nonprofit organizations), I believe the virtues of cooperation and commu-nity are too-little valued.

Social theorists often picture U.S. society as one in which individual-ism, competition, and large-scale organizations operating on universalistic criteria leave people searching for meaning and connectedness (Bellah and others, 1985). Family, neighborhood, church, and voluntary organizations have long been sources of social integration, personal meaning, and con-nectedness. All of these institutions are changing. As they change, will they continue to offer people the same opportunities to achieve social integra-tion, meaning, and connectedness? Will they continue to be the foundations of community? More particularly, if it is true that greater competition is the likely trend for nonprofit organizations, what can and should the leaders and managers of nonprofit organizations do to counteract that trend?

Obviously, I take the position that the nonprofit sector and the com-munities that nonprofit organizations serve will benefit from greater cooper-ation among nonprofit organizations. Not everyone will accept that view. For those who share my view, the key question is What can be done to weaken the forces toward competition and/or to strengthen the forces toward cooper-ation? Merely urging more cooperation will not be enough. Nonprofit ex-ecutives face long and difficult days in meeting their responsibilities to their own organizations. To suggest that they and board leaders commit addi-tional time and effort to participating in unstructured meetings that might enhance sector cooperation is unrealistic and irresponsible.

It seems to me that the institutions with the resources, interests, and perspective to promote and encourage more local intrasector cooperation are the foundations (especially the community foundation) and corporate giving programs. The funder segment of a local nonprofit sector can en-hance the capacity of local nonprofit organizations to act as a community by initiating and supporting a community planning process. The goals of the planning process ought to be to determine the larger community's needs, to assess the extent to which local nonprofit service providers are respond-ing to those needs, and to develop a plan (probably involving interorgani-zational collaborations) to more adequately respond to those needs. In car-rying out this planning process three design principles are crucial:

1.   Grant-makers will need to commit multiyear funding to the project and be willing to fund continuing operating costs for some organizations (rather than funding only or mostly innovative projects or start-up costs). I believe the commitment to fund continuing operating costs is necessary in order to ensure a consistent focus on meeting the larger community's identified needs. Stability of funding will permit nonprofit service providers to implement long-term strategies and avoid (to a large extent) chasing grant dollars.

2.   The process must be open to any bona fide nonprofit charitable organization in the locality. It cannot be limited to only nonprofit organizations already supported or known by the grant-making community.

3.   The process will have to be developed and approved by all who participate. Control will have to be shared by all. Grant makers will be required to give up unilateral control.

These design criteria are clearly a substantial departure from typical practices. Grant makers may feel that agreeing to these criteria will violate their trusteeship obligations. I believe grant makers can fulfill their fiduciary responsibilities yet implement the criteria by funding the process, participating in the process, and indicating a willingness to help fund whatever plan is developed as a result of the process. Final decisions on funding the resultant plan would not be necessary until the plan was developed. Such a process may lead to a multiyear community charitable budget and to additional collaborative projects. The community planning process probably should be a recurring one—on a three-, four-, or five-year cycle. Several different models of such community-building nonprofit sector planning need to be tried.

Some readers may think that I am advocating a process that duplicates (or replaces) the local United Way process. That is not my intention. The process I have in mind should certainly include the United Way, but I am not advocating a broader federated fundraising campaign. The process I advocate would not replace or restrict any fundraising efforts. I would hope that the major grant-makers would make their allocations on the basis of the resulting plan and, through publicizing the plan and its rationale, encourage other givers to consider donations consistent with the plan (perhaps channeled through the community foundation). Beyond not being a fundraising campaign, the process I envision would be open to and involve a much broader spectrum of the locality's nonprofit sector. It would emphasize creating a widely supported process of community needs assessment and the commitment of some significant level of grant-maker funds to allocations and projects consistent with the needs assessment.

This proposal may seem to some to be unnecessary. I believe it, or something like it, is necessary. If the trends toward greater intrasector competition are not counteracted, most nonprofit organizations will continue to make the important contributions they have been making. However, more of their time and effort will be devoted to maintaining or improving their relative position in the fundraising marketplace. The possibility of strengthening community by strengthening the nonprofit community may be lost. Others may believe this proposal to be unrealistic. I believe it is doable, at least in many communities. Efforts somewhat similar to what I have proposed are under way in many places, though on more limited, issue-focused bases. The step that is required to move to the next level of cooperation, admittedly a very big step, is to expand from a single-issue focus to a community focus, where many issues are included. The future of management in the nonprofit sector will be significantly affected by whether or how well we take that step.

References

American Association of Fund-Raising Counsel Trust for Philanthropy. *Giving USA: The Annual Report on Philanthropy for the Year 1989.* New York: AAFRC Trust for Philanthropy, 1990.

Bellah, R. N., and others. *Habits of the Heart: Individualism and Commitment in American Life.* Berkeley, Calif.: University of California Press, 1985.

Christy, M. T. "In Philanthropy, Rich Colleges Just Get Richer," *Chronicle of Philanthropy,* June 1, 1993, pp. 37–38.

Collins, R., and Hickman, N. "Altruism and Culture as Social Products." *Voluntas,* 1991, *2*(2), 1–15.

Gray, B. H. *The Profit Motive and Patient Care.* Cambridge, Mass.: Harvard University Press, 1991.

Hansmann, H. "The Two Nonprofit Sectors: Fee for Service Versus Donative Organizations." In V. A. Hodgkinson and R. W. Lyman (eds.), *The Future of the Nonprofit Sector.* San Francisco: Jossey-Bass, 1989.

Name Index

A

Abrahamson A. J., 27, 41, 83, 86, 97, 98
Acomb, B. L., 173, 174n, 183
Adams, C. T., 228, 231, 233, 235, 243, 245
Alchon, G., 16, 35
Alexander, J. G., 139, 151
Allen, N. J., 295, 299
Allio, R. J., 175, 183
Ambrose, S. E., 12, 35
Amenomori, T., 109, 114, 116
Ammarell, N., 326, 340–341
Anderson, C., 23
Andreason, A. R., 252, 254, 255, 263, 269, 272, 276, 277
Andrews, F. E., 20, 22, 23, 33, 35
Andrews, G., 515, 517, 528, 531
Anheier, H. K., 100
Anthony, R. N., 403, 404, 409n, 413, 416n, 427, 441, 442, 444n, 473n, 483
Aramony, W., 56
Argyris, C., 239–240, 243
Arnove, R. F., 107, 114
Atkin, R. S., 306, 317, 323
Austin, M. J., 233, 240, 246
Axelrod, N. R., 119, 138

B

Backoff, R. W., 163, 168, 170, 173, 183
Bagozzi, R. P., 251, 276
Bahrami, H., 535, 536, 556
Bailey, A. L., 29, 31, 35
Bailyn, B., 5, 35
Bakker, J., 193
Bakker, T. F., 193
Barber, B. R., 332, 340
Barnadin, H. J., 540, 542, 555
Barry, B. W., 165, 182
Bass, B. M., 149, 152
Bauer, R., 45, 62, 63
Bearley, W. L., 614
Beasley, W. H., III, 34
Becker, D. G., 288, 299
Bell, P. D., 120, 135
Bellah, R. N., 189, 206, 332, 340, 623, 625
Below, P. J., 173, 174n, 183
Bender, T., 14, 35
Bendick, M., 231, 243
Berger, P. L., 83, 97
Biddle, S. C., 110, 114
Bixby, A. K., 326, 327, 340
Blades, S., 234
Blau, P. M., 315, 323
Bloom, P., 259, 276

Subject Index